2/26

Minicomputers:

Hardware, Software, and Applications

Minicomputers:
Hardware, Software, and Applications

Edited by

James D. Schoeffler
Professor of Engineering
Case Western Reserve University

Ronald H. Temple
Manager, Advanced Automation Technology
General Electric Company

A volume in the IEEE PRESS Selected Reprint Series, prepared under the sponsorship of the IEEE Educational Activities Board

The Institute of Electrical and Electronics Engineers, Inc. New York

International Standard Book Numbers:

Clothbound: 0-87942-015-4
Paperbound: 0-87942-016-2

Library of Congress Catalog Card Number 72-86955

PRINTED IN THE UNITED STATES OF AMERICA

Foreword

The minicomputer is an important part of the computer revolution. It reaches into many areas of human life and has an almost unlimited spectrum of applications, from manufacturing control to traffic control, from business billing to inventory planning, and from checking income tax returns to determining authorship of disputed documents.

Scientists, engineers, managers, analysts, and persons in many other walks of life are all in a position to make good use of the minicomputer. In order to do so effectively, they must acquire a certain amount of in-depth knowledge of minicomputer technology. The IEEE Educational Activities Board is delighted to sponsor this reprint volume on a subject of such unusual interest and timeliness.

The literature on minicomputers is scattered among a large number of periodicals. In addition to the prominent journals in this area (*IEEE Transactions on Computers, Proceedings of the IEEE, AFIPS Conference Proceedings, Journal of the Association of Computer Machinery, etc.*), there are many other less obvious journals which have published excellent tutorial papers on this subject. Some of these papers deal with applications for the minicomputer; others treat its characteristics, its behavior, or its design. Articles of this kind have appeared in the *IEEE Transactions on Industry and General Applications, IEEE Spectrum,* and in a number of non-IEEE journals. It obviously would be difficult for the beginner wishing to learn about minicomputers to search this vast amount of literature to find the best articles and to critically evaluate them. We are greatly indebted to the Editors of this volume, Professor James D. Schoeffler and Dr. Ronald H. Temple, for carrying out this task and for putting the volume together. The articles have been taken from trade magazines and from journals of other technical societies as well as from IEEE publications.

The authors are authorities in the field of minicomputers and have participated in several successful minicomputer seminars to teach scientists, engineers, and managers how to make practical use of this powerful new tool. The articles chosen for reprint here have been selected at least partially on the basis of their usefulness as textual material for short courses. The book will therefore be used by the Educational Activities Board in bringing instructional programs on the minicomputer to the various IEEE regions. The volume, however, stands on its own merits. It constitutes a valuable text for anyone interested in the subject, whether or not he reads the material in conjunction with course offerings.

Glen Wade, *Chairman*
IEEE Educational Activities Board

Preface

The technical activities of the IEEE have for many years included meetings, conferences, and publications directed to extending the knowledge frontier in electrical and electronics engineering. Activities of this type will continue to make up a major portion of the IEEE technical effort.

Recent events, however, have caused us to reorder our technical priorities and to emphasize man's industrial, communications, and service requirements. In particular, specialized communication, control, and display are receiving increasing attention. Major effort is being devoted to developing more economical hardware and equipment and to providing adequate software to accomplish the desired information handling.

During the past few years minicomputers were developed to meet these needs for lower cost information processing, and each day they assume a more and more important role. It is the purpose of this book to provide a means for helping IEEE members and others obtain an improved understanding of the hardware, software, and applications of minicomputers.

The needs of industry for information and control, whether it be in fluid processes (such as chemicals and petroleum), solid material processes (such as steel, rubber, cement, and ores), or discrete-part manufacturing processes (such as automobiles, refrigerators, stoves, and electronics) are being handled increasingly by on-line computers. The minicomputer has achieved a fine performance record to date and has a very promising future.

The Technical Activities Board hopes that this book will help IEEE members and others to develop their skills and abilities so as to apply more minicomputers more effectively. We are pleased that this book is one of the first published by the IEEE Press.

Harold Chestnut, *1971 Chairman*
IEEE Technical Activities Board

Contents

Introduction

The minicomputer has opened the door to a large number of interesting and important applications that were not economically feasible in the past. These range from on-line computer control of industrial processes or laboratory experiments, where the computer is the central component in the system, to a special purpose computer for the replacement of hard-wired electromechanical relay logic.

The minicomputer represents a great opportunity to develop systems more economically, not simply because of decreasing hardware cost, but rather because the availability of low-cost high-computational capability permits the application of methodology and theories that could not previously be economically justified. For example, the rapid acquisition of data from a laboratory experiment was often done by recording and later reducing the data by eye or hand. In contrast, the use of a computer at the heart of a data acquisition system permits an experimenter to rapidly and easily acquire data and use the results to choose the next experiment to perform. Similarly, the fast response rate of the computer can be used in situations that heretofore had to be controlled with a special purpose machine or run in a mode that precluded the need for fast-response computational capability.

For example, a production line was most economically designed for large runs of identical products because special-purpose nonadaptive machines were used for sequencing and control. Adding a computer or several computers to do these functions gives a degree of adaptive capability that may permit the mode of production to change quickly in response to demand, thereby permitting economic production of short runs or customized items.

The organization of the reprints in this book is directed toward illustrating these ideas. The first two parts discuss computer hardware and software, basics of the minicomputer itself. This is, of course, critical to any application since minicomputers and their software vary greatly, as do the requirements of various applications. Consequently, the application significantly influences the choice of a particular machine and its associated software, and the papers in these parts are directed toward illustrating the important characteristics and differences.

The third part is concerned with the devices that are used for input and output of data to the minicomputer. These devices are often unique to the particular applications and are not characteristic of devices found on large-scale computers used for computation or business data processing. Interfacing of these devices to the computer becomes an important consideration in any application.

The remaining five parts are directed toward classes of applications, not to illustrate these applications, but rather to illustrate the basic theory and methodology used in solving the application problems. For instance, the methodology used in data acquisition systems includes filtering, control theory, sampled data theory, etc., and is quite different from that used in manufacturing systems where the dominant problems are handling large files of interrelated information, scheduling, optimization, etc.

The situation with minicomputer applications is analogous to the study of a foreign language. It is undesirable to learn a foreign language well but have nothing to say. In a similar fashion, it is undesirable to learn all about minicomputer hardware and software if one knows no theory or methodology to apply. The minicomputer is a tool to be used in the solution of problems. The various parts of this book are directed toward illustrating theory and methodology that have been successfully applied to various problems in the past with the hope that they will stimulate the reader to apply the theory and methodology of his own field of specialization in the solution of his problems.

Part 1
Minicomputer Hardware

Introductory Comments

Minicomputer applications place two major constraints on the hardware: minimum cost of hardware to carry out an application and maximum flexibility for interfacing to the large variety of devices found in applications. The first implies that only the minimum hardware necessary for the application be included in the system. This precludes the use of general purpose standard configuration computer hardware systems for many applications. For example, an application that does not require bulk storage cannot tolerate increased hardware costs due to unused high-speed memory access channels or bulk storage controllers. Consequently, such features must be modular in minicomputers so that they can be excluded when they are not needed. Even more important, certain computational capability may not be needed in some applications, and the economics then dictate a simpler, more special purpose machine.

The first paper in this part describes a special purpose computer suitable for a single class of tasks, a programmable controller. The application here is the replacement of large amounts of relay logic by a digital machine that repeatedly scans the status of a number of relays, performs logical computations, and controls the status of other output relays. Because of the application of such a device, normal arithmetic is not necessary, nor are many of the control instructions present in any general purpose computer. Moreover, the restrictive nature of the application permits a great simplification in programming. Typically there is a special purpose console that permits the description of the program in the form of a relay network. Such a "language" is most acceptable to users who are accustomed to such descriptions and who are not professional programmers. The net result is that the programmable controller is a very special purpose digital computer that is much lower in cost than a comparable general purpose device. This is a significant consideration in the selection of a minicomputer for any application because the future may provide the ability to specify special purpose machines for individual application very economically.

Available industrial electromechanical relays are highly reliable devices that are insensitive to the large noise conditions of the typical industrial power line. In reading the first paper, attention should be paid to the input/output organization that is specifically designed for high-reliability and high-noise immunity and particularized to the special high-voltage relays typically used in industry. The overall system is a highly reliable economic alternative to large banks of relay logic because reliability and maintainability are the dominant characteristics of the design. This makes the hardware of the programmable controller far from a typical minicomputer.

The second major constraint imposed by minicomputer applications is an ability to use almost any instrument or device as an input or output device. That is, minicomputers are normally only one component in a system and must interface to various instruments, operator communication devices, or other components in the application system. This is in marked contrast to data processing applications where input/output devices can be categorized very nicely and are usually supplied by the computer vendor himself. The consequence of this constraint is a general purpose input/output system that permits the economic implementation of interfaces between arbitrary simple or complex devices and the computer.

The three papers by W. H. Roberts, E. Holland, and P. M. Kintner describe the overall architecture of minicomputers and the problems of interfacing these computers to various devices. The fundamental problem is one of coordinating two devices acting concurrently. That is, input/output devices are often relatively slow in their response. For instance, an electromechanical relay may take from 5 to 10 ms to close after the voltage has been applied to the coil. A computer desiring to close such a relay cannot wait for this length of time before proceeding; it consequently initiates the closure with an appropriate command and then goes about its business. The result is the computer proceeding with its program while the relay is closing concurrently. Any further communication between the computer and the devices then must ensure that previous actions have been completed.

The control of concurrent devices is through the use of priority interrupts and a "handshaking" discipline in the input/output hardware system. The paper by M. K. Van Gelder and A. W. England describes the priority interrupt system that is characteristic of most computers today. G. A. Korn then describes the problem of organizing and designing an interface between a device and the computer that ensures correct concurrent operation. Low- and high-speed interfaces are considered as well as special problems such as control of simultaneous sampling of analog signals.

In the selection of papers in this part, note that emphasis has been placed on input/output operations rather than on basic instructions, registers, and special functions that various minicomputers may carry out. The importance of these latter quantities should not be underestimated. In fact, the computational capability and speed of response of the minicomputer is determined by these quantities. Selection of a minicomputer for a particular application must take into account the demands of the application in order to choose a machine with an appropriate instruction set, register organization, etc. Another major consideration not discussed is the organization of fast memory and the manner in which this memory is addressed. This includes considerations of direct and indirect addressing, indexing, use of base registers, and tradeoffs in various word-length machines. These too are critical factors in the selection of the minicomputer. The bibliography has been provided so that topics such as these can be pursued in more depth.

Because of the importance of reliable low-cost interfacing of special purpose devices to the computer, however, the organization of input/output is critical. Hence the last three papers were selected in order to illustrate the problem, the solutions available, and the actual systems engineering that is involved in mating a minicomputer to an application.

Bibliography

[1] "Macro modularity: a design concept to end computer generation gaps," W. L. Arbuckle and R. C. Mattson, *Comput. Des.*, Aug. 1970, pp. 69–73.

[2] "A new architecture for mini-computers—the DEC PDP-11," G. Bell, R. Cady, H. McFarland, B. Delagi, J. O'Laughlin, and R. Noonan, *AFIPS Conf. Proc., Vol. 36, 1970 Spring Joint Comput. Conf.*, pp. 657–675.

[3] "Comparative criteria for minicomputers," J. L. Butler, *Instrum. Technol.*, Oct. 1970, pp. 67–82.

[4] "Computer instruction repertoire—time for a change," C. C. Church, *AFIPS Conf. Proc., Vol. 36, 1970 Spring Joint Comput. Conf.*, pp. 343–349.

[5] "Evolution breeds a minicomputer that can take on its big brother," R. J. Clayton *et al.*, *Electronics*, Oct. 11, 1971, pp. 62–66.

[6] "The design of a 32 bit minicomputer utilizing LSI technology," W. F. Dawson and R. Edry, *Proc. Computer Designers Conf.*, 1971.

[7] "Nova can't lose its instructions," E. D. DeCastro, H. Burkhardt, and R. G. Sogge, *Electronics*, Dec. 9, 1968, pp. 76–82.

[8] "System ten—a new approach to multiprogramming," R. V. Dickinson and W. K. Orr, *AFIPS Conf. Proc., Vol. 37, 1970 Fall Joint Comput. Conf.*, pp. 181–186.

[9] "Microprogramming: future prospects and trends," M. J. Flynn, *1971 IEEE Int. Conv. Dig.*, pp. 318–319.

[10] "Security considerations in process computer interface design," J. W. Garrett, *Instrum. Contr. Syst.*, June 1971.

[11] "'Cache' turns up a treasure," D. H. Gibson and W. L. Shevel, *Electronics*, Oct. 13, 1969, pp. 105–107.

[12] "Standard LSI chips breed a fast new series of minicomputers," R. Gruner, L. Seligman, and J. Sutton, *Electronics*, Nov. 9, 1970, pp. 64–69.

[13] "How hardware responds to software," T. J. Harrison, *Contr. Eng.*, vol. 14, Dec. 1967, pp. 65–70.

[14] "The mini-computer—a new approach to computer design," D. C. Hitt, G. H. Ottaway, and R. W. Shirk, *AFIPS Conf. Proc., Vol. 33, Pt. 1, 1968 Fall Joint Comput. Conf.*, pp. 655–662.

[15] "Architecture for large computer systems," G. L. Hollander, *Comput. Des.*, Dec. 1967, pp. 53–59.

[16] "A standardized data highway for on-line computer applications," I. N. Hooton and R. C. M. Barnes, *AFIPS Conf. Proc., Vol. 33, Pt. 2, 1968 Fall Joint Comput. Conf.*, pp. 1077–1087.

[17] "Common bus structure for minicomputers improves I-O flexibility," P. Janson, *Contr. Eng.*, vol. 18, Jan. 1971, pp. 50–53.

[18] "Magnetic bubbles—a technology in the making," H. R. Karp, *Electronics*, Sept. 1, 1969, pp. 83–87.

[19] "What is a minicomputer," M. A. Keyes, *1970 Proc. Joint Automat. Contr. Conf.*, pp. 187–190.

[20] "Computer architechture for process control," R. A. Klososky, *IEEE Trans. Ind. Electron. Contr. Instrum.*, vol. IECI-17, June 1970, pp. 277–281.

[21] "A medium-scale hybrid interface," G. P. Marston and J. S. MacDonald, *Simulation*, May 1968, pp. 225–233.

[22] "A serial input/output scheme for small computers," J. D. Meng, *Comput. Des.*, Mar. 1970, pp. 71–75.

[23] "The technical ins and outs of computerized numerical control," P. G. Mesniaeff, *Contr. Eng.*, Mar. 1971, pp. 65–84.

[24] "Minicomputers," J. Murphy, *Mod. Data*, June 1971, pp. 58–71.

[25] "The system logic and usage recorder," R. W. Murphy, *AFIPS Conf. Proc., Vol. 35, 1969 Fall Joint Comput. Conf.*, pp. 219–229.

[26] "Maturing minicomputers," C. Newport, *Honeywell Comput. J.*, vol. 5, no. 2, 1971, pp. 31–35.

[27] "Portable computer process controller is self-contained," T. J. Pemberton and E. C. Miller, *Oil Gas J.*, July 19, 1971, p. 65.

[28] "State-of-art survey of current micro-programmed computers," C. V. Ramamoorthy, *1971 IEEE Int. Conv. Dig.*, pp. 312–313.

[29] "The input/output architecture of minicomputers," R. Rinder, *Datamation*, May 1970, pp. 119–124.

[30] "Peripherals expand your mini's capabilities," G. Saviers, *Electron. Des.*, June 10, 1971, pp. 72–76.

[31] "Making a minicomputer superfast," L. Seligman, *Electronics*, Nov. 10, 1969, pp. 116–119.

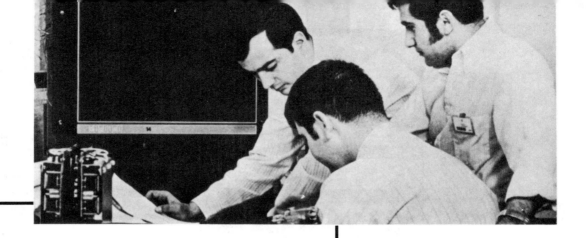

Repetitive control systems for assembly lines for mass-produced goods, for example, have traditionally used large relay panels for the control of machine functions. Some success has been had with solid-state controllers, but these are often special-purpose units, expensive to install and difficult to maintain. Still another approach is to use a programmable solid-state controller that operates like a general-purpose computer but is designed with industrial repetitive control in mind. The controller is easy to engineer and to program, and exhibits increased reliability over the relays it replaces.

The Black Box: Programmable Logic for Repetitive Control

JOHN M. HOLZER JR., DONALD E. CHACE, and ALAN W. RICKETTS JR., Digital Equipment Corp.

A little over a year ago the automotive industry indicated an interest in seeing specifications for a logical controller that would perform the functions of repetitive control that are now handled by relay panels. As a result of this interest, Digital Equipment Corp. recently introduced a solid-state programmable logical controller, the PDP-14 (CtE, March, p. 53). The purpose of this article is to show how the DEC logical controller performs repetitive control and to show how it can be engineered and programmed without specialized knowledge of computer programming or solid-state electronics.

The basic controller, Figure 1, resembles a computer in that it contains input-output interfaces, a control unit, and a memory. However, there are several important differences. First, the control unit is simplified so that programming is reduced to a few simple instructions. Second, the interfaces are designed to accept 120-Vac line inputs such as might be derived from limit switches, and the outputs are similarly 120-Vac with sufficient (500 VA) capacity to drive solenoids or contactors. Third, the memory is nonvolatile; that is to say, it is a read-only memory containing all the instructions for the operations un-

der control. It cannot be destroyed electrically but it can be altered by the insertion of a new set of wires.

Why solid-state logical control?

There are perhaps two major advantages of the logical controller over relays. Since it has no moving parts, a solid-state controller will be inherently more reliable than a relay panel. Because all the instructions are contained in a mechanically alterable read-only memory (ROM), alteration or expansion is a simple matter. With a relay panel the user must often install a completely new panel. The logical controller also has some advantages over the general-purpose computer in that it has a simple instruction set and no Teletype input-output, and the memory is not electrically alterable and hence not subject to interference.

The design of the unit reflects the DEC philosophy of only enough hardware to do the job, standard logic modules wherever possible, stringent production testing, and incorporation of the controller into a rugged enclosure, Figure 2. Extensive shielding effectively combats any possible radio frequency interference. The result is a unit that is relatively inexpensive ($4,900 for a basic controller), inexpensive to oper-

Reprinted with permission from *Contr. Eng.*, vol. 16, pp. 61–65, May 1969.

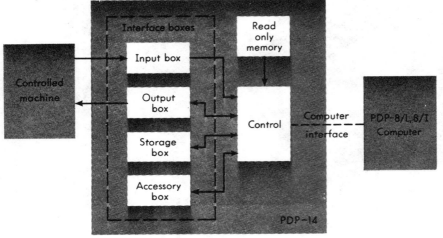

FIG. 1. The logical controller will control a repetitive machine through standard 120 Vac interfaces or boxes. The interface to a general-purpose computer may be used for supervisory control or for checkout of read-only memory programs. Intermediate storage is provided by a storage box containing flipflops. Timing functions may be handled by an appropriate accessory box.

FIG. 2. Basic home for the PDP-14 is a NEMA-12 standard enclosure. The controller is in the black box and above are the input-output and accessory boxes. Other equipment in in the upper half of the enclosure are customer-supplied motor-starters, contactors, and so on.

ate, and easily expandable by adding further modules.

An equally important part of the DEC philosophy is that engineering and programming should be such that the controller can easily be implemented by an engineer without experience in programming or solid-state equipment. Training time for a control engineer with no previous experience is expected to be about two or three days. Once trained, the engineer should be able to design a PDP-14 system, check it out fully, and have it operational in one quarter of the time necessary for a comparable relay system.

The hardware of programmable logic

The PDP-14 system can be regarded as consisting of three basic units: the input-output interfaces or boxes, the control unit, and the memory, Figure 1. The input boxes accept 120-Vac inputs from two-state sensing devices such as limit switches, pushbuttons, pressure switches, and so on. These inputs are converted by the input boxes into signals suitable for input to the control unit. The output boxes perform the reverse function in that they convert the output of the control unit into 120-Vac outputs capable of driving solenoids, contactors, small motors, etc.

The control unit, Figure 3, operates in a fashion analogous to scanning a relay diagram rung by rung. Each rung of the relay ladder contains a specific group of sensed input conditions that must be satisfied to cause a change in the condition of an output. Thus the ROM will contain several groups of instructions corresponding to the rungs of a ladder. The ROM directs the control to select each input in a group and test it. The ROM instructions also specify what the result of the test should be to effect a change in the

state of the outputs contained in the group. The control unit directs any required change in the output. The control then continues to the next group of inputs and outputs and repeats the process, Figure 4. Since the execution time for one instruction is nominally 20 microsec, one complete cycle through a 2,000-instruction program will only take 40 millisec, which is faster than the response of just one or two control relays.

For storage, the PDP-14 uses a braided-wire magnetic read-only memory developed by Memory Technology, Inc., Waltham, Mass., Figure 5. The memory is available in 1K blocks up to a maximum of 4K. The basic 1,024-word, 12-bit memory is built with 96 small, 1¼ by ¾-in. transformer cores, arranged in eight blocks of 12 bits each. Through each group of eight run 128 bit wires to provide the 1,024-word capacity. This means that readout is not by word but by groups of eight words. However, this technique reduces the number of wires threaded through each core and also the total number of cores needed.

Alterability of the memory is achieved by shaping the transformer cores into two sets of U-shaped halves that can be mounted in frames as the two "bread" sections of a sandwich, Figure 6. The bit wires are then woven on a special loom, potted in a silicone rubber, and placed between the two sets of transformer cores. The memory may be altered by clipping the ends of the bit wires at the edge of the braids, or by laying new wires over the potted set and leading them manually through the appropriate cores. However, for alternative programs, such as diagnostic routines, a completely new braid can be dropped into the sandwich in a matter of minutes. The cost is $290.

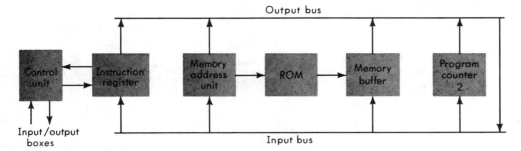

FIG. 3. In operation the memory address unit acts as a program counter to gate instructions to the instruction register via the the memory buffer. The control unit decodes the instructions and performs all the necessary gating functions. A second program counter controls the execution of subroutines.

Assembly Language Instructions

Instruction	Purpose
Test Group	
TXN 00	Test input X00 for the ON state
TXF 01	Test input X01 for the OFF state
TYN 02	Test output Y02 for the ON state
TYF 03	Test output Y03 for the OFF state
Set Group	
SYN 04	Set output Y04 to the ON state
SYF 05	Set Y05 to the OFF state
Jump Group	
JFN 40	Jump to location 40 if the test flipflop is on.
JFF 40	Jump to location 40 if the test flipflop is off.
JMP	Jump unconditionally to location 40. The
40	address of the jump-to location is stored in the location following the jump location.

FIG. 4. Control programs are made up of disjointed instruction groups. Each group solves a Boolean equation and sets an output either off or on. The last instruction in a group is a jump to the next group. The last instruction in the last group is a jump to the start of the first group, thus closing the loop. Cycles of the loop are made at high speed—1,000 instructions can be cycled through in a maximum of 20 millisec.

In addition to the low cost of changing the ROM, there is a particular advantage of the woven-wire memory for an industrial environment. The memory's output voltages are of the order of 2-3 volts, giving it an extremely high signal-to-noise ratio. Thus special rfi screening techniques are not necessary.

The ROM is tailored for a specific set of control functions by wiring it especially for those functions. This is analogous to programming a conventional general-purpose digital computer. The procedure is:

• Determine the machine functions required, develop a sequence chart, and list all input sensors and outputs.

• List all the testing and setting operations needed for control in a symbolic assembly language. This assembly is done on a PDP-8 computer.

• Check the assembly language program using a simulation program contained in the PDP-8. The simulation is both static and dynamic. Detected errors can be changed rapidly.

• Attach the PDP-8 to the PDP-14, which in turn is connected to the actual machine equipment. The PDP-8 functions as a ROM for the PDP-14, enabling a program check under actual working conditions.

• Generate a paper tape from the assembly listing contained in the PDP-8. This tape will control the loom that will weave the braid for the PDP-14 ROM.

• Manufacture of the ROM will be undertaken by DEC on a two-week turn-around basis. Upon receiving the wired ROM, the user can insert it in the PDP-14 directly and put the machine and controller into operation without further checkout.

Programming the black box

Three elements form the PDP-14 software package: a symbolic assembly language, a compiler that translates Boolean equations into machine instructions, and a simulation program for on- and off-line debugging. All three programs are used on a PDP-8 computer. The final output from the PDP-8 is a tape that controls the loom that in turn weaves the wire braid for the ROM of the PDP-14.

Most users will program with the compiler, BOOL-14, with only very sophisticated systems needing assembly language programming. The following description of the assembly language is included to show the simplicity of the PDP-14.

The assembly language, PAL-14, consists of three

FIG 5. All the controller modules plug into a large motherboard. At left are the connectors for the input-output boxes, in the center the controller logic (red modules), and at right the memory modules (green). The unoccupied slots are for further input-output connectors and memory modules.

FIG. 6. To change the read-only memory, the memory module is disassembled so that the wire braid (white) can be lifted off the cores and replaced by a new braid. The entire operation takes only a few minutes. The braid shown here is a mockup version and does not contain any wires.

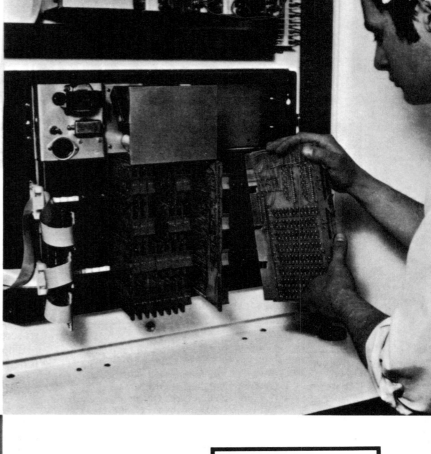

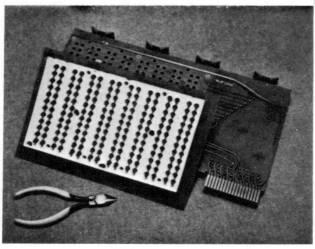

FIG. 8. The sequence of programming to generate the ROM braid starts with the Boolean equations specified by the designer (A). A compiler used on a PDP-8 produces an assembly listing of the ROM program (B). This program can be input to a simulator for checking. Here (C) a request was made for a truth-table output. The omission of X15 from the request caused an error message to be printed. The correct result appears below (D).

(A) Y6=(X6*X14)+(/X7*/X15)

(B)
Location	Content	Comment
0040:	TXF 6	
0041:	TXF 14	
0042:	JFF 46	
0043:	TXN 7	
0044:	TXN 15	
0045:	JFN 51	
0046:	SYN 6	
0047:	JMP	
0050:	40	
0051:	SYF 6	
0052:	JMP	
0053:	40	

(C)
SIM-14 output	Comment
.TA6	User types
.X6	request for
.X7	truth table
.X14	
.SA0	
A X006	List of
B X007	variables
C X014	
ABC	Incorrect
X015 E	truth table—
000=1	input 15
X015 E	not specified
001=1	
X015 E	
010=0	
X015 E	
011=0	
X015 E	
100=1	
101=1	
X015 E	
110=0	
111=1	

(D)
.TA6	Request re-
.X6	typed including
.X14	X15
.X7	
.X15	
.SA0	
A X006	List of
B X014	variables
C X007	
D X015	
ABCD	Correct
0000=1	truth table
0001=0	
0010=0	
0011=0	
0100=1	
0101=0	
0110=0	
0111=0	
1000=1	
1001=0	
1010=0	
1011=0	
1100=1	
1101=1	
1110=1	
1111=1	

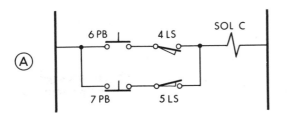

(B) Inputs:
$$\begin{cases} 6\,PB\,(n/o) & X6 \\ 7\,PB\,(n/o) & X7 \\ 4\,LS\,(n/o) & X14 \\ 5\,LS\,(n/o) & X15 \end{cases}$$
Output: SOL C   Y6

FIG. 7. Translation from a relay ladder diagram (A) is made by listing all switches as inputs and all actuated devices as outputs with symbolic labels (B). The switches become inputs wired as parallel normally open switches to the PDP-14. The outputs are also wired directly from the controller.

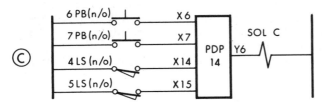

basic sets of instructions: test input or output, set output, and jump instructions (table, page 63). The test instructions sample the state of an input or output for the ON or OFF state. The set instructions direct the controller to set an output to either state. Only outputs may be set. Jump instructions cause a departure from the normal sequential execution to allow a program to branch and flexibly select groups of inputs. Conditional jump instructions transfer control to any memory location; they are normally used to jump from the end of one function to the beginning of the next function.

There are only nine instructions in the PDP-14 assembly language. But the programming may be simplified even more with the BOOL-14 compiler, which will accept control functions stated in terms of Boolean equations employing PDP-14 input-output symbols. Using a PDP-8 with Teletype input, the engineer types in the equations and receives a printout of the program in assembly language, Figure 8. BOOL-14 will be available in June.

The debugging aid for the controller is SIM-14, a PDP-8-based simulator. SIM-14 can be used in a local mode to check programs for errors by verifying equations and consulting truth tables. Most importantly, SIM-14 can generate the machine sequence that will result from the PDP-14 program. Thus the complete system design can be checked off-line. In an on-line mode the PDP-8 can connect to the controller and act as its memory. In this way the operation of the program and the machine can be checked to the designer's complete satisfaction before the memory braid is manufactured. No further testing is necessary.

In operation, SIM-14 is loaded into the PDP-8 before the user types in his PDP-14 program. To verify an equation, the user supplies the identity of the variables of the equation, their states, and the starting address of the equation. SIM-14 responds by typing the values of the output based on the inputs. To generate a truth table the user identifies the variables associated with the output and SIM-14 types a binary array to indicate the states of the variables that yield the output, Figure 8.

Once all the equations have been checked, suitable input values may be specified to run the complete program in a local mode. SIM-14 will type any resultant change in the state of an output. This process validates the user's control system design.

In the on-line mode of SIM-14 operation, the PDP-8 is connected to the PDP-14 as the memory of the controller. Both the PDP-14 and its attendant machine can be operated exactly as though the PDP-14 contained an actual ROM. This combination of on- and off-line testing will ensure that the manufactured braid will be free from design errors.

Programming in easy stages

As an example of programming the PDP-14, consider a simple solenoid energizing circuit, Figure 7.

Solenoid C will be energized if pushbutton 6 and limit switch 4 are on, or if pushbutton 7 and limit switch 5 are both off. Otherwise solenoid C will be deenergized. When wiring the PDP-14, no distinction is made between normally open and normally closed contacts. All contacts are wired normally open, and the normally open and normally closed states are accounted for by the programming.

Thus the first stage in design is to allocate an input to each limit switch and an output to each actuated device—in this case only solenoid 6, Figure 7B. Now output Y6 can be expressed in terms of the inputs as a Boolean equation, Figure 8A. Using the PDP-8, this equation is compiled to give an assembly language listing, Figure 8B. Note that normally open contacts are tested to see if they are off. The instruction TXF 6, for example, tests to see if pushbutton 6 is off. If pushbutton 6 were to be normally closed, the instruction would be TXN 6, which would test if the input were on. Similarly, pushbutton 7 and limit switch 5 are tested by TXN instructions. In this way the PDP-14 can handle normally open and closed contacts even though all switching devices are wired normally open.

After obtaining the program listing the user can call upon SIM-14 to check his program. In Figure 8C the off-line mode of SIM-14 has generated a truth table to check the original logic. If a mistake is made in using SIM-14 (as in Figure 8C, where the initial request for a truth table listing did not specify X15), the program will indicate the error.

When the designer is certain that the program is correct he may switch to the on-line mode and control the actual operation by executing the program contained in the PDP-8. Finally, when the program is dynamically correct, the PDP-8 will produce a paper tape from which the memory braid can be woven. All program checks are performed before any hardware is assembled, so that when the memory braid is manufactured it can be put in the controller and used directly without further testing.

Whither the black box?

Currently a PDP-14 is being used in a production environment to control an xy-table milling machine for an automobile manufacturer. It is expected to find wide application in any industrial process where the control operations can be expressed in terms of relay ladder networks or Boolean equations. The PDP-14 is in fact a black box that solves Boolean equations more efficiently, more reliably, and more economically than relay panels.

In the future this type of logical controller may lead to a machine-monitoring system wherein each black box controls its own bank of machine tools and keeps a computer informed of its progress. Thus an entire plant or assembly line may be placed under computer supervision. This is perhaps the first step along the road to a complete information and control system for discrete manufacturing processes. □

A minicomputer is a small, low priced general computer that is generally purchased outright (not leased) and used for a dedicated application. The "mini" in minicomputer is more descriptive of its price rather than its physical size or capability. Technological advances, permitting relatively powerful computers to be built and sold in the $3,000. to $20,000. price range, have created the large minicomputer market.

MINICOMPUTER ARCHITECTURE

By William H. Roberts

Reprinted from *IEEE Comput. Group News*, vol. 3, pp. 4–9, July/Aug. 1970.

Memories

As the prices of these computers continue to decrease, the size of the market will increase more rapidly as more applications evolve and computers enter fields previously untouched by digital computers.

The main factors which have helped to lower the cost of computers to the minicomputer category are the integrated circuit, the short word length, and a restricted instruction repertoire.

The advent of the integrated circuit and now MSI devices has done much to reduce both the size and cost of computers and at the same time increase their speed. Ten years ago, circuits equivalent to today's integrated circuit cost the computer manufacturer $10.00 or more and required ten times the mounting area. Computers with capabilities comparable to the CDC 160A which would require half of a rack, now occupy two or three printed circuit boards, such as in the case with the General Automation SPC-12. MSI devices which are just now beginning to be used will further reduce the size and cost of minicomputers.

The shorter word length, which is a characteristic of minicomputers, has helped to reduce the cost by lopping off a number of bits from the memory, registers, adder and transfer paths of the longer word lengths found in larger more expensive machines. Minicomputers rarely require the longer word length for data; applications such as process or machine control, data collection, and data communication can get along with word lengths of 16 bits or less. In cases where longer data word length is required, it is achieved by programmed double precision, at some loss of performance. The shorter word length does create a problem in the instruction formats, but ingeniously developed addressing techniques have helped to squeeze powerful instructions into the short word. Here again, performance is sacrificed when the short word length proves too confining for addressing by use of a second memory access for a full address. A small number of instructions also help to reduce the number of bits required in the instruction word.

Another important characteristic of minicomputers which aids in keeping the cost low is the small limited instruction repertoire. Floating point arithmetic, decimal arithmetic, searches, and byte manipulating instructions found in larger machines such as System 360 are not found in the smaller minicomputers. Multiply and divide are often missing, although sometimes they are provided as a hardware option. Some of the newer minicomputers provide only single position shift instructions rather than the more common multiple position shifts.

In general, minicomputers have the same basic elements found in their larger counterparts. A computer usually has a core memory, a central processing unit (CPU), input/output and a control panel. As ASR-33 teletype is the primary input/output device. The design of minicomputers is flexible and highly modular with a variety of optional hardware that can be incorporated to produce a system specific to a user's requirements.

Core memory for minicomputers is usually organized into 4K modules with word lengths of 8, 12, or 16 bits. Memory cycle times range between 1 and 3 microseconds. The maximum core memory size is usually 65K words, although sometimes limited to 16K or 32K by the format of the instruction address. Module sizes of 1K and 2K are generally available for OEM dedicated applications with small programs. Microprogrammed computers, such as the Micro Systems MICRO 800 require very little if any core memory because of the large number of operational registers and the fact that the program resides in a read only control memory.

Data is transferred between memory and the central processor via a memory bus. One or more Direct Memory Access (DMA) channels or controllers may also communicate with memory over this same bus. Memory request conflicts between the CPU and DMA are settled in favor of the DMA by some priority determination logic. Minicomputers cannot afford the luxury of multi-ports to memory and therefore have only a single memory bus. Memory timing is generally performed in the CPU, and with no overlap memory operations, instruction execution times are based on memory cycle times.

Most minicomputers being designed today make use of 3-wire, 3D organizations with 20-mil cores in a planar array. The current state of the art allows for packaging a one microsecond cycle time, 4K by 16-bit memory on as little as 200 square inches of printed circuit board. These one or two board designs permit easy field expansion of the memory system, merely by plugging the memory into board positions which have been prewired to the memory bus.

Many manufacturers provide one or two optional memory parity bits, but the trend seems to be toward designs which preclude this option. In some cases 16-bit memories are addressable to the 8-bit byte level which is very valuable for data communication applications. Byte addressing can be done by instructions which reference left and right bytes of the word or by treating memory as a byte memory with each byte having an address. The later method is the preferred method since it allows indexing of byte addresses.

Central Processing Unit

Until recent years, minicomputers have incorporated one or two accumulations with one or two index registers. Recently, there has been more variety available in the register configuration of the machine including machines without index registers (Computer Automation PDC-808) and machines with multiple general purpose registers such as found in System 360, Nova, and PDP-11. The low cost of integrated circuit scratch pad memories will probably increase the number of multi-register type of organizations, except for the very small minicomputers.

Most minicomputers are single address, binary, with negative numbers expressed in two's complement notation. Most 16-bit machines use one word instructions, but some of the new designs make use of a second or third word for data or full addresses. Most 8-bit machines operate similarly to the 16-bit machines by using two 8-bit words per instruction, but having the added flexibility of one and three word instructions.

The instruction format for machines having one or two operational registers contains a 4 or 5-bit operation code, a 3-bit addressing mode, and 8 or 9-bits of memory address. The memory addressing mode describes the variety of ways which can be used to determine the address of the data to be transferred to or from the core memory. The address field in most single word instructions is not large enough to directly address the complete contents of memory, but generally contains only 8 to 10-bits which describe some portion of the memory. Where a longer memory address of 15 or 16-bits is required, it is obtained from the contents of a register, the second word of an instruction, or an indirect address in memory. The latter two techniques usually add one memory cycle time to the instruction execution but permit addressing all of the memory. Some of the commonly used addressing techniques are categorized below:

Directed Addressing

Some computers divide memory into fixed pages of 256 or 512 words and allow direct addressing the first page.

Current Page

In addition to being able to address page 0, paging type memory addressing schemes also allow addressing of the page in which the current instruction resides.

Relative Direct

A technique which is coming into vogue, and is more popular than current page addressing, is to have a floating page which represents the 128 or 256 memory locations before and after the address of the current instruction. Such a scheme makes it easier to program because the programmer is not concerned with where his program resides relative to page boundaries; only that the memory reference is within range of the current instruction. This also makes it easier to relocate programs without extensive desectorizing at load time.

Indirect Addressing

Indirect addressing consists of reading a memory location which is directly addressable and using the contents of the location as the effective memory address. Indirect addressing may be used as a programming technique or merely as a means of obtaining a full length memory address.

Indexed Addressing

Indexing may be used in either direct or indirect addressing and adds the contents of the index register to the direct or indirect address. In some computers, such as the Micro Systems 810 and the DED PDP-11, the index register may contain the entire address, thereby eliminating the need of an addressing field in the instruction. In some of the newer computers, the contents of the index register may be automatically incremented or decremented. The auto-indexing used in the Data General, Nova and DEC PDP-11, for example, allows for efficient operation when operating with sequential locations and memory.

Immediate Addressing

A powerful addressing technique being used more often in mini computers places the operand in the address field of the instruction or in a second word of the instruction, thereby eliminating the need for an addressing field. Minicomputers involved in control applications can make good use of the literals contained in the instruction itself.

Minicomputers normally have a number of CPU options which will allow minimizing hardware necessary for specific applications.

REAL-TIME CLOCK is generally a counter in memory or hardware which

Panels

Input/Output

is decremented or incremented at rates such as 1KC or the line frequency.

POWER FAIL INTERRUPT provides a CPU interrupt upon impending loss of primary power, thus permitting a software routine to save all registers and perform any necessary shutdown.

AUTOMATIC RESTART, normally combined with the power fail interrupt, provides an interrupt for orderly startup of the computer when power is re-applied.

MEMORY PARITY provides one or more parity bits for checking memory read operations.

The CONTROL PANEL, which provides for register, memory entry, and display, is becoming more and more a processor option for OEM dedicated CPU's.

AUTOLOAD CAPABILITY, which provides for loading of a bootstrap program from an input device (or a communications line), is becoming an available option, especially with microprogrammed organization.

Interrupt systems for minicomputers are quite extensive because of the real time environment in which they are used. Internal interrupts include power fail, real time clock, memory protect, or some machine fault. External interrupts are associated with device controllers or are general purpose interrupt lines. Under program control, they can be individually armed and enabled. An armed interrupt allows an interrupt signal to be generated while one which is disarmed is not generated and therefore not remembered. An enabled interrupt signal allows interruption of the CPU when it achieves priority and, if disabled, must wait until the program enables it.

When the CPU recognizes the interrupt, it either executes an instruction from a memory location specified by the interrupt or uses the contents of the memory location as the address for a forced subroutine jump. In addition, all or a selected number of operational registers can be automatically stored in a reversed area of memory or in a pushdown stack (MAC 16, MICRO 812). Lower priority interrupts are locked out until enabled by the interrupt subroutine. Storing of the program counter and any processor status will allow for re-entrant interrupts (PDP-11).

The control panel is a major element of minicomputers which more and more are becoming expendable for dedicated applications in the interest of lowering system costs. Many new minicomputers have plug-in panels which are not needed for program running. The use of the control panel for program debugging is questionable since most computers have software debug packages which provide the same capability as obtained from the control panel. The panel is probably required for maintenance and could be plugged in by field maintenance personnel as required.

The capabilities available from the front panel include display and entry of selected operational registers and memory. The displays may include all registers, the program counter, and a selected register or selected registers. Control of single instruction execution, run, halt and panel interrupt are generally provided.

The I/O concept changes drastically as the size and cost of the computer are reduced. It is not uncommon in a minicomputer to find controllers for such peripheral devices as disks or tapes to be located a few board slots away from the CPU itself rather than in the next card chassis or "halfway down the room." Minicomputers require minicontrollers to keep the cost of peripheral interfaces in line with the cost of the computer. Quite often, these controllers consist of only a single printed circuit board which is housed in the same cabinet or card chassis as the CPU and its memory. This situation will become more pronounced as the size of the CPU and peripheral interfaces is decreased through MSI and LSI devices.

The architecture of a minicomputer should take this situation into account. A good example of how this can be done is illustrated by the DEC PDP-11 which treats registers in peripheral controllers as addressable memory and causes these controllers to interface directly with the computer's memory bus. This combined memory and I/O bus provide for CPU-memory transfers, CPU-peripheral device transfers for control and status, and peripheral device-memory transfers for direct memory I/O transfers. The use of a single I/O for peripheral devices, rather than one for control and one for DMA transfers, can produce significant cost savings in the peripheral controllers since bus interfacing is becoming a larger portion of the total circuitry required.

Future Developments

The minicomputer market will continue to grow at an ever increasing rate in the future years. Technological advances and volume production will cause further reduction in prices and/or increased capability. With decreased size and cost, it will be necessary to define a new category of computers: the "mini minicomputer" or the "micro computer" which will sell for $1,000-$2,000. The continual decrease in cost of these computers and their use as components in OEM equipment will cause the mini computer to look less like a portion of the general purpose computer industry and more like a portion of the electronic equipment market. Eventually, these computers will find their way into the consumer product market.

The architecture of mini- and microcomputers and their implementation techniques will change drastically during the next five years. Up to now, the organization of computer hardware has not been strongly dependent on the circuit, upon which it was implemented. With LSI and MSI semiconductor technology, this pattern must change. Computer designs must make use of these complex circuits if the price performance is to improve and be competitive. Registers, adders, shifters, and data path portions of the computer represent ordered arrays of logic and can be implemented with off-the-shelf MSI or LSI components. Even today, functional elements capable of producing all the required logical and arithmetic functions of two variables for a 4-bit slice are readily available. These elements also incorporate a full look-ahead carry scheme thereby reducing the addition and subtraction to that of logical operations. The computer designer's freedom is being constrained by the available MSI circuitry. This is especially true in minicomputer designs where the number of devices must be kept small and the required architecture closely fits that provided by available circuits. This fact will be compounded as MSI circuit complexity increases to include more and more of a computer contained in a single device.

The control circuitry of the minicomputer represents an entirely different situation. It is here that the manufacturer must exert his own individuality and supply a functional capability that sets him apart from his rivals. The normal control circuitry of a computer consists of very irregular hodge-podge logic which does not readily lend itself to taking advantages of off-the-shelf MSI and LSI circuitry. The minicomputer manufacturer could procure customized LSI circuitry but this would require that the semiconductor manufacturer be responsive to the customer with numerous low output production of highly specialized devices. The per unit cost to the minicomputer manufacturer would be quite high due to his inability to spread initial cost over many units. This would severely limit the off-the-shelf capabilities of both the user and manufacturer. Another severe problem would be that of providing second sourcing for the customized devices.

The use of a control memory technique appears to offer a useful approach to reducing the amount of random logic required in implementing the control section of a minicomputer. Even today, the off-the-shelf MSI components which will make up the data path of computers are ideally suited for microprogram control since they generally have coded control lines which can be driven directly from the output of the control memory. These lines control input selection, functional capability, register select, etc. Read only memories with 512 or 1024 bits per device are available today. It is predicted that by 1973 bipolar read-only memories of 4K bits and a cost of 1¢ per bit are achievable. Because of the ordered logic and the fact that specific patterns are generally handled as a final metalization process, the microprogrammed approach to computer architecture can take advantage of the LSI circuitry without the problems of customized control logic. Developments of electrically alterable read only memories will further help to promote the use of microprogram control and reduce the cost of read only memories. With such a memory semiconductor manufacturers will be able to produce and test memories containing all 1-bits, leaving the customizing to be done by customers.

Microprogramming should play a major role in future minicomputers. The advantages of microprogramming are seen as greater flexibility, more regular structure, and lower developmental costs. Although the basic hardware of many minicomputers may be similar in organization, they will differ greatly in their architecture due to the flexibility afforded by microprogram control. These computers will incorporate such features as push-down stacks, elaborate interrupt handling, multiply, divide, multi-precision, and floating point operations. Powerful instructions, heretofore not found in inexpensive computers such as moves, searches, translates, and floating point operations, will be found in minicomputers. I/O, other than high performance direct memory access channels, will also take advantage of read only memory control. In data communication applications, the I/O will be capable of handling data link protocol procedures, error checking, and encoding, data echoing, and code translation.

The microprogram organization of minicomputers will allow the computer architecture to be tuned for particular applications. A basic architecture and instruction set may have add-on capabilities which enhance the throughput and price/performance for a specific application such as mini-time sharing, data communications, laboratory automation, process control, etc. An interesting method of tuning the computer for a particular application is to allow the user to do his own microprogramming—either as an addition to the basic architecture or by creating his own architecture from the basic microprogrammable hardware.

Summary

In the past, the architecture of minicomputers has been dictated by the semiconductor devices only to the extent of the cost of the devices. Machines which will be designed in the next few years will be more constrained by available MSI devices. Looking into the future five years from now, the computer architecture will not be constrained by available devices since it will be implemented on a microprogrammed "inner-computer" which is supplied by the semiconductor houses. With this type of system, minicomputer architecture will be exciting and dynamic.

MINICOMPUTER I/O AND PERIPHERALS

by Ed Holland

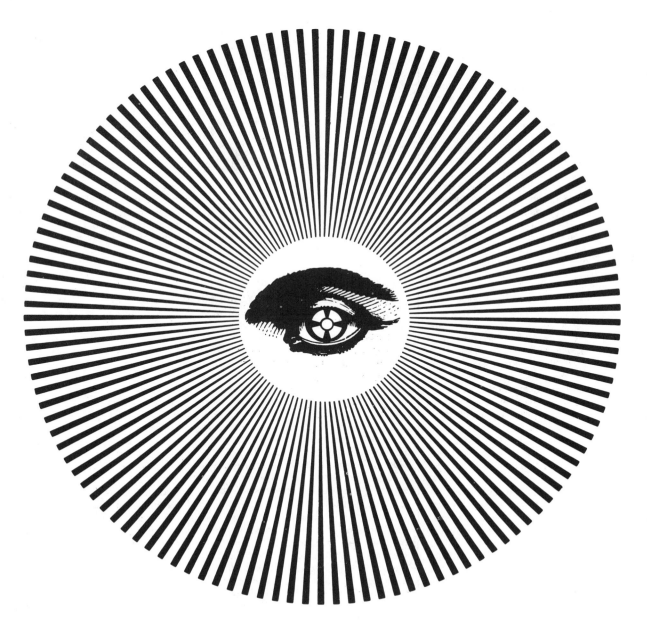

Reprinted from *IEEE Comput. Group News*, vol. 3, pp. 10–14, July/Aug. 1970.

MINICOMPUTER I/O AND PERIPHERALS

Most of the popularity of minicomputers is attributable to the ability of a minicomputer system to solve a problem with minimum total cost. The low cost of minicomputer main frames and typically low software costs are very important components of the total system. These subjects are covered in detail in other papers in this issue.

The cost of peripherals used in the minicomputer system, and the cost of interfacing the minicomputer to other system hardware (e.g., instrumentation, machine tools, etc.) are the remaining factors in the minimization of total system cost. This article addresses itself to the questions of minicomputers, peripherals and interfacing.

The I/O System of a minicomputer has an organization and implementation that is austere when compared to the I/O structure of an EDP computer. Much of the burden of I/O operations is carried by the programmer, since functions not done in hardware must be accomplished by software. However, this is not usually a big limitation in the use of a minicomputer system but instead often gives the user an advantage of flexibility when interfacing to a wide variety of devices. I/O software (I/O Drivers) are usually written once by the computer manufacturer and incorporated in the user's program as subroutines. Since much of the complex functions of device controllers are handled by software, device controllers are often contained on one printed circuit card, plugged into the computer mainframe. Usually these controllers are simple interfaces to a single peripheral device.

When considering peripherals for the minicomputer system, the cost/performance factor becomes a problem. There are "low-cost" peripherals having prices in the same range as minicomputer mainframes, but their information bandwidths are very narrow. High performance peripherals will often force system costs up to many times that of the mainframe. Tradeoffs between through-put and peripheral costs must be examined carefully.

MINICOMPUTER I/O CHANNELS

There are three methods of I/O transfer used in minicomputers. These are:
a) Programmed Data Transfer
b) Direct Memory Access
c) Multiplexer Channel

The direct memory access (DMA) is an option in most minicomputers but is not available in some of the lower priced units. The multiplexer channel is an option which is found in only a small number of minicomputers.

The programmed data transfer channel is the slowest but most flexible method of I/O transfer. Some form of interrupt system must be used with this method. Transfer takes place between an I/O Bus and one or more of the CPU registers. This is usually in the form of a parallel transfer of one computer word or one eight-bit byte. Because of the time required for subroutine overhead, a maximum of 30 to 40 thousand words per second is the upper limit for the highest priority device. Because of the probability of missed data, this form of transfer is not desirable for even medium-speed synchronous devices (i.e., magnetic tapes or card readers without full card buffering). Programmed Data Transfer is used for control of peripheral devices and for checking status. Its use is required where the computer must act on all incoming data as it is received.

Direct Memory Access (DMA) is usually an option costing in the range of 2 to 5 thousand dollars. The option allows one, two or sometimes more devices to make block transfers by "stealing" memory cycles from the running program at rates up to one word per memory cycle. Maximum DMA transfer rates from one half to more than one million words per second are typical.

Word count and memory address registers are usually contained in the DMA channel hardware, although sometimes they are located in the device controller. Transfer normally takes place between the device controller and memory without disturbing the CPU except that one memory cycle is lost (or "stolen") by the channel for each transfer. An interrupt is provided for the CPU when transfer of the block of data has been accomplished.

In contrast to standard practice in larger computers, chaining of block transfers is seldom found in minicomputer DMA channels; and scatter-gather operations are possible only on slow devices where the computer has time to initiate multiple transfers as the data is being transferred.

Medium to high speed synchronous devices like disks and magnetic tape often require the use of a DMA channel. In applications of analog-to-digital conversion and digital-to-analog output to a display (without storage), DMA is used extensively.

The Multiplexer or I/O Channel is much like the DMA except that 16 devices or more may be active and transferring at the same time. The word count and memory address registers are dedicated core locations. Maximum transfer rates are limited to 100 to 300 thousand words per second (total for all channels) due to the need to have up to three accesses to memory per word transferred. (One of the memory cycles is to decrement the word count and check if it has reached zero. Another memory cycle is to obtain the memory address and increment it and of course the third memory cycle is to transfer the data.)

Card readers, punches and line printers as well as slow magnetic tape may all make effective use of a multiplexer channel.

As we look at the history of small computers in the last ten years with the cost of hardware steadily decreasing, we see one type of register after another being removed from core (i.e., program counter, accumulators, index registers). This trend will probably soon extend to multiplexer word count and memory address registers. These registers will probably become part of future device controllers. In this way the user will pay for the hardware in proportion to what he needs. The number of memory cycles required will, of course, be reduced to one per data word transferred.

INTERRUPT SYSTEMS

A discussion of minicomputer I/O would not be complete without some consideration of the interrupt system.

In programmed data transfers, the main program execution must be interrupted to branch to a subroutine to process each word of I/O data. Since this is the dominant mode of I/O in the minicomputer, an order of magnitude more interrupts must be serviced to input or output the same quantity of data as in a large EDP computer where block transfers are the more common way to transfer data. Interrupt rates as high as one interrupt for each bit of data transferred over a serial interface have been used, although this is not common. With the heavy use of interrupts, one might expect highly developed interrupt systems; but in order to keep costs down, this is often not the case. As few as one hardware level of interrupt is used in some systems with priority being implemented by the order in which the device controllers are polled by the software service routine.

More than one level of interrupt priority is often an option, with between 16 and 256 allowed hardware levels. Transfer of command to the proper routine for service is accomplished by one or more of the following methods:

a) Polling device controller flags by software.
b) Execution of an instruction (usually a Jump Subroutine Indirect) in a dedicated location corresponding to the level of interrupt.
c) Device identified by a register containing the address of the last interrupting device.
d) Device controller identifies itself on software command by putting its address on an I/O Bus.

Hardware is included in the interrupt system to prevent other interrupts on the same or lower priority level until the level being serviced is released by command from the CPU. Also, all interrupts are held off during transfer of control both going into and coming out of a service routine. Temporary changes in hardware priority can usually be made by turning off one or more level for a time. When re-activating the level that has been suspended, the programmer might have the option to ignore or now recognize the request for interrupt generated during the period of suspension.

Automatic storing of the current machine status is included in some machines but in most cases the programmed service routines must save and restore the contents of all working registers used in the service routine.

INTERFACES AND TRANSMISSION LINES

Until very recently, people designing a device controller for a peripheral have had a real variety of interface circuits with which to communicate. With the freedom that discrete circuits allow, no two peripherals from different designers have used the same logic levels, or impedances; and certainly not the same signal definitions. Single-ended systems were used as well as balanced twisted-pair transmission lines.

As the latest generation of peripherals have been developed, the heavy use of integrated circuits in peripheral devices has rapidly brought about a change. A DTL or T²L gate is fast becoming a de facto interface standard for peripherals to be used with minicomputers.

If power gates are used in a system with twisted-pair lines terminated in a low impedance approximating that of the line, the length of cable normally required in a minicomputer system can be driven with a workable level of noise immunity. The small number of peripherals on a minicomputer system is a big factor in keeping the noise generated by the system down and keeping the cable runs short. The relatively small amount of power required by a typical mini system usually keeps the whole system on the same power circuit so that common-mode power line noise problems are reduced over those encountered in large EDP installations.

The integrated circuit manufacturers have been quick to realize that they can provide integrated circuit line drivers and receivers which for an additional price give much superior performance. The circuits are low-impedance differential drivers and differential amplifier receivers having good, common mode rejection. When used with twisted-pair transmission lines, cable lengths well beyond 100 feet may be possible. Some of the available circuits use "enable" inputs to both transmitter and receiver allowing the use of the circuits on a bus system.

How soon minicomputer I/O will make use of these improved circuits depends on the solution of several problems. The first is price. Minimum cost is one of the minicomputer's objectives. Current parts cost is several dollars more per signal pair. Another problem is the lack of a standard. Each IC manufacturer uses a different set of voltages for the logic levels transmitted and in most cases there are no second sources for the components.

TYPICAL PERIPHERAL DEVICES

Except for some computers built into dedicated systems, all computers have a need for at least four types of input/output.

a) Some form of (program and data) storage for output from the computer.
b) A method of reading this back as input to the computer. In addition, some method of off-line preparation of programs into this media is usually required.
c) A keyboard for input of commands and programs from the operator and/or programmer.
d) An output printer.

Teletype

A low cost solution to all four needs is the Teletype ASR-33. Price is the reason for the popularity of the ASR-33 (at least with people who prepare the budget when buying minicomputer systems). Performance leaves the programmer with Excedrin headache #33. At 10 characters per second, it takes: 27 minutes to load or dump 8000 words of core; about an hour to list a 1000 instruction assembly language program if it has many comments; and minutes to output a table of data the computer calculated in seconds. The Model 33 teletype was designed for intermittent operation at the rate of about one to two hours a day and in this kind of use is good for only about a year without problems. In the computer room the teletype repairman and the computer programmer have gotten to know each other well!

Figure 1 shows the cost of some of the alternatives to the teletype for data input-output. In this plot the total system cost (peripheral equipment, interface or controller, plus medium cost) are normalized by and plotted against the total amount of data stored off-line. For very large values of off-line storage, the cost of the media predominates.

Paper Tape

An optical paper tape reader and a paper tape punch, totalling together three times teletype cost, give a speed multiplication of 12 times for punching and 30 to 50 times for reading. This combination also has the advantage that paper tape punched off-line on a teletype can be read into the computer with the high-speed reader. (Of course no output printer is included in this alternative.)

Paper tape as a medium has a number of disadvantages. Handling is probably the biggest objection, although fan fold tape and newly introduced equipment which rerolls the tape during reading (and leaves it immediately ready for use), overcomes this to some extent. Perhaps the biggest shortcoming of paper is the fact that the reader and punch are separate devices requiring operator intervention if the medium is used as a temporary storage for data to be read back into the computer. Magnetic recording on tape or disks certainly is preferred for this type of use.

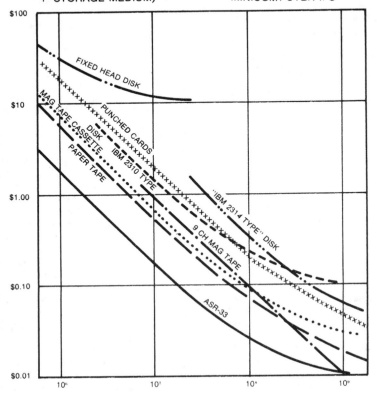

TOTAL SYSTEM
COST PER
1000 BYTES
(PERIPHERALS + INTERFACE
+ STORAGE MEDIUM)

TOTAL SYSTEM COST PER
1000 BYTES OF OFF-LINE
DATA STORAGE VS AMOUNT OF
OFF-LINE STORAGE FOR
MINICOMPUTER I/O

Total Off-line Storage Bytes

Magnetic Tape Units

For only a small increase in cost a large measure of performance and convenience can be obtained with some of the lower cost magnetic tape units available. At the present time 9-channel mag tape recorded in IBM format at 800 bpi is the most popular. This offers the advantage of interchange of data between the minicomputer and EDP systems. The need for compatibility will probably cause a shift to use of 1600 bpi recording in the future although the added electronics will raise the price by 50 percent or more. A disadvantage of mag tape is that it is more expensive to generate a tape off-line.

Disks

The next step up the line in cost and performance is the small, removable cartridge, moving-head disk (of the IBM 2310 or "System 3" type). The "System 3" type disk has a removable disk cartridge capable of storing a little over a million bytes and a fixed (non-removable) disk having an addi-

tional million byte capacity. Economy in production of this type disk is achieved by having one head positioning mechanism for the two disks. The non-removable disk is usually used to contain the system operating program and library subroutines in a Disk Operating System application. With average access time under 100 ms and two or more million bytes available at any time, the minicomputer which has been I/O bound up to this time can now take on some sophisticated computer jobs. The biggest limitation in the near future will probably be in the area of writing the software application packages to fully exploit the combination of the minicomputer and this type of disk.

One disadvantage of the small moving-head disk is in the off-line preparation of input. Here the cost of hardware (key-disc equipment) is too high for economical use except in a time-share mode. This may not be justifiable for the minicomputer used in a stand-alone configuration. Another apparent disadvantage of the disk cartridge is the high cost of the medium relative to the other types. Figure 1 shows, however, that up to about 100 million bytes, the cost of the storage

medium does not have a large effect on the total cost of the system for any of the removable types considered.

Two other types of disks used on minicomputers are the larger moving-head types (IBM type 2311 and 2314) and the fixed-head disk. The 2314 type is an advantage if 24 million bytes or more are needed on line at any given time. Figure 1 shows that for off-line storage of less than about 500 million bytes, the single disk type has a cost advantage.

The high-speed access (8.5 to 17 ms average) and transfer rate of the fixed-head disk is often necessary in time share and real time applications but the relative cost per byte is high (see Figure 1). Fixed-head disks as small as 32 thousand bytes are sometimes used to extend core memory capacity.

Punched Cards

Another medium used for input and output of data is punched cards. Disadvantages are the high cost of the reading and punching equipment and the bulk of the data medium. Performance is about equal to paper tape. The advantages are that cards allow easy editing; can be directly read by people; and may be conveniently circulated to pick up other data to be input to the computer. When used in computer systems where only a minimum of editing software is normally available, the punched card is the easiest medium to update or edit off line.

Card equipment manufacturers are giving a lot of attention to low cost card readers. These units are useful for remote batch terminals and are priced more in keeping with the price of the minicomputer. Card reading rates in the range of 200 to 400 cards per minute are typical.

IBM obviously feels that there is still a future for punched cards with the introduction of the new System/3 card. This card with small, round holes in a matrix of 18 rows by 32 columns can hold 96 six-bit characters in a card size about that of a credit card. If equipment becomes available at low cost to read and punch this type card, its use, may become more popular than the larger cards have been in minicomputer systems.

Another type of card which has some strong advantages as an input document is the mark sense card. With the mark sense card reader, punched cards may be read as well as cards which are prepared with a common pen or pencil. By proper design of the card form, marking the card can be as easy as filling out a coding sheet. This saves the entire step of having the program key-punched. The advantages are obvious in any situation where keypunching is a throughput bottleneck. The low cost of a mark sense card reader gives a further strong advantage to this medium.

Magnetic Tape Cassettes

The convenience in handling of the popular home entertainment cassette cartridge, has caused a large amount of interest in this medium as a direct replacement for paper tape. It seems reasonable that a two deck unit interfaced to a computer could cost about the same as the paper tape reader and punch it would replace. The media costs would be higher than paper tape, but the convenience should compensate for this. Two problems face the mag tape cassette. One is a matter of reliability. The other is the lack of standardization that now exists.

Although paper tape is easily damaged in the rewinding process, it is otherwise a very reliable medium. Even when damaged, the paper tape can often be repaired and the data stored on it recovered. Soft (recoverable) error rates higher than paper tape may be tolerated in the cassette system, but non-recoverable errors must be kept low to make the medium acceptable. Many systems proposed do not provide read after write checking. Redundancy in recording is often used in the attempt to obtain more reliable recording.

At the present time there are no two cassette products on the market using the same recording format on the tape. There are even a number of manufacturers who choose to design their own type cassette, although most are using the home entertainment cassette cartridge with some improvements in tape guiding and using computer grade tape. Lack of a standard recording format is going to be a major problem in the interchange of data, and cassettes will not achieve their fullest utility until standardization is accomplished.

Printer - Keyboards

Going up in price from the teletype there are a number of printer - keyboard alternatives in the speed range up to 100 cps. These include impact printers which make noise, as well as thermal devices which require special paper and are incapable of multiple copies. If a speed above this is required, there are three choices: A CRT/Keyboard, which does not make a hard copy; a printer using some type of ink squirting technique, which does not make multiple copies; or a line printer using either a drum or belt for printing. The line printer is hard to combine with a keyboard since the printing is not visible to the operator until after 4 to 8 lines have been printed. A CRT/Keyboard and a line printer is a very powerful combination but the total cost—in the order of 15 thousand dollars—seems high when compared to one-tenth of that for a teletype or one-half of that for the minicomputer.

OTHER "PERIPHERAL" DEVICES

The list of other items which have been and will be combined with a minicomputer are almost endless. Some of the more common items are:

a) Data communication interfaces to the telephone lines. This is a very active area since the minicomputer fits well into data communication systems as the front end of a large computer, remotely as a message concentrator, and as the data buffer and control of a remote terminal.

b) Analog-to-Digital Converter. Here almost every physical quantity which can be digitized directly or converted into a voltage has been or will be interfaced to a minicomputer. General software systems make programs for control of an experiment and logging of data as easy to write as the Fortran or Basic Program to process the data.

c) Digital-to-Analog Converter for limited graphics on CRT units, for power supply programming, and for analog inputs to control processes are common.

d) X-Y plotters.

e) Electronic and Scientific Instruments.

f) Medical Instruments.

The minicomputer manufacturer often provides a line of interfaces or modules which may be used to build device controllers for a wide variety of special items. General purpose interfaces which provide buffered logic-level outputs and inputs, contact closures, sensing of voltage levels or contact closures on remote lines are some of the building blocks available.

FUTURE TRENDS

The I/O structure of the lower priced minicomputer will probably not change much. Lowest possible cost will always be an objective. Medium priced minicomputers will probably develop much more powerful I/O architecture. The ROM controlled minicomputer processor of the future will probably be able to do context switching and operate as an I/O processor (multiplexer) as well as a device controller for such peripherals as moving-head disks or mag tape, and still have time to run programs as fast as today's mini CPU. In the higher priced minicomputer, we will probably find two complete processors; one processor with its special ROM will be a CPU and the other processor will be programmed by its ROM to be an I/O processor with the capability to do many of the functions of the device controllers.

Device controllers will increase their capability at little or no cost increase. Functions like code conversion through software table look up will be replaced by ROM and MSI hardware in the interface. Error checking will be included at no extra cost in the hardware. The size of device controllers will decrease, although cable interconnection problems will place a lower bound on this.

To minimize the interconnection problem, we may find data being converted from parallel to serial for transmission to the main frame where it would be reconverted to parallel. One LSI pack at each end of the transmission line should be able to do the conversion as well as provide error detection.

The crystal ball which shows us a bright picture when we look at the main frame, CPU, I/O structure, and device controllers of the future minicomputer, turns a bit dim when we try to look for major improvements in the price/performance ratios of future peripherals.

Certainly CRT/Keyboards will decrease in price and become more common. Perhaps we will see a few less teletypes. Mag tape cassettes may make some real inroads on paper tape, after a standard cassette tape format is devised. Paper tape will be in use for a long time to come. Printers will probably remain high priced and noisy although with the use of on line CRT/Keyboards the amount of printing done to accomplish a given job will decrease substantially. Perhaps an on line electrostatic copy machine will come through at low cost soon.

The cost per byte of data stored on a disk will decrease but may never reach the point that the software written for the minimum hardware configuration of a minicomputer system can depend on having a disk as part of every system.

With the price of some minicomputers below a 5 thousand dollar selling price, it's obvious a lot of attention must be paid to minicomputer peripherals. Each of the devices needed to make a usable system can cost more than the main frame (i.e., paper tape reader and punch or mag tape cassette, CRT Keyboard, and line printer). Perhaps it's time we took a look at the total problem minicomputer users are trying to solve.[1] Incorporating all of the basic I/O functions within the main frame might save more money for the customer than anything more that can be done to the minicomputer. After all, the price of a CPU can approach zero as an asymptote, but it can't go negative.

---

[1]Coury, Fred. "A Systems Approach to Mini-Computer I/O", SJCC 1970.

As more and more control computers become available, more is written and said about their advantages in specific situations and what they can do in general. There are certain fundamental things about control computers that a computer user must know. These have to do with how control computers interface functionally with the variety of devices they are supposed to control. This article discusses the two most common interfacing methods and how they work.

Interfacing a Control Computer
With Control Devices

P. M. KINTNER, Cutler-Hammer, Inc.

Recent years have seen an impressive invasion of the stored-program computer into areas formerly the province of wired-logic control systems. This is due to a remarkable reduction in the costs of the computer and to an increasing awareness on the part of control system designers of the inherent advantages of the stored-program concept for control.

The type of stored-program computer that has been developed, while characteristically small, has versatile interfacing provisions for controlled devices. This is not surprising, since the main function of the computer is to control external equipment. This article discusses the general characteristics of the functional interfaces available and the nature of the circuits the user is expected to provide to connect his own equipment.

Use program-control interfaces

Viewed functionally, control-computer interfaces fall into two classifications: single-word transfers under computer program control and direct-memory block transfers primarily under external control. The first type requires the least amount of hardware but gives the lowest transfer rate; the second requires more circuits but gives a high transfer rate.

All control computers offer as a standard interface a method whereby the computer itself controls the transfer of data and signals. The control is through program instructions, and data is transferred one word at a time. Depending upon the speed of the computer, transfer rates between 50 and 100 kHz can be achieved. The general features of program control interfacing are as follows.

• **Input-Output Data Bus.** The need to accommodate a widely varying number of external devices has led to the universal adoption in the stored-program computer of the bus or "party line" for controlling the data transfer. All devices are connected to a common data transfer signal line, Figure 1. It is usual to use one bus for both directions of transfer, though in some cases two buses are incorporated, one for each direction of transfer.

Typically, the input-output bus originates at the accumulator register of the computer. Data words can be taken from the computer's memory prior to an output action and placed in the register by program control, or they can be readily stored in the memory after an input action. Again typically, 15 to 20 devices can be placed on an input-output bus—an amount that can be extended by repeaters (signal amplifiers). The number of lines in the bus is usually fixed by the capacity of the accumulator register; sizes ranging from 12 to 16 bits are most common.

• **Device-Selection Bus.** It is clear that with a paralleled data bus some means must be provided to steer data to and from the right devices. This is accomplished by a second bus, called the device-selection bus, over which a code is transmitted to all devices but to which only a desired device can respond. A typical device-selection bus contains six to eight lines; it follows that a six- to eight-bit binary code can be transmitted, and that 64 to 256 device-selection codes can be generated for as many devices.

The device-selection bus originates typically at the instruction register of the computer, and is taken from the address portion of the register. A device selection is obtained by programming an input-output instruction whose "address" is the device code value.

An AND unit connected to each device serves as a device-selection decoder to detect assigned codes.

Reprinted with permission from *Contr. Eng.*, vol. 16, pp. 97–101, Nov. 1969.

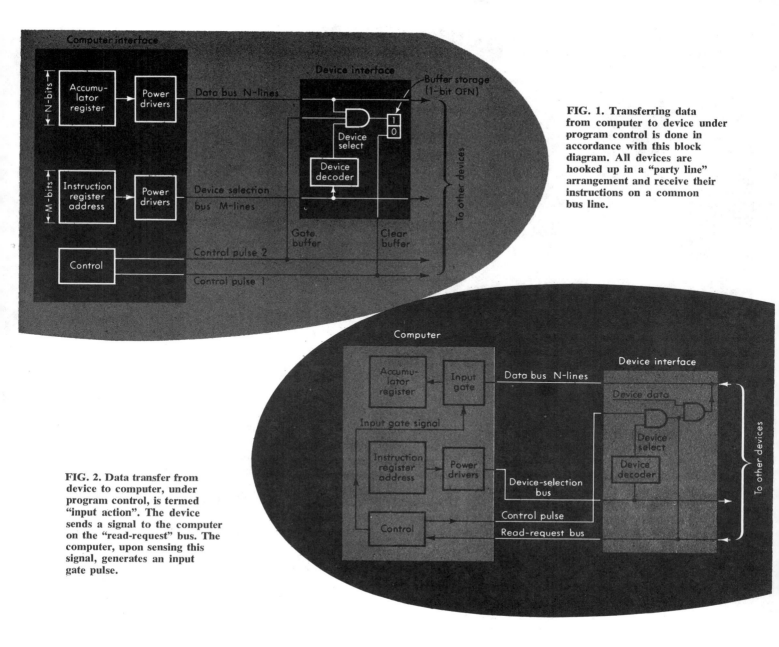

FIG. 1. Transferring data from computer to device under program control is done in accordance with this block diagram. All devices are hooked up in a "party line" arrangement and receive their instructions on a common bus line.

FIG. 2. Data transfer from device to computer, under program control, is termed "input action". The device sends a signal to the computer on the "read-request" bus. The computer, upon sensing this signal, generates an input gate pulse.

Many control-computer manufacturers offer a module for this purpose which can be readily connected for a given code by, say, clipping out diodes.

• **Control Pulse Bus.** Still another signal must be transmitted to the device: a control pulse. This signal informs the device that an input-output instruction and a device-selection code are present, thus further distinguishing the device for purposes of directing data to it or from it. The pulse also gives timing information—that is, it defines the time at which the device can safely take data from the data bus.

The control pulse signal may be considered to be generated by the order portion of the input-output instruction. The organization of the control pulse structure varies in considerable detail from one computer to another. One of the earliest and most widely used control computers—the PDP-8, manufactured by the Digital Computer Corp.—provides three control pulses spaced at equidistant intervals throughout the input-output computer cycle. These three pulses can be microprogrammed through the three rightmost bits of the input-output instruction. Microprogram-

ming is accomplished by making each of these bit positions "1" when a pulse is to be generated.

• **Output Action.** As shown in Figure 1, the user must also provide a buffer or register into which the data value can be gated, or "strobed", and thereby stored for use by different devices. Gate time is defined by a control pulse. If several control pulses are available, as with the PDP-8, it may be convenient to use one to clear the buffer just prior to the gate pulse, to simplify the gating hardware.

Action is then initiated by two program instructions executed by the computer, FETCH (memory location x) and INPUT-OUTPUT (device y) (control pulses z).

The first of these instructions transfers a data word from memory location x into the accumulator. The second transmits to device y both a device code and two control pulses z (a clear buffer pulse followed by gate buffer pulse, for example).

• **Input Action.** An input action starts when data from a particular device is gated onto the data bus with the help of a device-selection code and a control pulse. From the data bus the data goes into a com-

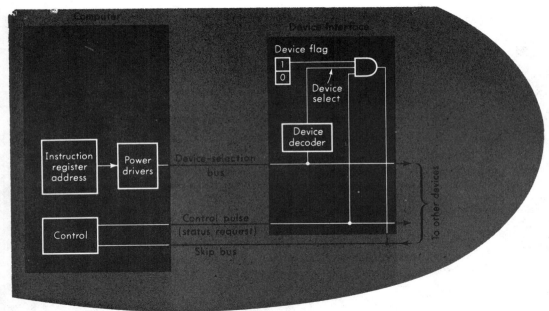

FIG. 3. Synchronizing the internal computer action with the device action can be accomplished by a step called status request. This signal, termed a "flag," is usually generated by a flipflop.

puter register (usually the accumulator), in an internal action generated by the computer control.

How does the computer "know" it must carry out this action? Computers with larger words and thus larger input-output instructions generate the required information through a bit in the instruction. Set to "1", for example, such a bit calls for the input gating action. Other computers, with short words and limited input-output instruction capability, require a signal sent from the device to the computer on what is termed a read-request bus. The signal is the same one that first gates the device data onto the data bus; the computer control, upon sensing this signal on the read-request bus, generates an input gate pulse timed to occur in the middle of the data-bus gate pulse. Figure 2 gives a block diagram of an input action based on this approach.

The computer program for the input action is then as follows: INPUT-OUTPUT (device y) (control pulse z) and STORE (memory location x).

• **Synchronization.** A computer executes instructions at rates of several hundred kilohertz, but almost all peripheral devices, while also cyclic in action, are usually much slower in rate. It is fundamental that there be a method of synchronizing. Data cannot be transferred out until a device is ready. Conversely, data cannot be transferred in until the computer is ready or until the device is ready to send. There are two synchronization methods used in connection with interfaces: (1) status request, whereby the computer asks the device if it is ready to send or receive, and (2) interrupt, whereby the device tells the computer without being asked that it is ready for action.

(1) *Status Request.* The status of an interfaced device is indicated at the device by a signal, usually termed a "flag," Figure 3. Thus it is said that the device "raises its flag" when it is ready for data transfer, after it completes an action, and so on. Generated by

flipflops, flags are set "high" or "low" by the device control to correspond to "ready," "busy," "done," and other states.

A status request is the action of determining the state of the flag. It is made through an input-output instruction that generates a device select code, and a control pulse that is ANDed at the device with the flag value and sent back to the computer. A signal is generated if the flag is high, and no signal is sent if the flag is low.

The status request reply could be placed into the computer's accumulator through a normal input action, and a response generated by the computer program using conditional program transfers. However, to reduce programming requirements, it is customary to provide a "device status bus" for the status request reply. The response of the computer control is then simple. The next instruction is skipped if the device status bus is raised but acknowledged if it is not raised.

A conditional program response to the device status is obtained by placing a "jump" instruction or program transfer instruction immediately after the device status input-output instruction. A program transfer is made if there is no skip. Otherwise, the program transfer instruction is skipped and the program sequences in order.

The following program illustrates the most common way of using the skip feature: JUMP -1; INPUT-OUTPUT (device y) (control pulse $z2$); SKIP ON FLAG (device y) (control pulse $z1$).

The first instruction is a device status request ("skip on flag" is a common designation). The next instruction (performed if there is no skip) simply returns the program to the first instruction. The result is a two-instruction program "loop" performed until the device flag is raised and the skip action is generated. The program then breaks out of the loop

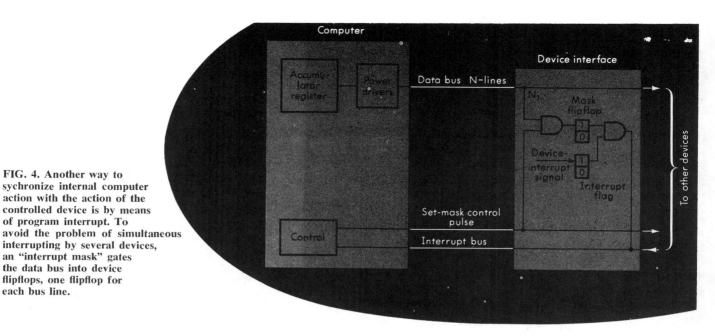

FIG. 4. Another way to sychronize internal computer action with the action of the controlled device is by means of program interrupt. To avoid the problem of simultaneous interrupting by several devices, an "interrupt mask" gates the data bus into device flipflops, one flipflop for each bus line.

and performs the input-output action on the device appropriate to the status in question. The effect is to force the computer to wait until the device is ready for the input-output action.

(2) *Program Interrupt.* The inverse of the status request method of synchronization is the interrupt. Here the device stops the computer program wherever it may be and demands immediate servicing, Figure 4.

This type of synchronization is useful in situations where it is not feasible to make the computer wait for the device because program time for a "wait loop" cannot be spared or the demand by the device is infrequent and unpredictable, such as is the case with an alarm action in process control.

The simplest interrupt arrangement is a parallel interrupt bus from all interrupting devices. One or more devices raising the bus will start the interrupt action in which the computer, upon finishing the current instruction action and storing the current value of the program counter (usually in a reserved memory location to be used for restarting the program after the interrupt is over), transfers the program to another reserved location. Here the computer begins an "interrupt service routine".

The interrupt service routine as usually written begins by storing away all register values to be retrieved when the interrupted program is reinitiated. The next step is basic: determining which device interrupted. The simplest way of doing this is to incorporate an "interrupt flag" on each device and poll the devices one by one, using the status request of skip on flag described in the previous section. The interrupting device will raise the flag.

But the polling process can be time-consuming and can require a rather extensive program. Some control computers have an "interrupt acknowledge" instruction that eliminates polling by requiring an interrupt-

ing device to place its device code on the data bus from which it may readily be identified. Possible simultaneous interruption by more than one device is avoided by blocking the interrupt acknowledge signal at the first device interrupting. The result is that the first interrupting device on the interrupt bus is the only one responding.

Simultaneous interrupting can be a problem especially if interrupts must be treated on a priority basis; i.e., if devices are ranked in importance as far as response is concerned and those with higher priority receive service before those of lower priority. An instruction on some computers facilitating priority ranking is an "interrupt mask" that gates the data bus into device flipflops, one flipflop for each bus line. Each device flipflop relates to an accumulator position, and when set to "1" inhibits interrupting. Through this instruction, and through appropriate "mask" words in the accumulator, devices of lower priority than the device being serviced can be prevented from interrupting.

Direct memory interfaces

The transfer rates available with program control are sometimes not sufficient for devices such as magnetic drums, magnetic tapes, and graphic displays. Most control computers offer faster transfer based on direct-memory transfers, wherein program control is bypassed, Figure 5. Direct-memory interfaces give transfer rates of above 600 kHz but at the cost of considerably more interface hardware than required for program control.

Direct-memory transfers are (1) completely device-controlled and (2) partially computer-controlled.

(1) *Device-controlled direct memory interface.* In device-controlled direct-memory transfers, the device interface must supply the memory address involved,

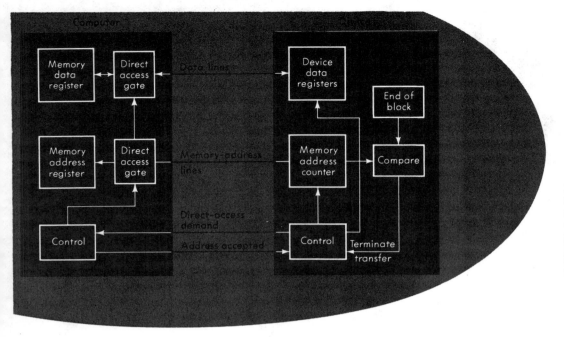

FIG. 5. Direct-memory access from device to computer is accomplished under either complete device control or partial computer control. This block diagram illustrates an interface for direct-memory transfer from a single device.

supply a data word to or accept a data word from the computer's memory register, and supply a control signal to initiate the action. In some cases, a signal must be supplied to indicate direction (in or out) of transfer. In turn, the computer supplies an "address accepted" signal to the device interface to indicate that an individual transfer has been consummated. This signal functions at the device interface to time and control the next transfer action.

Direct-memory transfers are sent in blocks of predetermined numbers of words into a set of sequential computer memory locations. Block control, if provided at the device, requires a counter for generating sequential-memory addresses and a register with comparison logic for recognizing when the end of a block —given by the highest memory location value—has been reached. An alternative to fixing the size of the block is to preset a counter with the block number and count in reverse until overflow.

It is customary to establish initial conditions—the size of a block and first memory address—through program control, using the interface hardware described. If these conditions are permanently fixed, the values are hardwired at the device.

The bus or party-line approach will not accommodate more than one device. To sequentially connect the data lines and memory address lines from several devices to the computer, a multiplexer or sequential switch is incorporated as an interfacing element—usually as an option by the computer supplier. Typically, six devices can be accommodated by a multiplexer.

There is also the problem of making sure the computer program "knows" when a transfer has been made. Two solutions are possible. One is to reserve a single memory location in the block being transferred, and to place a unique value on this location. The

computer program can then test the location to determine transfer status. Another approach is to have the device generate an interrupt when the transfer has been made, to place the interface under program control and provide the desired program link.

(2) *Partial computer control of direct memory interface*. At least one control computer (PDP-8) makes available what is termed a three-cycle direct-memory interface, wherein the block control described in the previous section is incorporated in the memory control of the computer. This is done by dedicating two memory locations to each device involved, one to define sequential block address locations and the other to generate an "end-of-block" signal by counting words as they are transferred from the computer's memory register.

Upon receipt of a "data transfer" request signal from the device, the memory control initiates three cycles. The first consists of reading out the word count, decrementing and restoring; the second reads out the block address count, incrementing and restoring; and the third either transfers data from the device to the current block address or reads data from the current block address and transfers the data out. The first of the actions also tests for overflow of the value passing through zero to find the end of the block. An overflow signal then is issued to the device to stop transfer action.

Two special versions of partial computer control of direct memory interfaces are available in some computers for special applications. One version consists of doing nothing more than incrementing by one the contents of a memory address defined by the external device, a feature useful for pulse-height analysis. The other adds the data value of the device to the contents of the memory location defined by the word counter, a feature useful for signal averaging. □

In any on-line system where several tasks are being handled, and are dictated by events external to the computer, two needs arise. First, the computer must be aware of the occurrence of the events as they happen, so that it can tell what demands will be made on its time; and second, some scheme should exist to make sure that the central processor in the system is always attending to the most important task. Designing such priority interrupt systems is the province of the computer architect, but the systems designer most certainly must understand their operation too. Here is an inside look at interrupt systems for the information systems designer.

A Primer on Priority Interrupt Systems

M.K. VAN GELDER and A.W. ENGLAND, Scientific Data Systems

In on-line computer applications, external events frequently determine the tasks the computer must perform. The computer must then be directed to the execution of each task as it comes up. If several tasks present themselves at the same time, the computer must choose the one it should perform—i.e., the most important task at that time.

To do just that, the central processor must be interrupted and its current state noted and stored, and then redirected to its new task. If several interrupts occur closely in time, then the system will have to establish a priority for each task. The computer's decision-making and ordering facilities are usually referred to as priority interrupt systems.

In almost any on-line application, whether it be airline reservations or continuous process control, the overall design—and frequently the computer too—is determined by the nature of the interrupt system. What follows in this article are some important criteria for interrupt systems, as demonstrated by three typical systems and an example of a dynamically alterable interrupt system.

Interrupt system criteria

Central processor response time to external interrupts will determine the maximum capability and, therefore, the value of an on-line system. To be effective, an interrupt system must react quickly to capture time-critical information and must operate efficiently so that noncritical tasks can be handled as well. In a well-designed system, additional levels and time can be available to accommodate an increased load without saturating the system.

Specific interrupt techniques have been developed during the last six years that satisfy many of the fast-response demands of on-line systems. The criteria needed to evaluate these techniques and, therefore, to measure the effectiveness of a priority-interrupt system, are:

● Response time—The time between the occurrence of a signal external to the central computer and the start of execution of the first useful instruction requested by the signal. An optimum response would be a reaction time of zero; but since digital computers cannot react in less than an instruction time, the optimum response is theoretical. How well a priority-interrupt system compares with the optimum is a measurement of its value.

● Overhead—The difference between the total time necessary to process the incoming request and the execution time of all useful instructions.

● Priority structure—The interrupt structure that allows the central computer to react with correct priority to incoming requests. If the most important interrupt, as determined by the current priority structure of the request lines, has been requested but is not being serviced at a given time, then the priority structure of the central computer is suboptimum.

● System saturation—A state reached when the on-line system cannot respond quickly enough to all

Reprinted with permission from *Contr. Eng.*, vol. 16, pp. 101–105, Mar. 1969.

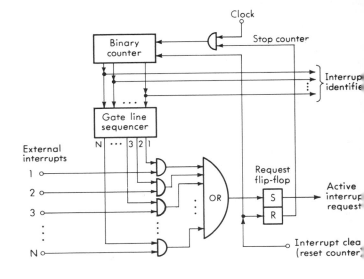

FIG. 1. In the search ring interrupt system the counter runs continuously until an interrupt is received and the appropriate output of the gate line sequencer is on. The request flipflop then stops the counter and the computer is informed that an interrupt has been received on the line identified by the stopped position of the counter. After the interrupt has been serviced the counter is reset and the search continues. This reset forces the next scan to see the highest priority lines first.

of the requests, and requests are essentially lost. The system is underdesigned if this state occurs.

At least three types of priority interrupt systems are in general use today. They are known as the search ring method, the single-level indicator method, and the matrix control method.

Search ring method is simple but slow

The search ring method uses an *n* position electronic stepping counter that continually scans *n* interrupt lines (Figure 1). The highest priority lines are scanned first so that if two requests, say, are received simultaneously, the higher priority line is recognized. The counter value associated with the position of this interrupt is then transmitted to the central computer as the address of the first instruction to be executed. The program address counter of the central processing unit (cpu) is automatically saved and restored at the end of interrupt processing.

What gives this method poor response time is the fact that if any interrupt is being processed, the computer is locked out from all other interrupts. In the worst case, the response time can be as long as the longest interrupt servicing routine in the system. Still another drawback is that true priority response is not present. The simple scanning technique prohibits a high priority interrupt from being recognized while one of lower priority is being processed. Overhead, however, is not excessive because the program counter is saved and restored. This method is single-level as opposed to true, multi-level priority.

The search ring method has limited capacity because of the time it takes to scan all lines. This time increases proportionately with the number of interrupt lines. Moreover, a fairly large *n* requires faster and more expensive components or an increased scanning cycle. The search ring method is frequently used with special-purpose computers, such as those in aerospace systems.

Single-level method is inexpensive

The single-level indicator method is the most common interrupt system, and the least expensive. It is used by several third-generation computers.

All interrupt lines develop an OR output, which serves as the interrupt request signal to the central computer (Figure 2). At the completion of the current instruction, the interrupt signal causes the program counter to be stored and an interrupt processing subroutine to be entered. This subroutine tests each interrupt line in sequence to determine which request caused the interrupt. Either by program or automatically, the interrupt line recognized is reset and program control is transferred to the correct routine.

The response time and overhead for this method are both very high due to the number of program steps that must be executed before the central computer begins to obey an interrupt request. While the system does test the highest priority requests first, its high overhead may make the lower priority interrupts ineffective. This method is single-level since no interrupt can be recognized while one is being processed. The combination of slow response time and high overhead, plus the lack of true priority response, make system saturation a possibility before the capacity of the computer has reached an economic level.

Matrix control uses a memory

The matrix control method uses a simple memory comprising two flipflops for each interrupt line. These flipflops provide the memory necessary to determine the current status of an interrupt level (Figure 3). The four possible states are:

• No interrupt will be allowed (1).
• An interrupt will be allowed, but no interrupt has been requested (2).
• An interrupt has been requested, but has not been recognized by the computer (3).
• The requested interrupt has been recognized, but processing has not been completed (4).

Each interrupt line is positioned into a matrix based on the order of priority. The highest priority is closest to the output, while the lowest priority is the farthest away. If no interrupt is allowed on a particular line—i.e., state 1—no action will be taken if an interrupt occurs. If an allowed interrupt request is received on a line, the level will shift from state 1 to state 3. If no higher priority level is presently in state 3 or state 4, the matrix will permit the interrupt request line to be activated to the central computer.

28

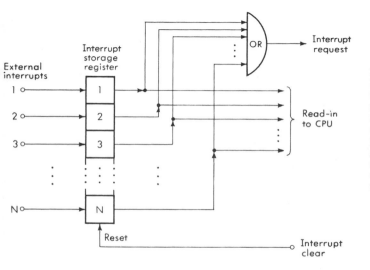

FIG. 2. When an interrupt is received by the single-level indicator system, the storage register will cause an interrupt request to be sent to the cpu. The request will initiate a program to start a subroutine to search each register position to identify the highest priority active interrupt line. When all the interrupt lines have been cleared, the interrupt clear signal will reset the storage register.

Simultaneously, an address unique to the requesting level is supplied to the computer.

At the completion of a current instruction, the computer transfers control to the memory location determined by the provided address. The cpu program counter is preserved and a signal sent to the priority interrupt system to change the state of the highest priority level presently in state 3 to state 4. By design, this will be the requesting interrupt level. At the completion of the desired routine, control is returned to the point of departure, with a signal to the priority interrupt system to change the highest priority level presently in state 4 to state 1 or 2.

The matrix control method provides both short reaction time and low overhead. Every allowed interrupt request is obeyed immediately, provided no higher priority request is presently in execution. A favorably low overhead is the result of not using program time to identify the desired routine.

The greatest advantage of this method, however, is a near-optimum priority structure. The most important interrupt is either being serviced or is about to be serviced at any instant of time. The matrix con-

trol method ensures that the next routine to be executed always has the highest existing priority regardless of how many lower-priority requests remain only partially completed.

Dynamically alterable matrix control

The fundamental component of a sophisticated matrix control interrupt system is the interrupt level (Figure 4). Several levels will exist within a comprehensive matrix control system.

With a dynamically alterable interrupt system, any interrupt level can be enabled, disabled, armed, disarmed, or triggered under program control. In addition, all levels or individual interrupt control groups within the system can be inhibited. Individual interrupt level control is accomplished by a single cpu instruction directed to the interrupt control system.

The interrupt logic is designed to operate on a request/acknowledge basis for external interrupt requests. When a given level is armed and an external interrupt is accepted, the interrupt enters the waiting state. Regardless of whether a level of higher priority is active, the new level activates an acknowledge line

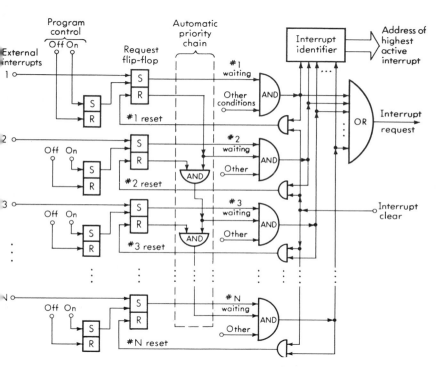

FIG. 3. The matrix control interrupt system is distinguished by an automatic priority chain that causes the highest priority interrupt to be acted on first. If, during the execution of an interrupt, a higher-priority interrupt is received, then the lower-priority interrupt will be deferred until it is again the highest. In this way the highest-priority interrupt always receives immediate service. The system here has a series of program-controlled flipflops for enabling any particular line.

unique to that particular interrupt. The acknowledge line will remain on as long as that level is in its waiting or active state, and will not go off until the cpu exits the service routine for the new interrupt.

Remembering processor status

With any interrupt system, a method is needed for storing the state of the machine registers at the time of an interrupt and returning the machine to that state after the interrupt is processed. A problem often arises when a routine executed in response to an interrupt request uses, or destroys, any programmable registers, such as accumulators, index registers, overflow indicators, etc. The problem is becoming more and more complicated as computers are being designed with more and more machine registers for greater flexibility.

The approaches available currently are:
- Let the program decide what to save and restore.
- Implement, through hardware, an automatic store sequence to save all registers in core memory and automatically restore them after completion.
- Maintain all registers in integrated-circuit fast memory and provide multiple register groups for use by interrupt routines and the main program. When an interrupt occurs, a pointer automatically will select a unique register group.

The first approach is the least expensive solution, and is generally effective if the instruction set is designed to allow many operations to occur without affecting too many registers. This is possible with those third-generation computers that allow arithmetic operations to take place in core memory. The programmer then has a choice of ways to keep the overhead low.

With the second approach, there is a fixed overhead no matter what functions are performed in the interrupt routine. The third approach adds flexibility to the interrupt system. The time saved by not requiring an automatic or programmed register-storage process helps to give much faster interrupt service.

Disabling of interrupts

In on-line applications, it may be necessary to defer recognition of certain interrupt requests while other functions are being performed. For example, a high-speed acquisition requirement, which may have low priority until the instant that an interrupt request is initiated, must capture most of the computer time. If the priority structure is allowed to stand, higher-priority items may interfere with the transfer and cause transmission errors due to loss of information. Then, too, certain critical interrupt lines may have to remain open at all times; in this case, the prevention of all other interrupts would not be desirable.

These situations can be handled by an interrupt enable/disable facility. A flipflop is placed on each interrupt level under control of the central computer. When the flipflop is set by the central computer, interrupt requests can be acted upon and the interrupt level is enabled. But when the flipflop is reset, interrupt requests are postponed and the interrupt level is disabled. To add flexibility, interrupt enable/disable flipflops can be controlled independently within convenient groups.

Selection of priorities

Assignment of priority-interrupt levels to particular functions in a given on-line system can be a perplexing problem. At first sight, it appears that request functions should be ordered on the basis of importance, and levels should be assigned accordingly. This, however, produces the most effective system performance only by accident. Priorities must be assigned using the interaction of functions with each other as a primary basis.

Consider a simple on-line control system with three major requirements: receive and modify input data, output the data, and maintain time in milliseconds. In this case, the maintenance of time is for future off-line processing and is the least important of the three functions. Since the output of data is possible only after data input and modification have oc-

FIG. 4. In a single level of a matrix control interrupt system three flipflops are used to define four states: disarmed, armed, waiting, and active. One flipflop is used as a level-enable, acting between the waiting and active state. In the disarmed state, no signal to that interrupt level is admitted. In the armed state, the level can accept and remember an interrupt signal. On a signal, the interrupt level advances to the waiting state and remains there until it is allowed to advance to the active state. If the level-enable flipflop is off, the level can not move from the waiting to the active state and is completely removed from the chain that determines the priority of access to the cpu. When an interrupt moves from the waiting state to the active state, the computer executes the contents of the preassigned interrupt location as the next instruction. An interrupt level remains in the active state until it is cleared by the execution of a special instruction.

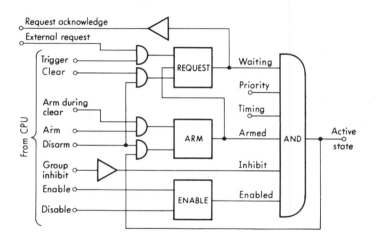

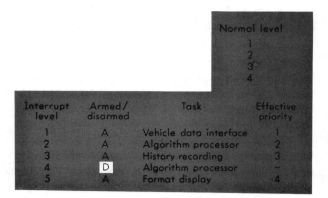

FIG. 5. Modification of the priority levels for four separate tasks (top) can be accomplished by using five actual levels, each with an enable line (lower). For the normal-level interrupt, level 4 is disarmed (left), and for the modified-level interrupt, level 2 is disarmed (right). In the Sigma series of computers this can be achieved by just one instruction.

curred, system input is the most important function. If the priorities were assigned strictly on the basis of importance, it is obvious that the time function would go unrecorded under certain conditions.

Yet, erroneous time measurement cannot be tolerated. If the time function is assigned the highest priority, no time information will be lost. More importantly, the net effect of this assignment is to prolong either system input or system output by only a few microseconds. Since worst-case conditions have been considered, no serious problem results and system saturation is avoided.

Dynamic priority allocation

As certain events occur, it may become necessary to reassign the priority levels of key interrupts dynamically under program control. This requirement is common in military command and control systems because of the fast-changing nature of tactical situations.

Dynamic reassignment may be implemented in a number of ways on different systems by using large banks of flipflops or core switching matrices. A large amount of expensive hardware is necessary if completely general flexibility is required.

If only a few different options of dynamic priority reallocations can be predicted or are required in an on-line system, however, it is cheaper to assign a given interrupt request line to two or three different priority levels in the interrupt system (Figure 4). Coupled with the ability to disallow an interrupt on each line will be the freedom to reassign requests to different priority levels as the situation changes. This method is generally less expensive than the more flexible approaches. It is offset by the tendency of on-line systems to grow.

Sophisticated systems often require that some portions of the interrupt routines not be interrupted during execution, although execution of instructions before and after the vital code may be deferred in favor of higher-priority routines. By allowing an instruction to be executed within an individual interrupt routine that inhibits individual interrupts or groups of interrupts, a system may make possible delayed processing.

Changing task priorities

A priority-interrupt system may be needed for real-time telemetry acquisition and analysis. For example, consider a system to be designed and implemented at a launch site where continuous monitoring of vehicle status is necessary through the countdown sequence and liftoff.

One of the more difficult functions of such a system will be to control task execution and establish task-priority-level assignments in real time. A really efficient system should be able to adapt the task priorities as a function of the type and severity of the load on the system. Listing the complete output of the reduction/analysis in real time is, of course, highly desirable. However, when conditions occur in which the load is greater than the ability of the system to adequately support it, the deletion of some of the less important tasks will generally reduce the load to within the system's capabilities. As soon as the load has decreased to a level that is within the system's capabilities, complete operation will continue. It is questionable whether such a requirement can be met without a sophisticated priority interrupt system.

Suppose priority assignments have to be changed according to Figure 4. In normal operation, the raw data acquired through the interface must be preserved. The history-recording task then will follow the task that allows for its input and authentication. But this time, due to system saturation, tasks with normal priority levels 3 and higher are not performed to completion. Data-history recording now must be accomplished prior to processing, and processing must be deferred to an off-line operation (Figure 5). Thus, by using one extra interrupt line two different situations can be handled. Such dynamically alterable interrupt systems are likely to find wide application in on-line computer applications. □

Digital-computer interface systems

by GRANINO A. KORN, *Professor of Electrical Engineering*
University of Arizona

This article was presented at the AICA meeting in Versailles.
It is printed here with the permission of Association interna-
tionale pour le Calcul Analogique.

ABSTRACT

Digital-computer interface design is of vital and increasing importance in simulation, control, instrumentation, and data processing. Hybrid-computer linkage design deals only with a small facet of the interface world, but reflects many of its problems. This tutorial report reviews the important techniques for transferring data and control signals between digital computers and the outside world and discusses, in turn, device selection and control for a party line I/O bus, device control, sensing, interrupts and automatic data channels with direct memory access. Interfaces for iterative analog computers, for combined simulation, and for simple graphic displays are described as examples. Finally, special interfaces for random-process measurements and interfaces employing an intermediate digital processor are discussed.

1. INTRODUCTION: THE INTERFACE WORLD

For something like a decade, our department at The University of Arizona has taught courses on analog/hybrid computation. Our research has been more hardware-oriented than that of most universities. We developed some very fast analog-computer systems with lots of free digital logic and employed them for statistical studies of dynamical systems and communications processes.[16] It was a natural development to link our hybrid systems to a digital processor or "laboratory computer" which would control experiments, perform optimizations, compute statistics, and help with accurate calculations. The small digital computer, readily accessible and even modifiable, proved to be much better at all these tasks than anyone had hoped; students began to play and experiment with the machine, as earlier generations had played and experimented first with radios and then with analog computers. As the processor was interfaced to hybrid computers, controls, and experiments, hybrid-computer experience paid off in the design of interfaces between digital computer and operator in the form of new displays and control consoles permitting on-line experimentation.

At the same time, all around us, in the University, in industry, and in aircraft and space vehicles, our hybrid-computer amplifiers, switches, and multipliers appeared as black epoxy cubes and monolithic chips: a hundred times as many as were ever used for simulation now interface the world of instruments and controls with dig-

ital processors. The digital computers themselves, large and small, no longer remain in computer-center basements. Computers in dust-proof boxes control quality and production in the plant; computers fly in air and space, supervise communications and, no larger than oscilloscopes, are wheeled into our laboratories to run experiments and to analyze data where the data are.[7-13] In turn, our hybrid-computer-design courses must now concentrate on a subject not taught before at a university, namely the design of interfaces linking real systems with digital computers.

Analog/digital-computer linkages reflect the larger world of system/digital-computer interfaces quite well, because hybrid-computer linkages are designed to do so many different tasks. Usually, one's first thought about such a linkage is about sufficiently accurate analog-to-digital converters (ADC's) and digital-to-analog converters (DAC's). A substantial body of sampled-data theory deals with the effects of conversion rates and digital processing delays on conversion accuracy and data reconstruction. In practice, though, correct interaction of analog, digital, and conversion operations also requires a fair amount of essential control and timing logic, and transmission of "discretes" or logic signals through the interface is usually of the greatest importance. Figure 1 indicates some of the tasks which may be accomplished by a digital-computer interface. This tutorial paper will outline the engineering problems of interface design.

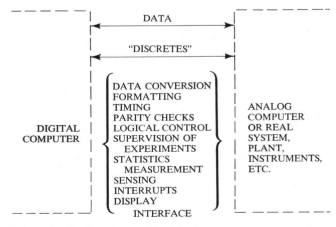

Figure 1—The interface and its functions

Reprinted with permission from *Simulation*, vol. 11, pp. 285–298, Dec. 1968.

It is best not to start our experience with a large scientific computer. Such a machine belongs to a computer-center manager, and it or he counts dollars per minute; the machine, moreover, speaks mostly floating-point FORTRAN and prefers to be interfaced only through buffers looking as much as possible like a tape deck or disk. "Laboratory computers," such as the PDP-8I, the PDP-9, the 3C-516, and many others are a much better start. They have neat symbolic assemblers with many different input-output statements; they are fast, and their 12- to 24-bit word length interfaces nicely with conversion equipment. [8,9,11,13] With a little extra memory and arithmetic, the larger laboratory computers can, moreover, be parlayed into quite respectable general-purpose computers if the need arises. New integrated-circuit hardware, indeed, permits refinements such as multiple addressable registers, byte manipulation, and even floating-point arithmetic at relatively very low cost.

2. THE PARTY-LINE I/O BUS AND THE USE OF PROGRAMMED I/O INSTRUCTIONS

The I/O bus. In the interest of processing speed, modern digital computers and linkage system handle data on parallel 8- to 24-bit buses, *i.e.,* all bits of each data word are transmitted simultaneously.

Hybrid-computer and instrumentation interface systems preserve this parallel mode of data transmission; serial data transmission is usually restricted to communication links and some special devices.*

In addition to the 8- to 24-data-bit lines, one requires, as we shall see, a comparable number of interface control-logic lines. To provide for switching (multiplexing)

lines to as many as 1000 or as few as 3 peripheral devices would compromise the processor design. Therefore, practically all computer interface systems employ a *"party-line I/O bus* of the general type illustrated in figure 2. Here, *all* "devices" (DACs, ADCs, displays, etc.) intended to receive or transmit data words are permanently wired to a *parallel I/O data bus* connected to suitable digital-computer registers and/or the memory buffer register. The data bus can be bidirectional, or separate input and output lines may be provided. Additional party-line wires carry *control-logic signals* for selecting a specific device and its mode of operation (*e.g.,* transmission or reception), and also synchronize data transmission with the digital-computer operating cycle. Control over device operation may be exercised by the central processor (through programmed I/O instructions), by a clock or external controller, or by requests from the devices themselves (sensing, interrupts, device-requested memory access).

Device selection and control with programmed instructions. For a minimum of linkage hardware, interfaces work with programmed processor instructions. This method permits flexibility and efficiency in analog and hybrid-equipment usage at the cost of some ingenuity in assembly-language programming.

Figure 3 shows how the parallel-connected device selection and control lines of a typical laboratory computer system (Digital Equipment Corporation PDP-9) correspond to the format of an input/output-transfer (IOT) instruction word in the processor instruction register.[9] Bits 0 to 3 of the instruction word inform the processor that an input-output operation is wanted. Bits 6 to 11 place levels (0 or 1) on five *device-selection lines* parallel-connected to all devices on the I/O bus. When

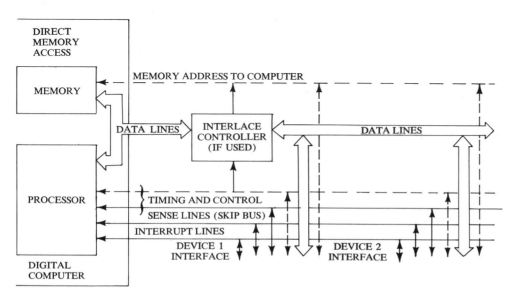

* The very smallest processors assemble 16- to 24-bit data words from eight-bit bytes.

Figure 2—An input/output bus

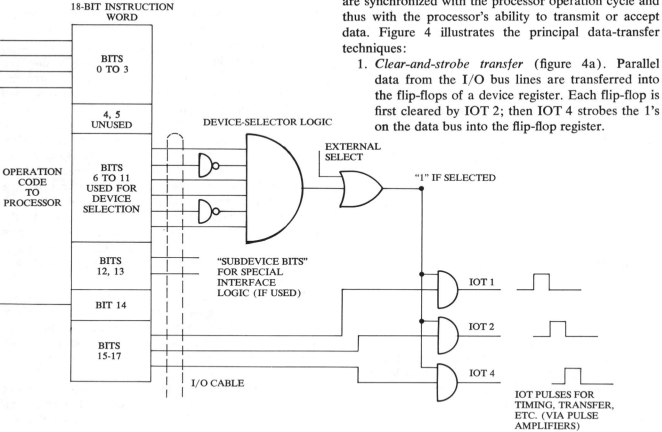

Figure 3—Program-controlled selection of device addresses and functions

are synchronized with the processor operation cycle and thus with the processor's ability to transmit or accept data. Figure 4 illustrates the principal data-transfer techniques:

1. *Clear-and-strobe transfer* (figure 4a). Parallel data from the I/O bus lines are transferred into the flip-flops of a device register. Each flip-flop is first cleared by IOT 2; then IOT 4 strobes the 1's on the data bus into the flip-flop register.

these lines carry the *device-selection code* associated with a specific device, its *device selector* (essentially an AND gate, figure 3) gates (and regenerates) a set of one, two, or three successive processor-timed *command pulses* (IOT pulses) used to effect data transfers and other operations in the selected device in accordance with instruction bits 15 to 17. Not all instructions and devices utilize all three pulses. Bits 12 and 13 of the instruction word ("subdevice bits") can similarly serve to select devices or subdevices or can further gate the command pulses to select device operating modes.

Other digital-computer input/output systems provide only a single command pulse on one, two, or three different lines similarly selected by different instructions; this method does not permit as complex control sequences, but reduces the time required for the execution of input/output instructions. In general, the selection and control logic for each device fits on an "interface card" associated with the device, and changes in the number or type of peripheral devices will affect the processor only to the extent of programming changes.[7,9]

Data-transfer operations. The most common application of the device-selector-gated command pulses is *data transfer* from and to the processor; note that the pulses

2. *Jam transfer* (figure 4b). A single command pulse (IOT 4) sets or resets the device-register bits in accordance with the data-bus levels. Jam transfers require slightly more complex electronics than clear-and-strobe, but need only one pulse period for transfer. Jam transfer *must* be used whenever the register resetting operation would disturb device functions. This is true, for instance, with DACs required to have a continuous voltage output, and also with control registers which continuously establish a device status.

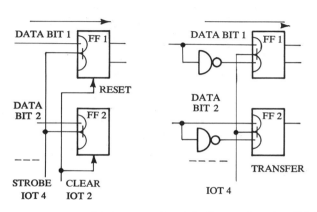

Figure 4—Parallel data transfer: (a) Clear-and-strobe, (b) jam transfer.

3. *Double-buffered-register transfer* (figure 4c). Data is transferred into the buffer register by either a clear-and-strobe or jam-transfer operation and is then jam-transferred into the device register. Double-buffered DACs permit simultaneous transfer ("updating") of the analog output of all DACs, *e.g.,* in an analog computer.

4. *Incrementing.* Figure 4d illustrates the use of command pulses to increment a counter. This type of operation, which does not directly involve the I/O data lines, is important for interfacing with incremental displays, plotters, numerically controlled machine tools, and incremental computers, such as those used in control and navigation systems.

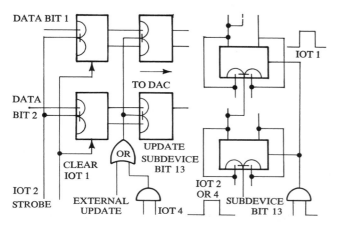

Figure 4—(c) transfer into a double-buffered DAC, and (d) incrementing of a (binary) counter

5. *Reading from a device into processor.* In figure 5, the correctly timed IOT 2 pulse gates data from a device into a processor register such as the accumulator; in the case of the PDP-9, the accumulator can be cleared at IOT 1 time if instruction bit no. 14 is a 1 (figure 3).

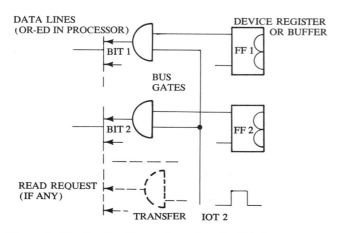

Figure 5—Reading data from a device into the digital computer

In I/O systems incorporating *parity-checking,* a parity-check bit is transmitted on an additional data line. Parity is then checked by simple logic at the destination, and the processor is interrupted when an error is detected.

Transfer of "discretes" (control signals, logic signals). If the subdevice bits in an input/output instruction word do not permit a sufficient variety of device logic control, one may employ either additional bits on the *data* bus or *complete control words transmitted over the data bus* to a *control register* in the device. Processor timing information is readily transmitted in terms of the IOT pulses.

In general, control registers require jam transfers. Examples of such control registers are found in the free-logic patchbays of analog/hybrid computers, where the control bits control analog-computer modes (COMPUTE, RESET, etc.), analog switches, etc. Perhaps the most important type of control register is the *multiplexer control register* selecting the multiplexer input channel for an analog-to-digital converter. Control registers may permit incrementation, *i.e.,* the control register is a counter reset to a given initial count by an I/O instruction and then incremented as needed; the variety of possible arrangements is endless.

EXAMPLE: A simple display interface. As an example of an interface requiring only program-controlled data transfers from the computer, figures 6a and b illustrate the design of a cathode-ray tube *display* for the PDP-9 computer. The display system shown in figure 6a positions a point (X, Y) on the oscilloscope screen through deflection amplifiers driven by 9-bit DACs. Similar delay feedback networks on the X and Y amplifiers cause both DAC outputs to approach new values

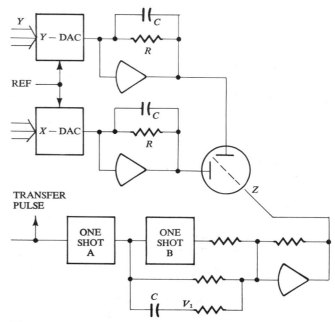

Figure 6a, b.—A simple graphic-display system

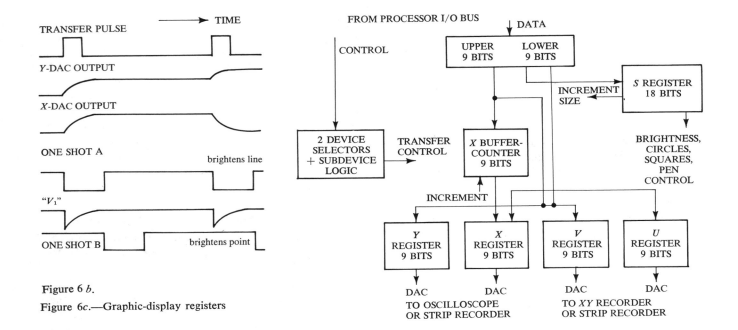

Figure 6 *b*.

Figure 6*c*.—Graphic-display registers

exponentially with a time constant of about 4 μsec. When the X and Y DACs are updated simultaneously, the point (X, Y) generates a straight-line segment useful for vector generation[3] and curve interpolation. Two one-shot multivibrators (A, B) permit selective brightening of each stroke and/or its endpoint (figure 6b).

Figure 6c shows the registers of the display interface, which employs two separate device selectors. The resulting combinations of six IOT pulses and four subdevice bits permit many different types of data transfers corresponding to different display instructions. The principal modes of operation are:

1. With Y in bits 0 to 8, and X in bits 9 to 17 of the I/O bus, transfer X and Y simultaneously.
2. Transfer X from bits 0 to 8 of the I/O bus into the X buffer. Then transfer Y from bits 0 to 8 into the Y DAC register, and transfer the X buffer simultaneously into the X DAC register.
3. Transfer Y, and simultaneously increment the X buffer, and transfer the incremented contents into the X DAC register (curve plotting with constant increments).

Various other instructions, with and without line and/or point brightening, permit one to draw X and Y axes, as well as separate X and Y displacements. Through the use of subdevice bits, one can, instead, load the 18-bit S register with combinations of 0's and 1's from the data lines. This S register is an example of a control register loaded from the data bus; the S-register bits can control point brightness, X—increment size, and also serve to add circles and squares of varying sizes about selected points (X, Y). Subdevice-bit logic steers the six available command pulses to effect data transfer

between different registers. The U and V registers shown in figure 6c serve additional DACs used to drive an XY plotter from the same interface. It is also possible to employ the X, Y, U, and V registers to drive four channels of a strip-chart recorder.

3. DEVICE-CONDITIONED TRANSFERS: SENSE AND INTERRUPT SYSTEMS

Flag sensing. The interface-system command pulses permit program-controlled data transfers at the correct processor-timed instants. Frequently, however, a device thus addressed might not be ready for a transfer; an important example is an ADC which has not completed a conversion. In such cases, program-controlled data or control-logic transfers may be preceded by a *sense-line interrogation or flag test.* The device status is indicated by a *flag* (logic level, usually a flip-flop output). A special instruction addressed to the associated device selector gates one of the command pulses (IOT 1 in the PDP-9) and, if the flag (level) is up, onto a *skip bus* in the interface cable (figure 7). The pulse on the skip

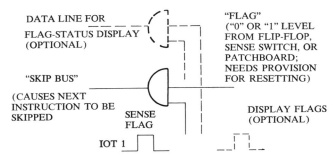

Figure 7—Sense-line operation

bus increments the processor instruction counter, which then skips the next instruction to produce a program branch. An example would be:

1. SKIP IF ADC FLAG IS UP
2. REPEAT LAST INSTRUCTION
3. READ ADC
. . . .

The program will cycle until the device flag is up, at which time the program continues, usually with a data-transfer instruction.

Instead of interrogating multiple sense lines in turn, one may have a special READ ALL FLAGS instruction which gates several flags onto the data bus (figure 7). The resulting "status word" can then be logically interpreted by the computer program; in particular, the data word may serve as an indirect address for the next instruction and thus permit multiple branching.

Interrupts and Priority Interrupts. While flag testing is an inexpensive way to have a device control the digital program, flag-testing instructions, and especially repeated skip-sense loops, can be a serious waste of computer time. In an *interrupt system*, a device-flag indication interrupts the computer program after the current operation cycle, causes the instruction counter and the active arithmetic registers to be saved in suitable memory locations, and starts a new instruction sequence (*interrupt-servicing routine*) from a specific memory location associated with the interrupt. The interrupt-servicing routine may be a data-transfer or data-processing subroutine. Again, an interrupt may generate input and output instructions for dealing with device or system malfunctions (shut a system down, replace a defective device); an important example is an *interrupt on an analog-computer overload indication.*

Interrupt operation would be simple if there were only one source of interrupt signals, but this is essentially never the case. Even a stand-alone digital computer usually has several interrupts corresponding to peripheral malfunctions (tape unit out of tape, printer out of paper), and flight simulators, space-vehicle controllers, and process-control systems may have hundreds of different interrupts.

A practical interrupt system must, therefore, contain provisions for "trapping" the program to different memory locations corresponding to the individual interrupts. A more difficult problem is to deal with *priorities* in case of simultaneous or successive demands from different interrupt lines.

The most primitive system is to OR all interrupt flags onto a single interrupt line, whose interrupt-servicing routine then tests all of the device flags in the sequence of their relative priority. As soon as the flag causing the interrupt is found, it will be necessary to disable transmission of all lower-priority flag levels. Such a system requires only simple electronics and disposes of the priority problem, but the flag-sensing program is time consuming (n devices may require $\log_2 n$ successive decisions, even if the flag sensing is done by successive binary decisions). A somewhat faster method might be to employ a flag status word for indirect addressing.

A true *priority-interrupt system* involves a number of additional lines in the interface (sometimes these lines are collected in a separate interrupt cable). In such a system, a device flag can cause an interrupt if

1. The interrupt is *enabled* (*armed*) by the digital-computer program, and
2. No higher priority interrupt is being serviced.

Each interrupt-line subsystem, then, has three states: it may be inactive, enabled, or waiting for service.[1,2] Figure 8 shows simplified hardware for one interrupt. An *interrupt request* (device-flag level) sets the *request flip-flop* in synchronism with a digital-computer-clock.

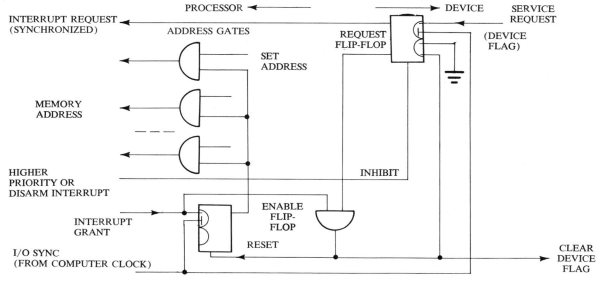

Figure 8—Interrupt logic for one device

output (I/O sync), unless the interrupt is disabled by the program or by a higher priority interrupt. The request flip-flop transmits an accurately timed interrupt request step to the processor, which then disables all lower priority interrupt lines and transmits an *interrupt-grant* level. The latter permits the processor-clocked *enable flip-flop* to gate the starting address for the interrupt program into the memory-address register at the correct time in the computer cycle. The device flag is cleared at the same time. The priority-deciding logic in the processor is not shown in figure 8. Several different systems exist, for instance:

1. The request flip-flops may be clocked in sequence of relative priority, so that the highest priority request wins. This method is practical only with a relatively small number of devices, because it involves a delay in servicing lower-priority interrupts.
2. With interrupt circuits similar to that of figure 8 physically associated with each device, the devices are arranged on the party-line interrupt cable so that the device closest to the computer has the highest priority and can inhibit the request flip-flops of devices farther down the interrupt bus.

Substantially more complex interrupt logic exists. It may be possible to arm or disarm individual interrupts or groups of interrupts under the control of the main digital-computer program or by the interrupt-servicing routines. In general, the program will revert to the next-

lower-priority interrupt-servicing routine and then to the main program after a high-priority interrupt has been serviced. Interrupts thus awaiting service in a queue produce very special programming problems in real-time computation if two or more interrupt-servicing programs require a previously interrupted subroutine (re-entrant programming, Reference 4).

Example of device-conditioned real-time operation: Simple iterative hybrid computation. Real-time operations are controlled by a real-time clock in the processor or, more frequently, in the interface, which is sensed or interrupts processor operation to synchronize the computation process. The following example involves both clock timing and waiting for successive ADC conversion cycles.

To compute statistics (averages, amplitude distributions, correlation functions) on timed samples of random-input analog-computer runs, or to obtain optimal parameters from such timed sample values requires only a very simple hybrid-computer interface. Referring to figure 9, a real-time clock in the analog-computer console controls the entire operation. The analog-computer *reset pulse* R places the analog computer in the COMPUTE mode and orders track-hold circuits to sample selected solutions at clock-pulse-counter-determined times. In our example, we assume that there are two independent ADCs; after each ADC is ordered to convert, its flag will be down until the conversion is completed. In our simple computation, the digital com-

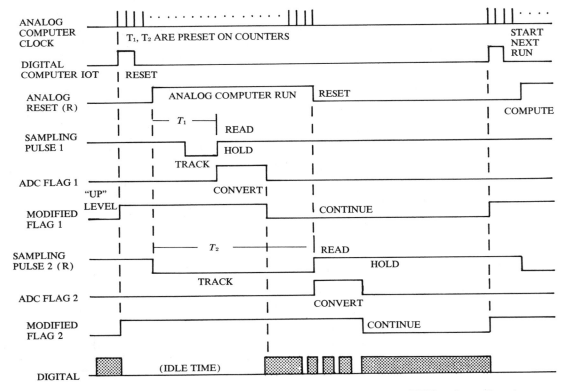

Figure 9—Timing for simple iterative hybrid computation. Negative flag logic is shown (*i.e.*, flags are "UP" at low voltage)

puter has nothing to do in the meantime, and can thus idle in a sense-skip loop until the first analog-to-digital conversion is completed. It may then do whatever work it can with the first sample alone, after which it tests ADC flag 2. When the second conversion is completed, the second sample is read, and the digital computation proceeds. The analog computer is reset after a predetermined number of clock pulses and remains in RESET until the digital computation is finished. The RESET period preceding the second analog-computer run may be either sufficiently long *a priori,* or the digital computer may start successive analog-computer runs by instructions at the end of the digital program.

With a more sophisticated hybrid-computer interface, the sense-skip cycles can be replaced by interrupts associated with the ADC flags. Note, however, that in this simple example the interrupt does not really save time over sense-skip operation, since the digital computer will not have any data to work with until the first conversion is completed. In many such applications, though, the digital computer may revert to a cathode-ray-tube-display routine during any idle time.[13]

4. DIRECT MEMORY ACCESS AND AUTOMATIC DATA CHANNELS

Cycle stealing. While our last example showed a practical and important application of simple program-controlled data transfer, the step-by-step implementation of separate input/output instructions limits data transmission rates and complicates programming. With modern, fast processors, the time wasted in alternate fetching or depositing of instructions and data is usually considered prohibitive. It is then preferable to interface our parallel data bus directly with the memory buffer register and to request and grant one cycle-pauses in processor operation for direct transfer of data to or from memory (*interlace* or *cycle-stealing* operation). In larger digital computers, a data bus may even access one memory bank without stopping processor interaction with other memory banks. To make direct memory access practical, we must be able to:

1. Address desired locations in memory
2. Synchronize cycle stealing with processor operation
3. Initiate transfers by device requests (this includes clock-timed transfers) or by the computer program.

Since two or more devices may request data transfers at the same time, one requires *priority logic* similar to that shown in figure 8. In figure 10, a *service request* (device flag), unless inhibited by a higher priority request, is answered by a *priority grant* which strobes a suitable memory address into the processor memory-address register while the device data are placed on the direct memory access (DMA) data bus by device or memory circuits. Levels on separate control lines implement the decision of reading versus writing. Note that

cycle stealing in no way disturbs the program sequence in the processor. The program simply stops for the data transfer and then resumes where it left off.

Automatic data channels. As just described, the DMA transfer was device initiated. A program-dependent decision to transfer data, even from or to memory, requires a programmed instruction. With a *single-word* transfer of this type, relatively little is gained by the direct memory access. The answer to this objection is that most DMA transfers, whether device or program initiated, involve not single words but *blocks* of tens, hundreds, or even thousands of data words.

Figure 11 shows how the simple DMA system of figure 10 may be expanded into an *automatic data channel* for block transfers. Data for a block can arrive or depart asynchronously, and the DMA controller will steal cycles as needed and permit the program to go on between cycles. A block of words to be transferred will, in general, occupy a corresponding block of adjacent memory registers. Successive memory addresses can be gated into the memory address register by a counter, the *current-address counter.* Before any data transfer takes place, a programmed instruction sets the current-address counter to a desired *initial address*; the desired number of words (block length) is set into a second counter, the *word counter,* which will count down with each data transfer until zero is reached after the desired number of transfers. As service requests arrive from, say, an analog-to-digital converter or data link, the DMA control logic implements successive cycle-steal requests and gates successive current addresses into the memory-address register as the current-address counter counts up.

The word counter is similarly decremented once per data word. When a block transfer is completed, the word counter may cause an interrupt, so that a new block of

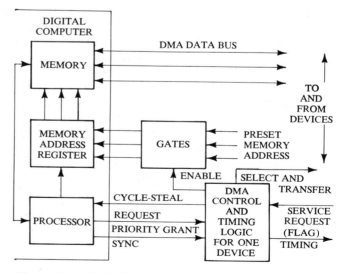

Figure 10—A simple direct-memory-access system

data can be processed. The word counter can also serve for device control or selection (*e.g.*, for selecting successive ADC multiplexer addresses).

A DMA system will, in general, involve several data channels of this type, each with a DMA control, address gates, a current-address counter, and a word counter, with different priorities assigned to different channels. For efficient handling of randomly timed requests from multiple devices (and to prevent loss of data words), data-channel systems usually incorporate *buffer registers* in the interface or in devices such as ADCs or DACs.

Efficiency of data-channel operation. Programming considerations. Direct memory access can transfer data blocks at very high rates (10^6 words per second is readily possible). To indicate the remarkable efficiency of cycle-stealing direct memory access with multiple block-transfer data channels, consider the operation of a training-type digital flight simulator employing a small 24-bit processor (3C DDP-224), which solves aircraft and engine equations and services an elaborate cockpit mockup with many controls and instrument displays. During each 160-ms time increment, the interface not only performs 174 analog-to-digital conversions requiring a total conversion time of 7.7 ms, but also 430 digital-to-analog conversions, and handles 180 24-bit words of discrete control information. *The actual time required to transfer all this information in and out of the data channels is 143 ms per time increment, but, because of the fast direct memory transfers, cycle-stealing subtracts only 3.2 ms for each 160 ms of processor time.[1]*

Direct-memory-access data channels will not only simplify input/output programming by substituting hardware for software, but also have an added advantage, especially in hybrid-computer simulation and in instrumentation. A hybrid-computer interface connected through a data channel looks, as far as the central processor is concerned, essentially like a standard digital-computer peripheral such as a tape deck or disk. As a result, interface data can be handled by simple extensions of ordinary FORTRAN read and write statements.

Simplified data channels. While data-channel systems of the type shown in figure 11 are usually options or accessories for digital computers, simplified data channels can be an integral part of the processor-system design. In particular, the word counter can be an index register in the processor, and the current address may be obtained through indirect addressing. Multiple data channels of this type are provided, for instance, in the Honeywell/3C 516 and in the Digital Equipment Corporation PDP-8I and PDP-9. In the PDP-8I and 9, individual memory registers can be incremented by external pulses; one such register serves as a data-channel word counter, and one serves as the current-address counter. Both registers are initialized by a program instruction depositing suitable words. When the processor honors a data-channel request, the respective device transmits the address of its assigned word-counter register. During the first cycle of the channel transfer, the contents of this word counter are incremented, and the address of the current-address register is established. In the second cycle, the contents of the current-address register are incremented to establish the effective address of the memory location delivering or receiving the data word. During the third cycle (or fourth cycle in the case of out-transfers), the actual data transfer occurs.[9] Because of the extra counting operations, such memory-imple-

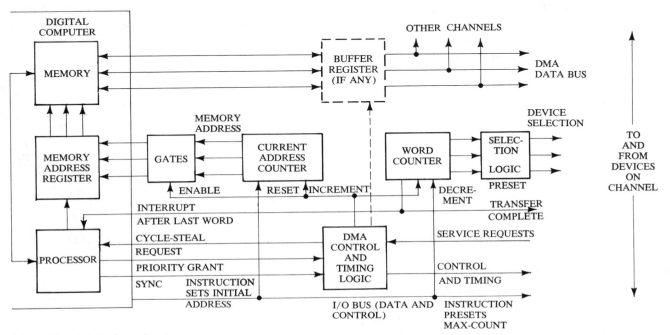

Figure 11—A data-channel system

mented data channels steal three or four computer cycles per data transfer, as compared to the single cycle required for externally controlled direct memory access with the same computer, but the built-in data channel still permits maximum word-transfer rates exceeding 200,000 words per second at very low cost.

Interfacing with satellite processors. When a digital computer requires an elaborate multiple data-channel interface, say, with several analog-computer consoles and/or other instrumentation, the data-channel control system and its associated buffers may well be replaced by a small, fast general-purpose digital computer (*satellite processor*), which can then take over many additional functions such as reformatting, scaling, fixed-to-floating-point conversion, display refreshing, etc., and may also have some stand-alone capability (figure 12a and b).

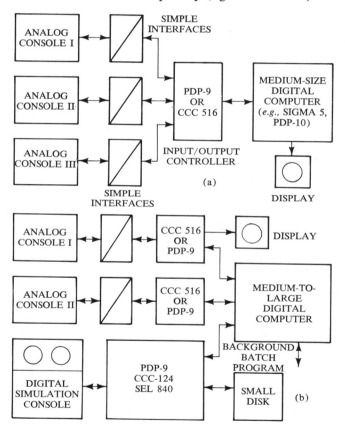

Figure 12*a, b.*—Use of satellite computers for I/O processing in larger hybrid-computer installations

5. SPECIAL DIRECT-MEMORY-ACCESS TECHNIQUES

Hybrid-computer function generation. Digital-computer interfaces with direct memory access permit a number of interesting hybrid analog-digital operations at high sampling rates with a minimum of digital-computer pro-

gramming. Perhaps the most generally useful of these techniques is *hybrid-computer generation of an analog function* in the form

$$F(X) = A_i X + B_i (X_i \leq X < X_{i+1} = X_i + \Delta X;$$
$$i = 1, 2, \ldots) \quad (1)$$

Here the argument X is an analog voltage, and A_i, B_i are tabulated digital words set, respectively, into a multiplying DAC (MDAC) and a DAC to produce the analog output (1).[15] *Our proposed implementation of this technique will perform the table lookup at high speed by means of simple DMA hardware rather than by programmed operations.* X is read with a fast and inexpensive ADC having only 6-bit resolution but 12- to 13-bit accuracy. The least significant ADC bit corresponds to the constant tabulation interval ΔX. The 6-bit ADC output, representing the "breakpoint coordinate" X_i just below X, is now applied to the digital-computer memory-address register in the manner of figure 10, with the addition of some higher-order bits indicating the origins of tables storing the A_i and B_i in memory. After the DMA circuits read A_i into the MDAC buffer, one of the extra bits is switched to read B_i into the DAC buffer.

Greater resolution (more ADC bits) can be obtained at the expense of extra memory without increasing the short time (1 to 8 μsec plus ADC conversion time) required to produce the desired function. Note that a small ($\$12,000$) digital computer and interface can replace 10 to 20 card-programmed diode function generators costing at least $\$2,500$ each, so that the function-generator application *alone* will pay for a small digital computer and interface. Moreover, functions of *two* variables X, Y can be similarly generated in the form

$$F(X,Y) = A_{ik}X + B_{ik} + (C_{ik}X + D_{ik})Y$$
$$\times (X_i \leq X < X_{i+1}, Y_k \leq Y < Y_{k+1}) \quad (2)$$

One simply addresses each interpolation coefficient with a 12-bit word (X_i, Y_k) where X_i and Y_k are 6-bit bytes read from two ADCs.

Hybrid-computer function storage and delay. A direct-memory-access data channel, if available, is a natural means for storing an analog-computer-generated function $X(t)$ of the time t in terms of successive samples $X(k\Delta t)$ for iterative hybrid computation[16] or transport-delay simulation. To read out a delayed sample $X(k\Delta t - m\Delta t)$ for the latter purpose, it seems best to provide a second data channel addressing the same successive memory registers. Reading and writing operations will alternate. A *constant* time delay $\tau = m\Delta t$ between the input and output samples is readily set up by suitable initialization of the current-address counters in the two data channels. Samples of two or more functions can be interleaved for storage, but separate output data chan-

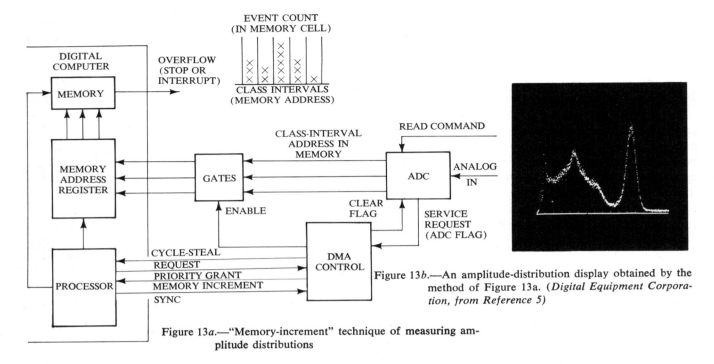

Figure 13*a*.—"Memory-increment" technique of measuring amplitude distributions

Figure 13*b*.—An amplitude-distribution display obtained by the method of Figure 13a. (*Digital Equipment Corporation, from Reference 5*)

nels will be required if the different functions are to have different delays. Simulation of *variable* transport delays (*e.g.*, variable flow velocity in a pipe) will require the design of special hardware for controlling the operation of the current-address counter in the data channel used for reading the delayed output, or program-controlled operation will be necessary.

Memory-increment technique for measuring amplitude distributions. In the Digital Equipment Corporation PDP-8I and PDP-9 computers, a special pulse input will *increment* the contents of a memory location addressed by the DMA address lines; an interrupt can be generated when one of the memory cells is full. When ADC outputs representing successive samples of a random voltage are applied to the DMA address lines, the memory-increment feature will effectively generate a model of the voltage-amplitude distribution in the computer memory: each memory address corresponds to a voltage class interval, and the contents of the memory register represent the number of samples falling into that class interval. Data taking is terminated after a preset number of samples, or when the first memory register overloads. The empirical amplitude distribution thus created in memory may be displayed or plotted by a display routine (figure 13a, b), and statistics such as

$$\overline{X} = \frac{1}{n}\sum_{k=1}^{n} X_k, \quad X^2 = \frac{1}{n}\sum_{k=1}^{n} X_k^2 \ldots$$

are readily computed after the distribution is complete. This technique has been extensively applied to the analysis of pulse-energy spectra from nuclear-physics experiments.[5,13]

As in the case of function-table lookup, *joint distributions of two random variables X, Y* can be similarly compiled. It is only necessary to apply, say, a 12-bit word (X, Y) composed of two 6-bit bytes corresponding to two ADC outputs X and Y to the memory-address register. Now each addressed memory location will correspond to the region $X_i \leq X < X_{i+1}$, $Y_k \leq Y < Y_{k+1}$ in XY space. Figure 13b shows a PDP-8 display of an amplitude distribution.[3]

"Add-to-memory" techniques.[5] Another command pulse input to the PDP-9 interface will *add* a data word on the I/O-bus data lines to the memory location addressed by the DMA address lines without ever bothering the digital-computer arithmetic unit or program. This "add-to-memory" feature permits useful linear operations on data obtained from various instruments; the only application well known at this time is to *data averaging*.

Figure 14 illustrates an especially interesting application of data averaging, which has been especially useful

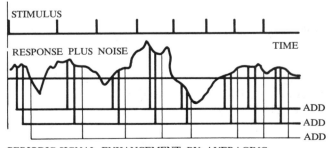

PERIODIC-SIGNAL ENHANCEMENT BY AVERAGING

Figure 14*a*.—Signal enhancement by periodic averaging

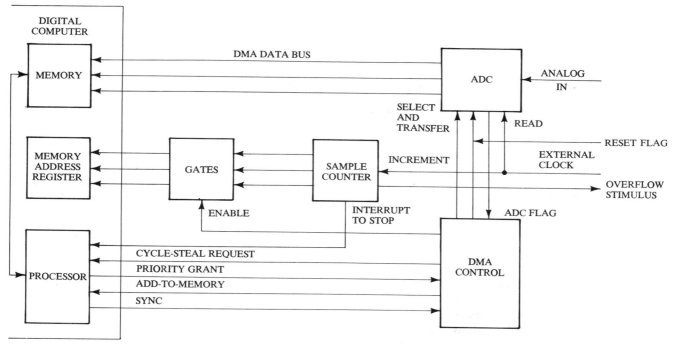

Figure 14*b*.—"Add-to-memory" technique for signal averaging

in biological-data reduction, (*e.g.,* electro-encephalo-gram analysis). Periodically applied stimuli produce the same system response after each stimulus, so that one obtains an analog waveform periodic with the period *T* of the applied stimuli. To pull the desired function $X(t)$ out of additive zero-mean random noise, one adds $X(t)$, $X(t+T)$, $X(t+2T)$, . . . during successive periods to enhance the signal, while the noise will tend to average out.

Referring to figure 14b, successive ADC samples $X(k\Delta t)$ are applied to the I/O bus to be added into memory, while the DMA address is determined by a clock counter whose output $k = 1, 2, . . .$ addresses successive memory registers during each period. The clock-counter is reset with each stimulus, so that the *k*th memory location accumulates the desired sum. Figure 14c shows a periodic signal obtained in this manner in about 40 db of additive noise.

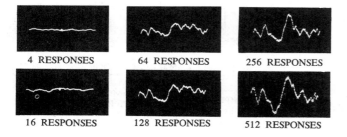

Figure 14*c*.—A damped sine wave extracted from additive noise by signal averaging (*Digital Equipment Corporation, from Reference 5*)

6. DESIGN OF A COMPLETE HYBRID-COMPUTER INTERFACE

Applications. Hybrid analog-digital computation has been applied successfully to many simulation problems. Perhaps the most appealing applications involve *iterative multiparameter optimization* and *Monte Carlo simulation of random phenomena* with fast analog computers and relatively small digital processors (see also figure 9). Provision of sufficient digital memory for *function storage* permits improved solution of partial differential equations and multiplexing of analog computing elements.[16]

In the so-called *combined-simulation applications,* especially in the aerospace industry, a larger digital computer may integrate some of the system's state equations, especially those involving only low-frequency components but requiring high accuracy (*e.g.,* vehicle trajectory equations). The important topic of digital-computer *function generation* for slow- and medium-speed analog computation has already been mentioned. In an increasing number of real-time flight simulations, the analog/hybrid portion of the equipment reduces essentially to equipment *interfacing a mainly digital simulator with real or mockup instruments, controls, and human operators.* Finally, *automation of analog-computer potentiometer setup and static checking procedures* is an important feature of small and large hybrid-computer installations.

A reasonably flexible hybrid-computer interface exhibits many of the features found in the actual interfaces of digital computers and the instruments and controls of real systems. For this reason, *a hybrid-computer with*

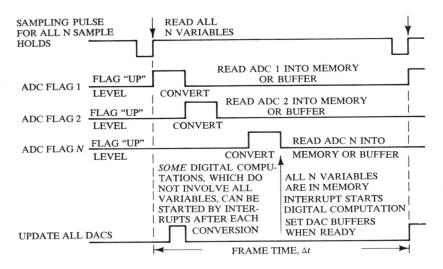

SAMPLING PULSE FOR ALL N SAMPLE HOLDS — READ ALL N VARIABLES

ADC FLAG 1 — FLAG "UP" / LEVEL — CONVERT — READ ADC 1 INTO MEMORY OR BUFFER

ADC FLAG 2 — FLAG "UP" / LEVEL — CONVERT — READ ADC 2 INTO MEMORY OR BUFFER

ADC FLAG N — FLAG "UP" / LEVEL — CONVERT — READ ADC N INTO MEMORY OR BUFFER

SOME DIGITAL COMPUTATIONS, WHICH DO NOT INVOLVE ALL VARIABLES, CAN BE STARTED BY INTERRUPTS AFTER EACH CONVERSION

ALL N VARIABLES ARE IN MEMORY INTERRUPT STARTS DIGITAL COMPUTATION SET DAC BUFFERS WHEN READY

UPDATE ALL DACS

FRAME TIME, Δt

Figure 15 — Timing diagram for combined simulation. N analog voltages are successively read by the interface. As digital processing proceeds, DAC outputs are successively read into the DAC buffers; then all DACs are updated simultaneously. Negative flag logic is shown, as in figure 9.

a suitably designed interface system is an excellent means for the design and simulation of instrumentation and control interfaces for process control, communication, and aerospace systems. In the following, we shall summarize our review by listing some of the features desirable in a flexible hybrid-computer interface installation; figure 15 illustrates a typical application.

Interface requirements: Data conversion. A useful interface system linking a modern fast 100-amplifier analog computer and a digital processor in the $70,000 to $100,0000 class with 16 to 32K memory (*e.g.*, PDP-9, DDP-124, Sigma 5) might comprise, depending on the specific application:

1. 4 to 40 channels of *analog-to-digital conversion.* Except with very slow analog variables (say below 10 Hz), a multiplexed ADC will require a sample-hold circuit for each channel. Most installations multiplex a fast (5 to 20 μsec) 13- to 14-bit ADC, but this should be weighed against the possibility of using *separate slower (and less expensive) ADC's,* which save the cost (and errors) of multiplexer and sample-hold circuits, provide separate buffers, and simplify the interface design. In combined simulation, 20 separate 100 μsec ADC's are just as fast as one multiplexed 10 μsec ADC. Such a trade off does *not* apply, of course, to fast data processing with one or two ADC channels (Figure 16a, b).

2. 4 to 40 DACs. *Only double-buffered MDACs should be considered for general-purpose hybrid computers.*

3. For high computing speeds and for programming convenience, ADCs and DACs should be interfaced to two *direct-memory-access data channels as well as to program-controlled device selectors.*

We have already discussed some of the operations possible with direct memory access which will, of course, add to the cost of the interface.

Interface timing and control. Interface patching. The design of practical and convenient *timing and control logic* is considered next. For maximum flexibility, *we recommend that much of the control logic be terminated in the analog computer digital-logic patchbay.* If the latter has insufficient space, a separate *interface patchbay* may be considered. The following terminations are desirable:

1. External READ command inputs and flag outputs for all ADCs

2. Buffer-transfer (update) command inputs for all DACs

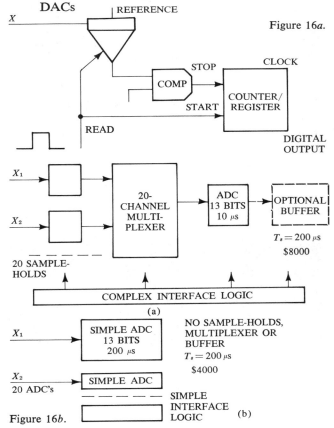

Figure 16a.

$T_s = 200\ \mu s$
$8000

(a)

NO SAMPLE-HOLDS, MULTIPLEXER OR BUFFER
$T_s = 200\ \mu s$
$4000

SIMPLE INTERFACE LOGIC

Figure 16b.

(b)

3. I/O data-bus terminations, with AND gates
4. 8 to 12 sense lines and 2 to 12 interrupt lines
5. Two or more ADC output registers for function generation and amplitude-distribution analysis
6. Terminations for the DMA address gates
7. Two or three 10- to 14-bit counter/registers with parallel, increment, and reset inputs. These counter/registers will serve for DMA addressing, and also as data-bus-preset clock counters which permit the digital computer to time analog COMPUTE periods and sampling pulses.
8. Select, command-pulse, and subdevice outputs for a special device selector associated with the control interface, and a 12- to 24-bit control output register loaded by the data bus and associated with the same device selector.
9. Miscellaneous control-pulse terminations, such as I/O SYNC (digital-computer clock), POWER-CLEAR, analog-computer clock, sampling, and RESET pulses, etc.

If a separate interface patchbay is used, it should be connected to the digital-logic patchbay by at least 12 trunk lines and may well contain some free digital logic (gates, flip-flops).

Static-check and coefficient-setting systems. An example of serial data transfer. The interface subsystem designed for accurate readout of all analog-computing-element output voltages and for analog coefficient setting can be useful enough so that it alone, too, can readily pay for a small digital processor and interface.[16] Especially in small hybrid computers, the static-readout system had probably best employ the analog-computer digital voltmeter rather than the fast ADC of the interface. The reason for this is that static readout requires less speed but, usually, greater accuracy than dynamic computations. Accurate readout of individual computing elements is usually achieved by a system of reed relays or FET switches set by a digital selector tree or matrix interfaced with the I/O data bus, which sets each address prior to reading the associated voltage. One usually provides for a digital-computer program which checks analog-computer voltages against precomputed static-check values.[16]

Servo-set coefficient potentiometers are set by servomechanisms actuated by a precision ladder network digitally switched by the I/O bus; each potentiometer must, of course, be addressed and set in turn. Much faster coefficient setting (plus freedom from maintenance of mechanical components) is achieved with *digital attenuators.* These are essentially FET MDACs set, in turn, by the digital computer. To avoid separate addressing of the 13- to 14-bit lines associated with *each* of perhaps 200 digital attenuators, an interface system developed at the University of Arizona sets each digital attenuator by a 14-bit shift register read *serially* at a 100-KHz rate from a central interface register. This method affords a considerable saving in hardware and maintenance at a negligible sacrifice in setting speed.

ACKNOWLEDGMENTS

The writer is grateful to the National Aeronautics and Space Administration for their support of this work under NASA Grant NsG-646.

REFERENCES

1 ANDELMAN S J
Real-time I/O techniques
Computer Design May 1966

2 BORGER E R
Characteristics of priority interrupts
Datamation June 1965

3 DERTOUZOS M L
Phaseplot: an on-line graphical display technique
IEEETEC April 1967

4 JOHNSON B
Real-time simulation
Proceedings of IBM Digital Symposium 1956 International Business Machines Inc New York 1967

5 KLERER M   KORN G A
Digital Computer User's Handbook
McGraw-Hill New York 1967

6 SCHMIDT W E
Methods for priority interrupts
Simulation July 1967

7 YAROSH N P et al
Interface optimization investigation
Technical Report AFAL-TR-67-152 Air Force Avionics Laboratory Wright-Patterson Air Force Base Ohio 1968

8 *Reference Manual for SEL 840 A*
Systems Engineering Laboratories Fort Lauderdale Florida 1966

9 *PDP-9 User's Manual*
Digital Equipment Corporation Maynard Massachusetts 1967 revised 1968

10 *Digital computers and the analog world*
Technical Information Series Note No 5 Redcor Corporation Canoga Park California 1967

11 *Data 620/i Systems Computer Manual*
Varian Data Machines Newport Beach California 1968

12 *1044 Hybrid Linkage Unit*
Publication 6030-1 Geospace Computer Division Houston Texas 1968

13 *Small Computer Handbook*
Digital Equipment Corporation Maynard Massachusetts 1968

14 PRACHT C P
A new digital-attenuator system
Simulation April 1967

15 RUBIN A I
Hybrid techniques for generating arbitrary functions
Simulation December 1966

16 KORN G A   KORN T M
Electronic analog and hybrid computers
McGraw-Hill New York 1964

Part 2
Minicomputer Software

Introductory Comments

One of the lessons learned from bitter experience during the past ten years or so is that the cost of a computer application is not simply the sum of the costs of the hardware, input/output devices, and their interfacing. In fact, successful implementation of a computer application usually results in as much cost in software as in hardware. It may not be obvious why this is so. In fact, it is often not clear why the often quoted rate of production of programmers of approximately four to eight instructions per man day should be so low. The answer is, of course, that no application is carried out by defining completely and definitively all details of the application, coding it, and leaving it alone thereafter. Rather, experience indicates that applications tend to be developed as they are programmed including major and minor changes in objectives resulting from testing of initial stages. The net result is a software system that evolves rather than being simply coded once and for all. Furthermore, the computer is only one element in the system and consequently must adapt itself to the application rather than vice versa. As a result, many applications require rather unique software, and the low production rate quoted before simply reflects the development time that is necessary in any application in which extensive systems engineering is required.

This does not mean, however, that we have to accept the high cost of software forever. Rather, the problem has been recognized and various approaches to its solution developed. The papers in this part have not been selected to illustrate basic programming techniques for minicomputers. In fact, no attempt has been made to include papers describing assembly systems, Fortran programming, linking loaders, problems of paper-tape, updating programs, and all the other details which arise in the programming of small machines. Many of the papers listed in the bibliography do discuss these problems as do most text books that introduce computer programming.

The objective of this part is to discuss software systems that have been developed to solve application problems economically. The paper by W. Diehl and M. Mensch discusses the use of a higher level language (real-time Fortran) for the programming of on-line control systems. They point out the difference between a scientific program written in Fortran and a real-time program that must interact with input/output devices and the environment in real time. In discussing the extensions to normal Fortran that are required for industrial process control programming, they illustrate very clearly the source of the complexity of real-time software. While reading this paper, consider the problems of implementing a real-time system either in Fortran or in assembly code from the point of view of a modification in the specifications of the system after it has been partially programmed. The complexity and interaction of various real-time tasks can result in a major effort to change once the structure has been set and the various modules programmed.

Just as important as describing concurrent real-time tasks is the problem of actually describing the application in the language. H. E. Pike and T. L. Willmott describe the problems of application programming in process control in the following two papers. In particular, it is noted that reliability, error recovery, speed of response, and extensive operation communication requirements preclude the straightforward programming of many applications even in a higher level language such as real-time Fortran. Rather, economics dictates the generation of special languages and software systems for various applications such as direct digital control, data acquisition, etc. These software systems are general purpose in that they can be applied to many applications of the same type but are very specific in that they are directed only toward those applications. The objective, of course, is the write-off of the software cost over many users as opposed to generation of unique software for each user. The software systems described by Pike and Willmott vary from table driven systems (the loop record organization for direct digital control and data acquisition described by Willmott) through "fill in the blanks" programming systems, as described by Pike. The latter should be examined carefully because the motivation for these systems comes from problems that are present in many computer applications. For example, documentation of software has always been a significant problem. "Fill in the blanks" systems are self-documenting in the sense that the application is completely defined by the forms which an engineer (as opposed to a programmer) fills in to describe his application.

The last brief paper by S. R. Amstutz has been included to illustrate the complexity of software requirements for many real-time minicomputer applications. He discusses communication executives or control programs, but the conclusions are the same for executives for process control, data acquisition, and other applications as well. Of particular interest in this paper is the problem of implementing software for a special purpose application such as this. Higher level languages such as Fortran are not really suitable for forming complex linked data structures of the type needed in this application. Assembly level programming is usually the solution, although it may not be entirely desirable. The alternative is a special purpose programming language for the implementation language in the literature today. These languages are more complex than languages such as Fortran because they are designed for a much more complex programming purpose. In reading the papers on minicomputer software, it is important to understand the difference in complexity between an application programming problem and a systems programming problem so that one can reasonably evaluate software aids provided by a minicomputer vendor, or languages that may become available, or special purpose packages for various applications.

Bibliography

[1] "Dataless programming," R. M. Balzer, *AFIPS Conf. Proc., Vol. 31, 1967 Fall Joint Comput. Conf.,* pp. 535–544.

[2] "The micro assembler, SWAP—a general purpose interpretive processor," M. E. Barton, *AFIPS Conf. Proc., Vol. 37, 1970 Fall Joint Comput. Conf.,* pp. 1–8E.

[3] "Prospro/1800," D. G. Bates, *IEEE Trans. Ind. Electron. Contr. Instrum.,* vol. IECI-15, Dec. 1968, pp. 70–75.

[4] "The design of computer languages and software systems: a basic approach," R. K. Bennett, *Comput. Automat.,* Feb. 1969, pp. 28–33.

[5] "PEARL—the concept of a process and experiment oriented programming language," J. Brandes *et al., Elektron. Datenverarbeitung,* Oct. 1970, pp. 429–442.

[6] "The ML/1 macro processor," P. J. Brown, *Commun. Ass. Comput. Mach.,* vol. 10, Oct. 1967, pp. 618–623.

[7] "Instrumenting computer systems and their programs," B. Brussell and R. A. Koster, *AFIPS Conf. Proc., Vol. 37, 1970 Fall Joint Comput. Conf.,* pp. 525–534.

[8] "Getting to know your mini," W. C. Carter, *Comput. Decisions,* Nov. 1970, pp. 17–21.

[9] "On the automatic simplification of source-language programs," E. R. Clark, *Commun. Ass. Comput. Mach.,* vol. 10, Mar. 1967, pp. 160–164.

[10] "Laboratory computers: their capabilities and how to make them work for you," P. B. Denes and M. V. Mathews, *Proc. IEEE,* vol. 58, Apr. 1970, pp. 520–530.

[11] "On-line simulation of block-diagram systems," M. L. Dertouzos, Martin E. Kaliski, and K. P. Polzen, *IEEE Trans. Comput.,* vol. C-18, Apr. 1969, pp. 333–342.

[12] "When user and vendor collaborate," V. V. Dobrohotoff, L. Silver, and S. Bacher, *Contr. Eng.*, Jan. 1969, pp. 124–127.

[13] "PL/1 as an implementation language," R. A. Freiburghouse, *1971 IEEE Int. Conv. Dig.*, pp. 64–65.

[14] "A computer system for automation of a laboratory," P. J. Friedl, C. H. Sederholm, T. R. Lusebring, and C. J. Jenny, *AFIPS Conf. Proc., Vol. 33, Pt. 2, 1968 Fall Joint Comput. Conf.*, pp. 1051–1060.

[15] "Computer languages for process control—their future," D. R. Frost, *IEEE Trans. Ind. Electron. Contr. Instrum.*, vol. IECI-16, Dec. 1969, pp. 189–192.

[16] "New process language uses english term," T. G. Gaspar, V. V. Dobrohotoff, and D. R. Burgess, *Contr. Eng.*, vol. 15, Oct. 1968, pp. 118–121.

[17] "Construction of multistep integration formulas for simulation purposes," W. Giloi and H. Grebe, *IEEE Trans. Comput.*, vol. C-17, Dec. 1968, pp. 1121–1131.

[18] "Compound data structure for computer aided design: a survey," J. C. Gray, *Proc. 1967 Ass. Comput. Mach. Nat. Meeting*, pp. 355–365.

[19] "Some techniques used in the Alcor Illinois 7090," D. Gries, M. Paul, and H. R. Wiehle, *Commun. Ass. Comput. Mach.*, vol. 8, Aug. 1965, pp. 496–500.

[20] "Toward a general processor for programming languages," M. I. Halpern, *Commun. Ass. Comput. Mach.*, vol. 11, Jan. 1968, pp. 15–25.

[21] "The minicomputer, a programming challenge," R. L. Hooper, *AFIPS Conf. Proc., Vol. 33, Pt. 1, Fall Joint Comput. Conf.*, pp. 649–654.

[22] "Segmented-level programming," M. Jackson and A. B. Swanwick, *Comput. Automat.*, Feb. 1969, pp. 23–26.

[23] "Some experiences with process control languages," P. H. Jarvis, *IEEE Trans. Ind. Electron. Contr. Instrum.*, vol. IECI-15, Dec. 1968, pp. 54–56.

[24] "Operating systems architecture," H. Katzan, *AFIPS Conf. Proc., Vol. 36, 1970 Spring Joint Comput. Conf.*, pp. 109–118.

[25] "Programs in Getel speak test engineer's language," G. Kierce, *Electronics*, Aug. 2, 1971, pp. 53–57.

[26] "Object code optimization," E. S. Lowry and C. W. Medlock, *Commun. Ass. Comput. Mach.*, vol. 12, Jan. 1969, pp. 13–22.

[27] "Standardization—a customer's view," A. C. Lumb, *IEEE Trans. Ind. Electron. Contr. Instrum.*, vol. IECI-16, Dec. 1969, pp. 192–194.

[28] "What to expect when you scale down to a minicomputer," J. J. Morris, *Contr. Eng.*, vol. 17, Sept. 1970, pp. 65–71.

[29] "Requirements for real-time languages," A. Opler, *Commun. Ass. Comput. Mach.*, vol. 9, Mar. 1966, pp. 196–199.

[30] "A base for a mobile programming system," R. J. Orgass and W. W. Waite, *Commun. Ass. Comput. Mach.*, Sept. 1969, pp. 507–510.

[31] "Some views on standardization," J. D. Schoeffler, *IEEE Trans. Ind. Electron. Contr. Instrum.*, vol. IECI-16, Dec. 1969, pp. 185–187.

[32] "Software organization for minicomputer systems," J. D. Schoeffler and R. H. Sherman, *1971 IFAC Conf. Comput. Contr.*

[33] "Role of minicomputers in process control," J. D. Schoeffler and H. E. Jordan, *Proc. 1970 Tappi Eng. Conf.*

[34] "Jovial—a programming language for real-time command systems," C. J. Shaw, *Annual Review in Automatic Programming*, vol. 3. Elmsford, N.Y.: Pergamon, 1963, pp. 52–119.

[35] "A specification of Jovial," C. J. Shaw, *Commun. Ass. Comput. Mach.*, vol. 6, Dec. 1963, pp. 721–735.

[36] "Small computer software," H. W. Spencer, H. P. Shepardson, and L. M. McGowan, *IEEE Comput. Group News*, vol. 3, July/Aug. 1970, pp. 15–20.

[37] "Computer displays," I. E. Sutherland, *Sci. Amer.*, vol. 222, June 1970, pp. 57–81.

[38] "Status of minicomputer software," R. H. Temple and R. E. Daniel, *Contr. Eng.*, vol. 17, July 1970, pp. 61–64.

[39] "Cyberlogic—a new system for computer control," G. R. Trimble and D. A. Bavly, *AFIPS Conf. Proc., Vol. 37, 1970 Fall Joint Comput. Conf.*, pp. 415–422.

[40] "Design and behavior of TSS/8: a PDP-8 based time-sharing system," A. Van De Goor, C. G. Bell, and D. A. Witcroft, *IEEE Trans. Comput.*, vol. C-18, Nov. 1969, pp. 1038–1043.

[41] "Design of a multi-level file management system," E. W. Ver Hoef, *Proc. 1966 Ass. Comput. Mach. Nat. Meeting*, pp. 75–86.

[42] "Programming the compacts," C. W. Walker, *Datamation*, Apr. 1966, pp. 31–34.

[43] "Importance of manufacturing software," S. Weaver, *Contr. Eng.*, vol. 15, Jan. 1968, pp. 61–64.

PROGRAMMING INDUSTRIAL CONTROL SYSTEMS IN FORTRAN

WANDERLEY DIEHL AND MICHAEL MENSH

(PRESENTED AT THE IFAC/IFIP SYMPOSIUM—TORONTO—1968)

The computer industry has éxperienced rapid technological developments that have, over the years, led to lower overall system costs. The development of solid state components, then integrated circuits in hardware and the increased use of compiler languages and operating systems in software have been major contributors to these decreased costs.

The industrial control field, while taking advantage of hardware improvements has been slow to accept new methods in software. Even though operating system software is now in general use, much of the applications programming in industrial control is done at the assembly language level.

The continued increase in complexity of control programming and the reluctance of both users and manufacturers to adapt compiler languages tends to maintain high programming costs. These costs can be brought into line with similar reductions in hardware through the increased use of real-time compiler languages.

Although early industrial computers were used primarily as data loggers, there were a few successful experiments in supervisory control. Machines such as the TRW 300 and GE 312, which used magnetic drum memories, were slow and extremely difficult to program. The only languages available were translators and primitive assemblers which were only a step removed from machine language coding. Because the rotation of the drum had to be considered when synchronizing input/output operations with computation, programming these machines became a nightmare of manual optimization and mapping.

The inherent difficulty of programming these machines meant that each software system had to be custom-tailored by the manufacturer to fit individual timing and hardware requirements.

The next generation of process computers used magnetic cores for working memories with drums for bulk storage and backup. These machines included the Honeywell H290 and H610, GE 412, IBM 1710 and the Bunker-Ramo 340. Faster execution times and sequential placement of instructions did away with laborious hand optimization.

Basic assembly language coding, using address control and data conversion techniques derived from scientific and data processing computing became common. Some primitive operating systems for control of input and output were developed. These operating systems were automatic interruption of programs for input/output processing and controlled the transfer or programs and data between bulk storage and core. Programming systems were still custom-built packages, but now could better handle supervisory (set-point) control and some optimization as well as data logging.

The introduction of third-generation, high-speed, integrated circuit computers has paved the way for the true economic justification of industrial computing. Such machines as the IBM 1800, GE/PAC 4020, Honeywell DDP-516, CDC 1700, and the SDS Sigma 2 for the first time, provide the ability to control many complex operations, optimally, at a reasonable cost.

The development of generalized software and comprehensive real-time operating systems has greatly simplified the task of building control programs. No longer is it necessary for manufacturers to hand-tailor each application. The problems of interfacing with the real-time world have been generalized to the extent that any user, with knowledge of his process requirements can write his own software for supervision, optimization and control.

"CANNED" AND "TAILORED" SOFTWARE

There are two basic approaches to application software. The "canned" approach provides generalized packages for each application which the user can modify in certain ways to fit his requirements. The other method involves "tailored" software created by the manufacturer specifically for one user's application.

Several manufacturers offer "canned" software for such applications as data logging and direct digital control. The customer supplies table parameters and other data to adapt the programs for his process. This approach works well if the "canned" package includes all features of the customer's specific problem. In many cases, there are additional functions which must be performed which require additions or changes to the standard package. Since these standard programs are usually written in assembly language, with economy of time and memory as a goal, they are often difficult for a user to understand. Changes or additions which have been anticipated by the designers of these standard programs are usually quite simple; others are nearly impossible for all but the most experienced programmers. Too often, the required modifications were not part of the original planning for the standard package and represent an unexpectedly large expense on the part of the user.

Reprinted with permission from *1968 IFAC/IFIP Symp.*

As an alternative to "canned" software, the manufacturer may assume responsibility for turn-key programming systems. Here, the customer imparts his knowledge of the process problem to the vendor, and the vendor programs the system to exact specifications. This method usually involves an extended definition period during which the customer educates the manufacturer concerning his process and its exact needs. Unavoidably, a certain amount of information is lost or distorted in the process of transferring it from user to vendor, and the results are often unsatisfactory to both.

The trouble with this "tailoring" approach is a basic incompatibility in knowledge between manufacturer and customer. The customer knows what he wants to do but can't program; the vendor can program, but doesn't understand what the customer wants to do. This approach has most of the disadvantages of the "canned" package and it is even more expensive to implement.

The solution is a compromise between "canned" and "tailored" programs, where the manufacturer supplies, for each system, only those functions which are truly general, and provides a way for the user to program his unique applications software in compiler language. This solution minimizes the information transfer problem between user and vendor and protects the user's confidential information. Compiler languages are easy to learn, quick to code and provide clear documentation. They have the further advantage of machine independence. Should the user decide to change computers, the applications software could be adapted to the new machine with a minimum of effort.

PROGRAMMING LANGUAGES AND PROCESS CONTROL

Today, although we have made great advances in hardware, operating systems and in the ability of programmers to deal with complex control problems, most of the coding in the industrial control area, is still done in assembly language. On a limited number of systems, background computations and performance calculations are programmed in FORTRAN. The use of compiler level languages in the industrial control field lags that of the general EDP and scientific fields by three to five years.

The scientific and business data processing segments of the computer business have already become compiler oriented. They have found that the use of higher level problem-oriented languages has reduced training effort, completion time and overall costs by significant factors. Why, then, haven't higher level languages been used more in industrial control programming?

The reasons for this lack of development can be found in the prejudices of the manufacturers and programmers involved.

They believe that compilers are wasteful of time and memory; that programs written at the compiler level will never meet the stringent timing and memory usage restrictions of the industrial control business. They feel that their processes are too complex and time-dependent for compiler level coding and that no standard industrial control language has been developed.

Although there may be some validity in some of these objections, few people in industrial control programming have made a real attempt to explore the possibilities of compiler level programming, even though many have talked about it.

It's about time that industrial control programming caught up with the rest of the computer business. Compilers can now produce code that is 80–90% as efficient as assembly language code in memory usage. The FORTRAN language has been established as a defacto standard for engineering computation and FORTRAN IV is in common use throughout industry. Because the general characteristics of industrial control systems are well established and understood, there is no reason why FORTRAN cannot be extended to support these characteristics. Cost improvements in coding and checkout of 5 to 10 times that of assembly level programming could be achieved with a real-time FORTRAN.

REQUIREMENTS FOR A PROCESS CONTROL LANGUAGE

As stated previously, the FORTRAN language has established itself as the standard programming language for scientific and engineering problems. Therefore, the advantage of selecting it as the basis for an on-line process control language is obvious. It is familiar to most engineers, and a considerable number of programs for data analysis and process studies already exist in FORTRAN.

FORTRAN, however, by itself is limited to a data processing environment and is not able to take care of all the requirements of a process control computer installation. Besides standard data processing input-output devices, such installations include a wide variety of digital and analog input and output signals as well as the handling of automatic interrupts and time intervals. To support the randomly-occurring needs of process conditions, several programs are normally in core, in different phases of execution, time-sharing the system resources.

It is not practical to handle this multiprogramming environment, the peculiar hardware of the process, the process interrupts and the control of time using FORTRAN, with only the addition of subroutine calls. This method suffers the disadvantages of more cumbersome coding and of not having syntactical error control for the calls and their parameters.

A true Real-Time FORTRAN has the required extensions added to its syntax for all input-output, interrupt and time control and disc-core management. Furthermore, in FORTRAN, statements are executed one at a time, sequentially. A READ statement can take a long time to execute due to the slow speed of the peripheral devices. During the input-output transfer the central processor is practically idle. In Real-Time FORTRAN, therefore, we require the option, in statements that may require a long time for execution, of non-sequentiality, i.e. control may pass to the next statement before the action of the previous command has been executed. Thus, in the case of a non-sequential READ command, input will be initiated, but program control will continue, in the calling program, at the statement following the READ statement. This technique allows double-buffering of I/O and other overlapping operations which increase I/O speed and central processor efficiency.

It should be emphasized at this point that only a language that allows all the above options in its syntax can be called Real-Time FORTRAN. Such a language will allow simple and natural programming even in a multiprogramming environment, with the added benefit of full syntactical error control by the compiler.

REAL TIME EXTENSIONS TO FORTRAN IV

Programs written in Real-Time FORTRAN may be divided into non-interrupt and interrupt blocks. The first portion of a program, which is initiated as the result of a request from another program is called the non-interrupt block. In many cases this is the entire program. Additional blocks of instructions that are executed due to a hardware interrupt or an elapsed time interval are called interrupt blocks. Interrupt and non-interrupt blocks of the same program can refer to common data and labels. The only separation between these portions of the program is in the manner of initiation of each. Coding of these blocks is done in USASI FORTRAN IV using any of the following typical extensions:

In the following statements, those labels or names which are intended as examples are underlined.

CONNECT

CONNECT INTERRUPT ACTION (3)

This associates interrupt 3 with the program's interrupt block ACTION and causes the block of "interrupt code" to be initiated whenever a computer response is required because of a specific change in the environment. Special cases of the interrupt blocks are the clock blocks. These are initiated as the result of elapsed or absolute time.

CONNECT CLOCK ACTION (14, 03, 11, 0)

This causes the interrupt block ACTION to be executed at 14:03:11 military time. If the last parameter were set to a nonzero value k, the clock block would be repeated every k seconds until the block was disconnected.

CONNECT TIMER ACTION (3, 12, 5)

This associates an interval timer with the interrupt block, ACTION. One-minute granularity is specified by the 3 (1, 2 or 4 would specify 1/60 second, 1 second, and 1 hour respectively). The block will be initiated every 5 minutes, starting 12 minutes from now.

CALL TIME (A, B, C)

The time in hours, minutes, and seconds is stored in the storage locations A, B, and C, as binary integers.

DISCONNECT

DISCONNECT ACTION

Removes the association between the interrupt block (ACTION), and its interrupt, block or timer.

SCHEDULE

SCHEDULE <u>200</u>

Causes the portion of the program starting at the statement with the label <u>200</u> to be scheduled for execution by the operating system. Since it is often undesirable to execute lengthy computations or input/output operations as a response to an interrupt, these operations may be deferred and executed later as part of the non-interrupt block by using the SCHEDULE statement.

REQUEST

The REQUEST statement causes the execution of another program to be scheduled. If the requested program is on disc, a copy is transferred to unoccupied core sections for execution.

REQUEST <u>PROGRM</u> (<u>AL</u>, ... <u>AN</u>)

PROGRM is the name of the requested program and <u>A1</u>, ... <u>AN</u> are arguments which are treated in the same way as FORTRAN subroutine arguments. Following the REQUEST statement, when execution of the program <u>PROGRM</u> is finished, control returns to the next statement in the calling program. It is a sequential statement.

REQUEST <u>PROGRM</u> (<u>A1</u>, ... <u>AN</u>) <u>100</u>

Causes the calling program to keep control until it encounters a TEST PENDING statement when control is transferred to the scheduler. The calling program will be restarted at label <u>100</u>, when the requested program is completed. This is a non-sequential statement.

REQUEST <u>PROGRM</u> (<u>A1</u>, ... <u>AN</u>) <u>100</u>, <u>2</u>

The calling program can assign a level to the requested program for the sake or establishing relative priorities. This is done by adding the assigned level number (e.g. <u>2</u>) to the statement.

TEST PENDING

The TEST PENDING statement is used to insure that all input-output and scheduled functions are complete before a program signs off. If any of these operations are incomplete, they will be finished before the program is terminated.

TEST PENDING <u>340</u> would be used where it is desired to continue the program at label <u>340</u> if all requested operations are complete.

READ/WRITE

READ (<u>READER,</u> <u>100</u>), <u>A</u>, <u>B</u>, <u>C</u>, . . . , <u>G</u>
WRITE (<u>TYPER,</u> <u>200</u>) <u>Z</u>, <u>Y</u>, <u>X</u>, . . . , <u>R</u>

These are the standard FORTRAN IV sequential input/output statements.

<u>READER</u> and <u>TYPER</u> are symbolic device names. Numbers may also be used to identify devices as in standard FORTRAN IV I/O statements. <u>100</u> and <u>200</u> are the numbers of the FORTRAN format statements; <u>A</u>, <u>B</u>, <u>C</u>, . . . <u>G</u>; and <u>Z</u>, <u>Y</u>, <u>X</u>, . . . <u>R</u> are variable names.

READ (<u>READER,</u> <u>100</u>), <u>A</u>, <u>B</u>, . . . <u>G</u>, <u>500</u>

The program keeps control until it encounters a TEST PENDING statement. The calling program will be restarted at label <u>500</u> when the input is complete. This is a non-sequential statement.

WRITE (<u>TYPER,</u> <u>200</u>) <u>Z</u>, <u>Y</u>, . . . <u>R</u>, <u>500</u>, <u>3</u>

Causes the editing to be performed at software priority level <u>3</u>.

The non-edited I/O statements INPUT and OUTPUT also provide direct communication with appropriate I/O devices.

DEVICE

This statement is used to identify I/O devices symbolically.

DEVICE (OPERIO, 1, 2)

Here OPERIO is the operator's I/O device, 1 indicates it as a typewriter and 2 specifies which typewriter. All peripherals which are referred to symbolically must have their names assigned through the DEVICE statement.

ATTACH/DETACH

ATTACH (OPERIO)

Assigns exclusive use of the device OPERIO to the calling program. No other program can use that peripheral until the command DETACH (OPERIO) is given. These statements resolve conflicting requests for a particular device and need not be used if there is no such conflict.

STATUS

STATUS (KEYBD, ITABLE)

Allows a program to determine the current condition of a device. Places the status indicators (attached, detached, ready, device address, etc.) for the device KEYBD into the integer array ITABLE.

STORE/FETCH

These statements provide access to named files on disc.

STORE TABLE (BLOCK (10), FILE (20) 1, 130)

Transfers 130 words from elements 10 through 139 of the array BLOCK in core to elements 20 through 149 of the first copy of FILE on disc.

FETCH TABLE (LIST (1), FILE (20), 5, 130)

Transfers 130 words from elements 20 through 149 of the 5th copy of FILE on disc to another array, LIST, in core.

Tables on disc may be private to a program or public to the whole system. They may be ALLOCATED and DEALLOCATED as required, to conserve disc memory. They may also be ATTACHed and DETACHed in the same way as I/O devices.

PROGRAM STRUCTURE

MAIN PROGRM (A, B, C, X)

Indicates the beginning of the block of non-interrupt code of the program named PROGRM. A, B, C, and X are parameters which are passed to the program PROGRM by the calling program.

INTERRUPT ACTION

Indicates the beginning of the block of interrupt code named ACTION.

ON LINE ADDITION OF NEW PROGRAMS

An on-line process control system, with multiprogramming capability would not be complete if the operating system were not designed to allow for:

1. On-line compilation
2. On-line loading of programs
3. On-line deletion of programs
4. On-line debugging
5. Protection of the running portion of the software from the undebugged programs.

The ability of the designer to write new real-time FORTRAN programs has to be complemented with the ability to compile them in the same computer without taking the computer off-line. This is required in order to avoid the delays associated with development approvals, computer center delays, etc. which are unavoidable if an outside machine has to be used.

The compiled object program is but one step. The new program has to be loaded and tested. The operating system allows the new program to be loaded on-line. The existing running programs are in protected memory and the untested program can be run without the risk of damaging the existing working system.

The operating system will also support debugging features including tracing, breakpoints or snapshot displays of variable contents or arrays at run time. The inclusion of TRACE cards in the FORTRAN program produces object coding which can be used for tracing either selected variables or all variables within a selected program area.

Process input and output signals can be simulated for debugging purposes by changing the device statement which identifies the hardware associated with a logical device name. For example, READER could be used, interchangeable, as the name of the analog input device or the card reader.

FEASIBILITY OF PROCESS PROGRAMS WRITTEN IN REAL TIME FORTRAN

Several of the programs that are mostly commonly used in process control applications have been coded in real time FORTRAN, such as Analog Scan, alarm program, etc. The coding efficiency appears to be about 80% of similar programs written in assembly language. Even if in some instances the efficiency is smaller, this is more than offset by the extreme ease of coding with FORTRAN.

As an example, an analog program was coded in a few hours by a programmer with basic FORTRAN knowledge, and no process experience. This type of program in the past has been left to very experienced programmers. Appendix I contains an example of a real-time program which shows the simplicity of using Real-Time FORTRAN.

CONCLUSIONS

It is our opinion that FORTRAN with real time extensions, supported by real time monitors that allow on-line program development will be the language that will be used in on-line process control applications in the years to come. Its useful life will be the useful life of FORTRAN. Coincidentally, many of the features we included in our language are also features encountered in PL/1.

It may be that some very specific applications, where memory and time are really at a premium will still be coded in assembly language. Also in some applications involving sequence control of slow processes, interpretative compilers may be used. But for the general on-line real time data acquisition and analysis, and process control, today's language has to be Real-Time FORTRAN.

APPENDIX I

Below is an example of a program written in Real-Time FORTRAN. This program counts and displays the number of interrupts that occur on hardware interrupt line 3 for 10 minutes.

```
C          START OF MAIN PROGRAM
           MAIN TEST
           I=0
           J=0
C          EXECUTE TIMER BLOCK EVERY MINUTE
           CONNECT TIMER INT (3, 0, 1)
           CONNECT INTERRUPT EVENT (3)
           TEST PENDING
C          CONTROL RETURNED TO SCHEDULER
20         WRITE (1, 50) J
50         FORMAT (22H NUMBER OF INTERRUPTS=, 16)
C          START OF INTERRUPT BLOCK FOR TIMER
           INTERRUPT INT
           I=I+1
           IF (I.LT.10) GO TO 100
           DISCONNECT INT
           DISCONNECT EVENT
           SCHEDULE 20
100        CONTINUE
C          BEGINNING OF INTERRUPT BLOCK FOR LINE 3
           INTERRUPT EVENT
           J=J+1
           END
```

Process Control Software

HERBERT E. PIKE, JR.

Abstract—This paper examines the nature of the software which is necessary so that a real-time computer may be used to control industrial processes. The general nature of a process control software system is discussed, and several methods for implementing such a system are examined.

This paper is divided into several sections. First, the general structure of process control software systems is examined, and the programming problems associated with developing such a system are discussed. Then several tools for doing this programming are discussed, including problem-oriented languages, "fill-in-the-blank programming systems," procedural programming languages, and the operating systems which are used to tie the different portions of a process control system together. This paper closes with a dicussion of future trends in process control software and recent activities in developing software standards.

It will be assumed that the reader is generally familiar with software with at least a passable knowledge of FORTRAN programming.

Manuscript received September 1, 1969.

The author is with the Information Sciences Laboratory, General Electric Research and Development Center, Schenectady, N. Y. 12301.

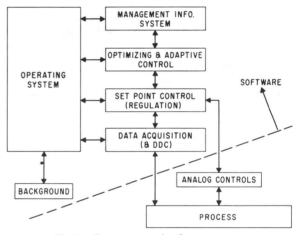

Fig. 1. Process control software system.

PROCESS CONTROL SOFTWARE SYSTEMS

AN idealized structure for a process control software system is illustrated in Fig. 1. The part above the dotted line corresponds to the computer and its associated software. The part below the dotted line corresponds to the process and the control hardware which is associated directly with the process. In this system breakdown, the software used for control is divided as follows. The operating system, or executive, is responsible for scheduling various other portions of the software system, maintaining communications between the various programs in use, and handling real-time input and output. The application software is divided into four levels which are characterized by the time requirements for response to outside events.

At the lowest level of control is a data acquisition and direct digital control (DDC) software package. The data acquisition software is responsible for controlling the input of data from the process into the computer. The DDC software system is responsible for the direct control of the process. (In DDC, the computer is used instead of analog control equipment [8].) The software at this level may be characterized as having to respond to changes in the process or other external events with a response time in the order of seconds or one minute for a typical chemical process.

At the second level in the system is the software which effects set-point control. This software generally consists of algebraic algorithms which examine the measurements

Reprinted from *Proc. IEEE*, vol. 58, pp. 87–97, Jan. 1970.

which have been made of the process and calculate from these measurements desired operating points according to some static algorithm. This set-point control is done less frequently than the control at level 1, perhaps at intervals of several minutes.

At level 3 are the optimization or adaptive control algorithms. These algorithms operate by varying the parameters of the algorithm used at level 2 to calculate set points. The purpose of the optimizing control is to improve the performance of the processes according to some predetermined criteria.

At the highest level of the system is a management information system and plant-wide control software. This software is used to generate operating information for management control, and/or to do production scheduling over long time intervals such as days or weeks. This function may be done on a process computer, or it may be done on a larger plant-wide computer.

The function of background computation also appears in most present-day process control software systems. When the process computer is not needed to do control at levels 1–4, the operating system goes to a job queue which determines if nonreal-time computing functions such as compiling or running scientific or EDP programs are required. Most process control systems include this function as an option.

When looking at the process control software development process, it is interesting to examine how standardized the various parts of the system (as shown in Fig. 1) might be. The operating system may be virtually the same from computer to computer, varying only with changes in the hardware configuration used and independent of the process which is under control. The data acquisition and DDC package may be estimated to be as little as 20 percent process dependent. Only DDC algorithms and the actual number of process inputs and their time dependence need to be specified in a data acquisition section, along with various constants such as those for conversion into engineering units.

At level 2, the set-point control algorithms are much more highly applications dependent, with possibly 50 to 90 percent of the software in this package varying from job to job. The optimization or adaptive control package is not as applications dependent as the set-point control, with perhaps 50 percent of the package consisting of general-purpose optimization algorithms such as linear programming or parameter optimization, and the rest consisting of specialized programming used to link these algorithms to the set-point control package.

Management information systems can be highly standardized. This is a data management problem and a program for the construction of a data base may be written in an applications-independent manner. Only the fine structure of the data base as determined by the applications needs to be specified. Thus, it may be estimated that only 20 percent of this package is applications dependent.

The Software Problem

Let us look at the problem associated with developing a process control software system. In such a system there are portions of the software which are almost totally applications independent and are, in general, supplied as standard software by the computer vendor. There are also portions of the software system, such as the data acquisition and DDC package and the management information system, which are highly applications independent. For these portions, the user hopes to have a general-purpose package supplied by the vendor or a software house, configuring it for his needs. In the optimization and set-point control area, a higher degree of custom tailoring of the software package is necessary, often requiring complete programming of these elements.

We will now examine in more detail the general characteristics of a process control software system. Since operating systems are generally supplied by the vendor, we will examine their general structure so that we may understand how the other parts of the system are controlled by the operating system. We will then look at various techniques for implementing the rest of the software system. Several procedural programming languages which may be used to implement the applications dependent parts of the system will be examined. We will give particular attention to the changes in the sturcture of FORTRAN which are being made currently in order to make it a useful language for process control programming.

In the next section we will examine several problem-oriented languages which are used in specific application areas to implement process control systems. Finally, we will look at several general software systems to which a user only adds parameters describing the characteristics of the control application which he is attempting to accomplish. These systems then are completely structured and have been called in the past "fill-in-the-blank programming systems." Note that we are going from procedural programming languages to fully implemented software systems to which a user just adds parameters.

OPERATING SYSTEMS

Fig. 1 shows that a typical process control software system consists of a number of programs which must operate together to control some external process. The program which co-ordinates the execution of all the other programs is called an operating system.

Programs making up the process control software system must, in general, be executed for one of two different reasons. The first is the occurrence of some external event. For example, when a program senses that a variable being measured by the process computer is out of normal operating limits, some sort of emergency action program may be brought into the computer and executed. This mode of execution is called event-oriented, and the process control software system must be capable of scheduling event-oriented program execution at completely random intervals. The second type of program execution is scheduled execution. A DDC and data acquisition program might cycle through a certain set of input points, reading the inputs and executing a DDC algorithm at one-minute intervals. This program is time-oriented because it is to be executed at fixed intervals of one minute.

A·complete process control software system is made up of many different programs, some of which are executed at fixed intervals and some of which are executed upon the occurrence of external events as signaled to the computer through its interrupt structure. In addition, some programs may be scheduled for execution by other programs which are within the system. Because of this random sequence of execution of programs, various programs are in control of the process at different times. Associated with this flow of control between various programs is a flow of information between these programs which also cannot be completely determined ahead of time.

The operating system which coordinates the execution of these various programs contains mechanisms for controlling the execution of programs in response to external events, the passage of time, or a request from another program that some program be run. The housekeeping required to do this is the responsibility of the operating system. In addition to these duties, most process control software systems require more core storage than is available in the computer itself. A bulk storage device such as a drum or disk is used to store portions of the software and data. The operating system also does the necessary housekeeping to swap various programs in and out of the computer according to some priority scheme, and allocate to core memory the programs which need to be run.

An additional function of the operating system is the scheduling of input–output activities. Since input–output equipment, in general, runs much more slowly than the computational speed of a computer, input–output activities must be overlapped with the execution of other programs. When one program has completed some phase of computation and requires an input or output operation, it requests that the operating system carry out that operation and, while the operation is taking place, the operating system allows another program to run.

What we have just described is a multiprogramming operating system. That is, it is an operating system which maintains the necessary housekeeping to control a software system of many distinct programs which operate in a random manner, being scheduled by external events, time passage, or requests of other programs. One useful way to consider an operating system's role in a process control environment is that the operating system is responsible for the control of the computer itself, allocating that computer to the various programs necessary to control the process. The operating system controls the computer while the computer controls the process. Most multiprogramming operating systems are similar. We will examine the operating system for the GEPAC 4020, RTMOS, to get some idea of

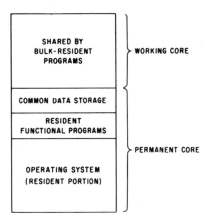

Fig. 2.   Core memory divisions for an operating system.

the structure of these programs [16].

The core memory is divided into two parts, permanent core and working core, as shown in Fig. 2.

Working core is the term applied to the area which is shared by all noncore-resident functional programs, and noncore-resident portions of the operating system.

Permanent core is the term applied to the core area which is *not* shared by bulk-resident programs. The following information is, typically, contained in permanent core:

1) *The Resident Portion of the Operating System:* A part of the RTMOS is core-resident. The remaining portions are transferred to working core as they are needed.
2) *Resident Programs and Subroutines:* Occasionally a subroutine or program is required so frequently by the process that it must be core-resident.
3) *Common Data Storage:* Data which must be transferred between programs, and must be rapidly accessed, is stored in this area. Where extremely fast access to the data is not required, common data may be stored on bulk memory.

Each program in the system is assigned a priority relative to all other programs. One copy of each program is maintained on bulk memory. Dynamic relocation permits these programs to be executed from any part of working core.

RTMOS decides what mixture of programs to have in working core, and which program to execute, on the basis of time, process events, and program priorities, reviewing this decision every time one of the following events take place.

1) A system time interval (usually $\frac{1}{4}$ second) passes.
2) A bulk–core transfer is completed.
3) A program finishes or delays.
4) A program temporarily terminates its execution until the completion of a certain input or output operation.

Programs are scheduled strictly on a priority basis within those programs which want to run.

If the highest priority program that wants to run is not in working core, its transfer to core will be started. While this transfer request is being served, some lower priority program that is asking to run and is already in working core will be entered. This program gets control of the central processor and keeps it until the operating system is re-entered as a result of one of the events listed above. At that point, a review of program priorities will again take place. If the program did not run to completion, the operating system will remember the point at which the program's execution was terminated. When the program is eventually restarted, it will be entered exactly at the point where its execution was previously terminated.

A snapshot of the computer's core memory at a given instant would reveal a combination of programs in various stages of completion. One might be using the arithmetic unit, one might be coming in from bulk memory, and the others would be either waiting their turn or using peripherals or process input–output devices. Normally, when a program runs to completion, it will release its working core area for use by other functional programs.

Occasionally it may be necessary to overwrite low-priority programs in order to obtain a core area large enough to run some high-priority program. Before overwriting a program, the program's intermediate results will be stored in bulk memory. Upon completion of the high-priority work, the operating system will reload the overwritten program from bulk memory, restore all intermediate results, and restart the program at the point at which the execution was previously terminated. The overwritten program may not have to come into the same core area to be resumed. If some other core area becomes available to the program, the program will be continued in that area.

Most multiprogramming operating systems used for process control are of this general nature.

PROCEDURAL PROGRAMMING LANGUAGES

Procedure: A series of steps followed in a regular, definite order.[1]

By this definition the earliest computer programming language was a procedural language—the language of the original computer itself. This language is procedural because the computer is a sequential machine, with instructions for it written in a clearly defined order with their proper execution dependent on the maintenance of that order. Since the early machine languages, more sophisticated procedural languages for programming computers have been developed. Symbolic assembly languages, the next step from machine language, were developed soon after the first computers. These languages provide for a symbolic representation of the instruction set and addresses of the computer which is being programmed, but are completely dependent on the computer for which the program is to be used. More recently, higher-level procedural programming languages have been developed which are independent of the target computer. For example, FORTRAN, ALGOL, and PL/I are procedural languages.

[1] Webster's New Collegiate Dictionary, 1965.

The most widely used higher-level procedural programming languages for process control applications software development are variants of FORTRAN. The nature of the changes and additions made to FORTRAN for process control programming is best understood by considering how the language is used [22], [24].

We have seen that the applications software system is broken into various independent segments which operate somewhat independently, passing data and/or control between various segments in response to either external events or the passage of time. Let us briefly examine the programming requirements for implementing such a software system.

The calculations to be done internal to a program segment may be characterized as: the definition of various types of data, arrangement of this data into various structures so that it may be found when needed for calculation, and the manipulation and transformation via algebraic formulas of this data into different forms. This may be done with a single program or a program consisting of a main program with several subroutines. These are typical functions which are easily programmed with FORTRAN IV. There is another type of calculation which must be done in a program: calculations which determine control actions as a result of looking at tables of logical variables which describe the status of external events. FORTRAN IV, as it has been defined for scientific purposes, is inadequate for these needs.

With some minor modifications, however, such as the addition of new data types and word packing capabilities, FORTRAN is useful for doing the calculations internal to the programs of a process control software system. Table I lists typical modifications of this type.

Serious weaknesses of FORTRAN occur in the area of communication between the programs of a software system and communication with the outside world. High-speed interprogram communication is often provided for by the extensions of the concept of global common for core-resident data. Lower speed communication of larger blocks of data may be provided through some type of file system which makes this data available from a bulk storage device. The additional input–output facilities provided in process control FORTRANS often include the ability to READ and WRITE storage devices such as drums or disks, the ability to READ or WRITE process input–output devices, and the ability to do this in a buffered fashion by initiating the input–output activity, going on to perform some computational tasks, and then checking for completion of the input–output event. Specific examples of these features previously discussed are given in Table I.

Another serious deficiency in FORTRAN is the lack of a mechanism for passing control optionally between various program segments depending on the status of external events. Because FORTRAN is a static language, designed to take a set of data and transform it into another set of data these concepts simply are not present in the language. It is in this area in which the most serious extensions of FORTRAN

TABLE I
Typical FORTRAN Extensions

1) Data
  a) Data Types
    Fixed point
    Bit
    Status
    Byte
    Binary
    Boolean (vector)
    Octal
    Hexadecimal
    Alphanumeric
  b) Data Manipulation
    Shifts
    Logical operators
    Bit and byte replacement
    Character manipulation
    String manipulation
    Bit testing
2) Communications
  a) Between Programs
    Global common
    External data
    Static file system
    Dynamic file system
  b) Input/Output
    Unformated I/O
    READ/WRITE Bulk
3) Program Control
  Schedule another program
  Link with interrupt
  Delay
  Look at clock
  Terminate execution
  Decision tables
4) Compiler Features
  Diagnostic trace
  Conditional compilation
  Reserved words
  Code optimization directives

have been made. Extensions for passing control rely mainly on an interface with the operating system. Commands which cause the initiation of the execution of other program segments either immediately or at some fixed time or in some time interval are often added. Also available are instructions which cause an execution of a block of code upon the occurrence of an external event by linking that code with an interrupt associated with that event. Typical extensions in this· area are summarized in Table I. Various compiler features that are sometimes included to assist programmers are also shown.

There are, of course, many other procedural languages—some, such as SPL IV and AUTRAN, also qualify as problem-oriented languages. However, the various FORTRANS (and assembly languages) are most popular at this time.

PROBLEM-ORIENTED LANGUAGES

One of the goals of the development of higher level programming languages or programming systems is to allow the potential user of computer control to implement his process control software system with less attention to the structure of the software system or computer hardware. One approach to achieving this goal is the development of problem-oriented languages. Problem-oriented languages are languages whose design is specifically related to some particular application. Examples might be the control of batch processes or the construction of a management information system. These languages are designed for a specific community of users with their characteristics and background in mind.

Problem-oriented languages are, in general, simpler to use than general-purpose procedural programming languages. A problem-oriented language provides the user with more systems structure than a general-purpose procedural language, and is more closely related to the application in mind. This is done by identifying the application area for which the language is intended, and its user. For example, if the end user is an engineer who is assumed to be familiar with the FORTRAN, the language might be given a FORTRAN-like structure to make it familiar and easy for him to use. If the user is an electrical engineer who thinks of control systems problems in terms of elements connected together in flow chart form, then the elements of the language may indeed be represented in this format. We will see examples of both of these cases. The question of whether a given problem-oriented language is good or bad cannot, in general, be answered. Pertinent instead is whether it matches the job to be done and the programmer's background. Therefore, the usefulness of any problem-oriented language must be considered strictly in the context of its intended application.

We will examine below two examples of problem-oriented languages. The first is AUTRAN, a FORTRAN-like programming language intended for use in process startup and the control of continuous processes. We will then look at BATCH, a sequencing control language oriented to the user who thinks in terms of flow charts.

AUTRAN

AUTRAN is designed for the control of continuous processes [27], [29]. A completed system includes user written application programs, a process input–output system, a direct digital control system, and an operating system.

The basic premise of the AUTRAN language is that the user would like to be able to specify the actions of his control system element by element, identifying these with the hardware elements of the system to be controlled. Furthermore, he would like to make this identification in English-like statements, with a structure similar to the statements of FORTRAN. The programmer develops his control program with statements of the following four types, examples of which are shown in Table II.

1) *Specifications:* A specification statement allows the user to describe the physical properties of objects such as motors, valves, and control loops such as direct digital control loops. These statements are used to describe to the software system the physical properties of the plant to be

TABLE II

TYPICAL AUTRAN STATEMENTS

Specification List

SPECIFICATION
CONTROL VALVE (CVALA (CLOSED, 3))
CONDITION SENSOR (ICCVA1 (2, 89))
VALVE (VALVA1 (CLOSED, 19))
CONDITION SENSOR (IOVAA1 (1, 8))
CONDITION SENSOR (ICVAA1 (1, 9))
VALVE (VALVA2 (CLOSED, 51))
CONDITION SENSOR (ICVAA (1, 31))
VALVE (VALVB2 (CLOSED, 52))
CONDITION SENSOR (ICVAB2 (1, 71))
MOTOR (PUMPA (OFF, 35))
CONDITION SENSOR (IPUMP1 (1, 17))
CONDITION SENSOR (IPCHPA (15, 19))

Alarm List

ALARM LIST (3)
NOTE. ALARM LIST 3 IS USED WHEN PUMPING FROM TANKA
     TO REACT 1
NOTE. ACTION LIST 42 CLOSES VALVES CVALA AND VALVA2
     WHEN (VALVB2 . ALARMS . OPEN) EXECUTE (42)
     WHEN (VALVB2 . ALARMS . OPEN) EXECUTE (42)
     WHEN (PUMPA . ALARMS . OFF) SCHEDULE
     (SHUTDOWN)
     END.

Action List

ACTION LIST (12)
NOTE. ACTION LIST 12 INITIATES TRANSFER FROM TANKA
     TO
NOTE. REACT 1 USING VALVE POSITION FOR FLOW SETTING
     CLOSE (VALVB2) CONFIRM
     WAIT
     OPEN (VALVA1)
     Wait (0, 10)
NOTE. 10 SECOND DELAY TO ALLOW PRIMING OF PUMP
     SCHEDULE (ALARM LIST (3))
NOTE. ALARM LIST 3 WILL CLOSE CVALA AND VALVA2 WHEN
NOTE. VALVB2 ALARMS OPEN
     START (PUMPA) CONFIRM, LOG
NOTE. LOG MESSAGE FORMAT. TOD PUMPA IS ON
     WAIT
     OPEN (VALVA2) CONFIRM
     WAIT (0, 15)
     POSITION (CVALA (VARIABLE))
NOTE. VARIABLE IS THE PERCENT VALVE OPENING
     SCHEDULE (SETLOG (1))
NOTE. LOG MESSAGE FORMAT. PUMPING FROM TANKA TO
     REACT 1
     END.

TABLE III

BATCH SYSTEM PROCESS TABLE (SPT) VARIABLE FORMATS

Type	Format	Usage	Typical Examples
1.0	ZRNNN	Word in SPT (System Process Table)	VA021 = 0
1.1	ZRXNNN	Indirect word in SPT	Initialize Counter → 46
2.0	ZYAANNN	Analog Point	
2.1	ZYXNNN	Analog Point Indirect	
2.2	ZYXNNN(OP)	Subscripted Analog Point	
3.0	ZRNNN	Bit in SPT	
3.1	ZRXNNN	Indirect bit in SPT	
4.0	ZAANNN	Contact output point	(C11200 = 1)
4.1	ZXNNN	Indirect contact output point	Start Product Pump → 202
5.0	ZAANNN	Contact sense point	
5.1	ZXNNN	Indirect contact sense point	
6.0	ZNNNN	Mode bit	J0027 = (0)
7.0	ZZZZZ	Subroutine Name	Initialize Feed Prep Mode Bits → 20

Z = Unique variable name
Y = Any alphabetical character except X. It must not be used
    by itself or in combination to form a term already defined.
A = System number
X = Indirect indication which is an X. This indicates the variable
    is common to other systems.
N = Code number
R = Any alphanumeric character

3) *Alarm Lists:* An alarm list specifies the action for the control system to take on abnormal conditions. For example, WHEN (PUMP A. ALARMS OFF) SCHEDULE (SHUTDOWN) instructs the computer to execute a shutdown program if pump A fails to operate properly.

4) *Display Lists:* Also available in the language are lists which are used to specify logs and displays shown to the process operator. These lists are used on-line to inform the operator of what is occurring in the process.

Thus, there are three separate concepts which are at the heart of the AUTRAN system: the specification which describes the hardware to be controlled, the action list which specifies how the system is to be controlled on the occurrence of external events, the alarm logging, and display lists which specify actions to be taken based on occurrences of external process events. Table II shows examples of the various types of AUTRAN statements.

BATCH

BATCH is a process control programming language used in the preparation of control programs for batch and semi-continuous processes. The format of BATCH is designed for the control engineer who likes to think in terms of flow charts.

There are two basic elements in this programming system: process variables, and basic instructions. On setting up a control system with this language, the user arranges the variables which describe his process in a system process table according to one of the seven possible formats shown in Table III. This table provides the definition of all the data which is known to the computational elements in

controlled. For example, CONTROL VALVE (CVALA (CLOSED, 3)) means that the valve to be named CVALA will be found closed, and is opened by a signal on line 3.

2) *Action Lists:* Action lists are used to define actions to be performed based on conditions of the plant; for example, START (PUMP A), CONFIRM instructs the computer to issue a starting command to a pump which has been designated in the specification statement as pump A, and to confirm when that starting command has been successfully executed by the pump. Other actions which can be called in the language include the opening and closing of valves, the opening and closing of switches, the activation and deactivation of DDC loops, setting or adjusting alarm-limits, and initiating other FORTRAN programs.

TABLE IV

STANDARD BATCH COMPUTATIONAL ELEMENTS

SETV	Set Value
ARIT	Arithmetic Operation
COMP	Compare
MESG	Initiate Message
TIME	Activate Timer
CONT	Contact Output Action
DCOM	DDC Communication
GOTO	Transfer Control Unconditionally
EXIT	Exit To Executive
SETR	Set Restart Address
CALL	Call Subroutine
RETN	Subroutine Return

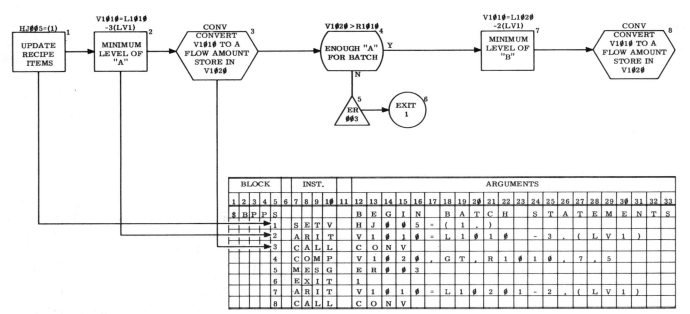

Fig. 3. Typical BATCH flow chart and related program sequence.

the system. The user then draws his control flow chart using standard computational elements shown in Table IV. These 12 elements provide the capability of exercising control over the process under consideration. For example, number two is an arithmetic operation which is used to perform calculations. It can do addition and subtraction with numbers stored in the systems process table. Element four, the message statement, will initiate the output of an alarm message on a logging typewriter. The other elements in the language have similar actions. Fig. 3 shows a section of a BATCH program showing the flow chart as used and the corresponding instructions on a coding sheet.

The software system functions by building the process table, compiling the instructions into an intermediate form which is then stored on bulk memory, and interpreting these instructions when the system is under control.

FILL-IN-THE-BLANK PROGRAMMING SYSTEMS

As has been mentioned previously, in this paper we are discussing programming systems for process control in order of increasing structure. The most highly structured

programming systems for process control are currently being called (for the lack of a better name) "fill-in-the-blank programming systems." These systems generally consist of separate preprogrammed subsystems for data acquisition, data management, general control actions, operator logs and console displays, and process output control. Within these subsystems, the user provides data according to some previously defined format. A predefined system uses these data to link up the data acquisition section with his process, configure the data base properly, specify control actions and timing, define the layout of logs and operator outputs, and link up the actual outputs to the process. These data are generally supplied to such a system on defined data sheets which form a very descriptive document of the control program. The real usefulness of these systems is determined by how well they happen to match the particular application for which their use is being considered.

We will examine two such process control programming systems—PROSPRO and BICEPS. The structure and general intent of these systems is very similar. The major differences are in the way control actions are specified. As we will see later, the PROSPRO user selects his control actions from

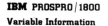 IBM PROSPRO/1800
Variable Information

 IBM PROSPRO/1800
General Action

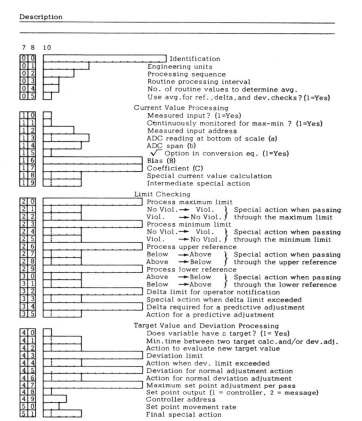

Fig. 4. PROSPRO variable information form. (*Courtesy of IBM Corp.*)

Fig. 5. PROSPRO general action form. (*Courtesy of IBM Corp.*)

a set of general actions which are available, and supplies parameters for these general actions. BICEPS is organized with a simple procedural programming language so that the user, after specifying the data he needs, actually writes his control algorithms as if he were writing a simple FORTRAN program.

PROSPRO

We will examine PROSPRO by looking at the five data sheets which are used to describe the desired control actions to this programming system [39].

The variable information sheet (Fig. 4) is used to describe and identify each process variable. After each variable has been identified with a name, various values associated with the variable may be referenced by appending an extra digit to the name. Possible values include the current or last computed value, the target value, the average value, the assigned maximum and minimum values, etc. If these values are not available, an error signal will result from an attempt to process them. The variable information sheet includes general information, input or current value development information, limit checking ranges, control output information, and special action information. For example, in the limit checking portion of the data sheet, the minimum and maximum limits are described, and special actions are specified to be taken when the value of the process variable exceeds these limits. In the target value

information, indications are made of what the target value is, where the controller is for this variable, and where its associated control actions have been specified to the system.

Fig. 5 shows a general action data sheet. When a general action of some type is needed which has not been provided as a preprogrammed control action, the user may write a small program in a special language or FORTRAN to provide this general action. For very simple actions it is easiest to use a language simpler than FORTRAN. The general action sheet (Fig. 5) shows the language provided. It is very much like the machine language of a computer itself. These actions can then be referenced by the variable information sheet; for example, a general action may be initiated when the process passes through a limit.

Fig. 6 shows a general equation sheet. This sheet is used to provide a calculated value of the form of the general equation shown. The calculated value may be used, for example, in a general action.

Fig. 7 shows the adjustment information data sheet. This sheet is used to specify the control actions used. The control actions must fit in the general form of the equation shown at the top of the sheet. On the data sheet the user specifies the specific variables to be used in this equation and the coefficients. Also specified are the actions to be taken under various unusual events such as the variable to be controlled being out of service, and the variable to be controlled out of limits. The frequency of the control action and the special actions to be taken if there is an unusually rapid change in the manipulated variable are also given on

IBM PROSPRO/1800
General Equation

X20-1753-0

Description

General Equation form: $X = A + B \left[C + (F/D) \right] E$

7 8	10 11 13	16	18	22
0 0	G E		-	1

13: Are values beyond MAX-MIN limits acceptable? (0=No, 1=Yes)
16: Temp. Stg. Loc. of X value when chaining Eqs. (-1 thru -7)
18-22: Next General Equation to be executed. (Chaining)

7 8	10	T	12 V' 16	18 V'' 22	24 Constant Coefficient 36	Remarks
0 1						
0 2						
0 3						
0 4						
0 5						
0 6						
0 7						
0 8						
0 9						

$$\text{Term}_T = 0.0 + \sum \left[(V')_T \times (V'')_T \times (\text{Constant Coefficient})_T \right]$$

Where T is A, B, C, D, E or F
(V) is the value of an identified variable V' or V'' as follows:
V = 0 (or omitted); Value assumed to be 1.0
V > 0; Contents of Identified Process Variable Value (iiiij)
$-7 \leqslant V < 0$; Contents of Identified Temp. Stg. Loc. (Chaining)
$-9999 \leqslant V \leqslant -10$; Contents of Identified Miscellaneous Data Storage

Constant Coefficient.

If omitted, the coefficient is assumed to be 1.0.
When specified, a decimal point (.) must be placed within the field;
all other significant characters must be a digit (0-9) except the first
which may be a minus sign (-) to indicate a negative value; and all
characters from the first to the last must be adjacent. The numerical
range of the Constant Field (24-36) can be extended through use of the
conventional exponential (E) format.

Fig. 6. PROSPRO general equation form. (*Courtesy of IBM Corp.*)

IBM PROSPRO/1800
Adjustment Information

X20-1752-0

Description

Adjustment Equation: $0 = F_1 \Delta T + F_2 \Delta M + F_3 \Delta U + F_4 \Delta V_1 + F_5 \Delta V_2 + F_6 \Delta V_3$
Simultaneous Equation Information. (Omit if single equation solution)

7 8	10	14	16	20	22	26	28	32	34
0 0	2		2		2		2		

☐ Re-solution acceptable? (1=Yes)

Definition and Development of Terms in Adjustment Equation.

7 8	10	14	16 Const. F$_n$ Coeff. 28	30	33	
0 1						T-Targeted Variable
0 2						M-Manipulated Variable
0 3						U-Uncontrolled Variable
0 4						V_1- ⎫ Other
0 5						V_2- ⎬ Variables
0 6						V_3- ⎭

Adjustment Equation Output Restrictions.

1 0		Action taken when Variable M Out of Service.
1 1		Action taken when Variable M Off Computer (On Operator).
1 2		Maximum allowable adjustment to M per pass.
1 3		Action taken when Target of M already at MAX-MIN limit.
1 4		Adjustment Reference List for Partial Loop Test. (2nnnn or Blank)
1 5		If Entry 14 specifies a Reference List, Entries 15-18 specify
1 6		sublists (-1, -2, -3, -4) referenced for all subsequent M's in
1 7		control loop. If Entry 14 is Blank, Entries 15-18 specify all of
1 8		the subsequent M Variables in control loop. Is Target of M set
1 9		to Average instead of Current for Partial Loop? (1=Yes)

Manipulated Variable Adjustment (Δ M) Output Control.

| 2 1 | | TIME in minutes (bXXXX) or as developed (-nnnn or 1nnnn). |

7 8	10 12 14 17	
2 2		10-12: %T = Cumulative elapsed time from present time
2 3		expressed as a percent of TIME.
2 4		14-17: % Δ M = Percent of Δ M change made after %T time.
2 5		

Special Action Initiated Upon Significant Change in Manipulated Variable (M).

7 8	10 Initiating M Change 22	24 Action	
3 1			Action may be specified as follows:
3 2			(a) Process Variable Special (0nnnn).
3 3			(b) Execute General Action (1nnnn).
3 4			(c) Feedforward Request Call of
3 5			Adjustment Equation (2nnnn).
3 6			(d) Execute Special Program (3nnnn).

Fig. 7. PROSPRO adjustment information form. (*Courtesy of IBM Corp.*)

IBM PROSPRO/1800
Miscellaneous Data

X20-1755-0

Description

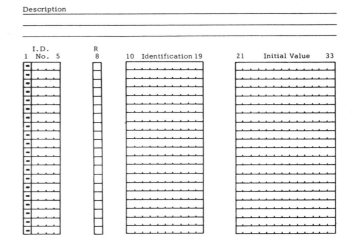

I.D. No.	R	Identification	Initial Value
1 No. 5	8	10 ... 19	21 ... 33

I. D. No.
Any number from -0100 through -9999 which is not duplicated elsewhere.

R-Restart Code
A number from 1 through 4 as follows:
1=Leave present value in storage unchanged.
2=Set present value in storage to equal zero.
3=Set present value in storage to "unavailable".
4=Set present value in storage to initial value.

Identification
Any combination of letters, numbers or special characters.

Initial Value
A specified value to be stored initially. It must contain a decimal point (.)
within the field; all other characters must be a digit except the first which may
be a minus sign (-) to specify a negative value; the range can be extended by use
of the conventional exponential (E) format. To indicate a value which is not to be
available until a value is determined by processing, the following notation is to be
used: UNAVAILABLE.

Fig. 8. PROSPRO miscellaneous data form. (*Courtesy of IBM Corp.*)

this sheet. The adjustment information sheet provides the control of the process linking together the rest of the information used.

Fig. 8 shows the miscellaneous data sheet. This sheet is used to provide process parameters, initial values, and other descriptive data to be used in the various computational algorithms.

BICEPS

BICEPS (Basic Industrial Control Engineering Programming System) is a programming system for supervisory control [38]. Included in BICEPS are: a control program for processing the control loops in their correct sequence, a console program for operator communication, and a programming language—BICEPS programming language (BPL)—for use in writing nonstandard calculations for control loops.

To put the process under control, the control engineer must build and modify storage files for each control loop and define the way loops are connected together. This is done by filling in the blanks on standard BICEPS forms (Fig. 9 and Fig. 10). Each loop is defined by a set of related values and algorithms. A six character process variable name is assigned to the loop to collectively identify the set of values. In the event that a process variable has no associated output or control action, it is called a type "M" variable and is defined by the first of the forms.

Other process variables are called type "p" variables and

GENERAL INFORMATION

M or P | Process Variable Name

0 0	Sequence Number
0 1	PV Value's Auto Source (1 = BICEPS, 2 = Scanner, 3 = None)
0 2	Manually Entered PV Value (0 = Not Permitted, 1 = Permitted)
0 3	Data Type (0 = Magnitude, 1 = Digital Contact)
0 4	Process Variable Description
0 5	PV Engineering Units
0 6	Group Code

INITIALIZATION INFORMATION

0 7	Initial Value of PV
0 8	Initialization Code (0 = Leave PV Unchanged, 1 = Set 'Bad', 2 = Set Equal to Initial Value)
0 9	Initialization Program

CONSOLE ASSIGNMENT

| 1 0 | Console Number |

DIGITAL SCAN

| 1 1 | Scan Class, DIS No., Group & Point Address, Bit-field Width, Sign Code |

ANALOG SCAN

| 1 2 | Scan Class, AIS No., Point Address, Full Scale Millivolts |

MAGNITUDE SCAN

| 1 3 | Instrumentation Limits Code |
| 1 4 | Filter Type (0 = None, 1 = 1st Order Continuous, 2 = 2nd Order Continuous, 3 = Burst); Filter Cutoff Frequency (Cycles per Minute) |

CONVERSION

1 5	Conversion Type, Sensor Point Address of Thermocouple's Reference Junction Temperature
1 6	A
1 7	B
1 8	C — Conversion Constants
1 9	D
2 0	P
2 1	T — Conversion PV's
2 2	G

PROCESSING INFORMATION

| 2 3 | Process Interval |
| 2 4 | Program to Calculate PV (Used If This Loop Calculates Its Own PV) |

LIMIT AND VALIDITY CHECK INFORMATION

2 6	Normal Digital Contact Position (1 = Open, 0 = Closed)
2 7	PV High Limit
2 8	PV Low Limit
2 9	Clamp Code (Blank = No Clamping, 1 = Clamp PV at Limit)
3 0	Deadband Code (Applies to PV and Setpoint)
3 1	Rate of Change (Delta) Limit
3 2	Suppress Standard Alarms (1 = Standard Alarm Messages Will Not Be Printed)

Fig. 9.   BICEPS process variable identification form.

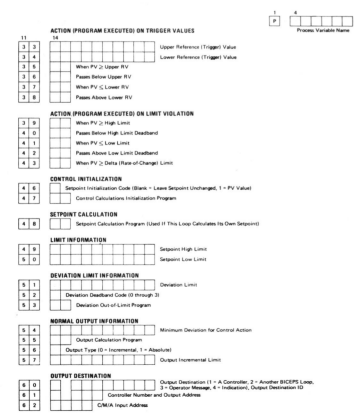

P | Process Variable Name

ACTION (PROGRAM EXECUTED) ON TRIGGER VALUES

3 3	Upper Reference (Trigger) Value
3 4	Lower Reference (Trigger) Value
3 5	When PV ≥ Upper RV
3 6	Passes Below Upper RV
3 7	When PV ≤ Lower RV
3 8	Passes Above Lower RV

ACTION (PROGRAM EXECUTED) ON LIMIT VIOLATION

3 9	When PV ≥ High Limit
4 0	Passes Below High Limit Deadband
4 1	When PV ≤ Low Limit
4 2	Passes Above Low Limit Deadband
4 3	When PV ≥ Delta (Rate-of-Change) Limit

CONTROL INITIALIZATION

| 4 6 | Setpoint Initialization Code (Blank = Leave Setpoint Unchanged, 1 = PV Value) |
| 4 7 | Control Calculations Initialization Program |

SETPOINT CALCULATION

| 4 8 | Setpoint Calculation Program (Used If This Loop Calculates Its Own Setpoint) |

LIMIT INFORMATION

| 4 9 | Setpoint High Limit |
| 5 0 | Setpoint Low Limit |

DEVIATION LIMIT INFORMATION

5 1	Deviation Limit
5 2	Deviation Deadband Code (0 through 3)
5 3	Deviation Out-of-Limit Program

NORMAL OUTPUT INFORMATION

5 4	Minimum Deviation for Control Action
5 5	Output Calculation Program
5 6	Output Type (0 = Incremental, 1 = Absolute)
5 7	Output Incremental Limit

OUTPUT DESTINATION

6 0	Output Destination (1 = A Controller, 2 = Another BICEPS Loop, 3 = Operator Message, 4 = Indication), Output Destination ID
6 1	Controller Number and Output Address
6 2	C/M/A Input Address

Fig. 10.   BICEPS control action form.

are defined by filling in both forms. Some of the blanks refer to programs written in BPL. The user writes these on a third form to define nonstandard functions and control calculations. The control program which processes the loops performs the following.

1) A data gathering function scans the set of sensors which interface with the process to read the various measured variables.
2) A data conditioning function digitally filters (if required), limit checks, and converts these values to engineering unit values.
3) The variable processor function sequences through the command files which specify the various loops. For each loop, it fetches the values associated with each applicable process variable from the memory in which it resides. It operates on these variables as specified on the forms (partly interpretively, but in directly executable code) when BPL programs are called for.

Different requests for communication between operator and computer can be initiated by the operator on his console, or through the I/O typer, such as

1) display any or all values associated with a process variable,
2) change status, set points, limit values,
3) set loops in or out of service,
4) read cards,
5) print date and time,
6) system binary load or dump,
7) transfer control, and
8) BPL program status.

BPL, the BICEPS programming language, is a FORTRAN-like algorithmic programming language. Among its features are the ability to end a programs execution, update systems variables, output messages, solve simultaneous equations, and output control actions.

SUMMARY AND FUTURE TRENDS

In this article we have outlined the general nature of a software system for process control, and have examined some basic approaches to developing this software. Since software costs are now at least equal to hardware costs for many installations, reduction of this expense is important to the economic viability of computer control.

When they match the requirements, prepackaged software systems such as PROSPRO and BICEPS will provide the most economical approach to obtaining process control software with a minimum of special programming expense. Problem-oriented languages also are very promising for the development of control software.

Work has begun on developing standards in an attempt to reduce the proliferation of different programming systems and to refine those which are currently used. A continuing workshop, sponsored by the Purdue University Laboratory for Applied Industrial Control, is attempting to resolve some of these problems—many hope it will do so.

Acknowledgment

D. R. Frost contributed significantly in the preparation of this paper.

References

[1] "Free-time system manual," G.E. Process Computer Dept., Phoenix, Ariz., FTS02/03, no. PCP 117, 1969.

[2] "Free-time system programming application guide," G.E. Process Computer Dept., Phoenix, Ariz., FTS02/03, no. PCP 121, 1969.

[3] "Minutes: workshop on standardization of industrial computer languages," Purdue University, Purdue Laboratory for the Applied Industrial Control, February 17–21, 1969.

[4] W. Diehl, "An integrated hardware/software approach for process control," presented at the ISA Conf., New York, N. Y., 1968.

[5] T. J. Harrison, "Hardware: a matter of logic, memory, and timing," *Control Engrg.*, November 1967.

[6] ——, "How hardware responds to software," *Control Engrg.*, December 1969.

[7] E. C. McIrvine, "Planning software for a manufacturing line," *Control Engrg.*, April 1968.

[8] H. E. Pike, "Direct digital control—a survey," presented at the ISA Conf., New York, N. Y., 1968.

[9] S. Weaver, "Importance of manufacturer software," *Control Engrg.*, January 1968.

[10] E. A. Weiss, "Needed: a process language standard," *Control Engrg.*, December 1968.

[11] T. J. Williams, "Software: more standard programs," *Control Engrg.*, September 1966.

[12] T. J. Williams and S. J. Bailey, "Software: critical factor in computer usage," *Control Engrg.*, October 1967.

[13] "IBM 1800 multiprogramming executive operating system introduction," IBM Corp. C26-3718-2, 1968.

[14] "IBM 1800 multiprogramming operating system, programmer's guide," *IBM Manual* C26-3720, 1968.

[15] "Alert programmers reference manual," Honeywell Computer Control Div., October 1968.

[16] "RTMOS manual," G.E. Process Computer Dept., Phoenix, Ariz., 1968.

[17] "American Standard FORTRAN," 1966 Am. Standards Assoc., no. X3.9, March 7, 1966.

[18] "FORTRAN IV computer reference manual for 12000 computer systems," Westinghouse Electric Corp., November 1968.

[19] "FORTRAN general information manual," Control Data Corp., 1965.

[20] "FORTRAN reference manual," G.E. Process Computer Dept., Manual YPG14M, May 1965.

[21] J. E. Clough and A. W. Westerberg, "FORTRAN for on-line control," *Control Engrg.*, March 1968.

[22] D. R. Frost, "FORTRAN for process control," *Instr. Technol.*, April 1969.

[23] R. E. Hohmeyer, "CDC 1700 FORTRAN for process control," presented at the Joint Automatic Control Conf., 1968.

[24] W. Kipiniak and P. Quiant, "Assembly vs. compiler languages," *Control Engrg.*, February 1968.

[25] M. Mensh and W. Diehl, "Extended FORTRAN for process control," presented at the Joint Automatic Control Conf., 1968.

[26] B. C. Roberts, "FORTRAN IV in a process control environment," presented at the Joint Automatic Control Conf., 1968.

[27] "AUTRAN training manual." Control Data Corp., La Jolla, Calif., 1968.

[28] "BATCH sequencing system," Foxboro Co., Foxboro, Mass., TIM-R-97400A-5-4, 1968.

[29] "Control Data 1700 AUTRAN process control computer system," Control Data Corp., La Jolla, Calif., 1968.

[30] "Supervisory programming system," Foxboro Co., Foxboro, Mass., TIM-R-97400A-5-3, 1968.

[31] "IBM process supervisory program (PROSPRO/1800)," *IBM Manual* H 20-0261-0, 1966.

[32] S. M. Fisch and S. J. Whitman, "An application of a process control language to industrial digital control," presented at the ISA Ann. Conf., New York, N. Y., 1968.

[33] T. G. Gaspar, V. V. Dobrohotoff, and D. R. Burgess, "New process language uses English terms," *Control Engrg.*, October 1968.

[34] O. Kircher and E. B. Turner, "On-line MISSIL," presented at the Joint Automatic Control Conf., Ann Arbor, Mich., 1968.

[35] G. W. Markham, "Fill-in-the-form programming," *Control Engrg.*, May 1968.

[36] G. W. Oerter, "A new implementation of decision tables for a process computer language," presented at the Joint Automatic Control Conf., 1968.

[37] J. A. Ralston, G. W. Oerter, and W. B. Schultz, "Simplified approach to steam plant computer programming," presented at the Am. Power Conf., April 27, 1967.

[38] "BICEPS summary manual/BICEPS supervisory control," G.E. Process Computer Dept., Phoenix, Airz., A GET-3539, 1969.

[39] "1800 process supervisory program (PROSPRO/1800) (1800-CC-02X) language specifications manual," IBM Corp., no. H20-0473-1, 1968.

A Survey of Software for Direct Digital Control*

T. L. WILLMOTT†

Beloit Corporation‡
Beloit, Wisconsin

▶ Since the scope of Direct Digital Control (DDC) has expanded considerably in the last decade, a review of the state of development of DDC systems is presented. Discrete and continuous control, and higher-level control as used in conjunction with DDC are discussed together with the multi-processor systems. To illustrate the most generally used structural technique in DDC programming—the parameter/variable table approach—a simplified example is presented and discussed with reference to the constraints imposed by real-time considerations. The most recent development in DDC—real-time executives for general application—is introduced and discussed briefly.

INTRODUCTION

THE PURPOSE OF this paper is to provide a tutorial overview of the "state of the art" of direct digital control (DDC) software. It is generally assumed that the reader has some basic knowledge of digital computer programs and process control, but is not generally familiar with DDC. Since this paper has been written as a companion to those of Bakke[1] and Zikas[2], details of the hardware and theory are assumed.

The scope of DDC has expanded considerably from that originally proposed in the late nineteen fifties. At that time, the fundamental concept was replacement of Analog (electronic or pneumatic) controllers to achieve reductions in capital cost. It was natural, therefore, that DDC programs should be organized in terms of modules corresponding to analog units. During the fifties, the concept of standard control functions was largely accepted in the process-control industry. Instrument and control vendors offered a series of "boxes", each of which performed some standard function, such as "proportional", "proportional plus integral", "ratio," and "cascade",[1] and it was generally understood that

such controllers were electronic or pneumatic analogs of mathematical computations. At the same time, equipment for converting electronic and pneumatic signals into digital (computer readable) form, and for converting back to analog, were becoming commercially available. Of course, the cost of digital computers was relatively high, but the incremental cost of implementing many control calculations on a digital computer was considerably less than the incremental cost of providing an individual analog controller for each computation. Hence, when computers with an adequately fast computational speed became available, computer control for a large number of loops was less expensive than an equivalent aggregation of analog controllers.[3] (And the increasing size of process units, as a result of "economies of scale" encouraged the increased use of automatic control.) Fortunately, this led to a computer program organization which envisaged a multiplicity of control "loops." It is the writer's opinion that this early insight was a significant factor which smoothed the way for development of large DDC systems.

TYPES OF DDC SYSTEMS

To consider DDC objectively, we should first briefly discuss the distinctions between "control" functions

---

*Presented at the 1968 ISA Annual Conference.
†Manager of Analytical Engineering.
‡Control Systems Division.

and "computers" as a hardware/software entity. Ideally, "control" can be described in terms of the operations to be performed on a process by a "box" (a control system), assuming certain information about the status of the process (measured variables) and goals (setpoints) are made available to the "box." The "box" is some sort of automata which may contain analog components, or a digital computer system, or various electronic, pneumatic, and electro-mechanical combinations of analog and digital devices.

Control Functions

Types of control can be distinguished by whether the process is discrete (manufacturing automobile parts, for example), or continuous (as in electric power generation), or batch, a combination of discrete and continuous, in which a process unit is first loaded, followed by processing (refining, polymerization, wood-chip digesting), and then unloaded and prepared for the next batch.[4] Plant start-up and product change-over (or grade change) are still another type of control problem.

Control characteristics can also be classified according to levels.[5] Assuming a process equipped with automatic measuring and actuator equipment, the first level of control, *direct control*, includes the basic control forms, such as single variable feedback, simple cascade, and ratio. It is also feasible and practical to implement more sophisticated forms of direct control, such as non-interacting multivariable, and multi-component blending, by "interconnected" combinations of the basic control forms.

Higher level control refers to methods of "directing" the operation of the first control level. Optimizing control, for example, may be used to change the first level setpoints to minimize product cost, with quality-control constraints. Adaptive control refers to methods by which lower level controls are adjusted to compensate for changes in process operating characteristics, such as, shifts in process dynamics resulting from deposits in vessels or lines.

In the first half of this decade, the term "DDC system" generally referred to a digital computer control system performing first-level control on a continuous process. The term "supervisory computer system" usually referred to either a data logging and monitoring system, or a computer performing higher level control on first-level analog controllers. This latter form of supervisory control has also been called (more accurately) "Digitally Directed Analog" control.

More recently, an increasing number of multi-level computer systems are being implemented which combine DDC and higher level control within the same system.[6]

In this paper, we shall refer to a computer system which has DDC as its primary function, as a "DDC only" system, and to a system which combines DDC and a significant amount of higher level control as a "multi-level computer control system." Systems which perform only data logging and supervisory systems are not within the scope of this paper.

Computer Configurations

Apart from the consideration of control functions, computer control can be implemented by a variety of equipment and program arrangements. Multi-processor systems, i.e., systems which include two or more interconnected computers, are not uncommon in DDC applications. The reasons for using multi-processor systems are not determined by DDC as such, but rather by attempts to improve system reliability and decrease programming complexity, at minimally increased cost.

One such system, for example, uses "twin" processors. One processor acts as a standby to take over if and when the other malfunctions.[7,9] Multiple processors are also used in a hierarchical arrangement in which there are one or more "slave" computers performing DDC and a "master" computer performing higher level control functions, as well as background, or off-line, compilation and computing functions.

Program Structures

As with hardware, the complexity of the complete program for a DDC or multilevel system (or for any on-line, real-time system) demands subdivision, so that the whole program becomes a set of interacting subprograms. Each subprogram must be a somewhat independent "module" with defined "linkages" to other subprograms. This collection of programs and their interconnections can then be viewed as a program system structure or configuration.

Viewing the total program as a set of modules, each with a unique function, it is important not only that each module perform its function effectively, but also that effective means of intercommunication among modules exist. For example, a good FORTRAN compiler may exist for "computer," as well as a satisfactory DDC program. This fact may be meaningless in terms of using FORTRAN to fulfill special requirements unless there is an operable program linkage between the DDC program and object FORTRAN programs.

The major structural parts of a (multilevel) DDC system can be categorized as:

1. DDC only: that part of overall program which implements first level control.
2. Higher-level control: the on-line control programs in a multi-level system (regardless of hardware configuration) which are not part of the DDC-only category.
3. Background system: the lowest priority task in an on-line system, which permits compiling and assembly of new programs, as well as execution of off-line programs.
4. Executive routine: the program which allocates computing time and memory to the various levels of on-line and background programs.
5. Input/output routines: the set of programs which provide an interface between the on-line and background programs and the input–output hardware, including drums and disks; in DDC,

process input, output, and communication with process operator's consoles are of prime importance.

Not all DDC systems include all these components. A DDC-only system may consist of only the basic DDC routines with a simple executive and minimal I/O (input/output) routines.[8] Such program configurations are typical in DDC applications where all or most of the software is supplied by the user. The background function is optional, although most users consider it imperative for multi-level systems, especially because they tend to require more debugging and consequent modification.

In the following section we will discuss the essential functions and characteristics of the DDC part, and consider the other categories as an expansion of this in later sections.

FUNCTIONS AND CHARACTERISTICS OF DDC ONLY

As stated previously, it is important to distinguish between the tasks performed by a system, and the organization of the hardware and software which perform these tasks (or more elegantly, functions). The tasks to be performed are determined by the process, the applicable control theory and the relevant economics. The organization of the hardware and software determines whether a particular computer system performs these tasks efficiently and reliably.

The essential functions of the DDC part of a system are:

1. Process input: direct reading of measurable process variables, through appropriate transducers and computer interface equipment.
2. Signal conditioning and checking: testing for validity of the input signal; linearization of raw values; digital filtering (which may be required in addition to the hardware filtering usually provided); checking measured or computed process variables for alarm conditions or return to normal (e.g., abnormally high pressure, low flow, rate-of change, etc.; note that this is different from signal validity).
3. Control and intermediate calculations: computing values for each manipulated variable under computer control, according to the algorithm and sampling interval specified for each loop; calculating intermediate variables such as compensated flows and cascade setpoints.
4. Process output: checking validity or reasonableness of output value or rate-of-change, performing any specified scaling, addressing the output to the proper output device (hold amplifier, stepping motor, DDC station, pulse-width-modulated-contact contacts, etc.).
5. Process operator communication: the equipment normally associated with this function consists of a display device such as nixie lights, back projection, or CRT, one or more output typers,

and push-buttons or dials for manual input). The functions provided include displaying current values of process variables and control parameters; changing setpoints, control gains, alarm, limits (usually restricted to engineering and supervisory personnel); changing loops from computer control to manual or back-up control, and vice versa; display and/or log alarm, or return-to-normal conditions, log occurrence of operator initiated changes in control status; on-demand or periodic logs of short-term process status or history.

As stated previously, the DDC system must be designed to accomplish these functions for a large number of loops, ranging from fifty to three hundred or more. Furthermore, it should be obvious that the system must account for a variety of subfunctions under each major function. In the case of process measurements, for example, various ranges of analog signals have to be accounted for, as well as counter-type inputs such as turbine flow meters and digital tachometers. Different types of digital filter routines and filter constants are required for various classes of inputs. Because a variety of final actuators is used on the process, it is common that different types of computer-actuator interfaces will be used on a system, each type requiring a different process output routine.

As illustrated in Bakke's companion paper,[1] no single control algorithm is satisfactory for all control situations, so the DDC system must include several algorithms (or a characteristic algorithm with several options). One of these is to be specified for each "loop," although many of the "loops" may utilize the same algorithm, each with its individual gain and time constant parameters.

Characteristics of the Parameter/Variable Table Approach

The structural technique most commonly used in DDC programs designed for generality, as far as can be determined, is an organization in terms of tables, or a set of tables, containing the values of various types of parameters; e.g., input address, type of filter, alarm limits, type of algorithm, ... and values of intermediate variables, such as must be retained in algorithms with time dependent terms. Most of the communication between programs, and between the computer system and its external environment, is carried out in relation to these tables. They are variously called "point tables," "loop records," "process variable records," and other names, depending on their function, and which "buzz-words" were most popular during the time the package was designed. We shall refer to these generically as parameter/variable tables (PVT's).

Example of PVT Method

To illustrate this tabular concept, we shall give a highly simplified example of the part, of a PVT relating to a control algorithm, ignoring for the moment such factors as filtering, alarming, and operator communications. Consider a simplified DDC system controlling 50 loops,* using only a proportional algorithm of the form:

$$Mi = Ki(Ri - Ci)$$

where

i = the index number of the loop
Ci = the input value (controlled variable)
Ri = the setpoint
Ki = gain factor
Mi = output (manipulated variable).

A straightforward PVT organization for this system would be to reserve 300 words of memory consisting of 50 blocks, each containing six words, as shown in Figure 1. The information to be stored in each block would be:

Word 1 : Ii = the *address* of the analog input multiplexer for the input to *i*th block
Word 2 : Ci = the most recent *value* of the input variable for block (i)
Word 3 : Ri = the *value* of the setpoint for block (i)
Word 4 : Ki = the *value* of the gain factor for block (i)
Word 5 : Mi = the most recently calculated output *value* of block (i)
Word 6 : Ai = the *address* of output device for block (i)

Assume that the system has a timer which initiates the control program once every five seconds (also assume the computer is fast enough to perform the described calculations in less than five seconds). The steps in the control program would be:

1. To reference the first PVT, set the index, i to 1;
2. Wait for the "start control" interrupt, which occurs once very five seconds, then proceed to Step 3. when the interrupt occurs;
3. Send Ii (from Word 1 of PVT (i)) to analog input multiplexer to read the proper input;
4. When the input conversion is completed, store the result as Ci (Word 2 in PVT (i));
5. Control algorithm: subtract Ci from Ri (Word 3 in PVT(i)) and multiply by Ki (Word 4 in PVT(i)), store the result as Mi (Word 5 in PVT(i));
6. Send the *value* of Mi to the output device (valve or other actuator) specified by Ai (Word 6 in PVT(i));
7. If $i = 50$, return to Step 1., otherwise perform Step 8.
8. Increase i by one and go back to Step 3.

If we now refer to the beginning of this section, it should be somewhat clear how such additional functions as signal conditioning and checking, selection of various control algorithms, and output checking could be implemented by expanding the PVT for each loop to include the requisite parameters and variables, and inserting the appropriate steps in the program.

*In practice, it is unlikely that all 50 loops in a system would use the same algorithm, but this serves the illustrative purpose.

MEMORY AREA CONTAINS 50 PVT'S (6 WORDS EACH, 300 WORDS TOTAL)

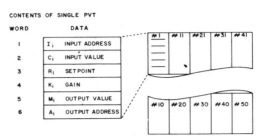

Figure 1. Organization of parameter/variable tables for example of PVT Method.

The reader should not be misled by the simplicity of the above example. In practice, the PVT's can become quite large. For example, Beloit Control Systems Division last year successfully started a 170-loop DDC system on a paper machine—stock preparation application for EasTex Paper Company,[9] using an IBM 1800 computer. The software system was one of the first to combine the earlier "stand-alone DDC program" the TSX executive (requiring 5 man-years of programming by the Beloit project team). The PVT's for this system occupy over 5000 words of core, and a typical PVT for a control loop contains 80 separate pieces of information encoded in 30 words (16-bits each). (The package announced by IBM in April of this year[11] is slightly more economical with space.)

It should also be clear that not all the information to be encoded in a PVT requires a full word. For instance, we need an indicator to describe whether the loop is presently on computer control, or on back-up. This requires only one bit of information, which would be included as one part of a word containing several such pieces of information. As a further example, we have to place an index in each PVT to indicate which type of control algorithm applies to that control loop. Suppose we provided 16 different algorithms (which can be indexed by a four-bit code). The appropriate algorithm code number can also be packed in a word which contains other information. We shall return to this subject later to discuss alternative approaches to PVT organization.

Real-Time Considerations

If one had to define the single factor which most complicates development of DDC software, it would surely be timing. Several types of timing constraints can be identified:

1. The sampling and output rate of the individual loops must be maintained.
2. Communications with the process operator must be responsive on the order of 5 to 20 s, and the information presented must be up-to-date within 2 minute at most.
3. Input and output devices, especially process I/O, must be operated at close to maximum rate, as dictated by computer system economics.

4. If higher level control is implemented, normally at a lower computer priority than DDC, time must be allocated to that function on the most favorable basis practical.

5. If the system includes background operations, enough computer time must be allocated to allow practical operation.

Furthermore, simple priority schemes do not meet the requirements. There is, for instance, a "hard" real-time constraint on control sampling rate, since any variation in sampling rate will affect the accuracy, and ultimately the stability, of control. Conversely, the constraint on response to process operator requests is "soft" because the response time can vary considerably without significantly affecting system performance. (The point at which the operator initiates input requests using a hammer is usually regarded as the upper limit.)

In the example program previously described, note that there is a considerable inefficiency between Step 3., which initiates an analog input, and Step 4., which waits for completion of the conversion and then stores the result. This operation typically requires 5 to 10 ms on presently available equipment. At 10 ms, for 50 loops, this wait would consume 0.5 s out of every 5 s, or 10 percent of the computer time. This might not seem inappropriate unless you consider it as 10 percent of computer lease rate. The solution ordinarily implemented is to "look ahead," so the multiplexer is converting the next input, while the computer is performing the calculations from the previous input.

This type of overlap problem generally arises with any I/O equipment. Of course, the above problem would be solved technically by using a multiplexer with a conversion time in the micro-second range, thus simplifying the DDC program. Unfortunately, the economics of this latter solution are presently vastly unfavorable. Hence, the phrase: hardware-software tradeoff.

Sampling Intervals and Loading

Not all loops in a DDC system are executed at the same sampling interval. The proper sampling interval for a given control "loop" depends on the time constants and transport delays of the process being controlled. With a few exceptions, sampling intervals in contemporary DDC systems range from 1 to 60 seconds. The upper end of the scale (60 s) is determined by the high through-put rates of processes on which DDC is presently being applied. There are, of course, loops such as drive-speed controls, which require sampling intervals of considerably less than one second. In these cases, the lower limit is established by the fact that the fraction of computer time required for control of a single loop becomes relatively large, consequently, reducing the total number of loops which can be controlled, and increasing the per-loop cost. Hence most system designers continue to use individual controllers for such loops. (Often such loops are thought to be too "critical" for computer control, but this is stated without regard to the relative reliability of the individual controllers.)

The sampling rate must be at least twice the closed bandwidth, by Shannon's theorem, but if too fast a sampling rate is used, significant changes in variables may be masked by accumulated truncation errors.

In practice, it is not necessary to sample each loop at its optimum rate (often the process parameters are not precisely determinable), but at some rate close to the optimum. A typical DDC program will provide for sampling at intervals of 1, 2, 5, 10, 20, 30, and 60 seconds. Another popular scheme is powers-of-two of the lowest sampling interval, e.g., 1, 2, 4, 8, 16, 32, and 64 seconds. The sampling interval is ordinarily encoded into the PVT for each loop. (See alternatives below.)

An important consideration is the distribution of loops to achieve a uniform system load. Depending on the computing speed of the central processor, the maximum rate of process I/O operations, and the program organization, DDC systems have an inherent maximum operating rate, which currently ranges from 50 to 200 loops/s. The major limitation, presently, is the operating speed of the input relays (as yet, high-speed solid state multiplexing is not in use). Examples of such standard systems include the "Controlware" package[11] developed by the Computer Control Division of Honeywell, Inc., which has a tested maximum operating rate of 190 loops/s. The Leeds & Northrup "Codil" system[12] on the LN500 computer, can operate close to 170 loops/s (although the multiplexer is considerably faster).

The maximum operating rate is related to the sampling rate for individual loops, in that the system will function properly only if the sum of the ratios of the total number of loops assigned to the sampling interval is less than the overall operating rate. Consider, for example, the following requirements for a 200 loop system:

Sampling Interval (sec.)	Number of Loops	Loops/s
1	10	10
2	50	25
4	40	10
8	20	2.5
16	80	5
Total	200	42.5

In other words, this system would require an overall operating rate of at least 42.5 loops/s. Moreover, the loading during each second must be distributed so that the requirements during any single second do not exceed the maximum. This can be accomplished, for instance, by solving during each second, all the one second loops, $\frac{1}{2}$ of the two second loops, $\frac{1}{4}$ of the four second loops, and so forth.

A more sophisticated method of distributing the loading is to define a separate list (PVT) for each sampling interval, e.g., a one second list, two second list, etc. The entry in each list is a pointer to the main PVT for each loop. The executive routine can then perform the distribution automatically. This type of organization has the further advantage that the sequence of solving loops, which is important in cascade, ratio, and other arrangements involving the interconnection of loops, does *not* depend on the relative memory locations of the main PVT's.

Alternatives in Organizing PVT's

From the discussion of the real-time considerations, it is apparent that the simple organization of the PVT's previously outlined has several disadvantages from a program structure viewpoint. With a well designed system, the end user need not be concerned with this problem, since he is mainly concerned with the existence of parameters and variables and how they can be accessed. The organization of PVT's, however, has a significant effect on the flexibility of DDC system for on-line modification and for inserting special purpose algorithms, or higher level control.

An extreme alternative, consisting of six tables, one for each parameter, each table containing one entry for each loop, is illustrated in Figure 2. This type of organization, since the input and output tables are separate, would have some advantage in that the programming to overlap input, output, and computation would be simplified.

Since a variety of algorithms are required, it is generally acknowledged that not all loops will require the same number of parameter and variable storage locations. Consequently, variable length records are commonly used. The length of the record may be fixed by categories of algorithms, or the length of record may be an additional parameter in PVT.

An advantage in the PVT organization is that it orders information in a uniform fashion. Some caution is required to ensure that flexibility in table organization does not leave a programmer's loophole for tabular chaos.

Figure 3 shows a third alternative, in which the input and output addresses are arranged in separate tables and the remainder are placed in tables on a loop basis. This organization is more typical of the arrangements used in standard vendor supplied DDC programs.

HIGHER LEVEL FUNCTIONS

Probably the only universal definition of higher level control is "everything which isn't DDC." More precisely, it consists of those on-line control functions which act upon the parameters of the first level controllers, based on the information received from the first. It includes such computations as determining optimum setpoints, by gradient or linear programming methods; and

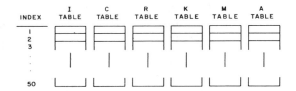

PVT AREA IN MEMORY CONTAINS SIX TABLES, 50 WORDS EACH

Figure 2. Alternative organization tables for example of PVT Method.

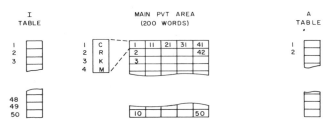

PVT AREA CONTAINS THREE TABLES

1. INPUT ADDRESS LIST
2. MAIN PVT (CONTROL TABLE)
3. OUTPUT ADDRESS LIST

Figure 3. Typical mixed organization of PVT's for example of PVT Method.

adaptive gain adjusting techniques, such as the control tuner developed by Bakke.[1] In applications where a single process is used to make several different products, such as various grades of paper, higher level control includes the function of automatic changeover from one product to another (grade change).

At present, higher level control is unique to each system, except in some cases of large users with several identical systems.

The programs for higher level control usually operate on a multi-programmed basis with DDC, i.e., when the higher level control program is operating, a real-time interrupt will periodically cause suspension of its execution to allow execution of the DDC functions. When the DDC cycle is completed, execution of the higher level control is restored until another interrupt occurs. The higher level control programs can read data from, and store results in, the PVT's. Thus, they can be programmed independently of the DDC programs. This is also advantageous in the hierarchical multi-processor type of system, since all communication between the "master" and "slave" computer can be performed via the data in PVT's. This eliminates, or at least simplifies, problems of synchronization between processors.

On a single computer system, the implementation of higher level control requires a real-time executive program with strong multi-programming capabilities.[13]

REAL-TIME EXECUTIVES FOR DDC

Until recently, executive functions for DDC only systems were generally built into the DDC programs. This was for two separate reasons. First, in those systems designed and programmed by the end user, there was not a strong enough need for a distinct general purpose real-time executive. Second, as regards vendor supplied standard DDC programs, both the vendors and end users agreed that the overhead time of the general purpose executives was too high for the rapid response required of DDC.

During the past year, four major vendors have announced tested DDC programs designed for general application, and operating under their standard real-time executive.[10–12,14] G.E. and Control Data have also implemented several DDC systems for particular customer applications, operating under their standard executives, but they have not yet publicized these as standard programs.

Three factors have mitigated for this change: speed improvements in computer and interface equipment; improvements in the programming and structure of executive routines; and most important, a strong user demand for systems with capability for multi-level control.

Figure 4 is a block diagram representation of the typical program components of a multi-level DDC system. The figure also serves to illustrate the concepts of multi-programming on a single computer. (In a multi-computer system, the blocks to right would be assigned to the 'master,' and the blocks under "DDC," with the PVT's, to the 'slave'.)

Multi-programming means using a single computer so that two or more independent programs appear to be executing simultaneously. This is accomplished under the control of an executive routine which allocates computer execution time and memory on a priority or "as requested" basis.

For the typical multi-level system illustrated, the independent programs are DDC, higher level control, operator communications, drum- or disk-file management, logging, and background, in that order of priority. The executive functions are: first, allocating program execution time to the highest priority program waiting to be executed (saving the status of lower priority interrupted programs, so that execution can be restored when the higher priority program is completed); and second, allocating available space in main (core) memory for programs stored on disk or drum.

Separate sub-executives are provided for the DDC programs and the background operations. Background operations are, by definition, the lowest priority job in the system.

Because of their "hard" real-time requirements, the DDC programs operate at a high priority. The interrupt handler routines operate at the highest priority, so that I/O operations proceed in parallel with the DDC execution. This can be done because interrupt response has a relatively short execution time—usually not more than 10 or 20 instructions.

Requests for execution of the intermediate priority programs such as higher level control, formatting, operator entry/display, and bulk, memory file management, are stacked on a straight queue basis, i.e., first-come-first-served. Some of the more sophisticated executives for process control computers now include several queues at different priorities. In this arrangement, all the requests in the highest priority queue are fulfilled before those in the second priority queue, and so on.

One of the important factors in multi-level systems is whether the computer has the capability for dynamic relocation of programs. The most common method of accomplishing this in small- or medium-scale computers is a relative addressing option on all instructions (except register reference). The importance of dynamic relocation is that it permits higher priority programs to be located in any available memory area, regardless of the status of execution of lower priority programs. Without this feature, a higher priority program may be inhibited from execution because the memory area allocated to it is already occupied by a lower priority program. One way around this, of course, is to provide separate memory areas for different program priorities. This solves the problem, but severely decreases the efficiency of memory utilization. The potential user should also be warned that some process computers have this capability in the hardware, but the vendor's executive software provides only minimal facilities for using it.

STATUS OF DEVELOPMENTS

DDC software is currently in a significant transitory phase. The feasibility of the concept of DDC systems is fully established, adequate hardware is readily available, and the gap between theory and practice has been successfully bridged, technically and economically. Standard DDC "packages" for first level control are available for several process control computers, and under development for others.

There is considerable justification indicated for various types of higher level control, but the theory appears to be well ahead of the software. It is doubtful that this kind of control can be standardized to the extent possible for first level control. We have concluded that a major factor inhibiting development of higher level control is the lack of availability of adequate programming languages.[13]

It is unfortunate that generally the facilities for intercommunication between DDC tables (or programs) and user-written FORTRAN programs are limited or nonexistent in several of the available "packages". (FORTRAN exists, and DDC exists, but they cannot communicate.) Some very creative efforts have been made to extend FORTRAN with bit manipulation, decision, tables, real-time statements, and the like. Overall, however, these are *ad hoc* solutions, at best, which solve a limited class of problems. From a user viewpoint, they

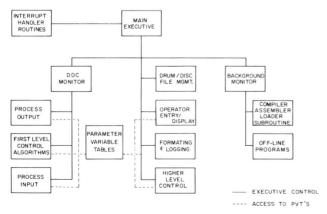

Figure 4. Program components of multilevel control system.

also have the disadvantage of being machine-dependent, since different vendors use various approaches.

One significant alternative (in which the writer is admittedly an accomplice) is the development of a language specifically designed for real-time applications.[15-17] This kind of language would include the basic scientific elements of FORTRAN or subsets of ALGOL or PL/1, such as integer and floating arithmetic and branching statements. In addition, it would include statements for handling interrupt operations, files of numerical or program data, interfacing with input-output devices, and for general conversion of character and bit string data.

With these facilities in a machine independent language, a user could more easily establish communication between his higher level control programs and standard first level control. It would also simplify the modification of executive routines, input–output routines, or DDC programs by either the vendor or the user, to meet special requirements. A good example of this need is the development of programs for special purpose process operator's consoles.

CONCLUSION

The availability of standard DDC programs for first-level control, with capability for multi-level control, continues to improve. The resulting decrease in implementation costs will have a positive effect on the acceptance of DDC, as evidenced by the amount of activity in this area by the major vendors of DDC systems. However, the clear trend to higher level optimizing and adapting control, made feasible by the first implementation of DDC, has introduced a new class of software problems, i.e., the requirement for higher level languages designed for real-time computation in an industrial process-control computer environment.

REFERENCES

1. Bakke, R. M. 1968. "Theoretical Aspects of Direct Digital Control." In *Proceedings* Part I, 23d Annual ISA Conference, paper no. 68-833, Pittsburgh: ISA.
2. Zikas, A. J. 1968. "Hardware Requirements for a Typical DDC System." In *Proceedings* Part I, 23d Annual ISA Conference, paper no. 68-832. Pittsburgh: ISA.
3. Farrell, R. J. 1966. "Pneumatic, Electronic Direct Digital Control." In *Proceedings*. 21st Annual Engineering Conference Technical Association of the Pulp and Paper Industry, Boston: TAPPI.
4. Lombardo, J. M. 1967. "The Place of Digital Backup in the Direct Digital Control System." In *Proceedings*, Spring Joint Computer Conference, pp. 771–778. Washington, D.C.: Thompson Books.
5. Lefkowitz, I. 1965. "Multi-Level Approach Applied to Control System Design." In *Proceedings*, Joint Automatic Control Conference, New York: Academic Press.
6. "DDC Workshop Highlights." July 1967. *Contr. Eng.* 14.
7. Amrehn, H. 1967. "Report on Two Process Computer Installations with DDC Applications." In *Proceedings*, 22d Annual ISA Conference, vol. 22, part 3, paper no. D2-1-67, Pittsburgh: ISA.
8. Markham, G. W., Johnson, D. O., and Dubinsky, A. n.d. *IBM 1800 DDC Direct Digital Process Control*. IBM 1800 General Program Library 23.5.002.
9. Gantzhorn, E. February 12, 1968. "Thoroughly Modern Mill Deep in the Heart of Texas-EasTex." *Pulp and Paper*.
10. Adler, L. S. *et al. IBM 1800 DDC-TSX, a Time-Sharing Direct Digital Process Control Program*. Contributed Program Library paper 1800-23.5.005.
11. "DDC System, Applications Reference Manual." Honeywell, Inc., Framingham, Mass. Computer Controls Division.
12. "CODIL, Control Diagram Language." Leeds and Northrup Company, North Wales, Pa.
13. Schoeffler, J. D. February 1966. "Process Control Software." *Datamation.* 12:33–42.
14. "CODPAC, Core/Drum Package," and "LAM, Loop Adder-Modifier." Foxboro Company, Foxboro, Mass.
15. Schoeffler, J. D., Willmott, T. L., and Dedourek, J. 1968. "Programming Languages for Industrial Process Control." Paper read at 2d IFAC/IFIP Symposium on Digital Control of Large Industrial Systems, 17–19 June 1968, at Toronto, Canada.
16. Willmott, T. L. 1967. "A Programming Language for Process Control Computers." M.S. thesis, Case-Western Reserve University.
17. "A Language for Real-Time Systems." December 1967. *Comp. Bull.* 10:202–212.

EFFICIENCY CONSIDERATIONS OF SEVERAL COMMUNICATIONS EXECUTIVES

Stanford R. Amstutz
Honeywell Information Systems Inc.
Framingham, Mass.

This paper describes the program structures and restart provisions of two turnkey message switching systems supplied by HIS, Framingham. Both systems are duplexed, based on two DDP-516 computers, each with 24K of 0.96 μsec core. Both systems have fixed head disc secondary storage, hereafter called drum. The program structures of the two systems differ significantly, and this paper will assess their relative advantages and disadvantages.

CYCLIC EXECUTIVE

The first system uses a cyclic executive, so called because the message processing programs are executed in a fixed cycle. During a cycle, the input programs are read from drum to core and then executed; the output programs are read from drum to core and executed; and last, the ledger is written from core to drum. The ledger consists of variables which must be saved on drum for restart. Overlapping the program executions are data reads and writes.

Figure 1 illustrates data chaining and output queueing. Free storage on drum is comprised of 128 word segments called chunks. Corresponding to each chunk is a word in the core-contained Drum Link Table (DLT). Messages which require more than one chunk are chained from the first, the SOM (start of message) chunk, via the DLT. Figure 1 indicates a three-chunk message with SOM in chunk 4, intermediate text in chunk 2, and EOM (end of message) in chunk 7. Routed messages are queued for delivery via a chained list of dynamically assigned "Queue Entries." Figure 1 shows that two messages are queued for delivery via line i: first the message with SOM in chunk 4, and last the message with SOM in chunk 57.

The DLT and the chain of queue entries are among the more important variables to ledger each cycle for restart, since their loss would make it impossible to deliver traffic received but not yet delivered before restart.

When restart is required, the drum(s) is switched to the offline machine, the most up-to-date ledger is read into the ledgered variables area of its core, and message processing is resumed. The read of the ledgered variables from drum is the converse of the per cycle ledgered variables write; it makes the core contents of the switched-to-machine indistinguishable from the core contents of the switched-from machine.

Advantage

Since the online machine leaves a trace of its processing status via the periodic ledger, the standby machine can be devoted to entirely different tasks, even while standing by.

Disadvantage

The ledger write takes about 20% of a normal cycle. Of this write only a small part (probably less than 1%) represents information changed since the last cycle's ledger. Thus the time duration of the ledger is not well utilized; little else can go on then, because of the need for a stable situation during the ledger write.

QUEUED EXECUTIVE

The executive of the second system is a queued executive, so called because the sequence of executions of message processing tasks is determined solely by position in an executive priority queue.

There are n task queues, corresponding to n task priorities. The tasks in priority queue k will be executed before those on queues numbered greater than k. Within a queue the tasks are serviced in a first-in, first-out order.

Each queue is comprised of task control blocks (TCBs), where each TCB represents a task awaiting execution. The TCBs are assigned from dynamic storage when a task execution is scheduled. Each TCB has a pointer to the next TCB on the queue; a pointer to the entry point of the routine which will execute the task; a pointer to data, if the task execution will process data; and any other parameters which must be passed from the program scheduling the task to the program executing the task.

Figure 2 illustrates data chaining and output queueing. The blocks comprising a message are chained together by pointers in the blocks on drum. That is, each block of a message points to its successor -- except the EOM block, which has a zero link field. Thus in this system, no DLT table is required in core.

After a message has been routed, Add-On-Header (AOH) blocks are written to drum to represent the message in the output line delivery queues, one for each required delivery. The AOH in this system corresponds to the queue entry in the first system; it includes a pointer to the first block of the transmittable message, and a pointer to the next message on the delivery queue. As indicated in Figure 2, there are two messages for delivery on line i, each of two blocks. Also note that the message in blocks c and f must be delivered via line i and again via line j.

Because the data block chains and output queues are dynamically maintained on drum, a

Reprinted from *1971 IEEE Int. Conv. Dig.*, pp. 238-239.

service interruption might produce unterminated chains, making restart from the drum image impossible. Therefore, the standby computer in this system tracks the online machine, fully processing the input traffic and maintaining the received traffic on its own drum. Only the online machine does output, however, informing the standby machine via an intercomputer link when a message has been delivered. Then, if switchover is required, the standby machine simply picks up the output functions, continuing the input function as before.

Advantages

1) The principal advantage of this approach is the flexibility of task scheduling and execution. There is no constraint as to whether a program is primarily an input program generating writes to drum, or an output program generating reads.

2) Because the data block chains are directly maintained on drum, this system has little requirement for a ledger write.

Disadvantages

This system has one principal disadvantage: a second machine must be fully devoted to traffic processing to achieve restart assurance. A standby machine could be put to many other uses even as it stands by if restart could be achieved from drum-contained information directly.

PROPOSED APPROACH

A system has been projected which combines some of the better features of the two systems described above. At the outset, certain salient features were deemed desirable to retain: (a) the system 1 feature whereby the online machine does the full message switching job, including checkpoint recording, leaving the offline machine

free to do other tasks until switchover and restart are required; (b) from system 2, the asynchronous queued executive and the direct recording of queuing information on drum, eliminating much of the need for a ledger write.

These features can be combined if the construction of chains and queues is carefully ordered. Two principles must be followed: (1) When a block is added to a drum chain, first the block must be written, and then the pointer to it. If the reverse order were followed and a failure occurred after the pointer write, an unterminated chain would result. (2) When a block is moved from one drum queue to another, the block must be added to the second queue before it is removed from the first. The reverse order would permit complete loss of a block if failure occurred immediately after the block had been removed from the first queue.

Since this proposed system has not been implemented, it is not known whether the write to drum of individual data items, each with its latency time, will in fact be more efficient then a single ledger write of largely redundant information but with only one latency time. However, the anticipated benefits of flexibility, without requiring the standby machine to be fully devoted to message processing, have inclined us to think that the proposed system is preferable to systems 1 and 2.

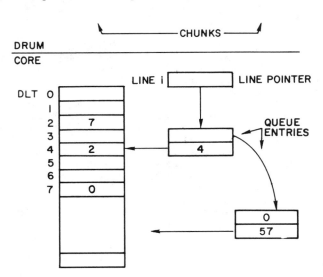

Figure 1. Data Block Chaining and Queueing --
Cyclic Executive

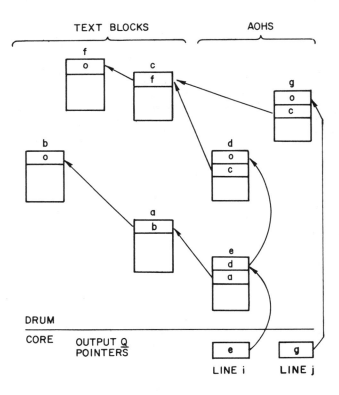

Figure 2. Data Block Chaining and Queueing --
Queued Executive

Part 3
Minicomputer Input and Output Devices Important in Applications

Introductory Comments

A significant characteristic of applications suitable for minicomputers is the type of input and output devices attached to the system. Large computer systems make use of many peripheral devices, but generally these are either manufactured or supplied by the vendor of the computer system and are integrated into the system. For example, controllers for individual devices are often part of the computer itself. In contrast, minicomputer applications are usually on-line and interactive, implying some connection to a physical device or process not normally associated with the computer system. These devices include instruments such as gas chromatographs, badge readers, credit card verifiers, A/D converters, and other special devices.

Applying a minicomputer then involves the interfacing of special devices to the computer. Today, the input/output structure is such that this interfacing is relatively straightforward. Nonetheless, it is important to understand the types of devices which must be interfaced, the problems associated with such devices, the elimination of electrical noise, multiple grounds, and common mode noise, plus the generation of the many control signals necessary to run devices properly and verify their correct operation.

The first two papers in this part review A/D conversion techniques, one of the most common problems in interfacing a minicomputer to any physical process where analog signals must be monitored by the computer. Connecting the sensor through an A/D converter and perhaps a multiplexor can lead to very significant noise problems implying that the choice of equipment for doing this job may depend on the noise present in the given application. Budzilovich, in the second article, reviews some of the standard means for effectively eliminating noise. Such considerations are most important in writing specifications for multiplexors, A/D converters, and sensor based systems, and also in evaluating various manufacturers' systems. This is a common source of large price differences in competitive systems.

C. G. Enke provides a general discussion of the problem of the conversion of the signal in a sensor into a form suitable for digital data processing including the types of sensors, transducers, and analog signal processing which must be done. He does this from the point of view of scientific instrumentation, stressing the minimization of measurement errors. He classifies the problem using examples such as pH measurement, gas chromatography, and so on.

The number of different manners in which variables can be sensed is very large and in fact is the basis of the entire field of instrumentation. R. H. Cerni describes a number of transducers that are currently used in industrial process control for the measurement of mechanical displacement, stresses and strains, temperatures, frequency, and the like. He emphasizes that present types of process sensors and transmitters are being challenged by new concepts and that we can expect many different types of sources for our signals in the future.

It is important to realize that any computerized data acquisition or control system still involves some human intervention by an operator or an engineer in almost all cases. As a consequence, the human engineering of the interface to the computer and the operator is critically important. That is, taking the computer off-line momentarily for maintenance or repair must be possible without shutting down most systems. L. M. Soule shows several alternate ways that computers, instrumentation, systems, and operator interfaces can be organized so that the human being can still maintain control of the system when the computer is not needed or available, and such that the system can be reliably switched from one mode of control to another. In reading this article, it is important to realize that this type of instrumentation is common in industry today. Notice that the role of the computer is much more than simply converting a signal from analog form to digital form. It includes monitoring the status of the interface (manual or automatic control, for example), the operation of the engineer, and the sensor itself in order that the computer can carry out the correct algorithms at the correct time. This additional complexity also affects the software and especially the organization of the software, as will be shown in a later part.

The actual interfacing of complex I/O devices to the computer is discussed in the paper by Kerr *et al.*, where problems of device addressing, signal and data line control, etc. are discussed in some detail. Notice in reading this paper that the problem of interfacing a device, or a set of devices to a computer, is really a systems design job. All uses of the device, problems of timing, problems of reliability, and problems of verification must be considered in the design of the interface. Conversely, standard interfaces available from minicomputer vendors must be considered from the same point of view: do they actually provide sufficient capability so that an application program can be sure that the data it is reading is correct?

The one unchanging aspect of minicomputer application is the constantly evolving hardware. All of the previous articles in this part discuss the interfacing of various devices to a computer. In many applications, however, the devices themselves must be located where they are used (badge readers at plant entrance points, machine status sensors at various manufacturing centers, etc.). The result might be a large number of signal leads being run to the minicomputer from distant locations. The common noise problem in this situation has already been discussed. An alternative solution, becoming feasible due to the decreasing cost of digital hardware, is the so-called line-sharing system described by R. L. Aronson in the last article in this part. Here, sensor signals are converted to digital form in the vicinity of the sensor itself. Similarly, other devices are digitized and formatted into standard form at the device itself rather than at the computer. Then a transmission line, which acts like a bus, is run through the plant, and all devices and sensors are connected to this single line. The result is that many sensors and input/output devices can share the same line so that only a single high-quality transmission line need be run back to the minicomputer itself. Of course, sharing this line implies some means of avoiding conflict among the devices, and this is discussed by Aronson. Several different organizations for line-sharing systems are discussed. In all cases it is clear that such systems provide a viable alternative to direct connection of devices to a minicomputer. This has significant implications in the choice of minicomputers and especially in the design of the supporting software. It must be emphasized again that the choice of the organization of the input/output devices, the way in which they are connected to the minicomputer, and the software to drive and control these devices is a systems problem in its own right. The manners in which this problem has been solved for various applications are essentially the content of the later parts of this book.

Bibliography

[1] "CRT terminals make versatile control computer interface," R. L. Aronson, *Contr. Eng.*, vol. 17, Apr. 1970, pp. 66–69.

[2] "Triple play speeds A-D conversion," H. B. Aasnaes and T. J. Harrison, *Electronics*, Apr. 29, 1968, pp. 69–72.

[3] "Materials handling control," S. J. Bailey, *Contr. Eng.*, vol. 15, Sept. 1968, pp. 81–89.

[4] "Hybrid computing: the hardware linkage problem," D. Block, *Comput. Des.*, Sept. 1968, pp. 59–61.

[5] "Interfacing communications lines with a computer," J. W. Conway, *1971 IEEE Int. Conv. Dig.*, pp. 234–235.

[6] "Assembly machine configurations," *Automation*, Jan. 1971, pp. 41–47.

[7] "Digital transducers: state-of-the-art report," *Comput. Des.*, Sept. 1967, pp. 26–42.

[8] "Interfacing programmers with process controllers," D. Johnson, *Contr. Eng.*, vol. 16, May 1969, pp. 79–82.

[9] "Analytical tools in process automation," F. W. Karasek, *Res./Develop.*, Dec. 1969, pp. 67–72.

[10] "Know your D-A converter's capability," J. J. Pastoriza and D. R. Weller, *Electronics*, Nov. 10, 1969, pp. 129–130.

[11] "15 ways to control moving materials," E. L. Ralston, *Contr. Eng.*, vol. 15, Sept. 1968, pp. 90–95.

[12] "General purpose systems for computer data acquisition and control," L. Ramaley and G. S. Wilson, *Anal. Chem.*, vol. 42, May 1970, pp. 606–611.

[13] "Graphic displays: matching man to machine for on-line control," D. E. Weisberg, *Contr. Eng.*, vol. 15, Nov. 1968, pp. 79–82.

*A study has been made of advantages and disadvantages of
basic A/D converters, which includes qualitative analyses
worth noting by potential users*

A Review of
Analog-to-Digital Conversion

Ephraim N. Aniebona

General Telephone and
Electronic Laboratories
Bayside, New York

Richard T. Brathwaite

Bell Telephone
Laboratories
Whippany, New Jersey

The need for analog-to-digital conversion has become increasingly important as more and more digital control and computation techniques are being
applied to commercial, military, and industrial systems. Most natural sources of information, such as
the human voice, air pressure, and changes in mass,
matter and motion are analog, and are therefore
easily transformable to analog electrical energy by
means of appropriate transducers. However, the rapid
development of high-speed digital computers, improvement in digital transmission in terms of noise
immunity, and the advancement of terminal equipment for encoding and decoding digital information
has resulted in a demand for higher quality and more
versatile A/D converters.

In principle, an analog electrical signal can be converted to digital form without loss of information by
sampling the signal at a rate of not less than twice
that of its most significant frequency. But because of
speed limitations in equipment due to energy-storage
devices and leakage of sample-and-hold components,
the rate of change of the analog signal to be digitized cannot be made arbitrarily large. In addition,
the accuracy of the quantization of a sample is limited
by the resolution and speed of the quantizer.

An example of the utilization of an A/D converter's
high performance characteristics was the investigation of the cause of the Electra plane crashes during
the 1950's. Tests were made on the planes for structural failure modes by vibrating the wings and recording the data on strip charts. The reasons for
failure were not found. In desperation, the investi-
gators utilized an A/D converter and fed in the outputs of the transducers measuring the vibration. It
was then discovered that there were high frequency
vibrations near the wing roots. The reason why this
was not discovered in previous tests was obvious: the
frequencies were higher than the capability of the
recording instruments, and as a result this data was
filtered out. These frequencies, however, happened to
be within the range of the A/D converter.

Reprinted with permission from *Comput. Des.*, vol. 8, pp. 49–54, Dec. 1969.

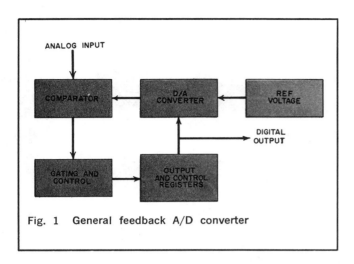

Fig. 1 General feedback A/D converter

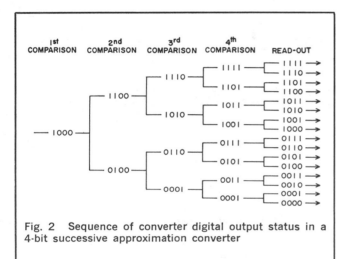

Fig. 2 Sequence of converter digital output status in a 4-bit successive approximation converter

Although A/D conversion seems to be the solution to many problems, it still has its disadvantages, one of which is that A/Ds are not compatible with the analog outputs of sensors or analog inputs to controls. The development of sensors and controllers having digital outputs and inputs, respectively, might be a solution. Research indicates that it is thus far economically unfeasible to have an A/D converter in every sensor. As a result it remains as a system component, which when used with sensors, accepts the analog sensor output and provides ON/OFF signals for operating digital control or computation circuits.

BASIC PRINCIPLES

In mathematical terms, an A/D converter is an encoder that accepts an analog input voltage, V_x and a reference voltage, V_r, and provides a digital output signal according to the equation

$$X \equiv [V_x/V_r]$$

The brackets indicate that X is the closest approximation to V_x/V_r within the resolution of X. For a clearer illustration, V_x/V_r is written in its binary approximate form,

$$\frac{V_x}{V_r} \approx [a_1 2^{-1} + a_2 2^{-2} + \ldots + a_n 2^{-n}]$$

In this equation, it is seen that the output signal X is a binary approximation of the ratio V_x/V_r.

Quantization errors are inherent in all digitization techniques and for A/D converters, the minimum quantization error is the smallest increment of analog voltage to which the ouput signal can be approximated. In mathematical form the smallest quantization error, ΔV_x is

$$\Delta V_x = V_x/r^n$$

where r is the radix and n is the number of digits in X.

Another type of error is sampling, arising from the fact that the converter uses the input signal value for a very short interval and ignores it for a very long period. Therefore, if the input frequency is high (or, the analog signal makes rapid changes) relative to the conversion rate of an A/D converter, the sampling error will be large. For example, to minimize the sampling error, a sinusoidal analog input is restricted in its maximum frequency by the relation

$$W \leq \frac{\Delta E}{E_p \Delta T}$$

where ΔT is the aperture time of the converter, or the time interval during which the converter must see a sample of the input for a complete conversion, and E_p is the amplitude of the sinusoid and ΔE is the resolution voltage of the converter.

The accuracy of conversion — or the ability to achieve the designed resolution under all operating conditions — is an important performance criterion. Common features and operating criteria of A/D converters include:

- Signals — all analog signal inputs (modified if necessary) are dc voltages with 0 V representing no signal, +10 V positive full scale, and −10 V negative full scale

- Power supplies — the number required for one A/D converter is normally three; two are used for amplifiers and comparators, the third for logic circuits

- Reference supplies — all A/D converters require reference voltages that are stable and accurate to at least ±.01%

A/D converters can be classified in several ways

depending upon the features of interest. They may be put into three major categories, namely, level-at-a-time, word-at-a-time, and digit-at-a-time. This categorization, however, is too broad to be suggestive of techniques used. We therefore choose a circuit-oriented, functional-block classification as used by Schmid.[1]

FEEDBACK METHODS OF A/D CONVERSION

A block diagram of a general feedback A/D converter is shown in Fig. 1. The analog input goes into a comparator device where one analog signal level is compared to another derived from the digital output of the converter. The comparator output is an error signal and indicates the conversion's status. Gating and control circuits channel the error signal (reshaped, if necessary) to the output and control registers, which then update and store digital representation of the input. The feedback path must be through a D/A converter, since the comparator inputs are analog. The feedback of the digital output may be either serial or parallel.

PARALLEL-FEEDBACK A/D CONVERTERS

The comparator consists of a summing circuit (for input and feedback analog signals) and a threshold circuit, which puts out a high-level error voltage of either polarity. The error voltage then drives a bank of flip-flops (or counters) that register and store the updated count. Particular circuits are mentioned here to illustrate two kinds of parallel-feedback A/D converters known as successive-approximation and servo.

Successive Approximation A/D Converter

If the number of bits in the digital output is n, this converter makes n successive comparisons at each conversion between the input analog signal value and a time-dependent feedback voltage. Thus whatever the analog input level may be (high or low), the same number of tests is made for each conversion. Consequently, the successive-approximation is a bit-at-a-time converter with the most significant bit generated first. Figure 2 shows the possible sequences of digits at the converter output prior to readout for a 4-bit approximation.

The conversion process is described with reference to Fig. 3. The input voltage V_x and feedback voltage $-V_f$ are summed at the dc amplifier. The sum is amplified and transmitted as V_a. If V_a is positive enough (up to 2.5 V for a 12-bit converter, 10-V reference, and 3-V Zener) it causes the bank of bistable latch flip-flops to enter a ONE in the ith position (counting from the left) of the 12-bit word output,

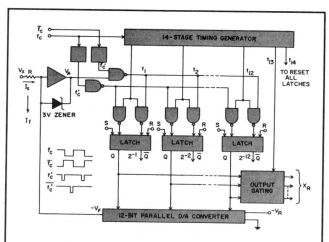

Fig. 3 12-bit successive approximation A/D converter. The timing generator output is properly sequenced to trigger bistable latches and inhibit readout until conversion is complete

corresponding to the ith comparison. If V_a is smaller than −0.6 V, a ZERO is entered.

The feedback voltage V_f changes in steps of $V_r/2^i$ for the ith comparison. That is, the first value of V_f used for comparison is $V_r/2$. If the comparator output is a ONE as a result of this first comparison, the next value of V_f is $V_r/2 + V_r/4$ (or $3 V_r/4$). If the comparator output is a ZERO for the first comparison, then the next value of V_f is just $V_r/4$. This process is continued until n comparisons are made. The ith feedback voltage, V_{f_i}, is generally given by

$$V_{f_i} = \frac{V_r}{2^n} [a_1 2^{n-1} + a_2 2^{n-2} + \ldots + a_i 2^{n-i}]$$

where $a_k = 0$ or 1 and the converter output after the $(i-1)^{th}$ comparison is

$$X_p = a_1 a_2 \cdots a_{i-1} 00 \cdots 0$$
$$| \longleftarrow n \text{ digits} \longrightarrow |$$

A numerical illustration of this procedure is:

$$V_r = 10V, \ V_x = 5.7V, \ V_f = V_r/2^i, \ V_e = V_x - V_f$$

Step 1. $V_f = 10/2 = 5V$;

$\qquad V_e = 5.7 - 5 = .7V$ $\qquad\qquad$ msb = 1

Step 2. $V_f = \dfrac{V_r}{2} + \dfrac{V_r}{4} = 7.5V$;

$V_e = 5.7 - 7.5 = 1.8V$ $\qquad\qquad$ msb = 0

Step 3. $V_f = \dfrac{V_r}{2} + \dfrac{V_r}{8} = 6.25$;

$\qquad V_e = 5.7 - 6.25 = -.55V$ $\qquad\qquad$ msb = 0

$\qquad\qquad \cdot$
$\qquad\qquad \cdot$
$\qquad\qquad \cdot$ etc.

81

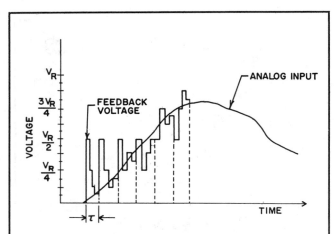

Fig. 4 Comparison of analog signal and feedback voltage in a 4-bit successive approximation converter. Readout occurs at the end of aperture time, τ

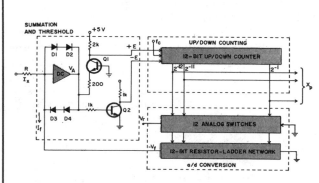

Fig. 5 Servo A/D converter. The up-down counter driven by summer and level converter circuit follows the input analog signal

X (in binary form) = 100101 where n = 6 converting back gives

$$X = \left(\frac{V_x}{V_r}\right)V_r = \frac{(100101)_2}{(1000000)_2} \times 10V$$

$$= \frac{37}{64} \times 10V = 5.758V$$

The end of the conversion interval is signalled by the 14-stage timing generator. At this instant, the digital output gate is opened, the digits are read out (or transferred), the flip-flops are reset and the cycle starts again.

From the foregoing, it is clear that the successive approximation can be grossly in error at the end of the conversion period if the analog signal is changing too quickly relative to the conversion rate. A histogram of the D/A converter output in the feedback loop of the successive approximation converter is shown in Fig. 4. The value of the histogram at the end of each conversion interval is the value of the converter's digital equivalent of the input analog signal value during the conversion period.

Servo A/D Converter

The behavior of the servo A/D converter is analogous to that of a servo system. Once a voltage difference is detected between the input voltage V_x and feedback V_f, the digital output will change in such a direction as to reduce the error, that is, to make $V_e = 0$. The description of the servo converter will be given with reference to Fig. 5. The three basic circuits of this converter are the summer and threshold detector, the up-down counter, and D/A converter. In this particular design the output voltage is limited to values between -1.2 and $+1.2$ V by diodes D_1, D_2 and diodes D_3, D_4, respectively. Except for the limiting action of the diodes the output voltage of the amplifier is the error voltage multiplied by its gain.

In the threshold circuits, transistors Q_1 and Q_2 indicate, respectively, whether the error is positive or negative. When the amplifier output voltage V_a is more negative than -0.6 V, transistor Q_1 is turned on and a high output voltage is taken off the collector of Q_2 indicating a negative error. If V_a is above 0.6 V, then Q_2 is turned on, and with Q_1 off (assuming good recovery time), the high collector voltage of Q_1 indicates a positive error. The on/off collector voltages of Q_1 and Q_2 provide a control drive for the up-down counter.

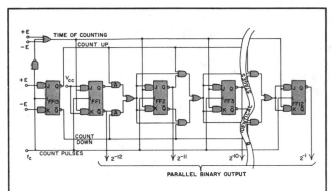

Fig. 6 Up-down counter used in the servo A/D converter (Fig. 5). Count-up occurs when error voltage +E is high and −E is low, and vice versa for countdown

The up-down counter used in this servo converter is the synchronous type shown in Fig. 6. The thirteenth flip-flop (FF13) insures that the up-down lines will not change simultaneously with flip-flops FF1 to FF12. Up-down control signals are generated by setting and resetting FF13 with positive and negative error signals, respectively. FF13 is designed to change only with the negative-going transition of the clock pulse, and it is seen that with the delay FF13 and AND gates, the up-down lines will always change after the counting flip-flops have changed. The error signals also control the duration of counting by ORING the error signals and gating the clock pulse with the input to the OR gate. The problem here is that negative transitions occur when error signals are low and clock pulse high, and additional undesirable counts result. This problem is avoided by ORING the error signals with an inverted clock pulse and the OR gate output is directly connected to the J and K input gates of the counting flip-flops. This also insures that signals will be on the J and K gates before the clock pulse goes negative, as the output of the OR gate can change only when the negated clock pulse is positive.

INDIRECT A/D CONVERTERS (Counter Type)

In this class of converters are those that do not go directly from the analog input to digital form but instead derive the digital form by an intermediate step that is partly or wholly analog. The parallel-and-serial-feedback converters, by contrast, are direct.

The ramp-comparison converter is indirect. The simple type shown in Fig. 7 converts the analog input signal V_x into a pulse-width signal, T_x. The pulse-width is then converted to a digital form by counting clock-pulses for the duration of T_x.

The ramp-generator consists of one dc amplifier, a precision resistor and capacitor (R and C) and an analog switch S_1. When the switch is closed, the capacitor discharges through it. When it opens, the capacitor is charged by reference voltage V_r through the resistor R. Thus the output voltage V_s is a ramp.

The dc comparator has two inputs, namely, V_r and analog input V_x. When V_s is greater than V_x, the comparator output is a positive pulse; otherwise, it is zero. The digital differentiator generates a narrow pulse at the end of the interval T_x, during which the ramp voltage is less than the analog voltage V_x. The differentiator output triggers the closure of switches for a readout of the counter output, which is the accumulated count in T_x.

The most significant stage of the 12-bit counter controls the ramp generator switch S1. The switch is kept closed for the period T_2, which is normally longer than one clock period because of the relatively low recovery speeds of the comparator and differentiator. The period T_1 should be just long enough for the 12-bit counter to count from zero to 4,095.

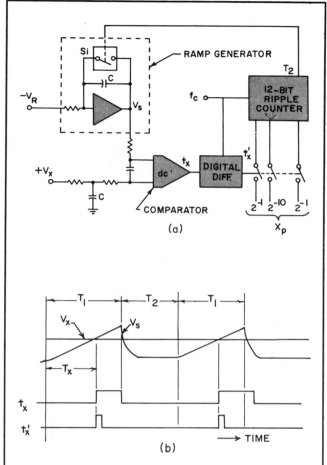

Fig. 7 Ramp-comparison A/D converter. The ramp generator in (a) requires precision components to give rise to the type of accurate timing in (b)

For a 10-MHz clock frequency, therefore, T_1 is 409.6 microseconds. The recovery interval T_2 is chosen on the basis of how quickly the linear circuits can recover.

OTHER TYPES OF A/D CONVERTERS

There are several other types of A/D converters, some of which represent slight modifications of those already described here; others are quite different. The simple-ramp comparison type can be improved upon by using a more accurate (precise) ramp generator and comparator. High-speed and high-accuracy converters have been built by paralleling $2^n - 1$ comparators and using an encoder to generate an n-bit word from the comparator outputs. Sample-and-hold circuits may be incorporated to increase the conversion rate and accuracy, but of course more than one comparator will be necessary with sample-and-hold circuits if the input signal is continuous for a long time. Also, sample-and-hold circuits play an important role in some time-division multiplex A/D converters.

COMPARISON OF A/D CONVERTERS

In all of the aforementioned types of converters, each has its own advantages and disadvantages. In the counter method, the converter simply counts the clock pulses. This method has the advantages of simple circuitry. The disadvantages, however, begin to outweigh the advantages when high accuracy and conversion rates are required. For example, to count from 1 to 2^{12} with a 500-kHz clock frequency requires 8,192 microseconds; this is a rate of approximately 122 conversions per second, which is slow compared to the successive approximation converter, as will be described later.

A modification of the counter technique is the continuous method employing the servo converter. It is simpler than successive approximation and employs an up-down counter to generate the binary output from error signals. The error signals indicate when the digital output does not fully approximate the analog input signal. The frequency response is beneficial because of its ability to follow small bidirectional input changes in one clock period; the disadvantage is a slow initial pick-up. With a clock frequency of 500 kHz and a 12 binary stage counter, the servo converter will follow the small changes in input within 2 microseconds.

The successive approximation converter is the most popular of all. At a clock frequency of 500 kHz and 12-bit words, this device requires 24 microseconds for the conversion of small or large values of the input signal. For the same clock frequency and signal voltage resolution, it is capable of converting faster varying signals than counter and servo converters. It also has a relative advantage in economy by more utilization of ICs.

CONCLUSION

This review of A/D converters, though far from being exhaustive, reveals a number of precautions worth noting by any purchaser or user. The first precaution is *caveat emptor*. To buy a "white box" called an A/D converter with manufacturers' labels of quality and performance is not acceptable. Because of the varied specifications and lack of standardization, one must be sure of what the provisions mean.

The second precaution is that a potential user must know exactly what the converter is expected •to do.

In other words, the relative importance of the following performance criteria must be thoroughly investigated: conversion speed, analog peak voltage, polarity of voltage, temperature range of operation and temperature stability, accuracy and linearity of conversion, noise effects, resolution (number of bits per volt), power consumption, and of course, cost. A major guiding thought should be of the end use of the digital data. For instance, if the data is for computer processing, then resolution and accuracy are quite important. On the other hand, if the data must be transformed back to analog by a D/A converter, then the converter may dictate the practical limit of resolution. Most current high-resolution A/D converters use 10 to 12 bits while a few have gone to 15.

Manufacturers of A/D converters number in the hundreds in this country, but most of the products are custom designed. This points to a possible path of growth of A/D converters, that is, toward more standardization and versatility. The state-of-the-art in A/D conversion technology, in general, seems to have made a fast advance within the last decade. In 1955[2], Epsco's Datrac A/D operated at 50,000 conversions per second, with .05% accuracy and 500 watts of power consumption, was mounted in a 2' x 2' x 3' space, and cost $8-9,000. An equivalent A/D in 1967 operated at 100,000 conversions per second, at about the same accuracy, consumed 2 watts of power, occupied a 5" x 3" x 1" space, and sold for $5-800.

Integrated circuit technology is playing an important role in improving the performance and reducing the cost of A/D converters. Digital ICs are being used for counters, digital filtering, and switching, while linear ICs find use in operational amplifiers. The problem with linear ICs is mainly temperature stability. It may be expected that improved ICs for A/D converters will evolve in the near future.

The multiplex capability of A/D converters is a cost-reducing factor and should make them attractive in future high-capacity channel usage, as in communication and large data processing systems.

REFERENCES

1. H. Schmid, "An Electronic Design Practical Guide to A/D Conversion," *Electronic Design*, Dec. 1968 Part I, II, Jan., 1969 Part III
2. G. Flynn, "Analog-to-Digital Converters," *Electronic Products*, Oct. 1967
3. R. Ruff, "Survey Evaluates Methods of A/D and D/A Conversion," *EDN*, Nov. 22, 1967
4. R. Stata, "Ray Stata of Analog Devices Speaks Out on What's Wrong with Op-Amp Specs," *EEE*, July 1968, pp. 44-49
5. D. Goodman, "The Application of Delta Modulation to Analog-to-PCM Encoding," *The Bell System Technical Journal*, Vol. 48, Feb. 1969, pp. 321-343
6. S. Wald, "Comparison of Analog-to-Digital Conversion Techniques," *Electronic Design*, August 1962, p. 82
7. *The Digital Logic Handbook*, Digital Equipment Corp., Maynard, Mass., 1968 edition

More often than not, discussions of electrical noise tend to be vague and general, reflecting the ambiguous nature of their topic. But at a recent meeting of the Milwaukee IEEE Group on Industry and General Applications, several speakers appearing before about 150 local engineers—most of them designers of machine tool and industrial control—were refreshingly specific and concrete in their treatment of the electrical-noise problem.

The following article briefly describes various ways to beat electrical noise—hopefully in as factual a manner as did the IEEE papers. Detailed references to two of these papers in particular will be made.

Electrical Noise: Its Nature, Causes, Solutions

P. N. BUDZILOVICH, Control Engineering

As solid-state logic becomes more and more common in industrial controls, problems associated with electrical noise grow. In a nutshell, the reason for this is semiconductor sensitivity to even very fast spikes and low-power disturbances. When a relay is replaced with an scr, for instance, the response time is changed by several orders of magnitude (say 10 ms for a relay, several microsec for an scr). Power levels undergo an even more dramatic change: An scr may require a firing signal of only a few milliamps, while a relay needs 15 or more VA (volt-amperes).

Consequently, when we speak about noise and transients reduction or elimination in a solid-state logic system, we are talking about maximum tolerable noise levels of less than a volt. Even the so-called high threshold logic, which usually requires input signals on the order of 6 or 7 volts and supply voltages of around 15 volts, has a noise immunity of only several volts more. And in a noisy industrial environment, where spikes of several hundred volts are encountered, the amount and type of protection required by both types of logic is about the same.

It is hoped that this article, with its several examples of "noisy" problems and solutions, will prove the cardinal rule on dealing with noise—never take anything for granted. Never assume, for example, that a wire is identical to a connection on a schematic. In short, always check out (with numbers) before signing a production drawing.

What's causing all the noise?

Among the most common noise sources are the following:

- Power equipment and lines
- Earth ground currents
- Common-mode voltages of several kinds
- Acoustical
- Thermoelectric
- Electrochemical
- Component

For the purpose of this discussion, which primarily concerns noise reduction in industrial controls, we will consider only the first three sources. This is not to imply that the other sources of noise are not important. But the others are more closer related to subsystem problems, while the first three are more properly the system engineer's domain.

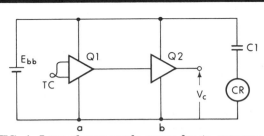

FIG. 1. Large thermocouple errors due to common-impedance electrical noise can occur in this typical circuit. The distance a-b here is assumed to be 50 ft and the relay coil is assumed to draw 0.5 amp.

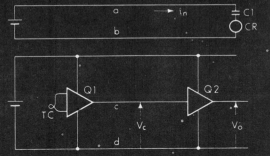

FIG. 2. Modifying the circuit of Figure 1 but placing all leads into a common raceway will not help. The thermocouple readings will still be in error, due to magnetic coupling among the wires.

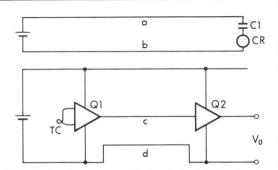

FIG. 3. Another cause of induced electrical noise is electrostatic, or capacitive, coupling. But a quick calculation will indicate that voltages of up to 6 volts can appear across the amplifier Q2.

Reprinted with permission from *Contr. Eng.*, vol. 16, pp. 74–78, May 1969.

Power equipment and lines constitute the most troublesome noise source for several reasons. For one, they are always present. For another, they are usually beyond the system designer's complete control: He may have to work from the same line that feeds high-current furnaces or large motors. And finally, about the only place for a control engineer's cables often is right next to a power-line conduit. (The control engineer may even be asked by the plant enginer to "play smart" and to use the same conduit to avoid an extra installation.)

How does noise get into a system?

This question was answered at the Milwaukee conference by Roy Hyink of Cutler-Hammer, Inc. Hyink listed four major ways in which noise can enter a system:

1. Common impedance
2. Magnetic coupling
3. Electrostatic coupling
4. Electromagnetic radiation

Common impedance noise can occur whenever two circuits share conductors, impedances, or—in extreme cases—power sources. Probably one of the most frequent reasons for common impedance coupling is the use of long common "neutral" or "ground" wires.

In Figure 1, two amplifiers, $Q1$ and $Q2$, amplify the output of an iron-constantan thermocouple, TC. A control relay, CR, operated by contact $C1$, is also part of the circuit. The lead a-b is 50 ft of AWG#12 wire, which has a resistance of 1.6 ohms per thousand ft, so that

$$R_{ab} = (50/1000)1.6 = 0.08 \text{ ohms}$$

If the relay coil requires 0.5 amp, the voltage between points a and b will be $0.5 \times 0.80 = 0.040$ volt. Of course, a good designer will place a differential amplifier ($Q1$) close to the thermocouple, TC, and amplify by 100 before transmitting to $Q2$. Then the 0.040 volt from a to b will appear to $Q2$ just like a 0.04/100 (or 0.4 millivolt) change in the input voltage to $Q1$. For an iron-constantan thermocouple, this would be equivalent to a 14 deg F temperature change near 100 deg F.

The effect of the self-inductance in line a-b should also be considered. The self-inductance of a single wire is, in this case, $L = (0.0152)(50 \text{ ft}) = 0.76$ microhenry. When the current through CR is interrupted, it could change from 0.5 amp to zero in less than 1 microsec.

$$V_{ab} = L(di/dt) = (0.76 \times 10^{-6})(0.5/10^{-6})$$
$$= 380 \text{ millivolts (an equivalent of 127 deg F at the } TC)$$

Of course this disturbance is a short-lasting spike, but it could cause trouble in the control circuit.

Magnetic coupling is often called inductive because it is proportional to the mutual inductance between a control circuit and a source of interference current. Its magnitude depends upon the rate of change of interference current. It is interesting to note that this type of coupling does not depend upon any electrical coupling between the noise source and the control circuit.

To illustrate this type of coupling, let us suppose that the engineer designing the wiring for the circuit of Figure 1 recognizes the common impedance coupling problem and rewires the circuit as in Figure 2. Now all four wires, a, b, c, and d, are placed in the same nonmetallic raceway, with a separation of 3 in. between a and b, 6 in. between b and c, and 1 in. between c and d. The mutual inductance between the noise producing circuit (a and b) and the control circuit (c and d) can be calculated from formula

$$M_{nc} = (61)(10^{-9}) \ln [(L_{ac}/L_{bc})(L_{bd}/L_{ad})](\text{length})$$
$$= (61)(10^{-9}) \ln [(9/6)(7/10)](50)$$
$$= 0.149 \text{ microhenries}$$
$$V_c = M_{nc}(di_n/dt)$$

If the rate of current decay is 0.5 amp per microsec, as before, the voltage induced in the control circuit would be $(0.149)(0.5) = 0.0745$ volt. This would be equivalent to a TC voltage of 0.745 millivolt (26 deg F at the TC).

Electrostatic coupling is often called capacitive coupling because it is proportional to the capacity between a control lead and a source of interference voltage. Its magnitude depends upon the rate of change of the interference voltage and the impedance between the common of the interference circuit and the common of the control circuit.

The same circuit as before can be used to illustrate electrostatic coupling, Figure 3. However, now we are concerned with the voltage between the wires and

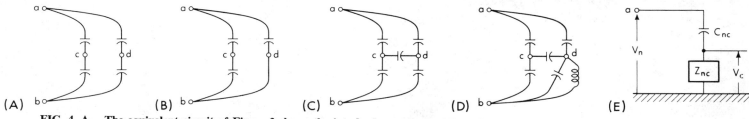

FIG. 4. A.—The equivalent circuit of Figure 3 shows the interlead capacitances. B.—Placing a short between two commons, b and d, results in close to 140 volts across the Q2. C.—A capacitor between lines c and d can reduce the voltage across Q2 to 0.12 volt. D.—The actual circuit also has some inductance. E.—A general circuit for computing effects of electrically induced noise.

the capacitance. The values for the capacity between two paralleled wires are

$C = (3.68) \log [(2L/d) - (d/2L)]pf/ft$
$d =$ diameter of wire (0.08 in. for AWG #12)
$L =$ distance between wires
$C_{ad} = (3.68)(50)/\log (20/0.08) = 76.7pf$
$C_{ac} = (3.68)(50)/\log (18/0.08) = 78.3pf$
$C_{bd} = (3.68)(50)/\log (14/0.08) = 82.1pf$
$C_{bc} = (3.68)(50)/\log (12/0.08) = 84.6pf$

While these are the important capacitors in this case, it must be realized that all objects have capacity to all other objects, resulting at times in unexpected "sneak" circuits. For instance, an isolated oscilloscope used for trouble shooting might have capacity to a conducting grid in a concrete floor of 150 pf.

When the current to CR is interrupted, it is conceivable that the voltage between lines a and b will rise to 300 volts in 1 microsec. This will induce a current in adjacent circuits, as shown in Figure 4A and by the values:

$i_c = C(dV/dt)$
$i_{acb} = [(C_{ac}C_{bc})/(C_{ac} + C_{bc})](dV_{ab}/dt) = 0.0122$ amp
$V_{bc} = (1/C_{bc}) \int i_{acb} dt$
$\quad = (1/C_{bc})(C_{ac}C_{bc})/(C_{ac} + C_{bc})$
$\quad = 138.8$ volts
$V_{bd} = 144.9$ volts

Thus a considerable voltage can be induced in leads c and d resulting in a difference voltage of 6 volts at the input to amplifier Q2.

It is interesting to examine some of the "cures" for this particular noise problem. One thought might be to connect line b and d common, Figure 4B.

This would result in little change in the voltage V_{bc}, but V_{bd} would be 0. This is hardly a "cure." A low impedance between line c and d, particularly a large capacitor, like 0.2 mf, is a possible cure, Figure 4C.

Since C_{cd} is more than a thousand times the size of any other capacitor, it will absorb any current pulses with very little change in potential. In this circuit

$C_{bc} = 84.6+ [(200,000)(82.1)/200082.1]$
$\quad = 166.7pf$
$C_{bd} = 166.7pf$
$V_{bc} = 95.9$ volts
$V_{bd} = 94.5$ volts

Thus, adding a capacitor from c to d will reduce

the induced voltage from 6 to 1.4 volts—still not enough. On the other hand, connecting b to d along with the capacitor, C_{cd}, will result in

$V_{bc} = (78.3)(300)/(84.6 + 200,000 + 78.3)$
$\quad = 0.12$ volt
$V_{bd} = 0$

This example assumes that the impedance between b and d can be made zero. In reality, the self-inductance of line d will be in series. This was previously calculated to be 0.76 microhenry. The real situation is shown in Figure 4D.

This circuit is too complicated to solve without knowing the exact waveshape of V_{ab}. However, it does illustrate a danger of assuming that a wire has zero impedance.

The process of electrostatically inducing a voltage in a lead wire, Figure 4E, can be summarized by the following equation:

$V_c/V_n = 1/[1 + (1/Z_{nc}\omega_n C_{nc})]$
$V_c =$ voltage induced in the control wire
$V_n =$ noise voltage source
$\omega_n =$ frequency of the noise voltage (proportional to di/dt)

In order to keep the ratio V_c/V_n as low as possible, the product $Z_{nc}\omega_n C_{nc}$ must be kept as low as possible. Thus anything that can be done to reduce coupling capacitance, C_{nc}, or return impedance to the noise voltage reference, Z_{nc}, will be helpful. A well-grounded shield will do both.

Voltage induced through magnetic or electrostatic coupling is sometimes called "near-field radiation," because this type of interference is produced close to interference sources. Further from the source, the same interaction causes radio waves. In general, radio waves are produced at distances greater than 1/6 wavelength from the source of interference. For reference purposes the following chart can be used.

Frequency	1/6 wave length
1 Mc	1970 in.
10 Mc	197 in.
100 Mc	19.7 in.
1 Gc	1.97 in.

This type of interference is generally not important until frequencies reach over 10 Mc. However, some high-speed computer circuits and fast-response mon-

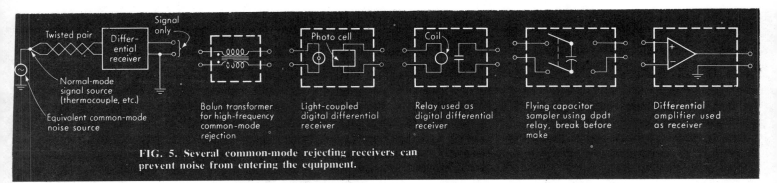

FIG. 5. Several common-mode rejecting receivers can prevent noise from entering the equipment.

olithic integrated circuits are making it necessary to reckon with this interference more frequently.

Noise prevention in control signals

Roy Hyinks' presentation was followed by a paper entitled "The Prevention and Treatment of Noise in Control Signals," by Frank G. Willard of Westinghouse. The major emphasis here was on equipment design and care in interconnections. Some of the points Willard made were:

■ Signal levels should be kept as large as possible, especially for digital signals. With signal voltages in the 24-to-48-volt region, line frequency related noise should not be troublesome.

■ Low-pass filtering should be applied at the receiver to reject switching transients. If available, a filter time constant of about 1 millisec should be used.

■ Two-wire differential receiver circuits should be used to permit normal-mode signal acceptance and common-mode noise rejection. The argument for this technique is that noise will be injected equally onto both signal wires, yielding no voltage difference between them, as long as the two wires are adjacent and symmetrical. Useful examples are shown in Figure 5.

Isolation of the receiver from local noise sources, such as power lines, local ground, and the like, becomes especially important where common-mode rejection forms the major information recovery means. Guard shielding of electronic circuitry may be essential, particularly with dc signals, Figure 6.

Low-noise interconnections

No matter how much care is taken by the equipment designer, inadequate installation wiring can ruin his work and make information recovery needlessly difficult. No mystery surrounds good wiring practice, but a few pointers about the wiring layout bear repeating.

Avoid series noise injection

Permanently gas-tight terminal structures will avoid loose or corroded connections. Chemically incompatible metals should not be used, nor should thermoelectrically dissimilar conductors. (If a section of iron conductor is inserted in an otherwise all-copper circuit, and if the ends of the iron differ by 1 deg F, a 25-microvolt signal error results.) A current carrying conductor should not be shared with another circuit.

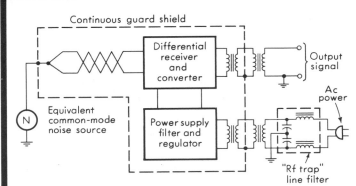

FIG. 6. Guard shields completely enclosing noise-susceptible modules and wiring are effective where system configuration permits them. Note that within the shield the circuit-to-shield voltage does not change with common-mode noise. Any stray capacitance to ground involves only the guard shield.

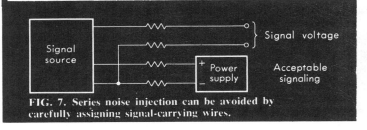

FIG. 7. Series noise injection can be avoided by carefully assigning signal-carrying wires.

(Ten ft of shared #18 AWG copper wire carrying 10 milliamps will insert a series drop of nearly 650 microvolts in the signal circuit.)

Avoid multiple ground connections

It is not unusual for several volts of potential difference to exist between grounding points in a typical industrial plant. If a conductor is connected to ground at two points, appreciable noise currents are likely to circulate through the conductor, unnecessarily obscuring the signal. Shields, return wires, and the like should be insulated from ground throughout their run.

Provide adjacent signal returns

Insulated conductor pairs for signal and return should be used for low-level signals. It is important that these pairs use immediately adjacent conductors, prefer-

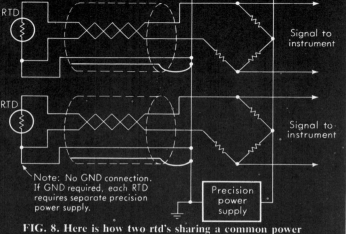

FIG. 8. Here is how two rtd's sharing a common power supply and a grounding point should be wired. Note that there is no ground connection at the rtd's. If a ground there is required, separate precision power supplies should be used.

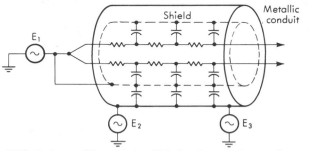

FIG. 9. A metallic conduit will help when used properly, i.e., by placing shielded (and insulated) cable within the metallic conduit.

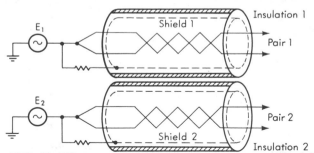

FIG. 10. When several shielded conductors are combined in a cable, each should be covered with insulation. Each shield here is at E_1 and E_2, respectively, thus preventing signal line-to-shield current.

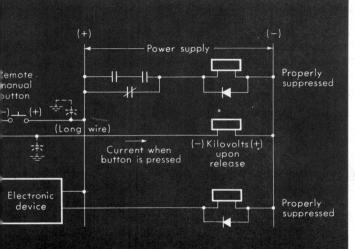

FIG. 11. Overlooking even a single discharge-producing load can result in seemingly unrelated failures of low-voltage electronic components.

ably twisted about twice in every foot to retain good symmetry. High-level signals usually need not be paired, though a common return conductor should be provided within each cable.

Shield cables properly

Shielding decreases the effective capacitance between conductors inside and outside the shield. The most effective shield is a continuous foil or metalized plastic. The shield should be insulated and equipped with a drain wire for convenient single-point grounding. Grounding of the shield and the signal inside it should be at the same point. Some exposure of signal conductors through the shield is usually unavoidable; and the point of greatest exposure (i.e., largest unguarded stray capacitance to ground) is the best place to locate the signal and shield-ground connection. Grouping of several signals within one shield is permissable if all signals have the same ground point and the capacitance between them is acceptable. In fact, high-level signals are usually grouped; low-level signals often require separate shields. In any case, the shield is not to be used as a current-carrying conductor to "save" an extra wire.

Separate incompatible cables

Signal cables may usually be run near each other without interference. However, wiring carrying appreciable ac or dc power, or driving unsuppressed inductive switching loads, should be separated by at least 10 cable diameters from the signal cables. Twisting these power wires helps reduce both capacitive and inductive coupling effects. High-current and high-voltage buses, induction heater cables, and the like can be quite troublesome; their distance from signal cables should be large compared to that of bus conductors (i.e., on the order of 100:1).

Examples of good wiring practice are shown in Figures 7 through 10.

Taming destructive transients

Quite apart from signal information problems is the damage to the equipment itself that can be incurred when transistorized electronic controls are connected to a process. Particularly when electronic circuits are used with conventional relays and contactors, voltage transients will be produced with sufficient amplitude to damage the semiconductors. Voltage spikes exceeding 5 kilovolts have been observed.

Protection against destructive transients requires that these transients be suppressed by limiting the decay rate of the originating magnetic fields or isolating them. Suppression can be accomplished by connecting a diode, resistor, or series RC circuit across the inductive load, which provides a path for current to flow during the discharge. Alternatively, a thyristor driving circuit for ac loads is quite effective. In Figure 11 measures for suppression were not taken because the switch and load involved seemed not to be related to electronic controls. Suppression, or power-supply isolation, was definitely needed in this instance. □

Data Domains—An Analysis of Digital and Analog Instrumentation Systems and Components

Data domains concepts offer a means of effectively utilizing new electronic devices which requires only an understanding of basic measurement processes. These concepts can be used to great advantage in designing or modifying systems and in assessing and minimizing the sources of measurement errors.

C. G. ENKE

Department of Chemistry,
Michigan State University,
E. Lansing, Mich. 48823

SCIENTIFIC INSTRUMENTATION is being revolutionized by the availability of an ever-increasing array of electronic devices which increase measurement speed, accuracy, and convenience while decreasing instrument size and power requirements. Integrated circuits and hybrid circuits have made many measurement techniques, which were previously only theoretically possible, a reality. The continual decrease in the cost of digital and linear circuits has made many sophisticated devices such as frequency meters, digital pH meters, signal averagers, and minicomputers practical for most laboratories. As electronic technology continues to advance, we can expect more and more of the sampling, control, and data analysis of scientific measurements to be performed by the instrument itself.

Digital instrumentation has been the scene of much development and interest because of its inherent accuracy capability, convenient numerical output, and potential digital computer compatibility. However, just "digitizing" an instrument does not insure these advantages. There are literally hundreds of data handling and digitizing devices available today and an unwise combination of units can actually degrade the output accuracy. Also, many digitized measurement systems, while providing excellent accuracy and convenience, are unnecessarily complicated.

Data Domains Concepts

The convenience and power of the amazing new electronic devices are irresistible to almost all scientists, but few are in a position to understand these new tools in detail. A means of applying new devices efficiently and effectively, which requires only an understanding of the basic measurement concepts, is needed for most. The data domains concepts described here are very useful in analyzing, describing, modifying, and designing analog, digital, and analog/digital measurement systems and devices and in assessing and minimizing the sources of measurement errors (1). In addition, a much better understanding of the instrumental data handling process is gained as a result of the study and application of the data domains concept. The first four concepts of data domains analysis are given below:

(1) Measurement data are represented in an instrument at any instant by a physical quantity, a chemical quantity, or some property of an electrical signal. The characteristics or properties used to represent the measurement data can be categorized in groups called "data domains."

(2) As the data proceed through the instrument, a change in the characteristic or property used to represent the measured data is called a "data domain conversion."

(3) All electronic measurement systems can be described as a sequence of two or more data domain converters, each of which can be analyzed separately.

(4) Methods of using electrical signals to represent measurement data fall into three major categories or domains: analog, time, and digital.

Since there are only three data domains for electrical signals, the electronic sections of complex measurement systems can be easily analyzed (or designed) as combinations of only a few basic interdomain converters. Also the hundreds of data handling devices available can be shown to be simply various methods of accomplishing the basic interdomain conversions.

Electronics-Aided Measurement

In an electronics-aided measurement, the quantity to be measured is converted into an electrical signal and then amplified or otherwise modified to operate a device which visually displays the value of the measured quantity. This process is illustrated for a typical case in the block diagram of Figure 1. An input transducer such as a photodetector, thermistor, glass pH electrode,

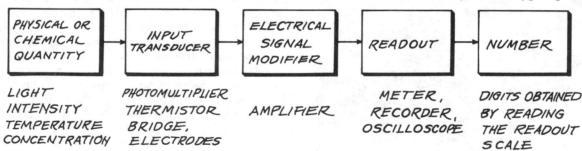

Figure 1. Basic electronic measurement

Reprinted with permission from *Anal. Chem.*, vol. 43, pp. 69A–80A, Jan. 1971.

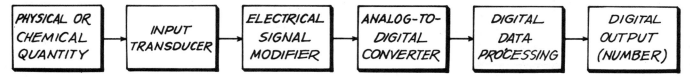

Figure 2. Basic digital electronic measurement

or strain gage is used to convert the quantity to be measured into an electrical signal. The current or voltage amplitude of this signal is related in some known way to the quantity to be measured. The electrical signal from the input transducer is then modified by an electronic circuit to make it suitable to operate a readout device. The electronic circuit is most frequently an amplifier with the appropriate adjustable parameters (zero, standardization, position, etc.) and sometimes with automatic compensation for nonlinearities, temperature variation, etc. of the transducer. The output is a readout device from which a number can be obtained, generally by observing the position of a marker against a numbered scale.

Using the data domains concepts, the basic electronic measurement of Figure 1 is described as follows: The measurement data exist first as the physical or chemical quantity to be measured. At the output of the input transducer, the measurement data are represented by an electrical signal and are thus in one of the three "electrical" domains. The input transducer is thus a device which converts quantities or translates information from a physical or chemical domain into an electrical domain. The measurement data remain in an electrical domain through the electrical signal modifier. However, the output device converts the electrical signal into some readable form such as the relative positions of a marker and a scale— *i.e.*, a nonelectrical domain. Thus the entire measurement can be described in terms of conversions between domains and modifications within domains.

In the basic electronic measurement, at least two converters are required; one to transfer into an electrical domain and one to transfer out. The characteristics of each interdomain converter and each signal modifier affect the quality of the measurement. To take advantage of special input transducers, particular readouts, and available signal processing techniques, an instrument may involve many data domain conversions and signal modifiers. The data domains concept allows each step to be blocked out and analyzed separately. This will be shown to be particularly desirable in assessing sources of errors and the relative advantages of various digitizing or interfacing possibilities.

Digital Measurement. A common form of digital measurement system is shown in block form in Figure 2. At some point after the measurement data have been converted into electrical amplitudes, an analog-to-digital converter is used (*2*). This is an electronic circuit which converts an analog electronic signal (where the measurement data are represented by the signal amplitude) to a digital electronic signal (which represents integer numbers unambiguously by coded binary-level signals). If the digitization was performed to take advantage of the great accuracy, power, and versatility of digital data processing, that will be done next. Finally, the numerical binary-level signal is decoded into a number which is displayed, printed, and/or punched.

Because so many advantages are claimed for digital techniques, many techniques have claimed to be "digital." In fact, any type of device which has dial settings or outputs which are numerals in a row is likely to be called digital. By that standard a decade resistance box is a digital instrument. Since the end result of any measurement is a number, all instruments could be called digital, but the meaning of the word in that sense becomes trivial. Some confine the use of the words "digital instrument" to those instruments which contain binary-level

electronic logic circuits of the type developed for digital computers. As will be shown later, it is common for measurement data to be represented by a binary-level electronic signal and still not be "digitized" or numerical. Therefore, in this paper, a digital instrument will be defined as one that uses a digital electronic signal to represent the measurement data somewhere within the instrument. The analysis and design of digital measurement systems necessarily involves an understanding of the ways electrical signals can represent data and how conversions from one form to another are accomplished.

Electronic Data Domains

There are only three basic ways by which measurement data are represented by an electrical signal: Analog, symbolized E_A, in which the amplitude of the signal current or voltage is related to the data; time, $E_{\Delta t}$, in which the time relationship between signal-level changes is related to the measurement data; and digital, E_D, in which an integer number is represented by binary-level signals. The characteristic signals in each of these domains and examples of their use are described in this section.

Analog, E_A. The measurement data in this domain are represented by the magnitude of a voltage or a current. The analog domain signal is continuously variable in amplitude. Also, the analog amplitude can be measured continuously with time or at any instant in time. Most input transducers used today convert the measurement data from the physical and chemical domains (P) to the E_A domain. Examples of P-to-E_A converters are: photodetectors which convert light intensity to an electrical current, a thermistor bridge which converts temperature difference to an electrical potential, a combination pH electrode which converts solution acidity into an electrical potential, and a flame ionization detector which converts the concentration of ionizable molecules in a gas into an electrical current. Figure 3 shows some typical E_A signals.

At each instant in time, the measured quantity is represented by a signal

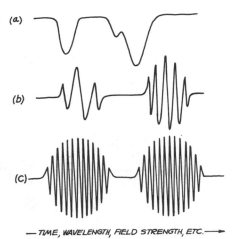

(a)

(b)

(c)

— TIME, WAVELENGTH, FIELD STRENGTH, ETC. ——→

Figure 3. Analog (E_A) domain signals

amplitude. The variations in the signal amplitude may be plotted against time, wavelength, magnetic field strength, temperature, or other experimental parameters as shown in Figure 3. From such plots, additional information can often be obtained from a correlation of amplitudes measured at different times. Such information would include simple observations like peak height, peak position, number of peaks, or more complex correlations such as peak area, peak separation, signal averaging, and Fourier transformation. The techniques of correlating data taken at different times must be distinguished from the techniques of converting the data taken at each instant into a usable form. It is the latter problem that this paper is primarily concerned with. The former problem is handled by data processing techniques, once the required instantaneous data points have been converted to a useful form and stored.

Signals in the E_A domain are susceptible to electrical noise sources contained within or induced upon the circuits and connections. The resulting signal amplitude at any instant is the sum of the data signals and the noise signals.

Time, $E_{\Delta t}$. In this domain, the measurement data are contained in the time relationship of signal variations, not the amplitude of the variations. Typical $E_{\Delta t}$ domain signals are shown in Figure 4. The most common $E_{\Delta t}$ domain signals represent the data as the frequency of a periodic waveform (a), the time duration of a pulse (b), or as the time or average rate of pulses (c). These are logic-level signals—*i.e.*, their signal amplitude is either in the HI or *1* logic-level region or the LO or *0* logic-level region. The data are contained in the time relationship between the logic-level transitions. The greater the slope (dE/dt) of the signal through the logic-level threshold region, the more precisely the transition time can be defined. Because the data in an $E_{\Delta t}$ domain signal are less amplitude-dependent than in an E_A domain signal, they are less affected by electrical noise sources. A common example of this is the FM radio signal ($E_{\Delta t}$ domain) *vs.* the more noise susceptible AM radio signal (E_A domain). The greater the difference between the average *0* or *1* signal-level amplitude and the logic-level threshold, the less susceptible the signal will be to noise-induced error. In these respects, the signal shown in Figure 4b is better than those of Figures 4a and 4c. The logic-level transitions of signals like Figures 4a and 4c are generally sharpened to those like 4b before the sig-

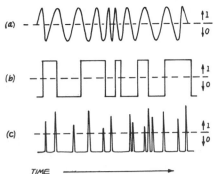

Figure 4. Time ($E_{\Delta t}$) domain signals

nificant time relationship is measured. This is accomplished by a *comparator* or *Schmitt trigger* circuit. Examples of converters producing $E_{\Delta t}$ domain signals from physical domain quantities are: a crystal oscillator that produces a temperature-dependent frequency because of the temperature characteristics of the quartz crystal, an oscillator which has an output frequency dependent upon the value of the capacitance used in the oscillator circuit, and the Geiger tube which converts level of radioactivity to a pulse repetition rate. An example of a E_A-to-$E_{\Delta t}$ domain converter is a voltage-controlled-oscillator or voltage-to-frequency converter which provides an output frequency related to an input voltage.

The $E_{\Delta t}$ domain signal, like the E_A domain signal, is continuously variable since the frequency or pulse width can be varied infinitesimally. However, the $E_{\Delta t}$ signal variable cannot be measured continuously with time or at any instant in time. The minimum time required for conversion of an $E_{\Delta t}$ domain

signal to any other domain is one period or one pulse width.

Digital, E_D. In the digital domain, the measurement data are contained in a 2-level signal (HI/LO, *1/0*, etc.) which is coded to represent a specific integer (or character) (*3*). The digital signal may be a coded series of pulses in one channel (serial form) or a coded set of signals on simultaneous multiple channels (parallel form). Representative digital signal waveforms are shown in Figure 5. The count serial waveform (a) is a series of pulses with a clearly defined beginning and end. The number represented is the number of pulses in the series. The count serial waveform of Figure 5 might represent, for instance, the number of photons of a particular energy detected during a single spark excitation. The count serial form is simple but not very efficient. To provide a resolution of one part per thousand, the time required for at least one thousand pulses to occur must be allowed for each series of pulses.

The most efficient serial digital signal is the binary-coded serial signal shown in Figure 5b. In this signal, each pulse time in the series represents a different bit position in a binary number. The appearance of a pulse at a time position indicates a *1*; the absence of a pulse, a *0*. The data are not represented by the exact time of the pulse as in the $E_{\Delta t}$ domain, but by the signal logic level present within a given time range. The binary number represented by the waveform shown is 101101011 which is decimal 363. A series of n pulse times has a resolution of one part in 2^n. Thus a 10-bit series has a resolution of one

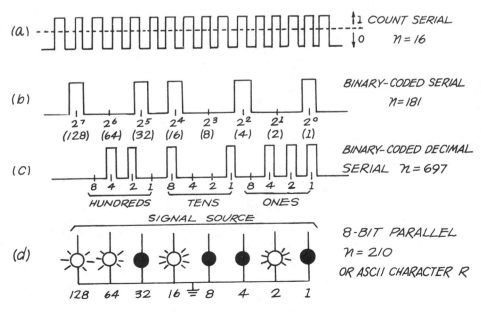

Figure 5. Serial and parallel digital signals

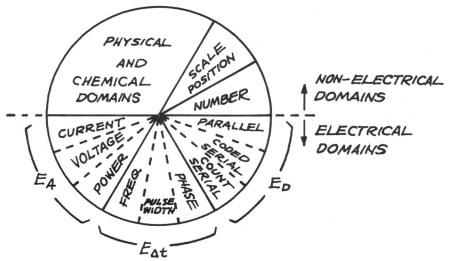

Figure 6. Data domains map

part in $2^{10} = 1024_{10}$, and a 20-bit series has a resolution of better than one part per million.

The binary-coded decimal serial form is somewhat less efficient but very convenient where a decimal numerical output is desired. Each group of four bits represents one decimal digit in a number. Twelve bits can thus represent three decimal digits and provide one part in one thousand resolution.

A parallel digital signal uses a separate wire for each bit position instead of a separate time on a single wire. The principal advantage of parallel digital data connections is speed. An entire "word" (group of bits) can be conveyed from one circuit to another in the time required for the transmission of one bit in a serial connection. An 8-bit parallel data source is shown in Figure 5d connected to indicator lights to show the simultaneous appearance of the data logic levels on all eight data lines. Binary coding (shown), binary-coded decimal coding, and others are used for parallel digital data. Parallel data connections are used in all modern, fast computers. Serial data connections are often used for telemetry and slow computer peripherals such as teletypes.

Mapping Domain Conversions

It has been pointed out that electronic instruments making chemical or physical measurements use no fewer than two data domain conversions. In fact, modern laboratory instruments frequently use three or more domain conversions to perform the desired measurement. Knowing the data domains involved in a particular instrument's operation can help in understanding its operation, applications, limitations, and adaptability as part of a larger measurement system. When analyzing an instrument it is helpful to use the data domains "map" shown in Figure 6. The path of the signal can be traced out on the map as it is followed through the instrument. This process will be illustrated for several chemical instruments of various types.

pH Meter. The block diagram of a conventional pH meter is shown in Figure 7. The combination glass/calomel electrode converts the hydrogen ion activity (chemical composition domain) to an electrical potential (E_A domain). This signal is amplified and converted to a current amplitude that is used to deflect the meter pointer. A number is then obtained by reading the position of the pointer against the calibrated scale. The signal path on the data domains map for the pH meter is also shown in Figure 7. Note that there are two instrumental interdomain conversions, one intradomain conversion, and one "manual" interdomain conversion. It will be shown later that interdomain conversions are more complex and error-prone than intradomain conversions. Recording and "servodigital" pH meters have essentially the same block diagram and domains path except that the servo system can be used to convert the E_A voltage signal from the combination electrode directly into the pen position in the case of the recorder or the position of the turns-counting dial (a rotary scale) in the case of the servodigital meter. Notice that even in the latter case the data are never in the digital domain.

Digital pH Meter. A digital pH meter (Figure 8) differs from an ordinary pH meter in that the meter is replaced by an analog-to-digital (A/D) converter and a digital display. A frequently used A/D converter for this application is the dual slope converter. As is often the case, this A/D converter does not convert directly from the E_A to E_D domains. The dual-slope circuit produces a pulse which has a duration proportional to the input signal voltage—i.e., a $E_{\Delta t}$ signal. The pulse width is converted to a digital signal using the pulse to turn an oscillator on and off, generating a count serial digital signal.

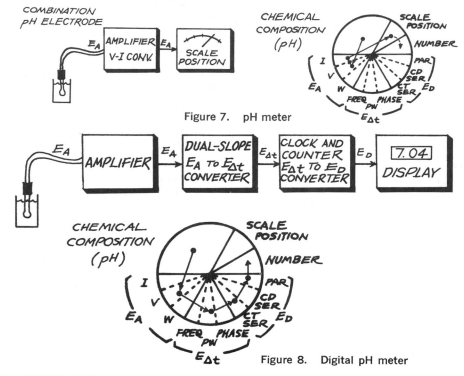

Figure 7. pH meter

Figure 8. Digital pH meter

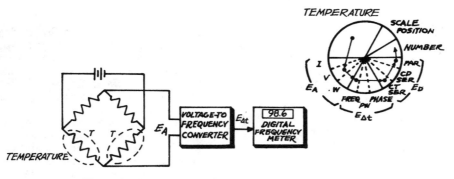

Figure 9. Thermistor-digital temperature measurement

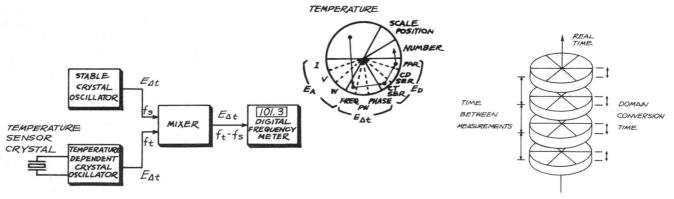

Figure 10. Crystal oscillator temperature measurement

Figure 11. Successive domain conversions

The count serial signal is in turn converted to parallel digital for the display by a counter. From the domains map it is seen that four interdomain and one intradomain conversions are involved in the measurement.

Digital Temperature Measurement. Two approaches to a digital thermometer are compared here. The first is a thermistor bridge connected to a digital voltmeter (E_D) as shown in Figure 9. The thermistor bridge circuit converts temperature to voltage. In this case the E_A-to-E_D (A/D) conversion is accomplished by a voltage-to-frequency converter and a frequency meter. The digital frequency meter operates by counting the number of cycles of an input signal that occur in a specific time. The resulting domain path is shown. There are four interdomain and one intradomain conversions.

The second approach is the use of a quartz crystal which has a temperature-dependent resonant frequency. An oscillator is used to convert the resonant frequency to an electrical signal in the $E_{\Delta t}$ domain. The block diagram is shown in Figure 10. A mixer is used to subtract a standard frequency, f_s, from the temperature-dependent frequency, f_t, to obtain a signal for which the frequency and temperature are related directly. This is an example of signal modification occurring in the $E_{\Delta t}$ domain. Note that this digital thermometer requires one less interdomain conversion than that of Figure 9. Whether

this simplification would result in greater accuracy, however, depends upon the accuracy of the converters involved in each case.

Conversions of Varying Quantities

The examples used in the previous section were measurements of steady-state quantities which were not expected to vary perceptibly over the interval of measurement. When the time variation of quantities in the various data domains is considered, a third dimension (time) needs to be added to the data domain map of Figure 6, as shown in Figure 11. Here each interdomain conversion is shown as a slice

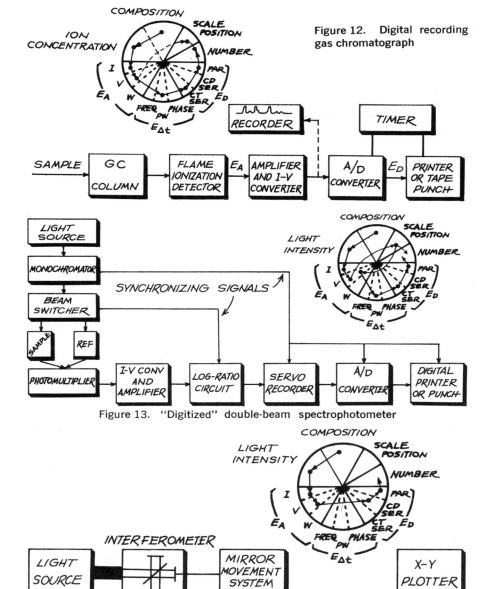

Figure 12. Digital recording gas chromatograph

Figure 13. "Digitized" double-beam spectrophotometer

Figure 14. Fourier transform spectrometer

intradomain conversion) which is then converted by the electric field in the detector to an electrical current (an interdomain conversion). The current signal is amplified and converted to a voltage amplitude suitable for A/D conversion and/or recording. The desired data are a record of detector current *vs.* time. The time relationship of the printed or punched values of the current amplitudes is generally obtained by having the successive A/D conversions performed at precise and regular time intervals. This is accomplished by the timer shown in the block diagram. The domain path for a single conversion (one time slice) is also shown.

Absorption Spectrophotometry. The block diagram of a digitized recording double-beam spectrophotometer is shown in Figure 13. A narrow wavelength range of light from the light source is selected by the monochromator and passed on to the beam switcher and cell compartment. The beam switcher alternately directs the monochromatic beam through the reference and sample cells to the photomultiplier tube detector. This produces an electrical current (E_A domain) which has an amplitude alternating between sample and reference beam intensities P and P_o. The desired output signal for the recorder is absorbance $A = \log_{10} (P_o/P)$, which is accomplished in the log-ratio circuit. This circuit performs a correlation between signal levels measured at two different times. It must, therefore, have a memory and a synchronizing connection to the beam switcher. The recorder is to plot absorbance *vs.* the wavelength of light from the monochromator. The recorder chart drive thus has a synchronizing connection to the monochromator wavelength drive mechanism.

This standard spectrophotometer was later digitized by putting a retransmitting pot assembly on the servorecorder. This converts the recorder pen position to a voltage amplitude which is connected to an A/D converter and printer or punch. Since the absorbance value recorded for precise *wavelength* (rather than time) intervals is desired, the A/D converter and printer are synchronized to the wavelength drive mechanism rather than a timer.

The data domains map for the resulting instrument is shown in Figure 13. It contains nine conversions; seven interdomain and two intradomain. The excursion into the scale position domain is unnecessary to the digitizing process and suggests that the A/D converter would have been better connected to the log-ratio circuit output, if possible. It is interesting to note that if photon

across the real-time continuum. If a quantity that varies continuously with time is to be converted to the digital domain, the resulting number can only be true for a specific instant in time. It is not possible, therefore, to make a truly continuous digital record of a varying quantity. What can be done is to measure the varying quantity at successive instants in time. The numerical result of each measurement is then stored in order in memory registers, or recorded on punched cards or paper tape, or by magnetic recording devices. If the measurements are made frequently enough for the varying quantity to change only slightly between each time, the digital record can quite

accurately represent the amplitude *vs.* time behavior of the measured quantity. Of course, the maximum frequency of measurement is limited by the time required to convert the measured quantity into the digital domain and record it. Successive data domain conversions will be illustrated by three examples of digitized measurement systems.

Gas Chromatography. A digital recording gas chromatograph is shown in Figure 12. The components in the sample mixture are separated by the column resulting in a flow of gas of varying composition through the flame ionization detector. The flame in the detector converts the hydrocarbon concentration into an ion concentration (an

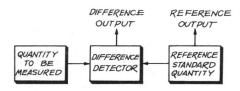

Figure 15. Basic measurement system

counting is used to measure the relative intensities, the number of interdomain conversions is reduced to three and a digital log-ratio circuit is required.

Fourier Transform Spectroscopy. A Fourier transform spectrometer is an example of a conceptually very simple data acquisition system connected to a complex data correlating and processing system. The block diagram is shown in Figure 14. To obtain the interference pattern, the A/D converter converts the detector output signal at constant increments of movement of the reference beam mirror. Each piece of data is stored for use in the Fourier transform calculation. The data domains map as shown is complete for each piece of data as it is acquired and stored. A successive approximations type of A/D converter has been assumed in this map. There are four interdomain and two intradomain conversions in all. After the transform calculation (which involves an intercorrelation of all the measured data points) is complete, a plot of absorbance *vs.* wavelength can be made.

This example demonstrates that Fourier transformation from amplitude *vs.* time or space to amplitude *vs.* frequency (or the reverse) is really an intercorrelation of analog signals which have already been "measured." It is essential to distinguish between the data domains involved in the methods of acquiring each data point and the methods of correlating and displaying groups of data points.

Errors in Domain Conversions

To understand the sources of error in domain conversion, it is helpful to review briefly the basic measurement process. Measurement can be defined as: *The determination of a particular characteristic of a sample in terms of a number of standard units for that characteristic.* The comparison of the quantity to be measured with standard units of that quantity is implicit in this definition. The comparison concept in measurement is illustrated by Figure 15. The quantity to be measured is compared with a reference standard quantity. The difference is converted to another form (domain) such as scale

position. The quantity measured is then the sum of the standard units in the reference quantity and the difference output calibrated in the same standard units.

All measurement devices involve both a difference detector and a reference standard, although they differ widely in the degree to which one or the other is relied upon in the measurement. As an example, three mass measuring devices can be compared in this regard. With a double pan balance, the unknown mass is compared with standard weights, whole units and fractional, until the difference detector (beam pointer) points to zero. In this case, the accuracy and resolution of the standard weights determines the accuracy of the measurement as long as the difference detector is sufficiently sensitive. No accuracy requirement is placed on the off-null calibrations of the difference detector. The other extreme is a spring-loaded scale, such as a fish or bathroom scale. In this case, the reference standard weights are used to calibrate the scale markings of the manufacturer's original prototype. In use, the measurement accuracy depends entirely upon the off-null markings on the scale. The reference standard quantity compared by the scale in this case is zero weight. In between these two extremes is the single pan balance with an optical scale for fractional weights. Balances of this type rely upon accurate standard weights for the most significant figures and upon off-null calibrations for the less significant figures.

Similar comparisons and analyses can be made for other types of measurement devices. A potentiometric voltage measurement depends much more upon the slidewire (standard voltage unit adjustment) calibration than upon the galvanometer null detector, while an electrical meter depends much more upon the difference detector calibrations than upon the standard. This kind of analysis is helpful in assessing the sources of errors in measurement devices and in choosing among available devices for a particular application. After considering a variety of measurement systems in this way, some basic concepts concerning measurement devices evolve which can be added to the four data domains concepts listed earlier.

(5) All measurement devices employ both a difference detector and a reference standard quantity.

(6) Either the difference detector *or* the reference standard can affect the accuracy of the measurement.

(7) The reference standard quantity is the same property or characteristic as that which is being measured.

A data domain conversion is the conversion of a number of units of some physical, chemical, or electrical characteristic into a related number of units of a different characteristic; for instance, the conversion of units of pH into Nernst factor potential units by a combination pH electrode. Devices for converting data from one domain to another are "measuring" one characteristic in terms of another. Therefore,

(8) Interdomain converters have the characteristics of measurement devices.

Using a combination pH electrode as an example of an interdomain converter to illustrate concepts 5–7: 5) The combination pH electrode itself is the difference detector; the reference standard is the standard buffer solution used to "standardize" the voltage output at a given pH. 6) The conversion error (difference between the predicted and actual potential/pH relationship) depends upon the accuracy of the standard solution and upon the accuracy of the electrode response. The greater the pH difference between the standard and unknown solutions, the more the conversion accuracy depends upon the electrode's characteristics. 7) The reference standard is pH, the units which are being converted to electrical potential.

Once one is accustomed to looking for the difference detector, reference standard, and accuracy dependence of interdomain converters, the basis of the conversion and the sources of error are easier to uncover. Every A/D converter contains a standard voltage or current source and every $\Delta t/D$ converter contains a standard clock oscillator, as expected from concept 7 above. In both cases the conversion accuracy depends directly upon the standard sources and, for various types, to a greater or lesser degree upon the other converter characteristics.

Conversions of data within domains can often be accomplished with high accuracy by simple transfer devices that require no comparison or reference standard. For instance, a resistor can be used to convert current to voltage or vice versa; the shift register will convert between serial digital and parallel digital domains.

Domain Converter Classification

A classification scheme for data conversion devices would seem desirable for two purposes: to categorize by function the great many devices available, and to provide a way to organize these devices into complete measurement systems. It is natural and useful to classify converter devices according to the domains which the device converts from

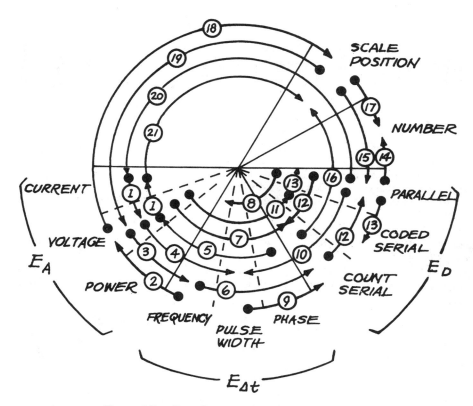

Figure 16. Domain converter classification map

1. Resistor, op amp circuit
2. Count rate meter
3. V-F converter
4. Dual slope A/D converter, ramp A/D converter
5. Phase angle meter
6. Counting gate timer
7. Staircase A/D converter
8. Programmable frequency divider
9. Gated oscillator
10. Preset digital timer
11. Successive approximation A/D converter
12. Counter
13. Shift register
14. Nixie tubes, printer
15. Shaft rotation encoder
16. Stepper motor
17. Mechanical shaft turns counter
18. Recorder
19. Retransmitting potentiometer
20. D/A converter (ladder or weighted sum)
21. Meter

and to. The domains map shows three electrical domains with three subdomains each, the scale position domain, the number domain, and the physical and chemical domains. For this classification, concentrating on electronic instrumentation, only the electrical, scale position, and number domains will be detailed. There are 110 possible interdomain and intradomain conversions among these 11 domains and subdomains. However, direct converters for most of these transitions are rare or unknown. Thus the number of categories required to encompass the common converters is not unwieldy.

The domains map is a very convenient means of organizing domain con-

verter categories. Figure 16 shows 21 categories of converters arranged by input and output domains. Examples of devices for each listed domain transition are given in the accompanying table. This map and table clearly show what direct transitions are possible and which specific devices will do them. In addition, Figure 16 can be used to obtain and compare many possible combinations of devices to achieve a given transition by following connecting paths. Thus voltage-to-parallel digital converters could be made by paths 3–6–12, 7–12, 4–9–12, 11–13, and 18–15. These five types of A/D converters are all currently marketed.

For any required conversion, that

path which has the fewest conversions should also be apparent from tracing the possible routes shown in Figure 16. However, the shortest path is not always the path of choice. For example, to go from scale position to parallel digital, the direct path is 15. However, absolute shaft rotation encoders with a high accuracy and ruggedness requirement could cost much more than the devices needed to take route 19–7–12.

Summary

The data domains and measurement concepts discussed here can be used to great advantage to analyze and describe available analog/digital instruments, to design or modify measurement systems, and to determine the sources of measurement errors. The data domains map can serve to show the data path from a block diagram or to devise a possible block diagram for instruments or modules, knowing only the input and output domains.

To analyze or describe an instrument, use the instrument description and block diagram to carefully follow the measurement data step-by-step through the instrument. Trace out the path on a domains map as shown in Figures 7–10 and 12–14. Now each converter corresponds to a line segment on the domains map. The conversion errors can be assessed by identifying and studying the reference source and difference detector for each converter. Modifications to instruments can be made by exchanging equivalent converters or by adding appropriate line segments to the instrument's domains map where new domains are to be included. New systems can be designed by completing a chart like Figure 16 for the devices available and comparing all the possible routes between the desired input and output domains.

Readers' comments, criticisms, and discussion on the concepts described in this article are welcomed. The author gratefully acknowledges the many helpful discussions he had with Dr. Howard Malmstadt, Dr. Stanley Crouch, Jim Ingle, and his graduate students during the evolution of these ideas.

References

(1) H. V. Malmstadt and C. G. Enke, "Digital Electronics for Scientists," W. A. Benjamin, New York, N. Y., 1969.
(2) D. Hoeschele Jr., "Analog-to-Digital-to-Analog Conversion Techniques," Wiley, New York, N. Y., 1968.
(3) H. V. Malmstadt and C. G. Enke, "Computer Logic," W. A. Benjamin, New York, N. Y., 1970.

Transducers in Digital Process Control

R. H. CERNI, Consolidated Systems Corporation

Expansion of digital computer control and automatic data logging in industry is increasing the need for versatile, economical, wholly electrical sensors. Present types of process transmitters are being challenged by advanced transducer concepts and by industrial versions of transducers originally designed for aerospace and dynamic measurement applications. Factors influencing the design, selection, and application of these new transducers are reviewed in this article. Digital transducers will speed the arrival of direct digital process control.

THE WAY in which transducers of various types are applied in systems is shown in Fig. 1. Most process variables are measured as electrical signals developed either by self-generating transducers or as a result of tiny mechanical displacements via suitable actuating mechanisms (Table 1).

TABLE I—TRANSDUCTION PRINCIPLES USED TO CONVERT MECHANICAL DISPLACEMENTS INTO ELECTRICAL SIGNALS

SELF-GENERATING TYPES
Piezoelectric
Photoelectric
Magnetoelectric
Electrochemical
Pulse Generators
Frequency Generators

PASSIVE TYPES
Variable Resistance (potentiometer, strain gage, thermistor)
Variable Capacitance (dielectric, position)
Variable Self Inductance (reluctance gages)
Variable Mutual Inductance (differential transformer)

Actuating mechanisms include the bellows, Bourdon tube, cantilever beam, proving ring, rotating shaft, spring-mass systems, and diaphragm. To sense the displacements produced by these mechanisms, strain gages (bonded and unbonded) and self- and mutual-inductance detectors (variable reluctance gage and differential transformer) are used widely.

Electromagnetic Transducers

Many conventional transducers for pressure and other variables already make extensive use of electromagnetic transduction means (differential transformer, reluctance, etc.). These devices have inherently high output-level and low source-impedance, factors which reduce the design and installation cost of long signal lines by minimizing problems of shielding, lead routing, and sensitivity to noise and ground.

A second reason for the use of these devices is that they are stable with temperature and time. Third, they are low in unit cost. Fourth, in digital system use, the fact that they can be scanned at high signal levels reduces the complexity of the computer input system and results in lower over-all system cost.

On the other hand, AC transmission must be used with these devices, except in units with self-contained demodulation. AC transmission produces line-capacitance and phasing-adjustment problems. Consequently, distance of transmission—especially beyond a few thousand feet—becomes a serious factor.

Strain-Gage Transducers

The *strain-gage transducer* already is used extensively in measuring pressure, force, weight, torque, vibration, flow, etc. This device works equally well on AC and DC (unlike differential transformers or reluctance gages, strain gages can be excited with DC, producing a DC output directly). They have enjoyed wide use for many years in aerospace applications, and industrial versions are also available. Wire, foil, and semiconductor types are in use and undergoing further development.

Unbonded strain gages are small, rugged units which have been used under severe environmental conditions for moderate-accuracy applications. As low-energy devices for industrial use, they are close to being inherently explosionproof. They offer high sensitivity (gage factor is typically 3 to 4), and low-impedance output. Over-all short-term total accuracies are in the order of 1%, although accuracies better than 0.5% have been produced. However, creep, temperature hysteresis, and mechanical hysteresis vary over a period of months, making frequent recalibration necessary. (These problems still persist, despite temperature cycling and aging, which aid in stabilizing unbonded strain-gage transducers.) In addition, zero tends to shift with long-term changes in strain-gage wire resistivity, creep, hysteresis, and stress relief. The excellent high-frequency response of this transducer type usually is not needed in digital process control.

Bonded strain-gage transducers, on the other hand, while suffering much less from long-term instability, are generally less sensitive (gage factor is about 2). Typical minimum full-scale range for this type is in the order of 100 psi. Over-all accuracy is about the same as that achieved by the unbonded type. The bonded strain-gage transducer has been produced in configurations suitable for process work, although they have been handicapped somewhat by

Reprinted with permission from *Instrum. Contr. Syst.,* vol. 37, pp. 123–126, Sept. 1964.

low output (in the millivolt range). Currently, efforts are being made to standardize sensitivities in order to make interchangeability in the field easier.

Semiconductor strain-gage transducers now being developed have high output voltage (in the order of volts) and gage factors of 200 for silicon (as compared to 2 for wire). While these types hold promise for heavy industrial use, especially with self-contained electronics, at present they exhibit poor long-term temperature stability and excessive nonlinearity. Mounting these devices in large industrial housings would achieve improvement over existing units by providing a stable thermal path, reducing thermal gradients and transients. Also, electrical compensating networks have been used to improve linearity.

Work on semiconductor strain gage transducers is progressing rapidly.

What can be expected in the next few years in the development of industrial strain-gage sensors? By eliminating the requirements for small, light-weight units with high-frequency response (requirements not pertinent to industrial applications), and by substituting goals of extreme stability and reliability, thermal gradients and mechanical shock effects can be reduced by increasing size. High reliability is much more probable in larger sizes because there are fewer constraints on the actuating mechanism. New unbonded and bonded gage supports for wire, foil, and semiconductor types are becoming available, leading to a higher degree of stability.

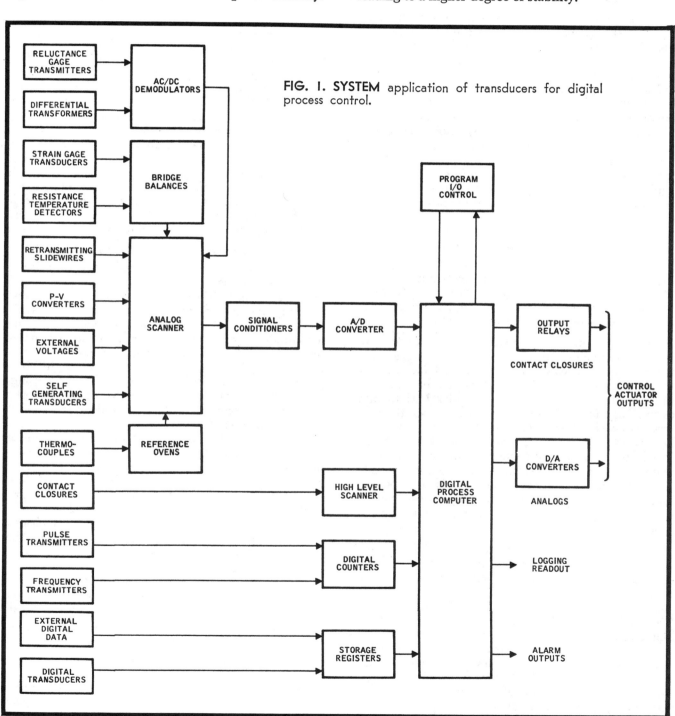

FIG. 1. SYSTEM application of transducers for digital process control.

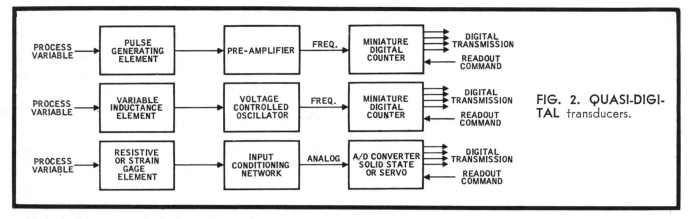

FIG. 2. QUASI-DIGITAL transducers.

Use of self-contained solid-state amplifiers and low-energy gage excitation is also tending to make possible industrial strain-gage transducers with less dependence on external zero or balance. Under these conditions, outputs can be in the order of 5 volts full scale. Industrial amplifier requirements also are less severe than military requirements, and proportionate economies can be expected. Over-all accuracy of 1% is now satisfactory for many applications, and this level of accuracy can be achieved in moderately priced transducers. (Transducers offering 0.5% to 0.1% accuracy can be expected at higher prices for applications involving optimizing control.) Elevated zero for fail-safe and alarm relay operation is easily handled.

High-Level Temperature Transducers

The common use of the thermocouple is being supplanted in some applications by temperature transducers providing higher outputs, such as the thermistor and resistance temperature detector, each with specific advantages for certain applications.

Thermistors have a large resistance change with increase in temperature, are small and rugged, extremely sensitive over short spans, and inexpensive. In bridge and other circuits they can be made to produce an output in the order of volts. Differentials as small as 0.001°F have been measured with thermistors. However, thermistors must be used carefully because they suffer from two significant limitations: First, the output is extremely nonlinear (approximately exponential). Second, as presently available thermistor semiconductor materials do not possess long-term stability sufficient for many process-control temperature measurements, frequent recalibration is required.

The *resistance temperature detector* (*RTD*), manufactured in full four-arm bridge configuration with internal balance resistances, represents a temperature sensor of great potential for process work. At present, single-element sensors are in common use. Their reliability is high and cost is moderate. Most single-element RTD sensors currently employ platinum or nickel. Platinum sensors are now priced comparably with thermocouples if the cost of the whole system is considered—that is, the cost of RTD and bridge balance is about that of a thermocouple, reference junction, and low-level preamplifier. Present RTD's are interchangeable to industrial standards, and exhibit a much lower linearity error than thermocouples (1% for platinum RTD's vs 13% for copper-Constantan thermocouples). RTD lead wires—up to 5,000 feet—may be copper when used with a proper bridge.

For applications where only a small span (such as 1%) of the entire temperature range constitutes the whole of the process input for a given channel, the RTD is definitely superior to the thermocouple. The RTD is inherently stable with time; in fact, it is used as a temperature standard. With suitable bridges and power supplies, the RTD has a high full-scale output range in the order of volts. One limitation, so far, is the restricted higher temperature ranges available; above 2000°F the thermocouple or radiation pyrometer is still preferable.

Frequency and Pulse Transducers

The prime application of frequency and pulse transducers to date in process work is to measure flow and speed. These transducers are of interest in computer control of processes for two reasons: First, a frequency or pulse signal representing the measurement can be transmitted relatively unaffected by noise and interference. Second, the frequency or pulse signal can be "counted" by the computer on an interrupt basis for further processing, or it can be totalized over precise time intervals with separate digital counters to produce true coded digital signals (Fig. 2).

The three most common forms for process control are the FM transducer, the photoelectric pulse detector, and the magnetic pulse pickup. The first finds application in pressure and displacement measurement, the second in counting objects, and the third in shaft speed and volumetric flow measurement.

FM transducers operate with oscillators which can be either separate from, or contained within, the transducer itself. Output is normally a high-level signal whose frequency deviates from a set point in proportion to the measured variable. While linearity is in the order of 1 to 2%, some types have good drift and repeatability characteristics. There is still considerable activity in the development of FM transducers for both military and industrial application.

RPM transducers of the pulse variety are simpler, more accurate, and usually less costly to install than AC or DC tachometer generators. When the pulse pickup is mounted adjacent to the teeth of a gear already within a machine, a pulse is generated by

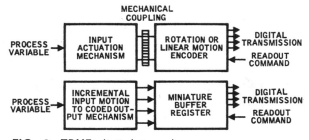

FIG. 3. TRUE digital transducers.

the passing of each gear tooth; the output pulse-repetition rate is proportional to average speed. Pulse-generating *turbine-type volumetric flow sensors* are well known and have been used with good reliability, generating an analog frequency proportional to flow rate.

Digital Transducers

Much has been said in recent years predicting the place of true digital transducers in aerospace as well as industrial applications. Aside from the present adaptation of shaft position encoders to sensing applications (either servo driven or direct acting), few true digital transducers—that is, transducers with digitally coded output—are yet available commercially (Fig. 3). Of those that are under development, the serial-output type shows most promise for process work. Parallel-output devices require 12 to 18 conductors per transducer. For long lines and many measurement points, this multiplicity of conductors is not desirable.

A unit that produces, on command, an internally generated serial digital scan for transmission, over a single line, is the most useful type. Commutating then can be done at the control pulse level, and the digital output can be high level, compatible with direct computer entry. A full-scale code of 100 increments will provide accuracy and resolution sufficient for most industrial applications. Digital signals can be expected (1) to be free from interference effects on long lines, (2) to preserve the initial transducer sensing accuracy, (3) to be self-checking for error in transmission, and (4) to require no analog-to-digital conversion or multiplexing before computer entry.

Several digital transducers are under development. For example, a nuclear type has been developed in which pulses produced by a weak radium source are detected with a silicon junction detector. The electrical pulses from the detector are totalized with an internal digital counter which provides an output in a digital code. The counter time base can be varied to produce output in direct engineering units. The initial measuring means can be one of the standard activating devices for converting process variables to a mechanical motion. The activating device moves a shutter which intercepts the radiation between source and detector, reducing the radiation in linear proportion to the movement of the shutter. Accuracies of 0.1% for a 1-second time base (1,000 increments) have been demonstrated. The disintegration rate of the source is independent of temperature.

Research also is being conducted on photo-optical methods of quantizing minute motions for application to digital transducers. Possibilities under study include polarization effects, photo-elastic effects, gratings, coded film shutters, and interference patterns. Magnetostrictive and other quantizing magnetic effects are also under investigation. True digital transducers using microcircuit electronic logic can be expected within three to five years. Cost per channel, while high at first, is expected, in time, to be compatible with industrial needs, especially considering the simplification of the rest of the computer control system which is in progress. The availability of digital transducers for use in digital subloops can be expected to speed up the arrival of direct digital control of industrial processes.

Selecting Industrial Transducers

Choosing the right transducer for a given process measurement or control application involves compromising transducer characteristics and cost against required over-all system performance and reliability. Transducer features most desirable for industrial process control and data logging applications are:

Field maintainability and disassembly
High-level output with low source impedance
Direct current transmission using unshielded cables
Moderate to low frequency response
High zero and span stability with both temperature and time
High reliability and low maintenance
Explosionproof construction or intrinsically safe design
Ability to withstand severe environments, rough handling and over ranging
Moderately low unit cost and low installation cost
Moderate over-all accuracy
Local indication for calibration convenience.

The use of advanced electrical industrial transducers designed and tailored for computer control is increasing, can be expected to grow rapidly in the future, and will affect the design of computer control systems.

References

1. H. K. P. Neubert, *Instrument Transducers*, Oxford, London, 1963.
2. J. L. Hyde, "Developing Digital Transducers," *ISA Journal*, June 1963.
3. Dean and Douglas, *Semi-Conductor and Conventional Strain Gages*, Academic Press, New York, N. Y. 1963.
4. *Transducers Compendium*, ISA, Pittsburgh, Pa. 1962.
5. T. Dickson, "Selecting Strain-Gage Transducers," *Automation*, Nov. 1962.
6. Cerni & Foster, *Instrumentation for Engineering Measurement*, Wiley, N. Y., 1962.
7. C. G. Carroll, *Industrial Process Measuring Instruments*, McGraw-Hill, N. Y., 1962.
8. F. A. Ludewig, "Digital Transducers," *Control Engineering*, June 1961.
9. K. S. Lion, *Instrumentation in Scientific Research*, McGraw-Hill, N. Y., 1962.
10. W. Kliever, "Principles and Techniques for Direct Reading Digital Transducers," *IRE Transactions on Industrial Electronics*, PGIE-5, April 1958.
11. E. J. Kompass, "What About Digital Transducers," *Control Engineering*, July 1958.
12. A. I. Dranetz, "Electro-Mechanical Transducers," *Machine Design*, January 9, 1958.
13. R. K. Jurgen, "How Transducers Measure and Control," *Electronics*, July 4, 1958.
14. D. M. Considine, *Process Instruments and Control Handbook*, McGraw-Hill, N. Y., 1957.

Control Instrumentation/Computer COMPATIBILITY

L. M. SOULE JR., The Foxboro Co

Data Logging Computers

COMPUTERS LOGGING DATA require inputs from transmitters and, occasionally, various types of logic signals from control equipment. Transmitters with signal levels as high as 10-50 ma, with low ripple contents and signals which may be grounded at the computer's input, are now standard equipment with most suppliers of instruments.

Feedback connections for all switch positions and other information concerning the status of control room equipment are provided either as standard or as low-cost optional extras.

Supervisory

Many supervisory computers provide signals to adjust the setpoints of analog controllers. Computer output depends on the manufacturer; it may be analog, pulse duration and pulse train output.

Analog

A supervisory computer may emit a 4-20 ma, 10-50 ma, or 1-5 vDC signal. For analog hardware this signal is essentially the same found in standard analog cascade control systems. In a supervisory system, however, the computer provides the signal normally supplied by a primary controller.

The control requirements for the secondary controller are the same in supervisory computer and cascade control systems. Operating procedures and feedback information required from the secondary controller may be quite different, though.

The secondary controller usually has some type of remote-local switch which allows an operator to adjust a setpoint manually or permits the setpoint to be adjusted by the computer signal.

In an analog cascade control system, transfer from remote to local setpoint on the secondary controller is rare. Thus, the switch is often located on the side of the controller.

But when a digital computer replaces a primary analog computer, an operator must know whether or not the process is under supervisory control. The remote-local switch should be on the front of the controller with the position of the switch indicating the mode of opera-

tion. Using switch position as an indicator eliminates lights which can cause maintenance problems and eye fatigue.

A remote-local switch should be standard equipment on electronic controllers to allow maximum interchangeability. Some simple method of switching bumplessly from remote to local setpoint, and vice versa, should also be provided.

Whether or not the controller's setpoint dial should be moved physically so that its position always corresponds to the setpoint calculated by the computer depends on economics and the desires of operating personnel. Movement may be implemented either by a servo or a stepping motor.

Grounding of measurements and feedback information on the status of operation mode are also important factors when an analog output signal is used.

When the remote-local and/or automatic-manual transfer switch is moved, it closes an extra set of contacts in the controller, thereby "telling" the computer whether or not it has control of the process.

The computer may transfer the controller from automatic to manual and freeze the controller's output in its last position. This is useful should a computer fail or a measurement signal from a primary transmitter be lost.

Setpoint changes should often be introduced into the process without proportional action and, almost always without derivative action to insure maximum process stability. The ideal controller permits setpoint changes without derivative action and with or without proportional action, depending on computer programming.

If a setpoint must be changed quickly, and overshoot is permissible, proportional action is advantageous.

To eliminate overshoot and instability, the fastest setpoint change should not exceed the reset rate of the particular controller involved.

Major advantage of analog output is possible system cost savings. System size and number of loops under supervisory control have a great effect on the relative costs of an analog output and a digital output system.

Major disadvantage is that a loss of output signal from the computer results in an analog controller reverting to zero setpoint unless some rather elaborate and expensive lockup system is provided.

Reprinted with permission from *Instrum. Contr. Syst.*, vol. 41, pp. 111–117, May 1968.

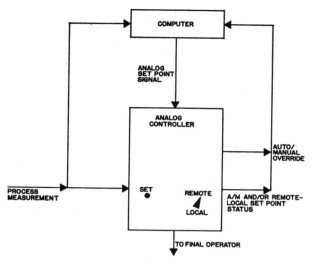

FIG. I. SUPERVISORY computer with analog output.

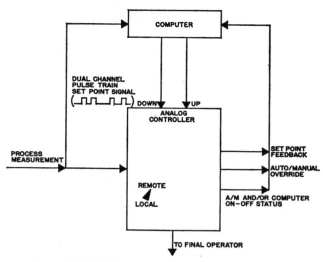

FIG. 2. SUPERVISORY computer with pulse duration output.

Pulse Duration

A second type of supervisory computer sends a pulse signal to the setpoint circuit of analog controllers (Fig. 2). The duration of the pulse determines the change of setpoint. Normally, two output channels are provided, one for upscale changes, another for downscale. A servo or stepping motor in the analog controller transforms these pulses into a setpoint potentiometer setting.

Since the computer produces an incremental signal, it must receive a feedback signal from the controller giving the position of the setpoint potentiometer. Probably the best way to provide this signal is to use a circuit similar to that in Fig. 3. The setpoint potentiometer regulates current flow through a fixed resistor. The voltage drop across this resistor is compared with the measurement signal to develop the controller error or deviation signal. The feedback signal is measured across another dropping resistor in the circuit. The feedback voltage level depends on the computer manufacturer, with 0.2-1.0 v, 10-50 mv, 40-200 mv, 100-500 mv and 1-5 v all being common.

With this method the setpoint feedback of the analog controller will be unaffected if anything causes a short or an open circuit in the wires which carry this voltage to the computer, or if a fault should occur in the computer. The method is superior to using two separate potentiometers—one for controller setpoint and the other for computer feedback—because calibration inaccuracies are virtually impossible.

Again, care must be exercised in grounding wires which carry information to and from the computer.

A controller receiving pulse signals should: (1) have provision for setpoint feedback, (2) be computer transferable from automatic to manual, and (3) allow setpoint changes without derivative response and with or without proportional response.

The elimination of derivative response on setpoint changes is especially valuable when using a pulse duration signal because the output from the computer is a step change. Derivative action would differentiate this step change and cause process instability.

Major advantage is that if the pulses are interrupted, the controller setpoint will remain in the last position

directed by the computer. The mechanically driven setpoint potentiometer provides drift-free memory.

Also, no balancing procedure is necessary when the operator transfers from computer-adjusted to locally-adjusted setpoint. The operator simply moves the remote-local switch and manually adjusts the setpoint dial. A clutch in the servo or stepping motor drive train shuts off the effect of any input pulses.

Major disadvantage is that the analog controller's setpoint can be driven off scale if the computer's output pulse remains on continuously. The direction in which the setpoint moves depends upon the particular output which malfunctioned. A sticking relay in the computer output equipment or a short circuit in the cabling between the computer and the controller can cause such problems.

Pulse Train

Some supervisory computers provide a train of uniformly sized pulses to adjust controller setpoints (Fig. 4). Two output channels are used. One drives the analog controller setpoint upscale, the other downscale. Each pulse moves the setpoint some given percentage. usually 0.1% FS.

A stepping motor is connected to the analog controller's setpoint potentiometer and provides the operator with a continuous display of setpoint position. A clutch in the stepping motor drive chain permits the operator to override the computer calculated setpoint.

Because the computer emits an incremental signal, it must be provided with a feedback voltage proportional to the analog controller's setpoint position. The system described under "Pulse Duration" is ideal.

All grounding and feedback signal considerations discussed previously should be investigated thoroughly.

Major advantage is that a malfunction in the computer output equipment cannot affect the analog controller's setpoint by more than one step, typically 0.1%. This also applies to any short or open circuits in the cabling between computer and controller. The pulse train system also maintains the computer setpoint on a pulse interruption and the operator can adjust the setpoint locally without using a balancing procedure.

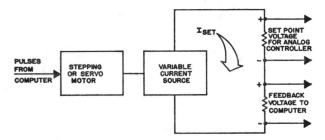

FIG. 3. CURRENT-regulated setpoint circuit.

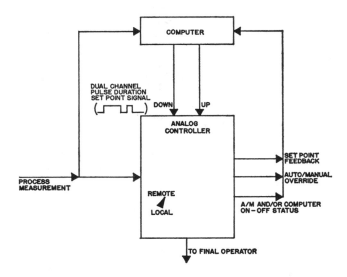

FIG. 4. SUPERVISORY computer with pulse train output.

Disadvantage. If the computer uses a contact to gate a common master oscillator into the selected controller, this contact may stick, causing the setpoint to be driven offscale. Computer manufacturers have devised systems which completely eliminate this problem.

The pulse train outputting system is probably the most common and the safest system recently employed in supervisory installations.

Direct Digital Control

No two computer manufacturers use the same outputting philosophy, let alone the same signal level for DDC. Thus, providing analog backup units for DDC computers is complicated. In all cases, however, the analog backup instrumentation must convert some type of analog pulse to a continuous current analog such as 10-50 ma. The types of DDC output signals used by some of the major computer suppliers are examined (Table 1).

Velocity Algorithm

Pulse Duration Output, Dual Channels

The Foxboro DDC system provides a varying width pulse output — the wider the pulse, the greater the change in valve position. Two output channels are provided, one for upscale operation, one for downscale. The pulses are of a constant amplitude (approximately -6.5 v) and of a width varying from 8 μsec to 1 msec. These widths correspond to valve changes of 0.1% to 12.5%. The output channel selected in the computer determines the direction of valve movement, the width of the pulse and the amount of change.

Table I—DDC Output Signals*

Supplier and Model No.	DDC Algorithm	Output Signal		
		Pulse Height and Equivalent ma	Pulse Length	Comments
Foxboro 97400A	Velocity	-6.5 v	Dual Channel 8 μ sec — 1 m sec 8 μ sec = 0.04 ma Δ 1 m sec = 5.0 ma Δ	Each pulse is capable of changing the valve position between 0.1 and 12.5%. Pulse duration determines valve movement. Channel selected by computer determines direction.
GE-4020	Velocity	0 — 1 ma $\pm$ 0 ma = 0 ma Δ $+$ 1 ma = $+$ 4 ma Δ $-$ 1 ma = $-$ 4 ma Δ	2 m sec	Each pulse is capable of changing the valve position between 0 and 10%. Polarity of pulse determines direction of valve movement.
IBM-1800	Positional	2 — 10 v 2 v = 10 ma 10 v = 50 ma	2 m sec	
Westinghouse	Positional	2 — 10 v 2 v = 10 ma 10 v = 50 ma	1 m sec	
	Velocity	0 — 10 v $\pm$ 0 v = 0 ma Δ 10 v = $+$ 10 ma Δ $-$ 10 v = $-$ 10 ma Δ	1 m sec	Each pulse is capable of changing the valve position between 0 and 25%. Polarity of pulse determines direction of valve movement.

* Standard signals reportedly being offered (Sept. 1967)

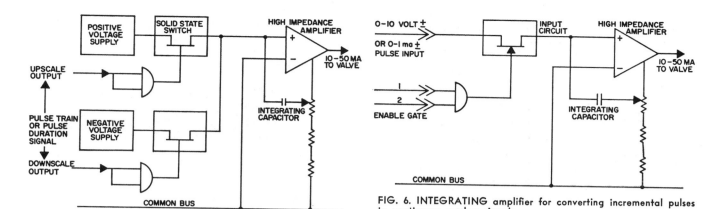

FIG. 5. FOXBORO DDC system—pulse duration

FIG. 6. INTEGRATING amplifier for converting incremental pulses to continuous analog signals.

The amplitude of the pulse is not critical because its only function is to turn on the solid-state switch mounted in the pulse-to-analog converter. When the pulse is present (Fig. 5), a voltage source mounted in the converter is connected to an integrating circuit. As long as the pulse is present, integration continues, causing the output of the converter to change. The converter's output ceases to change when the input pulse is discontinued. The solid-state switch (an FET), and the amplifier have a very high impedance which prevents the integrating capacitor from any significant leakage and the converter's output from drifting. Pickup in cabling between the computer and the converter cannot cause an error in the change of valve position calculated by the computer since the level of the pulse required to activate the FET is well above normal pickup levels.

Pulse Train Output, Dual Channel

Typically termed "General Purpose Output," this form of DDC output is the same as discussed in "Supervisory Control—Pulse Train" except that the pulses produce a change in valve position rather than drive a stepping motor for supervisory control. Each pulse is designed to change the valve position by a certain percentage, normally between 0.1% and 0.5%. The amount of change per pulse should be adjustable in the field to add flexibility in computer programming. One pulse channel provides upscale valve movement, a second provides downscale movement.

This outputting system is useful for computers designed mainly for supervisory control, but which have or plan to have a few DDC loops.

A pulse-to-analog converter uses an integrating circuit to transform each pulse into an equivalent valve position change (Fig. 5). Each pulse gates a voltage source to the integrating amplifier in a manner similar to the one described in the operation of the Foxboro system. The level of the interval voltage source determines the amount of valve position change.

Pulse Amplitude Modulation—Varying Current

In a system often used by General Electric on the 4000 series computers, a varying-height pulse changes valve position. Pulses emitted are of a constant width (approximately 2 msec), 0 to 1 ma high. A positive pulse, 0 to +1 ma, increases valve position from 0 to 10%. A negative pulse, 0 to −1 ma, decreases valve position from 0 to 10%.

A converter which has an integrating amplifier (Fig. 6) converts pulses to a proportional change in valve position. The particular controller to be selected may be determined by a selector circuit in the computer output equipment, or (Fig. 6) by using a solid-state matrix system which turns on the ENABLE gate within the converter. The area under each pulse is related directly to the calculated amount of valve change. The input impedance of the converter must be kept to a minimum to reduce pickup problems and prevent undue loading of the current source in the computer.

Pulse Amplitude Modulation—Varying Voltage

A system used by Westinghouse operates on the same basic philosophy as the General Electric system, except that the pulses are voltage variable rather than current variable. Each pulse is approximately 1 msec wide and 0 to 10 high. Positive pulses, 0 to +10 v cause an increasing valve position change of 0 and 25% FS. Negative pulses, 0 to −10 v, cause similar changes in the opposite direction.

An integrating amplifier may be used to change the pulses to an analog signal for the valve. The area under the voltage variable pulse is directly proportional to the desired amount of valve position change (Fig. 6).

The amplifier to receive the pulse may either be selected by a relay within the computer output equipment or by a solid-state matrix system located in the computer. The matrix system turns on the appropriate AND gate mounted in the converter.

Positional Algorithm
Pulse Amplitude Modulation—Varying Voltage

IBM and Westinghouse use a positional algorithm in DDC routines. A computer calculates a desired valve position, rather than a valve position change. The output pulse has a voltage variable amplitude of 0 to 10 v and a constant width (IBM, 2 msec; Westinghouse, 1 msec). A pulse 2 v high regularly corresponds to a 0% open valve to provide a live zero for positive shutoff. A 10 v pulse corresponds to a wide open valve.

To convert these pulses to continuous analog signals, a form of sample and hold circuit is used. The input pulse is impressed on a capacitor (Fig. 7). The charge on this capacitor drives a holding amplifier to the

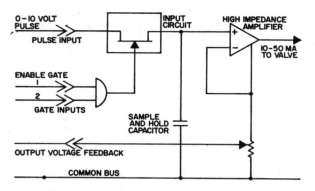

FIG. 7. SAMPLE and hold circuit for converting absolute value pulses to continuous analog signals.

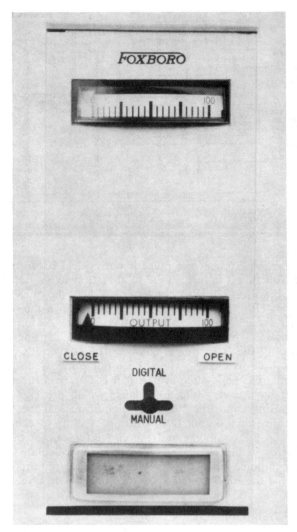

FIG. 8. FOXBORO M67 HD manual backup station for DDC.

corresponding value of valve output. When the pulse is removed from the converter, the valve remains essentially stationary. The converter which will receive the pulse is selected by a relay circuit mounted integrally to the computer or by a solid-state matrix system which actuates an AND gate mounted in the converter. The matrix system is in the computer's output equipment.

Since the computer calculates a new valve position at specified intervals, it cannot "know" the position of the valve if the operator has changed the valve signal manually. The computer must, therefore, receive feedback from the output of the converter to allow a bumpless transfer from analog to digital control. In this way the computer matches its initial output with that determined manually by the operator. Any change in this position will then be governed by the computer's program.

System Grounding

Great care must be taken in grounding a D-A system. Virtually all computer manufacturers require that all inputs to a computer be grounded. Several, however, specify that the ground used for signals—such as process variable, valve position and setpoint feedback signals—be isolated from logic signal ground (logic signals include switch contacts, alarm lights, stepping motor drive contacts, etc.). Although the grounds are eventually tied together, the computer vendor does this in his output equipment rather than risk inducing feedback signals into the computer's analog output modules. The pulse-to-analog converter should be capable, therefore, of providing two completely separate grounds which may be tied together in the computer.

Analog Backup for DDC

Manual Backup

A manual backup station (Fig. 8) converts the pulse from a computer into the appropriate valve position signal when the mode selection switch is in the DDC position. If the computer should fail, or if the operator wishes to regulate the valve manually, the backup station will function as a conventional remote manual loading station. Transfer from DDC operation to manual, whether manual or remote by the computer, is completely bumpless and balanceless. Upon a transfer to

manual, the output remains in its last position until the operator desires to change it.

A logic contact indicates to the computer that the operator has selected manual operation so the computer "knows" when it is controlling the process.

A green light on the front of the station warns the operator whenever the mode selection switch is in the DDC position and the computer has failed and the process is being controlled by the analog backup station. A red light may be activated by an external alarm unit to indicate an abnormal process condition. Foxboro Model 67 HD (Fig. 8) provides backlighted red and green nameplates. A lamp test pushbutton on the side of the instrument eliminates the necessity of an expensive external test circuit.

Other standard features provided with most manufacturers' manual backup stations include a process measurement indicator calibrated in % FS on either a uniform or a square root scale and a 0-100% output meter to indicate the signal being sent to the final operator.

Manual backup stations have been applied typically on control loops which require few changes in valve position or are essentially peripheral loops. In each

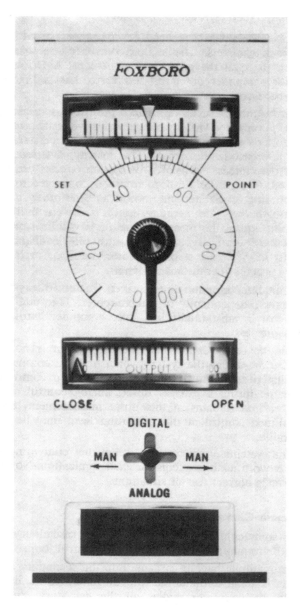

FIG. 9. FOXBORO M62 HD analog backup station for DDC.

case, it is permissible to lock the valve output signals in their last position when a computer fails. The operator can adjust the valve position on a periodic basis, perhaps hourly or even less frequently, to maintain the process variable within a desired range.

Automatic Analog Control Backup

Depending on the process, there are usually a number of loops in any plant which cannot or should not be controlled manually when a computer fails — loops which are critical from a safety standpoint and, usually, any loops which require frequent changes in valve position. In these loops a full two- or three-mode analog backup controller is desirable (Fig. 9). Besides converting the pulse output from the computer to a valve position signal, an analog backup controller provides both manual or automatic analog control backup. The field instrument engineer can change a jumper wire in the controller to select either.

If the manual backup mode is selected and a computer fails, the controller functions exactly as the station discussed in "Manual Backup." If the automatic control backup mode is chosen, the station controls the process using two- or three-mode analog control. Once the transfer is accomplished, the unit functions like any conventional analog controller. To transfer from DDC to manual or analog automatic, the operator moves the transfer switch on the front of the instrument or the computer opens a contact. Transfer from DDC to analog automatic is accomplished strictly as a function of the controller's reset rate if the two setpoints are different—there is no proportional step or bump introduced into the process.

Transfer, whether manual or remote to either manual or automatic control, or back to DDC, is completely bumpless and balanceless.

A logic contact within the backup controller indicates to the computer if the operator has selected either manual or analog automatic operation.

A green light indicates a computer failure whenever the operator has left the mode selection switch in DDC. A second light shows other alarming functions. A lamp test pushbutton is also supplied.

All analog feedback signals, process measurement, analog setpoint position and valve outputs are referenced positively to a common bus permitting the computer to ground all inputs at a single point. All logic signals, contact feedbacks, alarm lights, enabling gates, etc., are referenced to a second common bus which is grounded in the computer output rack. This prevents any logic data from feeding back into the computer's D-A converter and causing outputting errors.

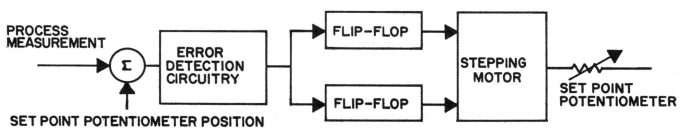

FIG. 10. SETPOINT tracking of measurement.

Panel Features

The uppermost meter in Foxboro's Model 62 HD (Fig. 9) may be a 0 to 100% process meter or a ±10% deviation meter. The latter, when read in conjunction with the setpoint dial, indicates process measurement. The setpoint dial may be calibrated in any engineering units desired. The analog controller setpoint mechanism has a calibrated accuracy of ±0.5% of span; this permits accurate control of the process in the event of long-term computer outage. The meter, located directly below the setpoint scale, indicates the 10-50 ma output signal to the final operator on a 0-100% scale. The cross-bar switch below the output meter allows the operator to select DDC, manual, or analog automatic operation. The nameplate is backlighted with the functions previously described. The backup controller provides adjustable high and low limits on the output to prevent undesired valve excursions.

On a few loops it may be impossible for an operator to preset on the analog controller a setpoint which provides safe or reasonable process control when a computer fails. One convenient way to eliminate this problem is to allow the backup controller to fail to manual. The operator then balances the controller setpoint by nulling the deviation meter and transferring to analog automatic control. If there are many such loops or if the operator is required to perform other functions immediately after a computer failure, some form of automatic setpoint tracking is advisable.

Setpoint Tracking of Computer-Calculated Setpoint

This is undoubtedly the safest, surest method of analog backup from a system viewpoint. A backup controller receives an output signal from the computer to physically drive its setpoint to equal the setpoint being used in the DDC algorithm. This output signal may be any one described under "Supervisory". It is most typically an analog voltage or a pulse train. The drive circuitry used to physically rotate the setting dial on the backup controller is the same in either system. Although a memory amplifier could be used for this function, it is better to use either a servo or a stepping motor. Use of the motor-driven approach offers advantages over the memory amplifier:

(1) Continuous, accurate indication of the analog controller and computer setpoints.

(2) Infinite setpoint memory, in the event of a computer failure, due to the mechanics of the driving system.

(3) Bumpless, balanceless transfer to operator setpoint control, since motor driven potentiometer and manually operated setpoint are the same.

(4) Standard 0.5% of span accuracy for analog control setpoint.

(5) A setpoint scale which can be calibrated in engineering units and easily changed.

This form of setpoint tracking does require computer output channels and input channels (feedback signals indicating setpoint position), however. Thus, it consumes valuable computer time and requires outputting hardware.

Setpoint Tracking Process Variables

This eliminates the need for computer output and feedback channels. The analog controller's setpoint is driven to equal the process measurement. A following memory amplifier or circuit similar to that in Fig. 10 may be used.

In the motor-driven approach, the process measurement is compared with a voltage indicative of the analog controller's setpoint. An error detection circuit senses any difference in the signals. The polarity of a resulting error determines which of two flip-flop circuits are energized. One of the flip-flop circuits is connected to the up-winding of the stepping motor, and the other to the down-winding. The stepping motor is driven until the setpoint equals the measurement, or is within a preset percentage of it. By allowing adjustable deadband of about 0.5-5%, the stepping motor does not cycle on noisy process measurement signals.

Valuable computer time is saved because the system operates independently of the computer. The total system cost is substantially less since computer hardware costs are less.

On the other hand, this tracking system is not as precise or safe as the system which tracks a computer-calculated setpoint. If transfer to a backup controller is made during a process upset, analog control commences and remains at this upset measurement level. Continued control at this abnormal level may be undesirable.

The systems engineer must weigh the relative merits of the two tracking systems for each application. No one answer is correct for all situations.

Cascade Control Backup System

In some control situations, an analog cascade system may be required to back up a DDC control loop.

In a simple backup cascade loop the secondary controller is a conventional backup controller. In the digital mode the computer makes all the necessary control calculations. The secondary controller converts the pulse output to a proportionate 10-50 ma valve signal. The primary analog controller does not enter into the valve calculation in DDC operation. Its function is simply to provide cascade control during a computer outage. The No. 2 measurement is fed to the primary as well as the secondary controller. The primary controller acts as a one-to-one repeater. Its output is the No. 2 measurement which becomes the setpoint of the secondary controller.

Upon computer failure, the second controller takes over control of the process. Since its setpoint is equal to its measurement, the controller assumes the last output value dictated by the computer. When the transfer to analog control takes place, the No. 2 measurement is disconnected from the primary controller, which then controls the No. 1 measurement at the setpoint indicated on the controller. If a difference exists between the No. 1 measurement and the primary controller setpoint, the error will be eliminated as a function of the controller's reset rate. Alternatively, the primary controller can be equipped to track the appropriate computer setpoint, so that there will be no change upon analog take-over.

A modular analog digital input output system (ADIOS) for on-line computers

by R. W. KERR, H. P. LIE, G. L. MILLER, and D. A. H. ROBINSON

Bell Telephone Laboratories, Incorporated
Murray Hill, New Jersey

INTRODUCTION

The most important single feature that allows a computer to be employed in a broad range of calculations is the fact that one can, by programming, in effect restructure the machine to perform the desired computational task.

It is not possible to retain the same degree of flexibility in on-line systems because of their need to be connected to specialized external hardware. Primarily for this reason the majority of on-line computer systems that have been constructed in the past have been designed to perform a pre-defined class of specialized operations. This situation is analogous to that which existed before the invention of the stored program machine when a computing device would be constructed to perform each new special task.

The system described here is the result of an effort to obtain a reasonable degree of flexibility in on-line computer controlled environments and is based on careful considerations of the factors that tend to limit such flexibility. The consequences of such problems in previous systems has been evidenced by difficulties of adding or reconfiguring hardware and interface equipment. Such difficulties have reduced the potential versatility of many existing systems in which the effort required to implement useful changes is uneconomic and such changes are therefore only rarely made.

It is possible, however, by the use of appropriately designed modular units interconnected by a common two-way analog and digital data-bus to obtain the desired degree of flexibility and power. The next section of this paper outlines the general consideration involved in the design

of such data-bus systems, while the remainder of the paper describes the implementation of these ideas for a specific small computer, namely a Digital Equipment Corporation PDP–8.

Design considerations

Of the many schemes whereby equipment may be connected to a computer perhaps the simplest division is between "radial" and "bus" systems. In the former, the interconnecting cables can be thought of as radiating like the spokes of a wheel to connect the computer to each external unit, while in the latter each external unit is connected to a common "highway," "party line," or "bus" cable system. In a certain sense this distinction is artificial since in the last resort even a radial connection is handled on a bus basis once the signals enter the computer hardware proper. However, the distinction is a valid one for the domain of equipment external to the computer itself and can serve as a starting point for comparing different systems.

The greatest single advantage in a radial system, from the user's point of view, is the fact that external equipment need only be plugged into a suitable connector to be on-line with the computer. The outstanding disadvantage, however, is that such systems are relatively inflexible and can become expensive if large numbers of external units are required. Furthermore, the user may become overly dependent on the computer vendor and his instrument division since only their equipment is automatically interfaced with the machine. In bus systems, on the other hand, the organization is different in that each external unit is connected to a common set of cables which

Reprinted with permission from *AFIPS Conf. Proc., Vol. 33, Pt. 2, 1968 Fall Joint Comput. Conf.*, pp. 1065–1075.

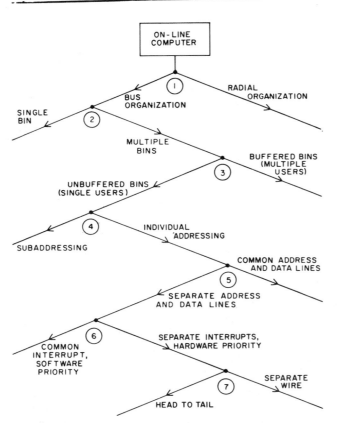

FIGURE 1—Logic tree indicating the major decisions involved in the design of a data bus system

carry address, data, and status information to and from the computer.

A feature of such bus systems that is worth noting is that the interfacing operation between the computer and the external world occurs only once, namely between the computer and the data bus. It is therefore possible to design such systems so that the same, or different, collections of on-line equipment can be connected to many different computers by changing only the bus-to-computer interface.

The differentiation into radial and bus systems is indicated by the node labeled 1 in Figure 1. Other important decisions follow at other nodes in this diagram and it is the purpose of this section of the paper briefly to indicate the major considerations involved at each branch. In order to forestall any misunderstanding it may be well to point out that though a particular design path was followed in the PDP–8 system described in the remainder of this paper, it is by no means claimed that the resulting system is ideal for every application. As will become clear the design of any system is dependent on numbers of factors, major ones

being, for example, the total size of the system envisaged (i.e., number of input and output units together with information on their spatial separation), and whether the system is to be employed by a single user or time shared by several non-interacting users simultaneously. Another important consideration is of course input/output speed and data-rate. Interestingly enough, however, in a number of actual on-line experimental environments that we have considered, it turns out that the bus approach imposes only a small time burden on the system. In the last resort this arises from two causes, first because operations proceed sequentially inside the computer, requiring a certain time to service each external unit, and second because external units are themselves often quite slow (e.g., ⌐50 μs conversion time for a typical 12 bit nuclear physics ADC). The result of this is that if reasonable care is exercised in the design of the bus system the access and I/O time for external units can become quite small compared with the sum of the device operation and computer servicing time. Obviously it is always possible to envisage situations where this is not the case, but we believe them to be only a small subset of most on-line situations. In those cases where I/O speed becomes an unavoidable limitation, e.g., CRT displays, it is usually worthwhile to consider the use of a separate dedicated piece of equipment (such as a disc with suitable DAC's, etc., for display) to perform the critical function at all times.

Returning to the general considerations indicated in Figure 1, the next question is one of system size. It is taken for granted that the user's hardware will consist of some form of modules which plug into bins (see for instance the European standard IANUS system or the ADIOS system described here), and the question is whether there will be one bin or several. This decision involves questions of how multiple bins are to be addressed, and what will be their physical separation and distance from the computer. This latter point is highly important though easily overlooked. Its importance can be seen in the following way. If the cable length is long then the cables must be terminated to avoid reflection. The logic levels employed for modern microcircuits are typically 0 and +4 volts. For 50 ohm terminated cable this means 80 ma/bit. Since on-line systems usually employ common grounds between analog and digital hardware it follows that the transfer of a 16 bit word can involve a current pulse at over 1.2

amperes in the ground return. The noise and crosstalk implications of this are obvious. (A new data bus system presently being designed at Bell Telephone Laboratories for a multi-user environment using SDS Sigma computers circumvents this problem by using balanced current-driven twisted pair. No such extreme steps were necessary for the relatively small PDP-8 system described in this paper.)

If multiple simultaneous users are envisaged it is advantageous to employ a buffer unit between each bin and the data bus. This has a number of advantages for large systems, not least being the ability to provide logical buffering between bins to prevent one user from wiping out another by, for instance, unplugging a module. This decision is shown at node 3 in Figure 1.

Again in large multi-bin environments it can be advantageous to provide a bin address with unit sub-addresses within each bin, (this is the route followed in both the European IANUS and BTL Sigma system designs).

At node 5 a difficult choice must be made regarding the extent to which the bus cables are shared by time, or other multiplexing arrangements. The advantage of multiplexing lies in its ability to reduce the number of cables in the system. The disadvantages are reduced I/O speed and added complications to unit hardware and system programming.

The way in which external units signal the computer via the interrupt system is also one of central importance. In this connection the major choices lie, as indicated at node 6, between using a single common interrupt line, or of employing a hierarchical or priority system. The latter can be organized two ways, either by using a separate physical interrupt wire from each external unit to the computer, or by connecting the external unit interrupts in head-to-tail fashion whereby priority is defined by position in the chain. Neither of the latter system is well suited to a flexible data bus system designed to accommodate a wide variety and number of external units since each time a change is made in the configuration of modules, numbers of separate physical wires must also be re-routed.

It will be appreciated that the foregoing discussion of general questions is of necessity superficial, though we believe it to indicate most of the major hardware considerations involved. Without going too deeply into details of software and logical design one other question regarding module addressing must be raised. This is the issue of what we term "generic" addressing and its importance can be seen with a simple example. Suppose the on-line system involves a number of external devices which must be turned on and off in exact time synchronism. Since any bus system is by definition sequential, in that only one set of address lines is used, it is not at first clear how this can be achieved. A solution to the problem can be provided by allowing units to recognize more than one address. Each unit or module recognizes its own unique address and having been so addressed one of the commands to which it can then respond is to *enable recognition of another address*. Such other addresses are termed generic addresses and they can be common to many different units. In this way the computer can issue generic commands which apply simultaneously to any subset of external modules, allowing them to operate in exact time synchronism.

By way of concluding this section on general design considerations it may be illuminating to consider a number of questions that can be asked regarding the logical organization of any on-line computer system. *Does it, for example, require special timing, logic and drive circuits to be added to an external unit before it can talk to the computer?* If the answer is yes then the chances are that considerably less experimental innovation will be carried out with the on-line hardware than would otherwise be the case.

Another important point to bear in mind is the ability of the system to check itself. *Can the computer tell what units are connected and whether they are operating?* This feature can be very important in systems employing many modules.

An area that is outside the scope of this account is that of programming, but it is obvious that the hardware and software of any on-line system must be harmoniously designed. Less frequently considered from the outset, however, is the question of the ease of debugging the operation of the entire on-line system. Our experience with the present system has shown the extreme desirability of being able to "force" external equipment to well defined conditions, by hand, as a check in debugging programs and hardware. This also is, therefore, a point to consider in comparing system configurations, *how difficult is it to debug the hardware-software interaction in preparing programs for the on-line system?*

A corollary to this point is the related one of investigating the degree to which the computer is able to exercise external equipment. In this connection it has been found extremely useful to prepare programs which operate all the computer-accessible features of a module sequentially. This approach allows convenient debugging of modules as they are produced since an operator can examine repetitive waveforms at his leisure, proceeding sequentially through a series of test conditions under programmatic control.

A final point involves the provision of an analog measurement capability within the data bus system. This has been found to be most useful in the PDP–8 system described here, and comprises a shielded twisted pair in the data bus cable connected to a central 12 bit ADC at the computer. In conjunction with suitable external modules this furnishes the ability to both measure and provide analog levels. Together with the digital capabilities of the system this provides a combined digital and analog capability which encompasses a broad range of applications.

The data bus

A diagram of the data bus system chosen for a PDP–8 and a single-user environment is shown in Figure 2. The logic of the operation of the data bus closely parallels that of the PDP–8 computer. Commands are sent to a particular module by placing the module address on the address lines and activating the instruction lines. The three instruction pulses in this system occur at 1 μs intervals and are .4 μs in width. Because one of the system rules is that the modules operate with instruction pulses of any length greater than $\backsim$.2 μs, there is no restriction on the maximum length of the cycle. (Thus the system may also be used with other computers of lower speed than the PDP–8 provided a suitable computer to data-bus interface is constructed.)

The type of operation performed with each instruction pulse has been standardized as follows.

Instruction Pulse	Operation
IOP1	Augmented Instructions
IOP2	and I/O Skip
IOP4	Input to computer
	Output to modules

Since it was useful to have many more than three instructions, a system for deriving a set of augmented instructions during IOP1 is used wherein the six low order bits of the computer *output* lines are each interpreted as a separate instruction. The six high order bits have been reserved to be used in coincidence to obtain 64 additional augmented instructions, should such a need arise in the future. IOP2 is used to generate all inputs so as to relax the requirement on the fall time of the input pulses which must be clear before the next instruction is executed.

A module requests attention from the computer by energizing a common interrupt line until it is serviced by the computer. The computer then interrogates the modules to determine which one is requesting service. (Since a priority interrupt system might be desirable when the system is interfaced to a different computer, four additional lines in the data bus have been provided, which may be used in this manner.)

The I/O skip line provides a means for a module to respond to interrogation by the computer. An affirmative response is signalled by energizing this line, which causes the PDP–8 to skip an instruction. If the system were connected to a different computer, the I/O skip line could set a status bit in the machine.

The distribution of the analog input lines to the module bins is performed with shielded twisted pair. The interface contains a parametric amplifier in a configuration which converts the

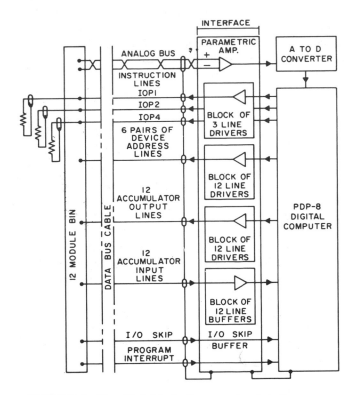

FIGURE 2—Simplified block diagram showing the computer interface and data bus cable

single ended 0 to —10V range of the analog to digital converter in the PDP–8 to a +10V to —10V differential system with good dynamic common mode rejection.

Since the logic of the bus system is compatible with the PDP–8, the interface is used simply to provide the level shifting and buffering that is necessary to communicate directly with the integrated circuits in the modules.

The interface unit converts the negative logic levels of the PDP–8 to standard microcircuit levels as used in the data bus system. In addition the interface input buffers provide noise filtering and an input threshold which can be varied in order to investigate noise margins. Tests have shown the data bus system capable of operating with cable lengths of more than 100 feet.

The data bus consists physically of 48 miniature coaxial cables, together with one shielded twisted pair, which interconnect the required number of module bins. Within the bins, the data bus loops through twelve 50 pin connectors into which the modules connect upon insertion into the bins.

The plug-in modules

Four general purpose modules were designed to operate in conjunction with the computer to assist in the operation and control of experiments and in the acquisition of the resulting data. Figure 3 shows one of each type of module installed in a module bin. A modified NIM power supply located at the rear of the bin provides local power for the modules.

The construction of all the modules is similar to

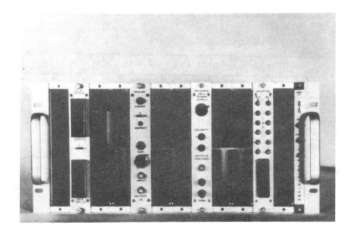

FIGURE 3—Photograph of one modified NIM bin containing one of each of the four modules

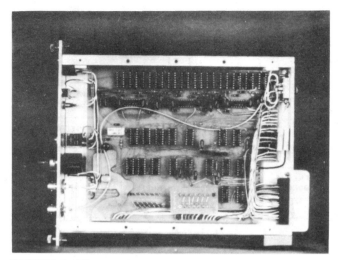

FIGURE 4—Photograph of a scaler module, showing the location of the plug-in address cards at the lower center of the printed circuit

that of the scaler, which is shown in Figure 4. The use of integrated circuits on a single special purpose board results in considerable reduction of cost and size over the more usual technique of using general purpose logic boards. The cost of the more complex modules is approximately $300 each.

In order to simplify programming and debugging, the module addresses are defined by small plug-in cards, visible in Figure 4, which may be changed at will. Removal of a unit for repair may thus be performed by switching its address card to a new module. A brief discussion of the structure and operation of each of the modules is given in the following sections.

Register

The register provides a general purpose interface for digital devices. It is capable of accepting a 12 bit word from an external device and inputting the word to the computer. It can also accept a word from the computer and present it, with buffering, to the outside world. The block diagram of this unit is shown in Figure 5. Table I lists the commands for the unit, most of which require no explanation.

The voltage levels for input and output are standard NIM and integrated circuit levels. The use of jam transfer makes resetting unnecessary, and allows alteration of selected bits of the register without even a momentary change in the other bits.

The use of master-slave flip-flops as buffers

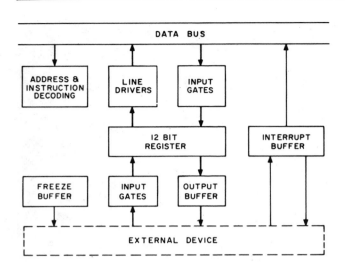

FIGURE 5—Simplified block diagram of register module

permits the register to be used as a hardware bit-reformatting device by connecting the outputs of the register to the inputs in the desired sequence. The word to be reformatted is sent out to the register and then read in as external data. This feature also permits use of some bits of the register as input and some as output, since by connecting a bit output line to the corresponding bit input line one makes the value of the bit independent of the Load Register from External Unit command.

The most serious stumbling block in interfacing an external device to a computer is not the compatibility of the input/output levels, but the necessity of establishing logical communication between the devices and the computer in a simple way. In the register the "freeze" circuitry allows the computer to command a device to remain stable while being read. The interrupt circuitry allows the device to request service from the computer. A busy line informs the unit of the status of its request.

Relay module

The logic of this module is shown in block diagram in Figure 6. It contains twelve single pole double throw high speed relays each capable of switching 3 amps. It is used in conjunction with a register module to handle signal and power levels which are inconvenient to handle electronically.

The relay driver commands are shown in Table II. The Test Unit Ready command allows the computer to test for the presence of the module.

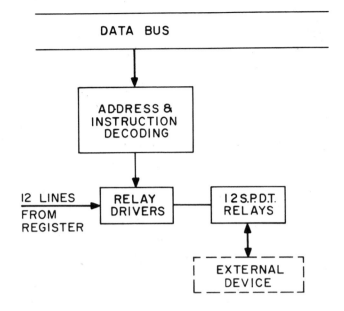

FIGURE 6—Simplified block diagram of relay driver module

Scaler

This module comprises a 12 bit binary ripple counter and the necessary logic to permit the module to function on the PDP–8 data bus system. In operation the module sends an interrupt to the computer for every 4096 input pulses. The system records the number of these interrupts and therefore functions as a scaler modulo 4096. At the end of the counting period the fractional count remaining in the scaler is added to the previously recorded total. Figure 7 is a logic block diagram of this unit. A unique feature in this design is the use of a two address command structure. The first of these is the generic address and the second the unit address. By use of

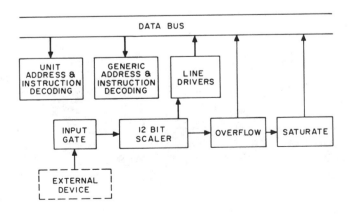

FIGURE 7—Simplified block diagram of scaler module

the generic address the computer can execute any one of three commands and have all scalers sharing that address respond simultaneously. The command structure for the unit is shown in Table III. Most of the commands are self-explanatory. While Increment operates in front of the input gate, Preset, which also increments, operates at all times. Enable Generic and Disable Generic permit the generic commands to be obeyed or ignored.

The overflow and saturate logic allow the computer to serve as the high order portion of the scaler in the following manner. When the high order bit of the scaler overflows, its overflow flip-flop is set and a program interrupt is sent to the computer. The computer then initiates a search using the Test Overflow instruction and thereby ascertains which module interrupted. Should a second overflow occur in a scaler before the previous one has been recorded by the computer then the saturate flip-flop is set. The computer can test this flip-flop, and thus either ascertain that the scaling has been performed without error or take appropriate action to insure correct scaling.

A rear panel switch connects the output of the most significant bit to either the overflow detecting circuitry or to a front panel connector, thus allowing the use of a second scaler module to form a 24 bit scaler if desired.

A discriminator is located at the input to the module and its level is adjustable from —5 volts to +5 volts. A front panel lamp indicates the status of the input gate.

A three position switch allows manual setting of the unit in either the start or stop condition, or returns this control to the computer.

Programmable power supply

The primary purpose of this module is to allow the computer to supply adjustable voltages to external devices. As shown in Figure 8, the computer controls the power supply voltage by causing rotation of a motor driven ten turn potentiometer which serves as an inexpensive analog memory. The series regulators, which operate by re-regulating the bin power, are built either as positive or negative supplies, and furnish 0 to 10 volts with overcurrent protection from 10 to 250 ma.

The control commands for this unit are shown in Table IV. The computer controls the unit by operating the potentiometer while simultaneously

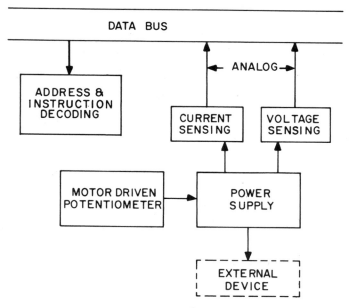

FIGURE 8—Simplified block diagram of power supply module

monitoring its output voltage, thus becoming part of a servo loop.

The front panel dial attached to the potentiometer indicates the supply voltage directly while also permitting manual setting of the voltage. In addition, the module may be used as an analog input from the operator, since the computer can, in effect, read the dial setting. Connection of the potentiometer shaft to other rotating equipment could also permit the computer to cause controlled motion in the external equipment should this be desired.

Sample applications

The system has been used to control, and process data from space experiments; to run nuclear analysis displays using DAC's; and as the data acquisition and control center for an automatic Hall-effect measuring system.

Figure 9 is a block diagram showing how experiments are connected into the system. Note that the computer output can control the experiment via the data bus. Computer input can store digital outputs from the experiment via the data bus, and make analog measurements via the analog bus and computer ADC.

Testing of a satellite charged particle spectrometer

A simplified block diagram of a satellite par-

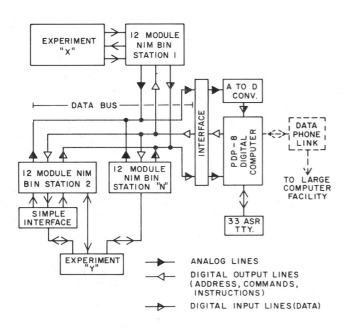

FIGURE 9—Simplified block diagram showing three bins connected to the data bus

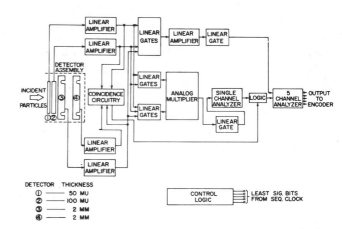

FIGURE 10—Simplified block diagram of a satellite experiment

ticle detector experiment is shown in Figure 10. Particles incident on the semiconductor detector assembly deposit their charge in one or more detectors. Coincidence logic applied to detector outputs determines the particle type, while the linear system sorts the energy of each particle type into one of five consecutive energy ranges.

Sixteen different particle identifying modes and the five channel energy ranges are controlled by the digital outputs from the spacecraft sequence clock in such a way that each mode lasts for approximately 10 seconds. For in-flight calibration the experiment contains a test pulse generator and two internal sources, each activated by certain states of the sequence clock once every six hours.

When tested in thermal vacuum in the laboratory by the computer system, outputs from a register unit simulated the sequence clock and thereby controlled the experiment modes. Calibration modes were arranged to alternate between the test pulser and internal source modes for every complete sequence of experiment modes, interspersed with complete sequences of no excitation. In this way a calibration cycle was repeated about once every 25 minutes, so large amounts of calibration data were processed in a relatively short time. The sequences of no excitation were useful for the observation of noise counts.

Scalers were used to accumulate the five chan-

nel outputs and to transfer the counts into the computer for printout.

Temperatures were also recorded. The outputs of temperature sensors were switched onto the analog bus using a relay driver and register combination, and were measured by the computer ADC.

Although not used in this particular test, it would be appropriate to use programmable power supply units in a test of this kind to investigate the effect of varying power supply voltages on circuit performance.

Automated hall-effect measurements

An ion implantation laboratory is in operation and many implanted diode samples will require extensive electrical testing. Each sample is expected to go through several stages of annealing, and following each stage measurements will be made to evaluate Hall coefficients, specific conductivity, carrier concentration and carrier mobility, over the temperature range 2°K to 300°K. Figure 11 shows a simplified block diagram of the electrical system.

A large number of voltage measurements from contact to contact are required at each temperature of interest, and the temperature stability at each measurement point must be carefully controlled.

Figure 12 is a flow chart showing the main steps in the computer controlled system. After the sample is mounted and ready to be lowered into the cryostat, the program starts with a comprehensive check of the hardware and a "FAULT" printout is generated indicating the nature of any malfunction. An "OK" printout in-

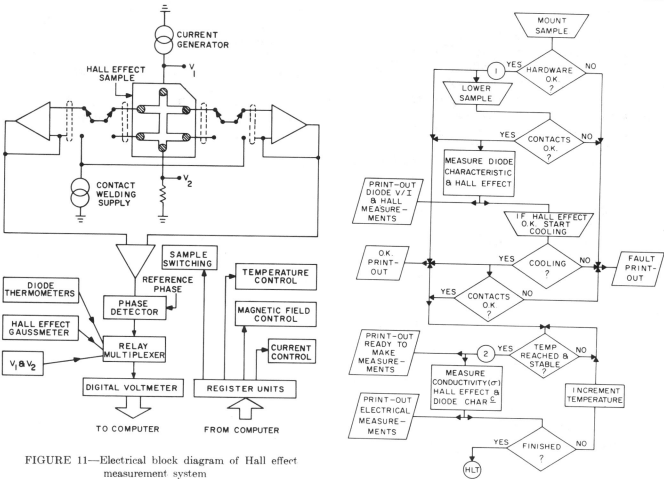

FIGURE 11—Electrical block diagram of Hall effect measurement system

FIGURE 12—Simplified flow-graph of Hall effect measurement

dicates the satisfactory completion of each test.

When the hardware test is completed the sample is manually lowered into the cryostat. The program continues by welding the sample contacts to ensure good connections and then checking that the voltage drop across each is within acceptable limits. The weld current and the contact test current paths are selected, by using relay units, so that they flow in the appropriate direction (depending on the diode junction type) and through any desired contact.

The next step is the measurement of a complete set of diode characteristics. These are made at several values of current, taken from a table in memory. A first set of Hall measurements is then made. Coefficients are processed and printed out. A manual decision is then made whether the Hall properties exhibited by the sample make continuation of the measurements worthwhile.

In continuing the test, the operator types in the upper and lower limits of temperature range and the increments at which measurements are

to be made, and opens the liquid helium valve on the cryostat. The computer selects the temperature values by interpolation from a table in memory, starting with the lowest specified temperature. The required temperature control is provided by the setting of a programmable power supply whose output controls the power applied to the sample heaters.

The computer proceeds in a similar way to control and check the remaining experimental conditions, as indicated in Figure 12.

The measurement of each of the many voltages is accomplished by using relay units as multiplexers at the input of a digital voltmeter. Two register modules are used to receive the DVM digital data and transfer it to the computer via the data bus. One of these registers is used to trigger, and also to recognize the end of each DVM measurement, signaling to the computer that data is ready for input.

Other applications

Many uses other than those already described have been considered. An example is that of automated sample liquid scintillation counting in which programmable power supplies can provide levels defining pulse-height windows. In conjunction with scalers this provides pulse height analysis, while relay/register combinations can exercise electromechanical control.

The system may also serve as a versatile, economical alternative to large multiparameter pulse height analyzers when used in conjunction with pulse analog-to-digital converters, and fast digital-to-analog converters for CRT displays.

When connected to an engineering breadboard, the system has been used as a versatile programmed pulser and circuit tester.

DISCUSSION

The point can be made, and with justification, that computer manufacturers realized years ago that peripheral hardware was best handled on a bus basis, which is all that is being achieved with the system described here. This is quite true. The differences that arise with on-line systems are primarily those of degree (with the exception of analog bus facilities) rather than those of kind. One example will suffice to make the point. The present system might be required to handle 60 scalers all counting at $\sim$1 MHz (e.g., a data rate of 6×10^7 bits/second) with the subsidiary requirement that various subsets of them be gated on and off in exact time synchronism. Such requirements are not encountered with standard computer peripherals for which supervisory control and timing can always be exercised in a logical sequential manner.

The major point being made here is really a different one, namely how to design a modular system with a small number of different types of modules to encompass a large number of on-line tasks. While examples of such tasks are endless it is hoped the outline of the rationale of the design, together with the sample applications given, demonstrates the flexibility that such an on-line modular analog-digital system can provide.

ACKNOWLEDGMENTS

It is a pleasure to acknowledge the many contributions of others to the work presented here.

Notable among these, have been E. H. Cooke-Yarborough and his associates at AERE Harwell in discussions of design philosophy and in providing information on their IANUS system, R. Stensgaard of the University of Aarhus in all phases of the work on Hall effect measurements, and W. L. Brown of Bell Telephone Laboratories for constant encouragement and support.

IOP	DATA BIT	COMMAND
1	6	Test Interrupt
1	7	Generate Interrupt from Computer
1	8	Disable Interrupt
1	9	Enable Interrupt
1	10	Set Freeze Output
1	11	Load Register from External Unit
2	—	Load Computer from Register
4	—	Load Register from Computer

TABLE I—Register module commands

IOP	COMMAND
1	Test Unit Ready
2	Enable Relay Drivers
4	Disable Relay Drivers

TABLE II—Relay module commands

A. UNIT ADDRESS COMMANDS

IOP	DATA BIT	COMMAND
1	6	Test Overflow
1	7	Test Saturate
1	8	Disable Generic
1	9	Enable Generic
1	10	Increment
1	11	Clear
2	—	Load Computer from Scaler
4	—	Preset

B. GENERIC ADDRESS COMMANDS

IOP	COMMAND
1	Start Scaling
2	Clear
4	Stop Scaling

TABLE III—Scaler module commands

IOP	DATA BIT	COMMAND
1	11	Motor Off
1	10	Measurement Off
1	9	Measure Current
1	8	Measure Voltage
2		Motor Counterclockwise (Lower Voltage)
4		Motor Clockwise (Raise Voltage)

TABLE IV—Power supply module commands

Line-Sharing Systems for Plant Monitoring And Control

RICHARD L. ARONSON, Control Engineering

Centralized monitoring and control is old hat in the flow process industries. Now many other industries are discovering major economic gains in detailed monitoring of the whole plant from a single control center: As a result, many users are developing a common complaint: cable congestion and soaring wiring costs.

Hence a new generation of control equipment is cropping up, combining sophisticated communication techniques with the monitoring and control function. All feature line sharing, which simplifies the rest of the control system as well as cutting down on wiring. Some are aimed at production control, some at process control, and several are universal systems which can be turned to a wide spectrum of in-plant uses.

No two of these systems are exactly alike, or address exactly the same problems in the same way. Here is a survey that looks at each application and its requirements, and details the available hardware.

General manufacturing is now following the lead of the process industries to centralized monitoring and control. It is becoming apparent that major economic gains are available from reducing machine and manpower idle time, reducing materials shrinkage and scrap, improving tool life, and quickly detecting production-rate drops on the plant floor. This requires close monitoring of materials flow, machine status, tooling conditions, and personnel activity. Getting the correct service—maintenance, lift truck, or tooling—to a machine fast when it halts for any reason requires that many details of shop and machine status be available in the control room. The progress of work orders must be monitored so people can be reassigned as needed and so the size of production runs can be controlled.

The result is an increasing number of manufacturing facilities with hundreds of "process points" fitted with sensors or manual input devices and wired to a central control room.

The centralized systems presently installed in both the process and the manufacturing industries can be called "first generation" in one sense: Each monitored or controlled point is separately wired to the control room. And therein lies a problem: wiring congestion—the costs and difficulties of connecting hundreds or thousands of in-plant points to the control center.

The process industries, as the leaders in centralized control, are also the leaders in discovering this problem, but other users are also finding that wiring costs are worth close study.

The basic labor and material costs of installing wire are considerable by themselves. Some figures from the process industries can indicate the general problems facing all kinds of users.

An instrument engineer who made a special study of the subject (Ref. 1) cited some costs (as of 1969 in the Gulf Coast area) that can serve as an indication of costs nationally. For multiconductor cable (12 to

Reprinted with permission from *Contr. Eng.*, vol. 18, pp. 57–76, Jan. 1971.

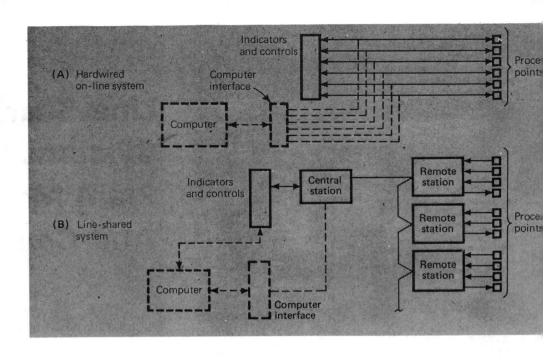

FIG. 1. In a hardwired monitoring or control system (A), every process point is separately wired to the control center. Part B illustrates a line-shared system (color) inserted between the process points and the control center. There may or may not be a computer.

36 pairs per bundle) he showed prices ranging from about 17 to 67 cents a pair-foot, depending on the type of conductor—whether individual pairs or the entire bundle is shielded; whether open trays, covered trays, or conduit is used; whether the routing is overhead or underground.

Since a typical centralized process control system will monitor as many as 500 to 1,000 points, often 1,000 or more feet from the control room, these rates imply basic wiring costs in the hundreds of thousands of dollars.

This finding is consistent with the wiring costs reported by other process users. One control engineer in petroleum processing said that wiring typically costs 17 percent of the total controls budget for a large centralized system (which can often run into seven figures). Another in the same industry said that installation costs (of which a major share is wiring) are typically 70 to 75 percent of the cost of hardware (instruments, computer, and accessories).

In discrete manufacturing, with fewer points monitored on any one production unit, there tends to be less use of multiconductor cables and more of individual wires or pairs, bringing the cost per pair-foot up considerably.

After the initial cost of installing the wire, the conductors must be "rung out" and connections verified—a considerable cost in direct labor and often also a penalty in production downtime.

Thus in many environments there is money available to buy equipment which significantly reduces the amount of in-plant wiring required for on-line monitoring and control.

This requires the sharing of communication channels by two or more process points, usually by time sharing in a fixed or variable sequence. (The term "process point" will be used broadly in this article to mean a process measurement or control point, a machine-monitoring point, or a remote data entry point in the production area.)

Single channel

Line-sharing systems of this type are now commercially available; 16 of them are surveyed in this special report. Although differing widely in features and applications, all correspond generally to part B of Figure 1, in which the portion in color is a line-sharing subsystem which has been inserted into the conventional on-line system illustrated in part A.

In the conventional hardwired system, all process points are wired separately to the indicators and control devices in the central location. In a line-shared system, signals to and from individual process points are passed sequentially along a single communication channel. This operation and the associated signal processing (e.g., multiplexing or conversion. between analog and digital) are performed by the central station and the remote stations of the line-shared system.

In some situations, the signal-processing circuitry in the central and remote stations are additive to the basic system—for example, if there are conversions to digital and back to analog in what would otherwise be an all-analog system—and the cost must be subtracted from the saving in wiring costs. The advent of medium- and large-scale integration of semiconductor circuitry is strongly affecting the economic feasibility of line sharing in a variety of industrial applications.

Each of the 10 by 13 by 5 in. boxes (see cover) in the I/C Engineering Corp. Uniplex system contains all the logic and signal-conditioning circuitry required to handle 30 channels of discrete and analog process data—roughly equivalent to the functions performed in a six-foot cabinet in a system using discrete components. (The A-to-D converters in the Uniplex system are each fraction-of-an-inch semiconductor chips costing less than $50.)

In certain environments there are other benefits besides wiring savings to be weighed against the cost of a line-sharing system. Where a computer is used for monitoring or control, interface gear—including, typically, multiplexers and A-to-D converters—is always required. The adoption of the line-sharing configuration can mean, in effect, moving this interface gear from the control room out to the remote location.

And the arrival of plant data in a formatted or controlled fashion on a common bus can considerably reduce the complexity of the control room wiring and panels, and reduce the cpu overhead required to get the plant data into the computer memory.

Each remote station is placed to serve a number of process points, typically in a single plant area or on one process unit. The number and location of remote stations are chosen to get the best tradeoff among the amount of wire laid down, the dollar cost of the remote stations, and the desired distribution of data traffic for readaround-time requirements and system security. (Readaround time, as it is used here, means the time required to complete one programmed scan of all process points and return to the first point in the scan cycle.)

Three types

Of the 16 systems surveyed here, no two are at all alike, and none is a true all-purpose system; the requirements in different environments are too dissimilar. A process plant, for example, requires the handling of proportional signals at relatively high accuracies and resolutions. A large discrete manufacturing facility requires provision for many manual inputs at remote points. And a wide variety of other special needs arise: security provisions (check-before-operate and automatic error detection), interrupt capability, and short readaround time for fast processes, for example.

Hence some definitions will be useful.

The systems presently available can be placed in three broad categories: process monitoring and control systems, production control systems, and universal systems.

Process monitoring and control systems emphasize the transmission of physical process measurements and physical control signals, discrete and proportional. These systems are characterized by medium to fast readaround time, good resolution and accuracy of proportional signals, provision for error checking, and provision for transmitting process interrupts to the control center.

Of the 11 process systems listed here (see Table I), six are complete systems (except for instrumentation), including the computer and the process interface equipment. Of these six, two (L&N Conitel and the Hitachi system) are designed fundamentally as computer systems; the other four (I/C Uniplex, Bristol Datamaster, General Electric GE-TAC, and AMS MUX 2000) incorporate hardwire scan-sequence control, with computer control as an option. Two more systems (IBM 1070 and CDC 1590/1591) are essentially multiplexing subsystems designed to be inserted into computer-control systems. Another two (Herco TDAS-2/A and the EMC Information System) are stand-alone analog multiplexing systems with optional computer interfaces. The eleventh system (Motorola Omnipoint) is a slow, low-cost system with limited capacity to handle analog inputs, oriented more to general monitoring and alarm surveillance than to process control.

Production control systems handle manually entered data and discrete inputs automatically sensed within the production machinery. The two systems in this category (IBM 2790 and General Electric CommanDir Factory Feedback) are oriented to production control in discrete manufacturing. They handle production and material quantities, machine status information, and labor reporting. Manual data entry is typically via badge or card readers,

Large-scale integration is a major factor in the economic feasibility of line-sharing systems. This 1/8-in.-sq chip contains all of the encoding, multiplexing, and serial transmission circuitry of a Larse Corp. "SEN" (Send-ENcode) station capable of serving 16 process points.

Desktop console of American Multiplex Systems MUX 2000, a process-oriented system which scans 3,000 points a second. Process points manually selected at bottom right are displayed as decimal digits. Lights at left are for interrupts and alarms; top numerical display at right is time of day.

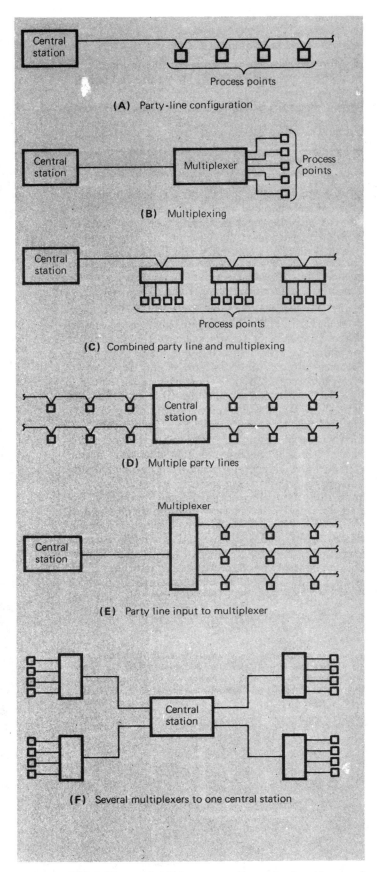

FIG. 2. Six ways in which a common line can be shared by several data sources (process points). The two fundamental configurations are the party line (A) and multiplexing (B). The other four are combinations of these.

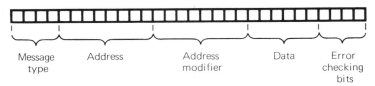

FIG. 3. Typical formatted digital word. This one is composed of 30 binary digits in five groups, each designated for a specific function in the message. This contrasts with an unformatted digital transmission, in which specific digits have no necessary function.

pushbuttons, and thumbwheel switches. The automatically sensed data is generally machine cycles or cycle counts, machine status (e.g., "down" or "running"), or digital outputs from such devices as in-line conveyor scales.

CommanDir can be configured as several separate small systems in different plant areas without a computer, or as a plant-wide integrated system using a GE-PAC 30 minicomputer. The IBM 2790 can operate off-line using a programmable special-purpose terminal, or it can interface with any of several process-control or edp computers.

The universal systems are inexpensive line-shared digital communication systems for in-plant use. They differ from the other two types of system in two ways: (1) Their remote and central station units are general-purpose designs not oriented to a specific application; and (2) the pulse stream is unformatted. The pulses are multiplexed and demultiplexed pulse by pulse, and the combining of pulses to create a formatted message is performed outside the communication system by the adjacent interface equipment and by the computer (if used). The universal systems are suitable for many types of production and process control, offering considerable cost savings and versatility in exchange for some system design effort to mate them to the application. Of the three, the CompuDyne Dynaplex requires and incorporates a minicomputer, the Larse Data Communicator has several free-standing modes of operation as well as optional computer control, and the Digicable is a very simple sequential-scan pulse multiplexer.

Party line and multiplex

All the systems accomplish line sharing by time division. There are two fundamental configurations: the party line (part A of Figure 2), in which a number of remote units in different locations are connected in parallel across a single channel (typically a twisted pair of wires); and multiplexing (part B), in which all the process points are connected to a single remote unit (the multiplexer). In both cases, messages to or from successive process points are transmitted through the common channel successively in time. This scan cycle may be programmed and timed from the remote locations or from the control center. Identification of the remote station may be by coded address (in the data stream or on a separate channel)

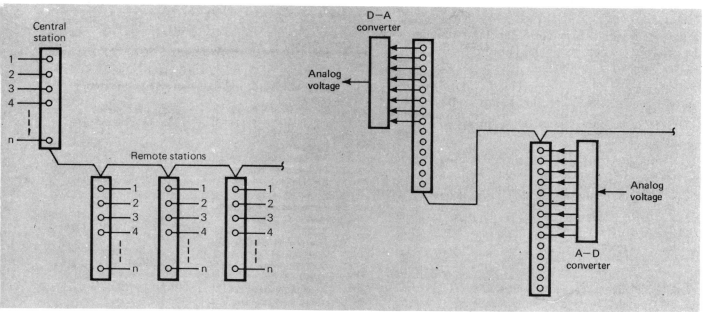

FIG. 4. In unformatted pulse transmission, the binary number impressed on terminal *i* at the sending station is reproduced at terminal *i* of the receiving station. The meaning of the pulse is defined outside the system.

FIG. 5. How pulses are grouped to transmit complex information through an unformatted system. The A-to-D converter uses eight terminals to supply the analog input in digital form. The binary number is reproduced on the corresponding eight terminals at the receiving station.

or by position in the scanning sequence.

A common configuration is a combination of party line and multiplexing (part C of Figure 2). Each multiplexer serves all the process points in its physical area, and the multiplexers in turn are on a party line. Time division of the remote points proceeds in this configuration just as it does in the other two. Some of these systems require that all points connected to one multiplexer be scanned before proceeding to the next multiplexer. Other systems, with more complex control provisions, can scan in any programmed sequence of points without regard to which multiplexers the successive points are connected to. In either case the multiplexers are generally each placed to serve a locality—one manufacturing area or one process unit, for example.

These basic combinations of line sharing and multiplexing are pyramided in the commercially available systems to form more complex configurations. For example, there may be two or more party lines from one control center (part D of Figure 2), or each input line to a multiplexer may itself be a party line connected to several process points (part E), or several multiplexers may be connected by separate dedicated lines to one control center (part F).

Note that a party line need not be one continuous conductor running around a plant. It can branch wherever convenient to minimize wire runs. As long as it is electrically a single channel or pair, it is effectively a party line. (Branching—especially if several branches radiate from the control center—increases reliability by decreasing the number of points dependent on one section of conductor.)

Types of signal

There are four fundamental types of signal used in the systems described here:

■ Formatted digital
■ Unformatted pulse
■ Character code (a special case of formatted digital pulse)
■ Analog voltage

Formatted digital messages can take any of a wide variety of forms, usually based on binary coding. There is generally a fundamental unit, called the "word" or "frame" (or both, in a two-level structure), with either a fixed number of bits or a fixed basic number of bits with additional word-elements of a fixed size.

In general, the meaning of a bit is determined by its position in the frame. Figure 3, for example, illustrates a typical format, with designated bits to indicate the type of message (interrogation, response, command, interrupt), the data address, the address modifier (e.g., to designate one of several process points served through the addressed remote station), the actual data (for example, a proportional variable in eight binary digits), and redundant bits for error detection.

The universal systems use **unformatted pulse communication**. This consists of multiplexing *n* binary discrete inputs (see Figure 4)—as impressed from outside the system onto *n* terminals at the sending station—onto a channel serially and then demultiplexing these binary signals to *n* corresponding terminals at the receiving station. Thus the binary value of, say, terminal 5 at the sending station is reproduced at terminal 5 of the receiving station.

These binary signals are not necessarily grouped in any specific way; they may represent the closure state of *n* unrelated contacts. To transmit complex information, the binary discretes are grouped outside the system. In Figure 5, for example, an analog voltage is resolved by an A-to-D converter to eight binary digits which are impressed onto eight terminals of a sending station. The corresponding terminals at the receiving station are connected to a D-to-A converter, which reproduces the analog voltage. The remaining terminals may be similarly grouped or may each be transmitting separate binary discrete information.

Of the three universal systems, the CompuDyne DynaPlex system includes options which structure the bit stream as required to transmit complex information. The Larse system is formatted for the purpose of error checking (34 bits for 16 data bits), but the verified data bits are available for grouping at the user's convenience.

Some systems oriented to manual inputs and business data processing use a format built on one of the standard eight-bit **character codes** (ASCII or EBC-DIC). Complex messages are transmitted by assembling strings of these characters, which make up the message header and the data.

Finally, as noted, three systems (Herco TDAS-2/A, Motorola Omnipoint, and the EMC system) multiplex **analog voltages** into time-shared lines.

Process Control Systems

The 11 process monitoring and control systems included in this survey fall into the five categories identified in Table I. Design details and specifications of each system are listed in Table II (page 64), and each is briefly described in the text which follows.

The first group, the fast systems, are capable of substituting for large numbers of hard wires in the dynamic control loops of fast processes. They can be used as a digital line-shared link in an analog system (part B of Figure 6), so that the analog controllers in the control room look and act as if they were hard-wired to the process points. If a computer is performing supervisory control, the process measurements are available in digital form for the computer. In effect, the computer-process interface (analog multiplexing, A-to-D conversion, etc.) has been moved out to the vicinity of the process points.

Alternatively, the fast systems mate very well with the direct digital control (ddc) configuration (part C), since for communication purposes they convert the process variables to the sequential digital form required by the ddc computer.

Of the three systems listed in this category, two are available in the U.S. (The Hitachi system, not presently exported out of Japan, is included for possible interest in its novel approach to line security.)

Of the two, I/C Engineering's Uniplex is a complete system, capable of stand-alone operation or interfacing with a computer as in parts B and C of Figure 6. It is implemented in medium- and large-scale integrated circuitry; at $400 a point for a large system it is competitive with direct-wiring costs without considering other benefits.

The second system, CDC's 1590/1591, is actually

Table I. Process-Oriented Party-Line Systems.

System	Analog points per sec (assuming no discretes)
Fast systems	
Control Data 1590/1591 (with 2 megabps option)	1,360*
Hitachi Data Highway	5,000
I/C Uniplex	5,000
Medium-speed systems	
AMS MUX 2000	325
Slow voice- and subvoice-grade modem-oriented systems	
ACCO Bristol Datamaster	10 per party line at 2,400 bps
Control Data 1590/1591 (with 2,400 bps option)	30 per party line
General Electric GE-TAC	33 at 1,200 bps
IBM 1070	5 at 134 bps; 22 at 600 bps
L&N Conitel	37.5 at 1,200 bps; 75 at 2,400 bps

*Control Data says this is limited by the computing time required to service each point. On the basis of line speed the figure would be higher, but CDC has not calculated it.

Analog multiplexing systems oriented to thermocouple monitoring	
Electronic Modules Corp. Information System	40
Herco TDAS-2/A	40 standard (1 to 200 optional)
Slow low-cost system oriented to alarm-limit surveillance and limited control	
Motorola Omnipoint	67

a subsystem option of the company's 1700 process computer line, which falls into the high-speed class when equipped with its 2-megabit per sec option. Implemented in discrete transistor circuitry, it has been available about four years. The remote unit, in a standard relay rack, has a special "ddc station controller" output—actually an amplitude-modulated pulse signal.

All three systems incorporate redundant bits in the transmission format and perform automatic error checking to protect the validity of information at the control center.

Note that the speeds given in Table I are for the special case of monitoring analog inputs only, with no discrete inputs or command outputs, to set a common basis for comparison. (This was necessary because each system differs from the others in the ratio of analog to discrete scanning rates, and in the penalty against monitoring rate imposed by control transmissions to the remote stations. To evaluate these systems in terms of an actual application, the performance specifications must be analyzed using a representative mix of analog and discrete inputs, and of input vs output traffic.)

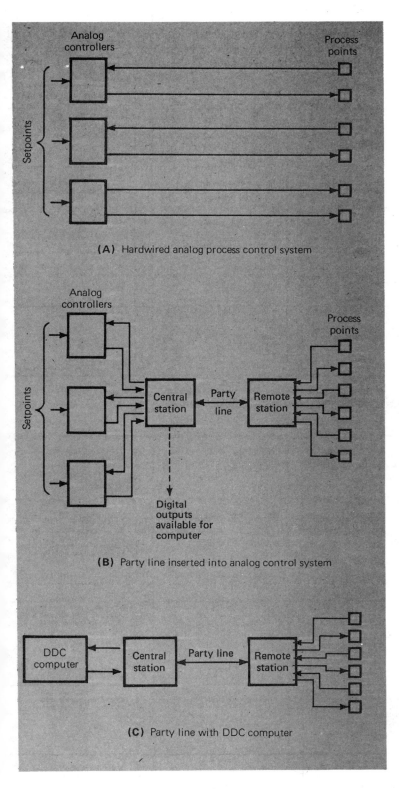

(A) Hardwired analog process control system

(B) Party line inserted into analog control system

(C) Party line with DDC computer

FIG. 6. Fast process-oriented systems can be used as digital line-shared links (B) in analog systems (A). In a ddc installation (C), the line-shared system can convert the process variables to the required sequential digital form at the remote station.

The second group, medium-speed systems (between 100 and 1,000 analog points per sec) contains only one entrant, the MUX 2000 System by American Multiplex Systems. Whereas two of the fast systems, the CDC 1590/1591 and the I/C Uniplex, use basic bit rates of 2 megabps and 500K bps respectively, AMS uses 150K bps. Interestingly, this system becomes more nearly comparable to the fast ones when a mix of discrete and analog points is considered; at a two-to-one mix, it scans over 3,000 points a second.

Since the manufacturer's stated price calculates to $37 a point on the basis of fully loaded remote stations, this is apparently a very economical system in applications mated to its speed characteristics.

(It should be noted that it has not been possible to check out exactly what has been included in each stated price. It is not always clear, for example, that necessary interfacing equipment is included, and in some cases it definitely has not. In addition, the system configuration on which the per-point price has been calculated varies widely in the ratio of discrete to analog points, although the latter are much more expensive to process. Thirdly, the per-point price of an actual system will depend heavily on how well the remote terminals are loaded—that is, how much idle capacity must be purchased in order to locate remote stations everywhere they are needed. And of course due recognition must be given to basic system differences: A multiplexing subsystem which requires an existing full control computer installation can't be directly compared in terms of dollars per process point with a free-standing complete system.)

The third category of process systems is the relatively slow systems which communicate through voice- and subvoice-grade modems, at bit rates ranging from 60 to 2,400 bps. Though too slow for most dynamic ddc applications, they are fast enough (10 to 75 analog points per sec) for many instances of setpoint control and for direct control where there are no significant dynamics.

With all five of the slow systems, two or more party lines can be run from the central station. This greatly increases the effective speed, since each line operates at the speed shown in the table. In addition, the multiple paths increase system security.

All five of these systems use the type of modem commonly employed to interface edp equipment to the common carriers, and all can easily be connected via leased lines to dispersed facilities.

Several of these systems were designed originally for supervisory control of dispersed facilities: pipelines, utility transmission lines, tank farms, etc. They are included here because process users or the vendors, or both, have determined that they fit the requirements of certain types of in-plant process control systems, in terms of computer compatibility, operating speeds, control capabilities, and the accuracy and resolution with which they handle analog quantities.

Table II. Details of Process-Oriented Systems

System	System size	Data structure and security	System speed	Communications and wiring requirements
American Multiplex Systems, Inc. MUX 2000	8 remote stations max (128 in Super MUX). 68 process points max per station. 544 max per system (8704 for Super MUX).	Addressing on separate channel from data stream. 8-bit word format. Self-test and security features.	240 millisec for 128 binary discretes and 64 analogs. Thus more than 3,000 points per sec with a mix of two discretes to one analog. Basic bit rate 150K bps.	Baseband modulation. Party line is 3 shielded twisted pair. 3,000 ft maximum distance.
ACCO Bristol Datamaster Div. Datamaster	64 remote stations max per party line. Each station can monitor or control 64 process points for 4,096 max per party line. Central station can handle two or more party lines for more points or faster readaround time.	Model 425: 33-bit word Bose Chaudhuri [1] code; 18 data bits per word. Model 325: 18-bit word includes address, data, and parity.	Bit rate determined by type of modem and transmission line. Readaround time determined by number of party lines.	Wide range of modems. Wiring specs determined by desired line speed.
Control Data Corp. 1590/1591 Remote Input/Output Subsystem	8 remote stations max. Each remote station can accommodate a max of 4,096 binary discrete inputs, 8,192 binary discrete outputs, 128 event-counter inputs, 3,072 analog inputs, 1,024 analog outputs, ASCII outputs to 12 typewriters, and 128 process interrupts.	32-bit frame Bose-Chaudhuri [1] code. Address, check bits, and 16 data bits per frame. Automatic retransmission on error detection. Special short 16-bit frame for acknowledge valid transmission and other special functions.	Optional basic bit rate 2 megabps or 2,400 bps. For 2 megabps, the effective data rates below are based on computing time per point (i.e., not line-limited). Points per sec: 2 meg bps 2,400 bps analog in 1,360 30 discrete in 57,600 500 analog out 592 19 discrete out 1,200 300 ASCII out 15.6 5.8	Wideband unit has internal 2 megabps modem and requires RG-8/U coax. 3.5 miles max. Voice-speed version uses standard modem—typically 2,400 bps binary synchronous, 4-wire, half-duplex operation.
Electronic Modules Corp. Industrial Information System	Remote multiplexer for 100 points min. Indefinitely expandable in 100-point increments.	16-bit digital address. Process variables multiplexed as analog voltages. Self-check (fault and calibration) before and after each transmission.	40 points per sec max.	Twisted pairs.
General Electric GE-TAC	29 remote stations max. Each can monitor 100 analog inputs, 1,000 binary discrete inputs, and control 100 setpoints or discretes.	30-bit word plus one sync bit, divided into 6-bit characters of which the sixth is a parity bit. Longitudinal parity checks. Select-checkback-operate on control functions.	Voice-grade speeds, depending on choice of modem. At 1,200 bps, reads 100 data points from one remote station in less than 3 sec.	Voice-grade lines. Modems separately procured.
Houston Engineering Research Corp. (Herco) TDAS-2/A	10 remote multiplexers max, each monitoring a max of 100 points; 1,000 points max per system.	Digital addressing. Inputs converted to compensated current signals for transmission. Zero and full-scale check and thermocouple fault check between points.	Optionally 1 to 200 points per sec.	Open pair 10,000 ft max. 22 AWG copper pair 5,000 ft max. With serial address option will work over two standard in-plant telephone pair: one for address, one for data (current) signals.
Hitachi, Ltd. Digital Data Highway System [2]	100 remote stations max per coax loop. More loops can be added for security or added capacity. Input, output, and interrupt stations count separately to make 100. 5 analog and 5 discrete points per station.	Address and data on separate party lines. 16-bit data word includes parity.	5,000 process points per sec, input or output, proportional or binary discrete.	Wideband. Requires two unbroken coax loops (inductive coupling; see text) per 100 remote stations. Max loop length 1 km.
IBM 1070 Process Communication System	Indefinitely expandable by adding communication channels and line-interface hardware. 26 remote multiplexers max per channel; 50 to 300 points per multiplexer. Analog input requires three points.	Built on asynchronous bcd character: Start B-A-8-4-2-1-Stop. Proportional signals are three decimal digits in this form. Address in data stream. Horizontal and vertical parity check.	Basic bit rate 134.5 or 600, depending on choice of line and modem, providing 14.8 or 66.7 characters per sec.	Leased voice or subvoice lines or comparable on-premises twisted pair. 8 miles max on-premises distance.
I/C Engineering Corp. Uniplex 500	256 remote stations max. Each can monitor or control 30 points, in an optional mix of proportional and discrete, for a total of 7,680 process points.	40-bit word: 4-bit message code (interrogate, response), 12-bit address, 12 bits self-test and priority, and 12 bits of data (one proportional or 12 binary discretes). Check before operate and check after operate.	Basic bit rate 500,000 bps. 5,000 analog or 60,000 binary discrete points per sec. In a typical mix, readaround time for 500 analog and 1,200 discretes is 125 millisec, or 8 times per sec.	Wideband FSK and phase shift keying. One interrogation and one response party line of Twinax cable.
Leeds & Northrup Co. Conitel 2050	128 switched party lines max. 512 remote stations max per line, or 65,536 remote stations. 15 analog or 180 discrete points monitored max per station; 1 analog or 12 discrete points max controlled per station.	Serial pulse-code modulation, address in data stream. 31-bit word; 26 data and address bits and 5 redundant bits in Bose Chaudhuri [1] code.	Basic bit rate is 30-2,400 bps depending on modem and line. Readaround time can be reduced by adding more lines, reducing points per line. One fully loaded remote station (15 analog or 180 discrete inputs; one setpoint or 12 discrete outputs) is scanned and controlled in 0.4 sec. at 1,200 bps.	Any type of line. Baseband modulation at lowest speeds, otherwise modem using FSK required.
Motorola Instrumentation and Control Inc. Omnipoint	20 area stations max per system. 50 remote stations max per area station. 10 process points max per remote station. Hence 10,000 process points max.	8-bit parallel address separate from data and command stream. Validity tests and check-before-operate on discrete monitoring and command signals. Monitoring of analog signals is an option requiring an additional pair of wires; signals are multiplexed to the control center in analog form.	15 millisec per point (67 points per sec), monitoring or control.	8-wire party line from central station to area stations. 14-wire party line from each area station to its remote stations. (10 and 16 respectively when analog voltages are to be handled.)

1. This is a cyclic code said to possess unusual error detection capability for its coding efficiency (84 percent, or 84 data bits for each 100 bits transmitted). According to Control Data, 100 percent of errors of burst length of ten bits or less are detected.

Computer role	Process monitoring provisions		Process control provisions		Costs
	Analog	Binary discrete	Analog	Discrete	
Self-programmed on internal seven-day digital clock. Interface available to computer for stored program control.	Remote station includes A-D conversion to 0.1% accuracy resolved to 8 or 10 bits.	Inputs from vendor-provided primary sensors or customer-provided contact closures.	Voltage	Amplifier or contact closure outputs.	MUX 2000 console, central terminal, and 8 remote stations: under $20,000.
Manual or hardwire programmed operation. Optional Bristol Meta-Logger computer for operator-guide process control.	Remote station includes A-D conversion resolved to three decimal digits.	Contact closures	Setpoint: 3 bcd digits.	Yes	Simplest central station about $8,000. One remote station handling up to 64 process points $5,000 to $6,000. Central station with computer and programs $25,000 to $100,000 depending on options.
This is a subsystem for CDC 1700 control computer systems.	Remote station includes A-D conversion resolved to 10, 12, or 14 bits including sign. Fast and slow conversion options.	Contact closures	Voltage. For ddc: amplitude-modulated pulse.	Register output. Process-latched contact closure.	Local adapter $16,000. One remote station with no process interfacing gear $16,000.
System can stand alone, operating on a hardwired or stored scan cycle program. Interfaces available to IBM 1800 and GE 4020.	Remote relay multiplexing and amplifying. Central station digitizes for logging, display, or computer input at 0.1% accuracy, 0.01% resolution.	Not applicable	Not applicable	Not applicable	Not available
Works stand-alone under hardwire program control or incorporates GE mini- or full-sized process computer.	Remote station includes A-D conversion resolved to ±1999 decimal.	Contact closures	Setpoint to 3 decimal digits and jog pulses.	Yes	Minimum system to monitor 20 analog points and control 20 discretes: master station about $10,600; one remote about $13,300.
Two modes: operator manually selects data point for digital display, or optional computer programs the scan cycle.	±2 deg F over 2,000 deg span accuracy including thermocouples and digitizing at central station. Resolve to 1/8 deg F.	Not applicable	Not applicable	Not applicable	1,000-point central station: operator panel and display, master station, and computer interface—$13,000. Five 200-point remote stations with compensation and conditioning—$35,000. Thus about $48/point for a large computer-interfaced system.
Requires one or more Hitachi HIDIC computer for system control.	Remote station includes analog multiplexing and A-D conversion.	Contact closure or other binary input.	D-A converter in remote station.	Static register	Not available
Interfaces to 360, 1440, 1460, or operates off-line to 1050 batch terminal.	Remote station includes A-D conversion. Resolves to 0-1,800 or optionally 0-7,800 in three characters by using A, B, and C bits. Overall analog accuracy 0.2% or 0.3%.	Stores momentary contact closures. Counts pulses and stores count. Accepts decimal input on 10 lines.	Pulse train of controlled number of counts. Pulse duration signal.	Binary discrete or 1-of-10 digital outputs, momentary or latching.	Typical remote 1070 installation $30,000 for one location. Price of required central-station equipment depends on configuration.
Stand-alone self-programmed or controlled by optional computer. Interface available for Varian 520i/620i.	Remote station includes A-D conversion, resolved to 12 bits. Accuracy 0.25%.	Accepts contact closures. Reed relay isolation provided internally in remote station.	Optional 4-20 ma or 0-5 volts provided by remote station.	Isolated contact closures	Typical 50-point system $1,000 a point all costs including installation. Additional points approach $400 a point in a large system.
Lockheed MAC-16 integral to system. All system functions under computer control. Software packages available for monitoring and setpoint control.	Analog scaling and A-D converters included in remote stations. Single (12-bit) or double (14-bit) precision with or without sign. Options for current, voltage, or resistance inputs. Balance in 1.0 to 1.7 millisec.	Accepts contact closures.	0-10 volts	Optional: reset, close, and trip, for circuit breakers; interposed relay: timed latch or customer latched.	Hardware, including central station equipment, should cost about $200 to $300 per point for a large system (1,000 points), not including wiring or installation.
Incorporates Motorola MDP-1000 Miniprocessor.	Alarm limits of analog quantities are handled as binary discretes. Operator can change limits from teletypewriter. Optionally, analog voltages are multiplexed onto extra pair in party line.	Accepts contact closures.	Change alarm-limit values. No actual proportional control.	Contact closures	$40,000 for a 200-point system not including wiring and installation. Designed for customer installation.

2. This Japanese system is not commercially available in the U.S., but some of its features are included here for their technical interest. The system is described in more detail in Ref. 2.

Large-scale integration in a process-oriented system. These two packages form the complete 12-bit A-to-D converter of the I/C Engineering Uniplex System, accurate to 0.25 percent.

General Electric CommanDir System continuously monitors machine status, counts production cycles. Operator can signal specific service required; key-operated switch is for foreman's use. Operator enters production data via thumbwheel switches.

Of the five systems, two (Bristol Datamaster and GE-TAC) can stand alone as self-programmed monitoring and control systems or interface optionally with a computer made by the vendor. A third (L&N Conitel) is a complete system incorporating a minicomputer. The two remaining systems (the 2,400-bps version of the CDC 1590/1591 and the IBM 1070) are multiplexing subsystems designed to be inserted into process computer control systems made by those vendors.

Four of the systems can be used in party-line fashion, with two or more remote stations on each communication channel. The CDC system requires a separate channel from the control center for each remote unit, in the configuration of Figure 2, part F.

These slower digital systems tend to fit best in situations where:

■ Dynamic control is less important than close, secure monitoring.

■ In-plant distances are great enough so that wiring costs are high and audio-modulated transmission is required to maintain signal quality.

This combination turns up where there are one or more remote process units, not requiring fast dynamic control from the control center, but which are to be unmanned, and hence require close, error-free monitoring and fast detection of alarm conditions.

In common with the high- and medium-speed systems, all the slow digital systems use redundant coding and automatic error detection.

Table III indicates the digital resolution of proportional inputs in the nine digital systems.

Two systems oriented specifically to thermocouple monitoring comprise the fourth group: analog multiplex systems. These are aimed at processes in which many temperatures must be monitored at high accuracies. Both systems use digital addressing; both are monitoring systems without control capabilities, and without provision for handling discrete data. Both are stand-alone systems with computer options for stored-program control. And both offer options to permit monitoring of other analog sensors besides thermocouples.

The remaining process system is the Motorola Omnipoint, a very low-cost system oriented primarily to binary discrete signals, and aimed at alarm-limit and operating-status surveillance of industrial machinery.

American Multiplex Systems MUX 2000. This is a medium-speed system of the party-line configuration shown in part C of Figure 2. It interfaces optionally with a digital computer; otherwise, alarm and status information appear in lights on a desktop console and the analog value of a manually selected process point appears in an illuminated decimal display.

Options include a digital clock which can program a seven-day monitoring and control cycle, and AMS lists a large number of remote-site options for input and output data manipulation (analog and logical) and amplification, as well as final control elements. Another option is the incorporation of a voice-intercom system.

Readaround time is faster than 3,000 points per sec with a mix of two discrete to one analog signals, using baseband modulation at a bit rate of 150K bps.

ACCO Bristol Datamaster. This is a subvoice/voice-speed system of the party-line configuration shown

Universal systems multiplex the binary discrete inputs on separate terminals to corresponding terminals at the receiving station. This CompuDyne DynaPlex remote unit has been fitted with interface modules to group the pulses conveniently for the application.

in part C of Figure 2, except that the central station is designed to handle several party lines, as illustrated in Figure 7.

Operation is manual (i.e., point selection by pushbutton at the operator's console), or automatic scan under a hardwire program, or scan under the control of an optional computer. Redundant coding is used in both models (33-bit word in one; 18-bit word in the other), with automatic error detection.

The system handles analog and discrete inputs and analog and discrete commands, but is not designed for closing the control loop through the computer. Bristol prefers operator-guide control, and provides for operator-guide displays and manual control signal inputs.

Line speeds listed in the product literature range from 30 to 2,400 bps. Each party line can handle 64 remote stations, each serving 64 process points, or 4,096 points per party line. Capacity can be increased or readaround time shortened by adding lines.

Control Data 1590/1591 Subsystem. This is a multiplexing subsystem in the configuration of part F of Figure 2, designed to be inserted into a CDC 1700 process control system. The remote multiplexer uses the 1500 Series process interface gear supplied for the 1700.

The system can be made slow or fast: One option incorporates a 2-megabps modem in the central and remote stations, and uses RG-8/U coax as the party line. At this line speed, CDC specifies a readaround time on the basis of a compute-time limitation in the 1700. The company states that the line-limited speed would be faster, but that no figures are available. On

this basis, each party line handles several thousand analog and discrete inputs and outputs per second, as noted in Table II.

The voice-grade version requires external modems at the central and each remote station; 2,400 bps units are cited as typical. With this modem the system is line-limited in speed; see Table II for details.

One central station can handle up to eight remote stations on eight communication channels. The remote stations are very large in capacity: Each can handle more than 7,000 inputs and 9,000 outputs. See Table II for a detailed breakdown.

The word format is a redundant 32-bit cyclic code with automatic error detection.

Two features of this system are the ddc and the teletypewriter outputs at the remote stations. The ddc signal is an amplitude-modulated pulse; the typewriter output consists of up to 12 channels of ASCII characters.

Electronic Modules Corp. Information System. This is an analog multiplexing system resembling part C of Figure 2. At each remote station, up to 100 thermocouple or other analog-sensor inputs are compensated, linearized, conditioned for transmission, and multiplexed in analog form onto the party line. At the central station, the signal is digitized for decimal display or computer input.

Each remote unit is equipped to handle 100 process points, indefinitely expandable in 100-point increments. Point addressing is digital; point selection may be manual, by hardwire scan program, or optionally by computer.

A self-check cycle is automatically initiated after

Table III. Resolution of Proportional Signals in Process-Oriented Digital Systems.

System	Resolution	Approximate equivalent binary resolution
AMS MUX 2000	8 or 10 binary places	8 or 10 binary places
Bristol Datamaster	3 decimal places	10
Control Data 1590/1591	10, 12, or 14 binary, including sign	9 to 13 magnitude
GE-TAC	$\pm1,999$ decimal	12
Hitachi Data Highway	Not available	
IBM 1070	0-7,800 decimal	13
I/C Uniplex	12	12
L&N Conitel	12 or 14	12 or 14

each point reading. Multiplexing speed is 40 points per sec.

General Electric GE-TAC System. This telephone-line-oriented digital system was originally designed for supervisory control of pipelines and other geographically dispersed facilities, but is now considered applicable in certain in-plant control situations—especially where extreme security (i.e., error-free communication) is a requirement, the number of monitored points is much larger than the number of controlled points, and high operating speed is not required. It is of the type illustrated in part C of Figure 2, with a maximum of 29 remote stations. Each remote station can handle 100 analog and 1,000 binary discrete inputs, and can control a maximum of 100 output points.

The data format is a 30-bit word with five redundant bits for automatic error checking, and each command output follows a select-check-operate sequence for security. Output control signals include both setpoints and jog pulses.

Operation is manual, hardwire scan program, or optionally controlled by a GE-PAC 30 minicomputer or full-sized control computer (GE-PAC 4010, 4020, or 4070).

Herco Temperature Data Acquisition System TDAS-2/A. This is an analog multiplexing system, oriented to thermocouple monitoring, in the configuration of part C of Figure 2.

The system accommodates up to ten remote stations, each capable of monitoring 100 process points.

The compensated thermocouple signals are transformed to current signals (for noise immunity) at the remote stations, and multiplexed onto the party line.

Point addressing is digital, with either manual point selection or program control by an optional computer.

There is a fault and calibrate check before and after each reading, and reading proceeds at a standard speed of 40 points per sec, with options from 1 to 200 pps.

Interface options are available to permit analog sensors other than thermocouples to be monitored.

Hitachi Digital Data Highway System. This system, newly introduced in Japan and not yet available outside that country, is included here mainly for the possible technical interest of some of its features.

It can use one or several party lines, in the configuration of Figure 7. Each party line consists of two unbroken loops of coax cable, which gives an unusual degree of security, Hitachi says. Any inputs to or outputs from the party line are inductively coupled by the transformer configuration illustrated in Figure 8, which transfers pulse signals through the unbroken outer conductor of the coax. Any one break in the loop does not interrupt communication, since a path is still available the other way around. And an open or a short at any one station has virtually no effect on signal quality at any other station.

There are three types of station: input, output, and process interrupt stations. Each station is quite small in capacity—five analog and five discrete inputs or outputs—and the system will accommodate as many as 100 stations on one loop.

The computer is coupled to the loop by the same method (shown in Figure 8) as the remote stations, and the system is designed so that additional computers can be coupled to the line in this fashion at one or more remote points.

The scanning rate is 5,000 points per sec, but the available information does not specify the mix of proportional to discrete signals this represents, nor the basic bit rate.

IBM 1070 Process Communication System. This is a multiplexing subsystem (Figure 7 configuration) designed to interface with a computer or a manually controlled batch-data terminal (IBM 1050).

The system is indefinitely expandable by adding party lines. Each line can handle up to 26 remote stations, each of which monitors or controls 50 to 300 process points.

It uses subvoice-grade lines at bit rates of 134.5 or 600 bps. The format is an asynchronous bcd character (six bits plus Start and Stop), at speeds of 14.8 or 66.7 characters per sec, respectively.

Two types of analog output or control signal are

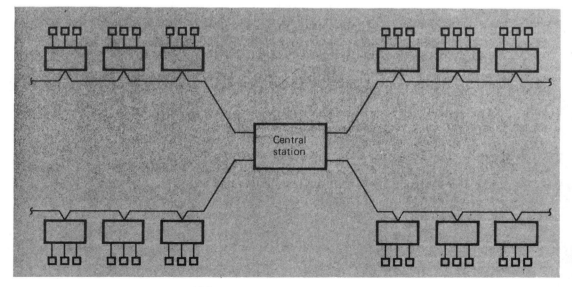

FIG. 7. Variation of the party line/multiplex configuration (part C of Figure 2) using two or more party lines.

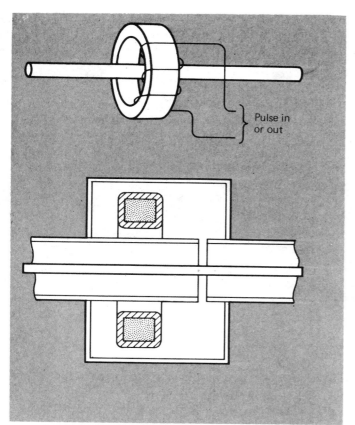

available at the remote station: a pulse train of a number corresponding to magnitude, and a pulse-duration signal. Discrete outputs are binary or one-of-ten decimal.

I/C Engineering Uniplex 500. This is a fast digital monitoring and control system of the party-line configuration (part C of Figure 2). This system and the Larse system (see p. 71) are the only two in the survey to make use of medium- or large-scale integration of semiconductor circuits. One result is a remote station 13 by 10 by 5 in., with good environmental tolerance, and easily installed where desired in the process. It is interesting to note that the other systems which incorporate roughly comparable functions in the remote station use six-foot cabinets to house the station.

The party line—one interrogate and one response channel, each a Twinax cable—operates at a basic bit rate of 500K bps, handling 5,000 proportional or 60,000 discrete signals a second (in a typical mix, 500 proportional and 1,200 discretes in 125 millisec).

The system can accommodate a maximum of 256 remote stations, each serving 30 process points in any mix of monitoring or control, analog or discrete.

The data format is a 40-bit word, including type-of-message code, address, self-test and priority, and data. In addition to parity checks, the system performs check-before- and check-after-operate tests.

The A-to-D and D-to-A converters are both low-cost single-chip devices. Analog inputs are resolved to 12 bits; outputs are optionally available as 4-20 ma or 0-5 volts. Discrete signals in both directions are isolated through reed relays.

The Uniplex system can be inserted between proc-ess points and analog controllers, as in part B of Figure 6 (in which case it time-shares the loops on an internally generated scan cycle); it can be used in a ddc configuration (part C of Figure 6), or in other stand-alone or computer-controlled configurations. Interfaces are available for the Varian 520i and 620i minicomputers.

Leeds & Northrup Conitel 2050. This is a large computer-centered subvoice/voice speed system of the general configuration of Figure 7. The central station is comprised of plug-in cards in a Lockheed MAC-16 minicomputer (see Figure 9). There are a maximum of eight line buffers, each connected through an associated modem to a relay multiplexer which selects one of up to 16 party lines under computer control.

Thus there is a maximum of 128 party lines, each capable of serving a maximum of 512 remote stations, for a system-wide maximum of 65,536 stations. Each station can monitor 15 analog or 180 discrete points, or a mixture, and can control one setpoint or 12 binary discretes.

A fully loaded station is scanned and controlled in 0.4 sec if served by a 1,200-bps line. (Each line buffer can serve a different type and speed of line.) Read-around time is determined both by the number of stations and the number of line buffers.

The computer can be used for closed-loop control, automatic scan and operator guide, or manual point-selection and control.

The data format is a 31-bit word in a cyclic error-detection code, with 26 data and address bits and five redundant bits per word.

Analog inputs may optionally be resolved to 12 or

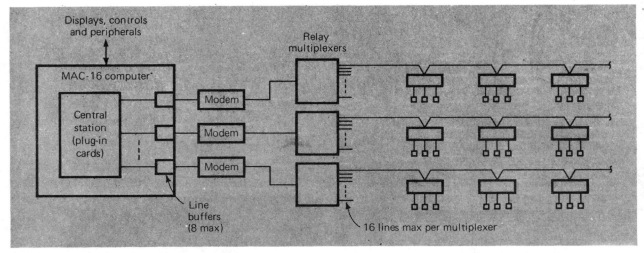

FIG. 9. The L&N Conitel central station is made up of plug-in cards in the MAC-16 computer cabinet. Each of the line buffers (eight maximum) can work at a different speed through a different type of modem. Each relay multiplexer scans 16 party lines under program control.

14 bits, with or without sign.

Motorola Omnipoint. This is a low-cost system designed primarily for alarm surveillance and the monitoring and control of binary discrete points. Applications are in machine monitoring, facilities and security surveillance, and limited process control.

Monitoring is of binary discrete and of analog points handled as discrete alarm-limit signals. As an option, analog signals can be multiplexed to the central station in analog form by adding an extra pair of wires to the party-line bundles.

The configuration is shown in Figure 10. A party line of six wires (eight in the first leg) connects one to 20 "Codepaks" to the controller, which incorporates a Motorola MDP-1000 minicomputer. A 14-wire party line connects each Codepak to as many as 50 "Logic Packs," each serving ten process points—a maximum of 10,000 points per system.

The Logic Packs in any one leg form a distributed shift register controlled by the computer. The status of each point sets a bit in the register, and the bits are shifted sequentially into the computer.

Each monitored bit is checked for validity, and each command signal is checked back before the command is executed.

The alarm limits are each entered separately at the control center and each can be altered to any desired value by typing an entry at the teletypewriter. System scan rate is 15 millisec per point, or 67 points per sec.

The primary operator interface is a teletypewriter. Process references at the typewriter are in Omnipoint rather than process terminology—e.g., "Leg 15, Point 86, ALARM," rather than, say, "Dryer No. 2 Overtemperature Alarm."

Universal Systems

Universal systems transmit pulses between stations on separately identifiable terminals (see Figure 4). They are essentially pulse serializer-deserializers with a one-to-one correspondence between the originating and the destination terminal, although the three systems described here (see Table IV) have a variety of operating modes and features oriented to in-plant monitoring and control.

These three systems take different fundamental approaches to system organization, data security, and plant or process interfacing. There is little to be said about them as a group beyond the fact that each delivers a binary digit from terminal i at an originat-

Area station of IBM 2790 System. Unit can be programmed to guide operator through transaction by illuminated displays. Badge and card readers are on right side.

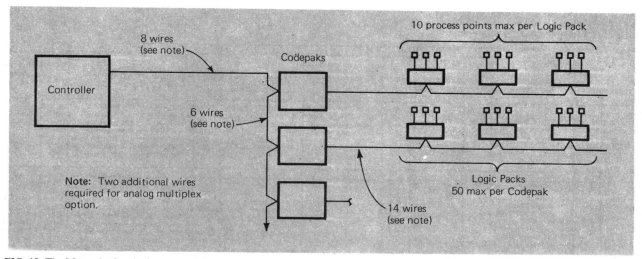

FIG. 10. The Motorola Omnipoint uses multiconductor wire bundles in party lines. A bundle of six connects the "Codepaks" to the central station. The "Logic Packs," which actually interface to the process, are connected to 14-wire party lines.

ing station to a corresponding terminal i at a receiving station, and that all three offer a range of optional speeds from tens to thousands of bits per second.

CompuDyne DynaPlex. This system corresponds generally to the configuration of Figures 4 and 5. The master station incorporates a minicomputer (Varian 620i preferred) which sequences the scan cycle, generates the interrogation and command messages, interprets the response messages, and chooses the bit rate for each message.

As each interrogation pulse from the master station is received at the remote station it enters an interface module which is connected to a corresponding terminal in the response sequence (see Figure 11). At any moment the module is either a short or an open circuit, and hence either does or does not pass the pulse to the opposite terminal. If it does, a "1" is transmitted back to the master station; if it does not, a "0" is transmitted back.

If the module is an input device, its state is determined by a local condition (state of a relay or contact closure, for example), and the value of the return pulse signals that condition.

If the module is an output device (a relay amplifier, for example) it produces its output upon receipt of a pulse, and the pulse sent back to the master station serves to verify that the output or command has been properly received.

Among the input interface modules are manually operated digital devices, multiple-bit momentary-contact storage devices (to, for example, accept a character from a teletypewriter or a punched tape reader), counters, discrete-voltage isolation devices, and A-to-D converters. Some modules, such as A-to-D converters, extend over several terminals and transmit or receive multiple-bit messages.

Among the output modules are pulse amplifiers, latching relay devices, momentary contact-closure devices, a transistorized relay driver, and a parallel digital-word output device.

The basic number of terminal pairs at a remote station is 16, expandable in increments of 16. Data is forwarded from expanded stations by two or more 16-bit cycles. A maximum of 256 remote stations are individually addressable.

There are four computer-selectable bit-rate oscillators in the master station, with a maximum bit rate of 10,000 bps.

Larse Corp. Data Communicator Modules. This sys-

(Table overleaf)
(Text continued on page 74)

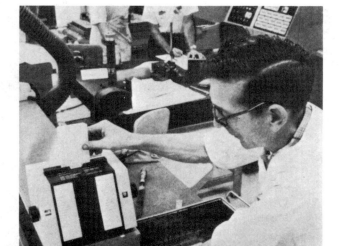

Data entry unit of IBM 2790 System, installed at work station. This version has two rotary decimal switches for variable data entry, a badge/card reader, and a phone jack. A larger variant adds more decimal switches and a key-operated switch.

Table IV. Universal Systems

System	Modes of operation	Maximum no. of remote stations	No. of points per station	Speed	Data structure and security	Communications and wiring requirements
CompuDyne Controls Inc. DynaPlex	Computer control of scanning sequence.	256	16 minimum, indefinitely expandable in increments of 16.	4 bit rate oscillators in master station are individually settable to any speed up to 10K bps. Computer can switch to any oscillator at any point in a message.	Addressing is by a redundant combination of tone-frequency identification and pulse code, for security. Message can be any length in 8-bit increments. 7,000 of every 10,000 pulses are data (the others being address). Data validity is checked bit by bit (see text).	Open pair. Three miles maximum.
Larse Corp. Data Communicator Modules	1. Sequential scan of all remote points. 2. Individual interrogation of remote points by tone or pulse-code address, manually, by computer, or other source of interrogation input. 3. Automatic time slot (synchronous sequential scan). 4. Automatic transmit upon change of status. 5. Single-word transmission, externally controlled.	64 sending and 64 receiving	16 minimum, indefinitely expandable in increments of 16.	Bit rates from 60 to 3,000 bps, depending on modulation option. There are 16 data bits in every 34 transmitted bits. Thus the number of data bits per sec is about 0.47 times the bit rate.	Unique "Larse Code" transmits 34 bits for each 16 bits of data. Check of "0"-"1" and "1"-"0" transitions yields unusual security for this degree of redundancy, according to Larse. Station addresses are required in the data stream only in the interrogation mode of operation. Where used, an address of six bits specifies a single remote station of any size.	Optional modulation schemes: AM tone (pulse-modulated audio frequency), FSK, line switching (telegraph style), line relay, EIA RS-232B standard modem interface. Wire requirements vary with speed and modulation; generally open or twisted pair or leased voice- or sub-voice-grade line.
Direct Digital Industries Ltd. Digicable	Monitor only. Straight sequential scan only.	31	8 minimum, expandable in increments of 16. 248 points max per station and per system.	200 points per sec standard. 25 to 20,000 points per sec on special order.	Pulses checked for width, shape, polarity, and phase, and spurious signals are rejected. Last valid always stored.	Baseband modulation or optional FSK. Open or twisted pair.

Table V. Production Control Systems

System	System size	System speed	Communications and wiring requirements	Computer role
General Electric CommanDir Factory Feedback	3 area stations max per 4-wire party line. 8 party lines max to computer center, or 24 area stations. 64 work stations max per area station. 1,024 fully loaded work stations max per system.	100 ASCII characters per sec on each party line. Read-around time for max system 6 sec.	Party line between area stations and to computer center is standard 4-wire telephone line carrying ASCII in FSK form. Multiconductor party line from area station to work station. Phone jack permits voice through party line.	Area stations can serve as stand-alone controllers for their work stations, or may be connected to an optional GE-PAC 30 computer for plant-wide control.
IBM 2790 Data Communication System	100 area stations max per system in one to four party-line loops. 32 data entry units max per area station, 1,024 max per system. 3 badge readers max per system.	500K bps line. 900 EBCDIC characters per sec.	Twisted-pair party lines. Data entry units also require twisted pair. Printers and badge readers use multiconductor cable.	Depending on the data processing load and on-line requirements, the following configurations are available: 360-2715 Transmission Control Unit-2790 Adapter; 1800-2790 Adapter; System 7-2790 Adapter; 2715-2790 Adapter (incorporates disc. Programmed to handle standard transactions and accumulate data off line.)

Input Interface		Output Interface		System components	Costs
Analog	Discrete	Analog	Discrete		
A-D converters	Manually operated digital input devices; single, 4-, and 8-bit parallel momentary contact storage devices; counters for contact closures or pulse inputs; voltage input isolation devices; parallel data-word-pulse input devices.	D-A converter	Pulse output device; latching relay output; contact closure output; transistorized relay driver; parallel digital word output device.	Central data unit; computer and its peripherals; remote data units; process interface modules.	A system to monitor 480 contact closures through 10 remote stations: $33,200 for all hardware including computer. Hardware to add 80 more points: $4,000. Thus about $66 per binary discrete point for a large system, including the computer.
Requires external A-D converter	Accepts voltages or contact closures. Incorporates memory for momentary inputs, with various resetting options.	Requires external D-A converter	Register output	Send ("SEN") and receiver ("REDE") units	Basic SEN: $600-$650 SEN expander: $400 Basic REDE: $700-$750 REDE expander $450 — Thus for a large system (10 SEN and 10 REDE, each with 4 add-on modules for a total of 800 points), about $20 a binary discrete point for SEN and REDE hardware.
Requires external A-D converter	Contact closures	Not applicable	Contact closures at master station only—one-way operation.	Basic transmitter and receiver and add-on modules.	Minimum 8-point system $800. Expandable at $100 a point. Discounts available for large systems.

System functions	Area station options	Costs
Monitors machine status and accumulates production information either manually entered or automatically sensed within production machines. Identifies machine-down reasons and communicates operator requirements. Transmits production schedules and other data to work areas.	Teletypewriter Card reader Badge reader Crt terminal	Typical stand-alone area station with 40-50 work stations, including system engineering and other nonhardware costs but not installation: $50,000. — Typical complete system with computer, 3 area stations, 150 work stations: $250,000.
Monitors machine status, work assignments, and production quantities of work in progress. Transmits production schedules and other data to work areas.	Printer Badge reader 21-key manual input and alphanumeric display Time-of-day display Key-operated switch	Basic units: 2715 Control Unit — $77,600 2791 Mod 1 area station — $ 8,245 2795 Data Entry Unit — $ 940 2796 Data Entry Unit — $ 1,140 2793 Data Entry Unit — $ 6,065

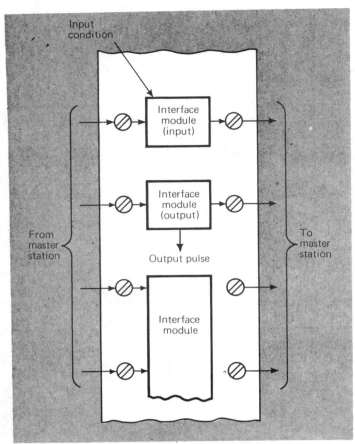

FIG. 11. DynaPlex System responds pulse by pulse. Each arriving pulse enters an interface module, which is either short- or open-circuit to the opposite terminal, and a "1" or "0" is transmitted back to the master station accordingly. The state of an input module is set by the monitored process point. An output module produces a "1" or "0" locally and sends a verifying pulse back to the master.

FIG. 12. Two ways the Larse SEN (sending) and REDE (receiving) modules can be used. In time-slot operation (A), successive SEN's transmit in turn. In the other mode illustrated, an address code in the interrogation signal from the SEN at the master station is detected by the proper REDE, which triggers a response from its associated SEN.

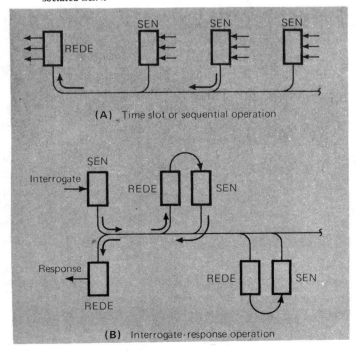

tem is made up of just two modules, a transmitting unit called "SEN" (Scanning ENcoding) and a receiving unit called "REDE" (REceiving DEcoding), plus expander modules for each.

The system has a great many optional modes of operation which can't all be traced here, but fundamentally it uses a SEN wherever a transmission is to originate and a REDE wherever information or commands are to be received. In either case this may be the master station or a remote location, or there may be no location designated as the master.

The SEN unit can be set to respond to an audio tone interrogation or pulse-coded interrogation, or to transmit within a given time slot. It can also be set to transmit whenever one of its own binary inputs changes state, or to transmit a continuous cycle of its 16 (or multiple of 16) inputs.

Thus numerous configurations are possible. Using coded addressing, any SEN on a party line can be used to transmit to any selected REDE. Or one SEN can broadcast to all REDE units. Or, using time slot operation, a REDE at a central station (see part A of Figure 12) can gather information sequentially from SEN units at different remote locations.

Or an interrogate-response configuration like that of part B of Figure 12 can be used. Here the first six bits of the 16-bit input to the SEN at the central station is the address code of the REDE at the selected station. Receipt of the correct address causes the REDE to trigger its associated SEN, which responds by serially transmitting back the data impressed on its 16 inputs.

The ten remaining digits in the interrogate transmission are available for commands or data outputs to the remote station. If more than ten are required, the REDE can be expanded in increments of 16.

As this is a universal system, the data pulses are not grouped into a character or word format, and may be grouped by the user in any convenient combinations. However, there is a format internal to the system: the "Larse Code," in which 34 bits are transmitted for every 16 bits of data. This code imposes exact constraints on the allowable transitions between "1" and "0" for each data bit, and is said by the Larse Corp. to yield an unusual degree of data security for the coding efficiency.

Data rates and modulation schemes are also available in a profusion of options: AM tone, FSK, line switching, and EIA RS-232B outputs to interface with standard modems. Bit rates vary from 60 to 3,000 bps.

The entire working electronics of the SEN or REDE unit is on an LSI chip about 1/8 in. sq. The SEN and REDE boxes are 7 ½ by 3 by 1 in., but this is mainly to permit convenient electrical connections and to make the units big enough to find (they are virtually empty inside).

The chips are Larse's own LSI design, and the company says they are an important factor in the price and reliability of the system.

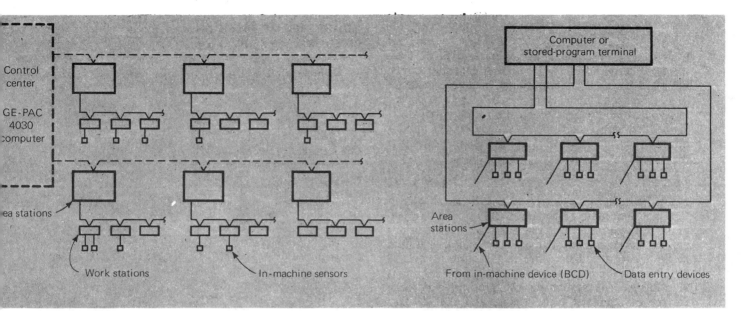

Direct Digital Industries Digicable. This is a very simple device intended primarily to multiplex pulses in one direction between two points, although the transmitter add-on modules can be located in more than one place. For two-way communication, a second system would be required.

The only mode of operation is a straight-through sequential scan, from the first input terminal to the last and then back to the first. The minimum system has eight inputs, and this is expandable in increments of 16 to a system maximum of 248. Standard speed is 200 points per sec, with 25 to 20,000 points per sec available on special order.

Production Control Systems

The two systems in this category (see Table V) are oriented specifically to the production control function: the gathering of information on machine status, production quantities, and employee attendance, and the distribution of work-order and schedule data.

There are a number of in-plant data acquisition systems commercially available (Ref. 3). The two included here are distinctive in three ways:

(1) They use line-sharing techniques to reduce in-plant wiring.

(2) They acquire information automatically from sensors in the production machinery.

(3) They provide for two-way communication, to the plant floor as well as to the control center.

The two systems perform many of the same functions, but approach them in somewhat different ways. The GE system places more emphasis on continuous close monitoring of machine status, while the IBM system permits more complex data entry at the work station.

The GE system is equipped to count cycles of pro-

duction machines automatically, as an independent check of manually entered data and as a means of sensing plant-floor conditions. (In a system using a computer, the lack of a production cycle for a specified period of time, or the slowing of the production rate, can be used to generate an alert signal for supervisors.) The work station of the GE system provides for manually setting in any of 11 reasons for machine outage (tooling required, electrical maintenance required, etc.), which aids in getting the needed service to the idle machine fast. A key-operated switch permits the foreman to confirm the "machine down" status, so that the "running/down" time data automatically acquired by the computer can be used to compute incentive pay.

Both systems use a two-level organization (see Figures 13 and 14): An area station provides for two-way communication and serves as a terminal point for work-station units located at the actual work sites.

It is interesting to compare the respective work station units (see photos) and area stations, which are markedly different in appearance and function in the two systems. The GE work station provides, as noted, for manually entering any of 11 separate requirements for service at the machine, and for independent confirmation of this status by key-operated switch. It also incorporates a phone jack into which the foreman can plug a portable hand telephone—also intended to help get the machine up fast. A three-place decimal thumbwheel switch is intended for manual entry of production-quantity data.

The IBM work station is built on a badge or card reader through which worker identity and job or lot number can be entered. It has as many as five rotary decimal switches (four one-place and one four-place) for manually entering data, and in one configuration has a phone jack and a key-operated switch. Thus the IBM terminal can also monitor machine status, but all of the status information is manually entered.

The operator interface at the GE area station is a teletypewriter, through which the foreman or workers in the area receive work schedules and similar information and enter worker assignments and other plant-floor information. Optionally the GE area station can incorporate badge or card readers or a crt terminal.

The IBM area station is quite different. One option is a blind unit which simply serves as a terminal point and controller for the adjacent work stations and an output printer. The other type of area station incorporates a badge reader and a card reader, 12 pushbuttons for manual data input, and alphanumeric displays. The system can be programmed for a variety of standard transactions, and the displays guide the operator through the transaction.

In the GE system, each area station can stand alone, acting as a controller and data acquisition unit for its associated work stations. Or the area stations may be connected by party lines to a central GE-PAC 30 minicomputer for integrated plant-wide control.

The GE system uses a standard four-wire telephone line as a party line connecting up to three area stations to the computer center. A maximum of eight party lines provide for 24 area stations. Connection from the area station to the work station is by multiconductor party line.

The IBM system, like the Hitachi process control system, makes a loop of the party line (Figure 14) so that all area stations are still in communication if there is one break in the loop. The system provides for as many as four loops to increase security of communication with the plant floor.

The system can have as many as 100 area stations, each serving a maximum of 32 work-station units, though the system-wide limit is 1,024 work stations.

All communications are by four-wire telephone party line except between the area station and the printer or badge reader, which require multiconductor cable.

The IBM system can interface directly to a large edp machine (i.e., a 360 or 370), to an 1800 process computer, a System/7 minicomputer, or an off-line controller equipped for stored-program control and with a disc unit for data accumulation. The choice of control room equipment depends on the data processing volume and on-line requirements.

REFERENCES

1. "Multiplex Systems Save Multibucks in Refinery and Chemical Plants," H. Simon, paper 70-564, ISA '70 Conference, ISA, 400 Stanwix St., Pittsburgh, Pa. 15222.
2. "A Digital Data Highway System for Process Control," F. Inose, K. Takasugi, M. Hiroshima, paper 70-510, ISA, '70 Conference, ISA, 400 Stanwix St., Pittsburgh, Pa. 15222.
3. "What's Available for In-Plant Data Collection," L. Walz, *Control Engineering*, Feb. '68, pp. 79-83.

ADDRESSES OF VENDORS CITED IN THIS SURVEY

American Multiplex Systems, Inc.
1515 Kraemer Blvd.
Anaheim, Calif. 92806
(714) 630-1481

ACCO Bristol
Datamaster Div.
85 Hazel St.
Glen Cove, N.Y. 11542
(516) 676-7300

CompuDyne Corp.
Hatboro, Pa. 19040
(215) 675-4100

Control Data Corp.
4455 Eastgate Mall
La Jolla, Calif. 92037
(714) 453-2500

Direct Digital Industries Ltd.
1570 Midland Ave.
Unit No. 6
Scarborough, Ontario
(416) 752-3243

Electronic Modules Corp.
Box 141
Timonium, Md. 21093
(301) 666-3300

General Electric Co.
Process Measurement & Control Div.
40 Federal St.
West Lynn, Mass. 01905
(617) 594-7271 (for GE-TAC)

General Electric Co.
Manufacturing Automation System Operation
Box 909
Charlottesville, Va. 22901
(703) 293-6117

Houston Engineering Research Corp. (Herco)
Box 35495
Houston, Tex. 77035
(713) 522-9703

Hitachi Ltd.
Instrument Div.
Mori 17th Bldg.
No. 2, Sakuragawa-Cho
Shiba Nishikube
Minato-Ku Tokyo 105, Japan

International Business Machines Corp.
Data Processing Div.
112 East Post Rd.
White Plains, N.Y. 10601
(914) 949-1900

I/C Engineering Corp.
3175 West Sixth St.
Los Angeles, Calif. 90005
(213) 380-5870

Larse Corp.
1070 E. Meadow Circle
Palo Alto, Calif. 94303
(415) 493-0700

Leeds & Northrup Co.
Sumneytown Pike
North Wales, Pa. 19454
(215) 643-2000

Motorola Instrumentation and Control Inc.
Box 5409
Phoenix, Ariz. 85010
(602) 959-1000

Part 4
Data Acquisition Applications

Introductory Comments

Of all applications of minicomputers, data acquisition is one of the most common. Data acquisition implies that the computer is monitoring a process, experiment, machine, or some other physical device by periodically converting one or more analog signals to digital form. In addition to simply acquiring the data, of course, some computation is usually performed, and perhaps there is some communication with the user of the system. The reason for the importance of digital data acquisition is rather evident. In the past, data were acquired and often recorded on either analog magnetic tape or on graph paper by a direct writing oscillograph or strip chart recorder. Any reduction of the data was done manually and usually, in fact, by eye. As a consequence, instruments were designed to provide data in a form that minimized the need for actual data reduction. Thus, if the sensor for one variable was influenced by another, the instrument was designed to remove that influence so that no further reduction of the data was required for its use once it was acquired. This resulted in more and more complex instruments.

Adding a digital computer's computational capability to a data acquisition system means that data reduction is very straightforward. As a result, data that is not directly in a form suitable for use can be acquired by the computer and processed until it is in a desirable form without increasing the cost of the instruments excessively. For example, a measurement of basis weight of a sheet of paper is influenced by the moisture content of the paper. Moisture, however, can be separately measured. Rather than combine basis weight and moisture measurement in a single instrument that removes the interaction between the two sensors, it is more straightforward to read both sensors directly into a digital computer and perform the necessary computation there. In other situations it is feasible to measure variables that are related to unmeasurable quality indicators of a process and through computation infer these unmeasurable quality variables (efficiency, for example). In addition to being able to acquire data at lower cost and without the need of more complex instruments, reliability of the data can also be improved by the digital computer, which can error-check measurements, instruments, and the like.

The articles in this part provide a number of examples of data acquisition systems and the way in which they are organized to illustrate the power of the minicomputer in this application. R. A. Henzel discusses industrial applications of minicomputers, all of which involve data acquisition and indicate the way that systems are organized for this purpose. R. D. McCoy and B. O. Ayers in one article, and P. P. Briggs in a second, discuss the use of on-stream analysis via a chromatograph under minicomputer control. The problem of measuring the concentration of components in a stream has long been an important one and only with the addition of computer controlled chromotagraphs has some success been achieved. It is a classic example of a data

141

acquisition system where the complexity of the data reduction problem shows clearly the value of the digital computer. Note that the actual acquiring of the data from the chromatograph is only a portion of the computer's task. The computer must also provide all the control signals to the chromatograph, all the timing signals, and the like, so that it is truly a computer controlled system even though the objective is data acquisition.

S. B. Wright and M. G. Silk discuss the design of a neutron spectrometer analyzer using a minicomputer. Notice in reading this article that the computer is fundamental to the data acquisition system and yet is really only one of the components in the system. The design of the electronics for acquiring the necessary counts and coincidences must take into account the manner in which the computer will acquire them. Similarly, the success of the system depends on the computer being able to do the necessary data reduction for the design. J. B. Pearce in the next article discusses another data acquisition application including problems of calibration, display, and control and recording of spectra. Again, a special purpose interface relating the computer to the device is the key to the system as well as the necessary software for reduction, display, etc.

Data acquisition systems often serve many devices, and the tasks of these devices may not be related. In this sense, a centralized data acquisition system for a laboratory or a process acts like a central computer with multiple time-shared users. The next two articles describe the use of computers in such systems. The first considers it from the point of view of a manufacturing test application where a number of test stands each requires digital data acquisition, display and storage but which operate independently of one another. The second is concerned with laboratory automation where a single computer is used to acquire data from a large variety of laboratory instruments, some of which have radically different data rates.

The remaining articles consider other specific applications that illustrate further the problems of integrating a digital computer into a data acquisition system. In summary, the problems are as follows: 1) interfacing a complex device, or a set of devices, to the computer; 2) providing adequate data and control lines to the device; 3) providing adequate status checking and error checking in the interface; 4) providing necessary data display and data storage; 5) providing the necessary software to reduce the data from its raw form to a meaningful form including engineering units, calibration factors, and so on; and 6) providing adequate operator or engineer interaction capability so that the many functions of the data acquisition system can be called upon in a natural and straightforward fashion. These articles illustrate further the importance of combining adequate hardware design with adequate software design.

Bibliography

[1] "Computer techniques for quantitative high resolution mass spectral analyses of complex hydrocarbon mixtures," T. Aczel, D. E. Allen, J. H. Harding, and E. A. Knipp, *Anal. Chem.*, vol. 42, Mar. 1970, pp. 341–347.

[2] "Atomic absorption with computer-controlled sampling," W. G. Boyle and W. Sunderland, *Anal. Chem.*, vol. 42, Oct. 1970., pp. 1403–1408.

[3] "Indirect measurement of process variables by minicomputer," A. B. Clymer, *IEEE Trans. Ind. Electron. Contr. Instrum.*, vol. IECI-17, June 1970, pp. 358–362.

[4] "An automated instrumental system for fundamental characterization of chemical reactions," S. N. Deming and H. L. Pardue, *Anal. Chem.*, vol. 43, Feb. 1971, pp. 192–200.

[5] "Computer controlled process chromatograph system," D. J. Fraade and L. Frost, *Instrum. Pract.*, Feb. 1968, pp. 127–131.

[6] "An automatic computer-controlled system for the measurement of cable capacitance," R. Fulks and J. Lamont, *IEEE Trans. Instrum. Measure.*, vol. IM-17, Dec. 1968, pp. 299–303.

[7] "Use of computers in a molecular biology laboratory," T. H. Gossling and J. F. W. Mallett, *AFIPS Conf. Proc., Vol. 33, Pt. 2, 1968 Fall Joint Comput. Conf.*, pp. 1089–1098.

[8] "Numerical deconvolution of overlapping stationary electrode polarographic curves with an on-line digital computer," W. F. Gutknecht and S. P. Perone, *Anal. Chem.*, vol. 42, July 1970, pp. 906–917.

[9] "Review of digital filtering," J. D. Heightley, *IEEE Comput. Group News*, vol. 3, July/Aug. 1970, pp. 22–24.

[10] "Application of an on-line computer to the automation of analytical experiments," G. P. Hicks, A. A. Eggert, and E. C. Toren, Jr., *Anal. Chem.*, vol. 42, June 1970, pp. 729–737.

[11] "Computer evaluation of continuously scanned mass spectra of gas chromatographic effluents," R. A. Hites and K. Biemann, *Anal. Chem.*, vol. 42, July 1970, pp. 855–860.

[12] "Computer control system realistically applied to oil and gas producing operations," M. G. Hubbard, *IEEE Trans. Ind. Gen. Appl.*, vol. IGA-7, May/June 1971, pp. 389–394.

[13] "Interactive electronic analytical instrumentation based on computerized experimental design," D. O. Jones and S. P. Perone, *Anal. Chem.*, vol. 42, Sept. 1970, pp. 1151–1157.

[14] "Computer applications for parameter control and data processing in a metrology laboratory," W. J. Layer, *IEEE Trans. Instrum. Measure.*, vol. IM-18, Dec. 1969, pp. 294–299.

[15] "Trends and advances in on-stream process analysis," B. Liptak, *Contr. Eng.*, Mar. 1971, pp. 61–64.

[16] "A miniature digital computer for reaction rate analyses," R. A. Parker, H. L. Pardue, and H. G. Willis, *Anal. Chem.*, vol. 42, Jan. 1970, pp. 56–61.

[17] "A computer operated mass spectrometer system," W. E. Plynolds *et al.*, *Anal. Chem.*, vol. 42, Sept. 1970, pp. 1122–1129.

[18] "Real-time computer prediction of end points in controlled-potential coulometry," F. B. Stephens, F. Jakob, L. P. Rigdon, and J. E. Harrar, *Anal. Chem.*, vol. 42, June 1970, pp. 764–774.

[19] "On-line digital computer system for high-speed single focusing mass spectrometry," C. C. Sweeley, B. D. Ray, W. I. Wood, and J. F. Holland, *Anal. Chem.*, vol. 42, Nov. 1970, pp. 1505–1516.

[20] "Computer-controlled gas chromatograph capable of real-time readout of high precision data," R. S. Swingle and L. B. Rogers, *Anal. Chem.*, vol. 43, June 1971, pp. 810–818.

[21] "Small computer magnetic type oriented rapid search system applied to mass spectrometry," L. E. Wanger *et al.*, *Anal. Chem.*, vol. 43, Oct. 1971, pp. 1605–1614.

[22] "On-line computer processing of stopped-flow data," B. G. Willis, J. A. Bittikofer, H. L. Pardue, and D. W. Margerum, *Anal. Chem.*, vol. 42, Oct. 1970, pp. 1340–1349.

[23] "Simultaneous kinetic determination of mixtures by on-line regression analysis," B. G. Willis, W. H. Woodruff, J. R. Frysinger, D. W. Margerum, and H. L. Pardue, *Anal. Chem.*, vol. 42, Oct. 1970, pp. 1350–1355.

[24] "Mulheim computer system for analytical instrumentation," E. Ziegler, D. Henneberg, and G. Schomburg, *Anal. Chem.*, vol. 42, Aug. 1970, pp. 51–61.

Some Industrial Applications of Minicomputers

By Russell A. Henzel

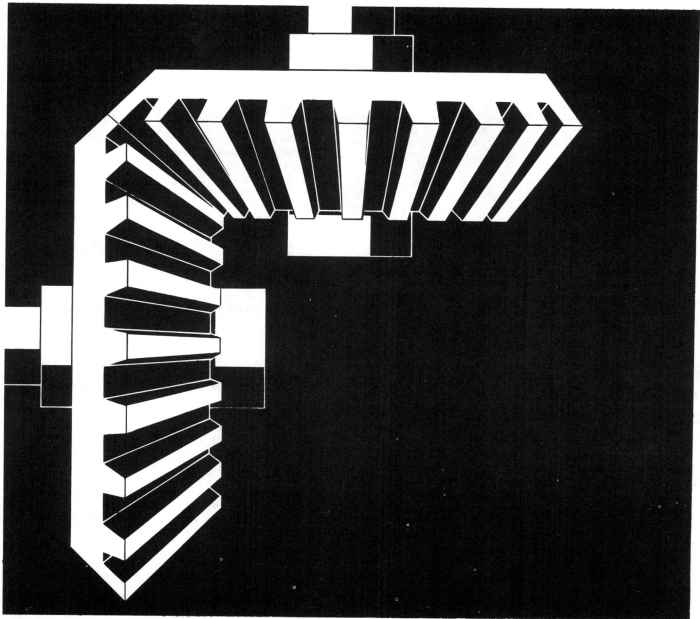

Industrial applications have been one of the key markets motivating the development of minicomputers. Some of the first small computers were designed specifically to perform tasks in process control, manufacturing and laboratories. Thus the history of industrial applications is as long and varied as the history of minicomputers themselves.

This article will attempt to describe only a few applications which have proven successful in this field, it is not intended as a record of all uses of small machines in a plant. The application of the machine will be described by listing the functions the machine must perform, the types of I/O equipment and devices needed in the system, and what features in the architecture of the computer are important. The size of the machine's configuration and the characteristics of the operating software will be described.

Reprinted from *Computer*, vol. 4, pp. 7–12, Sept./Oct. 1971.

DATA ACQUISITION

DATA ACQUISITION SYSTEM COMPONENTS

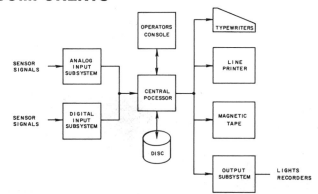

Figure 1. The data acquisition system is oriented toward acquiring sensor data and producing output information that is easily used by plant operators.

Data acquisition represents one of the very first applications of small digital computers in industrial plants and in fact one of the first applications of real time computers. Data acquisition takes many forms from missile monitoring to explosion testing with equipment and software tailored to suit; however, industrial data acquisition has achieved some standardization of configuration and application which can be discussed.

The primary functions performed by a data acquisition system are monitoring, alarm checking, and data logging. The CPU constantly scans a set of analog inputs which describe the state of certain variables in the plant such as flow, temperature, position, weight, pressure, angular velocity, etc. In addition to the analog inputs, a number of variables in the plant are two-valued and thus can be monitored by digital inputs. The machine checks the status of the digital inputs against previous readings, constantly looking for a change of state.

The alarm checking consists of determining when an analog input exceeds the boundaries set for this particular point. Since in general no two points have the same high-low limits, there is a requirement that a pair of values be maintained for each input in the system. Alarm checking on digital inputs consists of determining when a particular state change has occurred.

The system response to an alarm condition is obviously a function of the point which exceeded limits. Very commonly a message will be printed, or a light or audible annunciator will be activated to alert the plant personnel. In all cases, however, the output is to a human, no automatic corrective action is taken.

The third function of the system is data logging. This can be done after a critical event or periodically on a typewriter, a line printer, or on magnetic tape for future reduction. The data logging is ultimately for human understanding and therefore is always printed out in appropriate engineering units such as gallons/minute, degrees farenheit, pounds/square inch; not in binary, hexadecimal or other forms convenient to the computer.

Related to data logging is data reduction. Some applications require a fairly extensive computation of several data points to produce the appropriate figure of merit for the process. These calculations were formerly performed by a data processing machine from input data prepared on punched cards or tape, but the results were not timely. By having the data acquisition CPU make the calculation, the answers can be obtained fast enough for the operator to adjust the process.

The type of plants which tend to use the sort of data acquisition described above tend to be the continuous and semi-continuous process types, e.g., refineries, chemical plants, power generation facilities, jet engine testing and manufacturing process monitoring.

With the above application areas and system functions in mind, let us examine the configuration and needs of the minicomputer in the data acquisition system (see Figure 1). A system with a limited number of input points (~50), no data reduction, a few conversion routines to engineering units, and an output routine can be programmed in a 16 bit machine in 8 or 12K of core resident dedicated program with no mass store. However, where there are a number of different routines for engineering unit conversion, lengthy alarm messages or long data reduction programs, the need for an operating system with memory management is clearly indicated. The various programs would be disc resident and loaded into core when required; the several different programs utilizing the same core space at different times. Therefore data acquisition systems tend to run from small through rather large configurations.

Additional features required of the processor are hardware math capability if data reduction or much engineering unit conversion is to be done. This usually means hardware multiply and divide and double precision arithmetic. The interrupt response, however, does not have to be very fast. The output is ultimately to a human via message or light, therefore the CPU can be fairly slow before it is slower than human reactions.

The hardware requirements include the obvious need for analog and digital input systems. Not as obvious perhaps is the need for digital outputs to drive lights and other annunciators or the need for analog outputs for visual displays and strip chart recorders. Other output devices may include a magnetic tape for communications with a data processing machine or a communication line controller for direct connections. Data logging may require the use of continuous duty typewriters or a line printer.

If the system is small it tends to be placed in the environment of the process itself, which requires a wide temperature range machine or perhaps an enclosure sealed against corrosive gases. Because paper tape, magnetic tape and card peripheral device are incompatible with this environment, program development will probably be done elsewhere and system loading be the only function performed at the installation site. Larger systems having data processing type peripherals tend to be placed in control rooms or other air conditioned areas more friendly to the I/O devices. However, the output typewriter used for alarm messages must be placed near the person who can do something about the alarm condition. This often demands that the typewriter be placed remotely from the processor, perhaps in the process environment.

DIRECT DIGITAL CONTROL

Direct digital control utilizes the computer as the feedback element in the plant replacing conventional analog control devices. Analog control in a process plant involves the use of an analog controller as the feedback element for a particular part of the process. An example would be a device to maintain the temperature of a solution fixed by regulating the amount of fuel used to heat the container. The system has access to the temperature of the solution as an input and the control of the fuel flow as an output. A typical process is made up of many such feedback loops regulating temperature, pressures, flows, etc.

Each loop has a controller as the feedback element which operates by what is known as the three mode algorithm. The three mode algorithm produces an output which is made up of the sum of three parts: the first is a signal proportional to the error (the difference between the set point and the desired result), the second is a signal which is proportional to the time integral of the error, the third signal is proportional to the time derivative of the error. The loop is not analyzed for poles and zeros to determine the required transfer function of the feedback element but rather the controller is adjusted by trial and error for maximum stability and minimum error.

The market seemed right in the early sixty's for replacing all of these individual analog controllers with a single computer system which was time-shared among many loops. (The time constants of the loops ranged from tenths of seconds up which made time sharing possible). The plan was to build on the data acquisition base. By doing conventional scanning of analog and digital inputs and performing the alarm checks as usual, the appropriate data was available for processing by the control equation. The result from the equation was then outputted to the control device (usually a valve). Thus the three mode equation was implemented as well as some other control equations and direct digital control or ddc was on its way.

The systems tended to be large in scope and equipment, but the number of installations were few. The systems were too big, too complex, to hard to program and get running, and held to much of the control of the plant in one device. The entire plant could be tied up if the computer failed. Elaborate dual computer and back up schemes made these systems more acceptable but still the number of installations was not large.

In recent years minicomputers have enabled the implementation of much smaller systems which seem now to indicate that the projections of the early sixty's will be realized. Instead of a large central control system, the user installs several smaller systems dedicated to a particular part of the process. Thus the minicomputer seems to have made the market predictions for ddc achievable.

The industries that are using ddc are not only the continuous process ones such as the refineries but also the semi-continuous process industries which involve the start up of a machine or process which then runs for hours and finally is shut down. The machine can aid in this transition by actual control of the device, aids to the operator (reminding him to do a certain task) or checking on the operator (by telling him that he forgot to throw a certain switch or complete a certain task).

Related to ddc is supervisory control where the computer system is not the feedback element but provides the set point to the analog controller. Although error correction is now delegated to the analog controller, overall control is maintained by the computer system.

DDC SYSTEM COMPONENTS

Having reviewed the history and function of ddc systems, we can now list the requirements on the computer part of the system as compared with data acquisition. The CPU in ddc systems range from medium to large in configuration. As compared to data acquisition, there is more data for each input point such as history, set point, and control equation coefficients; therefore, systems tend to always have mass memory in addition to a fair amount of high speed storage.

Hardware multiply, divide and double precision is virtually necessary because of the amount of computation required by the control equation. Interrupt handling must be faster because the system outputs to a process with faster reaction times than the human in the data acquisition case. All of the above features are required in addition to what is needed for data acquisition because the requirement for scanning, alarm limit checking, alarm notification and data logging is still there. Direct digital control appears to be an extension of data acquisition systems.

The analog and digital input equipment remains relatively unchanged from the data acquisition case but additional output capability for operating control devices is needed. Because the system is large, it tends to be found in an environmentally controlled room, but the need for the remote alarm typewriter is still present.

The operating system requirements tend to be similar to those of the data acquisition system. There is the need, however, for a sequential control interpreter to provide the user with a vehicle to perform start-up, shut-down and other state transition oriented functions.

FACTORY DATA COLLECTION

The two previous applications of minicomputers in industrial control are principally directed toward continuous and semicontinuous processes. For several years machines have been used in manufacturing environments in a variety of ways from machine tool control to automatic component testing. A recently emerging application which has a great deal of promise is the collection of factory data in a manufacturing plant. The data to be recorded is not from sensors but from people, the factory employees.

The simplest of these systems is a time and attendance reporting system. This involves replacing the conventional time clock and punched card procedures with a simple terminal into which an employee inserts his identification badge. The terminals are placed at strategic entry and exit points to the plant. The terminal itself is very simple, consisting mainly of a badge reader and an interface to a communication line. Because most people want to know at what time they were logged in or out, a time display is sometimes specified, usually synchronized with the master factory clock. Several terminals need to have a key locked numeric keyboard to permit selected people (usually foremen) to log those employees in or out who have forgotten their badges.

The terminals are connected to the central computer via a multidrop communication line, i.e., a line on which more than one terminal can be connected. One method of accomplishing this is to assign each terminal on the line a unique address. The central computer then polls each terminal in turn asking if the terminal has a message for the CPU. If the terminal is inactive, it merely replies with a message indicating no activity. However, if an employee has entered his badge, the terminal responds with the employee's badge number. The computer then indicates to the terminal that the message was received with no apparent errors and the terminal finally indicates to the employee that the transaction was completed. This may be done by the terminal lighting an indicator or releasing the employee's badge from the reader.

The computer keeps the time display on the terminals current by selecting each terminal and sending a message which contains the following information. "This message is a time update, change your time display to read xx hours, xx minutes." If the message is received correctly, the terminals update their display and transmit an acknowledgement message.

What the central computer does with the time and attendance information ranges from simple to moderately complex. In the simplest scheme, the CPU merely blocks the messages onto a medium such as magnetic tape. At the end of the shift, the tape contains the times at which each employee entered and left and therefore is suitable for inputting into the payroll program which in turn generates the pay checks. A more complex function is for the central computer to keep on a disc file a record of permitted areas for each employee. Thus when employee attempts to enter an area for which he is not cleared, a security guard is warned. Such security systems could be popular not only in government and defense establishments but also with manufacturers in the soft drink, photographic supply, and other industries where trade secrets are important. A final use of the time and attendance data would be the generation of a report of those employees who were late or absent.

A time and attendance system of even the simplest proportion replaces the time clock with the terminal and computer hardware and has a payoff in terms of keypunching and timeliness of the information.

SHOP AND MATERIAL CONTROL

The time and attendance system is sometimes justified on its own and in other cases is an entry level system leading to a shop and material control system. In a manufacturing operation whose major cost is labor, the management is keenly interested in a timely and accurate labor cost reporting system. If the major cost is materials, such as a plant that deals in precious metals, the interest is more directed to material control systems. A labor reporting or operator's terminal can be made up of a badge reader for the employee's badge, a single card reader, a simple display and a keyboard. These terminals are placed at suitable points in the factory perhaps near clusters of machines or other places where employees work. The employee enters suitable data into the terminal at the begining or end of a job or both. For example, suppose the employee has a job card which specifies the quantity of parts to be produced, the part number and the order number to which his time is to be charged. At the completion of the task he enters his badge and the job card into the appropriate readers and then any other pertinent data into the keyboard. This data could be such items as: the required quantity completed; or less than the required quantity completed (and the number actually completed) because of material shortage, machine failure, or end of shift.

A material control system would be quite similar in that all entries and dispersals from the stock room would be accompanied by a terminal transaction. The part would be identified by a part identification card and the direction of transfer, order number, etc. could be entered on the keyboard. The identification of the employee would be via his badge.

The requirements on the terminals vary from application to application and there is a definite need for the system supplier to offer a modular terminal. This would be one design into which a varying mixture of devices can be configured. For example, customer number one might want the terminal with the display, keyboard, badge reader and card reader as described. Customer number two might want the addition of a card punch so that job cards could be punched remotely at the terminal. Customer number three might want a small strip printer and not need either the card punch or the display. It is to the system supplier's benefit not to design a custom terminal each time but to have a maximum configuration terminal from which devices can be gracefully deleted without destroying the operation of the remaining devices or the appearance of the terminal.

The communication line which services these operator's terminals obviously need more capability than the line which services a time and attendance terminal. For example, reading an 80 column card requires about ¾ of a second at 1200 baud using an 11 bit code. Near the end of a shift when many operators are trying to finish up and record tasks, it does not require many such transactions on a multi-drop line to make the apparent system response time intolerable. Obviously, data must be handled at a much higher rate in shop and material control systems.

A further requirement of the communication lines in the factory data collection system is compatibility with a suitable modem. Many manufacturing plants are distributed such that terminals would be located across public ways from the central portion of the system. In such cases, it is necessary to utilize leased telephone lines which are driven by standard modems.

The function of the CPU in the material reporting system is to interface with the terminals and log the data. As in the time and attendance system this is as simple as recording successive transactions onto magnetic tape. In addition, there are a number of variations to the method of getting the data to the central data processor. One popular system performs this function by storing one shift's transactions and then sending the data up a communication line to the DP machine. The reason for waiting until the end of the shift is that labor reporting programs on the DP machines run in batch mode, therefore, either the manual transportation of the magnetic tape or the transmission of one shift's results are just about equivalent in system results. The next step is for the labor reporting program in the DP machine to be rewritten and run on-line as part of some sort of management information system. This would require the minicomputer to pump terminal transactions up to the DP machine via a communication line as they occur. There exists some problems, however. MIS systems have not realized the level of performance which was promised by their promoters for several reasons, one of which would be evident if the direct connection were made. This problem is that errors in the transactions go more or less directly into the data base of the DP machine from which many reports are generated and a general data explosion takes place. If an operator makes an error in entering a number in the terminal, that error gets exploded into many places where it is not evident that an error has been made. For example, if a part number was entered incorrectly as being low in quantity, all sorts of material purchases might be triggered, or an alarm would be flashed because the incorrect part was a long lead item, or a large missing inventory report would be generated. The data that the MIS system uses must be verified and the person that can best do this is the foreman. By having the local operating management verify the data before it is distributed and removing the great majority of the errors, the final reports will be of acceptable accuracy. However, the direct connection to the DP machine running on-line is some distance off.

The need for local data verification requires the CPU to be equipped with suitably sized disc memories and a means for getting raw data into a meaningful form. This can lead to the inclusion of line printers or CRT's for data display.

FACTORY DATA SYSTEM COMPONENTS

The requirements of the CPU in such systems are that the machine be communication oriented. Obviously a machine whose data channels, interrupt structure and operating system cannot handle a lot of data swiftly is not going to function well in this application. On the other hand, the amount of arithmetic work is quite limited, and there is no need for multiply, divide or double precision hardware. The operating system's requirements are that it be able to schedule tasks efficiently and swiftly but there is no need for a bulk storage memory manager and overlay capability. These systems tend to require a simple user's language such that the details of a particular user's factory may be programmed easily while the part of the application program that deals with the communication line discipline and conversation with the terminal is not visible to the user of the language. Thus, the customer can specify the number of digits in his part number system, the types of transactions, the sequence of buttons the operator is to push, and other facets of the data flow without having to learn the communication procedure or other tasks down at the pithy, detailed level.

Of particular interest in this system is reliability. With so much of the operation of a large plant tied up in this system, including sensitive accounts such as payroll, large systems may have to continue to function even in the event of a hardware failure. This can be accomplished by dual CPU's and discs arranged in a fully redundant fashion. The terminals and communication lines are also vulnerable and it is necessary to deliberately run every other terminal in a particular part of the plant on different communication lines. In this way the failure of a line or terminal on that line means that the operator need only to walk to the next terminal to record his transactions. There is obviously a need for lateral and longitudinal parity checking and media read after write to insure hardware error detection. See Figure 2 for a typical factory data collection system.

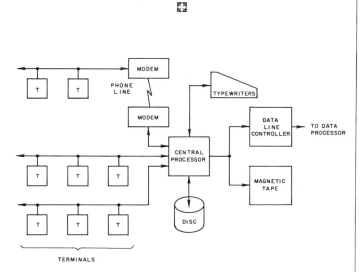

Figure 2. The factory data collection system accepts data generated by employees and stores it for future reduction and report generation.

DISTRIBUTED DATA ACQUISITION

Returning to the subject of data acquisition, one of the implicit assumptions made was that the signals from all of the sensors ran to the computer system which was located at a strategic point. In this era of rapidly rising labor costs and falling computer costs it is apparent that this will no longer be the case. In a typical large data acquisition system, as much as one third of the computer system budget can be allocated to the wire costs and the wire installation labor. A method of reducing this cost is to remotely concentrate signals onto a communication line and then run the coded information to a central machine.

The various system functions performed by the conventional data acquisition system are therefore separated. The task of data gathering, analog scanning, digital scanning, handling of interrupts, de-bouncing switches, digital filtering, etc. are delegated to the various remote multiplexing units. The task of data analysis, logging and reduction is handled by the central machine which is relieved of the data gathering tasks and the response time and I/O transfers requirements needed to do that task.

The concept of separating the data acquisition functions from the central system and distributing it around the plant in several remote multiplexers has a number of advantages. First, since the cost of a data acquisition system is not in the central processor but in the sensor interface equipment and peripheral devices, there is the potential of saving most of the wiring costs when the system is distributed without adding a great deal of computer equipment. If a system is installed to service 1000 analog points, the cost of the individual multiplexer points will be about the same regardless of whether they are all at one location or distributed in groups around the plant. The number of data processing peripheral devices will not increase as the system is fragmented because all of the rotating

memory, system loading, data logging and system control functions will still be located at the central site. There will certainly be an increase in electronics for communication line drivers, A/D converters, other controllers and power supplies, but the vast majority of the system equipment will not be replicated in the distributed system.

The second advantage gained by isolating the data acquisition function from the data reduction function is that each machine is simpler. Several operating system developments have shown that using the spare idle time of a on-line real time data acquisition system for data reduction calculations can be done but is expensive in memory and not entirely efficient in computer utilization. By separating the data gathering functions into remote units and by concentrating the data reduction at a central site, each machine can be configured to do its job efficiently.

The minicomputer plays a vital role in distributed data acquisition systems (see Figure 3). A large configuration of a 16 bit machine with communications ability can easily be the central machine. The peripheral devices are the same as discussed earlier in this article with the addition of communication line controllers and the deletion of sensor I/O equipment. The controllers at the remote multiplexer may be a hardwired device or a small minicomputer. The machine at this part of the system needs sensor I/O equipment and a single line controller and provides a great deal of signal conditioning and flexibility. For example, the analog and digital scans, thermocouple cold junction compensation, or even linearization are functions unique to the local hardware which can be handled by a remote machine to relieve the central machine of these troublesome, time consuming tasks.

Alarm conditions detected in either the remote multiplexer or the central processor may require the generation of a lighted alarm or a typewritten message. Since it is desirable that the alarm light or message appear close to the person who can best act upon the error condition, it is necessary for the remote multiplexer to support digital outputs and alarm typewriters. To eliminate the need for mass storage devices at the remote site, the message will be stored in the central machine and transmitted down the communication line when needed.

It should be noted that this hierarchical system concept can be extended to control as well as a pure data acquisition. There is even the added advantage in distributed control of having a small amount of control available at the remote machines to take over when the communication line or the central machine is down. In this fashion the system has a built in safety factor which limits the amount of damage a hardware failure can cause.

Figure 3. The distributed data acquisition system isolates the data gathering function into small systems to reduce wiring costs while the data reduction and outputting functions remain centralized.

CONCLUSION

The natural outgrowth of the communication technology and sensor based computer system has been the hierarchical distributed data acquisition and control system. The next evolutionary step in these systems will be the integration of the labor reporting terminal system and the distributed data acquisition system. Many problems can be seen because of the incompatibility of the sensor data rates and the human response requirements, but the potential for an integrated plant control system provides the motivation for their solution.

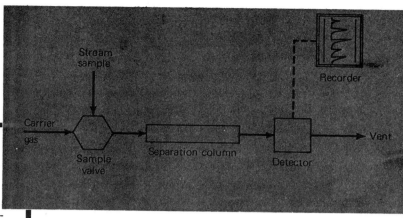

While not every process stream requires on-line identification of 100 or more components, it's nice to know that such identification can be accomplished routinely using the versatile equipment that is now available. Moreover, the authors point out that thanks to this equipment, it is also quite practical to set up a system to continuously analyze product composition where only a few components need be separated. Here is a detailed run-down on how on-line chromatographs operate when programmed by computers. Gasoline streams in a catalytic reformer provide the application example.

On-Line Stream Analysis With A Chromatograph

R. D. McCOY and B. O. AYERS
Applied Automation, Inc.

Conceptually chromatography is a simple technique, and that partially explains why it is becoming accepted so readily on line. The fact that it teams up so well with a computer affords, of course, further explanation of its increasing use. Finally, more and more engineers are finding that the chromatograph is more powerful than other instruments for making quantitative analyses of gases or volatile liquid samples.

How the chromatograph works

The basic components are a sample valve, separating column, and a detector, Figure 1. The sample is injected onto the column and carried through it by an inert carrier gas, commonly helium. Normally the column is either 1/8 or 1/4 in. in diam., and packed with a porous solid; or it is open capillary tubing of about 0.010 in. diam. In either case, the packing or the capillary is coated with a stationary liquid phase.

Sample components are continually dissolved and eluted (removed) from this liquid phase. Since the rate of elution differs for different components, they are separated in time, with the least soluble compounds reaching the detector first. Thus the key to the chromatograph lies in the fact that the detector need only analyze a two-component mixture—helium and one compound from the sample—at any one time. It follows under these simple analysis conditions, where one of the constituents of the mixture is always the same, that detectors operating on elementary principles such as thermal conductivity cells are often adequate.

New chromatograph profiles

During the 1960's, chromatographs for more complex applications were developed at Phillips Petroleum, Applied Automation's parent company. There were analysis instruments for optimization studies of catalytic crackers, a hexane isomerization unit, and a butane dehydrogenation process, Ref. 1. Other special chromatographs were designed and built to analyze and control a catalyst test unit and an experimental microreactor. Features included in one or more of these instruments that are not generally available in commercial instruments are:

■ Subambient column temperatures.

■ Multiple temperature zones.

■ Simultaneous parallel column operation to provide total analysis of complex samples in times compatible with process control requirements.

■ Computer compatibility for handling data reduction from complex sample mixtures.

Reprinted with permission from *Contr. Eng.*, vol. 17, pp. 44–49, July 1970.

FIG. 2. A chromatograph system with two temperature zones and an analog programmer which supplies analysis instructions. The separator columns, one in Zone 1 and three in Zone 2, look like coils of tubing. Reasons for using multiple columns and multiple temperature zones are given in the text.

Programmer

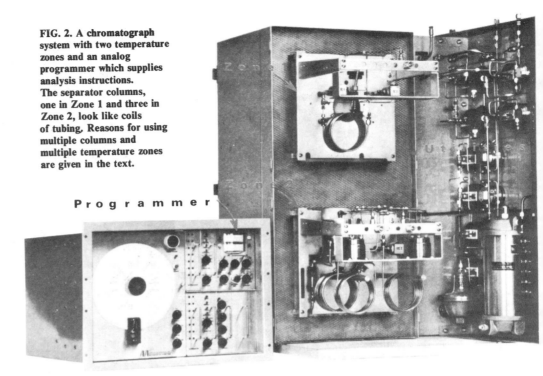

The upshot of this effort was a versatile commercial instrument with capabilities exceeding those of conventional instruments. Its major innovations were these:

■ Parallel columns in multiple, isothermal temperature zones.

■ Subambient column temperature capability.

■ Capillary column capability with back flushing.

■ Vaporization of liquid samples prior to sampling.

■ Computer compatibility such that an analog programmer could be replaced by a digital computer able to handle all chromatograph control functions plus any desired data reduction.

Figure 2 shows the 214 Process Chromatograph System, consisting of analog programmer, two-zone analyzer, and utilities panel. The two temperature zones normally have ranges between 40 and 300 deg F with stability of plus or minus 0.02 deg F under steady ambient conditions. The lower zone is shown with three parallel columns which may be capillary or packed. The detectors used may be either thermal conductivity cells that are insensitive to flow, or highly sensitive flame ionization units. Sample dilution prior to column injection is standard.

The programmer at the left in Figure 2 uses coded holes punched in a rotating plastic disc. The disc is read by phototransistors reacting to light sources. Over 200 event commands and 128 logic commands can be stored on one disc. Continuous outputs for 14 sample components are available.

For complex problems involving a great deal of data reduction, the analyzer subsystem is so designed that the analog programmer and output subsystems can be replaced by a digital computer. Program packages for controlling the analyzer and for gating and integrating the output have been essentially standardized. There is also the option of using a programmer (as shown) for analyzer control, and feeding only the output to a digital computer for further processing. Extreme flexibility is thus assured. Using the same basic analyzer, the system may be readily converted to handle applications with more than 100 components in the sample, rather than just a few.

Reasons for parallel columns and temperature zones

Many difficult separations may be accomplished in reasonable cycle times with parallel columns and multiple temperature zones. This is true even for relatively simple sample mixtures.

Example 1. Assume, for example, that an application requires separation of two components in a sample,

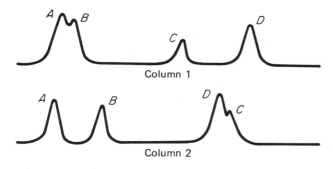

FIG. 3. Separations that are difficult to achieve with a single column may often be obtained easily with parallel columns.

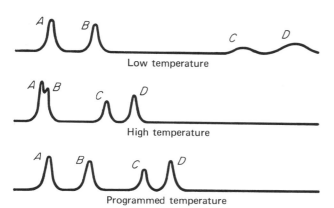

FIG. 4. Drawbacks inherent in the conventional technique of separating sample components by programming the temperature may be eliminated by using parallel columns and multiple temperature zones.

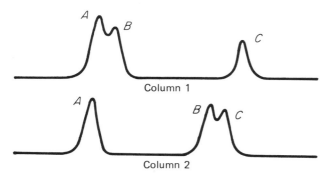

FIG. 5. Subtracting the contribution of C obtained on column 1 from the sum of B and C obtained on column 2 yields an analysis for B in a manner analogous to solving simultaneous equations.

only one of which can be resolved easily on a single column or on series columns, even when using temperature programming, Figure 3, and component peaks A and D. Using column 1, D can be readily resolved, while with column 2, A is clearly distinguishable. But if only one column were used, both A and D could not be clearly separated. Other components, B and C, make it impossible.

Various arrangements for switching series columns have been proposed, Ref. 2. But in order to obtain reasonable separation, longer cycle times are needed; moreover, the separation of peaks by the first series column is partially reversed by the second. In contrast, with parallel columns as shown, aided by multiple temperature zones, the outputs from both columns 1 and 2 are useful.

Example 2. The two components to be separated have very low and very high boiling points, Figure 4, A and D. The conventional solution is to accept the compromise of column length, temperature, and time required to resolve the components as illustrated in the upper curve. This procedure makes the elution time quite long.

The bottom curve illustrates the alternative approach of using programmed temperature. Here there is a nice separation of all components, but with attendant problems of gating, baseline stability, poor reproducibility, and more complex hardware.

Parallel columns and multiple temperature zones provide a reliable and reproducible means of accomplishing the same results in a much shorter time. The outputs from both the low-temperature and high-temperature columns of Figure 4 can be used, with C and D backflushed (discussed later) from the low-temperature column. In effect, this method is a way of simulating temperature programming without encountering its inherent problems.

Example 3. The next case involves separation of components A and B in Figure 5, where component C represents a sample complexity such that B cannot be resolved on any column. However, once it is noted that C can be analyzed on column 1, its contribution to the composite peak B+C on column 2 can be subtracted out, leaving an accurate value for B.

Although data reduction equipment is involved in this solution, it is parallel columns that make the approach practical. It is possible to make multiple analyses, normalizing between analyses, and use simultaneous equations to resolve peaks not distinguishable in any other way.

These examples show that even in simple separations of two components, parallel columns combined with multiple temperature zones can give valuable capabilities, such as:

Faster separations.

Analyses not obtainable on single columns.

Simulated temperature programming without the drawbacks of actual temperature programming.

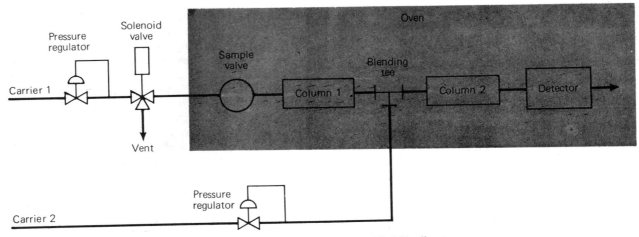

FIG. 6. Block diagram of capillary backflushing system. Use of pressure-controlled blending tee eliminates intercolumn valving, and prevents decrease in resolution that would otherwise occur.

Other chromatograph features

Three other important aspects of the 214 chromatograph are briefly discussed:

Subambient column temperature. Materials with low boiling points may be more easily analyzed when, as in this instrument, the columns can be maintained at temperatures below the ambient.

Capillary columns and backflushing. Backflushing through the detector during an analysis for the purpose of lumping the remaining heavier components as a single peak (or simply porting them to waste) is conventionally accomplished by additional valving—and thus added volume and reduced resolution. In the 214 chromatograph, however, a unique pressure changing system is used for backflushing through capillary columns, Figure 6.

Normally carrier 1 flows through columns 1 and 2. The carrier 2 pressure regulator is adjusted so that there is only a slight flow through the blending tee and column 2. For backflushing, carrier 1 flow is blocked while carrier 2 flow splits at the blending tee to flow through column 2 and simultaneously backflush column 1 to vent. Carrier 2 pressure regulator maintains a constant pressure at the blending tee so that the flow through column 2 remains constant with and without backflush. The result is backflushing capability without resolution loss.

Stated another way, the application engineer can consider the use of capillary columns without having to do a tradeoff between more analysis time (elimination of backflushing) and poorer resolution (inclusion of backflushing).

Vaporization of liquid samples. Automatic sampling of liquids for process chromatographs requires accurate metering of extremely small samples or some type of sample splitting as normally done on laboratory instruments. (The nominal sample size for capillary columns is of the order of 0.01 microliter.)

In the 214 system a large liquid sample of about 30 microliters is injected into a heated, evacuated chamber where it immediately flashes. It is then diluted with an inert gas to about 15 psig. This diluted vapor is then simultaneously sampled for each column in the instrument.

The rationale for this design is summarized as follows: (1) Materials with high boiling points can be sampled and vaporized at much lower temperatures. (2) Small quantities of a sample can be injected on capillary columns without requiring sample splitting. And (3) unstable samples can be handled at lower temperatures and at lower partial pressures if required.

Computerized process application

A 214 prototype is teamed with a PDP-8 computer to analyze five reformer streams on a time-sharing basis at Phillips' Sweeny, Tex., refinery. These gasoline streams contain over 100 compounds between C_3 and C_{12} carbon number. Four parallel columns and four temperature zones are used. The computer is essentially dedicated with 4K core and 32K disc memory. It performs these functions:

Stream selection and sample injection.

Scanning and storing of four chromatograms from four flame ionization detectors.

Gating and integration of the chromatograms.

Assembly and normalization of the four chromatograms into a single equivalent chromatogram.

Component identification and conversion to volume percent.

Printout of complete analysis as name versus volume percent.

Calculation from the analysis and printout of several parameters, including summed components of naphthenes, aromatics, branched paraffins, and normal paraffins; stream octane number; and stream

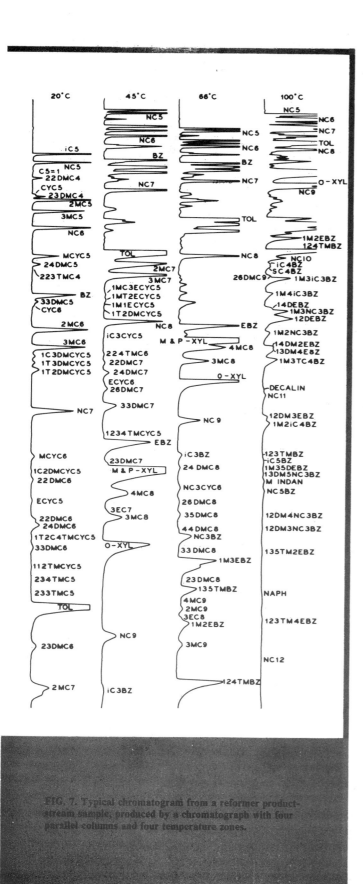

20°C	45°C	66°C	100°C
			NC5
		NC5	NC6
	NC5		NC7
iC5	NC6	NC5	TOL
	BZ	NC6	NC8
C5=1 NC5		BZ	
22DMC4	NC7	NC7	O-XYL
CYC5			NC9
23DMC4			
2MC5		TOL	
3MC5			1M2EBZ
NC6			124TMBZ
	TOL	NC8	NC10
MCYC5	2MC7		iC4BZ
24DMC5	3MC7	26DMC9	SC4BZ
223TMC4	1MC3ECYC5		1M3iC3BZ
BZ	1MT2ECYC5		1M4iC3BZ
33DMC5	1M1ECYC5		14DEBZ
CYC6	1T2DMCYC5		1M3NC3BZ
	NC8	EBZ	12DEBZ
2MC6	iC3CYC5	M&P-XYL	1M2NC3BZ
3MC6		4MC8	14DM2EBZ
	224TMC6	3MC8	13DM4EBZ
1C3DMCYC5	22DMC7		1M3TC4BZ
1T3DMCYC5	24DMC7	O-XYL	
1T2DMCYC5	ECYC6		DECALIN
	26DMC7		NC11
NC7	33DMC7	NC9	12DM3EBZ
	1234TMCYC5		1M2iC4BZ
	EBZ		
MCYC6		iC3BZ	123TMBZ
1C2DMCYC5	23DMC7	24DMC8	iC5BZ
22DMC6	M&P-XYL		1M35DEBZ
		NC3CYC6	13DM5NC3BZ
ECYC5	4MC8		M INDAN
	3EC7	26DMC8	NC5BZ
22DMC6	3MC8	35DMC8	12DM4NC3BZ
24DMC6		44DMC8	12DM3NC3BZ
1T2C4TMCYC5		NC3BZ	
33DMC6	O-XYL	33DMC8	135TM2EBZ
		1M3EBZ	
112TMCYC5		23DMC8	
234TMC5		135TMBZ	
233TMC5		4MC9	NAPH
		2MC9	
TOL		3EC8	123TM4EBZ
		1M2EBZ	
23DMC6	NC9	3MC9	NC12
2MC7	iC3BZ	124TMBZ	

FIG. 7. Typical chromatogram from a reformer product-stream sample, produced by a chromatograph with four parallel columns and four temperature zones.

FIG. 8. The prototype 214 chromatograph analyzer system installed in Phillips' Sweeny, Tex., refinery.

FIG. 9. Control room view showing the computer to which the chromatograph of Figure 8 is linked.

FIG. 10 — On-line printout

```
STAB BTMS DATA
    SPGR (ANAL) = 0.7948    API = 46.52
    OCTANE (+3ML) = 98.16
    VOL % CLASSES
        N-PARAF = 11.95
        B-PARAF = 30.24
        AROM    = 55.05
        NAPH    =  2.73
        UNKNOWNS = 0.00

C5+ YIELD = 84.15

UNIT 11 REFORMATE ANALYSIS

COMPONENT    CONC. (VOL. %)
```

Component	Conc.	Component	Conc.	Component	Conc.
IC5	2.99	22DMC6	0.14	NC3BZ	1.94
NC5	2.37	ECYC5	0.03	1M3EBZ	5.61
C5=1	0.05	25DMC6	0.25	23DMC8	0.32
22DMC4	0.28	24DMC6	0.55	135TMBZ	1.99
CYC5	0.06	1T2C4TMCYC5	0.05	4MC9	0.30
23DMC4	0.33	33DMC6	0.19	2MC9	0.61
2MC5	1.86	TOL	6.82	1M2EBZ	1.99
3MC5	1.44	23DMC6	0.61	3MC9	0.86
C6=1	0.06	2MC7	1.90	124TMBZ	5.65
NC6	1.78	34DMC6	1.03	NC10	1.23
2MC5=2	0.03	3MC7	2.63	IC4BZ	0.23
MCYC5	0.55	1MT3ECYC5	0.14	SC4BZ	0.48
24DMC5	0.24	1MT2ECYC5	0.17	1M3IC3BZ	0.91
BZ	0.95	1T2DMCYC6	0.05	1M3IC3BZ	1.04
33DMC5	0.41	NC8	2.28	SC4CYC6	0.10
2MC6	2.36	224TMC6	0.09	1M4IC3BZ	0.79
3MC6	2.04	22DMC7	0.16	1M3NC3BZ	1.38
1C3DMCYC5	0.13	24DMC7	0.34	12DEBZ	2.36
1T3DMCYC5	0.10	ECYC6	0.08	1M2NC3BZ	0.70
1T2DMCYC5	0.33	26DMC7	0.37	14DM2EBZ	0.42
NC7	2.00	33DMC7	0.96	13DM4EBZ	0.84
MCYC6	0.12	1234TMCYC5	0.11	1M3TC4BZ	1.51
1C2DMCYC5	0.03	EBZ	3.05	NC11	0.55
		23DMC7	0.34	12DM3EBZ	0.33
		XYL	8.65	1M2I C4BZ	0.95
		4MC8	3.05	1235TMBZ	0.04
		3MC8	2.28	IC5BZ	0.25
		O-XYL	3.88	M IND	0.18
		1T2ECYC6	0.13	NC5BZ	0.36
		NC9	1.62	12DM4C3BZ	0.22
		IC3BZ	0.62	12DM3C3BZ	0.13
		SC4CYC5	0.07	135TM2EBZ	0.12
		24DMC8	0.37	123TM5EBZ	0.03
		NC3CYC6	0.38	NAPTH	0.10
		26DMC8	0.26	1E3C4BZ	0.37
		35DMC8	0.39	NC12	0.08

FIG. 10. On-line printout from a reformer product stream analysis, produced by a 214 chromatograph system working with a PDP-8 computer.

specific gravity or API gravity, and distillation points.

A typical chromatogram from a reformate stream sample is presented in Figure 7. This is what the computer sees and stores in the disc memory. From these four parallel chromatograms, the above-listed data is calculated and made available for printout.

In addition to the chromatographic data, some 50 other measurements are made on the reformer units for input to the computer. These include temperatures, pressures, and flow rates, as well as outputs from other analytical instruments. Process operational criteria thus produced by the computer include actual yield, predicted yield, standard mass and volume flow rates, material balance, mol ratios of various components between feed and product, and percent conversion of various components from feed to product.

Three salient aspects of this installation are worthy of note:

■ The chromatograph was originally designed to be compatible with a digital computer.

■ It is estimated that the analysis that is made in 20 min would take at least an hour by other chromatographic methods, including use of temperature programming.

■ With the complete analysis available, it is practical to calculate physical parameters, a step that would normally be carried out with other instrumentation.

Figures 8 and 9 show the refinery installation of the 214 prototype analyzer and the computer, respectively. Figure 10 is a typical printout of a reformer stream analysis.

This system affords a splendid opportunity for detailed determination of the effect of operating variables and feed composition on the individual components of the product. In the past it was difficult to ascertain product composition on line in a routine manner. Hence it was customary to specify complex mixtures such as gasoline indirectly in terms of octane or vapor pressures. This procedure has sufficed, no doubt. But with the advent of air pollution abatement requirements, specifying composition detail may become a critical factor.

It seems reasonable to conclude from this documented experience that chromatographs may be on the threshold of an expanded phase of on-line utilization. Putting complete analyses of complex streams on a practical basis should yield greater latitude in the criteria used for determining the best methods of process operation and control. It should become practical to develop or recognize in greater depth the multitude of interactive relationships that could or do occur among manipulated variables and actual compositions along the process stream. Perhaps the most important single portent is that although the on-line composition detail will proliferate, it will still be practical to reduce it to tractable parameters for good control decisions. □

REFERENCES

1. "A Versatile Process Chromatograph," R. A. Sanford, M. L. Miller, and B. O. Ayers, *Analysis Instrumentation 1965,* Proceedings of the 11th Analysis Instrumentation Symposium, Plenum Press, New York, 1966, pp. 87-97.
2. "Process Chromatography Tips", L. Fowler, *Instrumentation Technology,* Sept. 1969, pp. 46-51.

Computer-Controlled Chromatographs

Chemical plant laboratories, which often keep several dozen chromatographs busy analyzing hundreds of routine samples a week, offer an ideal environment for computer control. Letting the computer monitor and control several instruments, reduce the data, and generate the final report saves a lot of time and manpower. Here's how Monsanto computerized its chromatography lab so that all the analyst needs to do is key in the test method, inject the sample, push a button, and tear off the analytical report.

P. P. BRIGGS, Monsanto Co.

Two separate trends of hardware development have recently merged to produce a happy pairoff for process control users: computers and chromatographs. Analytical instruments, particularly gas chromatographs, have found a wide acceptance over the past two decades in the petrochemical industry. The output from these instruments, an electrical analog signal, very seldom represents the desired analysis information directly. It must be edited and mathematically manipulated to convert it into useful information. For example, the output of a chromatograph is usually plotted on a strip chart recorder as a chromatogram, or series of peaks. The time at which each peak occurs helps to identify the component that the peak represents, while the area under the peak yields quantitative information on the amount of that component present in the mixture. Integrators, peak-pickers, and digitizers have been used extensively to partially reduce the chromatograph output data to numeric form, for manipulation by calculator or computer.

A number of small computer systems, recently introduced, are capable of multiple level operation while coupled with mass storage devices. The availability of these small on-line computers now makes it possible not only to do the integration and digitizing referred to above; but also to manipulate this data further in whatever ways are required to print out the desired component analysis directly. A single small computer can combine the functions of instrument monitoring and control, data reduction, calculations, and generation of the final report in its end-use form.

Furthermore, the ability of the computer to operate asynchronously with several independent real-time programs means that it can service a large number of instruments simultaneously.

Such a system has been in operation for more than a year at Monsanto's Chocolate Bayou plant laboratory near Alvin, Tex., where an IBM 1801 computer monitors, controls, and calculates results for 40 laboratory chromatographs and one mass spectrometer. As many as 20 chromatographs may be in simultaneous operation. Once the lab analyst injects a sample, the system requires no further attention from him until the report is typed. Data input and output stations are provided at two plant laboratories, remote from the computer. All program revisions, changes in constants, and similar operations are executed in the computer room, without disturbing the on-line laboratory operations. The time-sharing and bulk-storage capabilities of the IBM 1800 system have been taken advantage of to keep external documentation and filing systems to a minimum. New analytical methods or changes to existing methods are placed in the computer bulk memory by means of a simple fill-in-the-blank code sheet. This code sheet is oriented toward the lab analyst, who needs no knowledge of programming to set up the test method.

Samples in, reports out

The functional specifications that the system was designed to meet are to:
• Read on demand any of 40 chromatograph input

Reprinted with permission from *Contr. Eng.*, vol. 14, pp. 75–80, Sept. 1967.

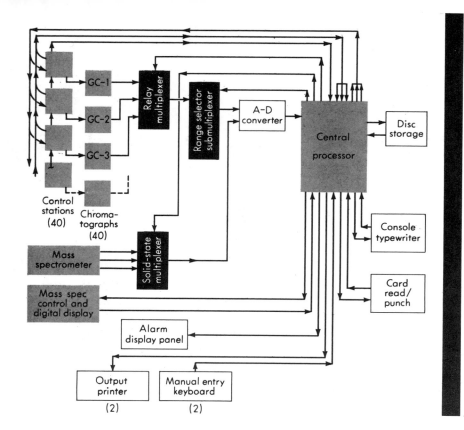

FIG. 1. IBM 1801 computer monitors and controls up to 20 laboratory chromatographs and one mass spectrometer simultaneously. Chromatograph outputs are scanned 4 per sec.

FIG. 2. Computer takes over after the analyst injects sample into a chromatograph and generates an interrupt by pushing button on the adjacent control station. On routine analyses, the analyst first specifies sample number and test method from a manual entry keyboard.

signals. Up to 20 of these may be in operation simultaneously. Once a reading is requested, each active input point must be read at least four times per sec.

• Convert signals having a dynamic range up to 5 vdc to digital form, with enough resolution to permit integration of peaks with an amplitude of 10 microvolts.

• Read and digitize each of three mass spectrometer signals 80 times per sec, without interfering with the chromatograph scanning.

• Provide programs and hardware to operate column switching valves, backflush valves, and other external devices which must be actuated in a definite time sequence to perform the chromatographic analyses.

• Provide a simple means by which the analyst may call from the computer memory all necessary labels, constants, and other information required to process the particular sample being analyzed.

• Provide communication between the analyst and the computer to indicate the current status of any chromatograph. The analyst must be able to tell the computer which instrument a sample is to be run on, and when to start scanning that instrument. Conversely, the computer must be able to indicate to the analyst which instruments are being scanned, and the time when scanning is completed.

• Edit the raw data at the completion of each analysis, identify each component, calculate compositions, and type out a complete analytical report.

• Provide maintenance programs to facilitate on-line revision of methods, constants, and similar data which is stored on the disc.

The block diagram, Figure 1, shows the hardware used to accomplish these functions. The main frame is the two-microsec version of the IBM 1801,

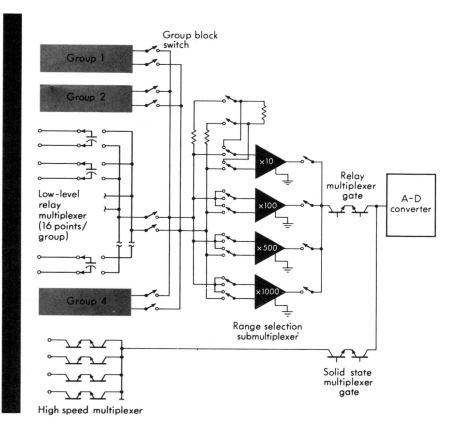

FIG. 3. Monsanto-designed sub-multiplexer provides a choice of four gain levels, under program control, to couple chromatograph outputs to A-D converter. Mass spectrometer outputs are read through a separate high-speed solid-state multiplexer.

with a 16K core memory and 12 levels of interrupt. An IBM 2310 disc storage unit provides random access to 512,000 words for bulk storage of programs and data. All output is typed on three Model 1053 Selectric typewriters. Manual entry of sample labels, job identifications, and chromatograph numbers is performed through modified IBM 1092 keyboard data entry units. Changes in computer programs and disc maintenance operations are processed through an IBM 1442 card reader-punch.

A small control station is located at each chromatograph, Figure 2. This station contains the contact closure switches that interface the instrument with the computer, and indicating lights to display the status of each chromatograph (active or inactive).

As shown in Figure 1, two independent multiplexers operate in an overlap mode into a single A-D converter. The standard IBM high-speed solid-state multiplexer scans the mass spectrometer inputs, and feeds the converter through one data channel. The entire input table for this multiplexer is scanned in the interval between two successive conversions on the second data channel.

The second data channel transmits the analog outputs from the chromatographs to the A-D converter, through a low-level relay multiplexer and submultiplexer, Figure 3. The submultiplexer, designed and built by Monsanto, operates under direct program control, and permits the computer to select the proper amplification range for the point being converted.

Coping with noise

Most laboratory chromatographs superimpose a considerable amount of noise on the useful output signal. Several different techniques were adopted in both installation and programming of the system, to reduce this noise to a tolerable level. Each chromatograph was reworked to eliminate ground loops and to suppress arcing switches and similar obvious noise sources. In some electrometer amplifiers, negative ac feedback was used to achieve a drastic reduction in noise level. All low level signal lines were run in individually shielded, twisted pair cables. Shield terminations were made at the low side of the signal source only. Low-pass RC networks were installed at the multiplexer terminal to reduce high frequency noise appearing at the multiplexer input. Each amplifier used in the submultiplexer includes a sharp cut-off active filter which eliminates most of the contact noise introduced by the multiplexer relays.

Common mode noise is rejected by both the "flying capacitor" multiplexer and the differential amplifiers used in the submultiplexer. A sharp discrimination against 60-cycle noise is achieved by external synchronization of the first entry in the multiplexer address table to the power line. The multiplexer is thus pulled back into sync with the 60-cycle noise every 200 millisec. This eliminates low frequency beat cycles produced by accumulated timing errors in the input rate. Although these measures will not remove the dc component of 60-cycle noise which may be present, this bias is not important because the programs must correct for baseline offset in any case, as described on the following pages.

Finally, the scanning program itself includes some digital filtering and logical checks which further reduce the effects of noise. These programming techniques are also described below.

159

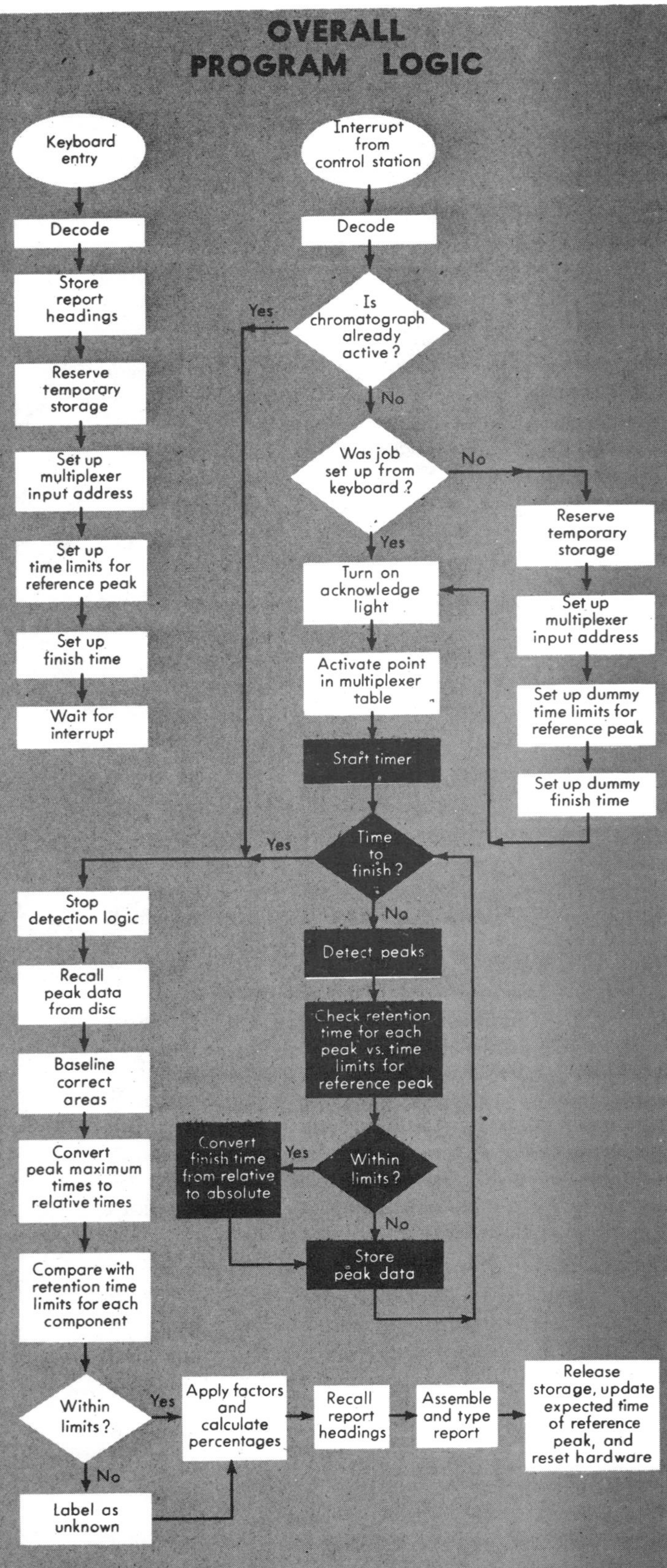

OVERALL PROGRAM LOGIC

Keyboard entry → Decode → Store report headings → Reserve temporary storage → Set up multiplexer input address → Set up time limits for reference peak → Set up finish time → Wait for interrupt

Interrupt from control station → Decode → Is chromatograph already active?

Is chromatograph already active? — Yes / No
No → Was job set up from keyboard? — Yes / No
No → Reserve temporary storage → Set up multiplexer input address → Set up dummy time limits for reference peak → Set up dummy finish time
Yes → Turn on acknowledge light → Activate point in multiplexer table → Start timer

Time to finish? — Yes / No
No → Detect peaks → Check retention time for each peak vs. time limits for reference peak → Within limits? — Yes / No
Yes → Convert finish time from relative to absolute
No → Store peak data

Yes (Time to finish?) → Stop detection logic → Recall peak data from disc → Baseline correct areas → Convert peak maximum times to relative times → Compare with retention time limits for each component → Within limits? — Yes / No
No → Label as unknown
Yes → Apply factors and calculate percentages → Recall report headings → Assemble and type report → Release storage, update expected time of reference peak, and reset hardware

FIG. 4. To conserve memory, the program does as much data reduction as possible while components are eluting (black blocks). After each peak is detected the computer integrates to obtain a raw peak area and stores this value along with time and voltage data for baseline correction. After all components of interest have eluted, the system recalls the information required to generate the final report.

The output of a typical laboratory chromatograph is a time-varying electrical signal that is related to the molecular fraction of each constituent eluting from the column by a proportionality factor K_n. Since each component elutes over a period of time, the output must be integrated over this same period of time to obtain the peak areas. If the area of the peak for the nth component of a mixture is given by A_n, then the mole fraction of the nth component is

$$X_n = \frac{K_n A_n}{K_1 A_1 + K_2 A_2 + \ldots\ldots + K_n A_n}$$

Analyses are run on standard samples of one type or another to supply the values for one or more of the variables or constants in the equation.

In applying a digital computer to calculate chromatographic analyses by means of this equation, a number of practical complications arise. The equation requires that all of the peak areas and constants be available at the time the solution is to be calculated. The computer must therefore store data which is acquired as each component elutes, but it cannot process this data until the analysis is complete and all components have eluted. Since storage capacity is limited, not all the raw data can be retained. An important objective of the computer programs is to limit the storage requirements by reducing the data as much as possible, immediately as it occurs. Thus, while the components are eluting from the chromatograph column, the computer detects peaks, integrates their areas, and stores the peak areas along with the time and voltage values which are required to make baseline corrections and to compute relative retention times. After all components have eluted, the computer retrieves this reduced data from memory and makes the final calculations. A generalized flow chart of the overall program logic is shown in Figure 4.

Peak detection logic

The computer program detects peaks as they occur by sampling the chromatograph output signal v 4 times per sec and computing slope and acceleration values of the output with respect to time. Digital data is inherently noisy, so running values for slope dv/dt and acceleration d^2v/dt^2 are calculated for each instrument by computing a least-squares fit through the last 13 readings of the chromatograph output. This digital filtering technique smooths the data and reduces noise still further than the hardware techniques described above.

A simplified logic flow diagram for the peak detection program, Figure 5, shows how peaks are detected from slope and acceleration values. A normal peak which starts and ends at the baseline causes the program to advance through the major loop. The two minor loops contain the logic steps to detect unresolved shoulder peaks on the front or back side of another peak. An imperfectly resolved or fused pair of peaks causes the program to cut across the major loop without a return to baseline status. There is no limit to the number of times the program can pass through any loop.

Although they are not all shown in Figure 5, a number of intermediate logic steps are included in the program. These steps require that changes in polarity of slope and acceleration be confirmed by a subsequent scan before the computer makes a logical decision on the existence of a peak. This programmed logic provides further digital filtering, and helps to prevent noise spikes from being reported as peaks.

Each time the scan program returns through the "on baseline" status, a time and voltage value is stored for use by a baseline correction routine. This routine interpolates between the stored baseline points to derive a baseline location for the start and finish of each peak. The area of the baseline trapezoid for each peak is then calculated and subtracted from the raw peak area.

For the final calculations of molecular fractions, each peak must be identified and associated with the appropriate constants for the component it represents. In the Monsanto system, relative retention times with respect to a selected component in the mixture provide the basis for identification. The selected reference component may be any component that is always present in the sample, and its peak is identified by the absolute retention time, within a specified tolerance. The absolute retention time of any component changes slowly, due principally to aging of the column. As the last block in Figure 4 shows, at the end of each analysis the computer program automatically updates the expected retention time for the reference peak to compensate for column aging.

When a new analytical method or a new type of sample is being set up in the computer, the analyst runs a typical sample through the chromatograph to obtain retention time data for each component. After the analysis, he feeds back to the computer the name of each component and its retention time in seconds, and specifies one of the components as the reference component. The computer then converts these absolute retention times to relative retention times for each component, and stores them on disc for use in subsequent runs.

The identification of peaks by relative retention times is limited to those components whose retention times have been previously stored in memory. When unexpected peaks occur, they must be assigned a proportionality constant if they are to be included in the normalization calculation. A constant for an unknown peak may be derived by interpolating between the constants for the peaks adjacent to it, or an arbitrary constant may be assigned to all unknown peaks. Some laboratory methods in use by Monsanto assign the unknown constants by interpolation, and others assign an arbitrary constant. Still others do not include unknown peaks at all in the calculations.

However, in all cases where unknown peaks are detected they are reported in the computer printout,

PEAK-PICKING LOGIC

FIG. 5. After each scan, peak detection program calculates least-squares fit through several data points, then calculates slope and acceleration of the equivalent chromatogram. The several logic loops shown will detect normal single peaks, fused peaks, and shoulder peaks.

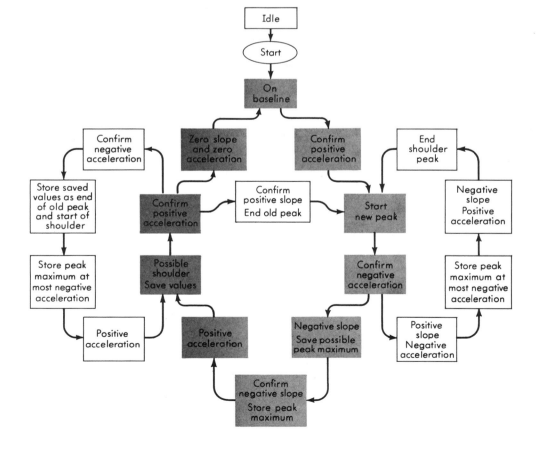

together with retention times and their percentage contribution to the total area. Whether or not the unknown peaks are included in the calculations, they are reported in this manner to indicate validity of the run. If an appreciable percentage of the total area is contributed by unknown components, the analysis is of doubtful value and should be checked.

Assembling the report

There are many ways in which the results of a chromatograph analysis may be reported. The general normalization equation assumes that the area and proportionality constant for each peak is available. In addition to calculation routines to solve this equation and to correct for baseline drift, the computer programs include routines for allocating areas between two or more components when shoulder peaks or fused peaks are encountered.

Many chromatographic methods, however, do not attempt to separate every component in the sample, or to include all separated components in the calculations. Some methods may normalize to a base other than 100 percent. Others may obtain sensitivity factors directly from the analysis of standard samples of known composition. These and other calculation routines are programmed into the computer for selection by the lab analyst when he is setting up an analytical method. The available calculation routines include all the common variations required for internal standards, external standards, normalization, and calculation of area correction factors from samples of known composition. In some methods, the analyst wishes the report to lump a group of peaks under one generic heading such as "total non-aromatics"; routines are available to group peaks in this manner. The peaks that are grouped do not have to be adjacent, but may be selected in any fashion as dictated by the elution order and the desired report format. Whenever peaks are lumped for any reason, the printout indicates the number of grouped peaks and their relative sizes.

The Chocolate Bayou laboratory presently runs more than 100 different chromatographic analyses. These methods are set up in the computer by choosing various combinations from 143 working subroutines stored on disc. In addition to the final calculation routines for various report formats, these subroutines cover variations in data acquisition and control actions required for different laboratory methods. For example, six parameters in the scanning program can be changed, including sampling rate and the values of weighting factors associated with the least-squares fit mentioned above. A gain change routine is also included, to select the proper amplifier in the submultiplexer. Other routines cause operation of external contacts to switch columns or backflush as required by the laboratory method.

The computer system also functions as a conventional digitizer for one-time analyses or to provide retention time data for the initial setting up of a new method. No keyboard entry is required when operating in this mode. The analyst simply injects the sample in a chromatograph and pushes the "scan start" button at the adjacent control station. When the last peak of interest has eluted, he terminates the scan by pushing the same button again. The printout in this case consists of a list of all detected peaks with their retention times and baseline-corrected areas.

Program maintenance

A control laboratory is a rather fluid environment. Methods and instrument configurations are constantly being changed to meet new analytical requirements. A very flexible program maintenance system has been provided to permit such changes on line by personnel who are not trained in programming. The lab analysts use standardized fill-in-the-blank forms to set up new procedures or modify existing ones.

The maintenance programs perform some rather sophisticated housekeeping, to eliminate the need for external documentation. For example, a table of variables that may be used by a number of different analytical methods is stored on disc. These variables are semipermanent constants that are associated with a particular column or a particular set of operating conditions. One example would be the absolute retention times for various components. Different analytical methods may use the same retention times, but require that they be referred to different peaks. If the chromatograph column is changed, the retention times must be revised only in the variable table rather than in the body of each analytical method. The computer will automatically search for every place the variable is used, compute new relative retention times against the proper reference peak, and replace the old value in each analytical method.

More precision, less time and manpower

The installation of the laboratory computer at Chocolate Bayou has resulted in a considerable improvement in precision in many routine control analyses. A typical example showed a change in standard deviation from 0.2 to 0.02 percent after the computer installation. In a large chemical plant, the ability to operate 0.1 percent closer to specification with confidence is worth many thousands of dollars each year.

The time required to generate a final report has, in some cases, been significantly reduced. This is particularly true of high speed capillary column chromatographs which may resolve a hundred or more peaks that were previously measured by hand. Some scans, which previously required two hours to measure and calculate, are now typed out in three minutes.

Analysts have been relieved of the chore of monitoring a recorder to determine cut points and attenuation factors, and reruns required because of missed attenuations have been eliminated. In the research laboratory, the computer-monitored chromatograph has become a vital tool that frees the researcher from monitoring and data reduction work and allows him to devote his full attention to the experiment itself.

A small computer as an on line multi-parameter analyser for a neutron spectrometer

by S. B. WRIGHT and M. G. SILK

A.E.R.E., Harwell
Berkshire, England

INTRODUCTION

The techniques in current use for the measurement of the neutron energy spectrum above a few kilovolts in the core of a reactor rely on the measurement of the energy of the secondary particles produced as a result of a neutron interaction with a nucleus. The most common reactions are scattering by hydrogen in which the energy of the recoil proton is measured, and the reaction between a neutron and Lithium-6 to produce an alpha particle and a triton which are detected in coincidence. In both these reactions the energy of the reaction products is a linear function of the neutron energy, and it is difficult to cover an energy much greater than a factor of ten in a single measurement with these techniques. This means that at least 4 and often 6 or 7 different measurements are required to cover the energy range from a few keV up to 10 MeV.

A neutron spectrometer which could cover this whole energy range in a single, or at least fewer measurements would be very desirable and such a spectrometer could be achieved by using the angle between the reaction products of the Li^6 (n, α)H^3 reaction as the measure of the neutron energy rather than their total energy. The reaction products of this reaction are emitted at 180° in the centre of mass system. If the incident neutron has zero or near zero kinetic energy this corresponds to the laboratory system. However, if the neutron carries significant energy the centre of mass system is moving relative to the laboratory system, and the angle between the reaction products is less than 180° in the laboratory system. As the reaction is isotropic relative to the direction of motion of the incident neutron the angle between the reaction products is not a unique function of the neutron energy, but the relationship is sufficiently simple for the neutron energy spectrum to be unfolded from the distribution of the angles. For energies below a few MeV the angle of the reaction products is a function of the square root of the incident neutron energy and so a spectrometer based on measurement of this angle should cover a wider range of neutron energies than one based on measurement of the total energy of the reaction.

Spectrometers based on this principle have been proposed by Beets [1] using a number of separate counters to detect particles at different angles. In the spectrometer discussed here the reaction products are detected in 3 position sensitive semi-conductor detectors, and a Honeywell DDP 516 used on line analyses the output of these detectors to give the angle between the reaction products. In this way data which are generated as 9 coincident parameters each of 8 bits are analysed and stored as a single parameter of 6 bits, and the data handling problem becomes manageable.

The spectrometer and the interface to the computer are in manufacture at the time of writing, and delivery is expected during September. The programme is basically written and awaiting the delivery of the computer. We therefore expect to have the first results available by the end of 1968.

The design of the spectrometer

In order to define the angle between the reaction products, the point of interaction and points on the tracks of both of the secondary particles must be determined. This can be accomplished using a set of three position sensitive detectors arranged in a stack as shown in Figure 1. The central detector, being coated with the lithium-6 carbonate target, defines the point of interaction while the outer detectors define the X and Y co-ordinates of the points of incidence of the secondaries. The Z co-ordinates are defined by the diode separation.

The position sensitive detectors used are of the type developed by Owen and Awcock.[2]. and are sensitive in two directions. The sensitive region of the detectors is a square of side 1.35 cms and it is anticipated that the spatial resolution will be better than 1/3 mm. Four

Reprinted with permission from *AFIPS Conf. Proc., Vol. 33, Pt. 2, 1968 Fall Joint Comput. Conf.*, pp. 1099–1103.

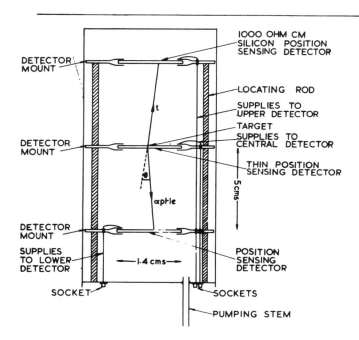

Figure 1—The design of the position sensitive neutron spectrometer.

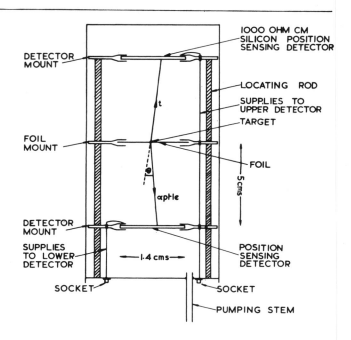

Figure 2—The design of the prototype neutron spectrometer.

pulses may be taken from each detector proportional to EX, EY, E(S-X), E(S-Y) where E is the total energy released in the detector, X and Y are the position co-ordinates and S is the side of the detector (1.35 cms). Adding the pulses corresponding to EX and E(S-X) produces a pulse corresponding to ES. Clearly

$$X = S(V_x/V_s) \quad Y = S(V_x/V_s)$$

Thus to determine the X and Y co-ordinates in each detector, three parameters (V_x, V_{ex} and V_y in this case) need be recorded.

The centre diode of the final spectrometer is a very difficult diode to make satisfactorily. A prototype spectrometer has therefore been designed in which the centre diode is replaced by a small spot of lithium-6 carbonate on a Mylar or similar film [3] (Figure 2). This prototype will require the an alysis of only 6 parameters, but all the electronics and programme design has been done allowing for the 9 parameters of the full spectrometer.

The expected range of angles for this device is 180° to 150° corresponding to a neutron energy range of approximately 10 keV to 10 MeV. This will be covered by 64 equal groups on a logarithmic energy scale.

Data collection

The fast neutron spectrum can be determined to a reasonable accuracy if about 10^5 counts due to fast neutron events are obtained. Thus, to determine the spec-

trum in a reasonable length of time, (say 25 hours) a count rate of about 1 fast neutron event/second must be obtained.

In thermal reactor systems only about 1 in 1000 of the recorded events will be due to fast neutrons; the remainder being due to the thermal and epithermal flux. These thermal events are indistinguishable from fast neutron events until at least a partial analysis has been carried out so the slowest acceptable storage rate in the recording system is about 1000 events/second. An event is defined by 9 parameters each of which is required to 8 bit accuracy. The storage rate required is thus 10^5 bits/sec. and the total stored data will amount to 7.2 10^9 bits which is well beyond the capacity of conventional multichannel analysers. Clearly the fact that only six parameters are required from the present prototype spectrometer eases the data handling problems but the general argument is not affected. In any case, it would be shortsighted to consider the prototype spectrometer separately from the final design unless the data handling problems were dramatically different.

Tape systems can be used and will handle data at the required rate with little difficulty although some derandomization would be required. However, the capacity of a typical 9 track tape is only about 2.10^8 bits so, even with the closest packing of data (impossible with events of a statistical nature) the data from one run will fill more than 35 full sized tapes. This technique is thus both cumbersome and expensive.

For these reasons, it was considered that the best means of storing the data was to introduce an on line data processor. This processor will reduce the data storage problems in two ways. Firstly a relatively simple test will eliminate the 'straight line' events due to thermal neutrons and to neutron reactions in the silicon of the detectors. The rapid elimination of thermal neutron events is very important since they are so much more frequent than fast neutron events. Thus the overall count rate is governed by the rate at which thermal events can be processed. Secondly those events not eliminated as straight lines will be analysed and the angle between the reaction products calculated from the recorded parameters. In this way, the quantity of data to be recorded is reduced by a factor of almost 5000. The calculations necessary are briefly described below. It is convenient to define an angle θ as being the supplement of the angle between the reaction products (Figures 1, 2).

The co-ordinates of points on the tracks of the secondaries will be calculated from the appropriate pulse heights. However, as the detector response is nonlinear the true values of these co-ordinates must then be calculated from a stored response matrix for each detector.

The elimination of thermal events is then accomplished by a simple test for a straight line for which

$$(X_1 - X_m) + (X_2 - X_m) = 0 \pm \delta$$

and

$$(Y_1 - Y_m) + (Y_2 - Y_m) = 0 \pm \delta$$

where the X and Y co-ordinates observed in the upper, lower and centre detectors are X_1, Y_1; X_2, Y_2; and X_m, Y_m respectively.

The value of δ will take into account the accuracy of the particular diodes used.

The value of θ is then obtained from the equation

$$\sin^2 \theta = \frac{(A_1 B_2 - B_1 A_2)^2 + (A_1 C_2 - C_1 A_2)^2 + (B_1 C_2 - C_1 B_2)^2}{(A_1^2 + B_1^2 + C_1^2)(A_2^2 + B_2^2 + C_2^2)}$$

where

$$A_1 = X_1 - X_m \qquad B_2 = Y_2 - Y_m$$
$$A_2 = X_2 - X_m \qquad C_1 = Z_1 - Z_m$$
$$B_1 = Y_1 - Y_m \qquad C_2 = Z_2 - Z_m$$

The values of $\sin^2 \theta$ obtained are compared against a table of values designed to correspond to equal intervals on a logarithmic scale of neutron energy.

The choice of computer was dictated by considerations of computing speed and word length. The word length must be great enough to ensure that potential increases in experimental accuracy are not limited by the computer and that rounding errors do not seriously contribute to the experimental errors. A word length of at least 14 bits is thus required and this eliminates 12 bit computers for which relatively slow double length arithmetic is required for part of the calculation. The computer used in the present experiment is the Honeywell DDP–516 which is a 16 bit computer with a core cycle time of 0.96 μsec. The best estimate of the mean total calculation time with this machine is 830 msec. which corresponds to a rate of acceptance of events of 1.25×10^3/sec. It seems likely that the calculation can be streamlined at many points once operational experience with these detectors has been obtained. The more usual and mathematically simpler formula for $\cos^2 \theta$ is not used in the calculation since at small values of θ the preservation of the overall accuracy would require parts of the calculation carried out to an accuracy corresponding to a computer word length of 18 bits.

It is estimated that less than 2000 store locations are needed for the program and the storage of the final data, so the size of store is dictated mainly by the response matrices for each detector. Present experience, which is limited to only a few detectors,[2] suggests that detector non-linearity can be allowed for to a high order of accuracy if 16×16 matrices are used for each detector. Thus a 4K store should be more than adequate for the present experiment.

The computer system described above has advantages both in cost and convenience over the alternative tape systems. In addition to this, it is more versatile since it can be readily applied to other experimental systems.

Electronics

A block diagram of the electronics is shown in Figure 3. Three signals are taken from each diode giving a total of 9 from the complete spectrometer (6 from the prototype). These signals are amplified and fed to separate gate and integrator circuits which give an output proportional to the integral of the pulse input when a suitable gate pulse is present. This gate pulse is generated by the coincidence circuit which demands a threefold coincidence between pulses from each detector to define a real neutron event. Threefold coincidence is adequate since it is clear that the release of charge in a detector will produce pulses at all three outputs. Cases where one output is not present due to a fault in the electronics are detected by program.

Sample and hold circuits based on a design by Kandiah[4] are used to store the integrated signals and these are then sequentially sampled and fed to a single

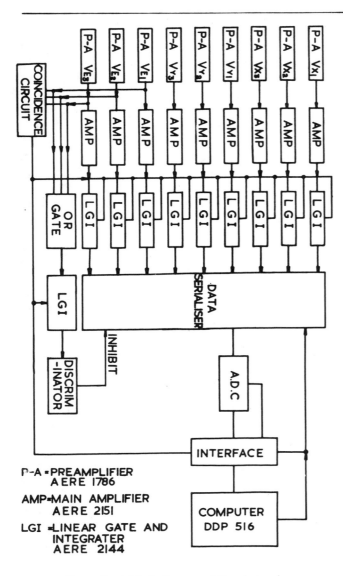

Figure 3—A block diagram of the electronics.

P-A = PREAMPLIFIER
AERE 1786

AMP = MAIN AMPLIFIER
AERE 2151

LGI = LINEAR GATE AND
INTEGRATER
AERE 2144

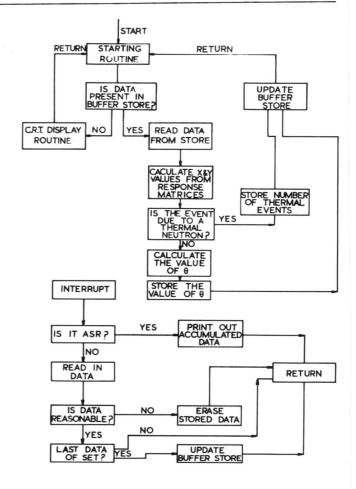

Figure 4—A flow diagram of the program.

ADC. The ADC conversion time in each case will be ∼ 70 μsec. maximum giving a total time of 630 μsec. which is well within the estimated computing time.

It is important that the data should be rapidly read into the computer from the interface. This is accomplished by means of the interrupt procedure using the I/O bus. It thus takes about 75 μsec. to read in each parameter which is quite rapid enough for the present experiment and which will not limit any foreseeable improvements in the data handling. The data output is provided by the teletype. A faster output than this is not required in an experiment of this nature in which a comparatively modest output of data is required at intervals of several hours.

Description of program

A flow diagram of the program is shown in Figure 4.

The basic steps shown are explained in the earlier sections on data collection and the electronics.

At the start of the program, and at the end of each complete logical sequence, control is returned to the starting routine. A test is made to see if data are present in the buffer store and if so the main sequence of calculations begins. These calculations may be terminated prior to the calculation of the angle if the event is judged to be due to a thermal neutron. In either case the buffer store is updated before control is returned to the starting routine.

A simple display routine is included which provides a display of the data input on an oscilloscope. This may either be a straightforward display of the spectrum of values of θ or may be partially corrected to provide an estimate of the form of the neutron spectrum. The routine comes into operation when no data are present in the buffer store.

Data input is carried out using the interrupt mode of the computer. Because of the sequential operation of the ADC, nine separate interrupts are used to input one complete set of data. The number of interrupts is counted and at the end of each set the data are transferred into the buffer store. The data are checked as they are read in to remove anomalous sets in which one of the detectors failed to record. If this happens consistently an appropriate message is printed out.

The print out of data is also governed by an interrupt from the teletype. This places the experiment under the control of the operator which is felt to be desirable at this stage. Similar control of the display will be provided.

Future development

The rate of acceptance of data is not as fast as we would like. It is estimated that the total computing time could be reduced, especially if the response of the detectors is predictable enough to enable the elimination of some thermal neutron events before the matrix correction is introduced. This would require a corresponding improvement in the total ADC conversion time, which could be accomplished either by the use of faster ADC's or by the use of two or more ADC's in parallel.

In the present system standard preamplifiers are used but, with nine signal channels, it is clearly impossible to mount the preamplifiers close to the detector inside a practical reactor system. The extra cable runs required may cause a deterioration in the signal to noise ratio and thus in the positional resolution of the detectors. In this case, it may prove desirable to mount the preamplifiers onto the base of the spectrometer. The use of integrated circuits makes this a practical proposition and it is not anticipated that the overall length of the spectrometer will be seriously increased.

It has been shown[2] that the calculation of X and Y for each detector may be carried out using an analogue system. This system reduces the number of signals taken to the computer from each detector from three to two and therefore enables the rate of data collection to be improved. An even more useful consequence, if the reproduceability of the detectors permits, would be the possibility of removing many thermal events before they are loaded into the computer. This would bring about a very significant improvement in the speed and efficiency of the system.

SUMMARY

A neutron spectrometer based on the measurement of the angle between the reaction products of the Li^6 $(n,\alpha)H^3$ reaction offers prospects of significant advantages over methods of neutron spectrometry in current use. However, the data handling problem is such that using conventional multichannel techniques the spectrometer would be completely uneconomic. The use of an on-line computer to reduce the data from 9 coincident parameters to a single parameter while the experiment is in progress reduces this data handling to such an extent that the experiment becomes straightforward. In addition to reducing the data to a single parameter so that multichannel analysis is possible the computer allows a crude analysis to be undertaken during the course of the experiment so that a display of the data in the form of a neutron spectrum rather than a spectrum of angles is possible. Thus the data are available to the experimentalist during his experiment in a form which allows him to judge the progress of the experiment.

The use of an on line computer has therefore made economic an experiment which would probably never be attempted using other forms of data handling equipment, and in addition has made it possible to provide adequate data to the experimentalist for him to have full control of the experiment at all times.

ACKNOWLEDGMENTS

The authors would like to acknowledge the assistance of Mr. M. Awcock and other members of the counters group of the Electronics Division who are undertaking the construction of the spectrometer. We would also like to thank Mr. K. Kandiah, Mr. F. D. Pryce and other members of the Electronics and Applied Physics Division for their assistance in the design and construction of the eletronic system.

REFERENCES

1 C BEETS   S de LEEUW   G deLEEUW-GIERTS
  Proc of a Conference on Radiation Measurements in Nuclear Power Berkeley 1966
2 R B OWEN   M L AWCOCK
  AERE R 5393 1967
3 M G SILK
  AERE–M 1850 1967
4 K KANDIAH
  Private communication

A MINICOMPUTER SYSTEM FOR THE ACQUISITION AND REDUCTION
OF DATA FROM THE MARINER VI AND VII ULTRAVIOLET SPECTROMETERS

J. B. Pearce
Laboratory for Atmospheric and Space Physics
University of Colorado
Boulder, Colorado 80302

A data handling system, designed for the acquisition, display, control and recording of spectra, based on a Digital Equipment Corporation PDP-8 has been in use at the University of Colorado's Laboratory for Atmospheric and Space Physics since 1967. The system has been used extensively during the calibration of the Mariner 6 and 7 ultraviolet spectrometers and for the reduction of the observations of Mars obtained by these instruments (Barth, et al 1969, 1971; Pearce, et al 1971).

During calibration the ultraviolet spectrometer is operated in a vacuum chamber where it is exposed to the ultraviolet light from a gaseous discharge lamp which is passed through a monochromator (see Figure 1). The output of the spectrometer is sent to the computer via a special interface which simulates the data system used on the Mariner spacecraft during flight (see Figure 2). This primary data, along with analog measurements of signals internal to the instrument, are assembled by the computer in buffers which are copied onto industry compatable tape for storage and later analysis (see Figure 3). Periodically during the calibration the operator selects an operating mode for standardization of the intensity of the source. In this mode a standard photo-multiplier tube is mechanically raster scanned through the beam and its output is recorded along with the output of two position potentiometers attached to the standard. These data are later used to obtain the beam intensity profile.

This system has also been used to interactively analyze the Martian ultraviolet data supplied from the Mariner project on tape. In this configuration an operator accesses individual spectra from tape under keyboard control. Selected spectra are continuously displayed on an oscilloscope. Using a specially written editor program various operations, such as scale shifting, display magnification, coherent addition, noise removal and integration under selected features, are accomplished. Analog potentiometers are used to enter selected variables. The operator may,

after manipulating his spectra, rewrite them onto tape or obtain a plot on a Cal-comp plotter.

The justification for this system, involving an initial purchase of $62,000, was not difficult since the magnitude of calibration data expected was overwhelming. The calibration data for the project filled about twenty-five 2400 foot reels of tape. The other alternative to a computer based system was our previous method, that of hand reducing strip chart records with their inherent inaccuracies for analog to digital conversion. Besides the obvious improvement in effort required to reduce the data, two other factors have been noted since putting the system in operation. First the computer based system is a much better record keeper than a human operator. By implementing keyboard requests for those conditions not directly recorded, such as dates and instrument serial numbers, a relatively complete data base was acquired. Secondly the operators were less inclined to skip steps in the procedure as they were using strip charts, since the data could be machine reduced instead of by hand. The concept of using the system as an interactive analysis tool was generated after the launch of the spacecraft and while they were in transit to Mars. An impetus was added by our inability to obtain satisfactory rates of analysis using the University's CDC 6400 in batch mode, although this facility was used for format conversion throughout the project.

The only hardware problems encountered, other than a few congenital defects which were quickly corrected, involved noise immunity. The system, when configured for a calibration run, had two separate a.c. supplies, a condition which was unavoidable. A good deal of trial and error testing was done to arrive at a modification involving the use of an isolation transformer for the spectrometer's bench checkout equipment and a procedure which forbid the use of a Xerox copier which shared a.c. mains with computer during calibration.

Software, however, was a different matter. DEC has, in the author's opinion,

Reprinted from *1971 IEEE Int. Conv. Dig.*, pp. 500–501.

a very serviceable software set for the basic PDP-8. For some of their more powerful, and therefore more expensive, and hence less frequently purchased peripherals, software can be hard to find. Only maintenance routines were supplied for the tape controller, the display controller and the analog to digital converter. As none of us were experienced in programing minicomputers a good deal of cut and try was necessary. Since that time DEC seems to have improved in this area. A second software problem is that of configuration control. The interactive analysis programs especially have undergone continuous development and modification. Control is being obtained through the purchase of a line printer and disk and by using the University's computer for file manipulation.

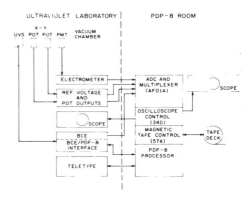

Figure 3. Computer and equipment configuration during a calibration.

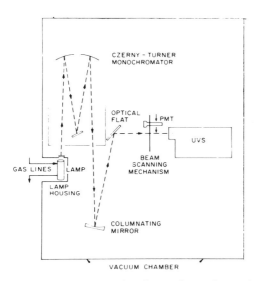

Figure 1. The optical path and equipment arrangement within the vacuum chamber.

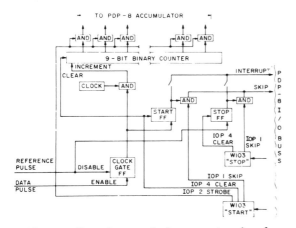

Figure 2. A special computerized spacecraft data system simulator.

REFERENCES

Barth, C.A., W. G. Fastie, C.W. Hord, J.B. Pearce, K.K. Kelly, A.I. Stewart, G.E. Thomas, G.P. Anderson and O.F. Raper, "Mariner 6: Ultraviolet Spectrum of Mars Upper Atmosphere", Science, 165, 1004, 1969.

Barth, C.A., C.W. Hord, J.B. Pearce, K.K. Kelly, G.P. Anderson, A.I. Stewart, "Mariner 6 and 7 Ultraviolet Spectrometer Experiment: Upper Atmosphere Data", J. Geophys. Res., 76, 000, 1971.

Pearce, J.B., K.A. Gause, E.F. Mackey, K.K. Kelly, W.G. Fastie and C.A. Barth, "The Mariner 6 and 7 Ultraviolet Spectrometer", Applied Optics, 10, 000, 1971.

ACKNOWLEDGMENTS

This work was performed under JPL contract JPL-951790.

Design of a Real-Time Central Data Acquisition and Analysis System

PAUL C. ABEGGLEN, WILLIAM R. FARIS, MEMBER, IEEE, AND
WILLIAM J. HANKLEY, MEMBER, IEEE

Abstract—A computer system is described for real-time data acquisition and servicing of 40 asynchronous inertial guidance system test stations. Some data are received automatically from the small guidance system computers at a maximum rate of eight words per second. Other data are input manually at each station via a mode selector and several 16-position thumbwheel switches. The data are received, partially edited and stored all in real time, and retrieved and analyzed with the highest "time-availability" priority at the time of completion of the guidance system test. The analysis results determine further testing or repair actions for each guidance system.

The central computer is a SEL 840-MP, a general-purpose 24-bit, 32K, 1.75-μs cycle-time machine with basic real-time monitor software. The special purpose system is implemented as a software/hardware interface with the real-time monitor and the test station hardware. A key factor for the real-time data processing is the use of random access blocks on mass storage discs to greatly augment primary memory without seriously degrading total accessing time. This also frees "background" core for off-line programs running in a low-priority interruptable mode and for the analysis programs which do not operate in the real-time mode. A disc allocation and cataloging scheme is presented along with a hardware and software description.

INTRODUCTION

THIS PAPER discusses the design and operation of a Central Data Acquisition and Analysis System (CDAAS) which has been installed at Newark Air Force Station, Ohio. The primary emphasis of this paper is on the data acquisition, storage, and retrieval, as opposed to data analysis. Design constraints required that the system be integrated into an operational maintenance facility with the very minimum of impact, that the system acquire data from up to 40 remote test stations in an asynchronous fashion, and that time be allocated on a lower priority basis to the analysis of the data and the running of routine tasks. Special hardware interfaces were designed to make the connection between the facility hardware and the acquisition computer. The computer used is the SEL 840-MP, manufactured by Systems Engineering Laboratories of Fort Lauderdale, Fla. The entire acquisition and analysis scheme selected revolves about the priority interrupt and multiprogramming capabilities of the 840-MP, which is discussed in some detail.

The maintenance facility is primarily concerned with

Manuscript received August 8, 1969. This paper is based on a thesis by P. C. Abegglen and W. R. Faris submitted to the Department of Electrical Engineering, University of Utah, Salt Lake City, Utah.

P. C. Abegglen and W. R. Faris are with the Guidance and Control Branch (OONEGS), Service Engineering Division, Ogden Air Materiel Area (OOAMA), Hill Air Force Base, Utah 84401.

W. J. Hankley is with the Department of Electrical Engineering, University of Utah, Salt Lake City, Utah 84112.

maintenance of the inertial guidance systems used by the Minuteman Weapons System and the Titan Weapons System. An inertial guidance system is composed of four major components or "black boxes" which are the gyro-stabilized platform, the on-board digital computer, and two electronics packages. Each of these is a separate hermetically sealed package, and system-level repair is generally accomplished by replacing suspected black boxes. The gyro-stabilized platform contains three accelerometers, two gyros, a gyrocompass, an alignment block, two mirrors, two level detectors, and various torquers, resolvers, and electronic modules. At the platform level of repairs, these individual instruments are replaced when suspected of failure.

Due to the complexity of these systems, they are, of course, subject to malfunction. Sometimes a gross failure occurs, and isolation of the faulty component is usually quite simple; however, marginal failures are much more difficult to locate. The first technique used to isolate malfunctions was to program the on-board digital computer to dump certain memory locations and pertinent data as the system simulated operational use. These data were then analyzed by hand, and the results compared manually to precomputed "patterns."

A later technique used an off-line computer system, and provided somewhat faster and more reliable results but still required far too many manual operations in preparing the data for input to the computer. Finally the on-line, real-time system, discussed in this paper, was designed and installed. The overall capability of the maintenance facility has been greatly increased by the use of this system through which data are acquired, stored, and analyzed. Although CDAAS was designed specifically to solve the inertial guidance maintenance problem, the techniques involved in the design have general applications in the design of any real-time data acquisition and analysis system.

The paper is divided into five major areas. First, a description is given of the basic machine and standard peripherals which are used in this application. The second section deals with the specialized interface hardware, and the third section contains a discussion of the data acquisition and storage software from a design point of view. The test sequencing and operator communication techniques are presented in the fourth section. The last section discusses the integration of all software under priority interrupt control and the overall system operation.

Reprinted from *Proc. IEEE*, vol. 58, pp. 38–48, Jan. 1970.

THE CENTRAL COMPUTER, STANDARD PERIPHERALS, AND STANDARD SOFTWARE

Central Computer

The computer selected to solve the CDAAS problem was the SEL 840-MP. This machine is a general-purpose computer having 32K words of 24 bits each. The memory access period for this computer is 1.75 μs per read/write cycle. The computer is a standard item with hardware fixed-point multiply and divide, three index registers, and the following standard "off-the-shelf" options:

1) extended arithmetic unit
2) 31 individual priority interrupt levels
3) power fail safe
4) stall alarm
5) instruction trap
6) memory protect.

The extended arithmetic unit allows hardware floating-point arithmetic and is used extensively by the analysis programs. Each priority interrupt is assigned a unique "level" which may be enabled or disabled under program control. During each instruction fetch cycle, the priority interrupt hardware is interrogated to determine if a higher priority, enabled interrupt has occurred. If an interrupt is detected, control is transferred to the program connected to that interrupt level; otherwise, the next sequential instruction is executed. This allows hardware external to the computer to influence the sequence of events within the computer and affords a very efficient means of performing real-time operations. The manner in which a program is "connected" to a particular interrupt level will be discussed in a subsequent section.

Each of the last four options in the above list requires one of the 31 priority interrupt levels. The power fail safe creates an interrupt when the line voltage drops below a safe level and allows reinitialization when power returns. The stall alarm causes an interrupt when the computer "hangs up" in an indirect loop or noninterruptable input/output (I/O) hold. The instruction trap interrupts when an illegal operation is attempted or when execution of certain "privileged instructions" is attempted from an unprotected location. The memory protect feature consists of a 25th bit in each memory word which, if set, does not allow that word to be modified by an instruction whose protect bit is not set. Transfer to a protected location from an unprotected instruction is also not allowed. Occurrence of any of these interrupts causes the offending program to be aborted, and the operator to be notified. These interrupts are very useful in keeping non-real-time programs from interfering with real-time operations.

Standard Peripheral Units

In addition to the central computer, the following standard peripherals manufactured by SEL were selected for the CDAAS application:

1) two console teletypewriters.
2) paper tape reader

3) paper tape punch
4) high-speed Mylar tape punch
5) card reader
6) card punch
7) line printer
8) two magnetic tape drives and controller
9) two disc drives and controllers
10) *X-Y* plotter
11) real-time clock.

With this set of peripherals, it is possible to solve standard data processing problems as well as real-time problems for which the system was designed.

Standard Software

The system is equipped with a real-time monitor program which is capable of handling all of the peripherals. The real-time monitor program is a batch processing system which permits the computer to perform general-purpose computation on a multiprogrammed basis while performing real-time data acquisition. It consists of both resident and nonresident components. The resident components are memory protected and reside in absolute lower core (foreground) while the nonresident components are loaded and executed in upper core. All real-time operations are performed in the foreground area in the protected mode.

The real-time monitor connects programs to specified interrupt levels, performs all I/O operations, and is deeply involved in the servicing of some interrupts. There are three types of interrupts available which provide the flexibility necessary to make real-time operation feasible. The fastest response time interrupt is the directly connected type which allows the servicing program to begin processing the interrupt about two machine cycles (or about 3.5 μs) after the occurrence of the interrupt. The second type of interrupt is connected through the interrupt monitor and requires a maximum of 125 μs to begin execution of the interrupt servicing routine. Although this has somewhat slower reaction time than the directly connected type, it has the advantage of saving and restoring the registers before and after servicing the interrupt. The third type of interrupt is the nonresident monitor-serviced interrupt, which is connected through the interrupt monitor. It requires approximately 100 ms of response time to load the service routine into memory before processing can begin. Programs can be connected to specified interrupt levels either at monitor generation time or at run time.

Provisions are made which allow a higher priority routine to release time to a lower priority program when the higher priority routine cannot effectively use the central processing unit (CPU). All I/O operations operate under this philosophy, so that while one routine is waiting for a peripheral device to complete an operation, a lower priority routine may use the CPU until an interrupt from the peripheral indicates that the I/O operation is complete. The monitor must therefore keep track of which level is using any particular peripheral unit at a given time.

If it is determined that the program connected to a given interrupt level may be of the nonresident monitor-serviced variety (with the inherent 100-ms delay), a checkpointing feature is available which allows the background core area to be copied onto a disc file, the background to be protected, and the nonresident routine to be loaded into the newly available core area. This is accomplished automatically by the monitor when it is determined that sufficient foreground room is not available for loading of the program.

Other standard software includes a FORTRAN IV compiler, an assembler, a link loader and cataloger, and various updating and debugging routines.

THE INTERFACE HARDWARE

In most real-time data acquisition systems, it is necessary to design and build special-purpose interface hardware to make the link between the data source and the general-purpose acquisition computer. To accomplish this, it is necessary to keep in mind several things. First, the interface must physically monitor the data source and be able to accept data in the form in which they are issued from the source. Second, it must transform the data without a loss of information into a form compatible with the acquiring computer. Third, it must physically transmit the data to the central computer. Finally, sufficient speed is required in order that these tasks may be accomplished without limiting total system performance. With these points in mind, it was decided that the CDAAS interface hardware should consist of 40 remote test station adapters (TSAs) and a central interface unit (CIU) to complete the data link. This section discusses in some detail the hardware which was designed to accomplish these tasks.

For the CDAAS application, the data are available in 4-bit packages, and nine of these 4-bit packages define one data message to be transmitted to the acquiring computer. Fig. 1 shows a high-level logic diagram of a TSA. A logic diagram of the CIU is shown in Fig. 2. The CIU is a special computer peripheral unit whose function is to receive data from the 40 different TSAs, format it into a form that the CPU recognizes, and output it to central memory. The TSAs must be capable of handling data at a rate of at least 17 messages per second (600 bits/s) while the CIU (since it is asynchronously monitoring 40 TSAs) must be able to handle worst case data rates of at least 680 messages per second (27 200 bits/s).

Since the basic philosophy of the TSA is to accept 4-bit packs, it was decided to serially shift these data packs into a 36-bit serial shift register exclusively reserved for data. The 36-bit register is actually the first 36 bits of the 40-bit shift register shown in Fig. 1. Circuitry was also designed to assure that only nine valid data packs were allowed to enter the 36-bit serial shift register at one time. This is accomplished by detection circuitry which enables the shifting process only after a "begin message" character is received and until an "end-of-message" character is received. Both the "begin message" character and the "end-of-message" character are generated by the guidance system computer. As each data pack is received by the TSA, parity (generated by the guidance system computer) is checked. If an error is detected, this fact is recorded by

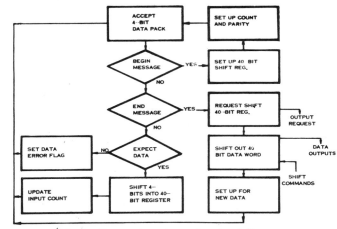

Fig. 1.   Test station adapter functional diagram.

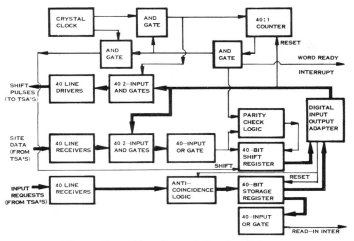

Fig. 2.   Central interface unit functional diagram.

setting a 1-bit shift register designated for notifying the CPU of a data parity error. As each bit of each data pack is serially shifted into the 36-bit shift register, a counting flip-flop keeps track of total data parity. When the "end-of-message" character is received, this parity bit is stored in another 1-bit shift register designated to notify the CPU of total message transmission parity.

If a data pack format error (not exactly nine data packs between a "begin message" character and an "end-of-message" character) is detected during the receipt of a message, this fact is stored in another 1-bit shift register designated to notify the CPU of a data format error. Upon receipt of an "end-of-message" character, the TSA unit initiates a signal to the CIU indicating that it has a message ready for acquisition and that it requests this message be accepted by that unit. When the CIU is ready for the message, it transmits 40 shift pulses to the TSA requesting the service. These shift pulses shift the 36-bit shift register and the four 1-bit shift registers 40 times in such a way as to output the 40 bits of information serially as one data message. Thus for input, the TSA appears to have only one 40-bit shift register.

The CIU is the piece of hardware which receives messages from the TSA, adds a transmission parity bit, and then transmits the data to central memory. Fig. 2 shows a block diagram of this hardware. As can be seen in this diagram, the unit is capable of receiving data from 40 different TSAs asynchronously but not simultaneously. The digital input /output adapter which is shown on the right of the diagram provides the digital inputs and outputs necessary for synchronization and timing between the CIU and the CPU.

When a TSA sends a service request to the CIU, one bit is stored in its respective position in a 40-bit storage register. In reality this register is a set of 40 different flip-flop circuits which correspond to the 40 different TSA units. When any one of these flip-flop elements is set, a "read-in-requested" priority interrupt signal is sent to the CPU. All 40 flip-flops are combined into a single line by a 40-input OR gate to create this input request. When the read-in-request interrupt is serviced by the CPU, the status of the 40-bit storage register is input into central memory. The CPU then determines which of the remote stations require service and using that information begins transferring data from those stations in numerical order.

The first step in the servicing operation is for the CPU to output a site selection message to the CIU. This enables one of the forty 2-input AND gates in the shift pulse lines, thereby allowing shift pulses to be sent to the remote station selected. At the same time, another 2-input AND gate (in the site data lines) is enabled, thereby allowing data from the remote site to be serially shifted into a 40-bit shift register in the CIU. This register is exclusively reserved to temporarily store the data from the selected site.

The data transfer from the TSA to the CIU begins when the site selection command is received from the CPU at the beginning of the service operation. A reset is applied to a forty-to-one counter used to count the input bits of data. An AND gate at the output of this counter had been disabling two other AND gates. These other AND gates provide a count pulse to the forty-to-one counter and shift pulses to the 40-bit shift register in the remote site. This is accomplished by connecting one of these AND gates to the crystal clock, thereby advancing the forty-to-one counter at each clock pulse until the counter again reaches the 40th or "hold" state. When this occurs, the AND gate on the output of the counter again disables the input to the counter and the counter stops counting until another reset pulse is received.

The other AND gate which is connected to the other side (180 degrees out of phase) of the clock allows 40 shift pulses to be applied to the shift input of the 40-bit shift register in the CIU. The delay between these two pulses is sufficient for the data from the remote site to be transmitted to the CIU. When all 40 counts of the 40-bit counter have been completed, the data contained in the remote site shift register will be contained in the 40-bit register in the CIU and will be ready for input into central memory.

When the 40-bit counter has reached 40, an interrupt is generated which notifies the CPU that the message is ready to be transferred. The same signal which generates the "message-ready" interrupt also initiates a parity check on the received data. If a parity error is detected, this fact is recorded as a part (one bit) of the data. At this point the

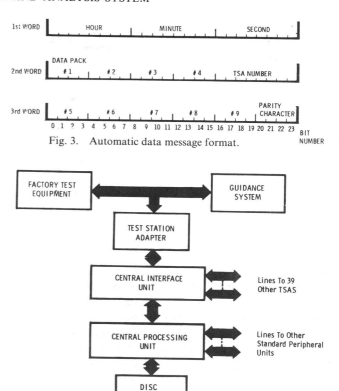

Fig. 3.   Automatic data message format.

Fig. 4.   CDAAS hardware block diagram.

CPU generates the necessary I/O commands to cause the data to be transferred to memory. After the data are received by the CPU, they are formated as shown in Fig. 3, and put into a first-in, first-out (FIFO) stack in memory. A block diagram of the hardware developed appears in Fig. 4. At this point, the special interface link is completed.

The interface hardware was designed and built by SEL using system and data specifications developed at Hill Air Force Base, Utah. These specifications were written in sufficient depth to provide an overall system concept as well as to satisfy basic hardware and software design constraints.

The next section of this paper contains a detailed presentation of the routines required to handle data after they have been received by the CPU. The connection between these routines and the priority interrupt system will be discussed in a later section.

THE DATA ACQUISITION AND STORAGE PROBLEM

Data Flow

In almost any computer application, there exists one fundamental tradeoff, i.e., storage versus time. In this regard, CDAAS is typical. Many of the decisions made with regard to the data buffers for CDAAS may be considered somewhat arbitrary, but final design was made by weighing storage and time together, and developing a workable compromise.

The acquired data come from the CIU under interrupt control into the CPU, where they are stored in core memory (as previously shown in Fig. 4). The buffer in memory is emptied at a lower priority on a first-in, first-out basis. This buffer is called the automatic circular buffer since the data enter from TSAs in the automatic mode (discussed below).

Using expected data rates and the fact that data are formated into three-word packages, it was decided that 201 words would provide sufficient buffering before the 40-way sort. An algorithm has been developed which creates the 201-word circular buffer in memory using a continuously updated input pointer and an analogous output pointer. If this buffer is ever overflowed for any reason, the program goes into a special routine which begins storing the data sequentially in background memory. This creates a FIFO stack in background which will allow the storage of up to 16K data words before the system is completely overflowed.

Since the volume of data to be acquired by CDAAS is significant, it is necessary to provide ample storage for these data. Providing this storage in core memory is undesirable in that background size is reduced, making non-real-time processing difficult, if not impossible. It was therefore decided that the bulk of these acquired data should be kept on random-access disc files. One complication with this plan is that disc access is only by a sector (62 24-bit words) at a time. Thus to write a word on the disc, the sector must be read in, the word added, and the sector rewritten. The data may be compressed to a certain extent by editing the data as they are acquired. One way to do this is to perform a 40-way sort and store the data to be kept in 40 individual buffers (one per TSA). Since the tests vary considerably in length (from one to approximately 20 sectors), these 40 buffers are dynamically allocated from a large disc file (called TEMP, which will be discussed shortly) and are called dynamically allocated disc buffers. To minimize disc accesses somewhat, these buffers are filled eight words at a time from 40 core buffers called simply TSA buffers. A word-count for each of these TSA buffers is kept in core, and each time one of them is filled, the data are transferred to the disc. This concept is illustrated in Fig. 5.

Disc Organization

Each disc is physically composed of 10 heads with 100 tracks per head, 16 sectors per track, and 62 words per sector totaling 992 000 words per disc. Although two discs are present in the system, the acquisition and analysis programs are written so as to use only one of them, leaving the other free for batch jobs and for use as a backup. Since the disc is the movable-head type and revolves at 2400 r/min, it has a maximum latency time of 25 ms and a maximum seek time of 145 ms. Thus the worst case disc access time is 170 ms. The data transfer rate is 52 082 Hz or one word per 19.4 μs.

Since all data for a given test on a given guidance system are to be linked together and since these tests vary considerably in length, the disc file for accumulation and temporary storage (TEMP) of these data is allocated one sector at a time. This file is designed to store all test data for a specific system until that system is eventually repaired and returned to the field. It is likely that data will reside in this file for a period of several weeks. As a result of this large

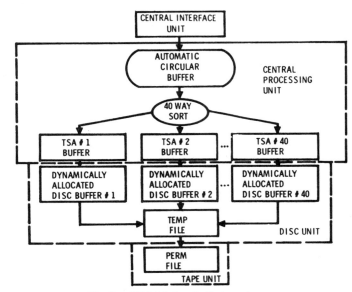

Fig. 5. CDAAS data buffering scheme.

volume of data, this temporary storage file consists of 48 cylinders (approximately 480 000 words). Since variable length records are needed, an explicit linkage system is used to connect various sectors of the same test. A cataloging scheme allows access to the first sector of a test, the first sector points to the second, etc., with the last sector carrying a terminate code to stop the chaining. The physical sector-to-sector linkage consists of one word containing the head, track, and sector (HTS) address of the following sector.

Disc Allocation

With a sector-at-a-time allocation scheme, an efficient method of locating empty sectors must be obtained. Keeping sector-busy information in each sector is simple, but requires that a given sector be read to determine whether or not it is empty, so that searching for empty sectors would require too many disc accesses and would be too time consuming. To overcome this problem, the following method is employed, using but one bit in a table to indicate a sector's availability for use.

Two separate storage areas are required for this disc utilization scheme, referred to collectively as the disc usage block. One portion requires thirty words in core memory, while the other is made up of ten sectors on the disc called usage sectors. This scheme is illustrated in Fig. 6. In each of the ten usage sectors, only the first 48 words are used. Each of the $10 \times 48 \times 16$ bits in the usage sector area implicitly indicates the condition of one sector in the TEMP file, using the convention 0 for busy, 1 for not busy. Each of the 48×10 bits in the core array indicates the condition of a whole word in the usage sector area, using the convention 0 for all implied sectors busy, 1 for at least one sector not busy. Each of the additional 10 words gives the HTS address of the corresponding usage sector.

An example should serve to illustrate the method. If a sector is desired, a search is made in the 20-word portion of the 30-word core area for a nonzero word pair. Assume that $i-1$ 48-bit groups in the core array are zero and that the ith

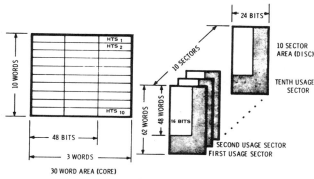

Fig. 6.   Disc usage scheme.

group is found to be nonzero. This means that there is at least one empty sector on the ith head. Then, obviously, there must be at least one 1-set bit in this 48-bit group. Beginning at the left, the bits are examined and counted, until the first 1-set bit is encountered. Assume that this is the jth bit in the ith 48-bit group. This indicates that there is at least one empty sector on the jth track of the ith head. To find which of the 16 possible sectors is empty, the sector at HTS_i, indicated in the 30-word core array, is loaded into core and its jth word is examined for the first 1-set bit. If the kth bit is set, then head i, track j, sector k is empty. Bit k is then reset and if word j on HTS_i is now zero, then bit j in the ith 48-bit group is reset and HTS_i is rewritten on disc. This scheme is programmed in a routine called GSEC (Get Sector) which formats i, j, and k into a standard HTS word and returns it to the calling routine. Thus two disc accesses are required to find one empty sector on the TEMP file.

One subtle problem exists with this scheme as presented above, namely, that it is nonreentrant. This means that undesirable consequences can result if this program is called from two or more different interrupt levels. As an example of this problem, suppose that a program at a low interrupt level calls GSEC and is then interrupted before the updated usage sector is rewritten on disc. If the interrupting program happens to call GSEC, it will find the same sector empty as the first program and will therefore use it. Upon return to the lower level program, the same sector will have been assigned twice. To eliminate this problem, the 48-bit group in the core array is copied into a non-volatile last-in first-out (LIFO) stack, and the 48-bit group in the 30-word array is cleared. All interrupts are disabled during this short time interval after which interruptions may occur. The net result is that an interrupting program will see the ith head as entirely busy and will search further down in the 30-word core array, thus accessing a different usage sector.

Another routine called RSEC (Release Sector) is used to return a sector to the "empty" state. This routine must also be reentrant, since it writes in the disc usage block. Again the physical 48-bit group is cleared after having been stored in a LIFO stack. Since RSEC and GSEC are reentrant, it must be realized that no instruction modification or data storage within the routine can be allowed. The registers, of course,

are restored after interruption. Since all of the programs which call GSEC and RSEC are themselves nonreentrant, storage can be done in an array provided by (and contained within) the calling program; 85 words are thus required for external storage by RSEC and GSEC.

Cataloging

In order to locate data for a given test, a cataloging scheme must be provided which is essentially a table of correspondence between storage addresses and lookup criteria. It is imperative that the lookup criteria be unique. The storage addresses in this application are head, track, and sector locations for the first sector of the given test data. To provide unique lookup criteria, the guidance system serial number is used along with a recycle number and a sequence number. The recycle number is upgraded each time the particular system is returned to the maintenance facility for repair. Within a given recycle, on a given guidance system, all test data are identified by a sequence number which is incremented as each new test is run on the system. This guarantees unique identification for any test, but is somewhat undesirable in other ways. There are several (approximately ten) different types of tests which may be run on a system for which data are to be retained by CDAAS. Each type of test is indicated by a test identification (ID) code. While this test ID code is not required to uniquely identify test data, it is very useful information, particularly for several searches which must be made during the system repair cycle. Therefore, a catalog entry consists of four lookup criteria (system serial, test ID, recycle, and sequence numbers) and a corresponding HTS address of the first sector of the test.

Generally fewer than 15 tests per system are required per repair cycle. The test ID, recycle, and sequence numbers can be packed into one word and the HTS address into an additional word, so that usually fewer than 30 words of catalog entries are needed for the TEMP file for each guidance system serial number. For this reason, catalog entries are entered into half-sectors on the disc in order to keep the catalog as compact as possible. Entries for a given system (same serial number) are stored in the same half-sector. Additional half-sectors are linked explicitly, if necessary, through the 31st word in the preceding half-sector. If the 31st word in each half-sector is not used as a HTS pointer link, then it is used as a word count to tell how many entries are in the half-sector. The catalog for the TEMP file is built to handle up to 600 systems at a time requiring 300 catalog entry sectors.

In order to avoid long catalog searches, an index consisting of ten sectors is employed. In the catalog index, system serial numbers are listed chronologically in the nth sector, where n is the last decimal digit in the system serial number, except that no entry is duplicated. The position of the system serial number in the index allows implicit location of the appropriate beginning catalog half-sector by counting that many half-sectors into the catalog file on the disc. Fig. 7 illustrates this cataloging concept. By searching for the system serial number in the proper index sector, calculating

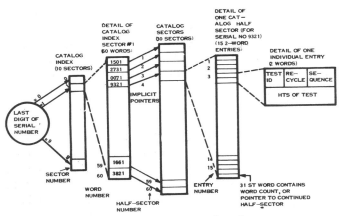

Fig. 7. Multiple level cataloging scheme.

TABLE I
TSA FUNCTIONS

Rotary Switch Position	Description
Guidance system serial number	Informs CPU of beginning of a guidance system test; enters guidance system serial number and test ID code.
Platform serial number	Informs CPU of beginning of a platform test; enters platform serial number and test ID code.
Delete test	Stops data acquisition on test in progress and releases all storage areas.
Test complete	Closes out test and makes catalog entry in TEMP.
Resume test	Restarts data acquisition after temporary stoppage.
Configuration	Enters subassembly configuration into the CPU.

the entry HTS address, loading that HTS, and searching (if necessary, linking to a new catalog sector), the given catalog entry is found from which the address of the first sector of test data is obtained.

When data are removed from the TEMP file (either by DELETE TEMP or TEMP to PERM, both of which are discussed below), it is necessary to release the sectors (through RSEC) and also to remove the catalog entry refering to that test. This is done in a routine called CATD (Catalog Delete). The proper catalog entries are simply cleared from the catalog. Another separate routine is used periodically to pack the catalog. This routine moves catalog entries into the zero-filled areas and corrects the 31st (entry count) word. If all entries for a particular system serial number are deleted, then that serial number is cleared in the catalog index.

In addition to identifying tests through the catalog, more test identification information is stored in the test data proper. This identification, known as a test tag, consists of system serial number, test ID, time and date that the test was run, recycle and sequence number, and the TSA number.

Permanent File

After a system is repaired and returned to the field, it is not generally necessary to refer to its test information until the system eventually returns for further repair. It is, however, desirable to keep these data for possible further analysis upon return of the system, or for statistical analysis of repairs, etc. Since it is not necessary to refer to these data as often as that for systems currently under repair and since the data tend to be quite voluminous, they are stored on magnetic tape files. These files are known as PERM (permanent) and are never destroyed but rather are kept for the life of the system.

OPERATOR CONTROL AND TEST SEQUENCING

Manual Remote Control

For the CDAAS application, acquisition and analysis of test data is not continuous and automatic, but rather it is a remotely controlled interactive process. In addition to acquisition of data, the central system collects and operates upon information which is input manually at each of the test stations. The manual input may be either configuration information or requests for service, both of which are handled by the manual data acquisition routine. Service requests are discussed first.

At the highest level, each TSA operator can request either "manual mode" or "automatic mode" by means of a special two-position switch. The central computer in turn conveys two bits of information to each TSA. These control two mode lights which indicate the current mode as either null, automatic, or manual. In the null mode, the TSA is off-line and with the exception of the manual/automatic switch it does not communicate with the central computer. In the automatic mode, the TSA monitors the guidance system computer and sends data to the CIU. In the manual mode, the operator selects various services by selecting positions of a 12-position rotary switch. These are listed in Table I. In cases in which the selected service requires a configuration or serial number, the operator enters the number into eight thumbwheel switches. When all switches are set, the service request is transmitted by pushing an "enter manual data" button. The positions of the switches are transmitted via the CIU to the central computer and stored in a manual data circular buffer. The manual data acquisition routine empties this buffer and performs the indicated task.

It is worth noting here the importance of the configuration and serial number information which along with the test data and test results are retained for each guidance system. With this information CDAAS maintains a complete chronological history of system repairs, component replacements, times to failure, etc. This information in turn allows systematic analysis of the total performance of the guidance systems and of the repair facility itself. While this is secondary to the primary CDAAS function of automatically acquiring and analyzing test data, the value of having test facility data available, most of which would not be accessible if recorded manually, should not be overlooked when considering any similar installation.

Control of the Test Station State

An important facet of design of an interactive man–machine system such as CDAAS is that the machine must retain final control over the sequence of actions requested by the remote operators. It cannot be assumed that the TSA operator will always request reasonable actions. Evaluation of the remote operator requests can be a deceptively complex task. Indeed, for the CDAAS application it required a significant part of the system programming effort. To handle this problem in a systematic manner, a modified state diagram was used, as illustrated in simplified form in Fig. 8. In the state diagram, circles represent the system states, the arrows represent legal changes in state, and the labels on the arrows represent TSA operator requests unless otherwise noted. For every state, all TSA operator requests which are not shown as a state transition label cause no change in state, although they do cause a message to be printed at a central teletype unit.

In constructing a state diagram, the state is interpreted as the minimal amount of information which, in conjunction with a service request, is sufficient to determine a legal action (a change in state). Hence, the transition label on each arrow identifies a service request and not previous states. In this sense, Fig. 8 is not a legitimate state diagram, although it does conveniently illustrate the legal state transitions. Since there are actually more states than shown in Fig. 8, each TSA state is represented in the central computer as a set of eight 1-bit flags. Each time the manual data acquisition routine is entered, the set of flags corresponding to the TSA which entered the manual data is tested to see if a legal state change has been requested. If the requested change is legal, the state is changed in the software, all necessary housekeeping operations are performed, and the appropriate flags are updated. If an illegal state change is requested, an appropriate message is typed on the console typewriter.

CPU Operator Communications

Since most real-time systems are extremely complex, it is essential that the CPU operator maintain control of the system. To accomplish this control it is necessary to know precisely what operations are occurring at any particular time. This information and control is furnished by a special-purpose operator communication routine. In this respect CDAAS is typical; therefore, a brief description of the operator communication routines has been included. This description is intended only to show typical communication and control functions rather than to be a detailed description of the existing routines.

During the normal operation of the CDAAS system, the operator of the central computer may desire to find out the status of the entire system or of some component of it. All communication with the operator of the central computer is done on two teletypewriters. These are standard computer peripheral units and are serviced by the real-time monitor

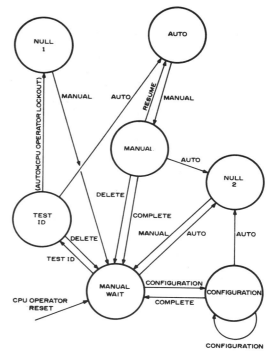

Fig. 8.   Test station state diagram.

and interrupts. The ASR-35 typewriter serves two communication functions, namely the real-time monitor I/O unit and the manual data acquisition routine output unit. The ASR-33 typewriter is the I/O device for the console request routine.

The console request routine is the program which handles communication from the operator to the central computer. It is connected to a normally disabled priority interrupt and is nonresident. To enter the routine, the operator closes a special switch on the ASR-33 typewriter. This causes an interrupt which is processed by the CPU. Servicing this interrupt causes background processing to be halted, the console request program to be loaded into foreground, and the message "CONSOLE REQUEST:" to be output on the typewriter. At this time, the computer waits for a request by the operator. It should be noted that although background is in a wait mode, the acquisition routines are not disabled since they are at a higher priority interrupt level and will interrupt the console request routine whenever the CIU has data waiting for acquisition.

In Table II, a list of the typical requests and a brief explanation of each is given. For the CDAAS application there are five basic functions performed by the console request routine. These are:

1) CPU operator information
2) CPU actions which require operator action (e.g., tape mounting, sense switch setting, etc.)
3) debugging tools
4) job sequence control
5) system initilization.

Almost any real-time system would require routines of these types to facilitate efficient real-time operations.

TABLE II
TYPICAL CONSOLE REQUEST COMMANDS

Command	Function	Description	Command	Function	Description
ASSEMBLY STATUS	1	Allows the status of selected TSAs to be typed out. The status consists of current serial number, test ID, and the time and date the test was initiated.	STORE SECTOR	3	Causes a test to be written on TEMP, given the starting sector address and properly set up linkage words.
CDAAS STATUS	1	Causes the status of the entire system to be typed out. This information includes the mode of all TSAs and the length of the analysis program backlog (job queue).	TEST DUMP	3	Allows a given test to be dumped on the line printer, given the starting sector address.
TEMP STATUS	1	Allows the status of selected serial numbers in the TEMP file to be typed out. The individual tests may be selectively listed to desired detail by options on this request.	MEMORY INSERT	3	Allows the operator to change the octal contents of any memory cell in core.
			MEMORY DUMP	3	Allows specified memory locations to be dumped on the line printer.
TEMP TO PERM	2	Allows selected test(s) to be moved in a sector-by-sector fashion from TEMP to PERM.	ENTER JOBQ	4	Causes the specified data to be entered into the analysis control job queue to cause the specified test to be analyzed.
PERM TO TEMP	2	Allows a selected test to be moved from PERM to TEMP. This is necessary since analysis can only be done from the TEMP file.	DISABLE AUTO	4	Causes future AUTO requests from the TSAs to be unconditionally denied.—
			ENABLE AUTO	4	Cancels DISABLE AUTO.
LOAD TEMP	2	Causes the specified test on TEMP to be loaded into a specified core area. This request may be used for updating and correcting small data errors.	DISABLE REDUCTION	4	Disables the interrupt connected to Analysis Control, and effectively causes analyses to be backlogged but not run.
STORE TEMP	2	Causes a specified core area to be moved into the TEMP file and cataloged for future references.	ENABLE REDUCTION	4	Cancels DISABLE REDUCTION.
DELETE TEMP	2	Allows the operator to remove the catalog entry to a specified test on the temp file and to release the disc area allocated to this test.	RESET CATALOG	5	Clears the catalog area on disc thereby allowing partial reinitialization of the system.
LOAD SECTOR	3	Causes a test to be loaded into a core buffer, given the sector address to the starting sector.	RESET DISCUSE	5	Resets the disc usage block area in both memory and on the disc thereby allowing reallocation of the TEMP file.

Using these routines in conjunction with the normal system messages which are output by the system routines, the operator is kept informed of exactly what is occurring throughout the system at any particular time and is able to maintain precise control of the real-time environment.

OVERALL SYSTEM INTEGRATION AND OPERATION

Priority Interrupt Connection

In a real-time data acquisition system the various software components must be integrated into one functional package which effectively acquires, stores, retrieves, and analyzes the data. This is accomplished through the use of the 840-MP priority interrupt system in conjunction with the real-time monitor. The selection of individual priority levels for each function is quite difficult and, in this case, was one of the final decisions made. The priority interrupt levels are indicated in Table III.

The selection of interrupt levels for the individual standard computer peripheral units will not be considered here. However, it must be realized that I/O operations which are already under way must be completed. For example, a punched card which is already in motion cannot be stopped without missing data. Another consideration is that the data acquisition routines must use certain I/O devices (disc, etc.). For these reasons, the standard peripheral unit interrupt levels have highest priority. This poses no great problem, since once the background and other lower priority routines are inactive, they will not call for initiation of further I/O operations.

The highest of the data acquisition interrupt levels is that of SCAN, which services auto/manual mode requests from the TSA operator. One way to generate this interrupt would be to OR together the requests from all 40 TSAs and allow the servicing routine to determine which TSA(s) required service. A more economical method which is only slightly less efficient was used in this application. An interval timer generates the interrupt every 120 ms, and the servicing routine inputs 40 bits (in two words) from the CIU. These

TABLE III
PRIORITY INTERRUPT LEVELS

Name	Function
Standard	All standard peripheral and environmental interrupts.
SCAN	Services all auto/manual requests.
MRDY	Transfers data from CIU to one of the CPU circular buffers.
IREQ	Transfers data from any TSA to the CIU.
ADAR	Transfers data from the auto circular buffer to the dynamically allocated disc buffers.
MDAR	Services all manually input requests from the TSAs, which are stored in the manual circular buffer.
CONR	Interprets and executes CPU operator requests.
ACRT	Loads and executes the appropriate analysis routine according to requests in the job queue.

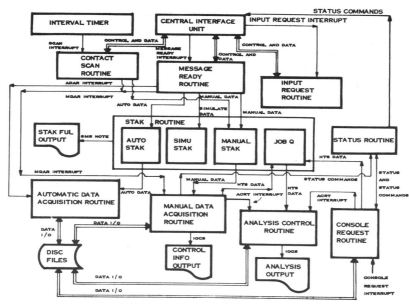

Fig. 9.   Real-time software system.

represent the current position of each of the auto/manual switches. These bits are then compared to 40 bits kept in memory which represent the previous auto/manual state of all 40 TSA requests. Messages for the manual data circular buffer are then formed for those TSAs requesting auto/manual mode changes.

The remaining interrupt levels shown in Table III are somewhat more self-explanatory. The next highest is the message-ready (MRDY) interrupt, generated by the CIU to cause the CPU to initiate data transfer from the CIU to the CPU. The read-in request (IREQ) interrupt is initiated at the TSA, comes through the CIU, and causes data to be shifted from the TSA to the CIU. The interrupts for the automatic data acquisition routine (ADAR), manual data acquisition routine (MDAR), and analysis control rou-

tine (ACRT) are present at all times; however, the interrupt levels are normally in a "disabled" state. When a message is placed into the manual or auto circular buffers by message ready, the appropriate level is enabled. The console request (CONR) interrupt originates at a switch on the computer console, and allows the CPU operator to make requests of the CPU. Finally, the analysis control routine interrupt level is enabled by the console request routine or the manual data acquisition routine. This routine is nonresident and overlays the background core area. It causes analysis to be performed on data given in the job queue. The routines for cataloging and disc allocating are reentrant service routines which may be called as needed by any routine.

Fig. 9 shows the total real-time software system including

interrupts and data transfers. The different priority levels are implied by the difference in level of the routines on the diagram.

General Operation

After a guidance system or platform has been mounted on a test station, the first event which happens is that the operator of the test station activates his TSA and informs the CPU of the upcoming test, system serial number, etc. He next requests the automatic mode (SCAN). Under a software decision, the CPU will normally change the mode of the requesting TSA to AUTO, inform the TSA operator by lighting the AUTO present light, and begin monitoring the data output lines of the guidance system (MDAR). The test station operator then initiates the guidance system test. As the test progresses, data are issued by the guidance system, picked up by the TSA, and transferred under software control to the CPU and disc (IREQ, MRDY, ADAR). At the completion of the test, the TSA operator requests and receives MANUAL mode and issues a "test complete" command (SCAN, IREQ, MRDY, MDAR). At this point, the CPU catalogs the test and makes an entry into the analysis job queue (MDAR). This activates the interrupt to analysis control which, upon becoming active, loads the data and the proper analysis routine into memory, and preempts background processing temporarily (ACRT). The analysis program is then executed, and background processing is continued. The TSA operator is free at any time to begin the cycle again.

Under normal operating conditions, the computer system spends about 5 percent of CPU time doing real-time data acquisition. The remaining time is used to execute analysis programs and to run general-type batch jobs in the background. Since this much background time is available, it has been found the system can be used as a highly effective general-purpose engineering tool.

SUMMARY AND CONCLUSION

The CDAAS system is designed specifically to acquire and analyze real-time data from a set of 40 remote guidance system test stations. Hardware has been designed to interface the central computer with the 40 remote stations. Several routines have been developed to supervise the total real-time environment of the system. These include data handling routines, disc allocation routines, control routines, and general-purpose operator communication routines.

The analysis software for the CDAAS system has required about eight man-years of effort. The executive routines which were discussed in this paper and developed at Hill Air Force Base, Utah, required about five additional man-years. Presently, the system is operational at Newark Air Force Station, Ohio. The hardware for the CDAAS installation was acquired from Systems Engineering Laboratories at a cost of approximately $750 000.

It is expected that the CDAAS system will improve the throughput of the maintenance facility by at least 40 percent, as well as provide an extremely valuable engineering tool. Provisions have also been made in the design for adapting the system to other uses in the future.

ACKNOWLEDGMENT

The authors are indebted to the many employees at OONEGS Hill Air Force Base, Newark Air Force Station, Systems Engineering Laboratories, and the University of Utah who have contributed to CDAAS.

A Laboratory-Based Computer System

Marvin Shapiro and Arthur Schultz

National Institutes of Health, Bethesda, Md.

A computer system for the acquisition of data from analytical instruments used in biomedical research was designed and is now operating in a laboratory environment. Six remotely located instruments have been interfaced to the computer, and data can be collected simultaneously from them while other programs are running in a background mode. Features of the system include a remote operator's console for communication between the computer system and the laboratory and additions to the manufacturer-supplied software to allow rapid interrupt processing.

WHILE A NUMBER of real-time computer systems have been implemented recently in support of laboratory research, no standard approach has been developed. Each laboratory instrument presents its unique problems when interfaced with a computer, and in an environment where a number of instruments are present, various approaches to the design of a computer-instrument system can be taken (*1, 2*). We are reporting here on a system which was designed to meet some of the computational needs of a group of scientists working at the National Institutes of Health on research in molecular and physical biology.

The desirability of such a system first became apparent three years ago when a number of scientists working in one building at NIH were making plans to request purchase of instruments or accessories which incorporated data acquisition hardware and digital recording devices. Data analysis was to be accomplished in the NIH central computer facility. With the high density of instrumentation in this building, the aggregate cost of this approach, if widely used, would have approached the cost of one centrally located computer-based data acquisition system. In many ways, this group of scientists located together presented an ideal opportunity for experimenting with such facilities at NIH because of the diversity of physical instrumentation and problems they were working on. The implementation of a computer system presented a more flexible approach than using any of the highly specialized devices which could have been purchased, and, in addition, provided sufficient capability to permit considerable data manipulation, signal averaging, and more complicated data reduction.

Over the past three years a computer system was designed and made operational. It is a time-shared system which acquires data simultaneously from a number of different types of analytical instruments while running one or more analysis programs in a background mode. The instruments currently connected are spectrophotometers, a spectropolarimeter, a Raman spectrometer, an analytical ultracentrifuge, and a computer of average transients (CAT). All of these instruments are located at distances ranging from 50 to 200 feet from the computer, which is centrally located in the building.

Two applications in the building utilize small dedicated computers that will be connected to the building computer to take advantage of its peripheral devices, principally mass storage. In one application a 16-bit computer with 4K core and high-speed (150 KHz) analog-to-digital conversion is used to capture transient signals. The other application is a commercially available X-ray diffraction system that both controls the diffractometer and acquires data.

With these research needs in mind, a system was designed around commercially available hardware and software components. A medium size real-time computer (Honeywell DDP-516) with 24,576 words of 16-bit, 0.96 μsec cycle time memory (later expanded to 32,768 words) was purchased, with the following peripheral equipment: two ASR teletypes, line printer (300 lpm), high-speed paper tape equipment, card reader (200 cpm), 10-inch, 10-mil step incremental plotter, nine-track magnetic tape, and 1.8 million word moving head disk. In addition, a digital I/O multiplexer for handling up to 576 bits, a 35 KHz, 12-bit A/D converter, sample-and-hold amplifier, and multiplexer, and three digital-to-analog converters were purchased. A standard foreground-background monitor, oriented around disk operation, was provided with the system. A diagram of the system components as currently configured is shown in Figure 1.

The principal additions which our own staff made to the system included: (a) Hardware: (1) a remote operator's console (ROC) for communication between the laboratory and computer was designed and built, (2) a data acquisition and display subsystem (DADS) for conditioning signals, for use in checkout, and for displaying system status, was designed and built, and (3) instrument interfacing and a data transmission system was designed and completed; (b) Software: (1) system interrupt response was greatly improved by specially written programs for data collection, and (2) a series of programs was written and incorporated into the operating system to provide interactive communication with remote operating consoles located in the laboratories. A staff of three programmers and two electronics engineers (with part-time help from an electronics technician for fabrication) worked for a total of eight man-years to bring the system to an operational status. Once the system was operational, staffing to support further additions and improvements was reduced to two programmers and one engineer.

The system was considered operational when it could support data acquisition and the scientist's use of the remote operator's console. However, until application programs were written to support the analysis of the data collected, the system attracted few users. General programs for data manipulation, plotting, and mathematical analysis of data have been written and work is continuing to provide specialized computations for specific instruments.

Essentially no knowledge of computers is required for the scientists to accomplish data acquisition, file management, and the initiation of programs from the laboratory. A short demonstration of less than an hour, plus a copy of the ROC user's manual, is all that is needed. Use of the system's FORTRAN capabilities, however, now requires that each user operate the computer himself, and, in addition, requires that he have some minimum knowledge about the system, including how the disk program storage is laid

(1) *IBM J. Res. Develop.*, **13**, No. 1 (1969).
(2) Proceedings IBM Scientific Computing Symposium on Computers in Chemistry, Thomas J. Watson Research Center, Yorktown Heights, N. Y., August 1969.

Reprinted with permission from *Anal. Chem.*, vol. 43, pp. 398–405, Mar. 1971.

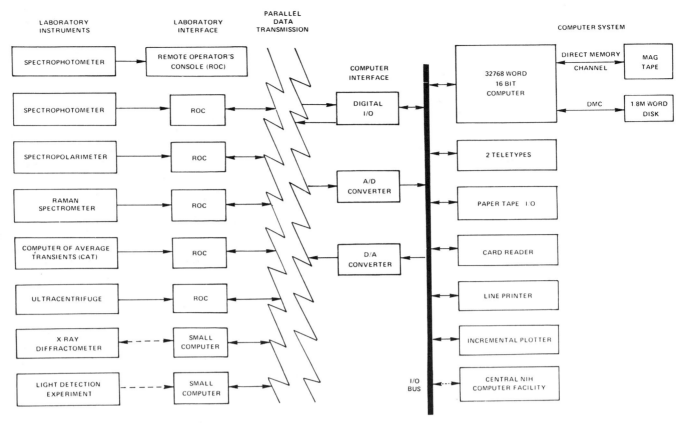

Figure 1. Diagram of the laboratory-based computer system

Dashed lines represent connections which have not yet been made

out. It generally takes a number of hours of hands-on use for a FORTRAN user to be able to use the computer without difficulty.

Generally, the system has been reliable for data collection. Each instrument was checked individually with specialized programs and with hardware tests for data transmission accuracy before being incorporated into the system. A number of software difficulties have been encountered in the form of system failures while running in a multi-programming environment. While most of these problems have been identified and corrected, it is expected that all such errors will be eliminated only after the system has seen heavy use for a long period of time.

The system has been operational for less than a year with a small, but gradually increasing, number of users. With this amount of experience in mind, this paper is directed toward explaining how a working system was designed and how it is used, as opposed to discussing long range effects on scientific research.

COMMUNICATION WITH THE LABORATORY

In designing a system for the acquisition of data it was clear that each instrument, although possessing similarities to another instrument, would require a unique interface. At the same time, the console that was adopted for entry of control information for each instrument could readily be standardized. The technique adopted combined within the same package a standard system for the entry of control parameters and sufficient space for the construction of an instrument interface. The package containing these elements is called the Remote Operator's Console (ROC), and one such console is associated with each instrument.

Each Remote Operator's Console (ROC) is composed of a Status/Control panel, a parameter entry panel, an X-Y storage scope, the instrument interface, and an intercom to the computer room. Figure 2 illustrates the functions that are implemented within a ROC. In addition to the indicator SYSTEM-UP, there are four button switches—SIGN ON, RUN, HALT, and SIGN OFF—on the Status/Control panel. In order to assure the operator that the switch action has been received by the computer and recognized by the operating system, each switch (except SIGN OFF) is backlighted, and is turned on by a signal generated by the computer. The correct operation of SIGN OFF is observed by the extinction of SIGN ON.

A parameter entry panel is also a part of the ROC and is the means of entering the specific information that will be used to condition the operating system for the particular data acquisition and/or processing task desired. A decade thumbwheel switch of six digits is used for parameter entry. The switch is divided into two sections, a two-digit control number and a four-digit parameter number. Two buttons, ENTER and CANCEL, are also a part of the parameter entry panel.

In order to provide the operator of an instrument with comprehensive information concerning the results of data acquisition and processing without requiring that he visit the computer room, a storage oscilloscope is included in the ROC. (In one case, two instruments located in the same room share a scope.) The Tektronix Type 601 Storage Display unit has been used for this application. To write a dot requires an analog signal on the vertical and horizontal axis to position the beam and, after the beam is positioned, a store signal to unblank the beam on the z axis. Alpha-

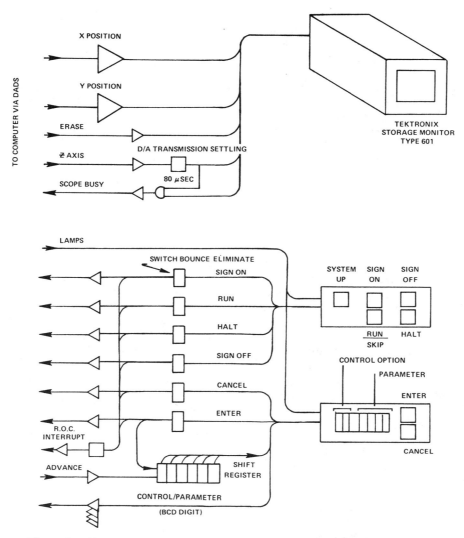

Figure 2. Simplified schematic of the interface to a remote operator's console

On the top, the storage display scope and below, the console buttons and thumbwheel digits

numerics and graphics are produced by the proper sequence of dots generated under software control. The scope can be erased either locally or under program control. Generation of beam position is by means of two digital-to-analog converters (DACs) located in the computer. Writing on a scope continues until either a message or plot is complete. Two DACs are used for the entire system. The output of the DACs is fed continuously to all connected scopes, but only the particular scope which is to write receives the signal to unblank its beam. The procedure for using a remote console is described later.

Interconnection between each remote console and the computer is by parallel transmission of signals, analog and digital, over twisted-pair shielded cables. This is a relatively simple approach from an engineering standpoint and also of low cost when all instruments are located in one building. Also, this technique does not require multiplexing/demultiplexing hardware and individual analog-to-digital converters at each instrument site. The cost of transmitting one digital signal is approximately $22.00, of which $9.00 is the cost of 300 feet of cable. In a situation where installation of cables is not easy or where large distances result in very large cable costs, this approach might not be practical.

All ROC cabling terminates within the computer room at the Data Acquisition and Display Subsystem (DADS). DADS is the focal point for both analog and digital data transmission and in addition contains timing logic and presents a visual display of the current system status.

A very useful feature of the DADS, for system checkout allows a local ROC, mounted in the DADS, to be substituted for any specific remote console. Thus, all the buttons, lights, and the scope on a standard ROC are built into the DADS unit. Other functions available on the DADS include an analog input channel for test data, one dedicated priority interrupt, and an intercom to the instrument areas. Since high current devices (including two elevators) operate within the building, the electrical environment between the ROC consoles and the DADS unit is relatively noisy. A differential signal was used for all signals (except lighting indicators) passed between DADS and the ROC to achieve maximum noise rejection. Analog signals are routed through individual low capacitance cable while digital signals are in multiconductor cables. Digital integrated circuit line drivers and receivers were chosen for this application.

Coupling of the digital signals from each ROC, via DADS, to the computer occurs at the Process Interface Control

(PIC). PIC functions as a digital input/output multiplexer which routes signals from the DDP-516 I/O bus to addressable external locations. The 576 bits in the PIC are divided into 48 addressable groups of 12 bits each. Each of the 48 locations may function as either an input or output. To meet the requirements for our system, two types of digital inputs, digital outputs, and two digital-to-analog converters were purchased as part of the PIC. Digital inputs with storage are used to record the occurrence of ROC button pushes, since the button may be released before the system responds. Digital inputs without storage are used for reading in instrument abscissa values (wavelength, wavenumber, etc.) and thumbwheel digit information. Digital outputs are used to turn on lights on the remote console and to synchronize some digital functions.

INSTRUMENT INTERFACES

The existing outputs of the instruments were modified by us to obtain signals for input to the computer rather than our attempting to modify the internal design of the instrument. Thus, data collection by the computer does not alter instrument performance.

Each remote console contains the electronic circuits to convert (or adapt) data from the form which exists within the particular instrument to a voltage signal suitable for transmission to the computer room. All the instruments involved have a stand-alone capability prior to any connection to the computer. The basic requirement for most instruments is to derive a sampling signal at some fundamental unit of the instrument (such as wavelength or wavenumber) and use this signal to direct sampling of the dependent variable. A dedicated external interrupt is used for this type of sampling. In some cases the dependent variable is sampled as a function of time. For sampling using a time base, a special real-time clock is used, and a rate is derived from its basic interval of 0.25 millisecond.

In most ROC instrument interfaces, both analog and digital signals are transmitted between the ROC and the computer room. When the value of the independent variable is known absolutely (e.g., via a shaft encoder), the selection of starting and stopping values for the data to be sampled can be specified in terms of this variable. The desired starting value is entered as a parameter; then during the instrument run, sampling begins automatically when this value is reached.

Cary 60 Interface. A block diagram of the Cary 60 spectropolarimeter interface is shown in Figure 3, and the functional aspects of this interface are presented below.

Wavelength range on the Cary 60 is from 1850–6000 Å. Scanning of wavelengths occurs in a linear manner at scan speeds between 0.2–30 Å second and is continuously variable. A shaft encoder was attached to the wavelength readout to give a direct wavelength reading in Ångstroms. Encoder readout is 4 digits of 8421 BCD, where 2 bits of gray code (0–3), repeated 50 times per turn (∴ 200 counts/revolution), are logically combined to create the low order bit of the units digit. As with all the shaft encoders, each increment of the units digit is used to create an interrupt which in this case directs the computer to sample the optical rotation. A linear slidewire, attached in parallel to the servo mechanism slidewire to acquire optical rotation, produces a voltage of approximately −7.5 to +7.5 volts over the 10-inch chart presentation. Three controls on the Cary 60 are available to allow scaling of the independent variable on the chart record. This scaling changes the interpretation of the voltage received

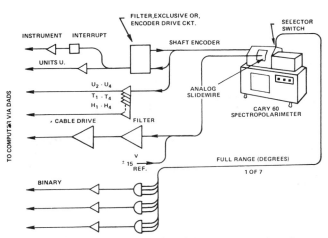

Figure 3. Simplified schematic of the computer interface to the Cary 60 spectropolarimeter

by the computer. Two of the control settings, zero offset and zero suppression, are entered through the parameter entry unit in the ROC. An addition was made to the third control, full-scale, to allow the computer to read its setting.

Cary 14 Interface. The Cary 14 spectrophotometer is a double beam optical instrument capable of operating between 2000 and 26,000 Å, thereby covering the ultraviolet, visible, and near infrared regions. The encoder is coupled directly to the Cary 14 such that its output reads directly in Å units. The electrical output of the encoder is presented in BCD and has a range of 0–39,999. The least significant bit (LSB) of the encoder units digit is delayed to allow discrimination against pulses of less than several hundred microseconds to reject noise. After passing through the delays, either edge of the LSB that is present is used to generate an interrupt. A potentiometer attached to the absorbance recorder produces a proportional voltage which is transmitted to the computer.

IR-7 Interface. The Beckman IR-7 produces a spectrum by varying the frequency in a linear manner over a part or all of the wavenumbers between 650 and 4000. A shaft encoder is attached to the wavenumber drive and a strip encoder to the absorbance recorder chart drive to acquire data. To define wavenumber, a shaft encoder of 100 counts per revolution is attached to the IR-7 wavenumber readout with gears establishing the ratio of one-tenth encoder revolution per wavenumber. Each revolution of the encoder generates a cyclic gray code of eight bits. Logical circuits within the ROC were designed to detect the encoder crossing 99-00 count up, and 00-99 count down. Since the encoder repeats every 10 wavenumbers, a counter external to the encoder is required to determine the scan position of the IR-7 relative to a starting point. In order to limit the initialization procedure, the counter has the capability of counting both up and down; therefore, once the ROC is turned on and the counter is initialized, the position of the encoder is known absolutely until power is turned off. An eight-bit parity circuit coupled to the encoder readout will produce an output for each shaft increment. This parity circuit output is used to develop the IR-7 instrument interrupt.

Much of the analysis done of the IR-7 depends on temperature. The sample area may be chilled or heated by circulation of fluids from devices external to the IR-7. Measurement of sample temperature is by means of a thermistor attached to a telethermometer. An analog signal available as an output and normally used to drive a chart recorder

Table I. System Software Priority Levels

Software priority level	Program function
8	Write data onto disk
7	Respond to console button push
6	Program initiated from remote console
5	Write remote scope
1–4	FORTRAN, assembly language programs

has been coupled to the ROC where it is buffered, amplified, and subsequently transmitted to the computer.

Cary 81 Interface. The Raman effect measured by the Cary 81 spectrometer uses a laser as the exciting source. Currently, the instrument is being modified to accept laser light from one of two sources. One source is a He–Ne gas laser with the major output of 50 milliwatts at 6328 Å (red). A second, more powerful Argon laser has for its most intense line 1.5 watts, at 5145 Å (green). A maximum of 4000 wavenumbers may be scanned beginning, approximately, with the laser excitation source. The Cary 81 has two mechanical wavenumber indicators, both of which are linear in wavenumber. One indicator denotes the current absolute wavenumber of the instrument optical system, the other is the displacement in wavenumbers from the excitation source, Δ cm^{-1}. A shaft encoder capable of defining 100,000 positions, 1000 per turn, 100 turns full-range, has been coupled to the instrument wavenumber drive mechanism. Gears added between the instrument drive and the encoder establish the ratio of 25 encoder counts per wavenumber. Therefore, the encoder range 0–100,000 corresponds to the instrument range 0–4000 Δ cm^{-1}.

It is necessary to adjust the relative wavenumber indicator for each change in the laser source that is used. An electric clutch under control of a toggle switch has been placed between the wavenumber drive on the instrument and the encoder gear drive to facilitate manual setting of the encoder to zero when the excitation source is changed. An analog representation of the Raman lines is acquired from a potentiometer attached to the instrument chart recorder.

Computer of Average Transients Interface. In this particular application, data are being accumulated in a Computer of Average Transients (CAT) used with a Varian HR-220 NMR spectrometer. After sufficient iterative scans have been accumulated in the CAT, the data are transferred from the CAT memory to the DDP-516 for analysis. A binary output of both memory address (10 bits) and memory contents (17 bits) is available from the CAT. An instrument interrupt is developed from each edge of the least significant address bit. Readout of the CAT memory to the computer requires enabling the instrument interrupt by the normal sign-on procedure, then placing the CAT in the readout mode at a rate selected by controls on the instrument.

Although the CAT is being used in this application with the HR-220, it has a general utility and is used in other applications. The interface deals only with the CAT in its readout mode and, therefore, may be applied in the other applications (disregarding problems of physical locations).

Analytical Ultracentrifuge Interface. Analysis of samples on the ultracentrifuge varies considerably from the instruments previously discussed. Multiple samples may be present in the rotor so it is necessary to have a positive identification of which sample is producing the analog data signal. Cell identification is continuously available to the computer

as a 3-bit binary number derived by sensing the centrifuge scanner. Rotor velocity is derived by counting a pulse signal, used internally for speed control, which is proportional to rotor velocity. This signal is counted in the interface for one second, then the total count is made available to the computer for the succeeding second. The counter is enabled by the computer and will continue to cycle every 2 seconds until disabled by the computer. Optical bench position is sensed via a potentiometer that has been attached to the bench drive mechanism. The optical density data signal resulting from the scan of the cell as a function of bench position is also transmitted to the computer as an analog signal. It has been acquired from the scanner electronics, a standard part of the instrument.

THE SOFTWARE SYSTEM

The software monitor, called OLERT (On-Line Executive for Real-Time), is a state-of-the-art system which provides scheduling, input-output, and FORTRAN capabilities. Up to eight software levels of priority are allowed for the running of programs (the highest level being eight). For our purposes this means that the foreground data acquisition programs will run at the highest priority level, the programs supporting data collection will run at lower levels, and the background FORTRAN and assembly language programs will run at the lowest levels. The use of the eight software levels is shown in Table I.

Any number of FORTRAN or assembly language programs can be running at levels 1–4, the only limit being the amount of memory available and the availability of I/O equipment. These programs are initiated from the computer console. The OLERT monitor does not (at this time) allow for program swapping so that no new program can be initiated until memory space is available. However, programs can be segmented. These segments reside on the disk and are requested and loaded as needed.

In order to make the input of laboratory data as fast as possible, the data are collected at a hardware interrupt level which has a higher priority than the eight software levels. Also, all interrupts are inhibited during the input of a laboratory data point. Software levels five, seven, and eight contain the programs which support data acquisition. Auxiliary tasks, such as emptying a data buffer to disk or identifying a console interrupt and responding to it, are scheduled for levels eight and seven, respectively. The actual driving of the scopes is done at levels five. All programs initiated from remote consoles are run at level six. One such program displays file ID information and plots data on remote scopes.

One major area of modification which was made to the monitor involves the method of responding to interrupts. Hardware interrupts can be initiated from one of the following six sources: (1) peripheral equipment (teletypes, card reader, paper tape reader/punch, printer, magnetic tape, or disk); (2) internal events (power failure, memory violation, etc.); (3) real-time clock; (4) another computer; (5) the independent variable associated with each instrument (wavelength, time, etc.); and (6) remote console buttons. The OLERT monitor handles the internal interrupts and contains the driving programs to handle the peripheral equipment and real-time clock, on an interrupt basis. Drivers to process external interrupts from experiment runs [types (5) and (6) above] could have been written, following the procedure used for peripherals, and incorporated into the system; however, this was not done. A rough breakdown

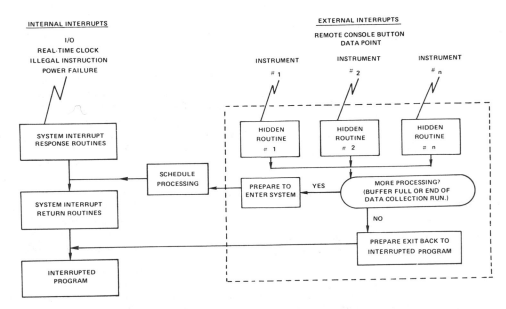

INTERNAL INTERRUPTS

I/O
REAL-TIME CLOCK
ILLEGAL INSTRUCTION
POWER FAILURE

EXTERNAL INTERRUPTS

REMOTE CONSOLE BUTTON
DATA POINT

INSTRUMENT #1   INSTRUMENT #2   INSTRUMENT #n

Figure 4. Diagram of software interrupt processing

Programs enclosed in dashes are not under system control

of the time required for executing an analog-to-digital conversion, using a standard system driving program, is the following: 150 μsec (approximately 150 machine cycles) to recognize the interrupt, 300 μsec to execute the A/D conversion and store the value, and 50 μsec to return to the interrupted program. (Actual A/D conversion time is only 35 μsec but the monitor requires that the conversion be scheduled, which results in a large software overhead.) This total time of approximately 500 μsec would limit the overall system data acquisition rate to about 2 KHz.

To allow overall sampling rates considerably above 2 KHz within the system, the executive program was modified to give faster response to data acquisition requests (3). This was done by incorporating into the system an interrupt program, for each instrument, which does not run under system control. That is, once it has gained control from the system through the initiation of a hardware interrupt, the special routine (called a "Hidden Routine," since it is hidden from the system) performs the necessary input (normally A/D conversion and input) and returns to the system in the same way a standard interrupt does. Since this hidden routine needs to save and restore only a very few registers, as opposed to the large number saved by the interrupt program provided by the system, and, in general, has much less overhead than that associated with general system interrupt response, it is possible to reduce the response and return time from 500 μsec to less than 100 μsec. Thus, using the Hidden Routine approach, an overall system data collection rate of about 10 KHz can be attained. Actual A/D conversion of data can be initiated as little as 13 μsec from the time of the interrupt as opposed to about 200 μsec using a standard A/D driver.

A hidden routine normally exits back to the system after each point is collected, but when a data buffer is filled the hidden routine branches to another path to first switch

buffers and write the last buffer onto the disk before returning to the system. A diagram of the relation between hidden routines and system interrupt processing is shown in Figure 4.

A typical foreground-background use of the system with two FORTRAN programs requiring, say, 1536 and 5120 words of storage, and running simultaneously with data acquisition, might find memory allocated as follows:

Location 0-12797 (25 sectors of 512 words each) OLERT operating system
    12800–13311 (3 sectors) FORTRAN program one
    16374–21493 (10 sectors) Data Acquisition and ROC communication monitor
    21494–26613 (10 sectors) FORTRAN program two

The OLERT and Data Acquisition Systems are permanently resident in the locations indicated, while FORTRAN or other programs are loaded into the remaining available memory as directed by the user.

APPLICATION PROGRAMS

Some basic programs have been written for general use in analyzing the data collected. In general, small scale calculations are done on the local machine and computations requiring a large amount of memory or time will be done on the NIH central computer system located in another building.

One of the programs for processing data gathered from an instrument performs linear operations on spectra, catenates spectra, and does smoothing. The results can be saved and/or printed. The user specifies the name(s) of the file(s) to be manipulated, the option desired, and the name for the resulting file. As with all application programs, this one can be initiated and run while data are being collected.

Other programs are available for further, more complex analyses of data. Once a spectrum has been normalized and a base-line spectrum subtracted, curve fitting calculations can be performed with another program which does a least

(3) J. Buzen, IEEE Computer Group Conference, Minneapolis, Minn., June 1969.

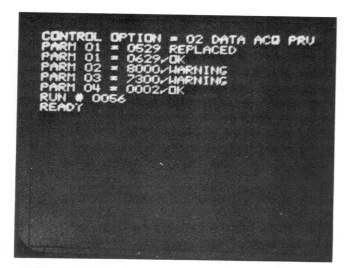

Figure 5. ROC displays during a data acquisition run

At the top, during parameter entry; at the bottom, at the completion of a run

square fit of specified spectra to another spectrum to determine its components.

Raw data or files resulting from the programs just described can be output using a set of general plotting routines which provides scaling and labeling.

There is a continuing effort in the development of applications programs and programs that support data collection. These programs range in complexity from the computation of standard formulas to, in the case of the ultracentrifuge, the detection of subtle patterns in the data. With the ultracentrifuge, some simple pattern recognition will be done in real-time to reduce the volume of data, while more complex analysis will be done after the data are collected.

USE OF THE REMOTE OPERATOR'S CONSOLE

A standard procedure is used for operating the remote consoles. Before beginning operation, the user must check that the SYSTEM UP light is on, which indicates that the console supporting software is operational. SYSTEM UP extinguishes unless refreshed at least once per second by the operating system. If the SYSTEM UP delay is not refreshed prior to timing out, it is assumed that the operating system is no longer in a reliable condition and the laboratory interrupts are disabled in the DADS (hardware). The remaining buttons on the console, SIGN ON, SIGN OFF,

Table II. Control Options Which Can Be Initiated from a Remote Operator's Console

Control option	Function
01	Data Acquisition Run with standard parameters
02	Data Acquisition Run with previous parameters
03	Restart run after Halt
21	Delete a data file
31	Display ID information from file
32	Display data from file
33–39	Initiate specified program

HALT, and RUN, are used, respectively, to initiate console use, to terminate console use, to stop data acquisition before the normal end of run, and to initiate data acquisition.

The parameter entry panel is used for entering (or canceling) control option and parameter information. The function of each run is specified by the two digit control option number entered. Currently the system allows the options shown in Table II.

The dialogue is begun by the user pressing SIGN ON. The system responds by asking (on the scope) for the scientist's user number. Each file of data collected is stored on the disk in an area reserved for the user number specified. Following entry of the user number, the system asks for the two digit control option. After the control option is entered, parameter values are requested, the number and meaning of each depending on the control option and laboratory instrument being used. Normally, for a data acquisition run (option 01, 02, or 03), the parameters consist of a file identification number, beginning and end values and sampling increment for the independent variable (wavelength, etc.), and instrument settings. For a data run, the user initializes the instrument properly, presses RUN on the console and starts the instrument scan. Values are collected from the beginning abscissa value specified, using the specified increment, until the final value is reached or HALT is pressed. When a buffer of 25 points is collected, it is displayed on the scope and stored on the disk. The dialogue from a typical data acquisition run, with four parameters, is shown in Figure 5. The figure shows also the display of data at the completion of a run. At the end of a run a new control option can be entered or use of the console can be terminated by pressing SIGN OFF.

The system software tests that parameter values are within an allowed range by comparing them with a table of values prepared for each instrument. If a possible error is detected in information entered from the remote console, a message is displayed on the scope and the CANCEL light is turned on. The message given is only a warning and can be ignored.

FURTHER WORK

Improvements to the present version of the system are being made to make it more responsive to the needs of the scientists and new work is being planned in a number of areas. The connections to other computers (the dotted lines in Figure 1) are now being developed. Communication with them will be controlled by background programs running simultaneously with data acquisition.

The system has the capacity for handling a number of additional instruments using complete parallel I/O techniques. The tables containing information for each instrument are at present permanently core-resident so that the main limitation to adding more instruments is the amount of available memory. In terms of hardware data acquisition capabilities, a total of ten instruments in the slow-to-medium speed range (say, less than 500 points/sec each) could easily be accommodated. When (and if) the number of instruments interfaced to the computer increases to the point where their table information begins to saturate memory, one acceptable solution (and one easy to implement) would be to restrict the number of data collection runs that can be made simultaneously. This number will depend on the characteristics (rates, amount of processing, etc.) of the particular instruments being run.

Instrument control via the computer presents another area for further development of the system. Monitoring and control of a single variable, such as temperature, could be done relatively simply with the present hardware but there is no immediate need for such control with the instruments now interfaced. The development of such control loops will depend on the particular instruments which will be connected in the future.

One complex area to be analyzed involves obtaining better system performance through modification of the instruments. In many instruments the mechanism for producing a chart record restricts the speed of scanning and, in addition, is a limiting part of the control network. In-creased speed and greater signal resolution, if obtained, could lead to the need for analog to digital conversion at the instrument.

Presently, only instruments located within the building can be connected to the computer because of the parallel transmission of signals. It is conceivable that a simple telemetering system could be designed and implemented that would allow the multiplexing of digital control and data signals over a low capacity telephone line or dedicated transmission cable. This would allow expansion of the system beyond the confines of the present location.

ACKNOWLEDGMENT

We acknowledge the contributions of a number of coworkers to the design and implementation of the system—in particular the contributions of William Holsinger, who designed the DADS unit; Jay Vinton, who wrote the software system for utilizing the remote consoles; Jeff Buzen, who wrote the programs for improving interrupt response time; and Mrs. Marie Chang and Dr. Richard Simon who provided much of the system and application software.

RECEIVED for review September 23, 1970. Accepted December 15, 1970.

FRED MOSES
SR. PROGRAMMER
INFANTS, CHILDREN, ADOLESCENTS AND ADULTS

23101 Honeywell Way   Burbank, California

Telephone: 340-1212

NAME _Alonzo Chavez_   DATE _9-26-71_

ADDRESS _____ CITY _____ CALIF.

Rx

Minicomputers # 30

In the Hospital

T. Ante hs

SIG: LABEL

     REP._____TIMES

     NE. REP. ☐

REG. NO. 22118   _____ M.D.

Reprinted from *Computer*, vol. 4, pp. 22–27, Sept./Oct. 1971.

The minicomputer's power to perform repetitive clerical tasks, monitor and control real-time processes, and perform scientific calculations has made it desirable in hospital systems. The minicomputer's inherent low cost has made it practical. Computer suppliers to the medical field are recognizing that they must collaborate with medical professionals to pinpoint well delimited problem areas.

The most ambitious undertaking has been the development of general hospital information systems[1] employing large minicomputer systems or, more often, medium or large scale computer systems. These systems attempt, with some limited success to date, to centralize patient records, take patient histories, schedule hospital facility utilization, provide fast data communication between sections of the hospital and perform various other medical, administrative and clerical tasks. It is envisioned

that as these systems mature, a central computer will be linked with more specialized satellite subsystems which will take advantage of common communication links and data entry, filing, and retrieval facilities.

This survey discusses several potential satellites which have been or are soon to be implemented as independent minicomputer packages. Automated clinical laboratory systems currently enjoy wide and increasing use. Intensive care units have begun to employ minicomputers for continuous real-time monitoring tasks. Radiation treatment planning systems, while highly specialized, display the significant computational power of a small computer. Some image processing applications, currently in the research or early developmental stage, show some of the most sophisticated, though currently restricted, tasks to which minicomputers are being applied.

CLINICAL LABORATORY AUTOMATION

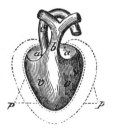

Approximately one half billion laboratory tests were performed in this country last year. This number is expected to double by 1975. Paralleling the massive increase in the number and variety of tests are demands for more rapid, accurate, and legible reporting of test results. To meet these demands, clinical laboratories have become the heaviest non-EDP medical users of computers.

To the typical on-line computer system,[2] the clinical laboratory presents a flow from the doctor's test requisition to detailed result reports for doctors' perusal and for insertion into a patient's permanent record. As requisitions are received by the laboratory, they are entered into the system by keyboard, mark sense reader, or punched card reader. The system generates "pick-up" lists of specimens to be collected. Gummed specimen identification labels are often generated.

As specimens are received by the laboratory, they are logged in and given internal identification numbers. Work sheets are printed assigning specimens to various automatic and manual test instruments. For most systems, specimens are not automatically identified although much effort is currently being devoted to developing machine readable test tube identification tabs and the like. The work sheets for computer interfaced testers generally define the order in which the system expects to see samples. If "stat" (emergency) tests are needed, most systems accept changes in the ordering. Manually derived test results generally are entered by keyboard or mark sense reader.

One of the prime tasks of laboratory automation packages is detailed error checking. While human error may be drastically reduced by computerization, error sources such as incorrect specimen labeling, instrumentation failure or drift, off-scale automated readings, reagent contamination, and incorrect entry of manually derived test results still exist. At each step of the process, the systems check for possible data invalidity, report questionable results immediately, and log instrument failures for quality control reports. A gross deviation from normal values, a radical change from a patient's previous test values, or an inconsistency with results from physiologically related tests may cause flagging of a test result.

The end product of the clinical laboratory system is a variety of reports. For internal laboratory use, daily and weekly summary reports provide quality control data. For external dissemination, interim reports give single test results or the current day's data for a given patient. Summary reports may contain all the results for a number of previous days. Graphical trend reports may be generated for some tests. All reports should flag abnormal values and may provide normal ranges.

Flexibility is a key requisite of a clinical laboratory package. Acceptance often rests on the ease with which the transition to an automated system can be made. Laboratory administrative procedures and available instrumentation vary from hospital to hospital. Printout formats must be extremely flexible since a hospital may wish to modify them several times before selecting a final format. New tests must be accommodated. Varying demand, instrument failure, and the addition of new test instrumentation make necessary the ability to reconfigure the device allocation and servicing portions of the software.

The technologist must be able to interface easily with the system. Most systems are carefully human engineered to avoid unnecessary or overly complicated keying in of commands or data. Some offer special-purpose terminals for individual areas of the laboratory.

The heart of a clinical laboratory package is its file handling system. Patient files, in addition to containing an accumulation of test results, generally contain patient name, identification number, age, sex, room number, test requested, tests with results pending, information needed for pick-up list printing, normal test result bounds checking, report generation, and billing. Often these files are tree-structured to provide ease of searching and efficiency of storage. Files for automated test equipment contain the expected values of calibration samples and samples used for drift correction in addition to the order of the patient specimens.

The central processors for stand alone systems generally range from 12 bit minicomputers with 8K words of main memory to 16 bit machines with 16K words of memory. Fixed head disks with .5 to 1.5 megabytes capacities generally provide file and program swapping storage. For automated test equipment interfacing, 16 to 32 multiplexed A/D channels and 16 to 32 digital input/output channels are provided.

AUTOMATED PATIENT MONITORING

Automated patient monitoring systems in intensive care units show the real-time processing power of minicomputers. Continuous monitoring of the critically ill, the post-operative surgical patient, and the recent heart attack victim provides the attending medical team with accurate and timely data on the progress of the patient. In addition, automated systems can immediately detect and signal many dangerously abnormal conditions.[1,3]

The primary monitored physiological indicator is the electrocardiogram. Many forms of heart malfunction appear as timing irregularities in this normally periodic signal. A major portion of a monitoring system's task is the detection, classification, and recording of these irregularities.

For surgical patients, it is important to monitor, in addition, blood pressure for signs of shock and other post-operative complications. From pressure transducers connected to tubes inserted into a patient's artery and heart chambers, not only pressure, but various derived measures of heart and circulatory system function may be calculated.

Respiratory system functions may be monitored through the basic measurements of respiratory rate, air pressure and flow, and the partial pressures of oxygen and carbon dioxide. Variables relating to lung mechanics and metabolic activity are derived from these. Other indicators of metabolic activity are calculated from internal and skin temperature and various blood chemistry tests.

Monitoring systems currently provide much of the information on which mechanical respirator adjustments, fluid infusion, and drug administration are based. In the future, monitoring systems may control these and other critical patient treatments in closed-loop operation.

Most computerized monitoring systems contain small to medium sized minicomputer configurations with analog signal conditioning front ends. CRT terminals provide graphic display of patient parameters, often both at the bedside and the nursing station. Strip chart recorders often provide permanent copies of monitored signals for patient records.

RADIATION THERAPY PLANNING

The radiation therapist may have at his disposal several different radiation sources with a multiplicity of beam shaping filters. He must decide which sources he should use and how he must aim them at a patient to provide optimal irradiation of the target, usually a tumor within the patient, while avoiding injury to nearby healthy, sensitive tissue. Hand calculation of the effect of a single treatment plan may take several hours.

With radiotherapy planning systems developed over the last few years, a therapist or technologist can enter and have saved on magnetic tape a library of beam characteristics. At a given planning session, he can enter, using a graphical input device, the outline of an appropriate cross-section of the patient. For reference purposes the target area and regions to be avoided may be drawn in.

With the outline and selected beams displayed on a storage scope, the therapist positions beams by turning potentiometers read by the system's A/D converter. By keyboard, he may add and remove beams and change beam strength factors. On command, the system computes and displays isodose contour plots showing the summation of the energy distributions of the beams. Reduction of the computation time to less than two minutes encourages the evaluation of multiple trial plans. When a satisfactory plan is obtained, the final beam parameters may be printed and the plan plotted on a digital plotter. The CPU is often a 12 bit minicomputer with 8K words of memory.

A PICTURE IS WORTH . . .

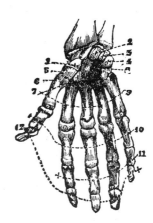

Much biomedical data is inherently pictorial in nature or has been transformed into images to take advantage of the human's prodigious image analyzing capability. Light and electron microscopy, radiology, and autoradiography provide examples of pictorial output spanning many clinical and research fields.

Many of the clinically valuable image processing tasks with sufficiently bounded scope yet high enough volume to warrant automation are classification problems.[4] These range from scanning individual chest X-rays for the differential diagnosis of rheumatic heart damage to characterizing and reporting the distribution of cell types in mixed populations, such as blood samples, containing thousands or millions of cells per sample.

The automation of differential white blood cell counts[5] is an area of high interest as this test is one of the most common and routine non-chemical laboratory tests performed. Its value is that variances in the relative numbers of the different white cell types are sensitive indicators of various disease processes, injury, general stress, ionizing radiation damage and some poisons. One of the test's major drawbacks is that it is tedious and requires a substantial time investment by a highly trained technologists.

This task is amenable to automation for several reasons. The standard preparation, a drop of blood smeared and stained on a glass or quartz slide, is a monolayer largely devoid of overlapping cells. This obviates the complex problems of focusing and distinguishing individual cells found in thicker preparations. The classification task is eased as there are only three major classes of white blood cells, one of the classes having three generally distinguished subclasses. The presence of red blood cells, platelets and possibly immature or pathologic white cell types complicates the classification processes slightly.

Visual classification of white cells relies upon the relative size and geometry of the nucleus, the presence and apparent texture of graininess outside the nucleus, and staining characteristics. Analysis of a blood smear, whether manual or automatic, is a two step process of locating white cells and then classifying those found. In an automated system, standard feature extraction techniques as boundary finding, relative perimeter and area calculation and convexity, concavity, and connectedness determination may serve to define points in a multidimensional property space for pattern recognition procedures. Another promising approach employs syntactic feature analysis as its classification tool. As a valuable by-product of its pattern recognition scheme an automated system can provide statistical properties of the cell populations not available from manual analyses.

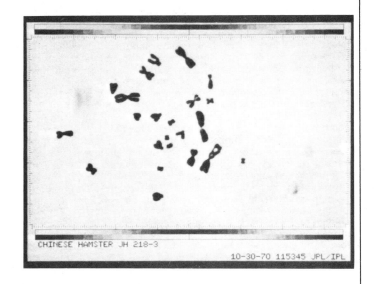

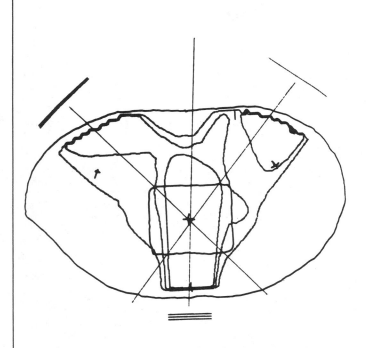

FIG 1 — Radiation treatment plan showing body outline, target area, and equal energy contours calculated for the three radiation beams whose central axes are displayed. (Photograph courtesy of the Digital Equipment Corporation).

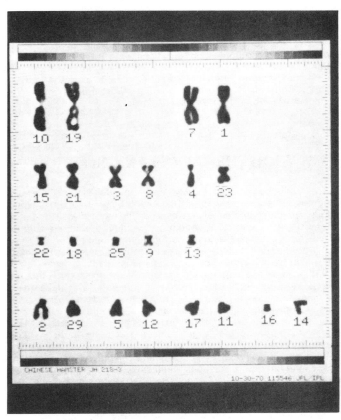

FIG 2 — Computer generated pictures of Chinese hamster chromosome spread. (A) Display reconstructed from automated microscope scan of the original specimen. (B) Display of these chromosomes ordered and oriented with their major axes vertical. Numbers refer to the order in which chromosomes were detected in a top to bottom scan of the original image. (Photographs courtesy of Dr. A. N. Stroud of the Jet Propulsion Laboratory).

Packages for computer assisted chromosome karyotyping may soon be available.[6] The karyogram, an orderly presentation of the chromosomes of a single cell, is generally prepared from specially cultured white blood cells. It can aid in the diagnosis of monogolism, various other genetic disorders, and chromosomal damage caused by ionizing radiation and some poisons. While it has been proposed that every newborn infant be karyotyped, this test now is performed infrequently due to its expense.

Manual karyotyping requires scanning a microscope slide to find and photograph cells whose chromosomes are well separated. The pictures of the chromosomes are then individually cut out, paired, and ordered into a standard sequence by size and relative position of the centromere, the cross-point in their X or H shape. In some cases, several such paste-ups are prepared from each slide. A newly developed staining technique yields more accurate classification and anomaly detection than earlier methods, but the manual preparation process remains time consuming.

Again, the task of an automated system is often two-fold. In configurations employing a computer controlled microscope, the system may scan the specimen automatically for cells showing good chromosome spreads or display selected cells for an operator to accept or reject. In biological dosimetry and toxicological studies scans for spreads containing fragments of chromosomes or ring structures are desirable.

Once a good spread is found, the chromosomes must be classified. Since chromosomes may vary in length and optical density from cell to cell, some systems calculate normalization factors by integrating these parameters over all chromosomes in a given spread. Measures such as area and variation of optical density along the length of a chromosome are used to find the centromere. After arm lengths are measured from centromere to tip, pairing and classification can be performed. Badly bent or touching chromosomes sometimes prevent proper karyotyping. Means for operator assistance may be provided or problemlatic portions displayed separately. To be most useful to the cytogeneticist reading the karyogram, the final pictorial output must preserve the spatial and density resolution of the original microscopic image.

Pattern recognition systems generally contain an image input device, a computer, and some form of graphical output device. In research applications, photographic film transports with flying spot scanners or image dissectors are in wide use because of their flexibility. For clinical use, they are appropriate for such data sources as X-ray films and autoradiographs. It is not unusual for the image to be broken up into a 1000 by 1000 point matrix each point readable with three to eight bits of grey level quantization. Point access times vary with the type of sensor used and the maximum I/O rate of the computor acquiring the data. They are generally in the 1 to 100 microsecond range. Since inordinate amounts of high speed memory and time may be required to read an entire frame with maximum resolution, sectional or low resolution scans are often available for gross feature detection or object finding.

For microscopically viewed specimens, film scanners interject an unnecessary processing step. A number of manufacturers now offer automated microscopes having digitally controllable stage motion and magnification. In some applications, illumination intensity and wavelength is also dynamically controlled. Most automated microscopes require specimens carried on the traditional glass or quartz slides which must be mounted manually on the stage. High volume continuous process systems have been developed which use plastic tape or a liquid as the specimen transport medium.

Most experimental systems employ a large scientific computer as their processor sometimes with a smaller machine for ancillary tasks as finding objects of interest and image input device control. Clinically oriented packages, if they are to be cost effective, will turn to minicomputers for their processing power. For applications such as differential white blood cell counting and karyotyping it is estimated that a small 16 bit machine with 16-32K words of main memory will suffice. Where high quality images must be retained, much of the memory will be devoted to data storage. For intermediate image store and program segment swapping, a small fixed head disk will generally be included.

To meet the high processing speed requirements of high volume continuous flow devices, special purpose auxiliary processors may be needed. LSI cellular logic arrays offer promise for parallel image point transformations leading to boundary detection, hole finding, concavity and convexity determination, and other basic feature extraction tasks.

Output device needs depend heavily upon the nature of the system's task. Pictorial output is needed for intermediate systems such as that described for chromosome karyotyping and those which will require operator guidance or verification of the image segment to be processed. A printing device or a link to a larger information gathering system is appropriate for fully automated configurations such as are proposed for differential white blood cell counts.

CONCLUSION

Minicomputers already are helping hospitals provide better health care. By automating clerical, computational, and repetitive tasks, minicomputer packages are reducing errors and speeding vital information. Reliability, ease of use by nontechnical personnel, and flexibility to meet the needs of diverse hospital environments are imperative attributes of hospital systems such as that described for karyotyping and those which will require operator guidance or verification of the image segment to be processed. A printing device or a link to a larger information gathering system is appropriate for fully automated configurations such as are proposed for differential white blood cell counts.

REFERENCES

(1) G. A. Bekey and M. D. Schwartz, eds., *Hospital Information Systems*, M. Dekker, New York, 1971.
(2) M. J. Ball, "An Aid to Diagnosis: The Use of Computers in Automated Clinical Pathology Laboratories," *Journal of Medicine: Experimental and Clinical*, 1, 265-298, April, 1971.
(3) J. O. Beaumont, "On-Line Patient Monitoring System," *Datamation*, 15, 50-55, May 1969.
(4) R. S. Ledley, "Automatic Pattern Recognition for Clinical Medicine," *Proceedings of the IEEE*, 57, 2017-2035, November 1969.
(5) M. Ingram and K. Preston Jr., "Automatic Analysis of Blood Cells," *Scientific American*, 223, 72-82, November 1970.
(6) K. R. Castleman, "Pictorial Output for Computerized Karyotyping," in *Perspectives in Cytogenetics: The Next Decade*, Charles Thomas Press, Springfield, Illinois, to be published.

Applications of digital computers to the long term measurement of blood pressure and the management of patients in intensive care situations

by JOHN L. CORBETT*

University of Oxford
Oxford, England

INTRODUCTION

Blood pressure is one of the most frequently measured variables in clinical practice[1] and is one of the most important in influencing treatment.[2] Measurements are normally made with an indirect method and since the first such techniques were described[3-5] progressive development has been made towards their automation.[6-18] Even in patients with normal blood pressures, however, these methods have been found to be inaccurate[19-23] and they are most liable to error with extremes of pressure—when high in severe hypertension or low in shock—and when peripheral vasoconstriction is present. It is in precisely these situations when it is often of critical importance to know the blood pressure, and at such times the direct measurement of intra-arterial pressure is the only reliable method. This approach is now used in many intensive care units and is likely to be implemented progressively more as the techniques are further improved and the usefulness of the results is more widely appreciated. The volume of data is potentially very large and there is the possibility of many derived results. Digital computers have been previously applied to the analyses involved,[24-28] the general approach being to compress the results of intermittent measurements made in real time on an arterial recording to a form essentially similar to standard nursing charts although considerably more comprehensive, and to leave interpretation to the attending physician.

The present paper describes a method based on a cumulative sum technique for demonstrating trends in the mean level and variability of the recorded parameter and its derivatives and for assessing the significance of trends detected. It has been applied to subsequent analysis at high speed of recordings made on a multi-channel F.M. tape recorder, but the basic programme could also be used for on-line analysis and the general approach is suitable for the analysis of heart rate, central venous or other pressures, some respiratory variables, and temperature.

Outline of system

Acquisition of data (Figure 1)

Studies have been based on continuous intra-arterial recordings made on over 50 patients for periods ranging from 2 hrs to 13 days. In these recordings a teflon cannula has been inserted percutaneously into either the axillary, brachial, or femoral artery or a teflon catheter has been introduced into the artery with the Seldinger[29] guide-wire technique, and connected to a strain gauge pressure manometer via a device for continuous perfusion and serial damping. The system for perfusion and damping has been developed in Oxford in the Electro-Medical Research Unit of the Medical Research Council for short and medium term measurements and has been fully evaluated in this use.[30-32] Subsequent modifications have been made to enable long-term measurements in intensive care situations to be made more effectively.[33]

---

*British Medical Association Research Fellow, and Medical Research Fellow of St. Peter's College, Oxford.

Reprinted with permission from *AFIPS Conf. Proc., Vol. 33, Pt. 2, 1968 Fall Joint Comput. Conf.*, pp. 1105–1114.

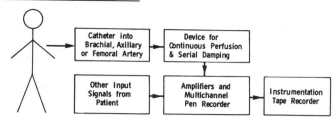

BLOOD PRESSURE RECORDING SYSTEM

FIGURE 1—Blood pressure recording system

The overall catheter system is critically damped and has a static and dynamic accuracy of about 1% and a frequency response of 30 - 40 Hz, these being considered adequate. [32,34-38] Analogue recordings are made simultaneously on a standard multi-channel penwriter and on a high class 14-track multi-channel F.M. instrumentation tape recorder (Sangamo) with excellent stability and linearity and long playing times (up to 16 inch reels of 1 inch tape can be accommodated). On-line computing facilities are not available and the tape recorder is therefore taken to a hybrid computing laboratory for subsequent processing of the records. This is done on a beat-to-beat basis at 16 to 32 times the original recording speed It should be pointed out that this is in effect an on-line system, since the signal from the tape recorder is a close reproduction of that from the patient, although the time base has been compressed. Although it is possible to deliver to the tape recorder an analogue of the blood pressure signal with a 1% accuracy, this is a very demanding accuracy level, and in long term recordings drift checks are necessary. In practice, an accuracy of about 1.5 to 2% would be more common, although attention to detail is required to achieve even this figure. A high class tape recorder can be expected to worsen linearity by about 0.5% and increase noise slightly (by about 1% at low speeds of operation).

Computing hardware (Figure 2)

The hybrid computing facility employed in this study consists of a standard hybrid computer, type TR48, made by Electronic Associates Ltd., in the United Kingdom, together with a sampling unit, analogue-to-digital converter, an interface and digital clock, and an I.B.M. 1130 digital computer with an eight thousand word memory and disc store of four hundred and eighty thousand words, and a punched card and paper tape output. An

English Electric KDF9 computer was also available and some of the results derived with the I.B.M. 1130 were transmitted to the KDF9 on paper tape, since the programme used for cumulative sum analysis was available only in KDF9 autocode. The hardware is illustrated in Figure 2 with input indicated from a tape recorder or patient and a display oscilloscope incorporated, and the overall system from patient to computer is shown in Figure 3. The maximum sampling rate attainable with the interface used was approximately one thousand per second and the analogue signal could be quantized to one part in 255 or one part in 2055.

Method of analysis

Normal blood pressure waveforms: General considerations for programming

In this approach analysis of systolic, diastolic, mean and pulse pressures, and heart rate (Figure 4) has been based entirely on the recording of intra-arterial pressure and it is therefore neces-

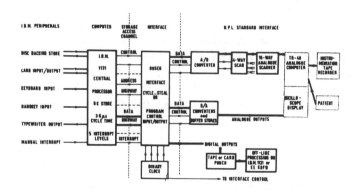

FIGURE 2—Hybrid computing facility

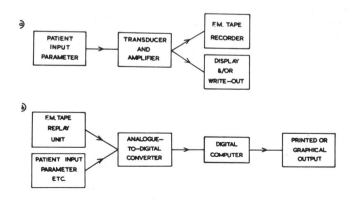

FIGURE 3—Overall system for computing of blood pressure recordings

sary to appraise the physiological and physical characteristics of the signal. As illustrated, the peak of the wave represents the highest pressure in the arterial tree as the heart contracts and is called the systolic blood pressure. The heart beats rhythmically, and during its relaxation phase, pressure is maintained by the elastic recoil of vessels, with back flow of blood being prevented by valves. The lowest pressure reached at this stage is called the diastolic pressure. Pulse pressure is the difference between these two values, and mean pressure is very commonly taken as the diastolic pressure plus one-third of the pulse pressure, on the assumption that the waveform is approximately triangular, although as the figure indicates, the average of the area under the curve is a more correct measure of it. The mean square value or the mean square about the mean may also be an important derivative. Heart rate is simply the reciprocal of the period, and when computed from beat-to-beat is usually referred to "instantaneous."

An aspect of the waveform which is important in digital computing is its amplitude/frequency spectrum (Figure 5) the illustration being taken from work by Patel.[38] Ninety-five per cent of the shape and amplitude of the wave comes from harmonics up to nine times the basic frequency, which varies roughly from 1 to 3 Hz, corresponding to a heart beat of 60 to 180 per minute. For accurate analysis, sampling should therefore be based ideally on a frequency of approximately 30 Hz, requiring a sampling rate of 60 per second or above to avoid aliasing.[39,40] In practice it has been found possible to use a sampling rate of 40 per second with little loss of accuracy since the contribution of frequencies above 20 Hz is usually small. This is equivalent to a sampling rate of approximately 600 per second when the time base of the record is compressed by a factor of 16. At this sampling rate an 8-bit word is adequate to keep quantization errors insignificant.[40]

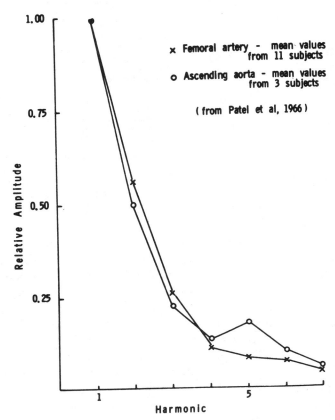

FIGURE 5—Amplitude-frequency spectrum of blood pressure waveform (From Patel, 1965)

"Problem" waveforms

While the classical shape of the blood pressure waveform is that illustrated in Figure 4, other shapes are frequently encountered. A sample of such shapes is shown in Figure 6, the records being taken from 6 different patients. All of the patterns shown are accurate recordings made with the same critically damp system as described above and the differences are therefore not due to arte-facts, although their explanation lies outside the purpose of this paper. Their importance lies in the fact that short periods of the overall wave during which a sign reversal occurs must not be recognized by the programme as new heart beats. Difficulties arise particularly when detailed predictions based on the exact shape of the waveform are to be made, especially since the pattern may not be constant even in one patient. This is demonstrated in the records shown in Figure 7 where the shape, DC level, pulse amplitude and rate of the blood pressure wave all change rapidly in response to a voluntary temporary increase in the pressure inside the subject's chest.[41,42] During this manoeu-

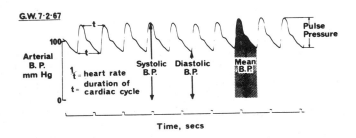

FIGURE 4—Blood pressure record—description of terms

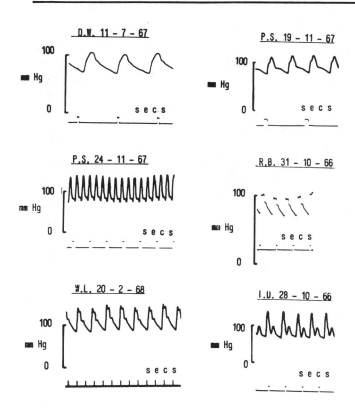

FIGURE 6—Varying blood pressure waveforms

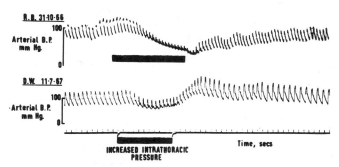

FIGURE 7—The effect on blood pressure and heart rate of a voluntary temporary increase in the pressure within the chest

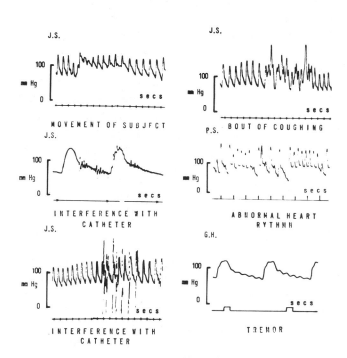

FIGURE 8—Noise in blood pressure recordings

vre, even in normal subjects, there may occur pulse pressure variations between successive heart beats of up to 20% and heart rate variations of up to 45%, while the mean pressure may vary by up to approximately 80% of its original value depending on how hard the subject "blows." Similar but less marked changes in the wave shape also occur with changes of posture and may be compounded by the presence of disease. A further difficulty is the frequent presence of noise (Figure 8) which has been interpreted here in a very wide sense. An example of a tremor in the patient, coughing, movement, interference with the catheter and an abnormal heart rhythm are shown, all of these events being common in clinical situations. It will be apparent that the frequency and amplitude of these events will usually distinguish them from a normal recording.

Programme for analysis of individual waveforms

Detection of the start of contraction of the heart (systole) has been found possible with a method based on the speed and duration of the rise of pressure during this period—probably the most

constant feature of the blood pressure waveform. The computer is programmed to recognize this event by searching for a number of monotonically increasing sample values, the number chosen depending on the sampling rate being used. The diastolic pressure is then taken as the immediately preceding minimum and the systolic pressure as the highest subsequent maximum occurring within a specified time. If this time is properly chosen the dicrotic notch, the "notch" seen during the downstroke of the wave in a number of the illustrations in Figures 6 and 7, will be ignored. Once systolic and diastolic pressures have been determined it is a simple matter to calculate the mean and pulse pressures and heart rate. Constraints are built into the programme to detect

197

high frequency noise and off-scale values, and limits are set for the maximum acceptable percentage variation between successive amplitudes and rates. When an unacceptable value is found the programme will either stop or register a fault count depending on which choice the user has made in a programme "option." Other features of the programme are an automatic calibration search, an initial scan to check that the signal conforms to the user parameters inserted, simple 5 point smoothing to remove high frequency noise, and options for the type of output and the duration of analysis.

The set of user parameters in the present version of this programme is indicated in Table I. The programme has been written in Fortran and also in machine code to increase its speed of operation. It will reliably accept samples at a rate of 600 per second to produce an analysis of the derivatives indicated in Figure 4 with an accuracy within 2%, enabling the speed of replay of the tape recorded signals to be increased by a factor of 16. When the tape speed is increased to 30 times the original and sampling rate is increased to a thousand per second, which is the highest of which the available hardware is capable, the accuracy of analysis decreases by a further 1 to 2.5%, depending on heart rate. It will be apparent that the amount of data will exceed available core store during analysis of long recordings since one track of a 16 inch spool can accept a continuous 20 hr recording at a speed of 1⅞ inches per second. The programme is therefore designed to automatically dump data on the disc store after every 320 heart beats and then return to the analysis. Incoming data is lost during this period.

TABLE I—User parameters for blood pressure analysis programme

1. Sampling rate of Analogue - to - Digital Converter.
2. Values of calibration signals (in mm Hg.).
3. Number of cycles, or period of time, to be analysed.
4. Permissible variation in a) amplitude b) heart rate between successive cycles.
5. Number of monotonically increasing points required to indicate systole.
6. Fall in amplitude after systolic point before beginning search for diastolic point.

At the end of the entire analysis further programmes are instituted for averaging set periods of the data and determining auto- and cross-covariances. Depending on the latter findings and on the nature and duration of the initial recording one or more selected derivatives are output on punched tape and occasionally on cards for cumulative sum or other subsequent analysis. For certain tests an example of which is given later, a "marker" signal is also recorded on the tape during the initial recording. Two types of marker have been employed, viz., a DC signal on an adjacent (unused) track which is then sampled alternately with the blood pressure signal during processing, and an AC signal of fixed amplitude and duration, superimposed on the data track itself. The latter method has been found more efficient for most purposes and the marker signal is detected by a separate loop in the programme. A similar method is used to indicate the end of a record.

Cumulative sum analysis

The beat-to-beat values derived from the foregoing blood pressure analysis constitutes in statistical terms a time series of nonstationary data in which the serial values are highly dependent and in which both the mean and root mean square vary with time.[40] If the degree of auto-covariance is known the initial derived series can be sampled at sufficiently infrequent intervals to convert it into a time series of independent samples. Present experience indicates that the degree of auto-correlation in the data varies considerably at different times in the one patient, and between patients. For the present illustration (Figure 10), serial half-hour-average values of heart rate, derived from a fifteen-day continuous blood pressure recording have been used. The method of time series analysis applied has been developed for another application by Woodward and Goldsmith,[43] and is illustrated in block form in Figure 9. Its purpose is to detect changes in the average level between groups of data in a time series and to determine the point of onset of such changes. The programme causes the computer to read in a time series, to calculate the cumulative sums of the series using the grand mean as a reference value, and to point out the occurrence of significant changes of slope in the cumulative sum chart. These changes can be determined at different probability levels, and the standard deviations of significantly different stages in the series are calculated. The output includes a graph of the

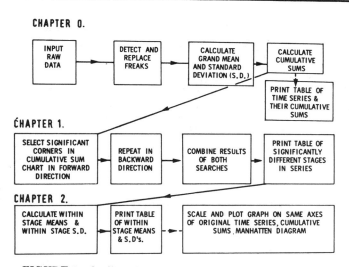

FIGURE 9—Outline of programme for cumulative sum analysis

original data, its cumulative sum or "cusum," and a "Manhatten" diagram, a term used to describe the graph of significantly different stages in the series.

It is obvious from Figure 10 that the initial series (a) is highly irregular and that trends of variation in the mean level are not very obvious. The cusum chart (b) however, gives a very clear indication of the overall trend, and visual inspection confirms the presence of a pattern in the original data which could easily have been overlooked. The Manhatten diagram (c) has condensed the scattered original data into a relatively small number of groups whose difference from their neighbors is significant, in this case at the 1% level. The within-group standard deviations, although available from the analysis, have not been included in this illustration. Differences produced by treatment of the patient with two anaesthetic agents, nitrous oxide and halothane, are clearly shown in both the cusum and Manhattan plots, the mean having decreased significantly. This method has also been used to test objectively the effects of various other treatments (to be published).

A further important application is shown in Figure 11, where an assessment has been made of the variability of the heart rate in the same patient over the same period. The difference between the highest and lowest values of instantaneous heart rate (excluding "freaks" produced by an abnormal rhythm) has been measured for each successive half hour period, and used as a primary measure of variability. These figures have then been proc-

essed in a fashion identical to that described above. The general comments already made on the type of output resulting from this analysis again hold true, and it is also clear that the changes in variability detected by this method do not closely parallel the changes in the average heart rate, although treatment with an anaesthetic agent has produced a clear decrease in the variability.

DISCUSSION

Blood pressure and heart rate are usually measured and recorded by a nurse. She is relatively cheap, easily understood, replaceable, reliable and compact. An automatic monitoring system must offer significant advantages over her to justify the increased capital cost and increased complexity. There is little doubt that most automated systems are indeed superior but there is equally little doubt that most currently available systems are much more effective in producing large volumes of unprocessed data than in efficiently compressing results—they tend to act rather as a team of nurses taking measurements more frequently. The presence of large volumes of potentially useful but unprocessed data in intensive care and research units is a growing problem, and blood pressure records of this type are in fact largely unprocessable, due to the time required for manual analysis. For instance, this may require up to 5 - 6 weeks for analysis of a continuous record lasting 7 - 10 days, and even after this time the analysis is limited. The need for computing is very real and will grow with time.

Reference has already been made to previous applications of digital computers to these problems. The present tendency is to make automatic comprehensive measurements and thereafter to compress the data simply by averaging over varying periods of time. Unfortunately, this is not always a particularly sensitive method of compressing the data without losing its information content. The point is illustrated in Figure 12, where five sections of a blood pressure record taken from the same patient at different stages of a disease process are shown. The duration of each of the traces is about 25 minutes, and a calibration signal is shown for each record. On the right hand side an approximate mean level is written, and the highest and lowest pressure during the period is indicated by a mark. It is immediately apparent to the eye that in the upper

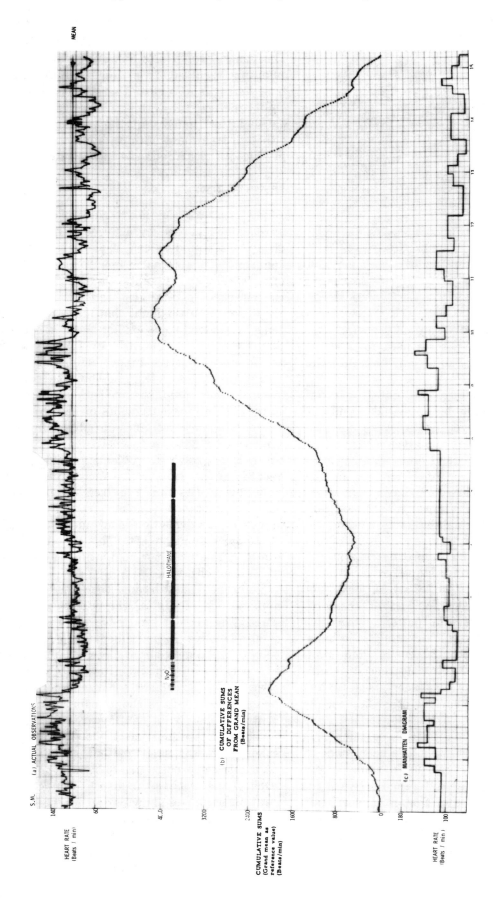

FIGURE 10—Cumulative sum analysis of half-hourly-mean heart rates during a 10-day period in a patient with tetanus (see text)

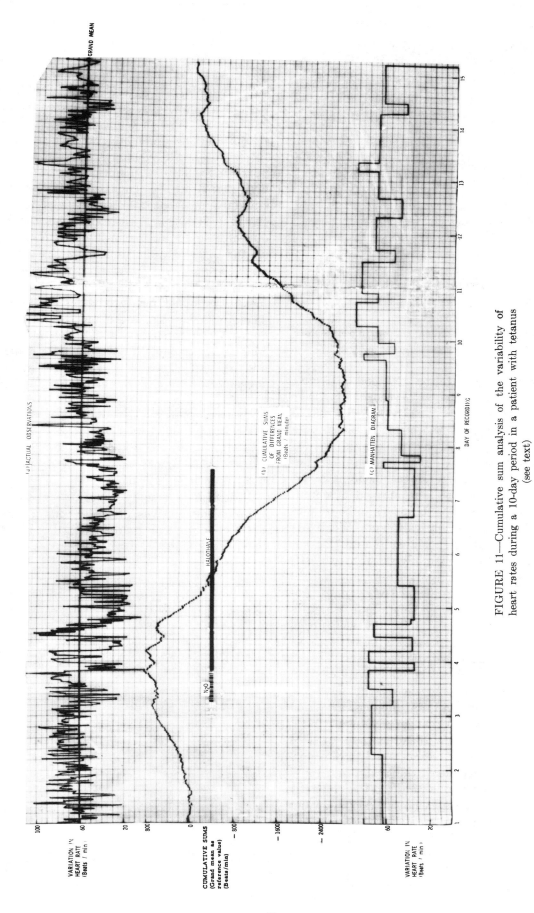

FIGURE 11—Cumulative sum analysis of the variability of heart rates during a 10-day period in a patient with tetanus

(see text)

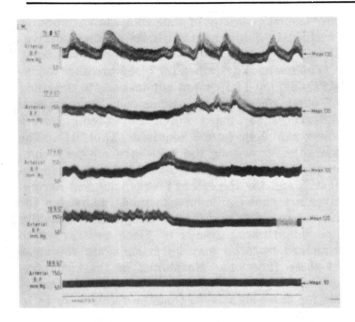

FIGURE 12—Blood pressure recordings taken on a pen recorder with a slow time base (see text)

record, there is great lability of blood pressure, while this decreases in the lower records. Neither the mean pressure however, nor the blood pressure range adequately reflect the various stages between a very labile and a very stable pressure, although these differences are very important in describing and interpreting changes brought about by the disease process.[33,44] The method of cumulative sum analysis described appears to be a more sensitive method for automatically and objectively describing and assessing such results and also approximates to what one normally attempts to estimate by eye. The in-built application of statistical methods of testing the significance of changes provides one means of assessing treatments which is free from observer bias and this may well prove to be one of the most important applications, as well as being a critical test of the method. Such assessments must at present be made with caution since a comprehensive analysis of the auto-correlation in such biological parameters as heart rate and blood pressure is not yet available.

It is to some extent a disadvantage of this method that the analysis is necessarily retrospective, since prior knowledge of the grand mean and overall standard deviation is required to determine the cusums. The analysis is however, rapid, and may prove convenient for many units which lack on-line computing facilities. It may also prove possible to develop a method based on the use of provisional estimates of the mean and variance or, in time, to define normal limits of these derivatives.

The methods described for blood pressure analysis should have important applications to the study of other physiological phenomena, the principal differences for many applications being that a lower sampling rate is required (Table II). The variables shown in the table are all very commonly monitored in clinical situations and in research and the important frequencies and derivatives are shown. Comments made above for the near impossibility of measuring the variability and quantitating trends of blood pressure with standard methods may be made again for some of these functions. Harmonics of the basic frequencies do not at present appear to require analysis for these signals, so that the frequencies to be analyzed are much lower than with blood pressure recordings. In addition, it is only the rate or the mean level which needs to be derived in most cases. The similarity lies in the fact that, each function being a time-series in which the degree of auto-correlation is high, they are statistically similar, and are all probably suitable for analysis and presentation by similar techniques, with the addition of cross-correlation analysis. The table is by no means exhaustive, and measurements could easily be extended to include the study of bladder and alimentary tract pressures and motility, some aspects of locomotor activity, and probably other body functions as well.

Research is also required to determine which primary derivatives of the blood pressure wave form have physiological significance and therefore need processing. The mean pressure, mean square

TABLE II—Frequencies and sampling rates for physiological variables suitable for study by techniques similar to those for blood pressure analysis

APPROXIMATE SAMPLING RATES REQUIRED FOR DIGITAL COMPUTER ANALYSIS OF COMMON PHYSIOLOGICAL SIGNALS

Physiological Signal	Frequence range/ min. in adults.	Derivatives usually required	Approximate sampling rate/ sec required for computer analysis in real time
Arterial Blood Pressure	45 - 200	Systolic Pressure Diastolic Pressure (Mean Pressure) (Pulse Pressure) (Heart Rate)	120
Central Venous Pressure	45 - 200	Mean Pressure	10
Heart Rate (from instantaneous ratemeter)	45 - 200	Heart Rate	10 for instantaneous rate 1 for average rate
Respiration	8 - 60	Respiration Rate	10
Temperature	0 (slowly varying D C level)	Temperature	1

pressure, and heart rate may provide as much information alone as they do in combination with systolic, diastolic and pulse pressures. The mean square pressure in particular is likely to be a powerful derivative, though its derivation has not previously been proposed. For certain applications it could also prove more suitable to derive such primary derivates with analogue techniques. Both in these research applications and in clinical practice cumulative sum techniques appear to have important applications. Above all the necessity for arithmetic processing of records must be affirmed. It is only in the critical analysis of a record that its worth or otherwise becomes apparent, and a great deal of information is likely to be lost if complete reliance is placed on simple visual inspection.

ACKNOWLEDGMENTS

I am grateful to Dr. D. Clarke and Mrs. H. Somner for substantial help with programming, Dr. A. Barr for advice on statistics, Dr. J. M. K. Spalding and Miss R. Williams for other support, and the Oxford University Systems Engineering Group for the use of their facilities. The investigations were supported by grants from the National Fund for Research into Crippling Diseases, the Nuffield Trust and the Wellcome Trust.

The programme for cumulative sum analysis has been kindly made available by Dr. P. L. Goldsmith, M.A., D.I.C. of Imperial Chemical Industries Limited.

REFERENCES

1 W H LEWIS JR
Procedures in measurement of blood pressure: a historical note
Practitioner 184 243 1960
2 W A SPENCER   C VALLBONA
Application of computers in clinical practice
JAMA 191 917 1965
3 S RIVA-ROCCI
Un nuovo sfigmomanometro
Gazz Med di Torino 47 981 1896
4 L HILL   H BARNARD
Simple and accurate form of sphygmomanometer or arterial pressure guage contrived for clinical use
Brit med J 2 904 1897
5 N S KOROTKOFF
Concerning methods of study of blood pressure
Tr Imp Mil Med Akad St Petersburg 11 365 1905
6 W E GILSON   H GOLDBERG   H C SLOCUM
Automatic device for periodically determining and recording both systolic and diastolic blood pressure in man
Science NY 94 194 1941
7 M B RAPPAPORT   A A LUISADA
Indirect sphygmomanometry physical and physiologic analysis and new procedure for estimation of blood pressure
J Lab Clin Med 29 638 1944
8 J C ROSE   S R GILFORD   H P BROIDA   A SOLER
E A PARTENOPE   E D FREIS
Clinical and investigative application of a new instrument for continuous recording of blood pressure and heart rate
New Eng J Med 249 615 1953
9 J H GREEN
Blood pressure follower for continuous blood pressure recording in man
J Physiol London 130 37P 1955
10 J H CURRENS   G L BROWNELL   S ARONOW
An automatic blood pressure recording machine
New Eng. T. Med. 256, 780 1957
11 R A JOHNSON
Model 16 atuomatic blood pressure measuring instrument
USAF Wright Air Dev Ctr Dayton Ohio Tech Rept 59–429 1 1959

12 T von VEXKÜLL   F KILLING
Ein apparat zur fortlaufenden unblutigen registrierung von puls and blutdruck
Münch med Wschr 101 380 1959
13 R W WARE   A R KAHN
Automatic indirect blood pressure determination in flight
J Appl Physiol 18 210 1963
14 A KAHN   R W WARE   O SIAHAYA
A digital readout technique for aerospace biomedical monitoring
Am J Med Electron 2 152 1963
15 R JONNARD chairman
Symposium on patient monitoring. 15th annual conference on engineering in medicine and biology
The Instrument Publishing Company Inc Pittsburgh Pennsylvania 1963
16 L A GEDDES   H E HOFF   C VALLBONA
G HARRISON   W A SPENCER   J CARRZONERI
Numerical indication of indirect systolic blood pressure heart rate and respiratory rate
Anesthesiology 25 861 1964
17 L A GEDDES   H E HOFF   W A SPENCER
C VALLBONA
Acquisition of physiological data at the bedside: a progress report
Ann NY Acad Sci 115 1091 1964
18 B L STEINBERG   S B LONDON
Automated blood pressure monitoring during surgical anaesthesia
Anaesthesiology 27 6 861 1966
19 W W HOLLAND   S HUMERFELT
Measurement of blood pressure: comparison of intra-arterial and cuff values
Brit med J 2 1241–1964
20 F H VAN BERGEN   D S WEATHERHEAD
A E TRELOAR   A B DOBKIN   J J BUCKLEY
Comparison of indirect and direct methods of measuring artierial blood pressure
Circulation 10 481 1954
21 L N ROBERTS   J R SMILEY   G W MANNING
A comparison of direct and indirect blood pressure determination
Circulation 8 232 1953
22 J M STEELE
Measurements of arterial pressure in man
J Mt Sinai Hosp 8 1049 1941–2

23 W F HAMILTON R A WOODBURY H J HARPER JR
Physiologic relationships between intra-thoracic, intraspinal and arterial pressure readings
J Am Med Ass 106 853 1936

24 R E JENSEN H SHUBIN P F MEAGHER M H WEIL
On-line computer monitoring of the seriously ill patient
Med Biol Engin 4 265 1966

25 H SHUBIN M H WEIL
Efficient monitoring with a digital computer of cardiovascular function in seriously ill patients
Ann Intern Med 65 453 1966

26 M H WEIL H SHUBIN W RAND
Experience with a digital computer for study and improved management of the critically ill
JAMA 198 1011 1966

27 S H TAYLOR H R MACDONALD M C ROBINSON R P SAPRU
Computers in cardiovascular investigation
Brit Heart J 29 352 1967

28 H SHUBIN M H WEIL M A ROCKWELL JR
Automated measurement of arterial pressure in patients by use of a digital computer
Med Biol Engin 5 361 1967

29 S I SELDINGER
Catheter replacement of the needle in percutaneous arteriography, a new technique
Acta Radiol 39 368 1953

30 F D STOTT
Medium term direct blood pressure measurement
Bio-medical Engineering 1 457 1966a

31 F D STOTT
Methods of assessment of variations of blood pressure
Bio-medical Engineering 1 544 1966b

32 A L MACMILLAN F D STOTT
Continuous intra-arterial blood pressure measurement
Bio-medical Engineering 1 20 1968

33 J L CORBETT
Long-term measurements of intra-arterial pressure in man
In preparation

34 A T HANSEN E WARBURG
Acta Physiol Scand 19 306 1949

35 A T HANSEN
Pressure measurement in the human organism
Teknisk Forlag Copenhagen 1949

36 D L FRY F W NOBLE A J MALLOS
An evaluation of modern pressure recording systems
Circulat Res 5 40 1957

37 H W SHIRER
Blood pressure measuring methods
IRE Trans BME 116 1962

38 D J PATEL J C GREENFIELD W G AUSTEN A C MORROW D L FRY
J Appl Physiol 20 459 1965

39 R B BLACKMAN J W TURKEY
The measurement of power spectra
Dover Publications Inc New York 1959

40 J S BENDAT A G PIERSOL
Measurement and analysis of rancom data
John Wiley & Sons Inc New York 1966

41 A M VALSALVA
De aure humana tractatus
G vande Water Utrecht 1707

42 G DE J LEE M B MATTHEWS E P SHARPEY-SCHAFER
Brit Heart J 16 311 1954

43 R H WOODWARD P L GOLDSMITH
Cumulative sum techniques
Oliver and Boyd Ltd Edinburgh 1964

44 J L CORBETT C PRYS-ROBERTS J H KERR
Cardiovascular disturbances in seven tetanus due to over-activity of the sympathetic nervous system.
Submitted for publication

Data Gathering System for Drilling Optimization Work

ROBERT J. ECKERFIELD

Abstract—A digital computer-controlled drilling data processing system has been developed which has the capability of monitoring drilling operations and storing information on magnetic tape. This data processing system is combined with a management information system which provides timely management-oriented reports on a spud-to-spud basis providing cost and time accounting for the entire operation while drilling and while off bottom. Capability includes casualty prevention routines which monitor drilling parameters and provide alarms for prevention of blowouts, twist-offs, and stuck pipe.

Paper 71 TP 7-IGA, approved by the Petroleum and Chemical Industry Committee of the IEEE IGA group for presentation at the 1970 IEEE Petroleum and Chemical Industry Technical Conference, Tulsa, Okla., September 14–16. Manuscript received January 22, 1971.

The author was with Technical Oil Tool Corporation, Glendale, Calif. He is now with Union Oil Company of California, Singapore 10.

INTRODUCTION

WHILE IT would be difficult to think of any industry today which does not use some form of data or information processing system to keep tabs on and improve its operation and profitability, the oil-well drilling industry has been reluctant to adopt such practices. This reluctance is due to several factors.

1) The drilling operation has traditionally been a "wooden derricks and iron men" operation, where a foreman or tool pusher performed his function with little guidance from upper management.

2) A general feeling exists among drilling people that the drilling operation is different from any other type of industry.

3) Application of data processing equipment to the drilling industry has been hardware oriented. Sophisticated

Reprinted from *IEEE Trans. Ind. Gen. Appl.*, vol. IGA-7, pp. 379–385, May/June 1971.

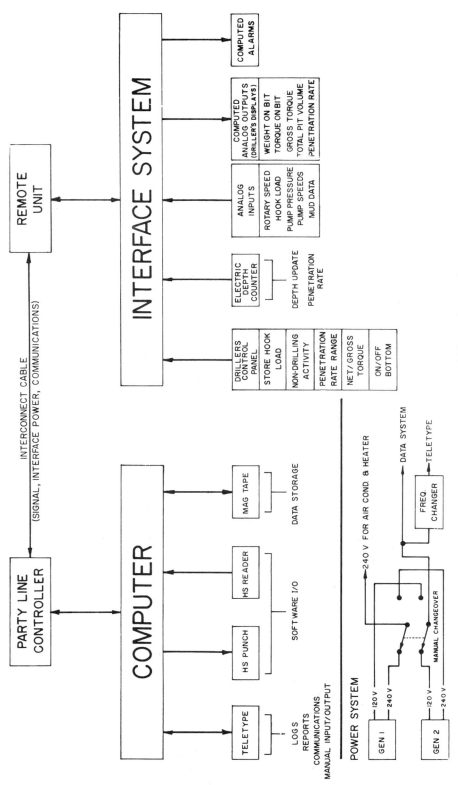

Fig. 1. Drilling information data acquisition and control system.

equipment was built with minimal thought given to the application of data being acquired. This has led drilling personnel to ask, "What am I going to do with the data?"

Before we can justify the application of a data processing system to drilling, the preceding assertions must be answered.

1) When we consider that a modern deep-hole or off-shore operation can cost $25 000 per day or more, it is shortsighted to assume that management is not interested in the progress of the operation. Conventional techniques do not allow for accurate or timely reporting of management-oriented information such as cost or inventory accrual and control. The drilling foreman has done a satisfactory job, and experience has shown that the vast majority of all drilling operations are smoothly and safely conducted. Increasing costs, however, require that more attention be given to improved operational efficiency at a minimum cost.

2) The drilling operation is composed of discrete functions which are extremely difficult to mechanize. As examples, a control system and actuators to automatically handle pipe and make connections is an extremely difficult problem; also, many solutions to the seemingly simple problem of accurately measuring pipe into the hole have been attempted, but a successful device is yet to be developed. However, drilling rig operating parameters can be reliably measured, recorded, and analyzed. Drilling time can be recorded and accounted for, drilling costs can be recorded and processed; in analogy, it may be mechanically impossible to automatically control a certain machine tool, but it would be a relatively simple task to measure the total time that the tool is generating chips.

3) Most attempts to date to apply data processing equipment have been directed to the goal of recording rig operating parameters, hook load, rotary speed, etc. Little attempt has been made to use the data to improve the state of the art. The data have been used mainly in attempts to "optimize" drilling operations. Drilling optimization in itself is a worthwhile and useful adjunct of drilling data acquisition but has limited value. For example, an analysis of rotating time versus total rig time for a number of holes will indicate that on-bottom rotating time on the average consumes about 20 percent of total time on a hole. This means that an optimization program which would cut rotating time by 20 percent (which is a good optimizing program) will reduce total time on the hole and subsequently total drilling costs only 4 percent. It is obvious that a hard look should be taken at the entire operation from spud to spud. The basic philosophy of the data acquisition system reported herein is to provide a management-oriented information service from rig up to rig down on a well. This entails two distinct but interrelated systems, a data acquisition system consisting of mechanical and electronic equipment for collecting and recording rig information and an analysis package which processes the recorded information and generates useful documents.

TABLE I
REAL-TIME ANALOG DATA INPUTS

Parameter	Input Form
Depth	Electrical 0–5 V
Hook load	Hydraulic 0–100 lb/in²
Pump (standpipe) pressure	Hydraulic 0–5000 lb/in²
Casing pressure	Hydraulic 0–5000 lb/in²
Pump stroke rate 1	Pneumatic 3–15 lb/in²
Pump stroke rate 2	Pneumatic 3–15 lb/in²
Mud pit level 1	Pneumatic 3–15 lb/in²
Mud pit level 2	Pneumatic 3–15 lb/in²
Mud pit level 3	Pneumatic 3–15 lb/in²
Mud pit level 4	Pneumatic 3–15 lb/in²
Mud pit level 5	Pneumatic 3–15 lb/in²
Mud pit level 6	Pneumatic 3–15 lb/in²
Rotary torque	Pneumatic 3–15 lb/in²
Rotary speed	Pneumatic 3–15 lb/in²
Mud density in	Pneumatic 3–15 lb/in²
Mud density out	Pneumatic 3–15 lb/in²
Mud temperature in	Pneumatic 3–15 lb/in²
Mud temperature out	Pneumatic 3–15 lb/in²
Mud flow rate (relative)	Pneumatic 3–15 lb/in²
Mud viscosity	Pneumatic 3–15 lb/in²
Mud yield point	Pneumatic 3–15 lb/in²

DATA ACQUISITION SYSTEM

The data acquisition system consists of field performance proven electronic and mechanical components normally used in drilling instrumentation, lease automation, and pipeline automation service. A block diagram (Fig. 1) describes the system configuration.

1) *End Devices:* All drilling rig end devices are reliable, time-proven products; no new sensors were designed for the system. The pickups all provide intrinsically safe hydraulic and pneumatic outputs which are linear and proportional to the measured parameter. Table I lists the existing analog pickups and their respective output formats.

2) *Interface System:* The interface system (Fig. 2) consists of pneumatic-electric transducers for converting the pressure signals from the pickups to appropriate electric signals of 0–5-V range. The hinged mounting plate provides for a maximum of 32 transducers. In addition, the interface contains electric-pneumatic transducers for operating the driller's displays which are system outputs.

Connector failures early in the program prompted a policy of using cable feedthroughs rather than electrical connectors wherever possible. Because of the multiplicity of conductors, connectors are used on the remote unit. On other equipment, cables are taken through panel feedthroughs to connector strips inside.

3) *Remote Unit:* The remote unit mounted on the interface is a multiplexer, analog–digital converter, and digital–analog converter which stores analog and binary signals from the interface until scanned by the party line controller. Table II lists the input and output card types which are available for use in the remote unit. Any combination of eight of the input–output cards may be

Fig. 3.   Driller's control panel and displays.

used. This allows flexibility and capability beyond foreseeable needs in the drilling application. The remote unit is ruggedly packaged in a heavy cast-aluminum enclosure suitable for the drilling environment.

4) *Driller's Displays:* The driller has four displays of the remote indicator type (Fig. 3). These displays present computed values of weight on bit, torque (net or gross), rate of penetration, and pit volume.

5) *Driller's Control Panel:* The driller's control panel (Fig. 3) is the driller's interface to the data system. The panel includes controls for the following.

a) *Store hook load:* With the pipe in the hole and the bit rotating freely just off bottom, the driller pushes the store hook load button. This stores in memory the total hook load and the free running torque, the values of which are used to calculate weight on bit and net torque.

b) *Nondrilleng activity:* The driller has a choice of 60 activities which are dialed in on a rotary coding switch. Time can thus be accounted for while in the off-bottom mode.

c) *Net/gross torque:* This switch controls the driller's torque display selecting either gross rotating torque or net bit torque.

d) *Rate of penetration range:* A six-position switch is used to keep the driller's rate of penetration display on scale.

6) *Party Line Controller:* The party line controller serves as the interface between the computer and the remote unit at the rig. The unit has the capability to handle 16 party lines with four remote units on each line for a total of 64 remote units (or rigs). Communication between the party line controller and the remote unit is via a single pair of wires. The data scan rate is currently

Fig. 2.   Interface system.

TABLE II

REMOTE UNIT INPUT–OUTPUT CARD TYPES

Input Card Types
    20 each 0–5-V analog voltage inputs
    10 each 0–50-mV analog voltage inputs
    20 each 1–5-mA analog current inputs
    20 each 4–20-mA analog current inputs
    20 each 10–50-mA analog current inputs
    20 each continuous contact closure inputs
    10 each pulse store contact closure inputs
    2 each 10-bit accumulator contact closure inputs

Output Card Types
    2 each 0–5-V analog voltage outputs (0.2 percent)
    2 each 1–5-mA analog current outputs (0.2 percent)
    2 each 4–20-mA analog current outputs (9.2 percent)
    20 each point select, continuous relay outputs
    20 each point select, continuous transistor outputs
    20 pairs point select, pulsed relay outputs (20 ONS and 20 OFFS)
    20 each parallel select, continuous relay outputs
    20 each parallel select, continuous transistor outputs
    Jogging or pulse duration set point control
    Teletype printer driver
    20 each point select, momentary transistor outputs with optional checkback before operate

Fig. 4. Data processing system.

Fig. 5. Power system trailer containing two 5-kVA diesel generators.

once every 2 s, producing a bit rate of 2400 bit/s. The rate may be altered by changing a card in the party line controller.

7) *Computer:* The computer (Fig. 4) currently in use is a Hewlett-Packard 2116B with 16K of core, allowing the operational program and several utility programs to be resident in core.

8) *Peripherals:* Peripheral equipment includes a heavy-duty teletype, high-speed paper tape punch and reader, and a magnetic tape deck. The high-speed paper tape punch and reader are used for input of the operational programs and for making assembly tapes. All data storage is on magnetic tape.

9) *Trailer:* The party line controller, computer, and peripherals are mounted in a 25-ft trailer which provides protection from the elements and a comfortable environ-ment for equipment and personnel. The trailer is towed to the drill site and may be located anywhere within 250 ft of the interface. The interconnect cable between trailer and interface includes conductors for voice communica-tion to the rig floor.

10) *Power Considerations:* Where the drilling rig utilizes municipal power or where rig power has acceptable quality (±10 percent on voltage, 50–70 Hz on frequency), the existing power can be used directly on all equipment with the exception of the teletype. The teletype is pro-vided with a frequency regulator which supplies well stabilized ac (±0.5 Hz). If rig power is unsuitable, a power supply trailer (Fig. 5) is available which includes two 5-kVA diesel engine driven ac generators capable of powering the entire data system and trailer support equipment.

SYSTEM OPERATION

Some novel hardware and software has been designed specifically for the data acquisition system and will be described here.

1) Depth Measurement: A conventional wireline and measuring wheel arrangement following block motion is used to drive an electrical pulser which operates an electric depth counter. A clutch operated by the driller disengages the depth counter when off bottom. When the driller makes a pipe tally, he manually updates the electric depth counter as he would his mechanical depth counter. The electric depth counter (Fig. 6) consists of a six-decade electric counter in cascade. Each digit supplies an analog voltage of between 0.5 and 5.0 V. The analog voltages are digitized by the remote unit. A software routine validity samples the output of each digit to prevent ambiguous readings.

2) Rate of Penetration: Rate of penetration is calculated by the computer using depth data received from the electric depth counter. Penetration rate is computed on a one tenth of a foot interval basis and is smoothed by a converging envelope averaging routine.

3) Weight on Bit and Bit Torque: The weight on bit and bit torque are calculated by subtracting the previously stored hook load and free running torque values from the hook load and rotary torque while drilling. This method is not precise but is adequate for most applications.

4) Teletype Inputs: Certain system information must be input manually via teletype. This information includes the scaling factors for all of the analog input data, dull bit grading information, and cost data, such as invoices and inventories.

DATA ANALYSIS PACKAGE

The hardware system previously described is capable of acquiring rig operational data and storing them in digital form on magnetic tape. However, to justify the use of this equipment, it is necessary to process the data in storage and produce printed information which is useable by and of interest to both operations and management personnel. A management information service has been developed which produces timely and valuable management-oriented information which heretofore has only been available through laborious analyses of tour sheets, analog recorder charts, and detailed accounting analysis.

1) Drilling Functional Cost Analysis: Reliable, accurate, and timely cost information has not been available to the decision maker due to current accounting methods which are normally practiced. Three to six months may elapse after a well has been completed before a reasonable estimate can be made of the actual drilling cost. Using the capabilities of the on-site computer, cost analysis can be made on a daily basis, which will present reasonably accurate information to the decision maker. All cost information (invoices) are collected by the data system technician at the rig, coded according to an identification

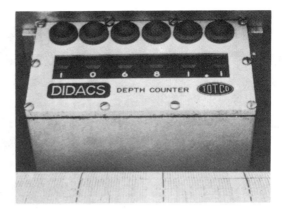

Fig. 6. Electric depth counter.

```
                COST REPORT  06:00   5/21/70

CONTRACTOR:                    WELL NO:

OPERATOR:                      RIG NO:

DATE:       5/21/70

DAY NO:     23
                                               TOTAL
                             DAILY   CUM      DAILY      CUM
100 DRILLING OPERATION                                   38000
    110 BIT TOOLS/TRIP                17000
    120 DRILLING AHEAD                19000
    130 DIR. CONTROL                   2000
200 MUD SYSTEM                                 500      47000
    210 MUD PRODUCTS            300   36000
    220 MUD MAINT.              100    8600
    230 AUX.                    100    2400
300 CASING INSTALLATION                      49000     105000
    310 CASING + ACC          34000   69000
    320 RUN CASING             6000   13000
    330 CEMENTING              5000   15000
    340 NU/ND                  3000    6000
    350 TEST CEMENT            1000    2000
400 FORMATION EVALUATION                                28000
    410 WL LOGGING                     5000
    420 CORING                        18000
    430 DST
    440 GENERAL                        5000
500 COMPLETION/ABANDONMENT
    510 DRILLOUT/COND.
    520 LOG/PERF
    530 STIMULATION
    540 ZONAL EVAL.
    550 WELL COMPLETION
    560 ABANDONMENT
600 SUPPORT SYSTEMS                            500      25000
    610 DRLG. PREP.                    22000
    620 RIG SUPPORT             300    2000
    630 TRANSPORTATION          200    1000
700 CASUALTY
    710 DRILLING OPERATION
    720 MUD SYSTEM
    730 CASING INSTALLATION
    740 FORMATION EVAL.
    750 COMPL/ABAN.
    760 SUPPORT SYST.

            TOTAL:                            50,000   243,000

    DEPTH 9500  PROGRESS  0

    DRILLING $/FT.  CURRENT: $0.00/FT      CUM: $4.00/FT

    MUD SYSTEM, $/DAY (AV. TO DATE)     $145.51/DAY
```

Fig. 7. Drilling operations cost report.

system, and manually input to core via the teletype. Inventories of mud, cement, casing, and other expendables are similarly coded and manually input to memory. The information stored in core is processed once a day and a printed form (Fig. 7) is generated which gives costs accrued to date, today's cost, cost per foot drilled, cost of individual expendables, and variance from planned cost where a cost versus depth or cost versus time plan has been prepared before spud. The results of the daily

```
                    OPERATIONS REPORT---06:00---6/16/70

WELL NO. B-17
CURRENT DEPTH 8514 FT
PROGRESS LAST 24 HOURS-- 124 FT
CURRENT STATUS-- NIPPLING UP

 MUD:
     8.9 #/GAL                45 SEC            16 PV            8 YP
     5# GEL                   3.1% SOLIDS       10.5 PH          2.0 SAND
     2% OIL                   8.5#/GAL OUT      2/32 FC          5.0 FL
     2500 SALINITY            AV WT IN 8.7#/GAL MIN WT IN 8.5 #/GAL
     MAX WT OUT 9.0 #/GAL
     DESANDERS 4.7 HRS
     DESILTERS 5.0 HRS
     GAIN 10 BBL IN 5.0 HRS
     LOSS 0.0 BBL IN 5.0 HRS


 BITS:
     NO. 3                    SIZE 9-5/8        TYPE Y3B         MAN. REED
     JETS 14-14-15            AV WT 60000 LBS   AV RPM 125
     DEPTH IN 7500            DEPTH OUT 8514    FOOTAGE 1024     ROT HRS 10.0
     BIT COND (T,B,G) 4,7,2
     AV PENETRATION RATE 102 FPH
     $/FT 6.50

 HYDRAULICS:
     PRESS 2100 PSI           #1 SPM 65         #2 SPM 0
     #1 LINER 6.5"            #2 LINER 4.5"     GPM 340
     ANN VEL 105FPM           JET VEL 350 FPS   BHHP 260

 OPERATION                   HOURS             % TOTAL HRS

 DRILLING                    5.0               20.8
 MUD COND                    3.0               12.5
 SURVEYING                   1.0               4.2
 FORMATION EVAL              2.0               8.3
 CIRCULATING                 2.0               8.3
 CASING                      4.0               16.7
 CEMENTING                   3.0               12.5
 WOC                         4.0               16.7
 UNACCOUNTED                 0.0               0.0

 COMMENTS:
     SLIGHT GAS CUT MUD WHILE CIRC PRIOR TO LOGGING.  WEIGHT UP TO 9.1#/GAL
     TO CONTROL GAS INFLUX.  BEGAN RUNNING CASING 17:00.  RAN 213 JTS, 38.0
     #/FT, XL; SHOE AT 8503 FT.  CEMENT W/350 SX CLASS B W/0.1% HR4 TO 15.3 PPG.
     BUMPED PLUG W/1850 PSI AT 02:00.  NOW NIPPLING UP.

     ORDER:  400 SX BENTONITE
             200 SX BARITE
```

Fig. 8. Drilling operations morning report.

analysis are stored on magnetic tape for future use in generating an after-the-fact cost breakdown at well completion. This breakdown is similar to the daily cost analysis, but is a summary of cost incurred over the entire drilling operation.

2) *Operations Reports:* All analog input information is continuously accumulated in core for 24 hours, at which time a daily operations report or morning report is generated. This report is similar to the traditional drilling foreman's morning report and is intended to serve that purpose. This morning report (Fig. 8) contains such information as current depth, depth drilled during the last 24 hours, physical properties of the mud system, bit information, average values of drilling parameters, and a chronological summary of all operations which occurred during the day. Much of this information must be input via teletype by the technician at the rig. Depth, drilling parameters, and the chronological operations analysis are extracted from core.

Another operations report is the bit record, which is generated at the conclusion of a drilling bit run. This is an operations breakdown for the particular drilling bit and includes such information as bit identification and condition, total rotating time, total footage made, and information relating to the formation being drilled, such as abrasiveness and drillability.

These operations reports are stored on magnetic tape for use in generating complete operations summaries at the completion of the well, which provide breakdowns of the same factors included in the daily reports but on a total well basis. These reports will save the operator the task of digging information out of tour sheets and can be easily converted into the traditional completion report. Where a slave teletype is tied into the data system at the rig, the above forms can be punched on paper tape and transmitted over a telephone line to a distant central office.

FIELD EXPERIENCE

At this writing, two systems have been operational; a data acquisition-only system has been operated in the Gulf of Mexico, transmitting data via telephone line from a drilling platform to a central office on the beach; a second system capable of acquiring and processing data has been built and checked out. This experience has pointed up some important lessons.

1) Electrical connectors have proven to be a reliability problem area because of the difficulty of selecting connectors which have the correct combination of oil field-type ruggedness, corrosion resistance, and acceptable cost. At present, most subsystems are hard-wired together for maximum reliability. It has been found that interconnects can be made quite rapidly if cable ends are prepared in advance with quick-disconnect terminals.

2) Communications have proven to be a more serious problem than originally anticipated. In the Gulf operation, the telephone network proved a highly unreliable link. This experience has shown that it is advisable for the computer and recording equipment to be at the rig, even for remote telemetering systems. A loss of the communication link will not jeopardize the operation of the data system or result in data loss.

3) The electronic equipment, namely, the computer and the data acquisition system, has proven more reliable than the mechanical components. Software routines are used wherever possible in preference to mechanical subsystems.

4) The driller's interface to the system must be as simple as possible for two reasons:

a) to simplify the task of personnel training and to reduce the possibility of human error;

b) input devices, such as thumbwheels and potentiometers, are difficult to package in a form which is ruggedized, weather-proof, and suitable for the drilling environment. The existing driller's control panel is enclosed in a rugged cast-aluminum box. The controls are sliding and rotating shafts which have ruggedized panel feedthroughs and are 0-ring sealed against fluid entry.

FUTURE DEVELOPMENTS

As in any new concept or system, lessons have been learned which will result in the evolution of improved hardware and software systems in the future. Modifications already envisioned include the following.

1) The software library will be expanded to include routines for casualty prevention.

    a) *Kick control:* A routine which, upon manual call up by the technician, will generate a printed program for safe control of an impending kick based upon operational information stored in memory. The output of this routine will be a recommended pressure, time, and mud density program for properly controlling the kick.

    b) *Lost circulation:* A routine which will monitor bit level, mud density, mud temperature, and mud pressure and sound an alarm when the symptoms of lost circulation are detected.

    c) *Washouts:* By careful monitoring of mud flow and pressure, potential twistoffs can be detected at the washout stage. Similarly, surveillance of the same parameters can indicate hole sloughing which is commonly a prelude to stuck pipe.

    d) *Blowout prevention:* A routine similar to the rate of penetration calculation will monitor the drill pipe and casing pulling and dropping rate to guard against swabbing or breaking down the hole and thus help prevent a major cause of blowouts.

These casualty prevention routines are natural extensions of the computer's ability to tirelessly monitor an extensive list of operational parameters both continuously and reliably.

2) It is expected that the addition of extensive software routines will require expanded memory capability, probably via disk.

3) As the application of modern technology is accepted in drilling, it is expected that the data system capability for closed-loop control will be applied to drawworks, rotary table, and pressure control choke operation.

Conclusions

A data acquisition system for drilling must be backed up by a data analysis system which provides timely and valuable information in hard-copy form. Such a system suitable for prolonged use in the drilling environment is both technically and economically realistic.

Part 5
Process Control Applications Including Direct Control, Supervisory Control, and Advanced Control

Introductory Comments

Automation in the process industries has been under way for many years. The variety of applications is extensive. Early systems tended to use a rather large process control computer to implement many applications in a single plant. The advent of the minicomputer has provided an alternative, namely, the dedication of a minicomputer to a single task or, at most, a small number of related tasks. This approach to automation has been termed "islands of automation" as opposed to overall or integrated automation of a plant. This leads, of course, to an alternate set of problems, intercomputer communication, since various minicomputer applications will be required to share information concerned with resources, orders, etc.

The papers in this part describe the various control applications that arise in industrial processes. They are selected in order to illustrate the variety of problems, the variety of control, theory, and technology that can be applied, and the problems of implementing such systems. The first paper by R. J. Mouly describes in some detail various applications in a typical process plant which provide opportunity for a great variety of different control theories to be applied. The organization of such a complex control system is important, for it may mean the difference between success and failure in any specific instance. Mouly describes the way plants are organized and how controls themselves must be organized in order to provide an effective system.

The second paper by J. M. Lombardo describes control at the lowest level, namely, direct control where the function of the computer is to directly manipulate valves, voltages, etc. in the plant. Of importance here is the integration of the operator into the control system as well as the constraints imposed by reliability. In particular, the design of the application must take into account the backup of the control system, the so-called set-point station, which may be used to switch between computer control and manual control and which influences greatly the organization of the direct digital control system. This paper also illustrates the variety of input/ output devices through which a minicomputer must communicate with human beings and the process. The third paper, by E. H. Gautier, M. R. Hurlbut, and E. A. E. Rich, gives an alternative

213

view of computer control. They stress the experience that has been gained from controls installed in over thirty cement plants and discuss operator communication, interfacing, and hardware and software problems in detail.

The last two papers look at smaller process control systems. E. B. Dahlin discusses the application of a minicomputer to the control of basis weight and moisture on a paper machine. The important result in this paper is that a dedicated application such as this still requires a rather complete hardware/software control theory system to make it effective. That is, in addition to the implementation of the feedback control algorithms themselves, additional techniques for determining appropriate parameters of the system and design of the resulting controller parameters are necessary ingredients in minicomputer software. This, coupled with operator communication requirements, implies that even in a dedicated application the overall system must be very carefully considered in the design. The techniques discussed in this paper are an illustration of one of the best applications of minicomputers in the process industries.

The last paper by C. P. Pracht illustrates the use of control theory in minicomputers, which cannot be economically applied without a digital computer. This is in contrast to many applications where the computer duplicates the function of an analog control system but perhaps at lower cost. Through the use of fast-time simulation, relatively complex problems can be solved readily in an on-line manner.

The overall intent of this part is to illustrate that the variety of applications that can be implemented with minicomputers in the process control area is limited only by one's imagination. However, successful implementation demands a rather thorough systems analysis of the hardware requirements, software requirements, operator communication, hardware and software, and the theory necessary to support the application.

Bibliography

[1] "In-plant sensors help schedule work and watch costs in brass rod mill," R. L. Aronson, *Contr. Eng.*, vol. 17, July 1970, pp. 40–43.

[2] "Control problems in papermaking," K. J. Astrom, *1966 IBM Scientific Symp. Control Theory and Applications*, pp. 136–161.

[3] "Goal: five paper machines under computer control," J. N. Bairstow, *Contr. Eng.*, vol. 16, Jan. 1969, pp. 120–123.

[4] "Dynamic control of the cement process with a digital computer system," T. Bay, C. W. Ross, J. C. Andrews, and J. L. Gilliland, *IEEE Trans. Ind. Gen. Appl.*, vol. IGA-4, May/June 1968, pp. 294–303.

[5] "Atlantic Richfield automates for safety and efficiency," W. B. Bleakley, *Oil Gas J.*, Apr. 19, 1971, pp. 110–113.

[6] "The digital computer in real-time control systems," A. S. Buchman, *IEEE Trans. Aerosp. Electron. Syst.*, July 1970.

[7] "Minicomputer grades steel strip on-line," H. S. Drewry and W. R. Edens, *Instrum. Technol.*, Jan. 1971, pp. 49–53.

[8] "True computer systems play a big role in pipeline control," *Oil Gas J.*, June 21, 1971, pp. 130–137.

[9] "Economic justification for digital control of a batch process," R. G. Fritchie and E. F. Schagrin, *Contr. Eng.*, vol. 17, July 1970, pp. 54–56.

[10] "On-line sampling saves valuable ore," F. W. Glow and S. J. Bailey, *Contr. Eng.*, vol. 16, Jan. 1969, pp. 117–123.

[11] "Direct digital control at Lone Star's Greencastle, Indiana, plant," D. L. Grammes, *IEEE Trans. Ind. Gen. Appl.*, vol. IGA-6, Sept./Oct. 1970, pp. 480–487.

[12] "Computer control of motor gasoline blending," R. J. Lasher, *1967 Comput. Conf. Proc.*

[13] "Automation in the steel industry," A. Miller, *Automation*, Nov. 1966, pp. 7–14.

[14] "Survey of real-time on-line digital computers," H. H. Rosenbrock and A. J. Young, *Proc. 1966 IFAC, 3rd Congr.*

[15] "Process performance computer for adaptive control systems," F. A. Russo and R. J. Valek, *IEEE Trans. Comput.*, vol. C-17, Nov. 1968, pp. 1027–1037.

[16] "Minicomputers rethink NC," J. E. Sanford, *Iron Age*, Feb. 18, 1971, pp. 53–57.

[17] "Sequence control for batch polymerization," F. H. Schreiner, *Contr. Eng.*, Sept. 1968, pp. 96–100.

[18] "Bumpless transfer under digital control," R. Uram, *Contr. Eng.*, vol. 18, Mar. 1971, pp. 59–60.

[19] "Modelling and programming for direct digital control," G. V. Woodley, *ISA J.*, Mar. 1966, pp. 48–54.

Systems Engineering in the Glass Industry

RAYMOND J. MOULY, SENIOR MEMBER, IEEE

Abstract—A survey of current trends of systems engineering in the glass industry is presented. The central theme is that systems engineering is the technique through which the process of our time—the information revolution exemplified by the digital computer—is exerting its impact on the industry.

Systems engineering is examined and basic concepts reviewed, and the production system is defined as a pyramidal, hierarchical structure. Process models which have been developed primarily for control purposes are reviewed; examples of theoretically or experimentally developed models are given. In computer control applications, a major trend is seen toward extensive integrated real-time information-processing systems consisting of several computers connected through a communication network. The development of the human components in the production system, particularly management structure, is considered as an essential aspect of the overall system development.

I. INTRODUCTION

ABOUT 200 years ago, the invention of the steam engine marked the beginning of the first industrial revolution. The mechanical age had begun, characterized by, in the words of McLuhan [1], "the technique of fragmentation that is the essence of machine technology," with its emphasis on the individual control of the fragmented parts without marked concern for their interaction and the behavior of the process as a whole.

The mechanical age is now receding. We are living in the "electric age." The information revolution—the process of our time—is taking place, forcing us to reshape and restructure our processes and to move inexorably from fragmented, slow, and informal control practices to a philosophy of global, instantaneous, and systematic control.

These statements provide the background for the survey that follows. It consists of three major parts. First, in Section II, some fundamental systems engineering concepts will be reviewed. Then, in Section III examples of the application of these concepts in the glass industry will be presented. Finally, in Section IV the role of human factors in systems engineering will be discussed in a general way.

II. GENERAL SYSTEMS ENGINEERING CONCEPTS

A. Definitions

What do the terms "systems and systems engineering" mean? There are almost as many definitions as there are writers on the subject. The concept of systems is an ancient one. An early reference can be found in this quotation from

Manuscript received December 21, 1968. This paper was presented at the 8th International Congress on Glass, London, England, July 5, 1968.

The author is with the Technical Staffs Division. Corning Glass Works, Corning, N. Y.

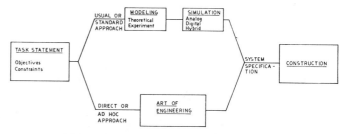

Fig. 1. Physical system design approaches.

St. Paul: "There are many members, yet but one body." A modern definition [2] reads as follows: "A system is any collection of interacting elements that operate to achieve a common goal." Systems engineering is the art or the technique of building systems. This, in itself, would not be a new activity were it not for two factors which characterize systems engineering and set it apart from conventional engineering. The first factor is the formal awareness of the importance of interaction between the parts of a system. The second factor is that systems engineering implies integration. It says that the whole is more than the sum of the parts.

Designing a system consists of translating a task statement into a specification of the system to be built. There are two fundamentally different approaches to the system design problem. They are, as defined by Athans [3], the direct or *ad hoc* approach and the usual or standard approach (Fig. 1).

The direct approach is often referred to as the art of engineering. It consists simply of building a system which does the job. The direct approach is acceptable for small systems, but as systems become increasingly complicated and extensive, it is frequently inadequate if optimum design is to be achieved. In addition, the risk and costs involved in extensive experimentation might be prohibitive.

The usual or standard approach is the technical or scientific approach; it begins with the replacement of the real world problem by a problem involving mathematical relationships. In other words, the first step consists of formulating a suitable model of the physical process, the system objectives, and the imposed constraints. Simulations of mathematical relationships on a computer often play a vital role in the search for a solution. Various alternative designs can be compared and evaluated. Then, and then only, a system is built.

Practically the design of a large and complex system is often achieved through the combined use of the direct and the standard approaches. The direct approach is likely to be used in the structuring of the whole system, whereas the standard approach will be taken for the design of

Reprinted from *IEEE Trans. Syst. Sci. Cybern.*, vol. SSC-5, pp. 300–312, Oct. 1969.

various components. The standard approach has been extensively used by engineers for the design of control systems.

The manufacturing process is the system we are interested in. I shall discuss its nature from a systems engineering viewpoint and particularly examine the role of the information network and show how it relates to the economics of process control.

B. Hierarchical Process Control [4], [5]

The manufacturing system, whether it be a major process, a plant, a multiplant operation, a company, or even a whole industry, can be looked at as the pyramidal structure shown in Fig. 2, consisting of two distinct elements: the physical process and the controller. The controller's function is to manipulate the plant in order to optimize the process with respect to the manufacturing system objectives.

Somewhat arbitrarily, a hierarchy of three interacting control functions can be identified. At the first level, we find the process control functions which include the single- and multiple-variable control activities usually associated with the control of process units. Production control, at the second level, is the guidance for the utilization of production facilities; it covers such activities as scheduling, inventory control, cost control, and invoicing. The management control functions at the third level include the setting of objectives to be achieved by the system within the constraints of policy.

Paralleling the hierarchy of control levels, we can identify a hierarchy of control functions—regulation, optimization, adaptation, and self-organization—as we move toward the top of the pyramid. It can also be observed that, as we advance toward the higher levels of control, the emphasis on the physical variables decreases as the economic variables play an increasingly important role in the decision-making or control functions.

Other important characteristics of the control system are the decreasing frequency of the controller action and the increasing complexity of the decision-making process as one rises through the hierarchy of control levels. It should also be pointed out that control problems at the lowest level are essentially those of a deterministic system, whereas as one rises through the hierarchy, the nature of the problems becomes increasingly probabilistic.

This hierarchical control structure can be identified in most industrial processes although not always in a systematic form. We find that machines, such as controllers, sequential control systems, etc., are carrying out automatically some of the control functions at the lowest level of control, but that most of the control functions are still exerted directly by human beings (process operators, supervisors, schedulers, and managers). All of these controllers, human beings or machines, have one common characteristic: they are processors of information and are part of the information network of the system.

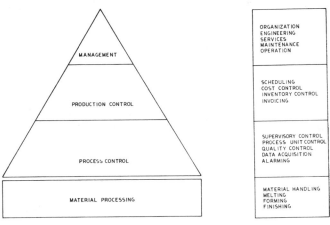

Fig. 2. Plant functions.

The importance of the information network within the manufacturing process cannot be overemphasized. It is the interconnecting tissue which relates the other five process networks: materials, orders, money, personnel, and capital equipment [6].

Efforts to automate process control functions took place initially at the first level of control with the application of process controllers. Little could be done at the higher levels until 20 years ago, when the invention of the digital computer marked the beginning of a new era. This second industrial revolution, the information revolution, which has already deeply affected our concepts of process control, has developed along two somewhat distinct paths. On the one hand, with the availability of data-processing machines, attempts have been made to automate part of the control functions at the third level. On the other hand, during the past 10 years, computers have increasingly penetrated the industrial process production control field at the first and second levels.

Today, the availability of reliable on-line process control computers makes it possible to affect in real time the entire information network of the production process and to implement integrated systems that will perform control functions at all levels of the hierarchy. Such systems are technologically feasible. Why should they be implemented? Technological feasibility is not enough. Powerful economic incentives must exist if the technique is to be applied extensively by competitive industries. In order to answer the question, we should examine the nature of the relationship that exists between the processing of control information and the economics of the process.

C. Process Control and Process Economics

We know, intuitively, that there is a relationship between these two subjects, but it is only recently, however, that the quantitative nature of this relationship has been established. Trapeznikov shows in a recent paper [7] that controlling a process consists in ordering information. Any process or system left to itself under natural conditions will tend to become increasingly disorderly; the

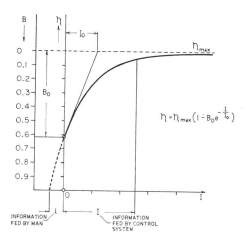

Fig. 3. Process effectiveness—control information curve.

entropy of the system will increase. The purpose of controlling the process is to counteract the growth of disordering. Control is work for ordering.

A fundamental relationship relates the system efficiency to the amount of control information I

$$\eta = \eta_{\max} \left(1 - B_0 e^{-(I/I_0)}\right)$$

B_0 being the measure of the degree of disorder in the system associated with the amount of control information I_0.

Efficiency should be taken here in a very general sense, and in particular, it can be looked at as profit. The relationship, illustrated in Fig. 3, can be looked at as a formal expression of the "law of diminishing returns" or of the "cost–effectiveness" relationship applied to control systems. It is quite similar to the familiar S-shaped relationship between return and effort expressed in monetary units.

Important practical conclusions can be drawn from these considerations:

1) Process effectiveness increases rapidly at first with increasing knowledge, but because of the basic nonlinearity of the relationship, the investment in control should not exceed a certain economically justifiable level.

2) In order to achieve the maximum overall effectiveness, it is necessary to attain the same degree of effectiveness at all levels.

3) So far, the automatic control of information at the higher levels has received little attention as, traditionally, the major function of instrumentation and control engineering has been to increase the ordering of information at the process control level, the first level of the control hierarchy. The automatic coordinated control of major units has not progressed as rapidly, basically because until recently no control tools were available to process reliably control information in real time. It should, consequently, be expected that the economic potential of automatic process control at the higher levels would be high because of the inherent, high information disorder usually found at these levels of control.

III. Systems Engineering in the Glass Industry

I shall now review specific examples of applications of systems engineering concepts in the glass industry. I shall focus on two subjects—process modeling and computer control systems.

A. Process Models and Modeling Techniques

The plant or process is the central and most fundamental issue. In process control, knowledge of process behavior comes first. Models which represent the essential aspects of the process are needed in order to apply the standard approach to systems design.

A model is defined as "a quantitative or qualitative representation of a process or endeavor that shows the effects of those factors which are significant for the purpose being considered" [8]. We shall not consider either physical scale models, such as tank models using viscous solutions [9]–[11], or activity models, such as PERT, but will discuss only models in which mathematics is used to describe the salient features of the process behavior and which are intended primarily for use in the synthesis of control systems. The mathematical relationships of interest are those which relate the process inputs, manipulated variables, and disturbances to the intermediate variables and outputs (Fig. 4). It is essential for process control problem applications that these relationships account for the dynamic behavior of the system.

Models can be classified as experimental or theoretical according to the techniques through which they are developed. Experimental modeling [12] requires the observation of the process variables in order that the state of the process may be recorded under a variety of conditions. Intentional perturbation of the process through the manipulated variables and inputs is usually necessary to obtain accurate relationships. The trend is toward the increasing use of automatic data acquisition and processing techniques to determine the quantitative relationships that exist between the process variables.

In theoretical modeling, the mathematical description of the process is built by writing the exact equations which govern the behavior of the process, such as conservation of mass, energy, and momentum, and the fundamental equations of heat transfer and fluid flow.

In any case, the validity and usefulness of the model generally depend heavily upon the ingenuity of the model builder, his clear understanding of the purpose of the model and his prior knowledge of the process.

Several examples of experimental and theoretical models developed for the design of control systems in the glass industry will be reviewed in the following.

1) *Vello Tubing Process Model* [13]: This first example is one of an experimental model. The problem is to develop an automatic diameter control system for a tube-drawing process used in the manufacture of fluorescent tubing.

The process is shown in Fig. 5. Glass is delivered to the forming process through a refractory ring placed at the

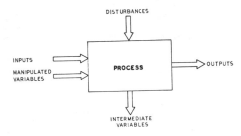

Fig. 4.   Basic process.

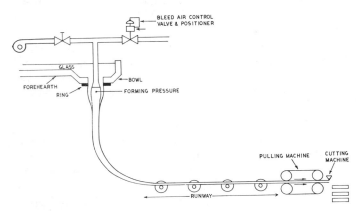

Fig. 5.   Vello tubing process.

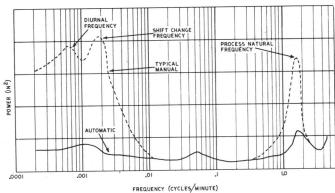

Fig. 6.   Power spectra—manual and automatic control of tubing diameter.

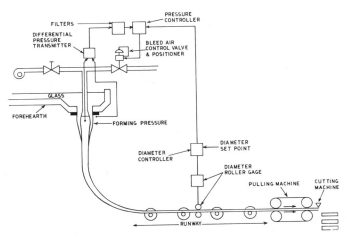

Fig. 7.   Vello tubing process with automatic diameter control system.

bottom of the bowl. Air is blown through a pipe in the center of the ring while the tubing is drawn by a pulling machine. At the end of the runway, a cutting machine cuts the tubing into tubes of proper length.

The experimental mathematical model used to describe this process consists of two parts. The first part is a set of linear, incremental, differential equations expressing the relationships between the manipulated variable, valve position, the intermediate process variable, forming pressure, and the controlled variable diameter. The equations given below were obtained by experimental step-response techniques.

$$\frac{\Delta \text{ forming pressure}}{\Delta \text{ valve position}} = \frac{T_1 s + 1}{\alpha T_1 s + 1} \frac{K_1}{T_2^2 s^2 + 2\zeta\, T_2 s + 1}$$

$$\frac{\Delta \text{ diameter}}{\Delta \text{ forming pressure}} = K_2 e^{-Ls}.$$

The second part of the model is the statistical description of the controlled variable. This description is in the form of power spectra and histograms. The power spectra, Fig. 6, characterize the way the diameter variations occur. Significant diameter variations still take place at the process natural frequency, 1.6 cycles/min. Consequently, an effective automatic control system must control diameter variations occurring up to this frequency. This information on the statistical behavior of the process provides a basis for the simulation of the process disturbances and a means for estimating the expected improvement in process performance that would result from the implementation of a given control system.

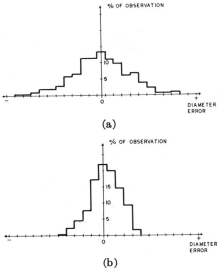

Fig. 8.   Histograms of diameter error (a) Manual. (b) Automatic diameter control. (Note: σ automatic $= 0.5\ \sigma$ manual.)

These process models, incremental differential equations, and statistical models were used in an analog computer simulation to evaluate a number of possible control system configurations. The control system of Fig. 7 was selected; it is a cascade control system in which the forming pressure is controlled by a high-gain, large-bandwidth loop, and the diameter is controlled by a low-gain, low-bandwidth loop.

The histograms, Fig. 8, characterize the performance of the system under manual and automatic control. It is seen that the automatic control system reduces the diameter variations by 50 percent.

2) Ribbon Machine Process Model [14]: Two models were developed in connection with the design of a computer system for the automatic control of the dimensions of bulbs made on a ribbon machine (Fig. 9). These models which account for the process behavior, including the quality control sampling procedures, were used in a digital computer simulation to evaluate alternate control strategies.

The first model is the matrix in Fig. 10. It was determined experimentally and represents the relationships that exist between the most significant process variables.

The second model was developed also for the analysis of the particular control problems resulting from the fact that only small, relatively infrequent samples of the end product quality can be obtained for feedback control. This problem was investigated in a digital computer simulation study of a one-variable control loop with quality data used as the feedback measurement and a long transport delay as the significant process dynamic element. The process disturbances were simulated by the sum of an assignable periodic disturbance and a random disturbance. This study indicated that the sample mean was the best indicator of average process performance and that the stability of the system in response to the assignable disturbance depended only upon the control system design parameters.

The computer process control system schematized in Fig. 11 was developed on the basis of these studies. The automatic control of the low-frequency components of the error signal resulted in a significant reduction of the variability of the product dimensions.

3) Glass Tank Model: Another example of experimental modeling is given by Hoetink in his investigation of the dynamics of a glass tank [15]. When the composition of the bath in a continuous furnace is changed abruptly, there will follow a change in the glass composition at the output of the tank. Comparing this change in glass composition to the step change in batch, the transfer function for composition of the melting furnace may be determined; two cases are considered with and without cullet return.

In general, the transfer function may be approximated by a transportation lag T_L and a first-order process with time constant τ. If all of the glass in the furnace were ideally mixed, the transfer function would have only one time constant T_{id}, which is also the mean residence time

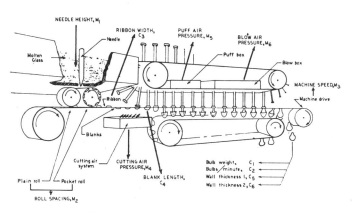

Fig. 9. Ribbon machine process.

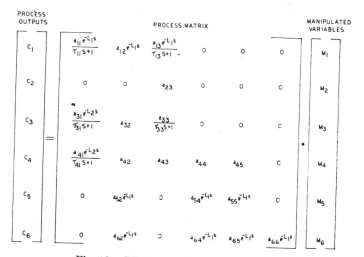

Fig. 10. Ribbon machine process model.

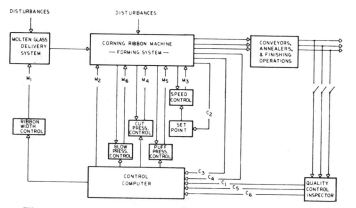

Fig. 11. Ribbon machine process computer control system.

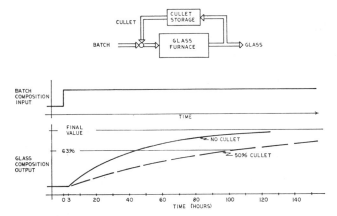

Fig. 12. Glass composition response to a step change in batch composition.

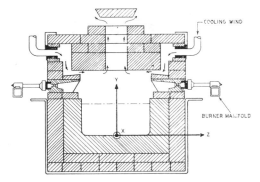

Fig. 13. Forehearth channel—cooling zone cross section.

of the glass in the furnace. The mean residence time can be estimated by dividing the furnace glass capacity M by the average glass output (pull) Q. Comparing T_L, τ, and T_{id} can give some idea as to what extent the glass is ideally mixed. The derivative of the step response gives the residence time distribution of the glass. Fig. 12 illustrates some experimental results.

For a furnace with a glass capacity of 200 tons and a pull of 96 tons/day, $T_{id} = 50$ hours; the transfer function without cullet return consisted of a transportation lag $T_L = 3$ hours and a time constant $\tau = 40$ hours. With a cullet return of 50 percent after 20 hours, the transportation lag was 3 hours as before, but the time constant increased to 100 hours.

4) Forehearth Model: The forehearth model developed by Duffin and Johnson [16] illustrates the methodology used to construct a theoretical model based on physical laws of nature. The development of a theoretical model usually involves the following steps: 1) formulate the system equations based on physical laws, 2) apply appropriate boundary and initial conditions, and 3) solve the equations by analytical or numerical means.

The forehearth delivers the glass in an open channel from the furnace to the forming machine and conditions the glass to a predetermined delivery temperature by means of wind cooling and gas heating as shown in Fig. 13.

a) Formulation of system equations: The basic energy equation—The general differential equation for heat transfer of a flowing stream of molten glass in a rectangular channel is derived based on the principle of conservation of energy. By taking an energy balance on a differential volume element of dimensions dx, dy, dz, the energy equation is

$$\underbrace{\frac{\partial}{\partial y}\left(k'\frac{\partial T}{\partial y}\right) + \frac{\partial}{\partial z}\left(k'\frac{\partial T}{\partial z}\right)}_{\substack{\text{rate of energy input by}\\\text{conduction and radiation}}} - \underbrace{\frac{\partial}{\partial x}(\rho C_p V_x T)}_{\substack{\text{rate of energy}\\\text{input by mass}\\\text{flow}}}$$

$$= \underbrace{\rho C_p \frac{\partial T}{\partial t}}_{\substack{\text{rate of accumula-}\\\text{tion of energy}}}. \qquad (1)$$

In deriving (1), the following assumptions are made.

i) Heat flow by radiation can be regarded as being due to a "radiation conductivity" of $8T^3/\alpha$, where T is the absolute temperature and α is the absorption coefficient for the energy of wavelengths corresponding to temperature T. The factor k' in (1) is defined as the true conductivity plus radiation conductivity.

ii) The effective conductivity k', density of glass l, and the specific heat of glass C_p are not temperature dependent (hence not a function of the space coordinates).

iii) The velocity V_x in the x direction (direction of flow) is not a function of x. Thus (1) reduces to

$$\frac{k'}{\rho C_p}\left[\frac{\partial^2 T}{\partial y^2} + \frac{\partial^2 T}{\partial z^2}\right] - V_x \frac{\partial T}{\partial x} = \frac{\partial T}{\partial t}. \qquad (2)$$

Equation (2) is applicable only in the interior of the glass. To completely specify the system, appropriate boundary and initial conditions must be supplied. These are the following.

i) The temperature distribution on the glass-refractory boundaries at the bottom ($y = 0$) and the sides ($z = W$) of the channel are assumed to be time-invariant and linear functions of the space coordinates.

$$T(x,0,z) = \phi_2(x,f) \text{ is specified}$$
$$T(x,y,w) = \phi_3(x,y) \text{ is specified.} \qquad (3)$$

ii) At the interface between the glass and the gas ($y = d$), the boundary is a radiating boundary where the glass is exchanging radiant energy with the channel enclosure (refractory crown). Further, the gas in the space between the glass and the crown also exchanges heat with the system through convection and radiation. The equation for the glass–gas interface is again derived based on energy balance

$$k'\frac{\partial T}{\partial y}\bigg|_{y=d} = \sigma F\,[T_{\text{crown}}^4 - T^4] - h(T - T_{\text{gas}}) \qquad (4)$$

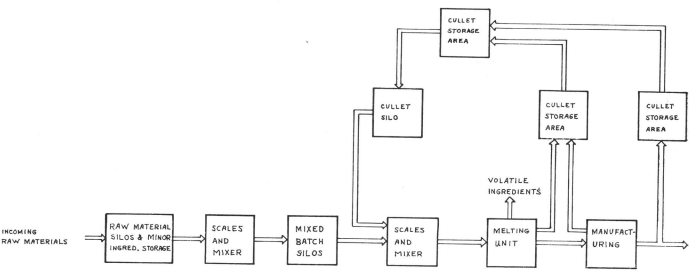

Fig. 14. Melting system schematic.

where

σ Stefan Boltzman constant

F view factor derived with the assumption that the glass surface and the crown are two opposite infinite parallel planes

h gas heat transfer coefficient

T_{crown}, T_{gas} these temperatures are inputs to the model and must be either assumed or determined by measurement on actual forehearths.

iii) Since glass temperature is symmetric with respect to the center of the channel ($z = 0$),

$$\left.\frac{\partial T}{\partial z}\right|_{z=0} = 0. \qquad (5)$$

iv) At time zero, the temperature distribution at some location X must be specified as an initial condition. Usually the temperature distribution at the inlet to the forehearth is given.

b) *Numerical solution:* Equations (2)–(5) and the appropriate initial conditions completely specify the system. The equations are partial differential equations of the parabolic type with nonlinear boundary conditions. Because of the complexity of the problem, an approximate numerical solution is the best that can be obtained. The equations are written in a finite-difference form and can be solved on a large, digital scientific computer.

c) *Application of the model:* This model is applicable to the systematic design of a temperature control system for an existing forehearth. Studies can be made with the model to evaluate control systems which will deliver glass at constant temperature to the forming machine in the face of disturbances in the inlet glass temperatures, ambient temperatures, and glass flow rate changes.

5) *Melting System Models:* One of the earliest examples of the application of modeling techniques to the analysis of

control system problems in the glass industry is given by Oppelt [17]. His paper presents a conceptual elementary multivariate dynamic model of a glass tank and suggests improved control strategies using feedback and feedforward techniques.

Our last example of theoretical modeling concerns the melting system illustrated in Fig. 14, consisting of raw materials input and storage, batch mixing and storage, melting, cullet recycle, and control systems. The study made by Sting [18] is important in that it develops models for process units, such as storage silos, mixers, etc., and demonstrates the use of these models in the analysis of systems design and operation through simulation.

The first step in approaching the problem is to construct mathematical models for all the process units by taking one of the most important aspects of the entire process into consideration: the physical transformation of granular material.

A general model is developed which, when specialized, can be used to model silos, mixers, and mixing tanks along with other process components. This general model will be described briefly for a silo.

A silo is defined as a temporary storage device whereby granular material is dumped into the top, stored, and at some later time removed from the bottom. The model was developed under the following reasoning.

a) The filled silo is divided into spaces of batch volume size (refer to Fig. 15).

b) Associated with each space is a corresponding batch and its describing constituent vector.

c) When a batch is removed from the bottom, all the batch constituent vectors above it move down one space.

d) When the material is either entered or extracted, it is done discretely in time.

e) Because of the mixing effect between adjacent batches, the output batch is some combination of any input batch.

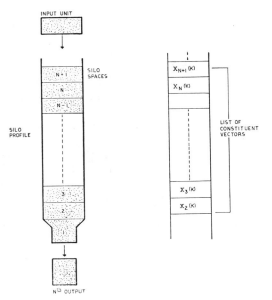

Fig. 15.   Schematic silo.

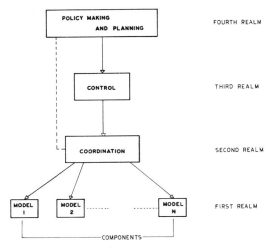

Fig. 16.   Activity realms.

f) All materials which are placed in the silo together have equal or nearly equal densities.

g) A batch of materials, or any part thereof, has a maximum and a minimum length of the silo to transverse, and this transversal occurs within some maximum and minimum number of output batches.

These assumptions, together with mass and impulse balance, yield the following set of equations:

$$Y(K) = \sum_{i=1}^{m} W_i(K) - X_i(K) \qquad (6)$$

$$\sum_{i=1}^{m} W(K) = 1 \qquad (7)$$

$$\sum_{i=1}^{m} W_i(K - i + 1) - X_i(K - i + 1) = X_1(K) \qquad (8)$$

$$X_1(K) = X_2(K - 1) = X_3(K - 2) = \cdots$$
$$= X_m(K - m + 1). \qquad (9)$$

By substituting (9) into (8), then rearranging it, there results

$$W_1(K) = 1 - \sum_{i=2}^{m} W_i(K - i + 1) \qquad (10)$$

where

$X_i(K)$ constituent vector of the material at the ith position in the compartmentalized silo, just prior to the kth output

$Y(K)$ Kth output batch constituent vector

m maximum range over which an input batch will be spread over the output batch

$W(K)$ the weighing value which designates the percentage of inputs that are in the output at time NT.

The weighing values are assumed to be of a statistical nature. The particular disturbance associated with the random variables of the model is dependent upon the particular silo to be modeled and the material to be stored. Thus the weighing values not only must satisfy the constraints imposed by (7) and (10), but also must be generated in accordance with the information extracted from the actual data obtained by conducting experiments on a particular silo. Once the weighing values are determined, (6) can be used to express the physical transformation taking place between input and output batches within the silo.

The second step is to combine all the component models into a "multiactivity system." Broadly defined, the model is composed of four activity realms (Fig. 16). The first realm defines the functions of the components of the process. The second realm defines the interactions and performs structure coordination. The third realm defines the supervisory functions (control), and the fourth realm defines the policy making and planning functions.

The complete system model for batch systems is amenable to digital computer simulation and has been used to investigate process design and control problems.

6) *Conclusions:* As is the case in other process industries, it appears that the lack of suitable process models still remains the major obstacle to the implementation of advanced control systems in the glass industry. As a rule, relatively unsophisticated control concepts are applied.

Although experimental techniques probably offer the best practical short-term approach to the problem of process modeling, theoretical modeling of process units offers very attractive long-term advantages, especially when the control system modeling can be combined with modeling for unit design. Although the cost of this approach is relatively higher and more time-consuming, the potential gains in the ability to synthesize optimally new process systems are very high.

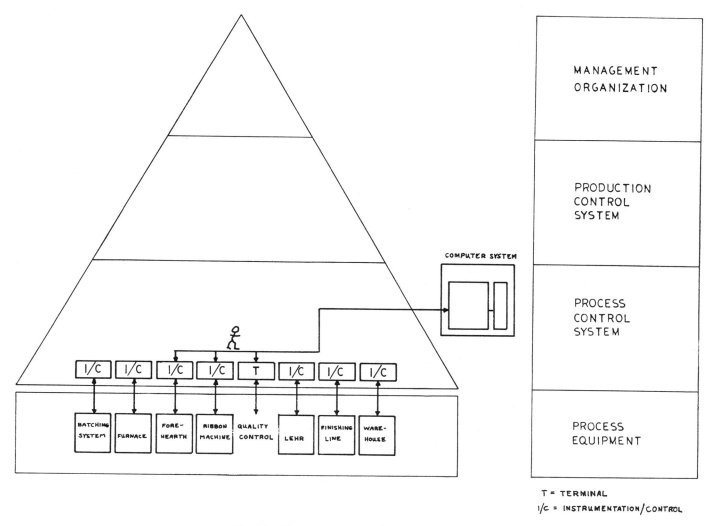

Fig. 17. Plant process control computer system.

Finally, much remains to be done in the area of modeling and control technology for large systems consisting of a number of process units. A particularly important problem is the incorporation in the model of the economic and information aspects of the process.

B. Computer Control Systems

The essential role played by the controller of the manufacturing process, the information network, was discussed in Section II-B. It was stated that the computer technology makes it now possible to automate control functions at all levels of the hierarchy. It is within this framework that we will now survey, on the basis of scarce published information, the status of the implementation of such systems in the glass industry.

One of the first computer control systems implemented in the glass industry was mentioned in the section on process modeling (Section III-A). It is the process computer control system developed for the automatic control of a ribbon machine [14]. This system performs control functions only. The structure of the system is depicted in

Fig. 17. Quality control information is entered manually and processed by a process control computer which in turn manipulates a number of variables on the forehearth and ribbon machine.

Another example of process computer control application is given by the control system used in the plants of the Owens-Corning Fiberglas Corporation. On the basis of published information, it appears that these systems are essentially process control systems performing first level control functions in the melting and delivery areas of the process, although some production scheduling might be effected in some instances [19]–[21].

Other supervisory control applications have also been announced recently by glass container manufacturers [22], [23]. Computer control systems are being used for the control of batching, melting, and inspecting operations at the Lakeland, Fla., plant of Owens, Illinois. The function of the computer is to supervise and monitor the entire process.

Recent publications indicate significant trends in the process control area. The trend toward central control

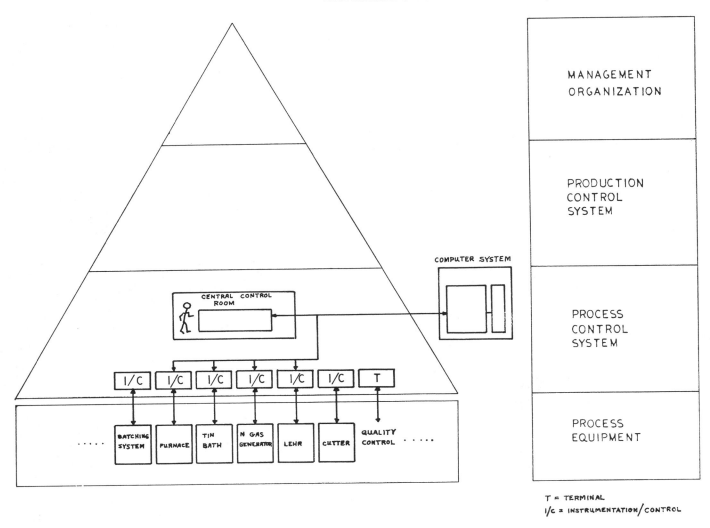

Fig. 18. Plant process control computer system with central control room.

rooms and centralized process control appears in the Ford Motor Company's process control computer system installed in Dearborn, Mich. The process computer control system controls a float glass manufacturing process [24], [25]. The system as illustrated in Fig. 18 handles approximately 80 closed control loops and monitors close to 500 process variables. The real-time, on-line control functions cover the melting furnace, tin bath, annealing lehrs, and gas generators. Monitoring of the batch house and the quality inspection is also effected. The system, which results in reduced manufacturing costs through improved quality and increased productivity, is also capable of handling background work such as generation of new programs, engineering calculations or nonprocess applications at the same time it controls the process. The central control room is represented in Fig. 19. The operator console, on-line printer, alarm typewriter, television display and recording devices, and graphic panels can be identified. The scarcity of recording instruments is apparent.

On the basis of these examples, it would appear that the glass industry, following the trend pioneered by other

Fig. 19. Central control room—Ford Motor Company (Dearborn, Mich.).

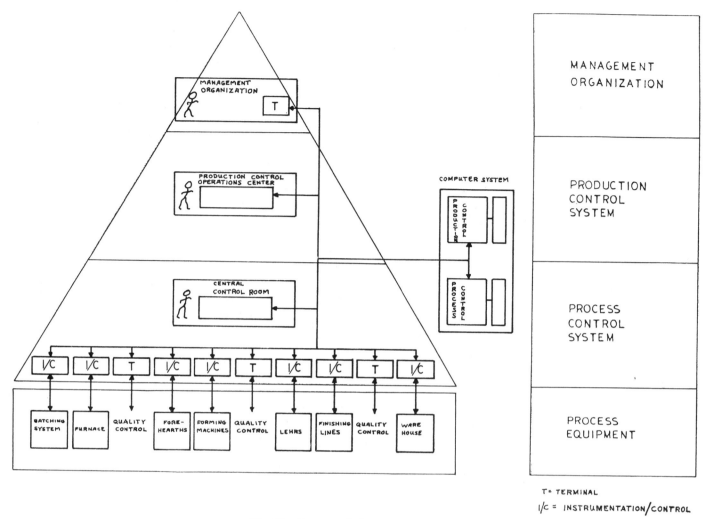

Fig. 20. Integrated plant control system.

process industries, is slowly moving, in an evolutionary fashion, toward computer-directed, central, process control systems.

It is believed that the trend toward integration will not stop at the process control level, but that production control and management control functions will progressively be included into the design of fully integrated on-line, real-time control systems. The diagram in Fig. 20 illustrates the structure of a possible integrated plant control computer system based on functional design. It is an integrated system because it performs both the process and production control functions on line and in real time. The information flow, data collection, and report generation are highly automated. The current status of the entire plant is available on a minute-to-minute basis. This permits the effective implementation of advanced management techniques with decisions made on the basis of quantitative information available where and when needed. There is no evidence that such integrated control systems are in operation today although, as we mentioned previously, some of the existing control systems might already have developed to include some production control functions.

The series of diagrams, the last one in particular, also suggests a clear trend toward making computing power available as a utility throughout the system in much the same way as electric power is available today.

The integrated control systems approach should naturally be expected to affect our basic concepts of plant design and operation. In particular, it should be expected to have a very significant impact on the management and organizational structure of the plant. This is the subject that will be discussed in the following section.

IV. HUMAN FACTORS [26]–[29]

The emphasis of this survey has been so far on the economic and technological aspects of systems development in the glass industry. We have discussed problems relating to the development of the automatic control loop represented by the diagram in Fig. 21, symbolizing the physical process controlled by an on-line computer. But manufacturing systems are man–machine systems, organizations whose components are men and machines, tied by a communications network, working together to achieve a common goal. Even in highly automatic computer control systems, the place of the human remains vital as Fig. 22

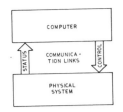

Fig. 21.   The automatic control loop.

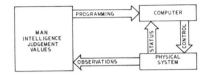

Fig. 22.   The man loop.

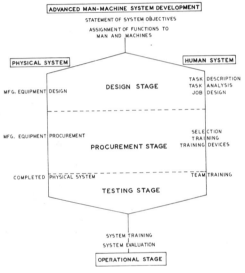

Fig. 23.   Man–machine system development.

suggests. Man communicates with the system through programming, manual data entry, and instrumentation. He further observes the process to evaluate, through the use of his intelligence, judgment, and values, the performance of the automatic control loop in relation to his criteria of adequate or optimal system performance.

Of particular concern today to those involved in development of integrated control systems is a need for an awareness of man as a component in man–machine systems whose developmental needs resemble those of the machine or hardware components. Planning for the design and development of human components of systems has not been as systematically pursued in the past as it might have been. Characteristically, systems were designed and developed first, and assumptions were made that the human components required either existed or could be found or could be trained to operate this system. Only in relatively recent years, especially with the advent of extremely complex military and aerospace systems, has an increasing awareness developed of the need for systematic design and development of human system components. In the

United States this is probably best reflected in the types of documents required of potential contractors for the development of complex man–machine systems. Qualitative and quantitative personnel requirements information (QQPRI) documents which specify the design and development of the personnel subsystem necessary for implementation, maintenance, and operation of these complex systems are required. This can no longer be an evolutionary development process. It must be planned and designed as the physical subsystem(s) is.

Fig. 23 schematically represents the man–machine system development cycle. Advanced system development involves the initial statement of system objectives and culminates in decisions leading to the assignments of operational functions to men and machines. From this point on, the human and physical systems proceed on parallel courses of development to the point at which the completed components are assembled for testing and training in preparation for operation. Although not specified in Fig. 23, the parallel development of the two major subsystems does not in any way imply independent development. One of the primary values to be gained from such a man–machine systems development approach lies in the repeated and ongoing interaction of the developers of the two subsystems at each point in the development cycle. In addition to assuming that all required components are available at a specified end point, the continuing interactions contribute immensely to preventing the need for costly and time-consuming retrofittings of components and major system modifications. To accomplish this, however, implies the development of an ability to communicate effectively and interrelate on the part of representatives of diverse disciplines. Compromises and trade-offs will be required. Ultimate optimization of each subsystem will undoubtedly not be possible, but total system optimization and effectiveness will be more closely approximated.

In light of what has been said about integrated process control possibilities in the future, what are some of the implications for human system components? The implications are numerous. Just a sampling would be the following: 1) Traditional organizational structures may be inappropriate for the management of integrated control complexes, either because they are too cumbersome or because their traditional control concepts are outmoded. 2) Routine, nonmotivating jobs may be eliminated entirely, resulting not only in a smaller, but in a more involved, committed, and motivated work force. 3) General technical and educational backgrounds of higher levels will be required, and programs and methods to prepare individuals for performance of the man functions in the system will have to be developed. 4) The relative status of various jobs, e.g., machine operators and maintenance employees may be modified with attendant needs for modifications of long-standing attitudes and opinions. 5) The traditional protection and security functions of labor organizations may no longer be required, leading to either a change of function or an elimination of the need for such functions entirely.

Whatever the end product of an integrated plant or company control system turns out to be, it is almost certain to require different approaches to the organization, management, development, and maintenance of the human components. What is implied in this paper is that planning for, and awareness of the need for, such an integrated approach to the human component development, along with the physical system development, must begin now if we are to achieve the higher levels of integrated control in the reasonably near future.

V. Conclusions

In this survey we have discussed some of the economic, technological, and human aspects of systems engineering. We see systems engineering as the technique through which the electric technology, exemplified by the digital computer, is being applied to our industry.

Several major trends that characterize the evolution of systems engineering technology in our industry have been identified:

1) There is a marked trend toward the increased integration of process control, production control, and management control functions.

2) Modeling techniques are playing an increasingly important role and should lead to the design of optimum systems through the integration of the design of the process and of its control system.

3) The importance of human factors cannot be overemphasized. Our understanding of these factors is one of the major elements, possibly the most important one, controlling the rate of implementation of modern technology in industry.

As engineers, we find ourselves increasingly moving in a position to influence directly social and human patterns. The nature of our work must change as our essential responsibility becomes one of education of the public in modern technology.

References

[1] M. McLuhan, *Understanding Media: The Extension of Man.* New York: McGraw-Hill, 1964.
[2] S. E. Elmaghraby, *The Design of Production Systems.* New York: Reinhold, 1966.
[3] M. Athans and P. L. Falb, *Optimal Control.* New York: McGraw-Hill, 1966.
[4] K. Chen, "Models for integrated control," presented at the 1965 Systems Engineering Conference, Chicago, Ill.
[5] I. Lefkowitz, "Multilevel approach to the design of complex control systems," presented at the 1965 Systems Engineering Conference, Chicago, Ill.
[6] J. W. Forrester, *Industrial Dynamics.* New York: Wiley, 1961.
[7] V. A. Trapeznikov, "Control, economy, technological progress," presented at the 1966 IFAC Cong., London, England.
[8] H. Chestnut, *Systems Engineering Tools.* New York: Wiley, 1965.
[9] I. M. Sheinkop and L. S. Belousova, "Modeling liquid for investigating glass movement in gas electron furnaces," *Steklo i Keramika,* vol. 23, pp. 23–25, February 1966.
[10] J. C. Hamilton, R. R. Rough, and W. B. Silverman, "Improved techniques for studying the design and operation of glass melting furnaces by means of models," *Advances in Glass Technology, Proc. 1962 Internatl. Cong. on Glass* (Washington, D.C.), pp. 190–195.
[11] J. D. McClelland, "Plastic flow model of hot pressing," *J. Am. Ceramic Soc.,* vol. 44, p. 326, 1961.
[12] P. Eykhoff, P. M. E. M. van der Gruten, H. Kwakernoak, and B. P. Valtman, presented at the 1966 IFAC Cong., London, England.
[13] R. J. Mouly and L. A. Zangari, "The development of an automatic diameter control system for glass drawing processes," *ISA Trans.,* vol. 3, pp. 158–164, April 1964.
[14] A. T. Bublitz, R. J. Mouly, and R. L. Thomas, "Statistical feedback squeezes product variations," *ISA J.,* pp. 55–60, November 1966.
[15] B. J. Hoetink, "Process dynamics of a glass furnace following a step change of one of the batch components," presented at the 1968 Internatl. Cong. on Glass, London, England.
[16] J. Duffin and K. Johnson, "Glass container process: forehearth simulation," IBM Corp., Systems Development Div., San Jose, Calif., Rept. 02-472-1, July 1965.
[17] W. Oppelt, "Regulating processes in furnaces and their representation with the help of block diagrams," *Glastechnische Berichte,* vol. 26, no. 5, pp. 146–150, 1953.
[18] D. Sting, "Granular batch process modeling," Case Institute of Technology, Cleveland, Ohio, Progress Rept. 19-9, October 1965.
[19] P. D. Griem, Jr., "Digital computers for glass process control," presented at the 1967 Am. Ceramic Soc. Meeting, New York.
[20] ——, "Direct digital control of a glass furnace," presented at the 20th Ann. ISA Conf., Los Angeles, Calif., 1965.
[21] R. R. Hudgins, "Fiberglas process control using DDC," presented at the 1967 IFAC/IFIP Internatl. Conf., Menton, France.
[22] "Computer operation in Owens–Illinois glass container plant," *Natl. Glass Budget,* September 25, 1965.
[23] "First computerized glass container plant dedicated at Dayville by Knox," *Natl. Glass Budget,* October 15, 1965.
[24] "Ford's computer controlled plant to operate non-stop for three years," *Natl. Glass Budget,* July 22, 1967.
[25] "Ford's flat glass plant hikes capacity, quality," *Automotive News,* May 1, 1967.
[26] R. M. Gagne, Ed., *Psychological Principles in System Development.* New York: Holt, Rinehart, and Winston, 1962.
[27] J. C. Kennedy, "Psychology and system development," in *Phychological Principles in System Development,* R. M. Gagne, Ed. New York: Holt, Rinehart, and Winston, 1962.
[28] I. L. Auerback, "The information revolution and its impact on automatic control," presented at the 1963 IFAC Cong., Basel, Switzerland.
[29] K. Davis, *Human Relations at Work: The Dynamics of Organizational Behavior,* 3rd ed. New York: McGraw-Hill, 1967.

The place of digital backup in the direct digital control system

by J. M. LOMBARDO

The Foxboro Company
Foxboro, Massachusetts

INTRODUCTION

The key to the success of direct digital control on large industrial processes lies in its flexibility in implementing everyday process control problems as well as advanced control at lower overall system cost. Control concepts for continuous processes use the computing, monitoring, information storage and analytical ability of the direct digital control computer. In the batch or discontinuous process the computer's logic capability is emphasized. To perform batching operations, a comprehensive logic system is necessary. Implementation of such a system using digital techniques provides many advantages over implementation using analog equipment with auxiliary digital logic circuits.

To fully appreciate these advantages, the reader must have a basic understanding of continuous control systems as well as the batch type systems. The fol-lowing will describe single loop control, several advanced control concepts and control of semicontinuous processes, as an introduction to digital computer application and backup.

Single loop control

Simple single loop feedback control is the most common control found in the process industries. It is used for controlling flow, level, temperature, pressure and many other variables. Both pneumatic and electronic devices are available which provide this type of control.

Basically, these controllers compare the measurement of a variable with its desired value or set point. If the two values are not equal, the controller adjusts a control value to minimize the difference (Figure 1).

In action, the controller is an analog computer which calculates a one, two or three term expression,

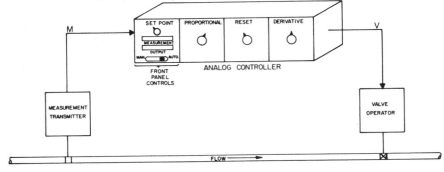

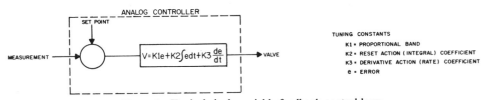

$$V = K_1 e + K_2 \int e\, dt + K_3 \frac{de}{dt}$$

TUNING CONSTANTS

K1 = PROPORTIONAL BAND
K2 = RESET ACTION (INTEGRAL) COEFFICIENT
K3 = DERIVATIVE ACTION (RATE) COEFFICIENT
e = ERROR

Figure 1 — Typical single variable feedback control loop

Reprinted with permission from *AFIPS Conf. Proc., Vol. 30, 1967 Spring Joint Comput. Conf.*, pp. 771–778.

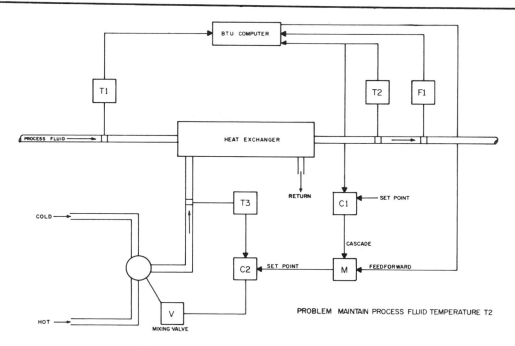

Figure 2 — Advance control techniques applied to a
heat exchanger

depending on the type of control action required by the process. The three terms define proportional, reset and derivative control action. During process start-up, coefficients of the three terms are manually set on the controller to provide the best response under normal operating conditions. If operating conditions change, or the process operator changes the set point radically, the coefficients are no longer at optimum values.

Advanced control concepts

As the control problem becomes more complicated, single loop feedback control is no longer sufficient. Figure 2 illustrates three types of advanced control: inferential, feedforward and cascade.

In the inferential control, a relationship is calculated between two or more measurements which is used to control the desired but unmeasurable variable. In Figure 2, the Btu computer performs a calculation based on the difference between the outlet and inlet temperatures to the heat exchanger (T2−T1) and the flow F1 of process fluid through the heat exchanger. This calculation — a measure of the heat transferred to the process fluid — determines the demand of hot or cold fluid needed to maintain process fluid output temperature T1.

Analog computing devices perform the necessary calculations and control can be executed with conventional analog control devices. Additional calculations may be necessary before some variables are combined. For example, the differential pressure signal provided by the commonly used orifice plate is proportional to the square of the flow. A computing element is therefore necessary to extract the square root of the differential pressure signal.

Figure 2 also illustrates feedforward control. The calculation of heat transfer (Btu) rate is "fed forward" to adjust the flow of heating or cooling fluid and change temperature T3. This feedforward calculation anticipates disturbances in both inlet temperature T1 and process flow F1. To provide more stable control of T2, the feedforward signal anticipates the change in heat input required. The magnitude of the feedforward action is usually determined by experimentation and may have to be adjusted periodically, since the heat transfer characteristics of the heat exchanger change with age.

A third control technique illustrated by Figure 2 is cascade control — a technique where one controller adjusts the set point of another controller. The output of temperature controller C1 is fed (cascaded) to the set point of temperature controller C2 through a multiplying device M. Hence changes in process fluid output temperature T2 affect the set point of controller C2 to ultimately maintain output temperature.

The control loops discussed have been applied to continuous processes which operate at near steady conditions with only nominal process or set point disturbances. Therefore, adjustment of the proportional, reset and derivative coefficients is rarely necessary and set point changes are nominal. In a steady, con-

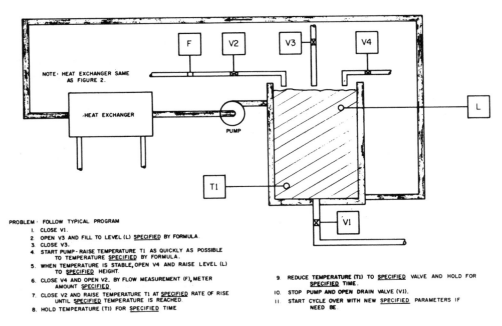

PROBLEM: FOLLOW TYPICAL PROGRAM
1. CLOSE V1.
2. OPEN V3 AND FILL TO LEVEL (L) SPECIFIED BY FORMULA.
3. CLOSE V3.
4. START PUMP-RAISE TEMPERATURE T1 AS QUICKLY AS POSSIBLE TO TEMPERATURE SPECIFIED BY FORMULA.
5. WHEN TEMPERATURE IS STABLE, OPEN V4 AND RAISE LEVEL (L) TO SPECIFIED HEIGHT.
6. CLOSE V4 AND OPEN V2. BY FLOW MEASUREMENT (F), METER AMOUNT SPECIFIED.
7. CLOSE V2 AND RAISE TEMPERATURE T1 AT SPECIFIED RATE OF RISE UNTIL SPECIFIED TEMPERATURE IS REACHED.
8. HOLD TEMPERATURE (T1) FOR SPECIFIED TIME
9. REDUCE TEMPERATURE (T1) TO SPECIFIED VALVE AND HOLD FOR SPECIFIED TIME.
10. STOP PUMP AND OPEN DRAIN VALVE (V1).
11. START CYCLE OVER WITH NEW SPECIFIED PARAMETERS IF NEED BE.

Figure 3 – Simple batch control sequence

tinuous well-behaved process, use of these adjustments would be very limited. Many high production petrochemical processes are in the continuous process category.

Control of semicontinuous processes

Figure 3 presents a process control problem where steady operating conditions are not maintained. This type of process requires a control system which changes operating conditions according to a preplanned event/time schedule. Batch or semicontinuous processes require controlled sequencing because: various equipment must be started and stopped frequently, product requirements change frequently and operating parameters change. It should be noted that most batch or continuous processes still use feedback control, but with programmed changes of control set point.

Figure 3 illustrates a simple chemical reactor. Ingredients are added sequentially and temperature is maintained according to various preset programs to provide the chemical reactions necessary for various products. The reaction within the vessel can vary from endothermic to exothermic during the production cycle. Hence in order to hold a set temperature, the control system may be required to switch from heating the reactor to cooling it when the reaction starts to generate its own heat.

In the typical chemical reactor or mixing vessel, different control sequences may be necessary for each new product. For instance, there may be changes in specified ingredient mix and heating and cooling

temperatures and temperature rates of change. Process control problems of this nature require more complex control than the feedback, feedforward and multivariable controls previously described. This control requires programmed sequencing of events, including equipment starting and stopping.

In Figure 3, the control of reaction temperature T1 is basically a feedback control problem. However, the problem is complicated, since T1 must change at the proper times, sometimes in step-wise fashion and other times at a controlled rate. Also, the sequence of events must be readily changed, depending on the intended product.

Combinations of special purpose digital and analog control equipment have been built which satisfy the demands of the discontinuous process. However, the programming of this equipment is relatively inflexible and the control cannot be well-tuned because of the cyclic nature of batch processes. Many of these systems are not used at full operating speed, since the control constants are a compromise.

Applying the digital computer

Digital computers are of significant interest to the industrial process control field due to their ability to store programs, calculate simple and complex control relationships, compute variables which are not directly measurable, monitor the process and take action according to a preplanned schedule. The digital computer easily performs tasks that the analog system finds difficult; it can be easily programmed to adapt the overall control system to changes in process dynamics, materials, equipment and production demands. Because of this versatility, digital computers are being designed and installed in continuous process plants as well as in batch process plants. Many of the installations use direct digital control techniques on all or some of the control problems.

Table I compares two systems, each using direct digital control exclusively. As shown, a continuous process application in an oil refinery has 530 analog measurements of which 275 are associated with control calculations, the other inputs are for performance monitoring and system operation analysis. Of the 275 control inputs, 180 are used for direct control of simple loops; the remaining 95 are used in advanced control. Therefore, approximately one-third of the 275 inputs associated with control are used to implement multivariable and advanced control techniques.

Table I — Comparison of computer system input/output between continuous and batch process control

	CONTINUOUS PROCESS	BATCH PROCESS
TOTAL ANALOG INPUTS	530	620
ANALOG INPUTS IN CONTROL LOOPS	275	240
CONTROL LOOPS		
SINGLE	180	225
CASCADE	30	70
FEED FORWARD	15	0
DIGITAL INPUT (CONTACTS)	210	1725
DIGITAL OUTPUTS (ON-OFF)	355	1300

Table I also shows the input/output distribution for a large batch control installation currently being implemented by a digital computer system. A comparison of the batch with the continuous process reveals a significant increase in contact sensing elements and on-off control outputs. In order to sequence events, the batch system must sense the status of process equipment and conditions. Also, more devices must be turned on and off. With the batch system, man-machine communication needs also increase. Increased number of push buttons, signal lights and the increased size of digital displays require more digital inputs and outputs.

It is also significant that the number of control outputs (295) can exceed the number of analog inputs (240) in the batch system. This situation occurs in batch processes because the same measurement can be used in control of different control elements and with different control algorithms, depending on the sequence of events and the starting and stopping of equipment.

The philosophy of DDC

With the introduction of the digital computer to the process control field, it became evident that relatively little was known about most processes. Most processes could not be adequately represented by mathematical models which would permit improved process control.

Early attempts at applying the digital computer emphasized supervisory control in which the computer adjusted the set point of an analog controller. In these systems, the analog controller retained the last computer control setting, if the computer failed. On continuous processes, this control was quite satisfactory; in fact, once the system was operating satisfactorily, it made little difference whether the computer was there or not. The operator could still adjust control actions, as he did before the installation of the supervisory computer. This made the process operators happy, but in many instances the process engineers and plant supervisors were not. There was no guarantee that the operators would achieve the optimum control settings for the plant.

What additional advantages did the computer provide? If so desired, the computer could make feedforward, cascade and inferential calculations which would optimize control set points for economic or production considerations. Economic constraints relating to material balance, throughput, inventory, etc., could be developed. In a sense, an economic mathematical model was possible, whereas a process model was still difficult to achieve, due to lack of process knowledge. In addition, the on-line process computer performed other useful work to aid operators, plant supervisors and process engineers: see Table II.

Table II — Some non-critical functions of an on-line process computer

● LOG OPERATING DATA IN ENGINEERING UNITS

● CALCULATE AND DISPLAY OPERATOR GUIDES

● INTEGRATION OF MATERIAL FLOW

● REPORT ON PROCESS STATISTICS - MATERIAL USED FUEL USAGE, THROUGHPUT, ETC.

● CALCULATE AND DISPLAY OR RECORD UNMEASUREABLE VARIABLES SUCH AS BTU RATE, MASS FLOW

● MONITOR AND ALARM PROCESS LIMITS

● RECORD PROCESS EVENTS DURING UNUSUAL DISTURBANCES

● MONITOR AND RECORD CHANGES IN SET POINTS, ALARM LIMITS, ETC. MADE BY THE OPERATOR

● PROVIDE ON DEMAND OPERATOR INFORMATION SUCH AS TREND RECORDING, ALARM STATUS REPORT, LOOP SET POINT AND PARAMETER DATA

Direct digital control was under consideration at the same time that the general purpose digital computer was performing process analysis, monitoring and some set point control.[1] It was reasoned that DDC would reduce the cost of a process control computer by eliminating the cost of the individual feedback controllers. Since the controller merely performs a calculation, why couldn't the computer perform the calculation? Several experimental ventures showed that the DDC concept was physically possible.[2,3] The feedback control law was calculated within a general purpose computer and the resulting signal outputted directly to the control valve.

At first, it appeared that the trade-off between individual loop controllers and a direct digital control (DDC) computer was in the area of 200 loops. There was a hooker, however. This trade-off did not include any provisions in case the computer system failed. For most installations this meant using analog controllers to back up the DDC computer on each loop considered critical.

The DDC equipment was designed so that, if the computer failed, each valve would remain in its last directed position unless backed up by analog control. Critical loops were backed by an analog controller which would maintain loop control on computer failure. Control valves of the other DDC loops were "locked in" at their last output, but the operator could manually position each valve from a console on which he could read valve position and process measurement.

Figure 4 shows two loops from a large system. The measurement M_1, fed to the manual control panel, enables the operator to manually operate valve V_1, in case of computer failure. The loop containing measurement M_n and valve V_n has an analog controller for backup since measurement M_n is fast acting and cannot be controlled manually by the operator.

With the evolutionary history of digital process computer equipment, it is impossible to more than estimate mean time between failures (MTBF). For the smaller digital computers, including input/output equipment, that have been applied to the process control problems, calculated MTBF has ranged from 1000 to 2000 hours. Advances in circuit design indicate that reliability will increase, but reliability statistics on integrated circuits are not yet available. However, regardless of the projections and the calculated claims, the time-shared single computer system will never be perfect and will sometimes fail. Therefore, control security must always be considered on any process installation contemplating a digital computer.

For continuous processes, involving less than 150 loops, it appears that the single computer with set point analog control or DDC with analog backup and some pure DDC on noncritical loops makes the most sense. However, the user must be fully aware that he will give up economic and process control optimization, as well as the functions listed in Table II, if the computer fails. Perhaps most important,

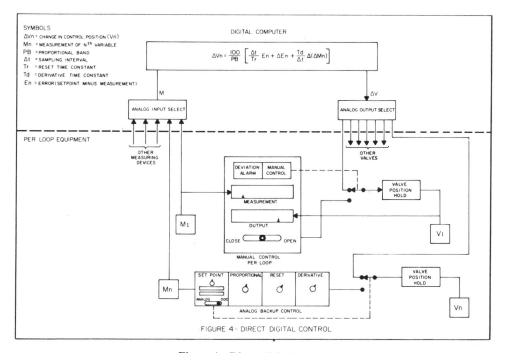

Figure 4 — Direct digital control

any advanced control that was dependent upon the computer, such as feedforward, cascade and multi-variable, will be lost during computer shutdown.

For the installation where control is not continuous, but where control sequencing is imperative, the use of computer set analog controllers is not sufficient. The computer provides sequencing and logic analysis which must have backup, if process operation is to be assured. The process control problem is not solved by keeping all control settings stationary upon computer system failure. In a chemical reactor, for instance, the contents can solidify or the reaction can "run away," if the process set point is not changed at the proper time.

A parallel DDC computer system

Figure 5 illustrates a parallel DDC computer system which not only provides computer backup but "backs up" the time-shared analog and digital input/output equipment which connects the computer to the various measurement and control elements. It also backs up all interloop controls, as well as all sequence control action.

In addition, this system can continue to perform the noncontrol functions such as those listed in Table II. It therefore permits control to continue even if one computer and/or its time-shared I/O equipment should fail. Note that if any of the time-shared equipment fails, process control is transferred to the backup subsystem.

Table III shows some interesting statistical data[4] which compare the availability of a single computer system with a parallel computer system. The table assumes that the MTBF of a single computer system is the same for each computer subsystem of the parallel computer system. Experience has shown that repair time for various failures, with on-site maintenance personnel, averages between 5 and 8 hours, depending upon the skill of the maintenance personnel, the availability of spare equipment, etc. With the parallel system, it appears that the average repair time can be maintained under 5 hours, since the system incorporates elaborate programs for self-diagnosis to ensure proper transfer to the backup

Table III — Availability — single computer vs. dual computer system

| | AVERAGE REPAIR TIME | MEAN TIME BETWEEN FAILURES | | | | | |
| | | 1000 | | 2000 | | 3000 | |
		AVAIL(%)	OFF[1]	AVAIL(%)	OFF[1]	AVAIL %	OFF[1]
SINGLE COMPUTER SYSTEM	2 HOURS	99.8	17.49 HRS	99.9	8.76 HRS	99.93	5.78 HRS
	5 HOURS	99.5	35.75 HRS	99.75	21.81 HRS	99.83	14.45 HRS
	8 HOURS	99.2	69.55 HRS	99.6	34.95 HRS	99.74	23.04 HRS
DUAL COMPUTER SYSTEM[2]	2 HOURS	99.9998	63 SEC	99.9999	31.5 SEC	99.9999	31.5 SEC
	5 HOURS	99.9987	6.83 MIN	99.99968	1.68 MIN	99.9998	1.05 MIN
	8 HOURS	99.996	14.2 MIN	99.9992	4.2 MIN	99.9996	2.1 MIN

SINGLE COMPUTER FORMULA

$$\text{AVAIL.} = \frac{\mu}{\mu + \lambda}$$

μ = REPAIR RATE (REPAIRS/HR.)
λ = FAILURE RATE (FAILURES/1000 HRS.)

DUAL COMPUTER FORMULA

$$\text{AVAIL.} = \frac{2\mu^2 + \mu\lambda}{2\mu^2 + 2\mu\lambda + \lambda^2}$$

1 TIME IN A ONE YEAR PERIOD THAT THE SYSTEM DOES NOT PROVIDE COMPUTER FUNCTIONS
2 ASSUMING REPAIR HAS BEEN STARTED ON FAULTY COMPUTER OF DUAL SYSTEM BEFORE COMPLETE SYSTEM FAILURE

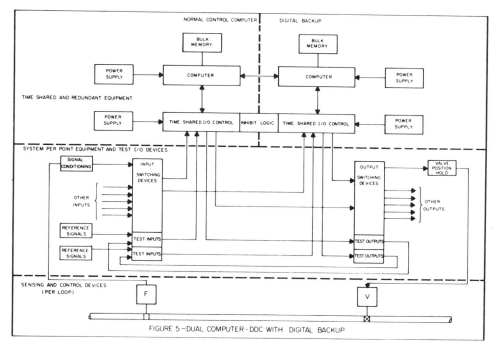

Figure 5 — Dual computer — DDC with digital backup

system. The failed computer subsystem is available for self-checking while the backup subsystem maintains process control.

Systems of this type can be economically attractive since they provide not only the essential control, but the system security essential to batch or start-stop operations. A parallel control processor using direct digital control techniques takes full advantage of the digital computer's process control capability without reservation and compromise. It can include advanced control techniques, such as self-tuning or adaptive control which cannot be obtained with set point control. The parallel computer processing system may provide these features and, in addition, may offer cost advantages over a conventional analog control system for the large continuous process.

For the continuous process in Table I, the computer contains the equivalent of 272 analog controllers. Implementation of a system of this size with DDC and analog backup could exceed the cost of implementation with the parallel or redundant computer scheme.

Input/output equipment

Figures 4 and 5 show that in DDC, as in all control systems, measuring elements and final control devices are still essential. Each measurement is individually conditioned before being fed to the multiplexer of the computer input/output system. Failure of any input or output therefore is similar to failure of a single controller and will not disable other loops. The system should be designed so that failure of any circuit element will not cause the loss of any common power supplies. Also, in case of a power failure, there must be battery backup or a redundant power supply.

Other cautions must be observed in the design of the parallel system interface equipment:

The system must be able to identify and diagnose the fault of any time-shared input/output equipment without disrupting control. The normal control computer and the backup system should both contain several inputs and outputs which can be used for automatic on-line testing of I/O operation, regardless of which subsystem is controlling the process. Some of these test inputs are connected to reference signals, others are connected to output test signals, closing the test loops through each subsystem.

All failed devices must be easily removed for replacement. Any disruption of normal functions during repair should be limited to the few inputs or outputs which share the same printed circuit as the failed element.

There also should be a diagnostic program which verifies correct operation, after the failed component has been replaced.

Output devices, for valve positioning or on-off control, which require power to maintain their status and/or output signal, should have at least a 30-minute battery backup system, in case of system AC power loss.

The system must detect the failure of any time-shared element in the input/output system control logic and automatically switch to digital backup. While operation is in the backup mode, the failed control logic must be electrically isolated and inhibited from operating input and output control devices. Repair can then proceed with no fear of accidental interference with process control.

In normal operation, with the control computer in command, the backup system must continually check its input/output operations to ensure that backup is available.

The inhibit logic must be fail-safe so that its failure will not disturb the system in control. It must be tested automatically to ensure that transfer to backup can take place if a transfer is commanded by a failure detection. If inhibit logic will not transfer the other computer automatically, the system should annunciate that fact and provide an independent manual override which forces transfer of the control of the input/output equipment to the other computer.

Other system design requirements

The system must have a computer-to-computer communication link which continually updates the backup program data and status on a periodic fixed time basis. The backup computer thus receives dynamic operating conditions within a short time period (in the order of seconds for a batch process).

Any program changes made on-line while the control computer is operating the process must be transferred to the backup control computer, at the same time. This updating must include operator changes to control settings as well as any on-line program changes.

A bulk memory must be used on both computer systems to retain the many formulas and programs that may be required. Bulk memory can also contain interpretive programs to simplify construction of a batch program, diagnostic programs for fault detection and programs to aid maintenance. Sophisticated man-machine communication programs, which involve lengthy message storage, can also be included.

Diagnostic programs for the computer-to-computer communications link should test for link failure, annunciate the failure and command the changeover to the backup system. A program system permits updating and on-line diagnostics while time-sharing the real-time programs in bulk memory.

There should be a system procedure and a system diagnostic program to assist in rapid repair of a failed subsystem. Another procedure and program is required to transfer all operating programs from the backup subsystem back to the repaired computer, without interfering with process control.

When the backup system is not on control, it is available for program compiling, debugging and problem simulation using the test inputs and outputs. It must also perform diagnostics to ensure operation is correct for takeover if necessary. When backup computer takes over process control, these programs are discontinued.

CONCLUSION

By using DDC with complete input/output control and computer backup, the parallel computer processing system permits unrestricted application of computer control techniques. It takes full advantage of the logic and computational ability of the digital computer, whereas a computer system which depends on analog set point control or analog backup cannot.

The parallel control computer system program storage ability, together with backup of logic control, program sequence and formulation, makes it ideally suited for complex batch or start-up and shutdown applications.

Complex continuous control systems would also benefit with this control system. Built with state-of-the-art electronics, the system should challenge the economics of computer set point control and single computer direct digital control with analog backup.

REFERENCES

1 J W BERNARD J F CASHEN
   Direct digital control
   Instruments and Control Systems Sept 1965
2 E VANDER SHRAFF W I STRAUSS
   Direct digital control - an emerging technology
   Oil and Gas Journal November 16 1964
3 J W BERNARD J S WUJKOWSKI
   DDC experience in a chemical process
   ISA Journal December 1965
4 R H MYERS K L WONG H M GORDY
   Reliability engineering for electronic systems
   John Wiley and Sons New York 1964

Recent Developments in Automation
of Cement Plants

E. H. GAUTIER, JR., MYRON R. HURLBUT, MEMBER, IEEE, AND EDWARD A. E. RICH, SENIOR MEMBER, IEEE

Abstract—Over a decade has passed since process computers were first applied to control parts of the cement manufacturing process. The path from there to the present has successes—and failures—along its way. Over 30 cement plants have installed such computers as part of their efforts to keep profit margins from shrinking. Progress in using these process control techniques has been largely evolutionary. Certain factors can now be identified more certainly as essential ingredients for success. Among these are the following. 1) "People factors" of the cement manufacturer stand as first in importance. These include management support, process know-how, training and supervision of operators, and an inner confidence and determination that "we can make it work." 2) Well-done interface jobs of adapting control room design and operators to each other, automation components with the process and its machinery, and plant design to fit automatic control fundamentals. 3) Designing the process to really be controllable. 4) Control hardware and software which fit the nature of this industry. Each of the foregoing factors is expanded with emphasis on how recent developments of better understanding, control functions, hardware, software, and of process and plant design are merging to help shape the future of automation in the cement industry.

Paper 71 TP 9-IGA, approved by the Cement Industry Committee of the IEEE IGA Group for presentation at the 1971 Thirteenth Annual IEEE Cement Industry Technical Conference, Seattle, Wash., May 11–13. Manuscript received June 10, 1971.

E. H. Gautier and M. R. Hurlbut are with the Manufacturing and Process Automation Business Division, General Electric Company, West Lynn, Mass. 01910.

E. A. E. Rich is with the Industry Sales and Engineering Operation, General Electric Company, Schenectady, N. Y. 12345

INTRODUCTION

OVER 10 years have elapsed since digital process control computers were first introduced in the cement manufacturing industry (cf references). Over 30 have been installed or soon will be. Some have achieved success. Some have not. Some are moderately successful.

During this period several distinct trends have emerged. Among these is the realization that the essential ingredients for successful process control systems, as shown in Table I, also apply to the cement industry. These ingredients were derived from a study of diverse process industries which had used process control computer systems. A further trend is increasing evidence that economic benefits of the more successful systems in cement plants tend to be at least equal to those shown in Table II.

Some additional trends are the following.

1) Increased awareness—and adjusting to the implications—of the essential importance of adequate "people factors" to operate and support such systems.

2) The spreading use of direct digital control (DDC) as part of the automation system as contrasted to computers using supervisory methods of loop control only.

3) The development of adequate interface concepts and hardware to adapt the automation system to the process and to the people using the control system.

Reprinted from *IEEE Trans. Ind. Gen. Appl.*, vol. IGA-7, pp. 458–469, July/Aug. 1971.

TABLE I
ESSENTIAL INGREDIENTS FOR SUCCESSFUL PROCESS CONTROL
SYSTEMS USING DIGITAL COMPUTERS

Ingredient	Accountability	
	Owner	Supplier
Management Support	X	
Process Know-How	X	C
Control Strategy	C	X
Equipment Specification	X	C
Interface Engineering	X (Part)	X (Part)
Standard Software		X
Programming	C	X
Installation	C	X
Maintenance	X	C
Training	X	C
Process Hardware, Operation	X	
Control Hardware	X (Part)	X (Part)

X—responsible, C—councils.

TABLE II
OPERATING BENEFITS

Item	Typical Percent Values
Reduced fuel consumption per unit weight of product produced	3-12
Increased annual production with same basic process facilities	7-15
Reduced maintenance of kiln linings, cooler grates, etc.	10-40
Reduced kiln chains wear.	10-40
Grinding power savings, plus less wear on liners and grinding media.	2-4
Extending quarry reserves, minimizing costs of purchased additives, better waste dust utilization.	*
Short term uniformity, as well as long term average uniformity, of quality.	*
Continuously produced production data, and production totals (for measuring trends of unit performance, management reports, etc.)	*
Labor	Some - No increase, Some - +1 to +2 men, one shift per 5 day week.
Investment where plant design is modified to better adapt to automation:	
Homogenizing (blending) facilities.	Less
Central Control Room, Central Operator's Panel and Associated Equipments	Less

* Figures not available.

4) The increasing awareness by many engaged in plant design that automatic process control principles provide a basis for making significant improvements in many aspects of plant design. In some cases the total plant investment required is favorably affected.

5) The large increase of total automatic control functions being performed where major consideration of such automatic control is taken in design and operation of new cement plants. This has been especially so for some plants designed by Europeans.

6) The increase of availability of automatic process control systems when the major components of the system are supplied with needed power by an isolated "clean" ride-through power supply.

7) The recent development of small or minicomputers, with adequate supporting interface hardware and software, makes possible economic automatic control of smaller segments of the process than was practical hitherto. In effect, a process segment becomes controlled by its own "dedicated" computer. The small computer provides the possibility of economically adding automatic control to selected parts of many existing as well as new plants. This is especially true where plant design and operating realities favor a stretched out step-by-step approach with a minimum of interaction between each new step and those already taken.

PEOPLE FACTORS

"People factors" are the major key in achieving successful profitable automatic process control. Even some slower first-generation process control computers are still earning their way when adequate people factors have been created and maintained in place over the years. The faster and more powerful third- and fourth-generation computers do not bring success where adequate supporting people factors are not designed and maintained in place. What are some of these people factors which can be considered vital to success?

A Favorable Environment for Central Control Operators: This favorable environment which is created mostly by plant management includes the following. 1) There should be no shame on, or threat to the security of, the operators if the automatic system controls the process better overall than the operators do. 2) There should be a desire on the part of each control operator and their supervisors in that they *want* the control system to succeed, they *believe* they can help make it succeed, and they *take* the necessary steps to make it succeed. Finally, this results in the realization that making the system work well is really a contribution to his company's profitability, hence to better job security. 3) There should be written and readily available operating rules. To be effective these must be simple, closely fit the local situation, and then be enforced fairly. Yet means must be retained for accepting and placing in effect valid suggestions for improvements coming from operating personnel.

Training Supplemented by Regular Refresher Courses: Ignorance and misconceptions about automation are a major source of apprehension about automation on the part of operators and their supervisors. This ignorance is often well disguised. Well-designed training and refresher courses, especially tailored to the needs and capabilities of these personnel, provide a tactful yet effective way to dispel sufficient ignorance about automation so that good progress is achieved.

The best training courses for operators generally result when prepared and administered by those having responsible charge and administration of control of the cement making process. Short courses of training in control system concepts and applications are also desirable for higher levels of cement plant management and for those supervisory personnel who, while not responsible for process control, significantly affect its results by the quality of support and understanding they give in discharging their duties. Training and practice in maintenance of automation components is also vital. Usually the highest availability on control has been found to exist where the owner does most of his own maintenance work on automation system components. Training in programming for 2 or 3 cement plant personnel is very useful. The nature of the cement making process is such that conditions often change. These changes may arise from wear, chemical or physical properties, and other sources. A reasonable proficiency in modifying the control programs to closely accommodate these changes, when they affect process control, does much to maintain good control efficiency. Equally important, a high confidence level in the processs control system itself is thereby maintained.

Adjusting Job Descriptions of Plant Supervisory and Process Control Personnel: The goal of this is to make the descriptions more closely fit the realities of automatic process control. For example, the four major continuous parts of most cement plants (raw grinding, homogenizing or blending, burning, and finish grinding) highly interact with each other, especially in the downstream direction. (Plants which use hot kiln gas for drying have even more complex interacting control problems.) How often does one see ball mill operators taking actions which influence chemistry, or vice versa, but without coordinating with the chemists to assure overall minimum perturbations to the process? Conceptually, the best arrangements, taking automatic control of the process into account, follow.

1) A single manager of process control who at least manages operating control of the grinding, blending, and burning operations. He is responsible for training and discipline of the central operators. He is also accountable for operation of the continuous parts of the process.

2) The chemical and other operating personnel act more as advisors to this Process Control Manager but with no direct autority over central operating personnel.

3) This single Process Control Manager usually will make minor program adjustments necessary to keep abreast of process changes and to make desired improvements. This can be delegated in whole or in part to others, but it is his responsibility to judge, install, verify, and finally determine the usefulness of such changes.

Some plants have modernized their supervisory and operating structures to achieve successful automatic process control with no overall increase of personnel. Some other plants have retained traditional job descriptions. The highest plant supervision has tended to stay busily, sincerely, and relatively aloof from addressing themselves to adjusting to the implications of automation. Frustratingly enough, most of the failures and moderate successes are found in this class.

People Factors of Automation Suppliers: Supplier's people are a key ingredient in assisting a user of automation to achieve successful control of the process, especially where application software for process control is purchased. Their know-how, combined with know-how of the owner's representatives, largely provides the basis for the later success or failure of the new control system. The trend is to better organize the planning, training, installation, and operation of automation systems to make success more certain.

DIRECT DIGITAL CONTROL

DDC time shares the digital computer to directly control the final element, such as a valve, damper, etc. Usually some form of backup hardware—computer manual station, as an example—exists on the central operator's panel for each final output device being controlled. This backup device also provides a means of manual adjustment of the final output device when the computer is out of service. It may even be in the form of a full analog controller.

Many of the earlier cement automation systems utilize conventional analog instrument controllers to manipulate those process variables which are within the capabilities of such analog controllers. Supervisory logic, often called "Level 2," calculates the output signals to cause manipulation of the set points of such analog controllers. Supervisory logic is used to handle those control situations where combinations of interactions with other control loops, nonlinearities, very long process delays, and highly involved calculations make usual analog controllers relatively useless. This system is also known as digital analog control (DAC); or digitally directed analog control (DDAC). As hardware, and especially as good supporting software, became available in the last half of the 1960's, DDC spread so that now it is first choice in many new installations. Among the advantages DDC provides, as compared with more conventional analog instrumentation, are as follows.

1) The DDC computer readily checks limits, provides digital filtering over long periods of time, makes mathematical calculations, and does decision making—many of which are difficult or impractical with analog instrumentation equipment.

2) In many instances more precise control results because the drift problem within the regulator itself is absent.

3) The use of DDC forces operators to be systematic in documenting all constants associated with each regulating loop. This is rarely done with analog regulating systems, although such systems would work better if such documentation was done and kept up to date, and used to maintain best adjustments.

4) DDC is comparatively easily arranged for bumpless transfer for different modes of operation, prevention of reset windup, and automatic failure detection.

5) With DDC addition and deletion of loops and changes in the control, equations to be used are easily done. This

Fig. 1. DDC operator's console.

Fig. 2. Minicomputer with CRT operator's console for cement process control.

is especially useful during automatic start-up and shutdown of major parts of the total process during which transient manipulation of control loops is often required.

6) In a DDC computer the overall higher level of process control (called Level 2 or supervisory control) tends to be more easily done since the computer must only communicate with itself to change set points, switch loops in and out, modify control equations, and so forth.

7) In analyzing several existing installations it is evident that a well-done carefully thought-through and well-operated digital computer system using analog regulators on loops for which they are suitable can provide essentially as good a control of the process as can DDC for many parts of the continuous process. However, this is not true during automatic start-up. As the complexity of the regulating loops increases (such as some cases where complex gas flow patterns exist between raw grinding and the kiln-cooler department), DDC provides significant advantages by readily permitting easy switching of regulating loops and modifying their forms to follow the variable gas flows which such plants have.

Fig. 1 shows one form of a DDC operator's console used for the man–computer interface in a DDC system. Fig. 2 shows a cathode-ray tube (CRT) input–output console more recently available for cement plant control. The use of CRT seems likely to spread.

INTERFACE CONCEPTS AND HARDWARE

Trends and experiences clearly show that essential ingredients for successful cement automation also include adequately interfacing 1) the central control room

design and the central operators to each other; 2) the automation components with the process and its machinery; 3) the plant design with the automation system; 4) the plant power distribution system layout with the automation system; 5) many drives and their control with the logic in the automation system where automatic start-up–shutdown is included in the automation system for selected parts of the plant processes.

Other factors exist. The foregoing are the most important. Discussion of each follows.

Interfacing Central Control Room with Central Operators

Simplification of the layouts of the central room and of the central operator's panel (COP) is worthwhile. Such simplification tends to lower initial costs for central control room equipment and wiring. Operating, troubleshooting, and maintenance procedures are greatly simplified if good concepts are used in such layouts. Among the factors which permit good simplification without sacrificing operability or reliability are as follows.

1) It would be wise to simplify the control room operator's job. A typical central operator is hard-pressed to effectively monitor and properly respond to more than a few hundred displayed items of information. Yet one sometimes finds a COP in a cement plant having 1000–2000 different indicating lights, 50–200 ammeters and indicators, 20–40 recorders, 200–600 push-button stations and selector switches, 30–60 controllers and set point stations, etc. Why so many?

2) In the design stage rigidly question whether it is necessary for each device to be in the central room. If it is an ammeter primarily intended for maintenance uses, it probably belongs on the motor control center for the motor in question. If it is an indicating light showing status of an individual drive, what can the operator do about that light? Often such status lights are better on their departmental motor control center or relay panel. Maintenance may be their primary purpose. If so, it is better done by having such lights at the motor control center or relay panel. If it is a recorder, would not the purpose of the central operator be better served if he were limited to charts of the critical variables only? Other analog variables can be recorded by switching to one or more shared recorders when special tests and observations are to be made.

3) Group starting of a **complete** grinding mill with its auxiliaries or of a subdepartment permits large reductions on the COP of push buttons and indicating lights. Group starting helps highlight the distinction in the design stage between those devices really needed at the COP and those devices needed for maintenance. Devices for maintenance are generally more useful—and less expensive overall—if located on their motor control center or the associated relay panel. The location of individual drive status indicating devices on the corresponding departmental motor

control center or relay panel permits quick fault finding by maintenance personnel when the central operator notifies them that a sequence of starting cannot be completed.

4) Where fully automatic computer-directed start-up and shutdown is being planned, including transient manipulations of regulating loops, arrange that the procedures for manual and computer start-ups and shutdowns be as similar as possible. This helps teach the operator correct procedures by having him observe computer start-ups. It also helps the operator sense and diagnose difficulties when something is amiss in the computer-controlled procedure.

Interfacing Automation with the Process and with Its Machinery

To control a process first requires reasonable knowledge by the process controller of process conditions. Since automatic process control digital computers are electronic devices, their process status knowledge comes from frequent monitoring of status of selected contacts and analog signals—all derived from process conditions.

Switches and their transducers help detect process limits, process flows, levels, starvation, and so forth, and provide the computer and the control operator vital status information. Some of these switches also provide part of the traditional process-flow sequence interlocking.

Process variables such as selected temperatures, flow rates, pressures, speeds, and so forth, provide process knowledge to the computer by using suitable transmitters to convert to suitable analog input signals to the computer. The clear trend for new construction is to at least make such feedback signals compatible with future process control computers.

The second major factor in remotely and automatically controlling the process is that all variables required to achieve process holdpoints must be physically available and remotely controllable. The trends discerned from applying automation show that this may mean: 1) substituting adjustable speed fan drives for damper controlled gas flow circuits in some cases; 2) assuring that all feeder drives and their feeding devices have adequate physical range of feed rates to meet actual process control needs; 3) providing sufficient number of independent raw feeders so that the chemical hold points desired can, in fact, be achieved without excessive dependence on downstream blending facilities to hopefully make up for deficiencies in this area; 4) selection of kiln, cooler grates, and other drives so that they are low drift, have preferably zero dead-band in control, have comparatively flat speed-torque curves, and can have vernier speed changes made of as low as 0.1 percent when required; and 5) arranging all such "commanded" variables with necessary components so that they are compatible with commands from the computer and its associated devices without requiring intervention by people; neither should excessive wear of the final mechanism result when subjected to large numbers of small control changes.

Interfacing Plant Design with the Automation System

The trend is to modify new plant designs (and operating procedures) and the automation system to better fit each other. For existing plants, some are so designed as not to be very compatible with automatic process control. Yet many existing plants are compatible with automation in certain parts of their process. For these, the trend toward using minicomputers tends to be a "good fit." Specific details of plant design interfacing with automation are elaborated in a following section of this paper.

Interfacing the Plant Power Distribution System Layout with Automation

A good trend based on sound engineering, but emphasized by automatic process control considerations, is to strictly departmentalize all power circuits. This means: let main power feeders serve the raw department from the raw-material feeders under raw silos to the inputs to raw homogenizing silos and nothing else. Let the cement grinding electrical power feeders serve that department and nothing else, and so on, throughout the plant. Automatic control helps highlight the importance of a well laid out power distribution system, especially when automatic start-up and shutdown are planned.

Part of the interfacing of the automatic process control systems with the power distribution system is to carefully consider in advance the effects, prevention, and cure of surges appearing in the power distribution system; of high-speed reclosing by remote utility circuit breakers; transient voltage dips and losses of whatever duration and origin; and just where power for the process control should actually be taken from the main power distribution system.

An X-ray analyzer in the laboratory that is responsive to welding somewhere else in the plant, or to spotting of a ball mill motor, tends to be relatively useless at those times. In fact, it may even give out erroneous data. A power supply for the process control taken from circuits which are subject to frequent outages or have severe switching transients, such as from cranes on them, tends to also be a poor choice. Transient overvoltages and severe short circuits in input–output wiring have each been known to "wipe out" large sections of automatic process control equipment in cement and in other plants. Good interface engineering of the power distribution system and of the automatic process control is a distinct trend and is worthwhile to do correctly. A specific solution to many of these problems is given in greater detail in a following section of of this paper.

Interfacing Drives and Their Control with Automatic Process Control When Automatic Start-Up and Shutdown are Included in the Automation System

Very few cement plants in the United States have included automatic start-up and shutdown of selected portions of the process in their process computer control system. Many are doing group starting and stopping of drives only by other means, with the operator manipulating the loops for the transient conditions during such start-up–shutdown. However, a few European-designed large throughput new cement plants have included such features. The work of doing this shows that rigorous attention must be paid to the process mechanical equipment and to its reliability when part of an overall system, as well as to the design of the automatic start-up and shutdown logic itself, if real success in executing this function is to result.

The implementing of this automatic start-up and shutdown clearly shows that first class interface engineering between machinery builders, plant designers, and automatic process control designers is best accomplished before the plant is physically built. Not only must complete possible sequences of start-up and shutdown and their variations be foreseen and accurately described ahead of time, but the performance and behavior of the various process flows and transient conditions must also be foreseen and described as accurately as possible ahead of time. Where such extra rigorous thinking is done completely during the design stage, automatic start-up and shutdown, including the transient manipulation of regulating loops, becomes more easily accomplished. When such rigorous thinking is not done ahead of time, then the actual implementing of the start-up and shutdown tends to be more protracted, unnecessarily expensive, and probably the function should not then be in the computer. An effect of applying this function already has been to contribute to modifications in process and machine design.

EFFECTS OF AUTOMATION ON PLANT DESIGN

Here is where a truly exciting aspect of automation begins to be evident. Good automatic process control finally provides a means of making raw materials into finished cement relatively quickly and accurately once the raw materials are committed into the raw grinding system. Certain other industries have noted and taken advantage of the ability of automatic process control to reduce the storage between successive following parts of the process. The cement industry is beginning to use these techniques more and more [4]. Selected aspects follow.

Raw Department and Control

Designers of one relatively new United States' cement plant understood and implemented the idea of minimizing time delays between raw mill feeders and quickly obtaining and acting upon chemical information about the stream going into their downstream homogenizer. By combining on-line X-ray chemical gauging techniques of ground raw composition with short times for transport, sample analysis, and corrective actions, they were able to utilize a single 8–15 h homogenizing vessel between their raw department and their kiln. Overall, they felt that this approach saved them an investment of approximately 1 million dollars.

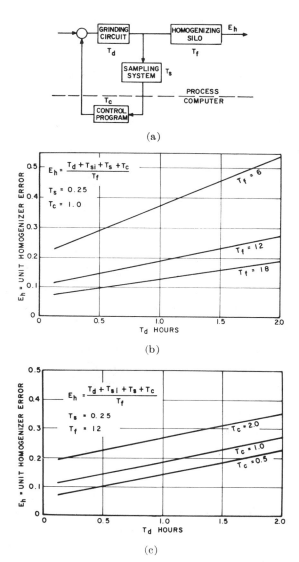

(a)

(b)

(c)

Fig. 3. Time delays and raw mix composition control accuracies. (a) Idealized raw mix control system for analyzing time delays versus homogenizer sizing. (b) Effects of time delays and homogenizer size on raw mix control. (c) Effects of control interval and system time delays on raw mix control.

Another plant in Western Europe combined good on-line gauging of raw mix chemical composition at the discharge point of the raw mill grinding circuit with short-time delays in making corrections and with computer control of their prehomogenizing pile building and computer guidance in quarry operation. By learning the techniques and performing them consistently well, they were able to completely eliminate downstream homogenizing equipment with the corresponding high operating expense of such vessels.

Another U.S. plant originally had planned to use large mill feed bins between the raw mill feeders and each raw mill. Analysis of the effects of the time delays such mill feed bins would have on decreasing possible chemical accuracies led them to eliminate such large feed bins and reduce the delays in that portion of the material transport circuits to about 10 min instead of the 2 h planned originally.

An analytical approach to assist in understanding the effects on reduction of process delay transport, sampling, analysis, and correction times in improving the accuracies of process control, is given in Fig. 3(a)–(c).

Fig. 3(a) is a block diagram of a simplified raw mix control system that can be used to calculate approximate worst case errors in the homogenizer analysis due to system transport times. The grinding circuit, the sampling system, the sampling interval, and the control interval are treated as causing simple time delays T_d, T_s, T_{si}, and T_c, respectively. The homogenizing silo has a filling time T_f corresponding to the actual "fullness" at which the silo is in fact operating. When an error occurs in the feed composition, the computer control program can do nothing until it detects the error at the output of the sampling system. It may take up to the sum of all these delays for the control program to detect the error and correct the feeders. During this time then, a total of $T_d + T_s + T_{si} + T_c$ h of bad material has gone into the system. The maximum error in the homogenizer composition will occur if the feed error occurs when the homogenizer is near full, and there is no time left to correct the error. Thus both the batch and continuous homogenizers may be considered the same, and the maximum fraction of the input error that will be present in the homogenizer output is then given by

$$E_h = \frac{T_d + T_s + T_{si} + T_c}{T_f}$$

where

E_h Unit homogenizer error, corresponding to a unit raw material feeder chemical composition error.

T_d Transport delays for time consumed by material traveling from raw material feeders to the sampling station, h.

T_{si} Sample interval, h (zero for on-line gauging in the example but is more for laboratory X-ray and manual chemical analyses).

T_s Sample preparation and analysis time, h (0.025 h used in example).

T_c Control interval, h (typically 3 min to 1 h).

Fig. 3(b) uses this equation to show the effect of grinding circuit transport times T_d on the homogenizer error E_h for homogenizers with 6-, 12-, and 18-h filling times and assuming a control program interval of 1 h ($T_c = 1.0$) and a 15-min sampling time ($T_s = 0.25$ h). To show the implications of these curves, consider a system with a delay of 1.5 h and a filling time of 18 h. If the delay were reduced to 0.65 h, the same results could be achieved with a silo of only 12-h capacity.

The results shown in Fig. 3(b) were obtained with corrections made at 1 h intervals. Fig. 3(c) shows the effect of increasing and decreasing the interval between corrections (T_c). It can be seen that decreasing the interval to 0.5 h

Fig. 4.   On-line X-ray chemical gauge in cement plant.

Fig. 5.   Laboratory X-ray chemical analyzer in cement plant.

shows small gain with a 12-h filling time, but that increasing the interval to 2 h causes a considerable loss in accuracy.

These results show the necessity of shortening the forward path and feedback path time delays in the raw mix system.

The possible implications of reducing investment in the "front end" of the plant by using principles shown in Fig. 3 represent a distinct and relatively new trend which will likely be used more in the future. Figs. 4 and 5 show views of X-ray chemical analyzers used in cement plants.

Improving Kiln-Cooler Design Concepts from a Control Viewpoint

Analyses of the trends show the following.

1) Increasing emphasis is being placed on keeping the arrangement of process flow and auxiliary devices in the kiln-cooler circuit as simple as possible.

2) The comments about characteristics and arrangements of kiln, cooler, grate, and selected fan drives previously given in this paper are applicable.

3) The larger grate type of coolers are more controllable if individual drives are provided to control air flow to each major compartment and for the cooler exhaust. The older practice of using very few cooler fans arranged with separate dampers to control air flow to each major compartment makes for a tough controllability problem. The trend is to provide separate fans for each function so as to permit the cooler to achieve its best performance as a heat recuperator *and* as a cooler of clinker [5].

4) When coal is used as a fuel, the trend is to try to reduce the variations in composition, especially the ash content of the coal. Such variations inevitably produce wide variations in chemical composition of the clinker where a

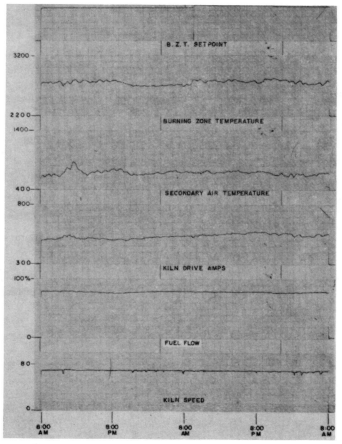

Fig. 6.   Two days of computer control of cement kiln.

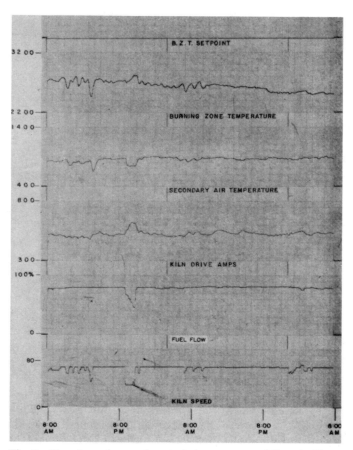

Fig. 7.   Two days of manual control of same cement kiln as in Fig. 6.

major component is the widely varying ash content of the coal as it enters the burning process. Blending of such coal may help. Purchasing higher grade coal may help. Some have even shifted to other types of fuel as the problems and costs of using coal have become more evident.

5) Another trend is to return dust to the kiln in a more uniform manner to improve controllability. Avalanching of dust in hoppers under precipitators or dust collectors and starving of dust feed at other times are factors tending to require violent control actions to respond to such kiln feed perturbations. The trend is to treat return dust as another separate kiln feed and install a return dust surge bin and return dust metering equipment arranged to gradually modulate the average return dust feed rate to fit the general level of return dust being generated.

6) Sizing all process components sufficiently large so as to provide "room" for control at top production rates is another trend. It is difficult to attain top qulaity control if the induced draft fan, fuel feeder, kiln drive, and so forth are operating "wide open" at their top limit, i.e., out of range.

7) There is more emphasis being placed on the recuperation aspect of the cooler by obtaining good secondary air temperature measurements and then using adequate logic to emphasize heat recuperation. Some have pioneered and

persevered in making good measurements of secondary air temperature.

Figs. 6 and 7 show good comparative but typical results with and without computer control on a kiln-cooler in a cement plant.

Grinding Mill Circuit Design and Automatic Process Control

The basic objective of grinding mill circuit control is to maintain fineness within a narrow band, usually at some maximum production level consistent with the existing process and machine constraints. Usually indirect measurements are required since not many fineness sensors are yet operating. Yet a trend does exist to apply and use more fineness sensors, particularly in cement grinding mill circuits [6]. Trends in grinding mill circuit design which are emphasized even further by considerations of automatic process control include the following.

1) Obtain good measurements of mill feed rates, either by weighing feeders or by a combination of total mill feed rate and selected weighing feeders for additives.

2) In closed-circuit grinding, sensing of input watts to elevators, separators, and ball mills is always preferable to attempting to obtain equivalent measurements using drive input amperes. Power system voltage affects drive input

Fig. 8. Process control computer installation in cement plant.

Fig. 9. Process control computer installation in cement plant.

amperes but only slightly affects drive input watts. Thus control based on ampere readings may, at times, be based no false information.

3) The trend is to place more emphasis on adequate sizing of all components of the grinding mill circuit. This especially applies to those handling recirculating load. Good control may be impractical if some of the recirculating load auxiliaries, or of other components, prevent adequate handling of the flow rate which may be inherent due to variations in the process materials actually used.

4) Some cement plants designed by Europeans are now being built and include features for closed-loop control of fineness using continuous fineness sensors.

Figs. 8 and 9 show a process computer installation in a cement plant.

TRENDS IN AUTOMATIC CONTROL FUNCTIONS BEING PERFORMED

The majority of United States' cement plants using digital process computer control techniques have applied them to the control of raw mix chemical composition, kiln-cooler control, sensor validity checking and alarm logging, production and trend data logging, and daily operating reports.

Grinding mill load control and DDC are also operating in a number of U.S. cement plants with DDC being more widely used in the last few years. Most new cement plants outside of the United States and Canada are designed by Europeans. In some instances selected European designed cement plants have been significantly altered in their design concepts to better interface with automatic process control principles and equipment. The purpose has also been to keep overall investment to a minimum. Thus a trend for such plants is to not only perform the control and other functions just listed, but to often include, as appropriate, additional functions of

1) quarry scheduling guidance;
2) prehomogenizing pile building control;
3) prehomogenizing pile building calculations;
4) grinding mill load control with maximizing as well as steady-state versions being utilized and with fineness loops, in some cases, being used based on continuous fineness sensors;
5) cement mix composition control;
6) cement silo monitoring and validity checking;
7) monitoring of drives for unscheduled shutdowns;
8) automatic start-up and shutdown of continuous process departments by programmed logic, including transient manipulation of regulating loops as well as ON–OFF control of drives themselves;
9) control of overall load coupling for departments between which relatively low surge capacity for materials exists.

A more detailed description of many of these functions is given in [5].

INCREASING AVAILABILITY OF AUTOMATIC PROCESS CONTROL SYSTEMS BY ADEQUATE POWER SUPPLIES

As briefly mentioned previously, a distinct need is to more thoroughly analyze the interrelation of the power supply for the automatic process control system and its major components and the power distribution system characteristics. The distinctive solution—and trend— found useful in many such automatic process control systems is to isolate the power supply for the process control computer and certain critical sensors (such as X-ray gauge and analyzer, oxygen analyzer, and selected instrumentation). This isolated power supply is often in the form of a separate induction or dc motor-driven alternator equipped with a flywheel and necessary control to ride through most power system transient disturbances. Such as isolated power supply, when properly designed, provides clean power to these control components.

The result of using such an isolated clean ride-through power supply is that the process control equipment is not harmed, or taken out of service, during momentary dips or voltage losses in the main power supply. In addition, the surges which sometimes get into the main power distribution system and its major components are kept out of the process control equipment.

As plants are designed which integrate automation and plant design together more carefully and include automatic start-up and shutdown of selected portions of the process, the isolated ride-through power supply concept is extended to also include power to the relays controlling the motor control centers themselves. This lays a basis for rapid restart of critical portions of the process following temporary shutdowns due to a short-term loss of voltage in the main plant power system.

In some instances the ride-through power supply becomes battery supported for, say, periods of from 5 to 30 min in order to permit standby auxiliary Diesel engine generator sets to be activated and take over the function of supplying critical loads for slow turning of the kiln, for operating pumps, fans, and cooler grates during loss of power from the normal main power source to the plant.

The ability to quickly restart the continuous process parts of the plant after a shutdown due to temporary loss of power system supply voltage is becoming increasingly important in another way. Most interconnected public utility power systems must use high-speed reclosing on their main transmission lines to keep separate generating stations in synchronism during short circuits occurring on lines which interconnect such generating stations. Unless the short circuit is removed promptly and the interconnection between generators restored promptly, the separate generating stations tend to swing apart sufficiently so that they cannot be safely reclosed together without elaborate time-consuming resynchronizing provisions.

The effects of this high-speed short-circuit interruption and subsequent high-speed reclosing, as seen at the cement plant bus, is that power is lost for typically 1/3–1/2 s, after which power comes back from the utility. During that short time, most drives shut down due to their using instantaneous undervoltage protection.

MINICOMPUTERS FOR CEMENT PLANT CONTROL

During most of the time in which digital process computers have been applied to cement plants, adequate software with interface hardware and necessary peripheral equipment have been available only with medium-sized process control computers. These medium process control computers have the capability of doing any or all of the functions listed in the preceding section of this paper, either individually or simultaneously. Because such medium process computers have substantial total capabilities, they tended to be uneconomic when being considered for a single particular control function such as, for example, control of raw mix chemical composition.

Small or minicomputers have been available for many years. Yet by themselves they are relatively useless on a real-time process control job unless an adequate library of standard software and good application software especially tailored for real-time process control are available. Moreover, the lack of adequate supporting interface hardware particularly suited to the industries to be served had reduced their usefulness in such industries.

Surveys of many existing cement plants in the United States concerning the possbility of applying automatic process control have disclosed that there is a need and a potential usefulness for minicomputers if they are adequately equipped with supporting standard and application software, necessary interface hardware, and supporting training and other installation services.

Such a recent development is shown in Figs. 10–12. These figures show block diagrams of a line of minicomputers backed up by adequate standard software, hardware, and services all aimed at serving this segment of the cement manufacturing industry.

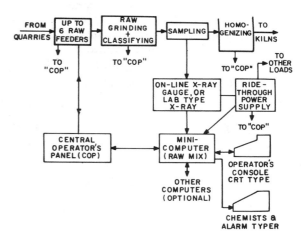

Fig. 10. Raw mix control with minicomputer package using X-ray sensing of chemical composition.

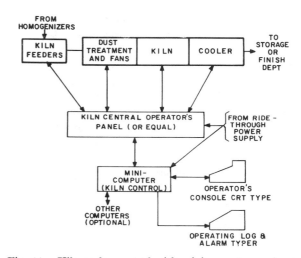

Fig. 11. Kiln-cooler control with minicomputer package.

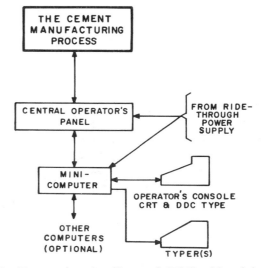

Fig. 12. Process data handling and DDC with minicomputer package.

The three minicomputer-based automation systems shown in Figs. 10–12 are for raw mix chemical composition control, for kiln control, and for extended digital capability (including generic DDC software). Each system has the following control equipment and operational features: they are all built around a minicomputer system of hardware and standard library programs designed to meet process control requirements; controls process through outputs to control devices typically on the COP; each utilizes modern reliable devices for interface with operator–video-type of operator's console plus typer for combination operator's log and alarm log; each is a complete and independent system; each is powered from a ride-through power supply; and each can communicate with other mini-computer-based systems belonging to its own family as appropriate.

The raw mix system shown in Fig. 10 includes an X-ray analyzer for elemental analysis of the raw mix stream samples. The functional control provided by the pre-engineered software will control up to six raw material feeders, correcting feeder rates as necessary to maintain the sample analysis at the proper chemical composition. The system will also control up to two homogenizers to be batch or continuous filled for a specific chemical composition by adjusting the chemical composition hold point for the raw mix stream. A chemist's log with paper tape punch and reader for dumping and loading programs are included, as is the capacity for various custom options.

The kiln-control system shown in Fig. 11 provides the basic functions of maintaining stable kiln operation through proper setting and adjustment of the primary kiln variables such as feed rates, speed, fuel flow, and air-to-fuel ratio. Cooler grater and gas flow are also controlled as appropriate to the type of clinker cooler used. The system has the capability of being able to control the various types of kiln-cooler combinations, dry and wet feed, with and without preheater. Kiln performance log is included, as in the capacity for various custom options.

The system for extended digital capability provides the capacity for extensive data acquisition, for monitoring and alarming, and for daily production summary, and other logging functions; and combined with the extensive data acquisition capacity is the availability of DDC software for digital control of any or all process loops. The set points for the DDC process loops are normally set at the operator's video-type console, although supervisory controls of those set points from another minicomputer system family member is also possible (Fig. 12).

In addition to the previously described equipment and operational features, the successful minicomputer-based automation system must continue to include the full complement of all organizational backing by both users and supplier, including awareness, training, and commitment by the user, and including adequate installation start-up assistance, and follow-on service availability by the supplier. The minicomputer-based system then is simply an extension of the latest automation technology to meet the evolving needs of the cement industry. All of the fundamental requirements for success still exist and must continue to be met for successful automation to result.

Conclusions

We may conclude the following.

1) The cement plant owner and his representatives have available even wider choices than before as to the sizes and capabilities of automatic process control systems which they can economically use.

2) This broadening of the base for process automatic control computers to also include the minicomputers, adequately supported by standard software and interface hardware, means that many existing plants can have automation applied to at least portions of their process which may not have been very economical hitherto.

3) Adequate people factors including appropriate job assignments of operating personnel and their supervision, combined with good initial and continued training remain vital for success in automatic control.

4) The possibilities of modifying basic plant design for new plants to better adapt to the possibilities of automatic process control are exciting. They lay a basis for significantly changing for the better total plant investment and operating profitability.

5) Success in achieving automatic process control is not an accident. Success is best designed-in from the beginning. To be attained, it principally includes owner involvement from the beginning and thereafter plus heavy supplier involvement from the beginning but tapering off as operation on control proceeds.

6) Principal essential ingredients for success with the typical accountability for each have now been identified for automatic process control systems in cement manufacturing plants. Typical economic benefits derived from successful automatic process control by digital computer installation have also been identified.

References

[1] Computer Users Symposium, "Scoreboard of process control computers for the cement industry," presented at the 1969 IEEE Cement Industry Technical Conference, Toronto, Ont., Canada, May 13–15.
[2] R. E. Evans and J. H. Herz, "Seven years of process computer control at California Portland Cement Company," *IEEE Trans. Ind. Gen. Appl.*, vol. IGA-6, Sept./Oct. 1970, pp. 472–475.
[3] S. R. B. Opie, "Direct digital control—a total system approach," *1967 IEEE Conv. Rec.*
[4] H. Egger, "Design and conception of integrated automated cement plants," *IEEE Trans. Ind. Gen. Appl.*, vol. IGA-5, Nov./Dec. 1969, pp. 752–758.
[5] M. R. Hurlbut, D. L. Lippitt, and E. A. E. Rich, "Applications of digital computer control to the cement manufacturing process," presented at the 1968 Int. Seminar on Automatic Control in Lime, Cement, and Connected Industries, Brussels, Belgium, Sept. 9–13.
[6] J. Warshawsky and E. S. Porter, "Automatic sampling and measurement of surface area of pulverized material," *IEEE Trans. Ind. Gen. Appl.*, vol. IGA-5, Nov./Dec. 1969, pp. 773–778.
[7] F. Lebel, A. Guy, and D. E. Hamilton, "Computer direction of quarry operations," *Rock Products*, Mar. 1967.
[8] S. Levine, "Sophisticated sampling systems optimize computer operations at Allentown Portland Cement," *Rock Products*, Apr. 1967.

[9] D. D. Bedworth and J. R. Faillace, "Instrumenting cement plant for digital computer control," *ISA J.*, Nov. 1963.

[10] J. R. Romig, W. R. Morton, and R. A. Phillips, "Making cement with a computer control system," presented at the 1964 IEEE Cement Industry Technical Conference, Pasadena, Calif., Apr. 14–17.

[11] J. R. Romig and W. R. Morton, "Application of a digital computer to the cement-making process," *IEEE Trans. Ind. Electron. Centr. Instrum.*, vol. IECI-13, Apr. 1966, pp. 2–9.

[12] E. A. E. Rich, "Cement automation—1965," presented at the 1965 IEEE Cement Industry Technical Conference, Allentown, Pa., May 12–14.

[13] J. Scrimgeour, "Instrumentation and control for industrial minerals—current and future," *Can. Mining Met. Bull.*, July 1967.

[14] C. J. Dick and R. G. Schlauch, "Large size clinker cooler operations," presented at the 3rd Annu. Cement Industry Operations Seminar, Chicago, Ill., Nov. 26–28, 1967.

The operation of a paper machine is critically affected by the complex interaction of subsystems that traditionally are subjected to independent control action. This article describes the design of a control system for a paper machine that takes into account such interaction, and shows how the design technique may be applied to a basis-weight/moisture-control system.

Interactive Control of Paper Machines

E. B. DAHLIN, Measurex, Inc.

Good paper-machine control must include coordination of such subsystems as refiner, headbox, and dryer, and speed and stock feed. Without such coordination, control actions that are taken in one part of the overall process may be major sources of upset in another part. Specifically, refiner adjustments may upset moisture control; speed changes may influence paper formation unless compensatory headbox actions are taken; setpoint changes in basis weight may cause both an upset in moisture content and a variation in sheet strength.

Effective handling of interactions among paper-machine subsystems may be initiated by constructing a control system that takes advantage of existing analog controls while employing the full power of digital computing techniques. The resulting control system is not too complex, yet greatly improves the output product, and at the same time keeps open as much digital computer capacity as possible for more sophisticated algorithm implementation.

For a general approach to mathematical modeling for the paper industry, Ref. 1 is suggested. Previous work by the author on certain algorithms appears in Refs. 2, 3, 4, and 5. The experimental data used in this article was gathered as described in Refs. 3 and 5.

Paper machine influences

The table on the next page establishes qualitative relationships among essential independent variables that may be either random disturbances or manipulation inputs, and an array of dependent variables. Variables preceded by an asterisk are normally manipulated and variables that can be observed are boxed.

Control objectives may be defined from a study of this table. The basic need for automatic regulation stems from the existence of the disturbance variables. Measured and manipulated variables afford possibilities for forming feedback control loops. The table also indicates simultaneous effects of manipulated variables upon variables related to specifications for the product quality, such as basis weight, moisture, and formation.

It is often useful to stabilize fiber flow by cascaded control around the stock valve. In the table, fiber flow is identified as dry stock flow (DSF), and is defined as the product of consistency and stock flow. The feedback loop, closed from calculated DSF to stock valve position, will be affected by consistency reading noise and temperature impact on the consistency meter calibration.

However, these steady-state calibration errors are not too critical to good control because the long-term behavior of fiber flow is determined by feedback of basis weight. The usefuless of the calculated DSF loop is rather to prevent short-term variation in consistency from upsetting the basis weight and the moisture content of the reel.

The feedback loop from steam pressure to steam valve position is normally implemented with analog pneumatic controllers. Within the dynamic range of this control loop, the effects of steam line pressure and flash tank pressure are prevented from propagating through the system to influence dryer heat flow rate and reel moisture.

Interactive computer control system

The block diagram of Figure 1 shows how a digital computer may be applied to a paper machine for the purpose of improving product quality through more sophisticated control of interactions among operating subsystems. The computer receives measurements of quality-defining variables and performs highly complex analysis of, for example, nonlinear calibration characteristics and calibration parameters for different paper grades. Production rates, fiber consumption per produced reel, and means and variances of quality-defining variables can be prepared regularly for management. The computer can calculate on-

Reprinted with permission from *Contr. Eng.*, vol. 17, pp. 76–81, Jan. 1970.

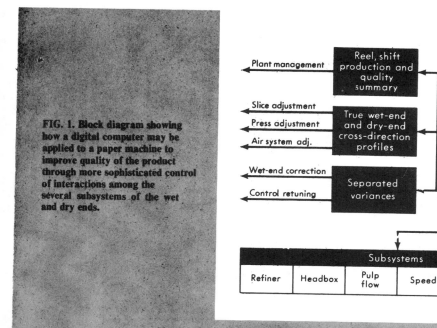

FIG. 1. Block diagram showing how a digital computer may be applied to a paper machine to improve quality of the product through more sophisticated control of interactions among the several subsystems of the wet and dry ends.

line the true cross-direction profiles of, say, basis weight, bone-dry weight, and moisture.

These and other complex functions are routinely performed as shown in Figure 1, where the computer implements algorithms to supplement the analog control of local operations. This system incorporates features that are not generally included in paper-machine control.

To illustrate the methods used, a relatively simple system for controlling basis weight and moisture will now be discussed (Figure 2).

The subsystem for pulp-flow control consists of a flowmeter feeding a signal to an analog flow controller, which then manipulates the stock valve position. A consistency meter transmits a signal to the digital computer. A program provides digital filtering for eliminating high-frequency noise associated with the consistency measurement. After noise removal, the program calculates flow set-point corresponding to fiber flow (dry stock flow or DSF). Implementation of this loop with a mixture of analog and digital hardware provides a profitable balancing between dynamic performance and cost.

The dryer-control system is a conventional pneumatic control loop regulating the steam pressure in a dryer section, usually the one directly ahead of the basis weight and moisture scanner.

The supervisory controller utilizes measurements of basis weight and moisture obtained (preferably) at scanning speeds between 500 and 1,000 in. per min. These speeds enable the computer to have better process information to work with in, for example, calculating cross-direction profiles.

Process identification

The objective of process identification is to determine process dynamics parameters—a must step in constructing the process mathematical model if an adequate control system is to result. The parameters are

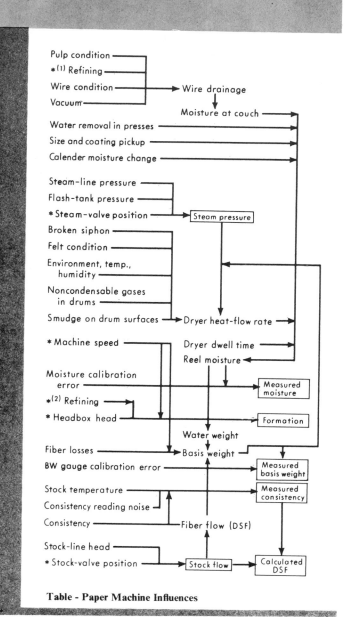

Table - Paper Machine Influences

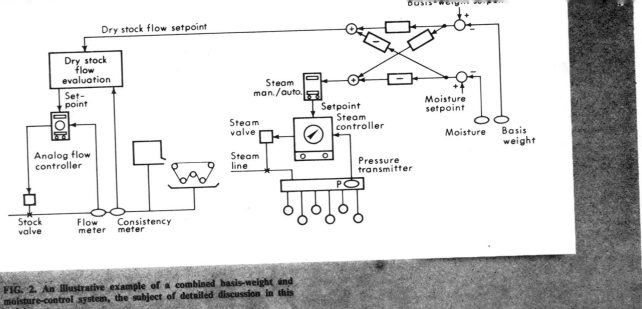

required for both the design and the tuning phases.

The procedure is to introduce small upsets in the manipulated variables and collect the response data in computer memory. After a small perturbation of the stock valve, for instance, a variation in stock flow, consistency, basis weight, and moisture will be observed. Again, a small variation in steam pressure setpoint will cause changes in steam pressure, moisture, and basis weight that are transmitted to the computer. The required parameters are obtained by analysis of such response data.

The criterion for a good model is that it provide the basis for good control-system tuning. The degree of needed accuracy of parameter estimation also depends on the loop sensitivity to discrepancies between assumed model structure with parameter values and actual process dynamics.

In the application being discussed, an adequate model structure can be derived from the wet-end model equations of Beecher, Ref. 1. Ignoring the head box time constant, the simplified linear model developed by Beecher is

$$\frac{\Delta BW}{\Delta DSF} = K_b e^{-s\tau} \frac{1 + \tau_2 s}{1 + \frac{\tau_2 s}{r_f}} \tag{1}$$

where ΔBW = basis weight change at the reel
ΔDSF = change of concentrated pulp flow to paper machine (gallons dry pulp per min.)
K_b = gain constant
τ = transport delay from stock valve to reel
τ_2 = mixing time constant in the wire pit
r_f = the fraction of fiber flow that does not circulate through the wire pit (retention)
s = Laplacian operator

This model being acceptable for the wet end of the machine, the dryer is next considered. The nature of a response to a small steam-pressure change is obtained from a heat-flow analysis of the drum, Figure

3. If the felt is the same temperature as the pocket air, the heat flow per unit area may be modeled as in Figure 4. The driving signal is the temperature on the inner surface of the condensate. The sheet is considered as having a wet and a dry section, the latter resisting water removal. The rate of water removal is

$$F_w = CU_{4w}(T_4 - T_w) \tag{2}$$

where C = reciprocal enthalpy of water evaporation
U_{4w} = heat conductivity per unit area between the wet sheet node
T_4 = temperature of the fibers in the sheet
T_w = temperature of the water in the sheet

With temperature as the analog of voltage, heat capacity as the analog of electric capacity, and heat-transfer numbers as analogs of electric conductivities, the transfer function for Figure 4 may be written

$$\frac{F_w(s)}{T_1(s)} = \frac{C\eta}{R_t} \frac{AB}{(s+A)(s+B)} \tag{3}$$

where

$$\eta = \frac{U_{4w}}{U_{4w} + \frac{1}{R_{45} + R_{50}}} = \text{incremental dryer efficiency} \tag{4}$$

$$R_t = R_{12} + R_{23} + R_p \tag{5}$$

$$R_p = R_{34} + \frac{1}{U_{4w} + \frac{1}{R_{4w} + R_{50}}} \tag{6}$$

$$R_{ij} = 1/U_{ij}$$

A, B = characteristic radian frequencies of the network

When the sheet is transported through the dryer section—all of whose drums are assumed to have the

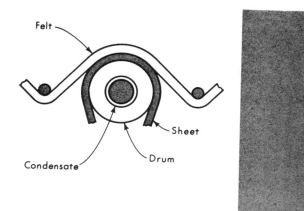

FIG. 3. Cross-section of dryer drum used to develop model, Figure 4.

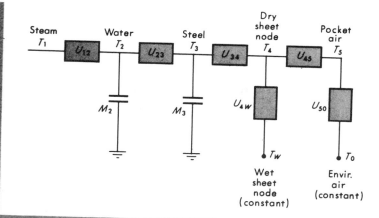

FIG. 4. Electrical analog network for dryer drum, explained in text.

same characteristics—the total water content of the sheet element is

$$w(t_1; t_0) = w(t_0; t_0) - \int_{t_0}^{t_1} \gamma F_w \, dt \qquad (7)$$

where $w(t_1; t_0)$ = weight of water per unit area at time of the element that entered the dryer section at time t_0.

γ = the fraction of the total dwelling time in the section during which the sheet element is in contact with the steam drums

From the concept of Equation 7, the water content seen by a fixed observer located at the end of the dryer section and watching the sheets go by can be expressed by the differential equation

$$\frac{dw(t)}{dt} = \frac{dw_0}{dt}(t - \tau_d) - \gamma \left[F(t) - F(t - \tau_d) \right] \qquad (8)$$

where $w(t)$ = water weight per unit area at dryer end
$w_0(t)$ = water weight pua at dryer entry
τ_d = dwelling time in the dryer section

Taking the Laplacian transform of Equation 8 and combining the result with Equation 3 yields the dryer-section transfer function:

$$\frac{w(s)}{T_1(s)} = - \frac{\gamma C \mu}{R_t} \frac{A}{s+A} \frac{B}{s+B} \frac{1 - e^{-s\tau}d}{s} \qquad (9)$$

The constants A and B depend upon the heat-transfer coefficients and the heat capacities of the system, and are difficult to estimate. In a typical dryer, A varies widely while B is relatively independent of the heat transfer to the drum, Figure 5. The A reflects the condition of the internal heat transfer of the drum. Analysis of heat transfer between drum and sheet, wet and dry sheet nodes, and sheet to air pocket shows that A and B are both fairly independent of these parameters.

Equations 1 and 9 define a reasonably adequate model structure for purposes of process identifica-

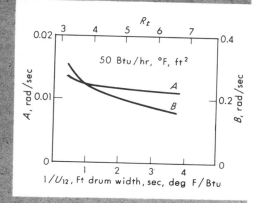

FIG. 5. Comparison plot of characteristic radian frequencies A and B of the dryer-drum analog of Figure 4.

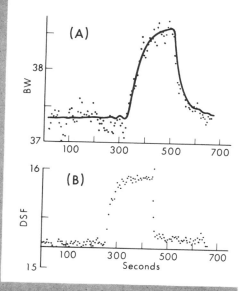

FIG. 6. Response to perturbations during an identification experiment of A (basis weight) and B (dry stock flow). The solid curve of Figure 6A is the response to the data in Figure 6B when used as a driver of the basis-weight model. Correspondence of this curve with the plotted data shows that a good model has been constructed.

tion. It is in practice feasible, Ref. 3, to combine these two structures into a single form:

$$Ke^{-s\tau} \frac{C}{s+C} \qquad (10)$$

where K, τ, and C are gain, transport delay, and pole, respectively. Each of these parameters is individually determined for the two transfer functions of Equations 1 and 9. If this simplified form is used, there must be very short intervals between perturbations on the identification process, Ref. 3. A method for determining K, τ, and C by analysis of the data from an identification experiment is given in Refs. 2 and 6.

Figure 6 shows the response to perturbations during an identification experiment of A, basis weight, and B, dry stock flow. When the input time series data of Figure 6B is used to drive the basis-weight model, the solid curve of Figure 6A results, indicating by agreement with plotted data that a good process model has been established in the computer.

Exposing the steam-pressure setpoint to perturbations yields the nonlinear behavior shown in Figure 7A, revealing the water-removal limitations of the steam drums. Figure 7B shows correspondence between observed response of moisture content and response obtained from driving the model with the data of Figure 7A.

The method illustrated here has been tested over many variables on a variety of paper machines. The conclusion is that effective tuning of larger systems can be accomplished by this method of process identification.

The control algorithms

For the system of Figure 2, algorithms are designed to obtain a specified response to setpoint changes in either moisture or basis weight. This response is overshoot-free and has exponential settling characteristics. Observations of closed-loop operation have been made on many installations, and the effectiveness of loop decoupling and transport delay has been verified, Refs. 4 and 5.

The process model of Figure 8 is used for controller design. The hold blocks maintain a continuous output signal updated periodically by the computer, which acts as a sampling device. The hold functions are incorporated in the steam manual-auto station and the analog flow controller shown in Figure 2.

The closed-loop dynamics of the steam-pressure loop are represented by a single pole, E. Crosscoupling characteristics are indicated by parameters α_1 and α_2. An illustrative example of crosscoupling networks is given in Figure 9 and discussed later in some detail.

The dynamic effects of scanning, and of the resulting control by the cross-machine averages for moisture and basis weight (alternately bone dry and conditioned), are included in the model of Figure 8. The averages are calculated from sums formed over the samples taken during a single scan. In the model, continuous integration serves as an approximation for this calculation. Such approximation significantly reduces the complexity of the final control algorithm without producing any effect on control-system tuning. The symbol z^{-1} indicates a time shift equal to the scanning time increment T.

In Figure 10, speed of settling is shown as being dependent on a parameter (λ) that is chosen as high as possible consistent with permissible frequency and amplitude for steam pressure and stock-flow changes demanded by the controller. Better control requires greater activity in manipulating variables. Often, however, the maximum value of λ is determined by overshoot characteristics generated by nonlinear phenomena not accounted for in the model.

As to decoupling, let it be assumed that a moisture setpoint change is made, Figure 9. The algorithm $C11$ will then see a positive moisture error d and call for a steam pressure decrease e. When steam pressure

FIG. 7. A—Plot of steam pressure variation obtained by exposing its setpoint to step perturbations. B.—Correspondence between observed response of moisture content and response obtained by driving the model with the data of Figure 7A.

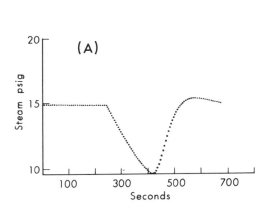

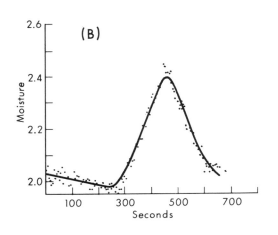

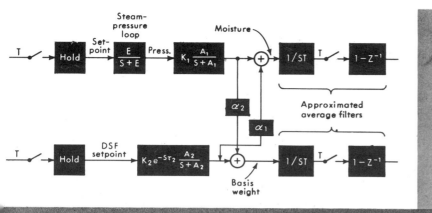

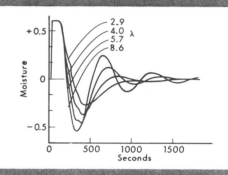

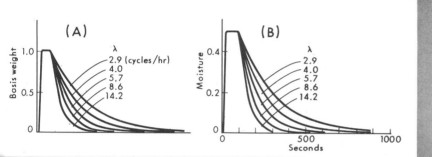

FIG. 10. Settling speed curves for basis weight (A) and moisture (B) shown dependent on the value of parameter λ explained in text.

FIG. 11. Response curves of the moisture side of the controller with all cross-coupling removed. Note the oscillatory results for various values of the parameter λ.

decreases, basis weight and moisture will be affected according to response curves indicated by f and g. Due to process interaction, not only is moisture changed but basis weight is also upset. Eventually the basis weight algorithm $C22$ would correct the basis weight error, but this needless upset is avoided by operation of the decoupling algorithms $C12$ and $C21$.

Algorithm $C21$ will have already seen the moisture error d that occurred with the setpoint change, and called for a stock-flow decrease h. This has resulted in a nullifying effect on moisture and basis weight as indicated by signals j and k. Proper selection of algorithm $C12$ can similarly offset the effect of a basis-weight setpoint change on moisture.

In addition to interaction-free setpoint change, the decoupled controller achieves much faster control action than do independent basis weight and moisture controllers, Figure 11. Using normalized units to indicate deviation from setpoint, the graph shows moisture response to an upset when the two controllers are applied without decoupling algorithms. The graph may be compared with moisture response in Figure 10B, where much tighter control is obtained with good stability.

The decoupled controller prevents unnecessary control actions. When a consistency variation causes simultaneous upset in basis weight and moisture, for example, the combined effect of the algorithms in Figure 9 will cause a stock-valve correction, leaving steam pressure unaffected.

It is hoped that this discussion of a combined basis weight and moisture-controller design has indicated how the basic principles may be applied to much more complex control systems.

REFERENCES

1. "Dynamic Modeling Technique in the Paper Industry," A. E. Beecher, *TAPPI*, Vol. 48, No. 2, pp. 117-120, February 1963.
2. "On-Line Identification of Process Dynamics," E. B. Dahlin, *IBM Journal of Research & Development*, Vol. 11, No. 4, pp. 408-426, July 1967.
3. "Process Identification and Control on a Paper Machine," E. B. Dahlin and I. B. Sanborn, IFAC/IFIP Symposium, "Digital Control of Large Industrial Systems," Toronto, Canada, June 17-19, 1968.
4. "Designing and Tuning Digital Controllers," Part I, E. B. Dahlin, *Instruments and Control Systems,* June 1968.
5. "Designing and Tuning Digital Controllers," Part II, E. B. Dahlin, R. L. Zimmer, M. G. Horner, and W. A. Wickstrom, *Instruments and Control Systems,* July 1968.
6. "Process Identification for Control System Design and Tuning," E.B. Dahlin, Measurex Corp., and D.B. Brewster, Westvaco Corp., *Control Engineering,* April 1969, p. 81.

THE MINICOMPUTER APPROACH TO
PREDICTIVE COMPENSATION

Conrad P. Pracht
Jackson Associates
4663 Executive Drive
Columbus, Ohio

Summary

The theory concerning the use of fast-time simulation to realize a near-ideal predictor for sampled control systems is discussed, and an evaluation is presented of its use as a method of compensation. A comparison is made between near-ideal predictive compensation and conventional compensation. When the approaches are combined they form a new and versatile approach to compensation.

Computer studies indicate that even when the fast-time simulation model of the physical system is inexact the fundamental advantages of near-ideal predictive compensation are retained. The ability of this technique to provide, in effect, a zero without a pole in the z-plane offers unique advantages to control of many systems.

This technique, easily implemented with modern minicomputers, provides the ambitious control engineer with a new approach to system compensation complete with analysis. The analysis assumes the fast-time simulation model is exact, yet for many practical situations it represents a realistic approximation.

Introduction

As long ago as 1954, Ziebolz and Paynter[1] recognized the possible applications of fast-time simulation in control systems, either to provide a predictive display to aid in manual control or to close a control loop through a time-scaling servomechanism. Their work was prompted by the realization that a manual operator generally "predicts" the system response and modifies his control parameter according to some "intuitive" criterion developed through experience. It was later demonstrated[2] that through use of a predictive display an operator can enhance his ability to control a system, if he is presented with an accurate "prediction" on which to base his "intuitive" correction. Since the prediction is made repeatedly in fast time, the operator need only change his control parameter until the predicted outcome agrees with the desired outcome. If the fast-time model is correct, this technique is quite effective. It has been used to aid manual operators in controlling submarines, and was considered for spacecraft rendezvous control problems. Unfortunately, when the number of degrees of freedom increases, the complexity of the display increases. More than two degrees of freedom are almost impossible for an operator to handle.

As pointed out by Ziebolz and Paynter, the process could be fully automated by programming a set of decision criteria to be used in selection of the desired control parameter. In 1955, Ziebolz et al[3] patented a fast-time simulation controller which

a) predicted the future of the variable, assuming no disturbance during the computation cycle,

b) controlled the fast-time model rather than the physical system, and

c) sampled the control action of the fast-time controller and drove the physical system with a servo which reduced the control valve travel rate of the fast-time controller by the ratio of the two time scales.

In the last decade, many engineers have attempted to use predictive techniques, some with success, others without. Predictive control had a purely intuitive foundation. It worked, sometimes, but was not supported by theory. Recent industrial results[4,5] indicate that a practical need exists for both theory and implementation of predictive fast-time simulation systems. Until clear guidelines are established to aid the control engineer, only the adventurous will attempt to apply predictive techniques.

Recent advances in two separate domains may help to bridge the gap that presently exists between theory and practice of fast-time simulation systems.

First, research in prediction theory[6] led to the inclusion of an ideal predictor in the forward path of a linear error-sampled system. Soon thereafter, this work was extended[7] to include a near-ideal predictor that could be realized using fast-time simulation. Thus, for at least one class of systems, the gap has been bridged between prediction theory and application.

During the same time period, advances in solid state and integrated circuit technology led to the second important development destined to aid predictive control, namely, the minicomputer. Minicomputers and stored-program digital controllers have become so plentiful that prices have dropped below $10,000, even to $5,000, making them quite practical for many control applications[8]. They are so fast that typical industrial processes can be simulated in a few milliseconds, allowing their use as a fast-time simulation of the process. The minicomputer is the necessary tool required to realize predictive control.

Reprinted from *IEEE Trans. Ind. Electron. Contr. Instrum.*, vol. IECI-17, pp. 272–276, June 1970.

Realizable Prediction

To examine realizable prediction, we must first define the term prediction. A device whose output represents its input T units of time into the future has the transfer function e^{Ts} and is called an ideal predictor. The Laplace Transform of the output is

$$F(s)e^{Ts} = F(s) + sTF(s) + \frac{s^2T^2}{2!} F(s) + \ldots \quad (1)$$

It can easily be seen then, that ideal prediction involves the generation of an infinite number of derivatives. Even the first few derivatives are difficult to generate in practice. However, if a system can be modeled exactly and a simulation performed in fast time, then the value of the system output at a future time can be determined from the simulated output. This, of course, assumes that the input will not change during the interval of prediction, and that there will be no disturbances. Allowing these assumptions, ideal prediction at discrete intervals of time into the future can be achieved, if the system can be modeled exactly.

Consider the system shown in Fig. 1. For the block labeled FAST TIME SIMULATION PREDICTOR to represent an ideal predictor with Laplace Transform e^{Ts}, it must accept an input from sampler S1 at time nT and provide the predicted error, the error that will appear at sampler S1 at time (n+1)T, at sampler S2 at time nT. This can be done with a single-parameter optimizer operating in fast time on the equation

$$e_p(nT) = e((n+1)T). \quad (2)$$

If the optimization could be performed in zero time, an ideal prediction of T seconds would be the result. Actually, because of the delay of optimization, dT, the ideal prediction realized is of T(1-d) seconds. Alternately, one could consider this an ideal prediction of T seconds, with the output of the predictor delayed by dT seconds.

The fast-time simulation predictor, Fig. 2, begins its operation by sampling the input and initial conditions of the system. As the output of the predictor will be delayed by the realization time, dT, the optimizer must begin its simulation runs at time (n+d)T. Thus, the first task to be completed in the fast-time simulation is the computation of the system conditions at time (n+d)T. These values must be used as the initial conditions for all optimization runs. The equation to be minimized is $e_p((n+d)T) = e((n+1)T)$. Almost any optimization routine may be used. For this type of function, use of optimization routines which insure convergence in a fixed period of time simplify the analysis. After the optimizer converges, the predicted error, $e_p((n+d)T)$, is available to drive the system. At each sampling instant the process is repeated. Thus, the predictor block can be described by the term $e^{(1-d)Ts}$, as in Fig. 3.

It should be recognized that, provided the input is varying slowly enough, the above process could be repeated to determine the error several sampling periods into the future. Then the predictor block would be described by the term $e^{(p-d)Ts}$, where p is the number of samples of prediction.

A Second Order Example

A typical second order system with two integrations and a realizable predictor is shown in Fig. 4. For a unit step disturbance, the output transform in the z domain can be expressed as

$$C(z,m) = \frac{A(1)z^2 + A(2)z + A(3)}{B(0)z^3 + B(1)z^2 + B(2)z + B(3)} \quad (3)$$

where

$$A(0) = 0$$

$$A(1) = KT^2m^2$$

$$A(2) = KT^2(1+2m - 2m^2)$$

$$A(3) = KT^2(1-2m+m^2)$$

$$B(0) = 2+KT^2(1-d)^2 \quad (4)$$

$$B(1) = 6-dKT^2(4-3d)$$

$$B(2) = 6+KT^2(1+2d-3d^2)$$

$$B(3) = -2-KT^2d^2$$

and the terms are defined as

K = gain of integrator

d = realization delay

T = sampling period

m = modified z-transform operator.

A root locus plot of this system in the z plane is shown in Fig. 5 for several values of d. For d=1 the locus is always outside the unit circle, denoting an unstable system if the predictor were not used. For d=0 the locus never leaves the unit circle, in which case the system is stable regardless of the gain K. Figure 6 demonstrates the response of the system to a unit step disturbance for varying realization delay d with T=1 and K=2. If d is greater than .5, the system is unstable. It is significant to note that for d=.2, the system response is quite satisfactory. An optimization time of two-tenths the sampling period is easily realizable for many systems.

It should be pointed out that predictive compensation techniques need not be used alone. When used in conjunction with conventional sampled-data compensation techniques, a notable improvement can be achieved. For this example system the use of a series compensator,

$D(z) = 2(z - .4)/z$, results in the step response shown in Fig. 7. The curve labeled D(z)=1 denotes the response without the series compensator.

Time Delay Systems

As might be expected, the inclusion of a block with a transfer function of $e^{(1-d)Ts}$ into the forward path of a system containing a time delay, e^{-Ts}, results in a significant improvement in the system response. In fact, the ability of this technique to provide, in effect, a zero in the z plane without a pole offers a complete cancellation of the phase shift of the time delay, leaving only the physical delay itself to differentiate the response from that of a system without a time delay; assuming, of course, that one can exactly model the system and that the input is constant from one sampling instant to the next.

It should be recognized that, even when the input changes between the sampling instants, the system response will generally be satisfactory; the only problem is that during that sampling period the analysis cannot be used to describe the system performance. This disadvantage is indeed minor, since analytical tools at best are merely approximations to the real world.

Use of this technique allows the stability of time delay systems to be controlled independently of the time delay. If a time delay of three seconds is added to the system shown in Fig. 4, the response, Fig. 8, is seen to be identical to that of the curve labeled D(z)=1 in Fig. 7 except for the time delay of three seconds.

Non-Ideal Simulation

The fundamental weakness of the analysis presented in this paper is that the fast-time model of the system will never be exact. While this is true, it has been shown[9] that as long as the simulation is a nominal model of the system, the analysis represents a valid approximation and will produce meaningful results. In fact, on some occasions, an incorrect model will result in a better response than an ideal model would have. This is true because no attempt was made to optimize system response to a particular performance index.

Simulation Via Minicomputer

Having described the advantages of predictive control, it only remains to explain the use of a minicomputer to generate the predicted error. Consider the system shown in Fig. 9. At the beginning of each sampling period, the analog-to-digital converter samples the analog set point and the condition of the system variables and converts them to digital. These digital signals are used, in conjunction with an optimization routine, to operate on a digital simulation of the physical system which is stored in the digital computer. At the end of the optimization sequence, at most a few milliseconds, the correct predicted error is available, which must be converted to analog and can be used to drive the system.

It is important to note that any other digital compensation techniques may be applied to the system in the same algorithm; however, if the analysis is to remain exact, it is necessary to include any digital compensation in the simulation model as well as in the control loop.

Conclusion

Although predictive control now yields to analysis only in a few special cases, the advent of the minicomputer should make this approach to system control practical in many situations. Particularly when the system to be controlled contains a time delay does predictive compensation stand alone as a new tool which offers a significant improvement in system performance.

Although this approach has not yet been tested in an industrial atmosphere, numerous simulations that have been performed tend to substantiate the theory. It is expected that as familiarity with these techniques increases, general guidelines will appear to aid the control engineers in industrial applications. Because of the striking advantages of predictive control in time delay systems, early applications will most likely appear in that direction.

With or without analysis, predictive compensation is a new tool for control of industrial processes, to assist those adventurous enough to use it.

List of References

1. H. Ziebolz and H. M. Paynter, "Possibilities of a Two-Time-Scale Computing System for Control and Simulation of Dynamic Systems," Proceedings of the National Electronics Conference, 1954, pp. 215-223.

2. C. R. Kelley, "Predictor Instruments Look into the Future," Control Engineering, March 1962, pp. 86-90.

3. H. Ziebolz et al, "Electrical Analogue Device," U.S. Patent Number 2,712,414, July 5, 1955.

4. C. R. Kelley, "Closing the Loop with Predictive Controllers," Control Engineering, May 1968, pp. 75-78.

5. P. G. Adams and A. T. Schooley, "Ada-Predictive Control for a Batch Reaction," Instrumentation Technology, January 1969, pp. 57-62.

6. W. R. Light, "The Behavior of a Digital Predictive System," D.Sc. dissertation, University of Virginia, Charlottesville, Virginia, 1967.

7. C. P. Pracht, "Realizable Digital Predictive Compensation," Ph.D. dissertation, University of Virginia, Charlottesville, Virginia, 1970.

8. J. R. Copeland and S. P. Jackson, "Analysis of Small Computers Available for Process Control," paper 69-510, 1969 ISA Conference,

October 27-30, 1969, to be published in Instrumentation Technology.

9. C. P. Pracht and E. S. McVey, "Near-Ideal Digital Predictive Compensation," submitted to IEEE Transactions on Automatic Controls.

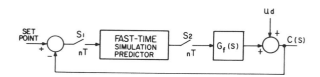

Figure 1   A Fast-Time-Simulation Predictive System

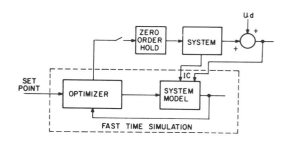

Figure 2   A Fast-Time-Simulation Predictor

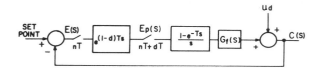

Figure 3   A General System with Near-Ideal Prediction

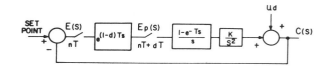

Figure 4   A Second Order System with Two Integrations

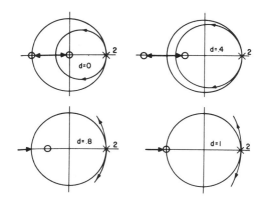

Figure 5   Root Locus of Second Order System with Near-Ideal Prediction

257

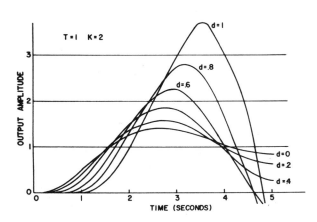

Figure 6   Response of Second Order Predictive System to a Unit Step Disturbance with K = 2, d varying.

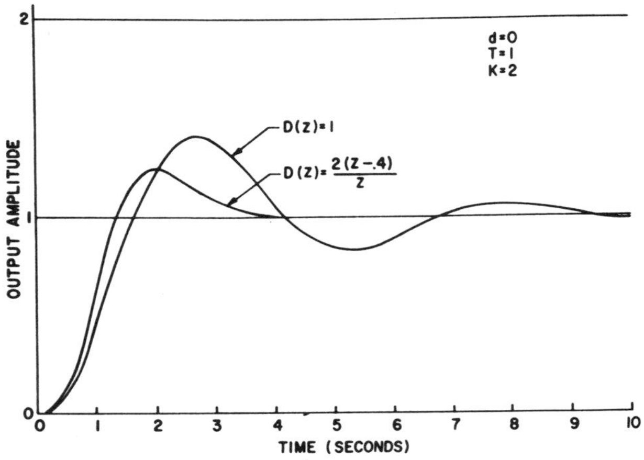

Figure 7   Second Order System Response with Both Discrete and Predictive Compensation

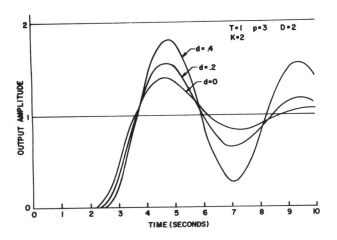

Figure 8   Response of Second Order System with a Time Delay

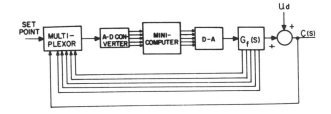

Figure 9   The Minicomputer Approach to Predictive Compensation

258

Part 6
Discrete Control Applications Including Testing, Production Control, and Manufacturing Information Systems

Introductory Comments

The applications discussed in previous parts were associated with more or less continuous systems where data was acquired from slowly varying analog signals and perhaps feedback control was used. Automation or control of discrete systems is a quite different but very important application of minicomputers. It appears that the greatest contribution to improved efficiency in manufacturing, testing, and other discrete operations will be through the use of on-line minicomputers. The impetus for this development comes from several directions, including the need to decrease costs in production, control production to meet delivery dates, and minimize in-process inventory. Equally important, however, is the demand for extensive quality control. This includes the need to test each and every item produced in contrast to sampling items for test purposes. This not only assures higher quality items, but also provides a greater degree of safety to the consumer in that most anomalies introduced in production can be eliminated by complete testing.

Similarly, the demand for mass production to minimize cost is often thwarted by the equally strong demand for variety in the product. It is only through computer controlled manufacturing systems that a large volume and variety of individual items can be combined economically.

The article by F. J. Clauss and R. M. McKay describes the total manufacturing control concept from design through production. They concentrate on a design system for numerically controlled machines and consider adaptive control of those machines, which is a natural computer application. In order to achieve the benefits of this system, however, it is necessary to have an integrated computer control system, as described by them.

C. A. Renouard describes the more complete manufacturing control system involving flow shops, job shops, and the information requirements needed to carry out inventory control, assembly, shipping, etc. It is important to note in these applications that the task carried out by the computer is far from trivial and may involve larger machines instead of minicomputers. Nonetheless, the minicomputer has an important role in smaller manufacturing systems, and the

259

ideas and techniques in these articles are then appropriate for such systems. Even in larger systems, however, minicomputers will probably be used throughout the plant to actually direct operations, receiving most of their own commands and objectives from a higher level computer. Consequently, to intelligently design such a system, it is necessary to understand the overall problem, including the task carried out by the higher level computer. This is most graphically illustrated in the article by J. E. Stuehler, who describes an overall manufacturing control system which has been implemented by the IBM Corporation and which has proved very successful in application. This article is concerned with the IBM System/360 implementation, but it should be noted that as a result of this experience the minicomputer System 7 was designed essentially for the discrete manufacturing control system on the plant floor and is tailored to economically implement the ideas and techniques developed in this system.

The remaining articles describe specific applications in more detail. For example, the two papers by D. M. Mueller and B. I. Zisk discuss the application of computers in warehousing and material handling. Much of the problem in manufacturing is keeping track of incoming material, material in process, and finished goods or inventory which involves, in a sense, control of the warehouse. Control in this case is not normal dynamic feedback control but rather ensuring that the right tools, the right parts, the right materials, the right people, and the right machine all come together at the right time and in the right place. The payoff here is, of course, on-time delivery, minimization of unused time of machines and people, and the capability of producing specialized items.

The last two articles describe minicomputer applications in the automotive industry, mainly the testing and adjusting of carburetors. This is an example of an application which is becoming more and more prevalent not only in the automotive industry but also in any industry producing consumer goods. Essentially the problem here is to test each device produced in order to ensure that it meets certain safety and pollution standards which have been set by law. If the device does not meet these standards, it is then adjusted so that the manufacturer can attest to the finished products meeting specified legal standards. Similar problems exist in tire manufacturing where it is necessary to detect any tire with a flaw or any tire that is out of round or not meeting other safety standards.

In all of these articles it is clear that the minicomputer is not the product but rather a tool which permits the implementation of a rather large and fairly complex systems application. The articles should be read from this point of view rather than merely as illustrations of minicomputer applications. In particular, it is clear that many of the techniques discussed in the papers on software are relevant here, and that furthermore, because each minicomputer is responsible for only one portion of a rather complex system, the integrated design is very critical.

Note, further, that input/output devices appropriate to discrete manufacturing applications are quite different from those for data acquisition or control. For example, important devices in manufacturing are logical input/output or relay position sensors for the detection of machine status, badge and card readers to detect the particular order or part passing the control point, and special input devices to automatically read identifying numbers on cartons, railroad card, pallets, or what-have-you, in the control of material handling. The fact that the input devices are radically different is a characteristic of most minicomputer applications, but it does not change the fundamental organization of the hardware and software.

Bibliography

[1] "Developing a long-term information systems strategy," J. F. Adham, *Automation*, Mar. 1971, pp. 44–49.

[2] "Production planning with the integrated Geamatic 1009 computer system," D. Anders, Allgemeine Elektricitates-Gesellschaft Aeg-Telefunken, UND 681. 14-52398:512

[3] "Central refinery computer control," P. N. Budzilovich, *Contr. Eng.*, vol. 16, Jan. 1969, pp. 103–107.

[4] "Closing the traffic control loop," D. L. Cooper and R. M. Knox, *Contr. Eng.*, vol. 17, Dec. 1970, pp. 34–38.

[5] "Using simulation to accomplish practical job sequencing," B. Z. Duhl and A. R. Stevens, *Automation*, Feb. 1971, pp. 62–65.

[6] "Storing and retrieving parts for production," *Automation*, Jan. 1971, pp. 38–40.

[7] "Liquid pipeline scheduling and control with on-line multiprogramming process computer," T. Flukinger and G. R. Smith, *IEEE Trans. Ind. Gen. Appl.*, vol. IGA-5, July/Aug. 1969, pp. 389–402.

[8] "Application of a minicomputer for control of dynamic analog simulation and diagnostic test techniques," S. Hardesty and F. Jones, *1971 IEEE Int. Conv. Dig.*, pp. 498–499.

[9] "Geamatic 1009 integrated computer system for real-time control of discrete manufacturing processes," W. Heusler and W. Hirsch, Allgemeine Elektricitats-Gesellschaft Aeg-Telefunken, UDC 681.14-523: 65.011.56

[10] "Company control via computer," B. Hodge, *Chem. Eng.*, June 7, 1965.

[11] "Plant automation systems," IBM Data Processing Application, IBM Doc. E20-0270-1, 1966.

[12] "Management information system for process plants," IBM Data Processing Application Note.

[13] "Minicomputer applications in the seventies," R. K. Jurgen, *IEEE Spectrum*, August 1970, pp. 37–52.

[14] "Expanding role of small computers," H. S. Kleiman, *Automation*, Aug. 1971, pp. 46–48.

[15] "IBM System/7 and plant automation," T. Harrison *et al.*, *IBM J. Res. Develop.*, Nov. 1970, pp. 652–661.

[16] "A look at minicomputer applications," G. Lapidus, *Contr. Eng.*, vol. 16, Nov. 1969, pp. 82–91.

Coming in the 70s . . .

Advanced computer-oriented techniques are turning into reality the dream of . . .

TOTAL MANUFA

By F. J. CLAUSS, Manufacturing Research Manager

R. M. McKAY, Automation Research Specialist

Manufacturing Research Organization
Lockheed Missiles & Space Co., Sunnyvale, Calif.

DURING THE PAST YEAR several aerospace, automotive, and machine tool companies have added direct computer control to their manufacturing operations. Direct computer control of manufacturing tools is also known as direct numerical control (DNC), computer numerical control (CNC), and computer - assisted manufacturing (CAM). This innovation represents a "quantum jump" of progress in the use of computer technology, rivaling the introduction of numerically controlled machine tools 15 years ago. But while direct computer control is a big jump in itself and provides immediate payoffs, its real significance is that it makes more practical many other sophisticated techniques such as conversational programming; in-process quality control; adaptive control;

and real-time management control. The 1970's will be a decade when computer technology will have as much impact on manufacturing as it has had on engineering, business, and financial management in the 1960's.

Each of the new computer techniques will provide capabilities that were not possible before. But the biggest payoff will come by integrating these techniques into a total manufacturing control system, *Fig. 1.* The various elements of such a system can be added in progressive increments as the needs and payoffs require and as the necessary company resources become available. To better understand how the various techniques work together, each one should be understood and evaluated separately.

Direct numerical control. With DNC, each machine tool or group of machine tools still has an operator and operator's console alongside it. The program instructions for the part being machined are still in digital form. But, instead of being on punched tape, the program is stored in a disc file provided for the computer. In fact, both the tape

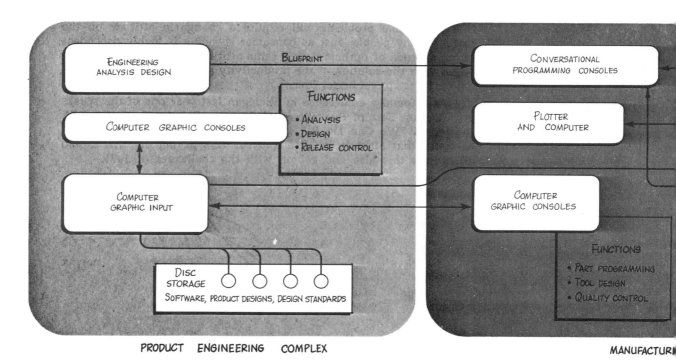

PRODUCT ENGINEERING COMPLEX

MANUFACTURI

Reprinted from *Automation*, vol. 18, pp. 34–37, Jan. 1971. Copyright 1970 by The Penton Publishing Co., Cleveland, Ohio 44113.

TURING CONTROL

and tape reader are gone, as is the significant cost of operating and maintaining such a system. The large cabinets of electronic gear for processing the digital inputs and feeding instructions to the machine tools are also gone from the operator's station. These inputs and instructions are now collected by a single computer and its peripheral equipment.

This type of operation is made possible by the fact that the computer's electronic capability for processing data and providing instructions is many times faster than the capability of machine tools to respond. Depending upon its main-frame capacity, a relatively small process computer can handle this type of work for a dozen or more multi-axis machine tools. Large, general-purpose computers may also be used. Their excess capacities can be utilized for other functions that require computational ability.

The cost of DNC can be less than the cost of hard-wired control equipment used with conventional N/C. Direct numerical control eliminates entirely the cost of tape and tape preparation. It

reduces the cost of maintenance, since the most susceptible items in conventional N/C systems (i.e., the tape readers) are eliminated, and the computer can be located at a remote site under better controlled conditions than exist in the shop environment. Direct numerical control increases machine tool utilization, since there is less downtime for maintenance. These are some of the immediate payoffs provided by DNC. While they are significant in themselves, much greater payoffs are possible because of the additional capabilities made possible by the use of DNC.

Conversational programming. This technique, *Fig. 2*, makes use of a cathode-ray tube display and a keyboard console on the shop floor. The part programmer can refer to the part program in disc

Fig. 1—Schematic diagram illustrates how various computer-oriented techniques can be integrated into a total, real-time, management control system. The idea is to provide minute-by-minute information to supervisors and managers so that corrective decisions and actions can be made more quickly and accurately than ever before.

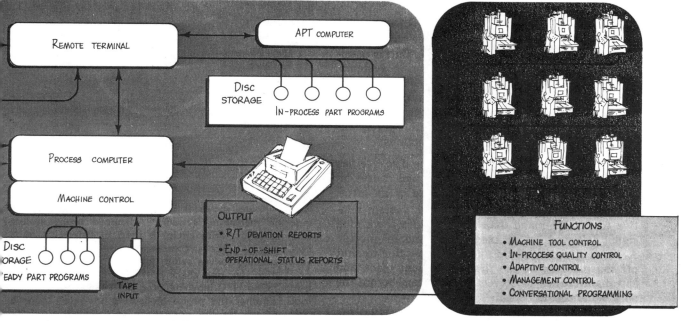

ENGINEERING AND CONTROL CENTER

MANUFACTURING COMPLEX

263

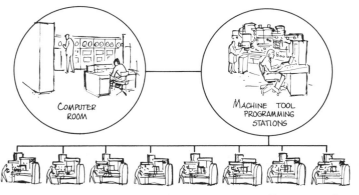

Fig. 2—Conversational programming technique makes use of a CRT and keyboard to allow a programmer to program a part on the shop floor. Once the part is programmed—and the program is stored in the computer—errors can be corrected and changes made at the machine tool.

storage. He can modify the part program in order to correct mistakes in geometry, eliminate wasted motions, and optimize cutting feeds and speeds. These changes can be made and the results can be observed instantaneously without leaving the machine tool. The capability for conversational programming depends on having the program accessible in disc storage rather than on punched tape, as is the current practice.

Conversational programming speeds the process of program proofing from several weeks to minutes or hours. It eliminates setting-up a job on the machine tool several times, only to find each time that the program is wrong and that another job has to be scheduled in the machine while the program is corrected. Conversational programming not only makes better use of the time of the programmer, operator, and machine tool, but it also improves the entire operation of production scheduling and control.

In-process quality control. In-process quality control consists of the following three subsystems: 1. Axis programmed path monitor. 2. Cutter monitor. 3. On-the-machine probe measuring system.

The purpose of the axis programmed path monitor subsystem is to guarantee that the machine tool axes move as programmed within the designated tolerances. This monitor contains three sections that perform the following functions:

• Verifies program data read from the disc, verifies data transmission and manipulation, and causes an axes inhibit with a diagnostic in case of an error.

• Monitors the response of the servo system relative to the command data and provides a warning signal followed by an axes inhibit and diagnostic. A warning signal would allow the operator to shut off the machine at the first convenient place and call maintenance to correct the problem before the part is damaged.

• Verifies its own operation. This verification would be done periodically by a program that would

exercise all functions of the monitor. By creating simulated faults, it would cause controlled system errors and actuation of the warning signal, the inhibit, and the diagnostics.

The second subsystem is a cutter monitor mounted on either the table of the machine tool or the workholding fixture. The cutter would be programmed through the monitor after being inserted into the spindle and before reaching the workpiece. The monitor would check the cutter's position relative to the theoretical programmed path, and reject the cutter if the cutter is the wrong length, the wrong diameter, or improperly present. The monitor would also reject the cutter if the cutter/holder assembly in the spindle is running out or if the machine tool alignment is off.

The third subsystem for in-process quality control is an on-the-machine probe measuring system. The probe sensor is inserted into the machine tool spindle in the same manner as a cutter, *Fig.* 3. The sensor can be programmed to measure from point-to-point on a master fixture to verify the composite positioning accuracy of all axes of the machine tool. The probe system can then be used to verify each production setup and to measure the part geometry at selected points during machining. Reference points on the workholding fixture would be used for verifying the system's performance before and after each set of measurements. The probe system indicates dimensional deviations from

Fig. 3—Photo shows a prototype of an on-the-N/C-machine measuring system. Advanced probe system (see inside of white circle) is used to determine each N/C machine tool's composite positioning accuracy, verify holding fixture setup accuracy prior to and after production run, and check part geometry on a selected basis. One N/C machine program controls the cutting tools, another the probe measuring system. There is little chance for the occurrence of common programming errors.

the nominal and, working with DNC, indicates when the deviations exceed acceptable tolerances. In all cases, the system provides a hardcopy printout of deviations, in analog or digital form, for a permanent inspection record. Added to conversational programming, this probe measuring system further speeds tool proofing.

The payoffs that can be foreseen from these subsystems of in-process quality control are less scrap, an opportunity to correct mistakes before it's too late, and a big reduction in inspection costs.

Adaptive control. The purpose of adaptive control, as applied to feeds and speeds, is to speed up or slow down the machine tool so that it is always being used to full capacity, consistent with part specifications. To accomplish this, the machine tool needs sensors at the machine spindle to sense parameters such as spindle deflection, vibration, or torque. The sensor signals are then compared to what they should be, as determined by such factors as workpiece machinability, cutter size, tool capacity, surface finish required, and the rigidity of the tool-holding fixture and part. The system then modifies the feed and/or speed to the maximum rate without damaging the cutter, stalling the machine, producing too rough a finish, or distorting the part.

Adaptive control makes these adjustments automatically, regardless of the depth of cut or even gaps in the cut. It can be programmed to adjust for the material and its metallurgical condition—even local variations in hardness can be taken into consideration. Adaptive control relieves programmers from the tedious parts of their jobs so that they can concentrate on providing correct geometries, and it optimizes feeds and speeds so that machine tools are used efficiently.

Real-time management. The direct coupling of a computer to manufacturing tools makes possible many refinements that add up to real-time management control. These refinements can be applied in scheduling, procurement, and other support areas as well as in actual manufacturing operations. By having the computer directly coupled to manufacturing tools, essential information is fed into the system automatically, independent of human responses.

A real-time management control system can be tailored to each company's particular needs. For example, *Fig.* 4 illustrates a particular manufacturing equipment utilization control system that might be part of the total management control system. Typical actions that the equipment utilization control system might perform include:

• Provide shop supervisors and foremen with a continuing report on the status of machine tools under their direction and alert them to corrective action whenever it is needed by management.

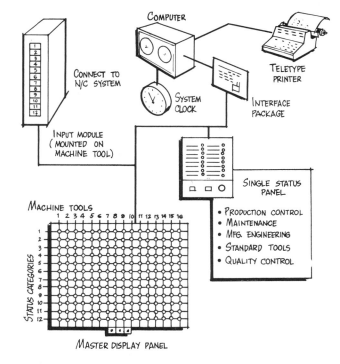

Fig. 4—Manufacturing equipment utilization subsystem of total management control system keeps track of machine tool status, alerts maintenance personnel when problems develop, and alerts supervisors when more work and/or equipment is needed.

• Alert maintenance personnel whenever a machine tool goes down, accumulate downtime records, and maintain histories of individual machine tools. This function can be extended to include a print-out at the operator's console of diagnostic information—if an in-process quality control subsystem is in operation—so that by the time maintenance personnel get to the machine tool, they will be advised of what the malfunction was, its probable cause, and what corrective action was recommended.

• Alert production control whenever machine tools are down for lack of scheduled work, fixtures, or tools.

A real-time management control system such as this does not, of itself, have the capability to prevent or correct problems. It provides real-time information on problem situations requiring management decision making which, in turn, results in the necessary corrective action. Its payoff depends upon how well management uses it.

In summary, advances in computer and sensor technology make possible a number of sophisticated applications in manufacturing. These applications will eventually overlap and provide a computer-based hookup between the manufacturing, engineering, and product functions. While this article concentrates on their use in relation to chip-making machine tools, many of these techniques will also be used on welders, riveters, and many other types of production equipment. Singly or collectively, they offer a tremendous potential for reducing manufacturing costs and scheduling lead time. How well this potential is realized depends upon how well management manages the system.

A Manufacturing Information and Control System Design

MIACS is a computerized approach to complete control of operations in manufacturing. Its heart is an integrated data store which allows many distinct functions to access a common data base in an application language. Any revision by one function automatically updates all affected files. MIACS controls the enterprise by constructing and controlling three data models: materials inventory, process, and resources inventory. Production is scheduled and inventory is controlled according to management-selected policy rules. A user creates a specific system incorporating decision rules, detailed models, and data files by programming in COBOL. Here are the basic system concepts.

C.A. RENOUARD, General Electric Co., Information Systems Equipment Div., Phoenix, Ariz.

New operating problems in industry are leading manufacturers to extend the concepts of automatic control beyond the physical process to management functions. An extensive study by the General Electric Co. shows that economic management by conventional methods is becoming difficult or impossible because of the proliferation of models and the growing complexity of products and processes. At the same time, customers are demanding shorter delivery times from suppliers.

As the output of a manufacturing enterprise grows more complex and varied, scheduling becomes both more important and more difficult. A time-table for the production of finished goods is required which meets customer needs, keeps inventory within stated bounds, and loads the production facilities with economic lot sizes or quantities. Each time such a time-table is set up or revised, all related procurement or manufacture of raw materials and subassemblies must also be scheduled. In addition, the detailed routing of work through the plant must be planned out to meet delivery commitments and make the best use of the available plant resources.

The study found these problems to be as significant in certain kinds of "flow shops" (table, right), which typically produce large quantities of standard products, as in job shops, which work on special order, and combination "flow/job shops."

Shape of an enterprise

General Electric concluded that most manufacturing establishments fit into a three-part framework:

- The shop.
- The main-line information system.
- The advance planning system.

The shop is the actual manufacturing arena, and includes work areas and process machinery. Typically, purchased materials—raw or finished—are shipped into the shop from vendors. After receiving, inspection, and possible warehousing, labor or machine time or both are applied at designated work stations. A completed product is formed and warehoused or shipped directly to the customer.

The main-line information system is traditionally a clerical-managerial function which processes quantities of customer orders, sales forecasts, and inventory data along with records of actual manufacturing activity from the shop, and generates purchase orders for vendors, requisition orders from inventory, manufacturing orders for the shop, and shipping orders for the distribution function.

It is this manual information system which the

Table—Typical Industries in Three Categories

Flow shop	
Chemicals	Metal rod
Paints	Light bulbs
Flow/job shop	
Appliances	Industrial equipment
Automobiles	Textiles
Automotive parts	Transformers
Electric motors	Aircraft parts
Job shop	
Aircraft	Steam turbines
Tool and diemaking	Earth-moving equipment

Reprinted with permission from *Contr. Eng.*, vol. 17, pp. 78–81, Sept. 1970.

computerized manufacturing control system is supplementing or replacing.

The third element of the enterprise, the advance planning function, is the creative, long-range direction of the business. It establishes product design data, new processes and facilities, and financial planning. It also involves materials flow engineering and establishes the decision rules, control parameters, and management policies which direct the main-line system.

Within this framework, General Electric evolved a concept for a Manufacturing Information and Control System (MIACS). A random-access-computer approach to integrated manufacturing control, it is designed to accommodate any degree of on-line operation.

Three models

The MIACS concept uses three basic planning and control models to completely describe material flow in the shop and the corresponding data relationships in the main line information system:
- Material inventory model.
- Process model.
- Resource inventory model.

Each of these models is a computer program which uses stored decision rules to plan, schedule, and control the respective function.

The *material inventory model* takes account of all items which enter and flow through the manufacturing process—bulk materials, parts, and assemblies; raw material, semifinished goods, and end product; items stocked and not stocked, and high- and low-cost items.

This model converts the schedule of manufacture of end products into a series of materials requirements. For each separately identified material, the model maintains a tabulation (Figure 1) of quantities on hand, and calculates the day-to-day quantities of future requirements on the basis of the manufacturing schedule, taking account of the time allocated to each manufacturing process. The model calculates purchase or fabrication quantities for each material from these quantity requirements, using management-supplied decision rules regarding economic order quantities, safety stock, and manufacturing lot size.

The *process model* stores the fabrication and processing details of each product made in the facility. It includes routing from one process to the next and the amount of time each increment of throughput occupies each process, thus modeling the actual manufacturing between inventory points. The model may separately detail such activities as receiving, inspecting, machining, punching, forming, treating, fabricating, winding, assembling, testing, packaging, shipping, and transporting of each material item.

The *resource inventory model* keeps track of the resources—manpower and equipment—required by the manufacturing process. Under the MIACS architecture, resources may be a single operator or ma-

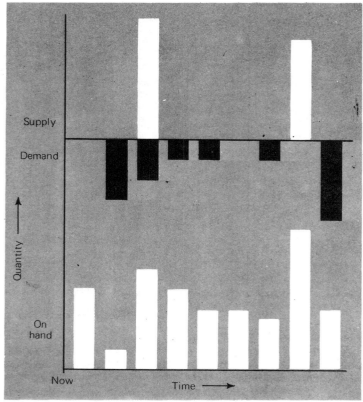

FIG. 1. Inventory model of one material. Each increment of demand is based on anticipated consumption by the manufacturing process on that day; each increment of supply is a replenishment scheduled according to programmed policies. These plans (and hence this tabulation) for future days are continuously modified as actual shop performance is fed back into the system.

chine, a group of operators or machines, or factory floor space or an assembly area. Resources are modeled in two ways:
- Gross capacity—the total number available of each separately identified type of resource.
- Time and quantity of withdrawals (loads) and replenishments.

The process model, responding to the manufacturing schedule, generates a series of resource requirements which then appear as withdrawals or loads against the resource inventory capacity. Resources, unlike materials, are not consumed by the process; machines and operators become available again after each scheduled activity. Each withdrawal and replenishment of a resource associated with an activity is assigned a quantity-time load against that resource (see Figure 2). The sum of all these loads provides a load profile.

Figures 3 and 4 show how the three models are integrated to form a main-line information system.

Integrated data storage

A system of this general architecture must store and relate data of several types, and often in rather large quantities. On each fabricated material item, subassembly, or end product, the identity and quantities of all constituent materials must be filed, along with the necessary process information and manufacturing resources. On each purchased material item, complete vendor information must be stored.

In a simple file structure this information must ap-

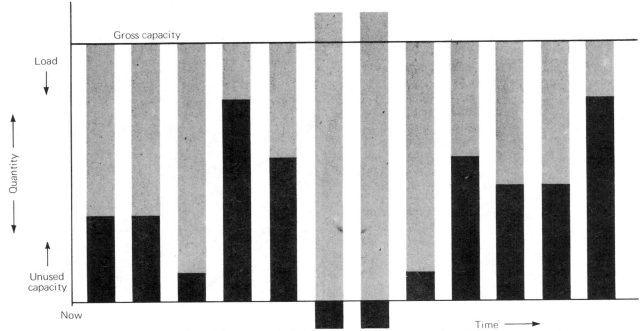

FIG. 2. Model of one resource. The horizontal "gross capacity" line indicates a constant quantity of the resource over the model period. Each light bar (top) indicates the load on that resource for one day; the dark (bottom) bar indicates the unused quantity available. This resource is loaded beyond capacity on the sixth and seventh day; work must be rescheduled or additional capacity made available.

pear many times in essentially redundant files. Work schedules, product documentation, and materials inventory, for example, all typically refer to the same in-process materials, But a file accessed by date (e.g., a work schedule) would have to be separately structured from a file accessed by product identity or by vendor.

This redundancy is costly in terms of disc space. More importantly, it can create enormous difficulties in file maintenance. An engineering change to product structure, for example, immediately affects production schedules, engineering files, product documentation, purchasing files and activities, and production control. If significant time is required to in-

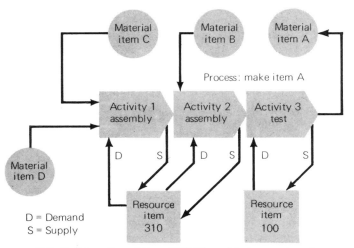

D = Demand
S = Supply

FIG. 3. Integration of three MIACS models to execute a shop schedule. In this simple network, activities—in the sequence and for the time period specified by the process model (center)—generate demands on the material inventory model (top), generate loads on the resources inventory model (bottom), and return resources to that inventory as each activity is completed.

corporate a single change in all the affected files, there can be costly waste and delay—and the file maintenance activity itself may actually fail or collapse in confusion.

The ideal file structure for an application such as MIACS is one in which each item of information is stored only once, and all required information in any transaction can be handled in one file access, using terminology oriented to the specific user interest. For example, a foreman at a remote terminal can retrieve the work schedule for his section for any specified day by keying in the required date and the identity of the station. A purchasing executive can similarly retrieve all back orders on a given vendor or he can enter a new purchase order. Note that all three transactions require accesses to interrelated data on product structure, work schedules, inventory, and vendors—although identified or structured differently in each case.

To fill this need in MIACS, General Electric developed the Integrated Data Store (IDS). This file management system maintains the integral files for the entire manufacturing control function, automatically updating all related information whenever new or revised entries are made, and supplying all required data in response to inquiries in user-oriented language.

The IDS technique will be described functionally in a subsequent article. In general, it uses "links" or pointers to establish all the required relationships among records. For example, the master file on a material item incorporates a pointer which leads to all material items required to fabricate the item.

IDS is presently in operation in a number of customer locations, and experience to date indicates that the elimination of redundancy saves 25 to 40 percent of the disc space required by the same file conven-

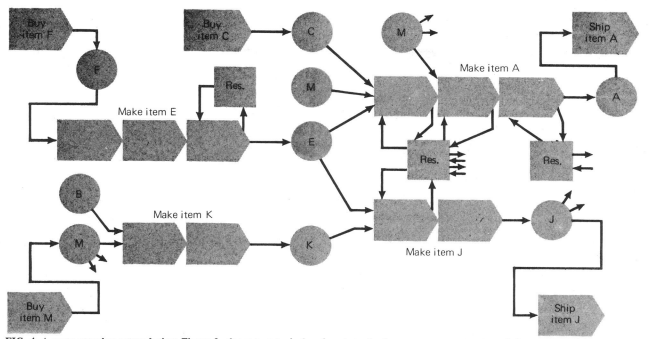

FIG. 4. A more complex network than Figure 3, closer to a typical real system. Again, squares are resources, circles are materials, and pentagons are processes. Note product structure: Item M, for example, is used at three levels of subassembly. And note effects of materials policy: When required for item K, item M is bought. When required for item A, in a different quantity at a different time —or when the shop is differently loaded—economic ordering rules call for item M to be fabricated from purchased item G.

tionally structured, as well as greatly reducing implementation time.

As an illustration, it is not uncommon for a material identification number in certain types of manufacturing industries to have as many as 18 characters. In an IDS file, this number appears only once, even if the item appears on a number of unrelated parts lists.

What the system is

The MIACS models, operating on current and historical data in the IDS, generate plans—approximations of future operations of the business. The models also serve as vehicles for recording these plans. The plans are communicated to the shop in suitable increments in the form of work orders. As work progresses, the shop feeds back the actual status of the work in terms of time and quantity to the computer system. Employees may enter data at on-line terminals through machine-readable documents. Throughput measurements may be made automatically by detectors in the process machinery.

Whenever there is any deviation from the shop schedule, or an activity must be rescheduled for any reason, all the associated material and resource withdrawals and replenishments are also rescheduled in a dynamic mode—the system is dynamically self-correcting. When exceptional circumstances occur (e.g., inventory of a specific item falls below the safety stock level), the system responds via dynamic reordering.

For these purposes, the total plant or enterprise is divided into "administrative centers"—groups of similar machines, specific floor areas or sections, or specific manufacturing processes—chosen for convenience in modeling and control. Each administrative center is separately scheduled and monitored by the computer system.

To help users implement system capabilities of the MIACS type, a variety of aids are available, ranging from preprogrammed modules to system design documentation. The modules might typically perform product structure control or inventory management; a design document might describe a subsystem devoted to scheduling or purchasing. In any case, a COBOL/IDS language is available for application implementation and modification, reducing the overall effort.

The approach has been adopted in varying degrees by several users. One, a large eastern industrial-equipment producer, has a satellite facility in the Midwest. Plant size doubled in two years, but customer delivery cycle has been cut from 28-32 weeks to 10-12 weeks. Engineering cycle time has been reduced 75 percent and engineering productivity increased 60 percent. The Midwest facility has on-line access to the central computer and engages in a degree of manufacturing control that would be cost-prohibitive if attempted locally.

In an integrated system such as MIACS, once a data base is set up, it can be accessed by many people and programs—including programs not yet conceived when the data base was set up. And this opens up the possibility of interfacing with process control computers, either directly through communications peripherals or through a manual link. This would enable the information system to track process-computer-controlled work accurately and take account of process conditions (equipment outages, for example) in scheduling. □

Future articles by this author will describe functionally the Integrated Data Store and the material inventory management components of the MIACS System.

Manufacturing process control at IBM

by J. E. STUEHLER

IBM Corporation
Boulder, Colorado

INTRODUCTION

IBM manufacturing facilities in both the United States and Europe have installed computer systems of essentially identical design to aid in the control of many types of manufacturing processes. The basic structure of the system is depicted in Figure 1. One or two central computer systems (IBM System 360) are attached to several satellite computers (IBM 1130, 1800 and 360 processors) via a high speed Transmission Control Unit (multiplexor).

The satellite computers attach to, and control, various types of manufacturing process and test equipment. The central computer system serves as a data bank, processor and shared input/output device for the satellite computers. It provides for storage and analysis of process data. The central computer minimizes the cost and size of the satellite computers by performing tedious calculations, providing the facilities of a large data base, and reducing input/output requirements. When used, the second central system provides backup, additional capacity, and a better response in a duplexed mode of operation.

This system structure was developed so that one basic design could serve several IBM facilities, thus reducing the hardware and software development costs that would be incurred if each facility were required to develop its own manufacturing process control system(s). In addition, the common design was able to draw upon the combined resources of several locations in order to make optimum use of critical skills.[1] Another major advantage of the common control system is in minimizing the cost of transferring products for manufacture from one location to another.

This paper will describe the requirements for, and development of, the common system. Also included are some of the problems encountered and the oversights, now corrected, that occurred during development and implementation.

HISTORY

The earliest major manufacturing process control system to be implemented in IBM was the system known as COMATS (Computer Operated Manufacturing and Test System).[2] This system consists of a pair of duplexed 1460 Data Processing Systems which are attached to numerous satellite processors through a high speed multiplexor (Figure 2). The satellite processors are specially developed computers which provide the control required to test most of the disk storage products for which the system was designed. The system was conceived to reduce the costs associated with developing, building and maintaining special test equipment to do a similar job.

After COMATS became operational, it was obvious that many other manufacturing facilities in IBM had control requirements that could be met by a similar approach. However, each IBM plant manufactures, in general, products requiring their own particular test and process control philosophies. COMATS, as implemented, would not meet all needs. Therefore, in order to save each manufacturing location the cost of developing a unique system, a system versatile enough to meet the needs of most plants was developed.

THE MANUFACTURING ENVIRONMENT

The types of manufacturing processes in IBM extend from the fabrication of microelectronic components through the assembly and testing of complex electronic processors; and involve tiny, precision machined parts through large, electromechanical data processing input/output equipment. The processes required to produce these and other IBM products can, however, generally be classified among five categories:

The first is a process which produces a large quantity of a single type of electrical or mechanical component such as a magnetic disk or core, or a tape or disk head.

Reprinted with permission from *AFIPS Conf. Proc., Vol. 37, 1970 Fall Joint Comput. Conf.*, pp. 461–469.

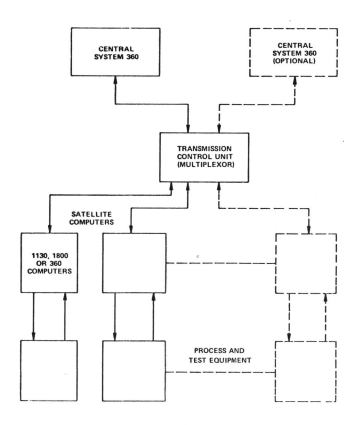

Figure 1—Manufacturing process control system used in IBM

the control computer can play is in testing.[3] The computer can supply customized diagnostic programs for assemblies under test, provide the control logic required to test electromechanical input/output devices, and retrieve and analyze test results to provide processed output for use in correcting assembly problems and controlling quality.

The fourth type of manufacturing process is general machining of mechanical components. The computer may be used to control the machining and measurement equipment. It is possible for the computer to feed back measurement data to machine tools to control and optimize the process. In addition, the computer is required to convert engineering information into tool instructions for each unique part to be machined.

The fifth type of process actually resides in development rather than manufacturing. An important step in the development "process" is in proving the product to be manufacturable. In order to experiment with process variables, a flexible and easily programmable control system is required. Furthermore, test data analysis is important to determine the effects of varying process parameters.

The manufacturing environment may be further characterized by considering that any one plant may employ more than one of the above types of processes.

The computer may be used here to control the mechanized operations. In addition, a great deal of process optimization is possible when the computer is used to collect and analyze data to determine the effect of each process variable.

The second type of process produces many "customized" variations of a single product. Examples include integrated circuits and printed circuit boards and cards. The computer can play an important role here by optimally controlling the process and test equipment. However, the computer must also supply information to the manufacturing process to "customize" the product. This requires obtaining and storing large amounts of engineering information as to how each component is to be made and tested.

The third type of manufacturing process produces mechanical and electrical assemblies and subsystems. Product examples include central processing units and input/output equipment such as printers, tape drives, displays, etc. The process consists of assembly and test operations. Most of the assembly operations are difficult to mechanize. However, the computer may be used to give assembly instructions. An important role

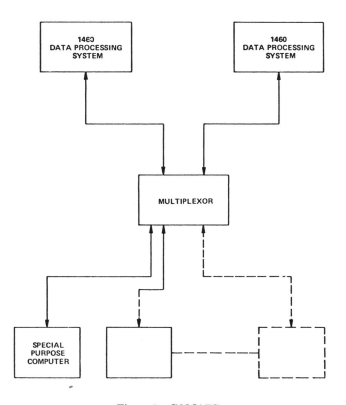

Figure 2—COMATS

Furthermore, a manufacturing process may be spread out in several buildings at distances of up to a mile apart. The processes continuously change to allow the introduction of new products or changes to existing ones. In general, each change must occur rapidly in order to keep pace with development and market requirements. Another trait of the manufacturing environment is that entire manufacturing processes are sometimes transferred totally from one location to another to balance work loads. Often a manufacturing process will be installed in two or more facilities for increased production and/or emergency production.

SELECTION OF A SYSTEM APPROACH

With an understanding of the manufacturing environment, the requirements for a common control system can be identified. The most significant of these includes sensor based input/output capability, extensive information handling and storing capability, modularity with the ability to easily and rapidly install new applications, the ability to mix and transfer all types of applications, and certainly not least important is the requirement for economy.

The satellite computer system concept,[4-9] as illustrated in Figure 3, best implements the above require-

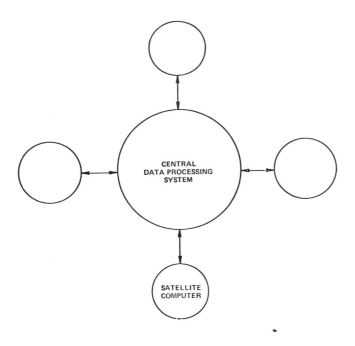

Figure 3—Satellite computer system concept

ments. The satellite computers interface to process and test equipment through sensor based input/output. These satellite computers may be transferred from one location to another and additional satellites may easily be added to expand an existing system. The central processor can provide extensive data analysis and large data banks, while minimizing the need for such capability at the satellite.

Two other possible approaches to developing a manufacturing process control system were considered and eliminated for the purposes described here.[10] A single, large central computer system would not provide the power, versatility and modularity required. This is because of the number of different types of control applications in a given IBM plant, and because each such application normally undergoes frequent change which would be difficult to cope with on a single computer system without affecting other applications. The use of a separate control computer for each process would not be adequate because of the expense in providing data banks and information analysis capabilities. In addition, the cost of duplicated input/output equipment and redundant programming would be much greater than with the satellite approach.

DEVELOPMENT AND IMPLEMENTATION

Central computer system

The IBM System/360 was considered the most practical system for use as the central computer. The primary considerations were growth capability plus the existence of many types of input/output equipment and commercially available programs. Only third generation data processing equipment was considered in order to provide state-of-the-art experience and motivation for the skilled programmers who would be needed to design the applications programs and implement an operating system. Other IBM data processing systems were considered which were generally lower in cost than the 360. These systems may have satisfied the needs of some types of processes where large data banks and a great deal of data analysis were not required (example: testing and process development). However, they had limited growth capability compared to the 360; and they did not have the larger analysis and input/output capabilities required in the other process applications. Therefore, at the expense of possibly "over computerizing" some very few locations, the System/360 was selected to maintain commonality.

Satellite computers

It would be desirable to use a single type of satellite computer in order to minimize programming and maintenance costs through familiarization. However, because of the diversity of control requirements at the process level, this was not possible without greatly increasing the average cost of each control application. The amount of control logic required for process or test equipment is inversely proportional to the logic capability of the product being produced or tested. That is, more "intelligence" is required to test components than is required to test input/output devices. Similarly, more intelligence is required to test input/output devices than is required to test systems. Thus, in general, IBM 1800 and 360 Systems are used to control process and test equipment which produces components (process types one and two) while the lower cost and lower powered 1130 System is used on products having higher intelligence (process types three and four). The 1800 Systems are interfaced to process/test equipment through digital and analog input/output channels. The 360 and 1130 Systems are interfaced via special hardware connected to the Original Equipment Manufacturers (OEM) channels.

System response

To keep the cost of the satellite computers low, it is necessary to minimize the data processing requirements (amount of core and speed) and the input/output equipment required at the satellite. Thus, the satellite computer will be heavily dependent on the central computer for these services. However, when the satellite computer requires data or programs from the central computer, or is required to send data to the central computer, it cannot wait for a long period of time as the process or test equipment may also have to wait (requiring more production equipment and higher implementation costs). Ideally, the satellite computer should be able to send or receive data from the central system as fast as the satellite could access its own files if it had them. Thus, a system design specification for simple data/program transfer was established at 500 milliseconds 95 percent of the time with the central system handling 3600 interrupts/hour (an average of one interrupt per second). This specification is the length of time the satellite computer must wait from the time it requests a program or data from the central system (or requests the central system to take data) until the program or data (an average of 2,000 bytes) has entered the satellite (or the satellite has sent 2,000 bytes of data). This specification places severe require-

ments on the communications system between the satellite and central computers as well as on the central computer's operating system.

Communications system

A multiplexor was required to allow communications between the satellite and central computers. The requirements of such a device included:

Modularity in the number of attachable satellites to allow growth (a maximum of several hundred satellite computers in some facilities was considered reasonable while other facilities might never have more than a dozen).

Distance capabilities for communicating up to one mile were required to be able to cover a plant site.

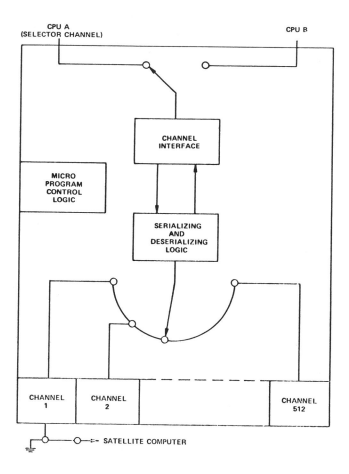

Figure 4—Transmission control unit (TCU)

Channel bandwidth for transmission in the megabit/sec range was needed to minimize satellite waiting time. That is, the channel bandwidth should be of the same order of magnitude as the central CPU channel and file transmission rates.

Serial by bit transmission was required to minimize cabling costs.

High reliability of transmission was required to allow operation in an electronically noisy factory environment.

No commercially available multiplexors were found to be suitable under the above requirements. A Transmission Control Unit (TCU) was, therefore, developed; this unit is shown schematically in Figure 4. The TCU is basically a micro-programmed, solid state switch which provides polling and allows the communication of either of two central 360 computers with any of up to 512 satellite computers (modular in groups of 64). The TCU also provides serializing and transmission logic which allows transmission of serial by bit data over a single coaxial cable at a rate of 2.5 megabits/ second. The number of bits in error is less than one bit for every 10 to the eighth bits transmitted. The TCU communicates with a satellite computer via a transmission adapter.

Central computer operating system

Some of the more important characteristics of an operating system in the central system include the following:

Response time to accept an interrupt from the TCU and begin processing should be of the order of a few milliseconds to provide the response required by the satellite computer which may be waiting.

Input/output support for many different types of devices is required to allow the system to be applied effectively in the different process environments. That is, one environment may require small, fast-access files while in another environment slower access to large quantities of information is required. Differences may also be found in the requirements for graphic terminals, printers, tapes (for history), etc.

Multi-programming is required to allow one or more satellite computers to receive service while file accessing or other input/output operations are pending for another satellite computer. This capability greatly reduces the waiting time due to queues for the satellite computers.

Support software such as compilers, assemblers, analysis routines, etc., is required to minimize programming costs and the need for programmers.

Modularity is required in order to minimize the price the small user must pay in core storage overhead which is required to obtain the sophistication needed by the larger user (examples include number of levels of multiprogramming, requirements for compilers, concurrent operation of peripheral input/output devices, types and amounts of input/output equipment, etc.).

Two approaches were considered to implement the above major requirements. One was to develop a special operating system and the other was to implement a commercially available one. The special operating system would be best from the standpoint of response and amount of core required since it could be customized to perform well in these areas. The disadvantages were that a great deal of development work would be necessary to provide the versatility required to support the varied input/output requirements at each using location. Furthermore, advantage could not be taken of already available compilers and utility programs designed to operate under a commercially available operating system. For these reasons, the decision was made to use a commercially available operating system.[11,12]

The best system available to provide multiprogramming capability was the IBM Operating System/ 360 (OS/360) which was augmented by a "Secondary Control Program" to provide a "real time" multiprogramming environment for supporting the satellite computers. This combination of OS/360, the Secondary Control Program and an input/output appendage to support the TCU is referred to as the **Process Control Operating System** (PCOS). The core map of the central computer is illustrated in Figure 5. TCU communications and TCU-detected errors are handled by the TCU appendage. All TCU interrupts are passed to the Secondary Control Program which invokes either a core or disk-resident Service Module (real time program) to handle the interrupt. The Service Module may (if required) initiate a background program to perform analysis on information the satellite computer has sent. The Service Modules always have priority in utilizing the central system resources. This allows a fast response to a satellite request for service.

Normally, the time required to enter a core-resident Service Module after the TCU posts an interrupt to the central computer is less than 25 milliseconds (if the service module is not active).

A drawback of using OS/360 as compared to a special purpose operating system is in the amount of core required. A Model 40 is the smallest system in the 360

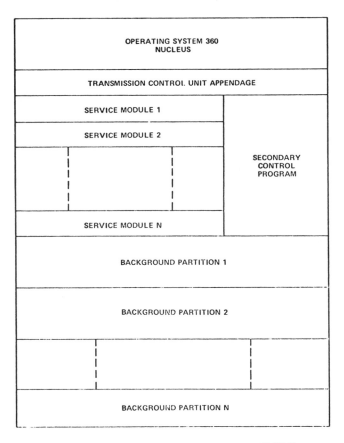

Figure 5—Process control operating system (PCOS)

line which can effectively run OS/360. This again is an expense to some locations which might have started off with a 360 Model 30 as the central computer if a "special" operating system had been developed.

CONSIDERATIONS IN RETROSPECT

Experience has revealed two problems that have now been solved but were not originally anticipated. One was a hardware design problem and the other a software problem. After the TCU specifications had been determined, any location planning on the first usage of a type of satellite computer (i.e., 1130, 1800, or 360) had the responsibility to develop the unique transmission logic adapter between that type of satellite computer and the coaxial cable which connected to the TCU. It was later learned that each designing location had developed an interface completely different from the others. As a consequence, common software in the central system could not be used to communicate with every type of satellite computer. This was because each type of transmission logic adapter presented different status indicators to the TCU or responded differ-

ently to TCU commands. Furthermore, since each adapter was designed differently, an engineering change placed in the TCU might affect some adapters adversely while not affecting others. This put a handicap on the TCU designers.

This problem was solved by developing a common transmission logic interface which could be used by every type of satellite computer. The common adapter was then uniquely interfaced to a particular type of satellite computer as illustrated in Figure 6. Now all satellite computers look the same to the TCU and central system software.

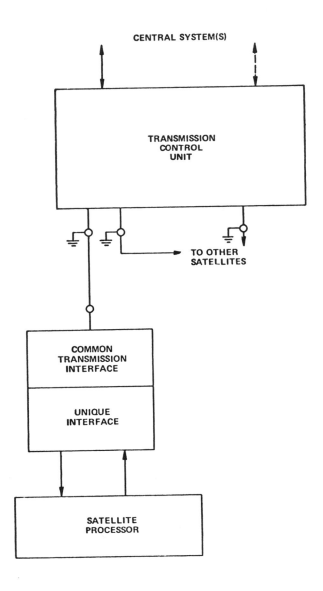

Figure 6—Transmission logic scheme

The software problem had to do with the definition (or lack of definition) of the Service Modules (real time programs) which reside under the Secondary Control Program. Most system users were developing Application Service Modules to be unique to a given application. As an example, a particular tester would require one or more unique Service Modules to completely support it; and these "Application" Service Modules could support no other application. Other using locations, however, began development of "System Service Modules." A single System Service Module could provide service to two or more applications. An example might be a System Service Module to retrieve information and store it on a file for any application, whereas each Application Service Module contained its own retrieval logic. The benefit of System Service Modules is that these routines, which can be common, would have to be developed only once. However, there is an initially high development cost for each such Service Module since they must offer a great deal of versatility.

The problem presented by having these two philosophies was that applications developed to be run on a system using System Service Modules could not easily be transferred to another location without also transferring the System Service Modules or rewriting the application programs. This problem was solved by defining and developing a common set of System Service Modules which can be considered an integral part of the operating system. Being able to change this philosophy of operating system function attests to the need for a great deal of operating system versatility. It is not unreasonable to expect that other conceptual changes will be made in the future based on knowledge not yet gained.

DEVELOPMENT AND IMPLEMENTATION

Architectural, as well as hardware and software specifications for the system were developed by representatives from each user location in 1967. Development responsibility for portions of the hardware and software were assumed by several of IBM's manufacturing locations. In 1968, the components of the system were brought together at a single IBM manufacturing facility in Boulder, Colorado, for successful system testing. The system is presently installed and operating in nine domestic and two European IBM manufacturing plants with plans for implementation at several other plants. The need for a versatile system approach can be attested to by looking at how the common process control system is applied at several IBM locations. At two locations, 30-50 satellite 1130 computers are being used for testing electromechanical

input/output devices. Both of these locations utilize the central system as the satellite's input/output device (storing programs, reporting, etc.). Furthermore, the central system performs test data and defect analysis and reporting for the Quality Engineering organization. Two other locations use the system heavily for controlling processes producing magnetic components. Here some satellite computers (e.g., 1800's) are used to control process variables while other satellite computers (e.g., 1130's) control test equipment. The central computer is used to store and correlate test results with process variables, thus allowing process optimization. As soon as enough history can be built up, process models can be designed and installed in the central system to better control the processes. Two other locations use the system primarily for supplying test programs to central processing units undergoing test. Here the central system stores and supplies large diagnostic programs to satellite computers. The central system collects test and diagnostic data for engineering analysis. One of these two locations uses its system to give assembly instructions via display units to assembly personnel working on complex electronic subassemblies. One IBM location uses its system to test complex integrated circuit memory modules. Here the central system must supply test data to satellite computers which control test equipment. Again, the central system receives, analyzes reports and stores relevant test data received from the satellite computer. Other IBM locations have combinations of the above applications installed on their systems. The number of satellite computers range from half a dozen at one location to over 50 at another. Central system configurations include a single System 360 model 40, a pair of model 50's, and a single model 65. All using locations appear satisfied with the flexibility the system affords.

SYSTEM PERFORMANCE

It is impossible to generalize any system performance criterion because of the differences in system configuration implemented by each using location (i.e., types of input/output, size of processor used, features of operating system utilized, etc.). However, a "representative" location has installed 22 satellite 1130 computers on a System 360 model 40 central system with 256 K bytes of core. They utilize the multiprogramming with a fixed number of tasks (MFT) version of the 360 Operating System and use a 2314 Disk Storage Unit as their bulk file. The observed response of their system closely follows the results of the simulation of their system which is depicted in Figure 7. This shows that 1890 messages per hour can be handled with a response of

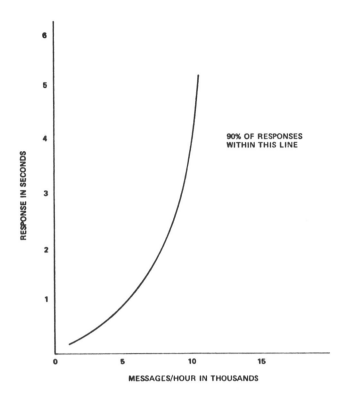

Figure 7—System simulation

THE FUTURE

With a common system structure established in these IBM manufacturing plants, it is now possible to develop additional common system services and applications.

A present concept is a high level **Process and Test Language** (PTL) which will allow an engineer with minimum programming experience to efficiently and rapidly apply a satellite computer to control process or test equipment using the central systems resources for compilation.[13] The test or process engineer can develop the control logic using macro statements in high-level languages he can easily learn.[14] Similar statements can be used to send process/test information to the central computer where programmer-written routines can analyze, store and report on the information.

Projected for the future are satellite computer driven machine tools with numeric control processors and post processors resident at the central computer and accessible by the satellite. It will be possible for machine parts programmers to directly enter macro program statements in the satellite computer or a terminal device to make a new part or modify an old. These statements will be sent to the central computer for checking and compilation. The result of the compilation will return to the satellite computer to cause execution by an on line machine tool.

Process Automation programs which reside in the central computer will be developed to directly accept raw development (engineering) information.[15] These programs will then interpret the design information and send process information to satellite computers which will be used to control process and test equipment. Among other benefits, this will allow a very fast response to product/process engineering changes.

A common quality assurance analysis programming system which will reside in the central computer is being considered. This will allow the Quality Control Engineer to easily use complex statistical methods in analyzing process information when a new application is installed on the system. It is possible that the Quality Control Engineer will, in the future, be directly entering high-level (macro) statements in a language like PTL into the satellite computers. These statements would specify data he would want collected and indicate to the central system what kind of analysis to be performed on the data.

Another important future aspect is the more sophisticated use of data management techniques. Such techniques will allow a user to directly access system data banks to retrieve test and/or process data without the aid of a programmer. The user will then be able to

300 milliseconds (90 percent of the time). The system performance specification of 3600 interrupts/hour being handled within 500 milliseconds is shown to be met. Other data show that with 1890 interrupts/hour, the system is 20 percent utilized (with no background processing). Input/output is one percent utilized. The Service Modules (application programs) servicing the interrupts had run times ranging from one to ten milliseconds with an average of seven milliseconds. There was an average of two file accesses per interrupt.

Another measure of system performance is central system availability. This again varies greatly from location to location. However, a representative system (as described above) reports that their system is available 423 hours out of approximately 429 per month. (The system is utilized on a two and a half-shift, five-day/week basis.)

Most using locations agree that the major cause of system down time is due to central system software problems. The causes of these problems include: operating system faults, PCOS faults and (most frequently) operator or programmer errors. This problem is being reduced significantly by developing better error handling and recovery routines into PCOS.

specify statistical programs to operate upon the data and methods for presenting the final output.

The process control central system will be interfaced to other manufacturing information systems which process information pertaining to production, warehousing, maintenance and in-process inventories. Information to be passed to those systems from the process control system includes production yields, equipment down time, units in process, units tested, etc. By completing the tie of process control systems to manufacturing information systems, plant automation becomes possible.[16,17]

SUMMARY

The justification for undertaking a common manufacturing process control approach in IBM was to reduce redundant hardware and software development and implementation costs at each IBM location. This has been accomplished. In addition, it was possible, by pooling ideas, to develop a system superior to that which a single location could have developed. This pooling of ideas and knowledge has ultimately led to a process control solution which, in general, reduces the costs of installing new manufacturing processes and of modifying existing ones.

Although the system as described in this paper is installed and operating at several IBM facilities, it appears to be only a first step toward automation. Almost daily, new ideas are born by one or more users of the system as to how new functions could be added to the system to either further reduce the implementation cost of new applications or to improve the quality of products being manufactured under control of the system. It appears that these ideas, which are born as a result of experience in using the system, are the real justification for the common system approach since many users can now benefit from a single idea and development.

ACKNOWLEDGMENTS

It would be lengthy for the author to acknowledge all individuals who contributed directly or indirectly to the success of the system. However, the key hardware developers were Messrs. R. Watkins, F. Thoburn and T. Rall all of San Jose, California, and Mr. K. Cisewski of Rochester, Minnesota. The primary software developers were Messrs. M. Mauldin and T. Reilly of Kingston, New York, along with Messrs. R. Henry, San Jose, California, and J. Calva, Rochester, Minnesota. Messrs. R. Boydston and C. Connoy of San Jose, California, developed the system simulator discussed in this paper. Special acknowledgment goes to Mr. W. Moore in Harrison, New York (IBM's System Manufacturing Division Headquarters), for the excellent job he performed in initiating and coordinating the entire project.

REFERENCES

1 W ANDERSON
Controlling processes with computers
Automation p 70 January 1969
2 J STUEHLER   R WATKINS
A computer operated manufacturing and test system
IBM Journal of Research and Development Vol II No 4
p 452 1967
3 J STUEHLER
Hardware-software trade offs in testing
IEEE Spectrum p 51 December 1968
4 N GAINES et al
Union carbide integrates multi-computer process control
Instrumentation Technology p 49 March 1967
5 J WAUGH   A YONDA
NSRL on line computer system
IEEE Transactions on Nuclear Science p 129 February 1968
6 R HORST
The justification of digital process control
Modern Data p 20
7 V LOSKUTOV
Computation technology in automatic control systems
Mekhanizatsiya i Avtomatizatsiya Proizvodstva, No 32p 442
1964
8 C BOND
A digital-computer system for industry
Industrial Electronics p 221 May 1966
9 M MESAROVIC
Multilevel systems and concepts in process control
Proceedings of the IEEE 58-1 p 111 1970
10 J STUEHLER
The devoted, shared or satellite approach for computer control of manufacturing processes?
Proceedings of Western Electronic Show and Convention
8-1 1969
11 J SPOONER
Real time operating system for process control
Instrument Society of America D1-1-DAHCOD 1967
12 P WEILER et al
A real-time operating system for manned spaceflight
IEEE Transactions on Computers C19-5 p 388 1970
13 E JOHNSON   J McCARTHY
Development of software systems for automated test equipment
Proceedings of Western Electronic Show and Convention
21-2 1969
14 *Special issue on process control languages*
IEEE Transactions on Industrial Control December 1968
15 R BOEDECKER
The computerized factory
Assembly Engineering June 1966
16 N CHIANTELLA
The systems approach to plant automation
ASTME Vectors 4 5 1968
17 F GUT
Operations control systems
Automation p 55 January 1969

APPLYING COMPUTERS TO WAREHOUSING

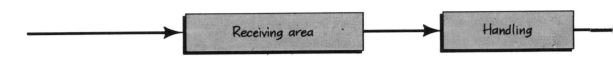

Receiving area → Handling →

By DALE M. MUELLER, Software Systems Manager
Ann Arbor Computer Corp., Jervis B. Webb Co., Ann Arbor, Mich.

ESSENTIAL FUNCTION of a warehouse is to supply a storage or float area for accommodating the short term imbalances between supply and demand on the items contained within the warehouse. Under consideration here is the warehouse normally storing a large number of different items with automated hardware for receiving and replenishing the storage systems, together with automated hardware for removing or shipping items from the warehouse.

▶ Major Warehousing Functions

The major flow components in the typical warehouse are shown in *Fig.* 1. In the receiving area of the warehouse, replenishment items arrive at the warehouse usually via either railroad or trucks. The major functions performed in the receiving area are the unloading of stock, verification of the unloaded quantities against the shipping invoice, inspection of the received material for damage, and entering the received material into the warehouse inventory.

Typically, the handling required to move the received material into the storage system involves the following functions: transfer to a palletizing area; palletizing the received stock; and transferring the pallet loads from the palletizing area into some relatively permanent location in the storage system. This movement into the storage system is typically accomplished by some kind of automatic conveyor.

The function of the storage area is to hold the material until needed. The design of the storage area is a fairly complex task, since items of many different shapes and sizes are involved.

Handling from one part of the storage system to another is minimal in most warehousing facilities.

Items in the warehouse which have the highest turnover should be located nearest the shipping area to minimize the amount of time expended in retrieving orders from the storage system. At the other end of the system, however, these items also account for a large proportion of the replenishment material. As such, one also wants to minimize the time required for storing these high volume items..

It has often proved to be true that one cannot minimize both storage and retrieval times simultaneously. A considerable amount of effort has been expended in the last year or two in developing fairly sophisticated storage movement algorithms for the purpose of optimizing the storage and retrieval times. It is one area of handling that promises to substantially increase the throughput capability of automated warehouses.

At the shipping area, orders are received which demand item retrieval from the storage system. The handling component from storage to shipping has several functions associated with it: There is the removal of the pallet from its storage location and its transfer to a de-palletizing operation (unless full pallets are shipped). The de-palletizing operation (whether manual or automatic) removes the required number of items from the pallet, deposits the de-palletized items onto another type of conveyor, and returns the partially unloaded pallet to the storage system. The de-palletized items or cases proceed either directly to the shipping area for loading onto trucks or to an order consolidation area where an entire order is accumulated prior to movement into the shipping area.

The functions of the shipping area include checking off the quantities for each item as they are delivered from the storage system against the shipping invoice;

What functions and problems are involved in today's automated warehousing systems? What benefits can a computer bring to warehousing over and above those which mechanized systems have already achieved? Is it easier (engineering-wise) and/or better (economically) to computerize an existing, mechanized facility than to plan, design, and build a computerized warehouse from scratch? Answers to these questions will aid potential users in evaluating the importance of computers to their own warehousing operations.

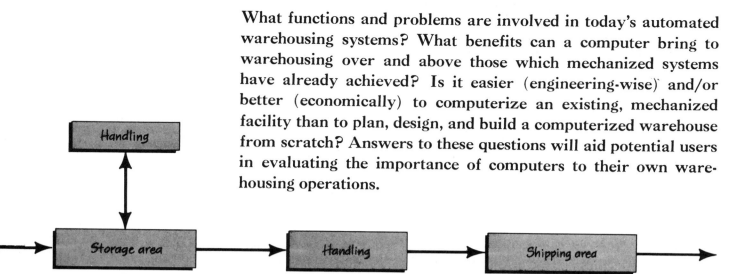

Fig. 1—Major flow components in a typical warehouse include receiving area, handling from receiving to storage areas, handling within the storage area, handling between storage and shipping areas, and shipping area. Operating such a facility efficiently involves controlling information about the items stored as well as the function of the materials handling equipment required to move, store, and retrieve them.

inspecting the material to be shipped for possible damage that may have occurred within the handling components of the warehouse; and verifying that the flow order has been received and loaded onto the trucks for shipment.

▶ Why Computer Control?

Reviewing the above description of the major functions of a medium to large scale warehousing facility, it becomes clear that the success or failure of a warehouse to perform these functions is embodied in the ways in which the problem of control can be solved. In a warehouse, the problem of control focuses on two areas. The first area is the control of information: i.e., the identification of the items and quantities needed for replenishment of inventory, the location of the items currently located in the storage system, and the destinations and times these items are needed for shipment.

The other major aspect of control is the control of the material flow, itself. It is in the area of materials handling that a revolution has taken place in the last 20 years. One can purchase telescoping roller conveyors which can be extended from a truck to deliver either pallets or individual items to a palletizing machine. On the palletizing machine, automation has developed to where one can select any of a number of stacking patterns, and the machine will automatically take the individual cases and stack them on the pallet in accordance with the selected pattern. From the palletizer, materials can be moved by way of an automated conveyor to the load points in the storage system.

At the load points, stacker cranes can be used to automatically pick up the pallet and insert it into the storage system. The same kinds of highly developed automated equipment are available for retrieving pallets and for order consolidation for shipping purposes. To this point in time, the development of this highly automated materials handling equipment has not required a computer for monitoring or control. Thus, it should be clear that most of the control problems of materials handling in a warehouse can and are being done without any kind of direct computer control.

Accordingly, the question is: If highly automated warehouses exist without computer control, then why incur the additional cost both in terms of initial development and maintenance to computerize the warehousing process? What, if any, are the incremental advantages of adapting computers to the already highly-automated warehousing area? There are three immediate performance advantages to computerizing warehousing:

1. The projection of demand and supply requirements which results in automatic scheduling of orders and the preparation of shipping invoices.

2. The relative ease of accessibility to current inventory levels by item. By means of data communications, corporate or warehouse management can interrogate current inventory levels concerning any one or a combination of the items in the warehouse. In addition, the warehouse supervisor can interrogate the computer system as to the storage location of each of these items.

3. Some warehousing installations are beginning to computerize various aspects of the maintenance area in warehousing. Primarily this consists of keeping track of the cost of maintenance (labor and material)

for the many portions of the materials handling system. Providing information on the history of equipment failures leads to a more realistic stocking of spare parts. Although "preventive maintenance" is a highly developed art in the computer world, it is almost unheard of in warehousing. The data contained in equipment failure histories promises to be an excellent source of information for the periodic scheduling of preventive checking and for the maintenance of the materials handling systems in a warehouse.

▶ Levels Of Computer Control

In considering the problem of utilizing the computer in warehousing operations, one needs to recognize that there are three levels of control. The first level might be termed strategic or computer scheduling control. This level of control is concerned with the management of the warehouse as a whole: namely, scheduled ordering, perpetual inventory management, and shipping. The second level of control is tactical: that is, computer direction of the flow through the warehouse. Here, the computer is involved in the decision concerning the flow of particular items through the materials handling equipment into and out of the storage systems. In this case, the computer is issuing commands to various portions of the materials handling system to perform selected functions. For example, the computer may supply the conventional stacker crane with the address in which to store an item currently at the load point.

The third level of control involves the computer as the integral controlling device for the materials handling system. In this case, every move that is made by the materials handling equipment is caused to happen by the operational or controlling computer. Instead of a command which causes certain sequences of control to take place, the computer program defines the sequence of operations that are to be taken by the materials handling equipment.

There are few, if any, truly computer-controlled materials handling systems in today's warehouses. Tactical or computer directed control is beginning to appear in a number of warehouses, particularly those involving stacker crane systems. In this case, when the stacker crane indicates to the computer that it is at its "home" position, the computer outputs a command (store only, retrieve only, or store/retrieve) to the stacker crane control system. Upon receipt of this command the stacker crane is made to carry out the direction by conventional relay control.

This is undoubtedly the first of many areas where the computer is moving inside the warehouse to become a part of the materials control of the system. The development of somewhat complex storage algorithms to substantially enhance the efficiency of both storage and retrieval promises substantial cost savings for the warehouse.

▶ Identifying Major Warehousing Problems

There are three main problems in the highly automated modern warehouse which the application of computers promises to considerably reduce. The first major problem is that of maintaining the integrity of the perpetual inventory that the scheduling control function requires for proper operation. Inventory-updating information can be lost for many reasons, but the principle reason is inaccuracy in identifying to the computer the item and/or quantity of material being received, shipped, or returned from shipment. Another reason is that extensive handling has led to high damage rates. For obvious reasons, damaged material is seldom identified properly to perpetual inventory maintenance. In short, inability to maintain the integrity of perpetual inventory leads to the periodic, expensive, and all too frequent re-inventorying of the total storage system. In a large warehouse the cost of re-establishing the integrity of the inventory is enormous.

A second major problem area in modern warehousing is the loss of items in the warehouse. It is this problem, more than any other, that has impeded the development of computer-directed stacker crane systems and optimal store/retrieve algorithms. The development of this kind of algorithm requires that the location into which a pallet is to be stored must be a decision totally under the control of the computer system. In short, a pallet is never assigned a permanent location but is moved from time to time as the efficiency algorithm dictates.

To guard against the substantial cost of having to re-establish the locations of all items, design people have usually specified that a computer system frequently produce some form of hard copy as to where all items are located in the system. Should the computer system or some portion fail in a way that the location information is lost, this hard copy is re-introduced into the computer system to once again establish the data base. Changes in the assignment that took place after the production of the hard copy are typically introduced by one-line commands via a keyboard.

The third major problem area in modern warehousing is largely a result of the high degree of automation that characterizes the warehouse. As the handling devices have become increasingly automated, the problem of maintaining these devices has also increased manyfold. The kind of maintenance man required in the warehouse of yesteryear is not comparable to the kind of man needed to maintain today's modern warehouse. The modern maintenance person is a highly trained technician. Since these individuals are hard to find and increasingly expensive, the problem of downtime on materials handling equipment has been considerably magnified as the degree of automation has increased.

The downtime problem has increased primarily for two reasons: First, the complexity of the control circuitry has considerably lengthened the time to diagnose the failure of the equipment. Electrical controls people have done an excellent job in making it easy to replace components that have failed, but they haven't been able to come up with designs that substantially reduce the time to troubleshoot a system failure. Second, the multipurpose character of this equipment has made it possible for a whole class of failures to go unrecognized.

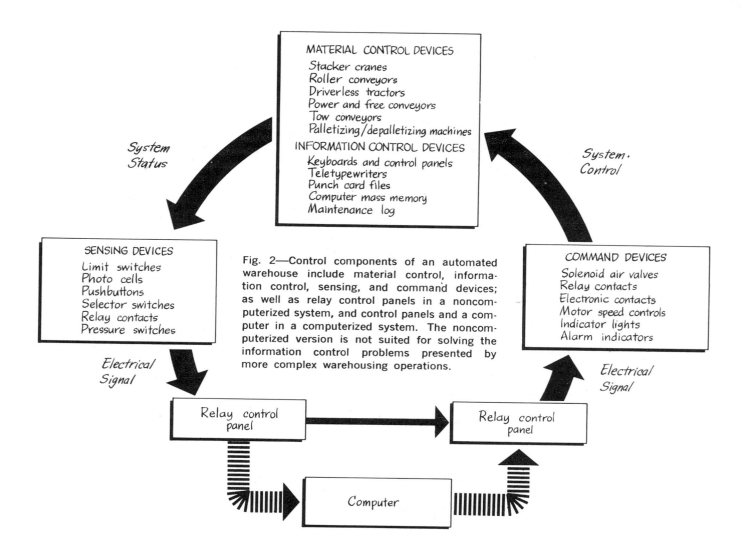

MATERIAL CONTROL DEVICES
Stacker cranes
Roller conveyors
Driverless tractors
Power and free conveyors
Tow conveyors
Palletizing/depalletizing machines

INFORMATION CONTROL DEVICES
Keyboards and control panels
Teletypewriters
Punch card files
Computer mass memory
Maintenance log

System Status

System Control

SENSING DEVICES
Limit switches
Photo cells
Pushbuttons
Selector switches
Relay contacts
Pressure switches

COMMAND DEVICES
Solenoid air valves
Relay contacts
Electronic contacts
Motor speed controls
Indicator lights
Alarm indicators

Fig. 2—Control components of an automated warehouse include material control, information control, sensing, and command devices; as well as relay control panels in a noncomputerized system, and control panels and a computer in a computerized system. The noncomputerized version is not suited for solving the information control problems presented by more complex warehousing operations.

Electrical Signal

Electrical Signal

Relay control panel

Relay control panel

Computer

Increased automation has meant the end of the man on the machine. He knew the machine better than anyone else in the warehouse and probably better than the original equipment designers. Experienced controls people tell many anecdotes about machine operators who, on the basis of subtle variations in the noise or vibration pattern of their machines, could sense that a failure was imminent. For many years, field service personnel relied heavily on the information supplied by the regular machine operators.

Since the machine operator is being replaced in the modern warehouse, a very important machine monitoring capability is also being lost. It is likely, therefore, that many failures of the system will pass without notice. Only those failures that are sufficiently degrading to system performance to draw the attention of operating personnel will be detected. Although not all system failures are necessarily cumulative in nature, many of them are. By the time a system failure is recognized under these circumstances, it is quite likely that substantial effort will be required to re-establish the integrity of the portion of the materials handling system involved.

The utilization of computers can go a long way toward eliminating these problems. Moreover, as will become clear, the computer need not be directly involved in materials handling control. A well designed materials handling monitoring system is all that is required.

▶ How Computers Upgrade Warehousing

The major components of control in a modern warehouse, and the role of the computer in directing materials handling control are depicted in *Fig. 2*. Removing the computer from the loop yields an example of a highly automated but noncomputer-controlled materials handling system. In the noncomputerized case, the relay control panels sense the requirements for exerting control. Signals are sent to the relay control panels which in turn cause relays to activate and operate various command devices such as solenoid air valves, motor speed controls, and alarm indicators. These devices cause the materials handling equipment to be energized and perform its functions, be it stacker cranes, conveyors, palletizing, or de-palletizing machinery.

As each of these equipments performs its function, sensing devices are used to monitor the operations being performed. The sensing devices may be limit switches, photocells, selector switches, or special pushbuttons. These sensing devices, in turn, communicate electrical signals back to the relay control panels.

The panels, in turn, initiate modifications to the original control. To a large extent, the size and complexity of the control panels are a function of the versatility and complexity of the materials handling hardware that is being controlled.

This system concept, however highly automated it may be, has two major shortcomings: First, it has been designed to handle materials control problems, not to process information. Second, it is unable to diagnose its own failures.

To understand the first shortcoming, one needs to distinguish between data and information. Information is the result of applying some kind of analytical strategy to data. Data might be compared to a set of relays in a control panel, some of which are latched, others of which are not. To the person who understands the operation of the circuits, the status of a particular relay provides him with useful information. Data is useless without interpretation.

It is the computer, and not the relay control panels, which is peculiarly suited to solving problems of information management or making information control systems viable. Information control and materials control are two equally important facets of the total control problem in a warehouse.

It can be seen that the three main problems in a modern warehouse as outlined above are primarily problems relating to information control. Concerning the problems of losing the integrity of inventory and losing the location of items in the warehouse, for example, the information control problem is primarily one of keeping track of what material is where. By utilizing the computer direction capability or, more simply, by just monitoring material flow, one can make available to the computer the kinds of feedback data it needs for verifying inventory levels and storage locations of the items. A computer need not be an integral part of the materials handling control system, but it does need to have sufficient data to monitor the flow of parts to the system.

For example, by providing a weighing capability to the computer, the operator who is checking pallets into a storage system can be checked for the entry of erroneous information. The computer is told the weight of each unit of each item. This weight becomes a permanent part of the computer's data base. When the operator enters the information on quantity, the computer can check by the weighing mechanism that the information is at least accurate in terms of weight. The same kind of checking can be implemented at the shipping end of the system. When the operational level, or special purpose computer, has verified that the information received checks out, it can communicate this information to another larger computer which has the responsibility of maintaining the perpetual inventory in the warehouse.

Information control cannot operate on faith. In the case of a computer-directed stacker crane system, for example, it is insufficient to tell the crane controller to store a pallet in a certain location and then simply assume that that location is where the pallet is stored. When it is important to system operation that information be accurately kept on the disposition of the material handled, it is essential to provide the information manager with data which gives him sufficient feedback to be assured that the records he has are an accurate reflection of the state of the real world. By applying computer technology to the monitoring of parts flow into, through, and out of a warehouse, one can do a great deal to mitigate the problems of losing the integrity of one's perpetual inventory and of losing the most essential information about a warehouse: namely, what items are where.

Once this kind of monitoring system is implemented, it becomes clear how the third major warehousing problem—the maintenance of highly automated equipment—can be considerably reduced. Verifying proper flow implies that the computer is already detecting violations of proper flow. By developing the fault detection concept further, computer monitoring can replace the man in the highly automated materials handling systems.

The computer can simultaneously monitor many hundreds of limit switches, relays, and materials flow controls. Moreover, it contains within itself the definition of what constitutes proper flow. It knows the sequence in which signals should be received in the relay control panels if they are to exercise proper control over material flow.

Since the computer is monitoring individual relays and individual control points in the materials handling system, it is fairly simple to add to it the capability of printing out what it diagnoses the cause of the failure to be. At least the computer can indicate to a maintenance man the particular relay or signal which led to the failure. In two industrial applications of this concept of diagnostic monitoring, it has been found that troubleshooting time for the vast majority of system failures has been virtually eliminated. Also,

---

TABLE 1—Functions of Computer Warehousing Controls

INFORMATION

- Identify the types and quantities of items needed for replenishment.

- Locate the items in the system.

- Determine the destinations and times these items are needed for shipment.

- Direct trouble shooting and preventive maintenance.

MATERIAL HANDLING

- Activate and de-activate handling machines.

- Direct each sequence of machine operation.

- Verify accuracy and completeness of each operation.

- Note and report suspected machine malfunctions.

the failure recognition time has been considerably decreased. Failure recognition time cannot be completely eliminated because it doesn't make economic sense to monitor every single relay in the entire warehouse.

The relays that are considered essential to operation are those relays that are selected for monitoring. Accordingly, until one of the critical relays is found to be in error, a failure which may have occurred in the non-critical area will go unrecognized by the monitoring system.

One very important feature has been discovered in these two industrial applications. The vast majority of electrical component failures are the results of performance deterioration. Since the monitoring computer verifies the integrity of each and every sequence that is performed by a set of electrical components, a single failure which might not occur for the next four thousand times will be recorded by the monitoring system. As the deterioration progresses, the monitoring system will, in like manner, record this progressive increase in failures. Accordingly, maintenance personnel tend to ignore the one-time failure and pay attention to the number of violations of a particular component per unit time. If, over a period of time, the proportion is increasing, attention is directed to the failing component. It should be noted that this kind of system may well prove to be a sufficient strategy of "preventive maintenance" in the modern warehouse.

On-line computer control of the materials handling system is not being exploited at the present time. The cost of minicomputers is low enough to compete favorably with the cost of large relay panels, particularly on highly automated machinery which offers the purchaser considerable flexibility. The cost of relay panels is substantially higher than the introduction of small special-purpose computers to do the equivalent control job.

Several materials handling companies are actively experimenting with direct computer control of their machines. It is to be expected that this trend will become more pronounced in the next few years. Most complex machines will be computer controlled. They will be multi-purpose and modular in design. By requesting a different program from the original vendor of the machine, the purchaser can easily meet changing requirements without purchasing a whole new set of materials handling machinery. By the changing of the program, and little else, the end user will have what today would be considered a totally new machine.

▶ Will A Computer Help Your Facility?

How can one decide when it is time to incorporate a computer into his warehousing operation? Is it necessary to plan, design, and build a totally new warehouse to reap the full benefits of computerized warehousing?

Whether or not one can profitably employ a computer at one or another level of control in a warehousing operation is fundamentally a question of system design. A computer should be viewed as one of the many tools available to the materials handling system designer. In smaller warehouses or those without a wide variety of differing items, it is likely that the benefits associated with computerizing will be minimum. If the nature of the demand on the warehouse is such that one can afford a one-to-two-day lag in updating the perpetual inventory, then the major advantages of computerization are not significant.

However, in most medium to large size warehousing installations, there is a wide variety of items, and the supply and demand requirements on the warehouse are such that management needs immediate and reliable information on the current inventory level. The advantages of computer scheduling control—which involves automatic demand projection, automatic ordering, and the preparation of shipping schedules— can be used to substantial advantage in terms of dollar savings. The computer can be used to detect shifting patterns of demand. Management can be alerted for the purpose of evaluating whether or not the shifting is a temporary or long-range phenomenon.

The scheduling level can also be exploited to advantage in the area of scheduled maintenance. The computer is used to maintain equipment failure histories and on this basis can derive statistics, such as mean time to failure, on particular components of the handling systems. It can be used to more effectively utilize the time of maintenance personnel in systematically checking portions of systems that are expected to cause trouble in the near future.

On the third level of control, the direct computer control of materials handling equipment, it is to be recommended that warehousing people rely on the equipment suppliers to exploit the potential. This level of control is really a question of machine design and operation. The companies that manufacture and market these machines obviously have the most experience in designing reliable equipment. Refitting an existing handling machine to run under computer control is likely to be more expensive than purchasing new machinery specifically adapted or designed with computer control in mind. It is unlikely that by applying computer control one can improve an existing machine's throughput.

Discouraging warehousing people from taking the initiative in applying direct computer control to existing machinery does not mean that existing warehouses should not begin to incorporate computers. As was pointed out earlier, there are fundamentally two control problems in a warehouse: the control of material and the control of information. Existing machinery has the reliable control and handling of material flow as its major function. In modern warehouses—particularly those that are highly automated—the problems of maintenance and inventory integrity are hard to cope with without resorting to some kind of computer application. The reason that computers are needed is because these problems are fundamentally problems of information control.

The computer is uniquely equipped for the gathering of data from many sources and the processing of this data to supply useful information to warehouse personnel. What is being suggested is that the tactical or computer direction level of control can be profitably exploited at the present time. It can be incorporated into either existing warehousing facilities or into newly designed facilities. Incorporating the computer in new facilities is likely to promise better payoff, since the computer's involvement is part of the basic system design. In the existing warehouse, it is likely that a certain amount of modification of electrical sensors (primarily relays) will be necessary to implement the computer monitoring system.

Obviously, however, the total cost of adding versus rebuilding is in favor of the concept of adding the computer to existing machinery. If the projected demand is insufficient to justify a new, computerized warehousing facility, it clearly does not make sense to build a new warehouse solely for the purpose of taking advantage of computers. On the other hand, if the demand is such as to require new warehousing facilities, it is unwise to put off consideration of computers until the new warehouse is installed and running.

A warehousing operation should be viewed as a total system. Each of the components of that system has its unique function to perform. The computer is an integral part of the total control problem in a warehouse.

Although some companies have been using the computer at upper levels of control for many years, computerized warehousing is still a largely undeveloped application area. Some of the reasons for this lack of development need to be considered here, since they are part of a management decision concerning whether or not to incorporate computers into warehousing operations.

The hardware technology is, without question, developed to the point where the computer is going to be the most reliable component in the materials handling system. The question still remains, however: what can be done in case of computer failure? How can the data base be recovered? No machine will be 100 percent reliable.

The answer to the problem is not the improvement of computer reliability. The problem is "solved" at the system design level. There is a propensity in the industry to boast about how many different things can be controlled with one computer. This is fine until the computer fails. Then one has considerably more downtime than was envisioned before.

What is being suggested is that the system design should be articulated in a way that several computers are used in warehouse control. The only really valuable information that is lost when a computer fails is the data base that it has been keeping. It is the data base that needs to be protected against computer failure.

The best solution for the small installation is to maintain this data base on a high-speed mass memory such as a disc or a drum. This mass storage medium should be interfaced to the computer in such a way that power loss on the system will not affect the data that is recorded on the device. In larger installations a better solution is probably to maintain the perpetual inventory on the mass storage devices associated with the strategic computer. Typically, this computer is not located at the warehouse site, but is located near corporate or division headquarters.

▶ Coping With The Programming Problem

A number of companies have experienced substantial difficulties in applying computers to industrial control because they have reassigned their business systems programmers to do the job of the real time system programmer. Over the last five years it has become increasingly clear that business type programming is largely unrelated, in concept and design, to programming for industrial control.

The industrial control programmer must have a good understanding of the functional characteristics of the machine that he is programming. He must have experience in the design of interrupt structures and the development of special-purpose monitoring systems. He must be adept at evaluating the timing problems which comprise the fundamental difference between real-time and nonreal-time systems.

A small proportion of programmers are familiar enough with these kinds of considerations to be able to implement a computer system in a warehousing environment. These individuals are in high demand. As a result, few companies want to pay the cost of full-time industrial systems programmers. Once the system is operating, a considerably less experienced individual can carry on maintenance and minor modifications.

New Developments in Automatic Warehouse and Material Handling Control

BURTON I. ZISK

Abstract—A review is presented of the "tools" now available to the materials handling control system designer for integration into control systems for material handling systems, from the limit switch to the programmed logic controller. The importance of coordination of electrical system design with that of the mechanical devices used in the system is discussed.

$\mathbf{A}$N exciting development in the field of automated material handling control has been the recent addition of convenient methods for accumulating large quantities of data in small hardware packages. We now have the capability of accumulating data for inventory control purposes within a control system that formerly provided only direction to the many machine elements that go into making up materials handling systems.

By making use of this ability to accumulate data, we can automatically maintain inventory records on every

transaction on every item being handled in the system at the instant the transaction occurs. It is, therefore, no longer necessary to keep inventory manually for entry into a data accumulation system of some sort when time becomes available.

A major problem encountered in the design of a system for the complete control of material flow through a plant is that if the need for inventory data accumulation is considered at all, it is considered as a problem completely divorced from the machine direction aspect of the system. This is a mistake that should not be made, since a great advantage will be realized when the total capability of an automatic control system is considered. It is much easier to economically justify the purchase and installation of a sophisticated control system when inventory data accumulation is included as part of the system design criteria. The sophistication of operation of modern handling systems has already progressed to the point where it requires, in most cases, little added cost to furnish inventory data accumulation as part of the control system, if this requirement is included as a part of the initial control concept.

Paper 69 TP 99-IGA, approved by the Rubber and Plastics Industry Committee of the IEEE IGA Group for presentation at the IEEE 21st Annual Conference of Electrical Engineering Problems in the Rubber and Plastics Industries, Akron, Ohio, April 14–15, 1969. Manuscript received September 3, 1969.
The author is with Cutler-Hammer, Inc., Milwaukee, Wis. 53216.

Reprinted from *IEEE Trans. Ind. Gen. Appl.*, vol. IGA-6, pp. 180–185, Mar./Apr. 1970.

Much of the data required for inventory control—location of parts in the system, quantity being handled, next destination, etc.—is the same information required for machine direction. Once it has been used to direct the action of our machines, why not store it and have it available for use later, either for machine direction or inventory information? Addition of the equipment to accomplish this purpose at a time after the system is built or even after design has progressed toward completion is not impossible, but is quite costly, in both time and money.

Data available regarding items being handled through a plant are current and accurate as they are changed whenever a transaction takes place in the system. This information is available on any—or all—items in the system at any time. No longer is it necessary to physically search through a number of locations in a floor stock area, handling—and obliterating the data on—many punched cards or assorted pieces of wrapping paper to find a tub of bolts or other parts vital to the operation of an assembly line. Wherever the parts are located in the plant, this location is "remembered" in our memory system and available quickly and simply by pressing a button. The data may be delivered in the form of a typed printout, punched cards, magnetic tape, or in a visual display for immediate action by an operator, if necessary. Integration of the inventory control function with machine direction will result in better system productivity since inventory information is immediately and accurately available at the point of use. There is no need to wait for inventory control information—at best hours old—which must come from time-shared data-processing machines (whose prime function is accounting) before we know how many parts of a given type are stored where in a system. Dialing in a part number and pressing a button will provide the required data in seconds or less.

The devices used for these integrated control and inventory systems are solid-state devices which store data in the form of binary numbers. The binary numbering system uses ones and zeros in a weighted manner to represent decimal numbers. It is a system of numbering to the base two, instead of base ten. Some form of the binary system is convenient to use with modern memory devices, since we can represent a digit one by a closed switch or magnetized "bit" of material, and a zero digit by an open switch, or demagnetized "bit" of material.

Switches and devices for converting decimal numbers (with which we are most familiar) to the binary system are simple to apply and readily available. These devices permit the system operator to "talk" to his machine in a language he understands—mainly numbers. Where necessary, it is not difficult to address the machine in a combination of numbers and letters.

A small, but important, dividend that may be realized by combining machine direction with inventory control data accumulation into the same equipment package is that the hardware used for these functions can be furnished suitable for installation virtually anywhere in an operating plant or warehouse. Most general-purpose data-processing machines—most often used for inventory control purposes when not part of an integrated system—require closely controlled temperature and humidity conditions and filtered air environment. Through experience gained in many on-line applications, our materials handling control designers have learned how to package all of the data-processing devices we use today as part of these integrated systems, so that they may be located at the point of use—that is, on the operating floor with the handling equipment.

A number of devices have been recently perfected that provide the "memory" capability necessary to provide these two features—machine direction and inventory data accumulation—in the same controllers for these automated systems. Magnetic core memories allow us to store, hold, and retrieve (at high speeds) data to control and provide instant inventory status on items in process or storage. The high speeds at which these memory systems operate permit complete random access to selection from storage on any basis required by the design criteria. Selection may be on a first in–first out basis, it may be based on model number, color, size, or any other recordable feature of the unit being handled. Inventory printouts may be provided so that selection from storage may be completely by storage location, at the discretion of the operator, based on information he gleans from the hard copy printout. Punched card readers may be provided that supply information to the system or storage machines. Tapes, both magnetic and punched, may be used to gain access to items stored in the system. Manual keyboards may be used by the operator to address his machine and deliver the required items to him or wherever he directs. And the more conventional switch and pushbutton arrangement may be used for directing items within the machines.

Information stored in any of the magnetic-type memories (cores, drums, magnetic tapes) of a permanent or semipermanent nature—such as part numbers that change when a model change is made—is easily revised by addressing the memory, and removing the data stored in the slot or position being changed. The new data are then inserted into the slot and held in memory until needed. This change may be accomplished by any of the means we have just mentioned; magnetic tape, punched tape, switch and pushbutton, or manual keyboard. The utmost in flexibility is available with these control systems.

With regard to speed of access to stored information, simple magnetic core memory systems operate in the microsecond range, while newer units and software programmed computers operate in the nanosecond range. The microsecond may be more meaningful to us if we consider the microfortnight (a fortnight being a period of two weeks)—a term jokingly referred to by our control designers—which can be shown to be a period of time equal to approximately 1.2 seconds. As we can now see, when we are speaking of conveyor and machine functions that take seconds to occur, these memory systems operating in the microsecond range can perform many functions and look up many things between conveyor functions and have loads of time to spare.

Data may be stored in various ways using punched and magnetic tapes, magnetic drums and disks, and magnetic core memories. Tape memories may be classified as either of two types: punched tapes or magnetic tapes. Magnetic tape printouts are frequently used for sending data on parts spread throughout the plant area to the data-processing department for accounting purposes, billing, shipping, scheduling, etc. The information now available to accounting and data processing is much more accurate and timely, since it now comes from the place where the parts are physically located. It is possible to present this information to the data-processing machines directly by wire link or data phone.

Magnetic drum or disk memories are usually used where a large bulk storage of data is required. Typical application for a memory of this type would be for a "table lookup" where a cross reference between a fairly simple intraplant PCN must be stored and compared frequently with a multidigit alphanumeric interplant part number. To store this table of data in a system main memory would require a great deal of space and time for lookup. Use of a drum or disk for this purpose releases the main memory for on-line operation.

Access time to data stored on a drum or disk is dependent upon the speed of rotation of the system. An attempt has been made to approach random access to the system by providing a number of read and write heads across the drum or disk surface to allow reading of a number of channels at the same time. One system, a so-called random access disk, has a read head for each channel, so that only one rotation of the disk is required to read all data on the disk. Since the disk rotates at about 3600 r/min, the access time is rather fast.

Magnetic core memories are made up of a large number of very small ferrite-filled ceramic doughnuts through which are interlaced a series of wires thinner than a human hair. Since these magnetic cores are so small, a great number of them may be enclosed in a very small package, permitting a very high bulk storage of information in a very small space. The magnetic core memory systems that we are interested in today are known as wired program memory systems, since the inputs to the memory device are based on a prewired set of inputs.

The modern digital computer, which in most cases use a core stack as a main memory section, is very similar in operation to the magnetic core memory system, except that they are software programmed machines—using a program written by an operator. In effect, the magnetic core memory systems are really hard-wired computers. Magnetic core memories provide random access to the data stored in them so that information can be loaded or unloaded from the memory in a matter of microseconds.

This is the range of speed required for real-time control of most of the systems now being furnished in the materials handling field by Cutler-Hammer. In addition to its fast access time to stored data, one of the greatest advantages of the core memory system is the fact that it is a static device without a single moving part.

Great advances are being made in the field of data storage and retrieval, the most important of which are in the area of access time to data stored in memory. Systems are now available with access time in the nanosecond range. As material handling systems became more complex and the amount of information to be stored for inventory control, for example, and for actual system real-time control becomes evident. It may be necessary that a memory device be suitable for handling the operation of a number of conveyors, operating in conjunction with a number of stacker cranes, operating in conjunction with a number of storage machines, all operating on certain cycle times. As access times to information in storage become faster and faster, it is possible to use the same data storage devices for control of quite a few elements in a mechanical system and include inventory data accumulation on the side. It used to be quite simple to worry about length of time only in months, years, days, hours, minutes—maybe even seconds—but the control system designer must break it down even further, into the microsecond and nanosecond range today. The nanosecond is approximately the length of time it takes light to travel one foot. To return to our original time reference, a nanofortnight can be shown to equal 1.2 ms or one one thousandth of 1.2 seconds. These speeds really have little reference to our everyday life but will become the standard until picosecond memories are fully developed.

There comes a point where the complexity of control and quantity of data to be handled becomes so great that we must consider the use of a number of our memory "tools" in combination to provide the control and data accumulation system we require. This had led to the addition of the digital computer to the control designer's "bag of tools." It has also brought with it a number of real psychological problems; just the mention of the word "computer," brings to mind the large, glassed-in complex of bookkeeping machines known as the data processing center. There is no question that data processing equipment has its place in the financial and bookkeeping end of the business; the least of the functions they perform is to handle the payroll. However, we cannot wait even seconds for the data processing machine (which we share time on with the accounting department) for access to memory for data required to control our conveyor system as a pallet approaches a point of diversion; a decision must be made to divert or not. We must apply *special-purpose*, not general-purpose computers to our control requirements so that we can have real-time, on-line control of, and memory for the materials handling system. Application of computers to data processing is as different from applying them to control problems as day is from night. Success of the application of computers to control problems depends upon the designer's ability to understand both the problem to be solved and the capabilities of all the "tools" available to him, including the digital computer.

In designing those control systems, we have established four basic design criteria: reliability, maintainability, simplicity, and compatability.

First, and most important, the control system must achieve an extremely high degree of reliability. The major factors affecting ultimate system reliability are the reliability of the hardware and components, the ratings applied to these components, the circuit design employed, and external disturbances which may affect the control system. All these factors must be taken into account if the final system is to achieve the necessary reliability. Manual backup modes are a "must" in any automatic control system. Since even the most reliable system can, and eventually will fail, the failure mode must be designed into the system so that it becomes "fail-safe." Usually this means that, in case of a control failure the controlled machine will not start, or if it is in motion, will stop.

When and if a failure occurs, our second and third design criteria become important. Simple, easily understood electrical circuits and diagrams allow maintenance people to locate trouble quickly. Since many logic control systems must of necessity become very complex, simplicity is achieved by breaking down the circuits into individual "building blocks." Now the maintenance man does not have to understand how the individual components and circuits operate, but only how each building block operates, and the overall system becomes easily understood.

Maintainability allows trouble to be easily located and corrected. Indicating lights, test points, and metering devices are some of the built-in trouble-shooting tools that are required to allow quick location of trouble. Plug-in components are the single most important aid in correcting trouble. Most properly designed control systems can be rapidly checked by trial and error, by simply removing and replacing "building blocks" until the system functions properly. Although this method is admittedly not very scientific, it does not require much understanding on the part of a maintenance man, and is sometimes the most expedient way to get back in operation.

Lastly, the control system must be compatible with the machine and/or process it is controlling and a memory or inventory device that is controlling it. This requires that the control system designer be intimately familiar with the machine and/or process. He must work very closely with both the machine builder and the inventory system designer during the design stages to assure compatibility of all elements in the overall system. Due to this intimacy of control and memory functions, it becomes more and more evident that a single source of design responsibility is necessary. Some of the most dismal failures in the material handling field have occurred when attempts were made to "marry" independently designed parts and subsystems into complete systems.

Probably the single most popular and widely discussed control element today is static logic. It is also one of the most important "tools" of the control designer. Basically, a static logic element is a solid-state electronic device that performs simple logic functions such as AND, OR, NOT, etc. Since control people have been performing these logic functions for years with relays, there is nothing new about the concept, but only in the hardware employed. However, these devices do offer some important advantages over relay systems. The two most important are life expectancy and speed of operation. Since they are solid-state devices, their life is not measured in terms of number of operations as a mechanical device is, and they operate in times several orders of magnitude faster than mechanical devices. Other important advantages include compact size and weight, low power consumption, and ability to perform complex logic functions. On the other hand, because of the low power level, static logic requires interface equipment for inputs and outputs, which is not required for relay systems. This, of course, adds to the price of static systems. Also, because of the lower power level and extremely high speed of operation, improperly designed static systems are subject to outside disturbances—electrical "noise" from nearby equipment. The effect of this noise can be completely eliminated, but it requires careful design and shielding techniques. Momentary power interruptions which last only microseconds do occur and are not noticeable in incandescent lighting, relay control systems, etc. can affect static systems, and circuit design must take these outages into account so that they do not disrupt system operation.

In evaluating the economics of relay versus static systems, several factors besides initial cost must be considered. In many instances, a higher initial cost system will result in lower operating costs and a lower overall cost. In general, a static control system is indicated when 1) the control system has an extremely high "cycle rate," resulting in many millions of operations; 2) the control system has a relatively small number of inputs and outputs with respect to its logic or decision making capacity; 3) the speed of operation required is extremely fast; 4) minimum space is available for control; 5) minimum maintenance is required because of control location or function.

An example of a logic module that employs all of the features previously discussed is the plug-in module which provides state indication lights for maintenance, and is repairable in case of an individual component failure. The boards are plugged into a compact "bucket," which is wired in the rear. The open construction provides maximum heat dissipation capacity, and the circuits feature easily understood English logic.

Up to now, he have discussed general terms and concepts. Now let us discuss a typical machine control system, and how these design concepts apply to the actual control system. Our example is a stacker crane control system. The job of the control system here is to accurately and reliably position the stacker in response to location commands from an operator or inventory device. Obviously, one of the most important criteria for this control system is position reliability. That is, it must always go to the designated address. Picture, if you will, visually searching for a "lost" load in a large rack system. If this type of failure were to occur with any frequency, utter chaos would result. As an example, 99.9-percent position reliability sounds like a fairly high number, but look at what this means in a typical storage system. A stacker operates on a 1-minute cycle, two shifts a day for 6 days a week. With our 99.9-percent reliability figure, approximately one load a day will be put away in the wrong location. At the end of the first week of operation, seven loads will be in the wrong location. In a short time, inventory control is non-existent and chaos results.

To eliminate this possibility, this control system employs a "positive address" system, which provides a reliability better than 99.9999 percent. Only the simultaneous failure of three components can make this system position in the wrong location.

Each horizontal and vertical location is coded, by means of a permanent magnet code bar with a binary code corresponding to the number of that location. A proximity reader "reads" these code bars as the machine moves, so that the control system always "knows" exactly where it is.

The control system merely subtracts the input information from the position information. The sign of this subtraction tells the machine which way to go, while the magnitude tells it *how far* it must go.

Static logic hardware is used because of the high cycle rate, large number of operations, compact size, and high reliability. A static stepper programmer steps the machine through the sequence of events required for each store and retrieve command.

The positive address system provides extreme flexibility; the pickup and delivery stations can be located anywhere within the confines of the system, and can be changed in the field by a simple wiring change. The binary address system is compatible with "machine language" used in the inventory systems described, providing ease of communication between inventory device and control device.

To allow the physical transfer of information from the stationary inventory control to the moving control on the stacker, a magnetic transfer head is used. The information is transferred magnetically across an air gap, and no physical contact is required.

A solid-state SCR drive provides smooth acceleration and deceleration and eliminates the possibility of spilling a load.

New developments in electronic components promise to provide the control designer with the tools for better and more reliable systems. The most promising of these new developments is the monolithic integrated circuit chip, which will provide logic elements to replace present-day designs at about one-tenth the size and at a much lower cost. These circuits are a reality now, and are being used on industrial control systems designed by Cutler-Hammer.

Developments in the field of transducers will allow better control by providing better feedback on machine status.

The combination of all these elements into a system that will fulfill all the requirements of the purchaser is not just a happening. Successful systems have *not* been those which are made up of a number of devices, both mechanical and electrical, chosen each to accomplish only one small phase of the overall picture without looking at the system as a whole. A prime supplier must be chosen whose function it is to combine all the handling and material flow problems into one concept and then choose the equipment to implement the concept in your plant. He may or may not actually build or manufacture the devices that he ultimately uses for the installation. He will take advantage of the many pieces of equipment that are available on the market to put this system together. The solution to your problem may indicate that getting the absolute best or least expensive or most expensive of each piece of equipment available will not necessarily provide the required operation as outlined by the functional specifications. Only analyzing the problem and equipment from an overall systems standpoint can answer all the questions that arise. It is possible to obtain electrical control apparatus with every mechanized piece of materials handling equipment available today. However, will this provide the control "system" we have in mind to monitor and control the flow of material as we have been discussing it? Chances are better than 99 to 1 that you will not get what you are looking for. The thing that ties all these devices or machines together into a system is the heart of the materials handling system, the design of the controls.

Each control system is unique within itself—a prototype, if you will! Chances of it ever being duplicated for another system are nil since no two systems have exactly the same requirements. This does not mean that the components used are new and untried, but that they are combined in some different way to fulfill your particular needs. As there are many mechanical devices available to provide the necessary functions of a system, many electrical devices are available to provide the various functions required to complete the control of the system. It is knowing what is required to make each individual mechanical component operate in harmony with each other component in the system that will make the system work.

The time to contact the control specialist is at the time when you contact your prime supplier of mechanical equipment or your consultant. The intermarriage of mechanical equipment with control has become so thorough that it is impossible to speak of one without involving the other. As the mechanical equipment dictates the type of control to be used, so the electrical equipment and control requirements may simplify or complicate that system due to certain data accumulation requirements set up by the ultimate user. Again, the successful systems have been those that closely coordinate design of the control with the design of the mechanical system; the most successful and least troublesome systems to design and run have been those where the control designer and mechanical equipment designer have been brought into the picture together, at time zero, before any decisions have been made that will have to be unmade or compromised upon to get even a semblance of a workable system designed. These two facets of the design must be worked hand in hand if we are to fulfill the concept requirements.

During the design phase of the project, our engineers use an analog computer to simulate the operation of various mechanical and electrical components for the system, so that interface equipment can be properly designed. After the controllers are built in our shops, they proceed to the systems test floor where all external devices, such as limit switches, motors, solenoids, etc., are simulated and wired into the system. The system is then run through its paces and does not leave the test floor until the design team and the customers are convinced that the control is operating per specifications. This method of design and test has saved many hours out in the field when the various components are finally merged into the overall system on the customer's premises.

FIG. 1. 102 tests stands check and adjust 20,000 carburetors per day as directed by a GE/PAC 4060 process control computer. Each operator loads and unloads carburetors from several test stands. The room is maintained at a barometric pressure of 29.5 inches of mercury, temperature of 75 deg F, and a relative humidity of under 50 percent.

A Computer Tests and Adjusts Automobile Carburetors

LAWRENCE B. BARNES,
Rochester Products,
Div. of General Motors

Anybody who ever watched a mechanic adjusting a car carburetor would say that the day when carburetors will be tested and adjusted completely automatically will never come. Yet this is what the GM test facility in Rochester, N. Y. has been doing automatically for better than a year at the rate of 20,000 carburetors a day. Here is the description of this system, how and why it came about, and what contributed to its success.

An operator lifts a carburetor from an overhead conveyor, puts it on a test stand, clamps it down and walks to the next stand. A GE/PAC 4060 process control computer does the rest: It demands proper amounts of air flow and measures fuel flow, makes all the necessary adjustments (yes, it actually commands stepping motors that turn the carburetor adjustment screws), makes sure that the carburetor performance is within a 3 percent tolerance over its complete working range, and signals the operator when it is through. If the computer can adjust the carburetor, the unit gets a "pass" stamp and goes to the shipping room; if not, it tells the operator which test was failed, and the faulty carburetor is sent back for repairs or rework.

This testing facility, Figure 1, houses 102 test stands in a pressure, humidity, and temperature controlled "clean" room 420 ft long and 50 ft wide. It tests and adjusts 20,000 carburetors of more than 120 models—single, two, and four-barrel—each day. Before getting into a detailed description of this sys-

Reprinted with permission from *Contr. Eng.*, vol. 16, pp. 95–99, Jan. 1969.

tem, let's talk about the reasons for testing carburetors this way.

How it all began

In 1966 the state of California adopted an Exhaust Emission Standard stipulating that motor vehicle exhaust gas concentrations must neither exceed 275 ppm total hydrocarbons by volume nor 1.5 percent carbon monoxide by volume when tested in accordance with the standard.

To meet this requirement, General Motors decided to tighten carburetor performance tolerances. Prior to this, carburetors were adjusted to fall within 6 percent of the optimum carburetor flow curve, Figure 2. But an exhaustive study revealed that the same carburetors adjusted to lie within 3 percent of this curve can meet the California standard. So the decision was made to start producing "3 percent" carburetors. Prior to 1968 (the year when the California standard was adopted nationally) limited quantities of 3 percent carburetors were made for California cars. The experience gained in producing these carburetors indicated the need for much more accurate test instrumentation; it was also learned that testing time approximately tripled. With production forecasts of 20,000 units a day in 1968, it was obvious that a better way was needed to test the 3 percent carburetors. General Motors engineers were given 18 months to come up with an economical testing method. A fully automatic facility was conceived, designed, built, and put "on line" within this time and has been in operation for better than a year with 99.5 percent availability.

The system and its operation

At the heart of the system is a GE/PAC 4060 process control computer with a 24K core and 128K bulk drum memory, Figure 3. Additional peripheral equipment includes a line printer, 6 typewriters, a card punch, a card reader, and an operator's console. The system employs 136 low-speed scan (200 pps) and 226 high-speed scan (20,000 pps) analog inputs, 1,200 digital inputs, 106 analog outputs, and 4,272 digital outputs. It uses 248 pulse channels (124 forward and 124 reverse), and it has 64 automatic priority interrupts.

The major computer functions that were planned and installed are as follows:
- Data acquisition, logging, and operator's display
- Performance calculations
- Supervisory setpoint control and calibration
- Direct digital control
- Machine sequencing

The computer is completely dedicated to the task of testing and adjusting carburetors. 50 percent of the on-line software was prepared by GM personnel and the other 50 percent by GE. The total programming time by GM was 70 man-months and presently 12 man-months a year is spent maintaining the system software and improving programs to reduce test

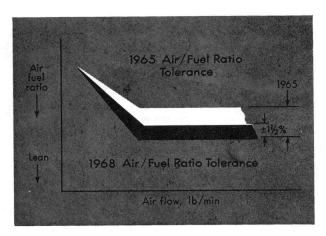

FIG. 2. 1968 Federal Exhaust Emission Standard is met by tightening tolerances on the carburetor air-fuel ratio to air flow characteristic from 6 to 3 percent. Manual testing and adjustment of the 3-percent carburetors would be much more costly than for the 6-percent carburetors. Computerized testing proved to be both economical and superior to manual.

cycle. During the first three months of operation there were 33 hardware and 13 software failures. Since that time the average has been 2 hardware and 6 software failures per month.

Testing a carburetor essentially means testing its ability to mix air and fuel at desired rates under all anticipated road conditions. In all cases a carburetor takes in metered quantities of air and fuel and the computer-controlled testing system monitors and adjusts the carburetor for proper flow of the mixture.

Each test stand, Figure 4, is equipped with fuel and vacuum measuring instrumentation. The fuel is fed to the carburetor under pressure while air is drawn through it in the same way as in a car, that is, by establishing a vacuum underneath it, Figure 5.

Each carburetor is subjected to the following tests:

Code	Test
01	wide open I
02	wide open II
03	snap cycle
04	minimum air
05	choke vacuum
06	early spark advance
07	early spark retard
08	idle
09	off idle
10	late spark advance
11	late spark retard
12	part throttle
13	set idle air screws
00	pass

Since the carburetor's performance covers a range of about 100:1 from no-load to full-load conditions, metering of both fuel and air is carried out by means of several precision orifices and nozzles. The vacuum (or sonic) chamber, for instance, has nine sonic nozzles of different dimensions, Figure 6. Proper air flow for each test is established by selecting a nozzle (or any combination of nozzles). Since the air flow through the nozzles is sonic, measuring the pressure

FIG. 3. With the routine testing and adjustment of carburetors well under control, further program and test improvements can be carried forward. Here Bernard Frank, Manager of Manufacturing Development, and Cliff Mashall, Senior Test Engineer, exchange views on what can be done next.

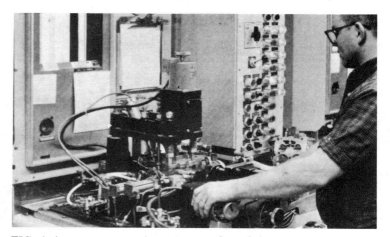

FIG. 4. A computer puts the carburetor through its testing and adjustment sequence as an operator is looking on. Note that while the testing is fully automatic, the shafts of the stepping servomotors are equipped with knobs for manual adjustment of the fuel screws should a system failure occur.

in the sonic chamber accurately indicates the amount of air flow.

The fuel chamber uses six orifices to meter fuel, Figure 7. The fuel flow is then determined by measuring the pressure drop across the orifices.

Empirically it has been established that all the measurements have to be done with an accuracy of 0.25 percent or better to produce a 3 percent carburetor. This degree of accuracy is assured because all fuel orifices are made to a tolerance of one-millionth of an inch. Furthermore, the computer stores a "personality" curve of each orifice for each test stand. Such a curve is obtained experimentally.

Referring to Figure 8, each sonic nozzle is described by a general equation, *y* equals *A + Bx,* where *y* is the pressure transducer output voltage, *x* is vacuum in inches of mercury, and *A* and *B* are constants whose values depend on a nozzle geometry. Once the computer knows these constants, it can calculate what the transducer voltage should be for each nozzle for each value of pressure.

A similar procedure is used for the fuel metering orifices. The only difference here is that these orifices are described by a more involved expression:

$$y = A + Bx + Cx^2 + Dx^3,$$

where y = volts

x = lb per min of fuel flow.

The calibration of both fuel and air systems is checked automatically at regular 8 hr intervals. Transducer zero shift is checked and compensated automatically after each five carburetors tested.

As soon as an operator places a carburetor on a test stand and presses the start buttons, the computer begins testing.

First, it performs several preliminary steps such as filling the carburetor's fuel bowl, erasing the test

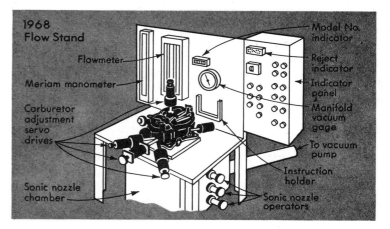

FIG. 5. A schematic of a carburetor test stand demonstrates its major components: a carburetor holding fixture with the adjustment servodrives, sonic nozzle chamber and the display panels. Not shown is the fuel orifice chamber. Also see Figure 4.

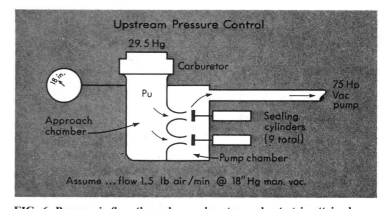

FIG. 6. Proper air flow through a carburetor under test is attained by selecting a sonic nozzle or nozzles as required by the test and the carburetor type. Sealing cylinders seal off those nozzles that are not used. This system essentially simulates normal operating environment of a carburetor where the air flow is established by creating a vacuum within the engine cylinders.

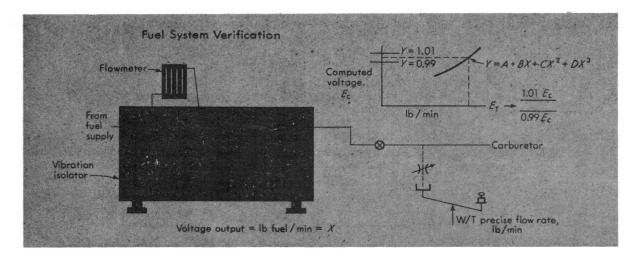

Fuel System Verification

Flowmeter

From fuel supply

Vibration isolator

Computed voltage, E_c

$Y = 1.01$
$Y = 0.99$

$Y = A + BX + CX^2 + DX^3$

lb/min

$E_T \rightarrow$

$\dfrac{1.01\,E_c}{0.99\,E_c}$

Carburetor

W/T precise flow rate, lb/min

Voltage output = lb fuel/min = X

memory and checking the fuel pressure. Then it begins the wide open I test, see Figure 9.

During this test air- and fuel-flow through the carburetor are checked under wide-open throttle conditions. The computer selects the sonic nozzle and fuel orifices, commands the throttle servo to open, and measures and compares the air- and fuel-flow with specified values. Then it stores either a reject or accept code and proceeds to the wide open II test.

During the wide open II test air- and fuel-flow are checked out through a carburetor under maximum wide open throttle conditions. The sonic nozzles and fuel orifices specified for a test on this specific carburetor type are selected, and pulses are sent to the appropriate stepping motor to bottom the off idle, or part throttle fuel screw. The bottoming of the screw is sensed electronically by observing electrical behavior of the motor. The pump vacuum is read and compared with a low limit to determine whether or not the air-flow through the sonic nozzles is sonic in velocity. Then the off idle, or part throttle fuel screw is preset to a calculated value based on the carburetors passed on this stand. Air- and fuel-flow is read and compared with predetermined high and low limits.

The rest of the tests are conducted in a similar manner; for example, the computer issues a sequence of commands in accordance with specifications for the particular carburetor on test. Failure of any test results in rejecting the carburetor. An operator is called to the stand, and the failed test number is displayed. The operator removes the carburetor, attaches a reject tag to it with the appropriate test number, and sends the carburetor to the repair area.

Why the gamble paid off

When the decision was made in late 1965 to design a completely automated, computer-controlled testing facility, there was no place to turn to for advice —this was to be the first such facility. All that was known for sure at GM was that 3 percent carburetors had to be produced economically.

First all the operations that constitute testing and adjusting a carburetor were noted. With this in hand, the GM Electronics Dept. at Manufacturing Development assisted in formulating specifications for the computer system. By May 1966 GM was ready to solicit bids. The vendor (GE) that was awarded the contract in July 1966 was chosen for several important reasons such as price, fast delivery, and agreement to conduct on-site system acceptance tests.

The following months were hectic. Detailed performance specs were drawn up, reviewed by GM, changed, finally approved. While a prototype test stand was being designed by GM's staff, control algorithms were simulated by the vendor to verify the approach. Debugging a prototype test stand under computer control (and continuous redesign) took nine months. This work was done using a computer facility at GM's manufacturing development center in Warren, Mich.

By the fall of 1966 production test stands were ordered. The deliveries started in Spring and continued into Fall of 1967. The system was fully operational by December 1967.

Some of the major factors contributing to the success of this operation were vendor cooperation and personnel selection.

Vendor personnel put in many long hours during troubleshooting programs and hardware. All GM personnel were selected from people with solid backgrounds in carburetor production and testing.

If it had to be done over again, GM would like to have more time for the job and even a better process definition at the start.

The over 99.5 percent system availability experienced to date has been primarily due to a rigid preventive maintenance program and a large supply of spare parts: GM has a full complement of spare parts for the computer system on hand (about 10 percent of the price of the computer system); preventive maintenance requires 8 hrs per week of computer "off-line" time.

During installation, great care was exercised to

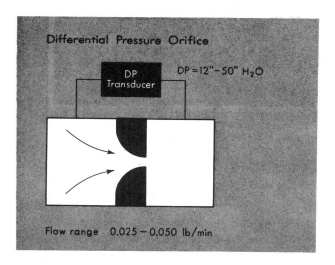

Differential Pressure Orifice

DP Transducer

DP = 12" – 50" H₂O

Flow range 0.025 – 0.050 lb/min

FIG. 7. Proper amounts of fuel for each test are delivered to a carburetor by selecting precision orifices, see diagram, right. The characteristics of each orifice for each test stand are measured and stored in the computer memory. The computer then solves the equation given in the lefthand diagram and compares the specified voltage with that put out by the pressure transducer.

reduce and eliminate electrical noise. All stands, for instance, are grounded to the fuel tank that is buried near the test room. The computer was grounded to the building structure which has a ground system common to the fuel tank. All signal paths are individually shielded twisted pairs. There was no attempt made to save on wires by providing a single common return wire for several circuits, As a result, noise problems were non-existent in spite of many motors and solenoids operating in the test room.

Data logging for production and quality control is now completely automatic. The computer keeps track of production, compiles causes and numbers of carburetor failures, records duration and causes of test stand downtime. Specifications for more than 120 different carburetor models are stored in the computer memory. Any time a stand is used to test a different carburetor, the corresponding program is called up and testing proceeds without any further delays.

In addition to frequent scheduled calibration checks of stands, the computer monitors testing accuracy and reliability in other ways as well. For instance, if five carburetors in a row are rejected on any given stand, the computer shuts down the stand and alerts the operator. The accuracy of the analog-to-digital conversion of the analog scanners is continuously checked. The system also continuously monitors the environment within the "clean" room and prints alarm messages for out-of-limits conditions.

For anyone contemplating the design of a similar large-scale, computer-based control system adequate memory is an important factor. Sufficient memory provides a means of program testing and trouble-shooting as well as the addition of new programs. Any additional program, for instance, can be stored in the spare memory and put on line as desired without the need for modifying or relocating existing programs. This gives the ability to experiment with further system improvements without disrupting the regular carburetor production.   □

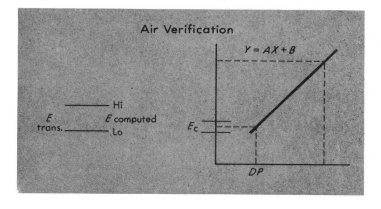

Air Verification

$Y = AX + B$

E trans. Hi E computed Lo

E_c

DP

FIG. 8. During any test the computer predicts the value of the air flow transducer voltage by solving the equation given above. Then it compares the predicted value with the measured one.

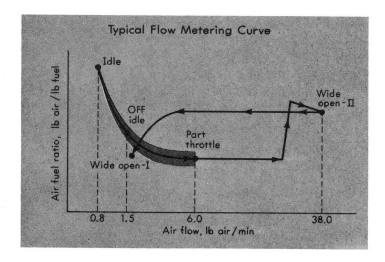

Typical Flow Metering Curve

Air fuel ratio, lb air / lb fuel

Idle

OFF idle

Wide open - I

Part throttle

Wide open - II

0.8   1.5   6.0   38.0

Air flow, lb air / min

FIG. 9. The meaning of several carburetor tests is demonstrated in this diagram. The computer makes sure that each carburetor flow curve is within 3 percent of its ideal shape.

THE AUTOMATION REVOLUTION IN
AUTOMOTIVE COMPONENT TESTING

H. W. Albert
Industry Engineer - Testing Systems
Manufacturing Industries Engineering
Industrial Sales Division
General Electric Company
Schenectady, New York

(Fig. 1)*

Why automate?

The needs for today's economy are placing greater and greater demands with more and more complexity, and at an ever accelerating pace, upon the industrial manufacturer. Customers demand greater variety and better performance; labor demands increased wages and fringe benefits; government demands greater reliability and increased safety; international competition is becoming increasingly vigorous. In such an economic climate, it is necessary for the industrial manufacturer to automate in order to maintain a profitable position in the marketplace.

During the past few years, major advances in control and computer technology, coupled with major economic factors, have set the stage for significant advances in automation of manufacturing operations. It is from these factors-- these Forces of Change--that we will derive the economic justification for the new automation systems and products which are emerging.

Let's review some of these Forces of Change.

Productivity Gap

We are facing a productivity gap. Total labor costs, both direct and indirect, are rising much faster than productivity. As an illustration, let's look at Fig. 2. In 1900, the rate of interest on a million dollars was 6%, or $60,000. A worker cost approximately $600 a year. The wages of 100 workers equaled the interest costs per year. Today, the interest cost on a million is $75,000. A worker costs $7500. Ten workers equal the interest charge. The ratio of workers to capital cost changed from 100 to 1, to 10 to 1 today. Ten years from now, the cost of a worker will be $15,000--and assuming capital will cost the same as today, the ratio will fall to 5 to 1. Capital investments to improve productivity are becoming more and more profitable.

Labor Shortage

We face a persistent labor shortage (Fig. 3). Labor shortages in both professional and factory people are showing up. People must be used more efficiently and more effectively.

Product Proliferation

Today there is product proliferation such as the world has never seen. (Fig. 4) As people's standards of living have improved, they have come to expect a wide variety of products and models--and at mass production prices.

Time Compression

Time compression is a fundamental characteristic of an industrial society. (Fig. 5) In the past 20 years alone, we have seen more technological change than in all recorded history. Changes in methods and procedures are taking place at an accelerated pace.

Reduction in Trade Barriers

A continuing reduction in trade barriers (Fig. 6) is increasing the international flow of goods and is compelling everyone to compete in a world-wide market. And this is a healthy stimulus to business.

It is precisely these Forces of Change that are requiring the adoption of these new automation techniques in the manufacturing area. Automation techniques, as applied to a typical manufacturing plant, might take the following general form:

Production Planning & Schedules are based on orders, forecasts and product structure data. These functions are usually performed by business or EDP computers. (Fig. 7)

Production Control involving detailed work schedules, material and finished goods inventory control, and work and materials status reporting are normally performed by a manufacturing process control computer.

Digital Controllers (or computers) of the medium and mini size perform the functions of:

-- NC machine control and direction
-- materials handling control
-- test and inspection control
-- production monitoring

The Basic Plant Equipment consists of the NC machine tools, stacker cranes and conveyors, test stands and production machines, and their associated work stations.

However, today, we want to discuss only one aspect of manufacturing automation--and that is testing. Testing is an important part of all product manufacturing. Testing is conducted at many phases of the manufacturing cycle--from components to sub-assemblies, to completed

Reprinted from *IEEE Trans. Ind. Electron. Contr. Instrum.*, vol. IECI-17, pp. 363–368, June 1970.

products. Testing can be regarded as a sub-system, or sub-set, of the manufacturing cycle.

Let's take a look at the average computer automated testing subsystem in today's manufacturing environment.

The control computer is the central part of the system (Fig. 8). The computer CPU acts as the director, decision-maker and general clearinghouse for the testing subsystem.

The digital and analog I/O channels are the main control and communications links to the test stand. The test stands provide the physical structure for housing the unit under test. In addition, the mechanical, hydraulic, pneumatic, and electrical interface equipment, as required for the application, is included in the test stand package.

Computer peripherals usually consist of such items as bulk memory for test programs, data analysis programs and data storage; line printer; I/O typer and X-Y plotter.

The detailed economic justification for any computer system should be done by the user's manufacturing, engineering, and finance representatives. There are, however, three areas of savings to which specific dollar values can be assigned. (Fig. 9) These are reduced labor cost, higher production volume from each test stand, and improvement in product quality and uniformity.

The Cost of Labor is Reduced because:

- fewer operators are required
- lower skilled workers can be used
- training time is reduced
- maintenance and repair manpower is reduced
- manpower to collect, compile, and generate reports is reduced.

Higher Production Volume is Achieved from each test stand because:

- test and adjustment time is reduced
- test setup time is reduced
- total down-time is reduced (computer can notify and diagnose down-time reason).

Improved Product Quality and Uniformity are Achieved because:

- more rigid specs can be implemented
- computer will not make intuitive decisions
- tests and adjustments are repeatable and consistent
- if any sensors are not working, tests will not be conducted
- computer can advise if a quality reject trend has been established.

In summary, you will obtain:

- higher production
- lower per unit costs
- better quality

What are some examples of computer automated testing of automotive components?

Automatic Transmission Testing

Automatic transmission testing by computer control is currently in operation at a number of manufacturing plants and scheduled for an additional facility this year. (Fig. 10)

A three-dimensional view of a transmission test facility shows the major test area components:

- input drive and control system
- transmission test stand proper
- output drive system
- interface hardware
- operator's communications console
- process control computer
- operating software

All automotive transmissions receive a final test before shipment to a vehicle assembly plant. A dynamic, running test is performed to determine proper transmission shifting, correct control pressure levels, correct operation of the mechanical gear shift lever mechanism, unusual leaks, noises and proper signal actuation. Such a repetitive test is a logical choice for automation.

Distributor Testing

Distributor testing under computer control is also currently in operation. Fig. 11 schematically depicts a typical installation. Distributors are adjusted for the correct primary and secondary spring tension to provide the desired advance angle for proper firing throughout the engine speed and load range.

Power Steering Gear Testing

Power steering gear testing is another computer controlled application. (Fig. 12) This application involves the control of a highly sophisticated test stand at which the proper adjustments are made, measured, and the final assembly drilled and pinned in place.

Carburetor Testing

Carburetor testing has been one of the most successful and well-known applications of computer automated testing. (Fig. 13)

The need for improved carburetor testing methods resulted from governmental regulations concerning exhaust gas emission composition. To meet these requirements, carburetor adjustments and tolerances had to be improved 100 percent. Manual testing methods were no longer acceptable from a standpoint of accuracy, repeatability, reliability and economics. Computer automation was the only practical solution.

The initial pioneering effort of computer automated carburetor testing was made by Rochester Products Division of General Motors Corporation. A number of technical articles have been written about this installation--and perhaps the most complete and comprehensive of these was the article, "A Computer Tests and Adjusts Automobile Carburetors," by Lawrence B. Barnes of RPD.

As a brief overview--the RPD facility consists of 104 test stands, all under the control of a single process computer, operating in a real time, multiprogramming environment, and testing 20,000 carburetors per day. There are approximately 120 different models of carburetors tested by the system; and at any one time, as many as 20 different models can be tested.

Carburetors arrive at the test stations in a strictly random mix. (Fig. 14)

The duties of the test operator are (Fig. 15) to load and unload the test station, to identify the carburetor by model number, and to apply the proper reject tag if the unit fails test.

The testing cycle is completely automatic-- under computer control. (Fig. 16)

Testing a carburetor essentially means testing its ability to mix air and fuel at desired rates under all anticipated road conditions.

A schematic (Fig. 17) of the closed loop control of carburetor testing is depicted.

The computer stored program contains a listing of the desired value of air-to-fuel flow under the full range of carburetor operation:

> idle
> off-idle
> part-throttle
> wide-open throttle

- For each condition, the computer compares the test value (transducer signal) with the computer-stored digital value.

- Depending upon the comparison results, the carburetor metering screw is turned backwards or forwards until the test value is within an allowed tolerance.

- The positioning of the metering screw is accomplished by a stepping motor controlled by a computer outputted pulse train.

- This is known as adaptive feedback control.

- And in this manner, Rochester Products is able

to test and adjust 20,000 carburetors per day, with a remarkable improvement in product quality.

The results at RPD are:

- 100% test and inspection
- Faster testing
- More accurate testing
- Reduced labor cost
- Summary report printout every hour on accept/reject status

As with all successful, complex installations, the practical solutions of the technical problems involving adaptive feedback control, system response, transducer accuracy and calibration and instrumentation raised many stimulating challenges.

System control algorithms were simulated to verify systems approach, prove technical feasibility, and measure systems response.

Transducer accuracies were optimized by storing in computer memory the calibration curves of individual pressure transducers, orifi and sonic nozzles, and using these data for correction of linearity of reading of the test transducers. Zero checks of primary transducers are automatically made by the computer after every five consecutive readings, and appropriate corrections are made.

The effects of electrical noise and stray pick-up are minimized by using individually shielded, twisted pairs for all signal wires. A superior grounding system was also established.

And, an operations quality control check was implemented that would shut down a test stand after five consecutive carburetor failures have occurred on that particular stand.

In view of this highly successful installation, it is certain that other mass production operations of all kinds will eventually come under the unbiased and untiring eyes of the process control computer.

*Note: Figs. 1, 3 - 6, and 9 were part of an audio-visual presentation and are not included in this paper.

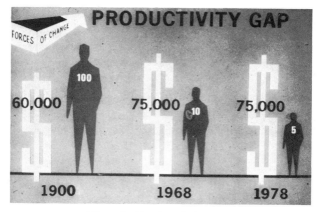

Fig. 2. Productivity gap.

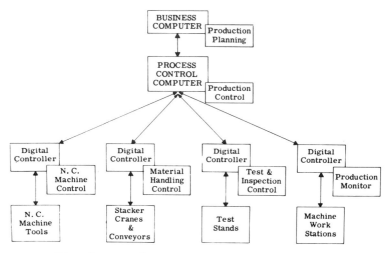

Fig. 7. Manufacturing automation system.

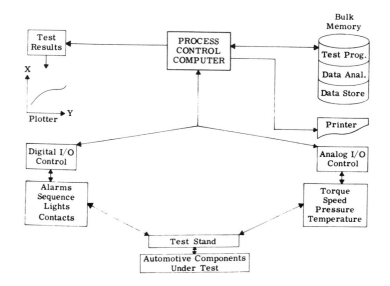

Fig. 8. Testing subsystem.

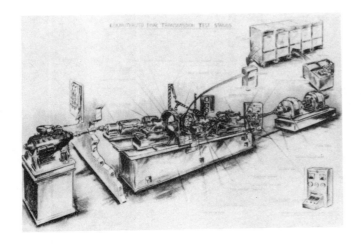

Figure 10.

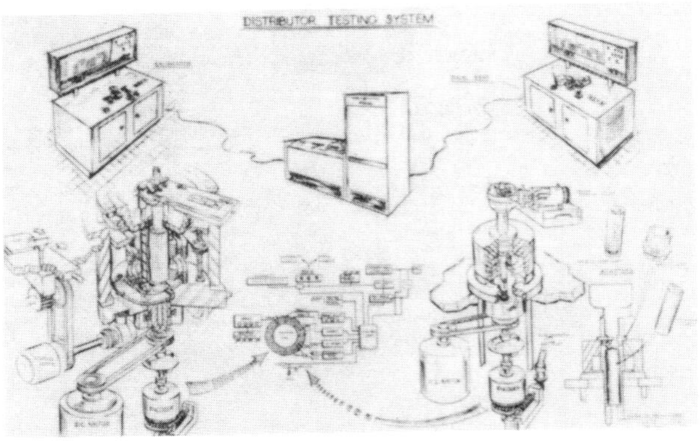

Figure 11.

- **Automatic Testing & Adjustment of**

    - Correct & equal torques
    - Correct pressures
    - Correct centering

- **Automatic Drilling & Pinning of Complete Assembly**

- **Automatic Final Check & Inspection**

Fig. 12. Computer automated power steering gear testing.

- **Automatic Test & Adjustment of Carburetor for Correct Air/Fuel Ratio**

- **100% Test and Inspection**

- **Faster Testing**

- **More Accurate Testing**

- **Summary Shift Reports**

- **Accept/Reject Status Reports**

Fig. 13. Computer automated carburetor testing.

Figure 14.

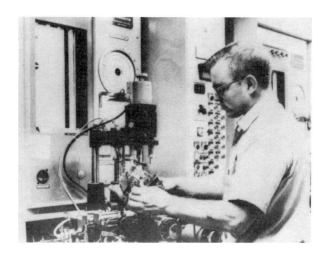

Figure 15.

Figure 16.

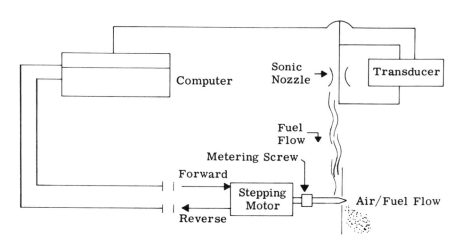

Figure 17. Computer closed loop control.

Part 7
Minicomputer Applications in Communication and Message Switching

Introductory Comments

Not all applications of minicomputers involve input/output devices for direct connection to a process, special consoles for communication with operator, and the like, but rather use the minicomputer as a hidden component in the system. The papers in this part illustrate this use of the minicomputer by concentrating on its application to communications and message switching. The problem here is a rather common one, namely, the control of a large volume of digital data whose origins and destinations are not all close together. An obvious example in the manufacturing system is the problem of order entry where the sales offices in which orders originate are scattered throughout the country. In this case, messages from each of these sources are created and must be transmitted to any of a number of sources, including other sales offices, manufacturing plants, or warehouses that may be scattered throughout the country. Moreover, a message originating at one source may be directed toward many destinations. It may be uneconomical to connect all sources and all destinations by direct wires so that a message may be sent directly from any point to any other point. Rather, it is convenient to have all messages transmitted to a computer which then controls where and how the message is transmitted to the appropriate destination. This has great flexibility, as is discussed in the first few papers of this part, permitting messages to be stored until a terminal is available to receive them, generation of duplicate messages from a single message, and the like.

This type of application will be more and more common in the future. For example, a university with multiple laboratories each with minicomputers doing data acquisition and a large central computer facility requires some control over the way data is transmitted from the mini-computers to the central computer and output back again into the laboratory for display and final use. This is essentially a message switching system and has even more stringent control requirements than the order entry system described above. Essentially, minicomputers can be used to control this traffic flow so that no data is lost, facilities are available when needed, and channels and telephone connections do not become too abundant and hence uneconomical. Even within a manufacturing plant where a large number of minicomputers are used to directly control machines, there is a communication problem that can be solved effectively with mini-computers. It is worthwhile to point out in these applications that the task carried out by the communication minicomputer must be carefully designed, keeping in mind the overall system and its constraints. That is, like most applications of minicomputers, the system is not "stand alone" and is not capable of being designed to be independent of the application, the other computers in the system, etc. The minicomputer is another component in the system.

Many other similar applications of minicomputers are discussed in the papers listed with the bibliography. For example, a minicomputer can be effectively used as a component in a graphic terminal that interfaces to a large computer. The so-called "smart terminal" in effect uses the minicomputer as a hidden component to reduce the hardware requirements in the terminal or to relieve the load on the central computer. It can be used to do many of the complex operations required in pictorial display.

One can imagine many similar applications, including a minicomputer in a check-out line in a supermarket, minicomputers controlling stacker cranes for automatic warehousing, and so on. Input/output devices in these applications are less important since they are more often part of the system rather than the computer. Communications with the external world are usually through modems or other communication line equipment that are readily available even for the smallest minicomputers today. The software problem in these applications can be considerably different since the computer is embedded in the product and not often reprogrammed for specific applications. As a consequence, the tendency today is to use assembly language programming in order to minimize memory requirements in these applications. As indicated in the papers on software, however, higher level languages for application such as these are becoming more feasible, especially as the cost of memory decreases. In reading these papers the software problem should be kept in mind as well as the problems associated with integration of the computer into the larger system. The different hardware requirements (lack of display consoles, compatibility with a variety of peripherals, etc.) can affect the hardware organization so that special purpose minicomputers for these applications become more economical.

Bibliography

[1] "An advance data handling system for environmental testing of satellites," P. E. Muller, *IEEE Trans. Ind. Electron. Contr. Instrum.*, vol. IECI-17, Aug. 1970, pp. 384–391.

[2] "A real-time command and control concept for vehicle dispatching," N. H. Shepherd, *Proc. 1968 Commun. Symp.*, General Electric Paper ECZ-522.

[3] "Minicomputer system for dial-a-ride," M. J. Zobrak, *Proc. 1971 IEEE Computer Soc. Conf.*

Communications and the Minicomputer
by Christopher J. Ball

The technical literature dealing with computing and data communications contains advertisements today for a tremendous variety of data communications hardware; terminals in almost every shape and size, modems, multiplexers, communications pre-processors, and so on. Applications and software packages to be used with this hardware are being described and programmers everywhere are learning how to optimize data transmission to and from their computers.

The reader will appreciate that a data communications revolution is under way that some feel will continue to the point where every housewife will be able to communicate her domestic requirements to a computer from the keys of her Touch Tone®

Telephone and the daily newspaper will be produced in the home on a low cost printer[1]. Already, experiments are underway to enable utility companies to read electricity or gas meters remotely, by a connection to the telephone line, and the portable time-sharing terminal, with which the computational power of a large computer is available anywhere there is access to a telephone, has been with us for some years.

This is the background to an explosive increase in the use of communications for data transmission. More and more frequently we find a minicomputer as a key element in the data communications network, and it is this relationship that will be discussed here.

Telephone Network

One of the most notable aspects of data communications has been the almost universal use that has been made of the telephone network — a system originally designed for voice transmission, not data. It has been the convenience of the existing telephone system, built up over many years and available from coast to coast and worldwide, that has been so attractive to the user of data communications.

Users with a very heavy volume of traffic to transfer between two points — between two computer installations for example — may rent a private line and have uninterrupted use of a high speed connection. A different requirement may be for only occasional use, such as a time sharing terminal, and here the switched network is the obvious solution. The connection between computer and terminal will be made by a caller dialing the required number, exactly as if it were a person being called rather than a computer. The dialogue that follows will be between computer and terminal and, on completion, the call will be concluded in the conventional way, by hanging up the telephone hand-set.

These two opposing requirements, for dedicated and switched lines, are handled economically and reliably by the telephone network, the only requirement being that digital data be suitably modulated on to a carrier for transmission over the voice network. Modems for the modulation and demodulation process are provided by the telephone companies and by many independent vendors, with models suitable for a wide range of data speeds.

Applications

The flexibility of systems configurations, made possible by use of the telephone network, has encouraged applications to evolve rapidly. Early data transmission was primarily used by the railroad companies, while the stock exchange services made heavy use of ticker tape machines. We now have expanded the areas of interest to include credit card verification, airline and hotel reservations, computer timesharing, worldwide message switching systems and complex networks of computers interchanging data between themselves.

In this rapid evolution, the minicomputer, because of its low cost, high reliability and programmability, has recently become a key element in many communications systems. We will examine a few of the more widely found applications of the minicomputer, but the examples given must in no way be considered exhaustive, since new uses are being found for minicomputers almost daily and they lend themselves easily to special system designs.

®Registered Services Mark of A. T. and T. Co.

Message Concentration

The simplest form of data communication to and from, say, a computer complex may be as illustrated in Figure 1. Remote terminals are each connected by individual communication lines to the central computer complex in city "A" and data are exchanged between computer and terminals in accordance with the job to be performed. The terminals may be of many types; Teletype, CRT display with keyboard or remote job entry are just a few examples, and they may be inter-mixed in any order and quantity on the one central computer. This arrangement works well providing that the distance between computer and terminals is not great. As long distance lines become the data transmission media, however, the line rental becomes a very significant part of the total operating cost and it becomes economic, instead, to concentrate the data originating in the distant cities on to one medium or high speed line. Such an arrange-

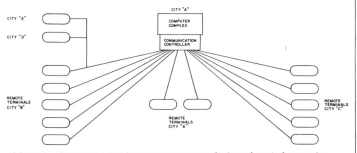

Figure 1. Communication between remote terminals and central computer complex — no concentration.

Reprinted from *Computer*, vol. 4, pp. 13–21, Sept./Oct. 1971.

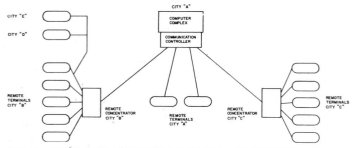

Figure 2. Communication between remote terminals and central computer complex using concentrators.

ment is shown diagrammatically in Figure 2 and represents the terminals in city "B" and those in city "C" being connected by local lines to the Message Concentrators. Each concentrator will accept data from the low speed terminals and concentrate this traffic on to one higher speed line, for the long distance section of the line. The reverse direction of data flow is handled in the same manner for information following from computers to terminals. The remote terminals in city "A" are connected by local lines to the computer in the same city, as before.

The reduction in the number of long distance lines has very significant economic advantages. For example, if cities "A" and "B" are 1000 miles apart and there are 10 terminals in city "B" each of which has a need to communicate with the central computer for 40 hours a week at a transmission speed of 150 baud, the dial-up line charges would be approximately $7960 per month. By installing a leased line between the computer and concentrator with a capacity to handle the same terminals, the line rental will be approximately $1095 per month, a saving of $6875 per month with a one-time multiplexer cost of approximately $8500.

Where does the minicomputer fit in this picture? Traditionally, the concentrating function has been performed by Frequency Division or Time Division Multiplexers. However, the plummeting cost of the minicomputer with some simple communications adapters has made it a very powerful tool with which to multiplex communications data. The added flexibility of a programmable concentrator, as opposed to the fixed configuration of the multiplexer, further enhances its usefulness. The way in which the minicomputer concentrator operates allows a higher concentration ratio than the fixed multiplexers. For example, if the 10 terminals mentioned in the previous example were 150 baud keyboard devices used on a typical inquiry-response system, input traffic would occupy about 10% of the line capacity and output traffic about 60%. A frequency division multiplexer can make no use of the fact that line utilization is low and allocates a fixed bandwidth to the terminal, whether or not data are being transferred. The programmable concentrator, on the other hand, assembles complete messages, or blocks of characters if the messages are very long, in its memory before making any transmission on the medium speed line. Consequently, the data rate on the concentrated line is the product of data rate and utilization factor on all the lower speed lines. The result of this feature is that a larger number of lines can be concentrated onto one line of given data capacity, or alternatively, a lower speed concentrated line can be used for a given number of terminals, than is possible with a simple multiplexer. In the example given, 16 terminals could be multiplexed on to a voice band line using a multiplexer but 33 terminals would be accommodated using the minicomputer concentrator.

Additional Advantages

TABLE I

SUMMARY OF COMMUNICATIONS TASKS THAT CAN BE PERFORMED BY REMOTE CONCENTRATORS

COMMUNICATIONS TASK	TERMINALS CONNECTED INDIVIDUALLY (AS IN FIGURE I)	TERMINALS CONNECTED THROUGH MULTIPLEXERS	TERMINALS CONNECTED THROUGH CONCENTRATOR (AS IN FIGURE 2)
BASIC MULTIPLEXING	NONE	REMOTE MULTIPLEXERS	RMC
CODE CONVERSION	CCC	CCC	RMC
LINE SPEED CONTROL	CCC	CCC	RMC
LINE POLLING	CCC	CCC	RMC
ERROR DETECTION AND CORRECTION	CCC	CCC	RMC

CCC — CENTRAL COMPUTER COMPLEX (includes business data processor and communications controller)
RMC — REMOTE MESSAGE CONCENTRATOR

While the cost of a minicomputer-based message concentrator is somewhat higher than that of a multiplexer at present, there are many additional advantages to be gained from adopting this approach.

The introduction of a minicomputer into the communications network at a site remote from the central computer complex allows us to take advantage of its capacity to perform additional functions, which would otherwise have taken up time in the main computer. Any work that can be offloaded from the central computer is usually valuable, since it is the function of the main machine to perform some revenue-producing or cost-saving task. General communications housekeeping merely diverts the machine from its primary work into a non-productive overhead task. At the same time, the minicomputer is likely to be quite lightly loaded and have spare capacity, at no additional hardware cost, to perform tasks such as code conversion, adaptive line speed control, line polling, error detection and correction. A detailed account of each of these items is given here and a summary appears in Table I.

Code Conversion

Communications terminals are characterized by their multiplicity of codes, line speeds and line disciplines. Early keyboard machines, for example, used the 5-bit Baudot code with one "start" bit and one-and-a-half "stop" bits appended to each character. Since that time, other codes have been introduced based on 6-bit, 7-bit and 8-bit codes with one "start" bit and either one, one-and-a-half, or two "stop" bits. Probably, the two most popular codes used for communicating with keyboard terminals today are USASCII[2] and EBCDIC[3], but many other codes, specific to an industry or to a user, are to be found, and the older codes are still with us because the equipment using them continues to function adequately.

The central computer performs character manipulation with only one preferred character set, however. At some point in the system, code conversion must be performed if the terminal code is different from the native code of the computer. In many communications oriented systems, a variety of terminals will coexist and code conversion is a task specific to each line.

In the basic system of Figure 1, the central computer complex must undertake code conversion, both on input and output for each line, by program reference to look-up tables in memory. If a multiplexer is used in the network, the same is true since the multiplexer is completely transparent to the computer and terminal. Where a minicomputer data concentrator is located at the remote site, all code conversion can be performed simply and the concentrated data flowing in each direction will be in the main computer's native code. In addition, the message arrives from the concentrator as "blocked" information; that is a block of information which originated from one terminal arrives correctly assembled into a message or mesage segment. In contrast, the data transmitted over individual lines or simply multiplexed lines, is in the form of individual characters arriving at different speeds and they must be assembled into blocks by the main computer. This task, usually performed by a combination of software and hardware scanning, is very time consuming and it is of great benefit to perform this function in the message concentrator.

In a similar manner, other terminal-specific characteristics will be handled completely by the concentrator, and be invisible to the main computer. In this category would be included not only the code and code length, but also parity generation and checking, deletion and addition of the correct "start" and "stop" bits, detection and generation of special character sequences which have unique interpretations and, of course, maintenance of the correct data speed on each line appropriate to the terminal in use. This last item would, naturally, have to be performed by any communications controller, but adaptive line speed control is yet another area where the minicomputer flexibility is apparent and can provide assistance to the central computer.

Adaptive Line Speed Control

It has been already noted that the range of keyboard terminals in use today means that a variety of codes must be accommodated by the system. The same is true of data transmission speeds. Low speed data rates most commonly in use today are 75, 110, 134.5, 150 and 300 baud. When the computer communications system allows dial-up operation, the type and speed of the caller's terminal is not immediately known and some method is, therefore, necessary to insure that terminal and computer are each using the same data speed. The simplest method of achieving this is to restrict all terminals on a system to one speed. However, this approach allows the customer only a limited choice of terminal and is not, usually, acceptable. A second approach is to dedicate a block of telephone numbers to 75 baud users; another block of numbers to 110 baud users and so on. The caller merely dials the number appropriate to the type of terminal he possesses. While this is a great improvement over the single speed system, it suffers from the disadvantage that all lines in, say, the 110 baud block may be busy with customers waiting, while there are 75 baud lines unused.

The best solution is to make any line adaptable to any speed, under program control. The initial dialogue between terminal and computer will allow the speed and identity of the user to be determined, the software will set the necessary parameters into the communications controller and the terminal and computer can then communicate. This function, when performed in the remote concentrator, can be carried out entirely independent of the central computer and only when the first message is ready in the concentrator will the main computer be aware of the new user's presence.

Line Polling

So far no mention has been made of yet another method of multiplexing a number of terminals on to one line, the poll and select method. Illustrated on the diagram of Figures 1 and 2 as the terminals in cities "D" and "E", this method allows several terminals to share one communication line. Each terminal is allocated a unique address code and contains sufficient circuitry to make automatic responses when its address code appears on the line. In this way, the central computer can "poll" each terminal in turn by issuing the address code and then waiting for the terminal's response. The reply from the terminal will be of the form "I have a message for you" or "I have no message for you". The absence of any reply at all indicates that the terminal has been switched off or is malfunctioning, and the central computer will make note of this fact.

When all messages to and from the selected terminal have been completed, the computer will proceed to poll the next terminal, and so on until all terminals on the multidrop line have been polled and the cycle will start again. This polling activity can be a significant overhead to the computer and serves no functional purpose other than to economize on communication line charges. The existence of a remote concentrator can ease the situation by undertaking the entire polling and selection sequence, thus relieving the control computer to perform more useful work. The polling sequence, when performed by a remote concentrator, can be modified at any time by commands from the central computer so that control is always maintained by the main processor.

Error Detection and Correction

Remote Environment

The preceding descriptions have explained the functional tasks that can be performed by the minicomputer as a remote message concentrator. The very fact that the concentrator is remote from the main computer site means that it frequently operates unattended, in a basement or small equipment room for example. Reliability is obviously an absolute requirement and here the minicomputer is outstanding. Its small number of circuits, all integrated and all digital, give a mean time between failures in excess of a year in many cases. Maintenance, when it is required, is usually rapid due to the small number of circuit boards in the system, and heat dissipation is low so that closely controlled air conditioned environments are not required.

When software changes are needed, for example to improve or alter a class of service performed by the concentrator, it is usual to "down line load" the new program rather than visit each remote site in turn with a reel of punched paper tape! Down line loading is a special communication mode in which the main computer commands the remote concentrator to consider a message to be an executable program rather than a message to be sent on to a terminal. By this means, the main computer can exercise complete control over all concentrators, the software in each remote location can be updated in minutes instead of days and recovery from power failure at the remote location is easily accomplished. An extension to the usefulness of down line loading is expected to appear in future remote concentrators as remote diagnosis of faults. Here, if a hardware failure at the remote site is reported to the central computer, a diagnostic program can be down line loaded and the results communicated back to the central site. In this way, the field maintenance engineer could be informed of the cause of the fault before he leaves his office and can then be certain he has the correct replacement parts with him.

Another of the many tasks that a communications oriented processor must perform is that of message validation. On today's telephone lines, bursts of noise, clicks, distortion and high background noise are sometimes experienced but are, in most cases, acceptable during voice conversations. However, if a bank is conducting a transaction from a branch office terminal to an account maintained on a central computer file, any error introduced by a click on the communications line is definitely not acceptable. Elaborate means are used, therefore, to check the accuracy and validity of data before allowing the transaction to proceed.

The particular techniques of error detection are highly application dependent, ranging from visual detection by the operator, in non-critical situations, to the use of redundant codes with an infinitesimal probability of an error passing undetected. Error correction usually is accomplished by re-transmission of the character or message containing the error. Although the use of error-correcting codes and subsequent correction of detected errors by the computer is quite feasible, it is not normally economic when re-transmission of the message is so simple.

The error detection and correction procedure is terminal dependent, in the same way as the code procedures described earlier. The computer must, therefore, maintain tables of appropriate procedures for message checking and correction on a line-by-line basis. Again, this is an overhead function that can easily be undertaken by the remote concentrator, which then passes only completely validated messages to the central computer. The main computer complex now, instead of having to accommodate procedures for every type of terminal that may be connected, has only to detect errors introduced between the remote concentrator and the central site and requires only the one correction procedure.

These, then, are the functions of a remote concentrator and the reasons that they are built around minicomputers. As computer-based communications expands, the number of such devices is expected to increase rapidly, due both to their relieving the main computer of significant overhead and to the rapidly falling prices making them competitive with the more traditional multiplexers. Already, large networks are operating successfully with unattended minicomputer concentrators as nodal points in the system and are proving to be a very successful tool in reducing operational costs.

Front End Processors

It was noted previously that the voice-oriented telephone network has become the primary medium for data communications today. It is interesting to note that, in a similar way, the majority of business computers presently in use were not designed to handle data communications efficiently and that the capability was added later rather than being an integral part of the original architecture. Yet it is in data communications that the biggest growth is predicted during the present decade.

It has been pointed out at some length how the message concentrator can assist the business data processing computer by performing communications tasks at a remote location. But why should it be restricted to remote locations? The minicomputer with its communications adapters and operating software can be placed adjacent to the main processor and can undertake all the tasks associated with handling a number of lines, terminals, codes and procedures. The routine and non-productive overhead can be offloaded from the main processor to the communications front end processor, which handles these tasks in a very cost effective manner. Again, fully code-converted and verified messages can be assembled and queued in the front end processor memory, then transferred to the business processor like data from any other peripheral device. Figure 3 shows diagrammatically the front end processor configuration. The normal way in which messages are handled in this environment is to initiate a high speed data transfer across the input/output channel, passing from the core memory of the communications processor and being queued for storage on the business machine's mass storage discs, from whence it can be subsequently retrieved for processing.

Can the available computing power inherent in the front end processor be used to further reduce the housekeeping necessary in the business machine? One such method, used in some larger systems, is to allow the business processor and the front end processor to share access to the disc files. This arrangement, known as the delta configuration, is shown in Figure 4. Reference to other peripheral devices has been omitted from the diagram for clarity, but naturally they remain connected as before.

When the delta configuration is used, the verified and blocked messages assembled in the front end processor are queued for transfer to the disc directly. The connection to the main I/O channel is used for passing control information only, and will be used to notify the main processor of the location and type of message most recently stored on the disc. Messages to be transmitted are handled in the same way, being stored on disc by the business processor and read directly from disc by the front end processor following a control interchange.

This configuration has an added advantage in the area of system availability. When the main data processor experiences an interruption in service due to a malfunction, messages will stop being processed immediately. However, messages can continue to be received by the front end processor and stored on disc ready to be processed when full service is restored. Receipt of messages can continue in this manner until all the available disc storage has been filled. Equally, completed messages already on the disc and waiting for transmission can continue to be sent during the break in service. Finally, it is possible for the communications processor to inform remote terminal stations of the degraded service instead of cutting them off abruptly, thus avoiding much telephoning and customer dissatisfaction which usually accompanies unscheduled interruptions.

The minicomputer front end processor is sometimes added on to data processing machines of another manufacturer by systems houses or communication specialists, or may be designed in as an integral part of the original architecture.[4] The potential advantages of this approach are being ever more widely recognized and it is expected that the next few years will see more of the major computer suppliers incorporating communications front end processors in their product line.

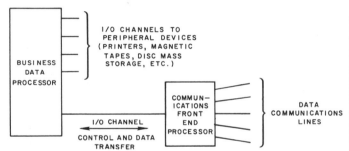

Figure 3. Communications front end processor configuration.

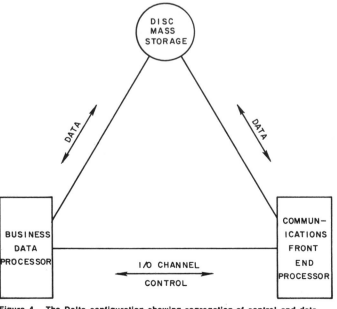

Figure 4. The Delta configuration showing segregation of control and data.

Remote Terminals

Networks

Let us now look at the other end of the communications line — to the remote terminal. Terminals might be broadly classified as (1) teleprinters, (2) CRT displays, (3) remote batch and (4) others, including remote data entry and industry specific (e.g., banking, insurance, etc.) terminals. Some of the smaller remote batch terminals and some of the remote data entry terminals include a minicomputer, although not primarily for communications control. However, the picture would not be complete without at least a mention of these devices.

A remote batch terminal allows a user to perform data processing jobs at a site remote from the main computer, but using the computational power and data base of the central computer. A typical medium size terminal of this type would include a card reader, line printer, keyboard printer, communications channel and a controller. The controller may be a fixed-function device but programmable controllers, often based on a minicomputer, are becoming the most popular type. The programmable approach means that one terminal design can perform several different functions merely by changing the stored program. In one mode, for example, punched cards can be read, the data transmitted to the central computer for processing, the results transmitted back and printed. In another mode, the punched cards might be read and directly printed, without any communication involvement. Other modes include a combination of these, for example, when printing standard forms. Here the fixed information and printing format is maintained at the remote site and added to the computed data arriving over the communications line to form a composite printed output. Other uses are easy to find and the scope can be greatly extended as the number and type of peripheral devices at the remote terminal is increased. It may be noted that the largest suppliers of this type of equipment find it economical to design a special-purpose processor for the programmable terminal, optimized around the specific tasks to be performed. Smaller suppliers often assemble a group of peripheral devices around a general-purpose minicomputer, write the application software and sell a very competitive product.

Remote data entry terminals use minicomputers in a rather different way. The office full of keypunch operators punching cards on noisy machines is beginning to give way to the office having a number of keyboards attached to a magnetic tape or disc store. The keyed data is coded, formatted and stored on the tape or disc. Usually, the completed reel of tape or disk pack is physically sent to the data processing center where the information is needed, although in some installations a communications line allows the tape or disc data transfer without physically shipping the storage medium. In this type of terminal, a minicomputer may be found performing the task of formatting and recording the keyboard inputs on to the magnetic storage device, and controlling the communications line to the central computer. As in the previous examples, it is the low cost, flexibility and reliability of the minicomputer which makes it so attractive as a component in the data entry system.

All the discussion up to this point has assumed a communication arrangement controlled by one central machine with the lines and terminals connected radially from it. This is by far the most common configuration of computers with remote terminal attachments. However, the full possibilities afforded by the marriage of computers and communication network is not realized until a further step is taken. This is the concept of an open-ended, infinitely expandable network with no single central control. The prime example of this approach is, of course, the telephone network itself which can be expanded at will by adding elements such as switching offices, trunk lines, local lines, and so on.

The adoption of the network principle allows many computers, often of different types, to perform jobs and to communicate with any terminal on the network. Thus, a terminal operator may have access to a business batch computer, a scientific computer, a time share computer, or to any other remote terminal connected in to the network. Expandability is a key feature of this arrangement. When any element of the network approaches its point of saturation, another element can be added to provide the necessary additional capacity. The computers in the network may be geographically concentrated — in one room if necessary — or may be distributed across a continent or worldwide, such is the flexibility of the system.

A good example of such a network is that under development by the Advanced Research Projects Agency (ARPA) of the U.S. government. The objectives of this network are to allow persons and programs at one research center to access data and use interactively programs that exist and run in other computers on the network.[5] The principle of operation is to provide a high-speed communication path between all computers in the network, and to use minicomputers to standardize all the network control procedures. Figure 5 illustrates the way in which the initial part of the network has been implemented using Interface Message Processors (IMP's) inter-connected by 50 kilobaud communication lines.

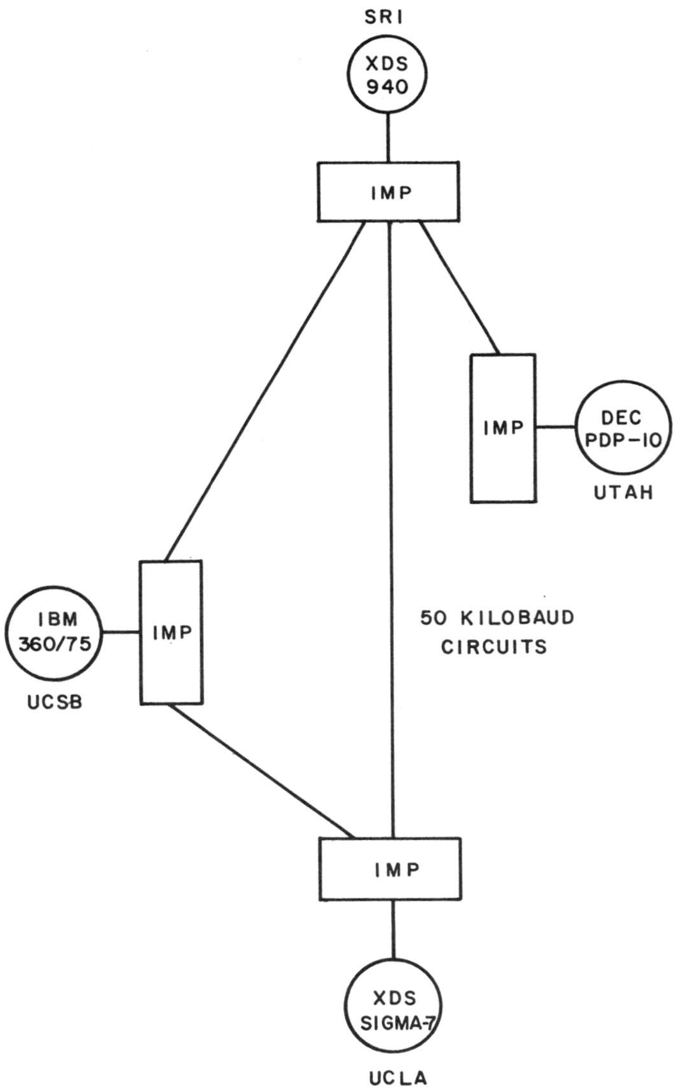

A Host computer is associated with each IMP in the network. Each Host has its own instruction repertoire and word length, and would be mutually incompatible without the minicomputer IMP's. When one Host processor communicates with another, it prepares a message that includes a header with the destination computer address and the requesting user number. This is passed to the IMP which then transmits the message in segments, called "packets". The message passes from IMP to IMP on a store-and-forward basis, being checked for errors at each stage, until it reaches an IMP that recognizes the destination address as being its own Host. The final IMP then strips the network control information from the packets and passes the validated messages to its Host computer. The information may pass through several IMP's on its way through the network and is dynamically routed by each IMP to minimize the total transit time. Updates to the routing information tables in each IMP occur frequently, to take into account very heavy traffic congestion or a malfunctioning IMP or communications link. The average time that a short message is in transit is approximately 0.2 seconds. Consequently, an operator at one machine and calling for processing to be performed on another machine would hardly notice the additional time due to the network. He would, however, have access to a greatly increased computing capability than if he were not connected to the network. Figure 6 shows how the network expansion is planned to include Midwest and East Coast computing facilities in addition to the West Coast centers.

The network principle is a very powerful tool in many environments. A distributed data base, for example, can improve communications efficiency by locating the data where it is most frequently used. Assume, for example, a hypothetical airline with coast-to-coast service and a reservation computer in Denver, Colorado. However, 70% of the airline's planes leaving Boston are going to New York or Washington, D.C. It is not efficient line utilization to transact all the Boston-New York-Washington, D.C. reservations over a long distance line to Denver. A computer on the East Coast to maintain all the local reservations and connected to the main Denver computer would mean a significant reduction in the long distance communications traffic. Each computer would have access to the data files of the other for passengers making through reservations.

Large corporations with decentralized facilities can also use networks and distributed data bases in a similar manner. File integrity is crucial in this environment to insure that only qualified users can obtain access to the computers and the data, much of which is company confidential and of a sensitive nature. One of the advantages of network operation is that computing redundancy exists, with the prospect of still being able to perform useful work even when the local processor is temporarily out of service. This is a particularly valuable feature which is further enhanced by the use of a network having several paths through it from source to destination. Thus, even in the presence of line or network processor failures, traffic can still get through, perhaps with some slight additional delay.

The minicomputer plays its usual role in the network environment of handling the data communications checking, routing, formatting, transmitting and converting of messages in a cost-effective manner. It has won for itself an enviable reputation for reliability when operating unattended 24 hours a day, 365 days a year, and as more users come to appreciate the power of the computing network, more minicomputers will be integrated as critical network processor elements.

Figure 5. Initial ARPA network configuration.

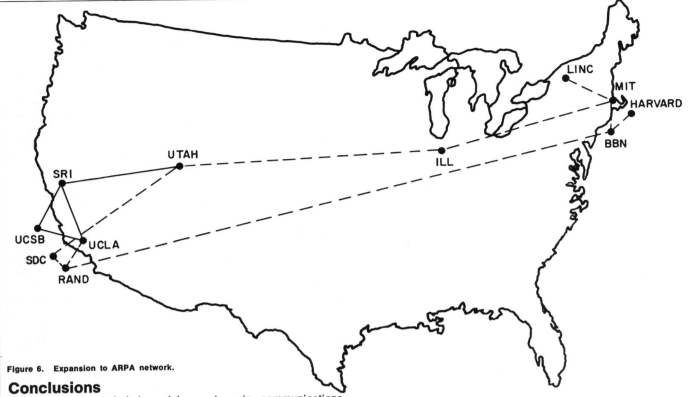

Figure 6. Expansion to ARPA network.

Conclusions

The place occupied by minicomputers in communications today has been illustrated by many and varied examples. Although the examples given here of data communications systems have all been computer-centered, it is not intended to imply that this is the only type of system for which the minicomputer is suitable. Indeed, minicomputer based message switches are in use by common carriers and large corporations for the routing of teleprinter messages both nationally and internationally. However, this application may be considered as a specific example of the general techniques described under networks. The future applications of the minicomputer are expected to be as broad as human ingenuity can conceive, because the costs are coming down, performance is going up and communications is becoming the growth area of the decade. The communications line characteristics are expected to change, as independent common carriers provide competitive data transmission services and the Bell System introduces its own digital data network.

If a specialized communications minicomputer were to evolve to perform the type of services illustrated here, probably the major differences that would be noted from the general purpose machines in use today would be an input/output structure that handles several hundred lines efficiently and further enhancements to the reliability and availability features. The usual technique to achieve high up-time in critical applications is to duplicate equipment and to incorporate either manual or automatic change over when a malfunction is detected. The switches required to achieve the change over are generally specially engineered, however, and are not a part of the original architecture. The ability to remotely diagnose malfunctions of an unattended system is also required in the communications oriented minicomputer. That further development will take place is certain. The power, flexibility of application and low cost insure that communications networks of the future will require an ever increasing number of minicomputers as an integral part of the overall system. Technological improvements will make the machines smaller and will make the communication line interfacing simpler so that they will become a building block in every system designers tool kit.

References

1 Advertisement by McGraw-Hill Publishing Company appearing in October 12, 1970 edition of Electronics, agency Ries Cappiello.

2 USASCII — United States of America Standard Code for Information Interchange.

3 EBCDIC — Extended Binary Coded Decimal Interchange Code

4 C. B. Newport, "Applications and Implications of Mini-Computers," AFIPS conference proceedings, vol. 36, pp. 691-695, Fig. 3, 1970 SJCC.

5 F. E. Hart, et al, "The Interface Message Processor for the ARPA Computer Network," AFIPS conference proceedings, vol. 36, pp. 551-567, 1970 SJCC.

Small computers in data networks

by C. B. NEWPORT

Honeywell, Inc.
Framingham, Massachusetts

Small computers, costing between, say $10,000 and $50,000 each, are rapidly proving to be very important elements in data communications networks. The value of these machines lies in their high speed data manipulation capability rather than in their computing power; in fact, the direct arithmetic capability rarely exceeds simple binary addition and subtraction.

The uses of these small computers can be grouped into two main areas:

1. Remote message concentrators and terminal controllers, and;
2. Communication interfaces for larger machines.

The primary function of remote concentrators is to reduce line costs by multiplexing the data from many low speed lines, up to 150 Baud, on to one or more medium speed lines. This function, by itself, can be achieved by many hardwired devices as well as by a stored program computer; however, the use of a computer with significant storage and data manipulation capability immediately brings many other advantages. Data can be blocked before transmission over the medium speed line, thus, normally eliminating demultiplexing at the large computer site, code conversion and data editing can take place, and various terminal control functions such as automatic answering, polling and error control can be implemented quite flexibly.

The system that Honeywell has implemented in conjunction with American Airlines on the Sabre reservation system is a good example of both concentration and terminal control (see Figure 1).

DDP-516's with two Data Line Controllers interface to the two 2400 Baud lines used for data transmission and hub polling on the Sabre network. On the low speed side up to 60 IBM 1977 agents sets operating at 148.5 Baud are interfaced to the DDP-516 via a multi-line controller. The DDP-516 handles the functions of assembling data blocks, editing out meaningless blanks, responding to polling messages, and the generation and checking of error control information. A number of these remote concentrators have now been in operation for more than six months and they have demonstrated an improvement in response time of about 30 percent over the previous IBM 1006 hardwired terminal control units. This is largely due to the data editing taking place in the DDP-516 so that redundant information does not have to be transmitted to Sabre or to the agents sets.

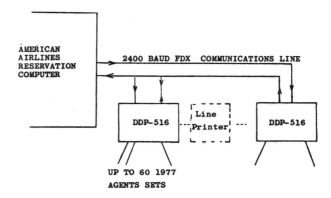

Figure 1

As an indication of the flexibility of the system it was found desirable to add a line printer since some of the reports required on a daily basis from Sabre took an inordinately long time to print on the IBM 1977, 15 character/second agents sets. The standard DDP-516 line printer was, therefore, added to the system, but since this is only an output device, it was not possible to treat it simply as a higher speed version of the 1977 terminal. The Sabre system always responds with a message directed to the terminal that made the request, so "output only" terminals are normally excluded. In this case, with the DDP-516 as the terminal controller, it is possible to monitor input messages from the appropriate agents sets and look for the code indicating that reply is required on the line printer. The message that is actually passed on to Sabre is then a modified version of the request which makes it appear to Sabre as though it had come from the line printer. Sabre then makes its reply back to the apparent originating terminal as usual, and the print-out appears as required on the line printer. This kind of modification would be a major undertaking with a hardwired controller.

The price of the DDP-516 system, with 12K of core, was approximately half that of the corresponding hardwired system. Price comparisons are, however, misleading and need to be considered in each individual situation. In particular, the programming costs need to be considered in relation to the design costs of a hardwired system and general comparisons only tend to be useful when significant quantities are being considered, say, above 10 or 20, so that one-time costs become minimal.

The second use for small computers in data communications, interfacing to larger computers, is illustrated by a number of applications in which DDP-516's and 416's have been interfaced to IBM 360/50 and 360/67, Honeywell H-1200 and 2200 and, perhaps, more interestingly, large scale DDP-516 systems.

The Honeywell H-1648 Time-Sharing System (see Figure 2) illustrates the use of a 4K DDP-416 computer to provide the communications interface to a pair of 32K DDP-516's which are providing a time-sharing

Reprinted with permission from *AFIPS Conf. Proc., Vol. 34, 1969 Spring Joint Comput. Conf.,* pp. 773–775.

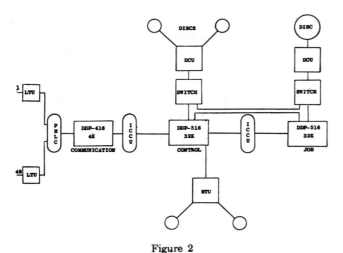

Figure 2

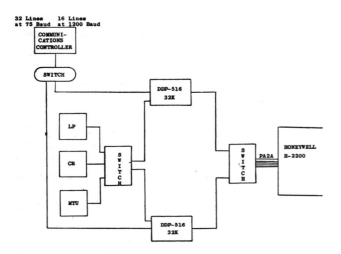

Figure 3

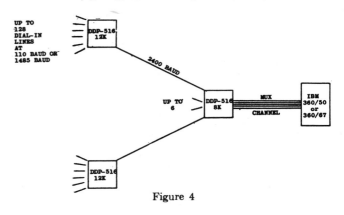

Figure 4

service for up to 48 simultaneous users. The two DDP-516's, the Control Computer and the Job Computer, are normally fully occupied providing the time-sharing and computing operations required by users, while the DDP-416 is dedicated to handling the communications lines. The control computer is the heart of the system and provides the terminal users with the ability to create and manipulate files on the disc complex. When computing operations are required (rather than control or editing functions) such as compilation of a file or the running of an already compiled file, then the control computer schedules these tasks, provides core allocation and disc references for the job computer and initiates operation via the ICCU (Inter-Computer Communications Unit). The job computer allocates a predetermined time period (between 100 ms and one second) for the running of each job and if it is not completed within that time, swaps it out on to the disc and starts the next job. The I/O structure on the DDP-516 allows processing concurrently with transfers to and from the disc so that delays due to disc access time are not important.

The DDP-416 handles all communication functions and simply presents the control computer with strings of characters and an indication of the terminals from which they have been received. The DDP-416 is used as a bit sampler and is continually scanning the state of the incoming lines at eight times the bit frequency. The interface is designed to be able to receive signals from both dedicated lines and from the switched network. The samples of the incoming lines are processed to determine the state of the line, and if in the character mode, successive samples are used to assemble the character.

To achieve complete verification that the DDP-416 has received the character correctly echo-back checking is used. At each terminal the teletype keyboard and printing mechanisms are connected respectively to the transmit and receive sides of the full duplex communication line, and each character received by the DDP-416 is immediately echoed back to be printed. The user can then be sure that if the teletype is correctly printing the characters which he types, the characters will have been successfully received by the computers.

The DDP-416 is capable of handling at least 64 lines at 110 Baud and if a DDP-516 is used this can be expanded up to 128, although in this time-sharing application the remainder of the system is not designed to handle more than 48 simultaneous users.

The use of a small computer as the communications interface provides cost saving and an increase in flexibility over a hardwired interface. Perhaps, the most significant feature in a system that is subject to high peak loads is the ability of the communications processor to provide flexible buffer storage which can be dynamically allocated to the busy lines, and temporarily suspend the passing of data to the larger computer. In addition, if echo-back is used, the input from the terminal can be slowed down by simply delaying the echo-back. In a system with many random inputs, peak loads will only last for a very short time, so these buffering and delaying techniques are very useful in increasing ultimate system capacity without causing noticeable effect to individual users.

The use of a small computer as a terminal controller for a large computing system

by H. B. BURNER, R. MILLION, O. W. RECHARD
and J. S. SOBOLEWSKI

Washington State University
Pullman, Washington

In the spring of 1967 Washington State University began investigating the possibility of replacing or supplementing its IBM 2702 terminal control unit with a small computer. We hoped to realize four significant advantages from such a move:

1. A small computer—being programmable—offered the opportunity of increased flexibility in the control of remote terminals.
2. The prices of small computers had decreased to the point that it seemed reasonable to expect such a system to cost less than the IBM 2702.
3. Since IBM required that each TTY line be connected to the 2702 via a 3233 line adapter and a 103A or 103F data set, we felt that significant

savings might be obtained through lower incremental costs per line, achieved by providing either direct TTY connection or the use of lower cost data sets on leased private lines.
4. By handling as many communication problems as possible in the small computer, we hoped to reduce substantially the amount and complexity of system modifications in the large computer.

We should emphasize that our primary concern was the internal campus network which involves only local communication lines. There was no thought of using the small computer at a remote location as a data concentrator in order to minimize long distance line costs. This is, of course, an application of small computers to which many companies, particularly time sharing services, are addressing themselves.

During the past 18 months we have been working closely with the Interdata Company on a system designed to meet the above objectives. The system is being delivered in two stages, the first of which has been operating successfully for some months. The second stage is being installed at the time of writing.

Stage 1 consists of an Interdata Model 3 processor,

Reprinted with permission from *AFIPS Conf. Proc., Vol. 34, 1969 Spring Joint Comput. Conf.*, pp. 775–776.

a Multiplexor Control Unit and an interface to the IBM 2870 Multiplexor Channel. The Multiplexor Control Unit connects 32 low speed terminals to the I/O bus of the Model 3 through four data line units each of which by using appropriate couplers can accept data from or send data to 8 remote terminals via direct telegraph lines, TWX lines, and switched or private telephone lines.

To facilitate handling of the multiplexor data, Interdata has provided a special BIM (branch of multiplex) instruction implemented in the read-only memory of the Model 3. This instruction, which is executed as a result of a clock interrupt every 1/7 of a bit time, assembles and disassembles the characters bit by bit stripping or adding the start and stop bits. By interrupting 7 times per bit time, we are able to ensure a sample close to the center of each bit pulse. When a character is completely assembled, it is placed in a fixed location in core memory corresponding to the terminal from which it was sent. Similarly, on output a character is taken from a fixed location in memory and sent out to a given terminal.

The interface between the Interdata system and the IBM 2870 was designed initially to make the Interdata appear as much like an IBM 2702 as possible. Thus, for example, each terminal attached to the Interdata is treated as one of the possible 256 devices that can be attached to the 2870. Also, transmission to and from the 2870 is always in byte mode. However, as a result of early tests with the system, several changes were made to the interface including the addition of extra command and status bits to provide more control to the program operating in the Interdata. This enables us to use the system as a controller in either a polling or contention situation.

When operating in a polling environment, the program in the Interdata is controlled by the 360/67 via interrupts. When the 360 requests data from a given terminal, an input switch is set for that terminal. The program continually scans the one-character-per-terminal buffers for input. When input is available, that is, when a character has been typed, it is converted to 360 format and placed in a line buffer for the terminal provided the input switch is set. If a backspace or line delete character is received, the line is appropriately edited and when the terminating character (x- off) is typed, the edited line is sent to the 360.

When the 360 has data to be sent to a terminal, the data is read, converted, and placed in the line buffer for the terminal. In addition, an extra carriage return and line feed are inserted after the 72nd character to allow printing of full printer length lines. An output switch for the given terminal is then set. Once per character time, the output switch is checked. If set, a character is transferred from the line buffer to the one-character-per-terminal buffer for transmission to the terminal.

With this system all of our objectives have been realized. However, in an attempt to gain even greater flexibility and lower the per line cost, we plan to expand the system in January 1969 with the addition of a second processor—an Interdata Model 4. All of the processing with the exception of the BIM instruction will then be done on the Model 4, a processor which is seven to ten times as fast as the Model 3. The Multiplexor Control Unit and the read-only memory of the Model 3 will be altered to accommodate 64 lines, and we anticipate that virtually all of the available time on the Model 3 will be taken up in executing the expanded BIM instruction. However, there should be relatively little interference with the Model 4 so we expect to have available 15 to 20 times as much processing capability as we now have. Between 5 and 10 percent of this capacity will be used in servicing four 2400 band lines connected directly to the Model 4.

It is clear that a terminal controller such as we have described can simplify the organization and operation of the operating system within the primary computing system. Differences among terminal devices and codes can be accommodated within the controller so that all devices appear the same to the primary system. In addition, control characters such as backspace and shift can be recognized by the controller and appropriate editing action taken before the information is transmitted. In fact, we expect within the next few months to be able to provide immediate syntax checking of each statement of a FORTRAN program as it is entered from a terminal into our remote-job-entry batch processing system, thus providing one of the most useful features of conversational programming in an essentially batch processing environment.

A Programmable Data Concentrator for a Large Computing System

H. BLAIR BURNER, RICHARD P. MILLION, OTTIS W. RECHARD, AND JOHN S. SOBOLEWSKI, MEMBER, IEEE

Abstract—Most large time-sharing computers require some sort of a data concentrator or multiplexor to accept inputs from a large number of low-speed remote terminals. Two major disadvantages of most of these concentrators are that they are nonprogrammable and relatively expensive. This paper describes the use of a small microprogrammed computer with a special instruction wired into the READ-ONLY memory to perform the multiplexing action. This approach has resulted in a programmable terminal controller which will handle up to 32 remotes, and provides enough processing capability to do code conversion and editing. This not only relieves the main computer of these routine tasks, but also reduces the amount and complexity of system modification within the main computer.

A dual processor system with a common memory is also proposed. This system will handle 64 low-speed lines and four 2400-baud lines, yet will have 15 times the processing power of the previous system. This will allow more sophisticated preprocessing, such as syntax checking, in addition to the code conversion and editing. The cost of this system is less than that of some currently available nonprogrammable terminal controllers that will handle a similar number of lines.

Index Terms—Character assembly and disassembly, code conversion, communication line, editing, interface, large computing system, multiplexor system, programmable terminal controller, remote terminals.

Manuscript received June 9, 1969. This work was supported by the Office of Naval Research under Contract N00014-68-A-0410-0001, NR 049-259. This paper was presented at the 1969 IEEE Computer Group Conference, Minneapolis, Minn., June 17–19, 1969.

The authors are with Washington State University, Pullman, Wash.

INTRODUCTION

THIS PAPER describes an approach to the use of a small-scale general-purpose computer as a front-end programmable terminal controller for a large-scale computing system. Most terminal controllers for large-scale systems have involved hard-wired logic and buffer registers designed to assemble characters arriving serially by bit from a number of communication lines and transmit them to the computer, and alternatively to disassemble characters arriving from the computer and place them bit by bit on the appropriate communication line. This approach has required that programs be available in the large computer to handle two or three different character codes and to carry out any character-by-character or line-by-line processing that might be necessary or desirable during the construction of an input file or the printing of an output file. Moreover, in order to accommodate changing terminal types or variations in requirements, one is frequently .faced with complex modifications to the operating system of the large computer. Finally, hard-wired terminal controllers can constitute a major item of expense in a large multiterminal system.

The above facts coupled with a drastic decrease in

Reprinted from *IEEE Trans. Comput.*, vol. C-18, pp. 1030–1038, Nov. 1969.

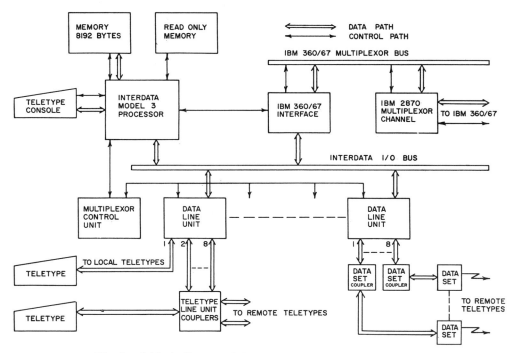

Fig. 1. A block diagram of the programmable data concentrator.

cost of small but relatively powerful processors have led several laboratories, manufacturers, and systems houses to consider the possibility of replacing hard-wired controllers with small computers [1], [2] in the hope of achieving increased flexibility at lower cost while at the same time relieving the large computer of some of its housekeeping chores.

Our own investigations along these lines began in the Spring of 1967 in collaboration with the Interdata Corporation and have been carried out in two stages. During the first stage, a single Interdata model 3 processor with an interface to the 2870 multiplexor channel of our IBM 360/67 was used. This system had a capacity of 32 low-speed (110 baud) lines with a moderate amount of processing capability left over. The second stage of our investigation is now in process and involves a dual processor (model 3 and model 4) system capable of servicing 64 low-speed lines and four voice-grade lines (2000 or 2400 baud) with approximately 15 times the residual processing capability of the earlier system. Also, as a result of earlier experience, the interface has been greatly improved to provide more flexibility and control.

A unique feature of our system is the use of a specially designed READ-ONLY memory instruction to service the multiple low-speed lines. Other systems have utilized the standard instruction set of the computer in order to control the line sampling and character disassembly [1]. The result of our approach has been that a significantly larger percentage of the total capacity of the small computer has been available for processing.

DESCRIPTION OF THE SYSTEM

A block diagram of stage 1 of the system is shown in Fig. 1. It consists of an Interdata model 3 computer

with a special READ-ONLY memory (ROM), 8K bytes of memory, a multiplexor control unit (MCU), and an interface to the IBM 2870 multiplexor channel. The multiplexor control unit connects 32 low-speed lines to the I/O bus of the model 3 through four data line units (DLU), each of which can accept data from or send data to eight remote terminals via direct telegraph lines, TWX lines, and switched or private telephone lines by using appropriate couplers.

Each model 3 instruction that a programmer may use is implemented by a small routine in the READ-ONLY memory. These routines, along with a control program, form what is called the "firmware" of the machine, i.e., they are programmed like software, but for a given machine are wired into the READ-ONLY memory, like hardware. Special-purpose instructions may, therefore, be implemented by coding and wiring a special-purpose READ-ONLY memory. To facilitate handling of the multiplexor data, Interdata has provided a branch if multiplexor (BIM) instruction implemented in the READ-ONLY memory. This instruction, executed as a result of a clock interrupt every 1/7 of a bit time, assembles and disassembles the characters bit by bit, stripping or adding the start and stop bits. By interrupting seven times per bit time, we ensure a sample close to the center of each bit pulse. When a character is completely assembled, it is placed in a fixed location in core, corresponding to the terminal from which it was sent. Similarly, on output a character is taken from a fixed location in core and sent to a given terminal.

All communication between remote terminals and the data concentrator is under control of the Interdata multiplexor system. Communication between the data concentrator and the 360/67 takes place through the 360 interface and is initiated by the 360/67. The interface and the multiplexor system hardware will now be described in more detail.

THE 360/67 INTERFACE

The 360/67 interface enables communication with the IBM 2870 multiplexor channel by changing the channel I/O sequences into model 3 I/O sequences and vice versa. Data transfer may be in either direction and is in the multiplex mode. Sixty-four addresses are recognized over the interface; thus, each terminal attached to the model 3 is treated as one of the 256 devices that may be attached to the channel.

The interface consists of the following functional blocks.

1) *Address decoder–encoder:* These send or recognize the addresses of the specified terminal to or from the channel. Once an address is recognized from the channel, it allows the control logic to recognize further control sequences for that terminal.

2) *Command decoders:* There are two of these. The first decodes the commands sent by the channel and sets the appropriate status bits presented to the model 3. The second decodes commands from the model 3, sets the correct status bits presented to the channel, and controls the response of the interface.

3) *Status registers:* One status register contains the status byte for the model 3, the other presents status to the channel.

4) *Data gating logic:* This controls the gating of status, address, command, and data bytes to and from the model 3 and the channel.

5) *Interrupt control logic:* The interrupt control logic sends an interrupt to the model 3 after each successful initial selection. Whenever a device has been selected by the channel and is ready to send or receive data, the REQUEST-IN line is raised to the channel.

6) *Parity generator and checker:* This generates parity on all the bytes sent to the channel and checks parity of all bytes received from the channel.

7) *Control logic:* This recognizes the various I/O sequences from the channel and changes them to model 3 I/O sequences. Similarly, it changes the model 3 sequences to the channel I/O sequences.

To initiate a transfer, the channel must first go through an initial selection by addressing one of the terminals attached to the model 3 and issuing a command. If the interface is not busy, the device address and the command are saved and an interrupt is sent to the model 3. The device address and the command are then accepted under program control as a result of processing the interrupt. Transfer of data is then initiated by the model 3. When data from the selected device is available or when the device is ready to accept data, the interface raises the REQUEST-IN line to the channel. When this request is serviced by the channel, the interface sends the proper device address and the channel responds by sending or reading the data, depending upon the command pending for that device. In addition to data transfer and initial selection, the interface recognizes control sequences such as proceed, stop, stack status, command chaining, interface disconnect, and reset. Means are also provided for setting and resetting the busy status bit to the channel under program control. This is to prevent an initial selection of a device by the channel while the model 3 is handling an interrupt resulting from a previous initial selection of another device. This is necessary since it takes 150 μs to process an interrupt, while the channel can start successive initial selections in much less than that.

THE MULTIPLEXOR SYSTEM

The multiplexor system provides the interface and control to enable up to 32 teletypes to communicate with the model 3 computer in the full duplex mode. It assembles serial data from each device into characters, and similarly, output data is serialized before being sent to each terminal. The data may come directly from a teletype or from a data set, depending upon the distance of the terminal from the model 3 computer. Synchronization for serial input and output is provided by a clock of fixed frequency, and hence only devices of one speed may be attached to the system. In a later version there will be two clocks to enable devices of two different speeds to be used. The multiplexor system is made up of three major parts; the hardware, the "firmware," and the core buffers, as shown in Fig. 2. The hardware consists of four data line units and a multiplexor control unit. The "firmware" is a fixed program wired into part of the READ-ONLY memory of the model 3. It is this microprogram which controls the operation of the multiplexor control unit and performs the character assembly and disassembly as well as the multiplexing operation. The core buffers are used by the fixed program to perform the necessary bookkeeping. Let us now look in more detail at these individual parts and the way the system operates.

As shown in Fig. 2, the hardware consists of a control unit and four data line units, each capable of servicing eight teletypes via a dc loop or data sets. Local teletypes can be plugged in directly into the data line units, while remote teletypes require either a teletype line unit coupler to permit signalling over the longer loop or a data set coupler. These couplers provide the necessary level shifting and impedance translation between the lines, data sets, and the rest of the hardware both for input and output. Each data line unit provides the interface between eight couplers and the multiplexor bus of the computer. It contains single bit buffering for each line for both input and output, as well as a filter to minimize any noise that may have been generated on the input lines. During output, the contents of the WRITE buffer (8 bits, 1 bit per line) appear on the I/O bus and set the eight transmit buffers. When these are set, their contents are gated to the eight couplers and

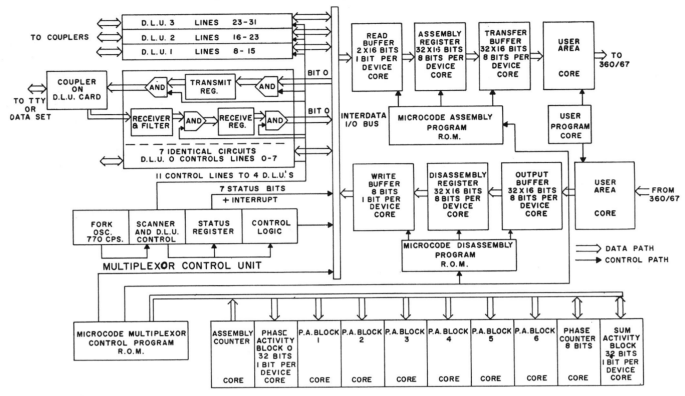

Fig. 2. A block diagram of the Interdata multiplexor system.

hence sent to the eight teletypes attached to that data line unit. On input, the eight single bit receive buffers are set from the receive side of the respective couplers. The receive buffers are then gated onto the I/O bus and into the READ buffer. All the gating and setting of these buffers is under hardware control of the multiplexor control unit, which in turn is controlled by the microprogram in the READ-ONLY memory.

The multiplexor control unit consists of a scanner, status byte register, control logic, and a fork oscillator. The oscillator provides the interrupts to enter the microprogram controlling the multiplexing action and provides the necessary control for the data line units to enable the serial data to be transferred to and from the core buffers where the characters are assembled or disassembled. Since the timing is fixed *within* a character, synchronization is provided by running the oscillator at 770 Hz or seven times the bit rate of the serial data coming from the teletypes. Each of the seven interrupts occurring per bit time is denoted by a phase, the first interrupt being phase 0, the last being phase 6. This scheme allows sampling of the serial data within 7 1/2 percent of the center of the bit time.

The 32 input lines are divided into four groups of eight lines each (each group corresponding to a data line unit); group 0 being lines 0 to 7; group 1, lines 8 to 15; group 2, lines 16 to 23; group 4, lines 24 to 31. The scanner can be set by the microprogram to any of the four groups and can thus generate the proper gating signals for that group to output or input data. Each data request or data available signal received by the multi-

plexor control unit results in the transfer of eight bits to or from the I/O bus. These represent the input or output bits for the eight lines corresponding to the group set by the scanner. The sequence of control signals to the multiplexor control unit for each phase of the clock is given below.

1) *Attention:* This is the interrupt generated by the multiplexor control unit clock at a rate of 770 per second. It causes the multiplexor program (BIM instruction) in the READ-ONLY memory to be executed if interrupts are enabled. The rest of the sequence is under control of this program.

2) *Address:* The CPU addresses the multiplexor control unit.

3) *Status request:* The multiplexor control unit sends its status to the CPU. If it is indeed the multiplexor control unit requiring attention, the multiplexor program is executed.

4) *Command:* This sets the scanner to the group address which corresponds to the eight lines that are to output on this phase.

5) *Data available:* One byte from the WRITE buffer, corresponding to one bit per device, is sent on the I/O bus and gated into the eight transmit buffers. It is then sent to the eight devices by gating it to the eight couplers. The scanner is then set to zero.

6) *Data request for group 0:* With the scanner set at zero, lines 0 to 7 are sampled and sent via the I/O bus to the READ buffer for group 0. The scanner is then incremented to 1.

7) *Data request for group* 1: With the scanner set at 1, lines 8 to 15 are sampled and sent to the corresponding READ buffer. The scanner is incremented to 2.

8) *Data request for group* 2: Lines 16 to 23 are now sent to the READ buffer for group 2 and the scanner is incremented.

9) *Data request for group* 3: Lines 24 to 31 are sent to the READ buffer for group 3.

Upon completion of the data manipulation portion of the microcode program, control is returned to the user program. Before describing the user program, however, let us take a more thorough look at the BIM instruction.

THE BIM INSTRUCTION

The branch if multiplexor (BIM) instruction, a simplified flow chart of which is shown in Fig. 3, is the special-purpose instruction which provides the multiplexing and conversion. It is designed to be executed once per multiplexor control unit clock count. If, when BIM is executed, the MCU is not ready, i.e., a clock count has not occurred since the last execution of BIM, no processing is done, and "return" is made to the instruction following the BIM instruction. If processing is done, the address specified by the BIM instruction is taken as a branch address and control is passed to that point in the user program. If more than one clock count has occurred since the last execution of BIM, an overflow status is set. No processing and hence no branching is done but the overflow indicator is cleared, so that on the next execution, processing will (presumably) be done.

An area of core memory is assumed to be available for use by the BIM instruction routine. This area (100_{16}–281_{16}) is used for buffers, indicators, and counters. Specifically (see also Figs. 2 and 3):

1) A phase counter (P) which takes on values 0 through 6.

2) An assembly counter (A) which runs from 0 to a maximum value, seven times the bit/character count of the remote device type. Both the phase and assembly counters are incremented on each (processing) execution of BIM.

3) Seven 32-bit (1 bit/line) indicators, called phase activity blocks.

4) One 32-bit indicator, called a sum activity block. This is effectively the logical OR of the above seven blocks.

5) A 32-bit READ buffer (called DATA on the flow chart).

6) An 8-bit WRITE buffer (DATA 8).

7) Thirty-two (1/line) 16-bit assembly register buffers.

8) Thirty-two 16-bit input buffers.

9) Thirty-two 16-bit output buffers.

10) Thirty-two 16-bit disassembly register buffers.

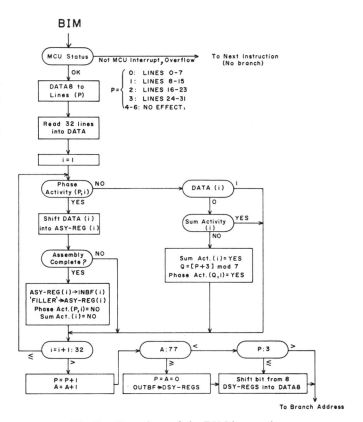

Fig. 3. Flow chart of the BIM instruction.

Although both input and output processing are done on each execution of BIM, explanation of the processes should be simplified by considering them separately.

Output to Remote Terminals

Output activity is forced to be synchronous with the assembly counter (which might more properly be called the "disassembly counter"). A character is started when the counter is reset and finished by the time the counter reaches its maximum value. Data must be sent to a terminal once every seven entries of BIM, i.e., once per terminal bit-time. The phase counter is used to determine when to send data and to which lines it is to be sent. Fig. 4 illustrates this process.

The data to be sent to the terminals is obtained from the disassembly registers. Typical operation, say at phase count 2, is to make up a byte of data by shifting one bit from each of the eight disassembly registers corresponding to lines 16 through 23. On the next entry to BIM, this data is sent to the terminals via the multiplexer control unit. When the assembly counter recycles, the disassembly registers are refilled from the output buffers and the process repeats.

Input from Remote Terminals

The general scheme for input is to sample each line in the middle of each character "bit-time" and to take that reading as the value of the "bit." The phase counter and the activity blocks are used to determine when the sampling should be made. Initially a line is idle and the

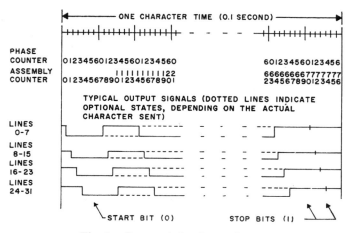

Fig. 4. Output timing for a teletype.

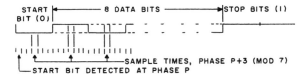

Fig. 5. Input timing for a teletype.

activity blocks indicate "not active." When a start bit (zero) is detected, the sum activity block is set to indicate that the line is active, or to be sampled, during some phase. The phase activity block for the phase three phase times later is also set. This indicates that the line is active and is to be sampled at that time (see Fig. 5). For example, if a start bit is detected on a line at phase count 2, the phase activity block for phase count 5 is set active for that terminal, indicating the line is to be sampled during phase count 5.

Referring to the flow chart, the input processing is the following. All 32 lines are sampled (read). Phase activity for the current phase is determined (for each line). If a line is "not active," the line state is checked. If the line is "1," either the line is idle or it merely should not be sampled during this phase. If the line is "0," the line might be going active, i.e., this might be the first appearance of the start bit. A check of the sum activity block will determine this. If the sum activity block indicates "active," then it is merely the wrong time to sample and the data will be ignored. Otherwise, the start bit is indicated, and the activity blocks are set, as described above.

If the phase activity test were "active," the sampled data value is used as part of the input character by shifting it into the assembly register for the given line. When the character is fully assembled, it is transferred to the input buffer, the sum and phase activity blocks are set "not active." A "filler" value is placed into the assembly buffer. It is the filler value, which consists of all 1's except a zero in an appropriate place, that indicates when assembly of a character is complete. When the zero "pops out" of the end of the assembly register, a character is completely assembled.

Programming Considerations

A number of things may be inferred from the above description with regard to programming for multiplexor operation. The most obvious concerns are the input and output buffers. When a character comes from a terminal and is placed in the input buffer, it remains there until it is overwritten, either by the user program or by another character from the terminal. It is up to the programmer to insure that he examines the input buffers in such a way that the characters are recognized before being overwritten by the following character. At the same time he must insure that he does not try to process the same character more than once. The latter can be accomplished by storing some noncharacter value, e.g., zero, in the buffer after reading a character from it.

The programmer has two responsibilities concerning the output buffers. He must insure that a character has been transferred from the buffer to the disassembly register before placing another character in the buffer. This may be done by examining the assembly counter. When it recycles, the transfer has been made. The second concern is that when he has no more characters to send, the programmer must place an "idle" character in the buffer. Otherwise, the last character is repeatedly output indefinitely.

Another basic responsibility of the programmer is to insure that BIM is executed sufficiently frequently to permit the characters to be assembled/disassembled properly. This can most easily be done on an interrupt basis.

TERMINAL CONTROLLER SOFTWARE

The system described here is a very simple system merely providing character transfer between the IBM 360 and the remote terminals. Additional capabilities are outlined below. The system consists of three major sections: an interrupt handler, which might be considered two sections, handling the 360 interrupts and the multiplexor interrupts; a program which for want of a better name will be called a scanner; and a background program, which for the simple case is merely the wait state. In addition, there are routines which are called upon by the scanner. Flow charts of the interrupt handler, the scanner, and two I/O routines are given in Fig. 6. Briefly the system works as follows.

On multiplexor interrupts (770 per second), the multiplexor interrupt handler is entered. First of all, this routine executes the BIM instruction which does the actual multiplexing operations. The assembly counter is then examined. If it is nonzero, return is made to the background program (wait state). A zero assembly count implies that characters have been transferred from the output buffers to the disassembly registers, and hence the output buffers may be filled again. In this system it is also used to trigger a scan of the input buffers.

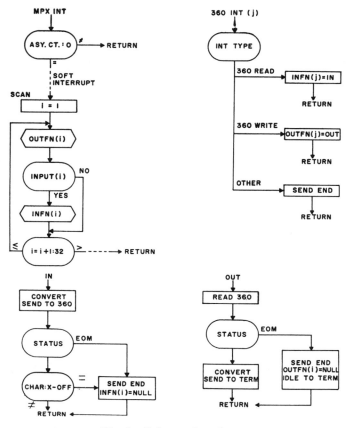

Fig. 6. Software flow charts.

The scanner program is entered from the multiplexor interrupt routine via what might be called a "software interrupt." The original interrupt point is saved and interrupts are reenabled. Thus the multiplexor interrupt routine may be entered while the scanner is working. When the processing is completed, return is made to the saved interrupt point, i.e., to the background program.

Scanner processing is the following. For each terminal, an output routine is executed. Start and stop bits are added to the character returned from the routine (if any), and the modified character is placed in the output buffer for the given terminal. The input buffer is then checked. If not empty, a zero is placed in the buffer (indicating empty), the extra bits left from the BIM processing are stripped off, and the character is passed to an input routine. The input and output routines to be executed are determined by two arrays with routine location entries corresponding to each terminal. When all terminals processed, the scanner is finished.

The two routines used in this simple system are called IN and OUT. IN converts the character to IBM format and sends it to the 360. If the status returned from the 360 is END OF MESSAGE or if the character sent was "x-off," an END command is sent to the 360 which signals completion of the I/O sequence and will usually mean a 360 interrupt will be forthcoming. If END is sent, the input routine array location is set to a dummy routine which does nothing. A similar operation in reverse is done by OUT. In addition, on END OF MESSAGE, OUT sets an "idle" character into the output buffer.

The system, which is used for remote job entry to the IBM 360 is controlled by the 360. Initially, the arrays are set to the dummy "nothing" routines. The 360 will interrupt the Interdata with READ or WRITE requests when ready to transfer data. Associated with each interrupt is an address which can be correlated to a particular terminal. The interrupt routine sets the array associated with the proper terminal to IN or OUT depending on the type of interrupt.

SOFTWARE CONSIDERATIONS

The basic consideration in an application such as this is timing. Some of the questions which need to be answered are the following. How many terminals can be processed? How much processing can be done for each terminal? What happens when desired processing time exceeds time available?

For 32 teletype terminals running at full speed (ten characters per second), it is estimated that approximately 100 Interdata model 3 instructions can be executed per terminal in each character time. Taking into account system overhead, interrupt handling, some sort of "safety factor," etc., we are left with perhaps 50 to 80 instructions that can be executed by an input or output routine. This is more than adequate for the simple system described above. It should also be adequate for a line buffering and editing scheme.

A buffering/editing system has been implemented. The major problem encountered was a possible "overflow" situation if we tried to send several complete lines to the 360 during the same character period. Approximately 10 ms are required to transmit a full line; thus if ten terminals terminated their lines at the same time—a very unlikely situation, but possible nevertheless—the complete character period would be used up and characters coming in from other terminals could be lost. A way around this problem is to put the scanner program in the background and let it run continuously, i.e., continuously check for terminal input or output or for transmission to the 360. Terminal-output time is indicated by a flag set by the multiplexor interrupt routine at assembly count zero. Transmission to the 360 is done by sending one character per terminal per scanner cycle. This is somewhat slower than trying to send the entire line in a block, but has the advantage of being interruptible so that the terminal transmissions can be adequately handled.

This system also solves a fault of the basic system not previously mentioned. If a terminal is transmitting at ·full speed, i.e., from paper tape, and if sampling of the input buffer is done only once per character period as in the basic system, it can be shown that it is possible to miss characters, i.e., that the input buffer can be overwritten by an incoming character before the system has "read" the previous character. Sampling of the input buffer more than once per character time eliminates the problem. In fact, it can be shown that twice per character time, if the second sampling is fixed in relation to the first, is sufficient.

A slight sophistication was added to the output routine to "fold" the output lines. This consisted of reading the 360 and sending characters to a terminal once per character time as in the basic system, but also counting the printable characters as they were sent. When the count reached 72, a carriage return and a line feed were sent on successive character times before reading from the 360 was continued.

System 360 Software

The terminal controller described above has been tested successfully in connection with a remote job entry (RJE) system developed originally at Washington State University for terminals (IBM 2741 and model 33/35 teletypes) connected to the IBM 360 through a 2702 transmission control unit. The bits, which arrive at the 2702 serially, are assembled into bytes in the line control word (LCW). A 32-bit LCW is associated with each line on the 2702 and each LCW is identified by a line address. The 2702 is connected to the multiplexor channel via the input/output interface. An input–output operation is initiated by a start input/output operation (SIO). This operation selects the input/output device by specifying its address. A channel address word (CAW) in lower memory points to a channel program which contains a sequence of channel command words. The CCWs are presented to the multiplexor channel one at a time. Each CCW specifies the operation to be performed, the number of bytes to be transferred, the main storage address of the buffer, and certain control flags for possible modification in command execution.

A maximum of three terminal types can be installed on a 2702. The terminal types are specified by line speed, number of bits per character, the transmission code used, etc. At system initialization time, the proper terminal type must be defined for each operational line on the 2702. Once performed, this is maintained until the power is turned off. This procedure involves the issuance of the set address command (SAD). This command is part of the channel program addressed by the CAW. When this command is accepted, the 2702 assigns the proper control and speed to the line specified by the SAD command.

The SAD command is issued by the remote job entry software for the teletypes and the 2741's. Since the Interdata does not recognize the SAD command, the RJE software does not issue the command for terminals attached to the Interdata. A test is made in the IBM 360 to determine if the terminal is attached to the Interdata, and if this is the case, then the first five CCWs in the channel program are overlayed, thus replacing the SAD command. In the software being developed for the system proposed below, the CCWs will be checked and the SAD command will be ignored; therefore, the IBM 360 software will require no changes for terminals attached to the Interdata.

A Proposed Dual Processor System

If the system is to be useful as a programmable data concentrator, it is imperative that the model 3 can execute an adequate number of instructions between multiplexor control unit interrupts. While there is enough processing power in the system described to do

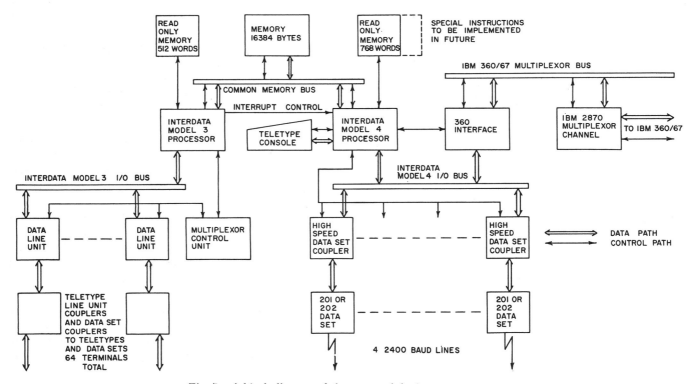

Fig. 7.   A block diagram of the proposed dual processor system.

code conversion and limited editing, there is not enough for more sophisticated processing such as syntax checking. To increase the processing power of this system, it is proposed to expand the present system to include dual processors sharing a common memory as shown in Fig. 7. In this scheme the model 3 will be dedicated to perform the multiplexing action on 64 devices. There will be two clocks in the multiplexor unit, each corresponding to 32 devices. These clocks may be of the same frequency or of different frequencies, enabling the system to work with devices of two different speeds. The model 3 computer will use the lower common core to perform the data manipulation as before. The model 4 computer will have access to the transfer and output buffers to enable communication between the devices and the IBM multiplexor channel. Since the model 4 will be executing exclusively the user program, the data processing capability of the system is virtually the processing capability of the model 4 since there will be less than 4 percent interference by the model 3 accessing the common core. Since the model 4 is approximately seven times faster than the model 3, the new system will increase the present processing capability by a factor of 15 to 20 times. Between five and ten percent of this capacity will be used in servicing four 2400-baud lines. These will be connected to the model 4 I/O bus via high speed data set couplers and 200 series data sets as shown in Fig. 7.

ACKNOWLEDGMENT

The authors are grateful for the help and cooperation of the management and staff of Interdata during this project. Many of the ideas presented here can be attributed to H. Hidu, E. Nestle, and W. Shunaman of Interdata. The authors would also like to thank L. Wheeler for making the necessary changes in the RJE package to support the Interdata controller on our 360 system.

REFERENCES

[1] C. B. Newport, "Small computers in data networks," *1969 Spring Joint Computer Conf.*, *AFIPS Proc.*, vol. 34. Montvale, N. J.: AFIPS Press, 1969, pp. 773–775.
[2] H. B. Burner, R. Million, O. W. Rechard, and J. S. Sobolewski, "The use of a small computer as a terminal controller for a large computing system," *1969 Spring Joint Computer Conf.*, *AFIPS Proc.*, vol. 34. Montvale, N. J.: AFIPS Press, 1969, pp. 775–776.

Data Terminal Control and Partial Retransmission by Mini-Computer

HANS J. BREME, MEMBER, IEEE

Abstract—Described is the use of a mini-computer for the communication control procedures, error detection, and data buffering of one to four on-line data terminals. The interface hardware is general and minimal. The character synchronization and control logic is done by software. An error correction scheme of partial record retransmission is developed. The resulting thruput is compared to that of the Idle-RQ system.

I. INTRODUCTION

DATA TRANSMISSION, particularly over the telephone line, is always susceptible to errors. The raw error rate is generally not acceptable. Therefore, some scheme of error detection and correction is employed. In most applications, this is accomplished with special dedicated hardware. The rapid evolution of error detection and correction schemes suggests that general purpose computers may be used instead of the special hardware. The stored program in such a control computer can perform the error detection and correction as well as the control of the interfaces, modems, and data sources and sinks. The core memory can also serve as buffer for data records for retransmission in case of errors.

II. SYSTEM CONFIGURATION

In our particular system, the computer is a PDP-8 and controls four half-duplex data transmission links as shown in Fig. 1. The PDP-8 interfaces to four 201A data sets (modems), a high-speed paper tape reader and punch, and two magnetic tape drives. The interfaces to the modems are very simple, since the stored program performs most of the control logic. Besides some drivers and gating logic, only one 12-bit shiftregister (SR) is needed for half-duplex operation. The two 12-bit buffers in Fig. 2, one each for the input and the output to the PDP-8, are optional. The 12-bit SR allows the maximum parallel data transfer to the accumulator (AC). If the interface is double-buffered, it allows a delay of up to 12 bit periods in the transfer of words to and from the computer after the computer has received such a service request. The exception is during the synchronization of a receiving station, when only 1 bit period of delay is permitted.

The software control allows data communication with other types of terminals such as the IBM 2700 and 7700

Paper 68TP448-COM, approved by the Data Communication Systems Committee of the IEEE Communication Technology Group for publication after presentation at the 1968 International Conference on Communications, Philadelphia, Pa., June 12–14. Manuscript received January 29, 1968.

The author is with the Engineering Research Center, Western Electric Company, Princeton, N. J. 08540.

series. Furthermore, transmission may take place to different types of terminals simultaneously. The same control computer with its connected interfaces, modems, data sources, and sinks may be changed to a different communications system by loading a different control program. Half of the 4096-word core memory of the computer is used to store the software logic, and the other half is assigned as 512-word data buffers, one to each of the four transmission links.

III. SYNCHRONIZATION

One of the major controls required in serial data transmission systems is the character or word synchronization of the receiving station with the sending station. If the words at two terminals differ in length, then at least their relative offset must be known at any time. The bit synchronization is provided by the modem. With transmission links using modems such as the 201A data set, the start of the first word cannot be directly indicated. Instead it is accomplished by starting the data string with a particular sync character and scanning the beginning of the received string for that sync character. That process must be repeated after each turnaround of the transmission link.

In the interface to the modem the same SR is used for the sending, receiving, and counting of bits per word. That allows the synchronization at the receiving station to be established under software control. While receiving data, the SR shifts the bits to the right at the rate provided by the modem or external clock. After 12 bits have been received, stages 1–12 of the SR are read automatically into the inbuffer, stages 2–13 of the SR are cleared, and stage 1 is set as indicated in Fig. 2. Now 1 shifts to the right in front of the received bits, and when it reaches the stage 13, stages 1–12 are again read into the buffer.

The word in the inbuffer is transferred into the AC under software control. The computer appends that word on the right of the preceding word and forms a 24-bit string. Then it searches that string for a substring which is the sync character. If unsuccessful, it tries again with the next word, forming another 24-bit string. Once the sync character is found, the number of bits k that are to the right of the rightmost bit of the sync character is determined, see Fig. 3. Immediately after the next word has been read from the SR into the inbuffer and into the AC, 1 is loaded from the AC via the outbuffer into SR stage number $k + 1$. The next word is read into the inbuffer and into the AC as a $(12 - k)$-bit word. So far 24

Reprinted from *IEEE Trans. Commun. Technol.*, vol. COM-18, pp. 646–650, Oct. 1970.

328

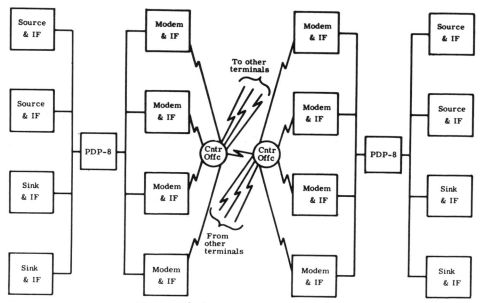

Fig. 1.   Hardware system configuration.

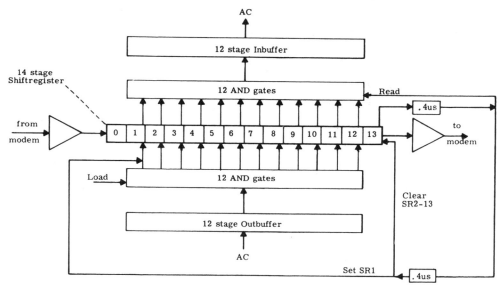

Fig. 2.   Simplified logic diagram of interface to modem.

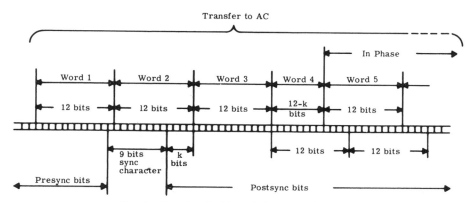

Fig. 3.   Synchronization of character phase.

post-sync bits have been transferred into the computer. They are appropriately assembled into two words which are in phase. All subsequent words are automatically in phase.

IV. Error Detection

The 63,51 Bose–Chaudhuri–Hocquenhem (BCH) code is used. It has a minimum distance of 5, and hence detects all errors involving up to 4 random bits per string. It detects also all error bursts up to 12 bits long, and better than 99.95 percent of all other possible errors as stated in [1]. For greater computer efficiency, in our system the code operates only on 48 bits of data without changing the effectiveness of the code. The checkword and the active portion of the generator polynomial are each 12 bits long, thus utilizing the parallel operation of the computer maximally.

The coding operation is explained very well in [2]. Let the 48-bit data string, the 12-bit checkword, the 13-bit generator polynomial, and the quotient be represented by polynomials $d(x)$, $c(x)$, $g(x)$, and $q(x)$, respectively. The constants of each power in x are either 0 or 1. The power in x is indicated by the position in the string: the zero power at the right, and increasing toward the left. The arithmetic is performed over the field of two. The check word $c(x)$ is arrived at by the formula

$$d(x)x^{12} = g(x)q(x) + c(x)$$

where the lowest power of $q(x)$ is zero. The multiplication by x^{12} is performed simply by appending 12 zeros on the right of $d(x)$. The division by $g(x)$ is equivalent to an exclusive-or operation bit by bit over the 12-bit words in parallel. Otherwise it is similar to ordinary long division. The divisor is

$$g(x) = x^{12} + x^{10} + x^8 + x^5 + x^4 + x^3 + 1$$

or a binary string 1 010 100 111 001. The dividend is $d(x)x^{12}$.

The computer algorithm simulates long division and the exclusive-or operation. See Fig. 4. The quotient is ignored. Because the high-order bit (first in time) in the computer memory and AC is on the right, the operation of the algorithm proceeds from right to left, i.e., opposite to manual long division. The identical algorithm is used for encoding at the sending station and for decoding at the receiving station. The algorithm operates on the 48 data bits and 12 low-order bits. For encoding, the low-order word is zero, representing x^{12}, and the remainder is the checkword $c(x)$. For decoding, the low-order word is $c(x)$, and the remainder is zero if the block is correct. The algorithm requires 47 core locations and two auto-index registers, excluding the data storage. In order to convey a feeling of how a 12-bit computer with only 6 memory reference instructions and without an exclusive-or instruction can perform the coding, the actual program and its flowchart are shown in Figs. 5 and 6. The upper bound for the execution time to code one block is 2.15 ms, or 15818 computer cycles. To receive one block at 2000

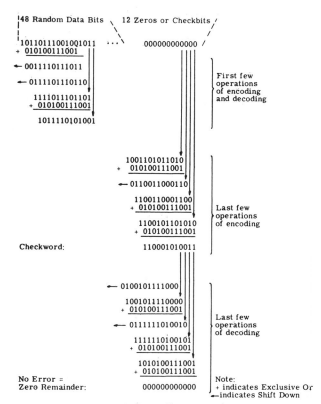

Fig. 4. BCH coding operations.

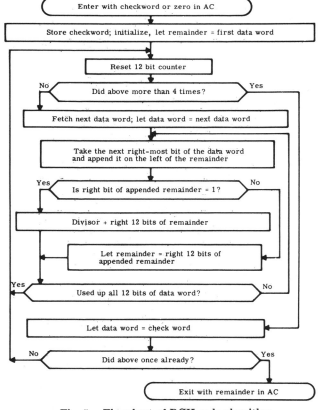

Fig. 5. Flowchart of BCH code algorithm.

```
                / BCH CHECK OR ENCODE
0200    0000    BCH, 0/AC=CKWORD OR ZERO IF ENCOD.
0201    3255    DCA CKWORD
0202    1260    TAD M4/BEGIN INITIAL.
0203    3251    DCA CTR4
0204    1261    TAD M2
0205    3250    DCA CTR2
0206    1414    TAD I R14
0207    3254    DCA REMAIN
0210    5234    JMP RESET/END INITIAL.
0211    1414    WORD, TAD I R14/FETCH NEXT DATA WORD, 3 TIMES
0212    7410    SKP
0213    1253    SHIFT, TAD DATA
0214    7110    SHIFT1, CLL RAR
0215    3253    DCA DATA
0216    1254    TAD REMAIN
0217    7010    RAR
0220    7420    SNL
0221    5231    JMP NODIV
0222    3254    DCA REMAIN/BEGIN XOR
0223    1254    TAD REMAIN
0224    0256    AND DIVISO
0225    7041    CMA IAC
0226    7104    CLL RAL
0227    1254    TAD REMAIN
0230    1256    TAD DIVISO/END XOR
0231    3254    NODIV, DCA REMAIN
0232    2252    ISZ CTR12
0233    5213    JMP SHIFT
0234    1257    RESET, TAD M12
0235    3252    DCA CTR12
0236    2251    ISZ CTR4
0237    5211    JMP WORD
0240    7040    CMA
0241    3251    DCA CTR4
0242    1255    TAD CKWORD
0243    2250    ISZ CTR2
0244    5214    JMP SHIFT1
0245    7200    CLA
0246    1254    TAD REMAIN
0247    5600    JMP I BCH/END OF BCH PROG, AC =CHECKWORD
                / BCH RREGISTERS
0250    0000    CTR2, 0
0251    0000    CTR4, 0
0252    0000    CTR12, 0
0253    0000    DATA, 0
0254    0000    REMAIN, 0
0255    0000    CKWORD, 0
0256    4712    DIVISO, 4712/HIGHEST ORDER ON RIGHT
0257    7764    M12, -14
0260    7774    M4, -4
0261    7776    M2, -2
                *14
0014    0000    R14, 0/INDEX REGISTER
```

Fig. 6.   BCH code algorithm in PAL 3.

bit/s requires 30 ms. Hence the computer can easily control four transmission links simultaneously and transfer the data to and from the sinks and sources.

Each time an error is detected, the computer stores the relative address of that block within the record. These error block addresses are transmitted as part of the reply signal.

V. Error Correction

The error correction is by retransmission. Hence, the sink station must send a reply to the source station to indicate an error. In our system, the data transmission pauses after each record, and the reply signal is sent in the opposite direction. It consists of a variable number of blocks. In case of errors in the previous record, the reply includes the error block addresses. The reply signal is also checked with the BCH code. In case any error is detected in it, the source station sends a "reply error" character to the sink station and retransmits the whole previous record. This is necessary to avoid multiple nesting of errors in replies. In case of a reply indicating errors in the record, the first word indicates the request for a repeat, and subsequent words are the error block addresses. The reply signal is always an integral number of blocks for BCH check, and fill-in words are used if necessary. The addresses are stored at the source station. After the reply signal ends the correction procedure begins.

In contrast to the Idle-RQ system the whole record need not be retransmitted but only those blocks in which an error was detected.

The error block addresses received with the reply signal are used to repeat the corresponding blocks of the previous data record, which is still stored in core at both stations. At the sink station, the retransmitted blocks are simply written over the corresponding error blocks within the last record. The retransmission string is encoded with the BCH code. Any detected error causes the sink station to send a control character requesting the retransmission of the whole record. In that way the multiple nesting of errors in retransmissions is avoided. After a record has been received error free or has been corrected properly, the sink station sends a reply requesting the next record. It also transfers the record in core to the data sink device. Then the old record is erased in the core buffer at both stations.

For applications where frequent turnaround of the channel for replies is not practical, the resulting long records may have a high probability of at least one detected error. This probability is just as high for the repeat with the Idle-RQ system. But for the partial scheme it may be reduced by two orders of magnitude, since only a few blocks are repeated.

VI. Comparison of Thruputs

The partial scheme will be compared with the Idle-RQ system, where the whole record is repeated in case of any detected errors. The evaluation builds on the results of [3] for the Idle-RQ system. Consider a record of m blocks. Each block has n bits, k information bits, and $n - k + r$ check bits. The efficiency of the code is $(n - r)/n = e$. The reply is encoded as one block. The combined delay due to the turnaround of the channel in both directions is t block-transmission times and is assumed to be of the order of one block. Then the thruput for the Idle-RQ is

$$R = \frac{em}{(m + 1 + t)E}. \tag{1}$$

E is the expectation of the number of retransmissions required. It is shown in [3] that

$$E = \sum_{i=1}^{\infty} id(1 - d)^{i-1} = \frac{1}{d} \tag{2}$$

where

$$d = (1 - P_d)(1 - P_E') + P_d P_u'. \tag{3}$$

d is the probability that the record is not repeated after the current transmission because of no detected errors in the record and no errors in the reply, or because of detected errors in the record and the undetected change of the RQ signal to the OK signal in the reply. P_d, P_u are the probabilities of a detected and an undetected error in the record $P_E = P_d + P_u$, and the prime indicates the same for the reply signal, except P_u' refers to the probability that the RQ signal is interpreted as an OK signal.

For the partial scheme, only the c blocks detected in error are repeated in the second transmission. In that case the first reply contains the addresses and is b blocks long, where

$$b = \lceil (1/k)(c\lceil \log_2 m \rceil) \rceil. \tag{4}$$

If any errors are detected in the first reply of the b blocks or the first repeat of c blocks, the subsequent replies and repeats consist of 1 and m blocks, respectively, until the record is accepted by the receiver. Rewrite (1) as $R = em/D$, where

$$D = (m + 1 + t)(d + 2d(1 - d) + 3d(1 - d)^2 + \cdots \tag{5}$$

and E has been expanded. For the partial scheme the thruput is written as $R_v = em/D_v$, where D_v is obtained from D by expanding d and making the appropriate changes

$$D_v = (m + 1 + t)(1 - P_d)(1 - P_E')$$
$$+ (m + b + t)P_dP_u' + (c + 1 + t)2d(1 - d)$$
$$+ (m + 1 + t)\sum_{i=3}^{\infty} id(1 - d)^{i-1}. \tag{6}$$

The second and third terms of D_v are the ones that differ from D to account for the b block reply and c block repeat in case of a detected error in the initial transmission of the record.

Let $q + p + u = 1$, where p is the probability that any one block is detected to be in error, u denotes that a block has an undetected error, and q denotes that a block has no error. For the sake of comparing thruputs, it is assumed that $p \leq 10^{-2}$ and $u \leq 10^{-3}p$.

To compare D_v with D, only the second and third term in (6) differ from the corresponding ones of D, namely

$(m + b + t)P_dP_u' + (c + 1 + t)2d(1 - d)$ versus $(m + 1 + t)P_dP_u' + (m + 1 + t)2d(1 - d)$. Note that $1 \leq b \ll m$, for m of the order of 100. Also, $P_dP_u' \ll 2d(1 - d)$ because

$$P_u' < u, P_d = \binom{m}{c}p^c(1 - p)^{m-c}$$

which has its maximum at $c = \lfloor (m + 1)p \rfloor = 1$, and $P_d < 0.5$, for $c = 1$, $m = 10^2$, $p \leq 10^{-2}$. Therefore, the comparison reduces to $(c + 1 + t)$ versus $(m + 1 + t)$, where $1 \leq c \leq m$. Clearly $D_v < D$ and hence $R_v > R$, as is to be expected.

VII. SUMMARY

An attempt has been made to show the advantages of using a low-cost high-speed mini-computer for controlling and buffering of several data terminals and transmission links. The character format and synchronization is flexible due to the simple SR and software logic. The error correction by retransmission of only the incorrect blocks within the record is possible due to the random access memory data buffer. As a result the thruput is improved over the Idle-RQ system. The software logic and random access data buffer may seem complex, but at present considering computer speeds and costs, this is to be preferred over inflexible and hence soon obsolete special purpose hardware.

REFERENCES

[1] H. O. Burton, R. N. Watts, W. J. Wolf, and L. P. McRae, "Error control systems for use on the switched telephone network," *1965 IEEE Int. Conv. Rec.*, pt. 1, vol. 13. pp. 144–149.
[2] W. W. Peterson, *Error Correcting Codes.* Cambridge, Mass.: M.I.T. Press and Wiley, 1961, ch. 7.
[3] R. J. Benice and A. H. Frey, "An analysis of retransmission on systems," *IEEE Trans. Commun. Technol.*, vol. COM-12, pp. 135–145, December 1964.

Part 8
Organization of
Computer Projects

Introductory Comments

Each of the preceding seven parts has indicated that a minicomputer application requires a thorough systems analysis in order to yield an economical application. The papers in this part are directed toward the carrying out or organization of the project so that the objectives of the overall systems analysis can be obtained. Although one of the advantages of the minicomputer is that it permits piecewise rather than integrated automation of a plant, nonetheless, the resulting computer control system is a part of a larger system, and thus the problems of scheduling and management are still critical. The paper by J. T. Yakas discusses the physical planning which must start at the beginning of the project in order that appropriate equipment will be in the right place at the right time and not cause excessive delays and cost overruns later. The various tasks which must be carried out are detailed, and it is of interest to note that all of these are present in any computer control system whether it be a very small or a very large one.

N. Roistacher and D. M. Steelman discuss project organization in a direct digital control system. In particular, they discuss the problem of dealing with vendor proposals and related problems of documentation, maintenance, and the like. Finally, W. E. Block and J. A. Bodine describe similar problems in petroleum production systems. Although the application is quite different, the organizational problems are similar. They discuss responsibility of various teams working on the project from preparation of instructions for bidding through software specifications, functional specifications, responsibilities of the vendor, and the problems of coordination between the user and the vendor. The petroleum system that they describe in this paper is an excellent illustration of a rather complex system that provides many alternative organizations for its control system. The function of the computer control systems design is to select a feasible alternative and then organize the project in such a way that the objectives can be economically obtained.

In addition to the general references on project organization in this part many of the papers in previous parts and bibliographies discuss similar organizational problems for specific industries. This may be very important because the ultimate user of the system can vary from an exceedingly well educated professional (in perhaps a laboratory automation application) to an untrained user who has no knowledge or understanding of computer control (as, for example, an operator in the process industries). These add additional organizational constraints because of the need for acceptance and cooperation of the ultimate user and must be considered during the project stages. An excellent example is process control software and process operators' consoles that have been discussed in several papers in the several parts. The entire rationale for these systems lies in the need for documentation and ease of operator communication in an on-line environment. The design of such systems is not straightforward and usually involves some interaction with the user that must be included in the project planning to prevent slippage of delivery dates or the design of an unacceptable system.

Bibliography

[1] "Maintenance of computers and instrumentation," R. F. Carney, *IEEE Trans. Ind. Gen. Appl.*, vol. IGA-5, Nov./Dec. 1969, pp. 720–726.
[2] "A minibased system takes careful planning," C. W. Eggers, *Electron. Des.*, June 24, 1971, pp. 56–60.
[3] "Automation of system building," D. Teichroew and H. Sayani, *Datamation*, Aug. 15, 1971, pp. 25–30.
[4] "How to contract for the use of computer programs," E. B. Turner, *Chem. Eng.*, Sept. 6, 1971, pp. 83–85.

Physical Planning of a Glass Plant Process Control Computer Installation

JOSEPH T. YAKAS, MEMBER, IEEE

Abstract—A strong foundation for the successful implementation of a process control computer system is the result of careful and thorough planning of all physical equipment in the early stages of the project. This was accomplished during installation of the existing float glass process control systems at both the Nashville and Dearborn glass plants of Ford Motor Company.

Since the installation represented one of the largest and most ambitious process control efforts ever attempted within Ford Motor Company, specific objectives and schedules were developed in detail and followed step-by-step during the planning and execution of the entire project. The installation proceeded with relative ease and performed extremely well when placed on line within the anticipated schedule.

The success of any particular process control system built around a computer can be virtually assured by judicious application of established and proven techniques of project planning, organization, and scheduling. Furthermore, utilization of a task force or working group will provide an effective channel for regular involvement of delegated personnel and the ultimate attainment of desired objectives within established schedules.

Paper 70 TP 7-IGA, approved by the Glass Industry Subcommittee of the IEEE IGA Group for presentation at the 1969 IEEE Industry and General Applications Group Annual Meeting, Detroit, Mich., October 12–16. Manuscript received February 10, 1970.

The author is with the Ford Motor Company, Ypsilanti, Mich. 48197.

INTRODUCTION

THE EVOLUTION of the digital computer approximately twenty years ago has created numerous applications in many diverse industries. The majority of these applications, however, have been devoted primarily to data processing and accounting functions. Recent advances in appropriate computer interface circuit developments have transformed the digital computer from a mere data acquisition and processing device into a powerful and highly sophisticated industrial control instrument.

The utilization of digital computers for centralized process control has become commonplace only within the last decade. The last five years have evidenced a proliferation of large centrally oriented computer control systems in such industries as petroleum, cement, and public utilities where the need for such capability has existed for many years.

The first application of direct digital control in the glass industry using a process control computer was performed by Owens-Corning Fiberglas Corporation in 1964 [1]. At that time a cooperative effort with IBM was undertaken to develop a glass furnace control system using a digital

Reprinted from *IEEE Trans. Ind. Gen. Appl.*, vol. IGA-6, pp. 205–215, May/June 1970.

335

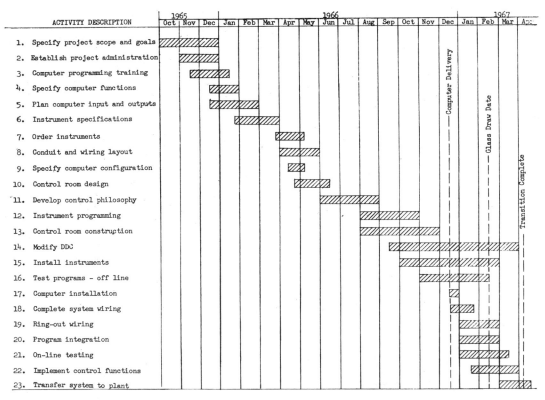

Fig. 1.   Process computer installation planning schedule, Dearborn Glass Plant.

computer to directly operate process valves and other operators. The recorded success of this undertaking is now history. Undoubtedly, such an effort required many hours of detailed physical planning before and during the successful venture.

Owens-Corning's experience with digital control was formally announced as a successful contribution to improved furnace control in March 1965. Shortly after, in June 1965, Ford Motor Company Glass Division initiated a feasibility study to evaluate the potential advantages of a centralized process control system for utilization in present and future float glass operations.

Through the courtesy of both Owens-Corning Fiberglas Corporation and IBM, a visit was made to the Owens-Corning computer control system which uses IBM computer equipment. After the visit, a decision was made by Ford management to proceed with plans to incorporate the direct digital control principles proven in the Owens-Corning Fiberglas project into a complete control system for the entire float glass manufacturing line. Several factors prompted the ultimate choice to install the rather new technique of direct digital control in the float glass operation. Among these were 1) the flexibility of altering control modes through software; 2) the recent development of computer designs dedicated specifically for process control applications; 3) the increasing availability of computer-to-process electronic interfacing equipment; and 4) savings inherent in the elimination of analog controller equipment.

INSTALLATION PLANNING AND SCHEDULING

One of the first steps in establishing a coordinated and organized effort to insure definite results compatible with plant erection schedules was the formation of a Computer Working Group. It was composed of the following personnel.

1) A group leader whose specific assignment consisted of organizing and coordinating the group's activity, implementing the group decisions, arranging regular meetings, and communicating with divisional management on all levels.

2) A software expert with programming experience and knowledge of software systems and organization. This person's responsibility was primarily to organize all the software programs required to utilize the computer effectively as the central element of the process control system. Since the computer programs provide the orders or directions for computer action, this individual must translate the desire of plant operating management into software commands which the computer can readily understand. Consequently, the software effort must be constantly monitored and coordinated with plant personnel to prevent costly errors and delays during the planning stages of the project. On the other hand, the extreme flexibility permitted by a software controlled computer does allow some alterations to specified control techniques without any hardware modifications. This is important since occasionally plant operating personnel may not have adequate past experience with a new process and, there-

TABLE I
KEY TO POINTS LIST CODE

First character: process area
1 inputs (batch house, cooling water, atmosphere generator)
2 furnace (melter, refiner, canal)
3 bath
4 lehr

Second character: process variable or input signal
C current output station feedback signal
D digital signals (status indicators, pulse counters, contacts)
F flow signals
I process interrupts
M multiple type character (amperages, analyzers, manual inputs)
P pressure signals
R radiamatic and radiation temperature signals
T thermocouples
U thermocouples

The third and fourth characters are numeric and may indicate 1) subarea, 2) associated process variables or signals within an area. They may also simply complete the 4-character code without particular significance.

fore, cannot specify detailed control procedures until such experience is gained at a later date.

3) A hardware expert whose background included computer circuit design, electronic process control circuits design, and instrumentation and transducer circuit knowledge. The specific assignment of this individual included such areas as computer-to-process interface circuit design, instrumentation electronics, and computer physical planning requirements. In addition, this individual was assigned the responsibility of coordinating all wiring layouts, planning and specifying efficient equipment grounding and signal shielding techniques to improve system reliability, and developing simplified hardware checkout equipment and maintenance procedures.

4) A plant representative, a manufacturing engineer from the plant where the computer system was to be installed. This person provided the vital and necessary function of liaison and communication between the plant and the Computer Working Group. He was responsible for redirecting the Working Group activities, as required, to insure compliance with changes in plant control requirements and objectives. In addition, he was specifically directed to update plant personnel on activities of the Working Group in all phases of the subject. Specific information on plant instrumentation equipment and process transducers was obtained from him.

Once the Computer Working Group was organized, project objectives and schedules were established to provide a yardstick for measuring the progress of the group during each weekly meeting.

Fig. 1 shows the detailed planning required during the Dearborn Glass Plant installation. Critical path network techniques were utilized to check progress, define project milestones, and establish permissible parallel activity to save time during the project.

Actual physical planning of the installation began with activity 4 (specify computer functions) and continued until activity 19 (ring-out wiring) when all wiring and interconnections were checked point-by-point before insertion of computer programs on on-line testing of the complete system.

One of the important initial objectives of the Computer Working Group was to request a detailed, written description of control philosophy from knowledgeable Process personnel who were to be responsible for various operating areas of the float glass line. From this data, a computer "points list" was created to provide detailed tabulation of every process point that would be monitored or controlled to enable implementation of the desired control philosophy. The computer points list evolved for both Ford Motor Company float glass plants utilizes a specific and unique four-character code to identify each point on the list, as described in Table I.

The coding format, once established, accomplished two important objectives. First, it provided a method to distinctly identify each of the input and output signals at their origin and terminating points within the entire process. Second, the code designation was easily converted into an equivalent binary value suitable for use by the control software to select and activate the correct conversion subroutine program at the appropriate time.

A typical computer points list sheet is shown in Fig. 2.

Control limits may be specified if they are well defined and determined before startup. In some areas, however, control limits, are dependent upon existing process operating modes. For example, lehr temperature limits may be specified according to desired strain characteristics for a particular glass thickness. The normal procedure for handling control limit settings is to set the limits wide enough to eliminate spurious alarms during startup of the float line and then close them in after operating experience has been gained and closer control is desired. The capability for changing control limits was provided by the direct digital control program through the loop record tables.

If a transducer is required to convert a process variable into a voltage or current suitable for computer input, the type utilized (P/I, DP/I, E/I, etc.) is found in the column headed "Trans." The column "Wire Loc." refers to identification of the input signal terminating point on the computer backplane. This provides a method of associating each point code with the physical location of its corresponding input signal wire termination. The last two columns provide software data to permit coordination of control action as requested by the computer program with computer hardware capabilities and limitations. "Scan Freq." specifies the polling interval and phase period values to permit definition and control of the scanning rate for each process variable. The phase value was required to prevent poll overloads which could occur if more than 100 process points demanded software servicing during any one polling cycle of 1-second duration. The "MPX/R Addr" column was used to record the input multiplexer address

Code No.	Description	Sensor	Eng. Units	Range	Limits		Trans	Signal	Wire Loc.	Scan Freq.	MPX/R Addr	Comments
					Hi	Lo						
4T13	Flue Control Zone #1, Bottom, Sec. #4	C-A	°F	500-1400	1261	378		0-50 my	1851 HH-29	4/2	477	
4T14	Sec. #5	"	"	"	1261	378		"	HH-30	4/1	478	
4T15	Sec. #6	"	"	"	1278	257		"	HH-31	4/0	479	
4T16	Sec. #7	"	"	"	1261	378		"	HH-32	4/15	480	
4T17	Sec. #8	"	"	"	1243	343		"	HH-33	4/14	481	
4T18	Furnace Control Zone #2, Top	"	"	"	1797	170		"	HH-34	4/13	482	
4T19	Flue Control Zone #2, Top Sec. #1	"	"	"	1209	188		"	HH-35	4/12	483	
4T20	Sec. #2	"	"	"	1157	188		"	HH-36	4/11	484	
4T21	Sec. #3	"	"	"	1174	292		"	HH-37	4/10	485	
4T22	Sec. #4	"	"	"	1209	222		"	HH-38	4/9	486	
4T23	Sec. #5	"	"	"	1209	205		"	HH-39	4/8	487	
4T24	Sec. #6	"	"	"	1191	170		"	HH-46	4/7	488	
4T25	Sec. #7	"	"	"	1209	257		"	HH-41	4/6	489	

Fig. 2. Typical computer points list.

for incorporation into software programs. This address permits actuation of the correct multiplexing relay at the proper time as specified by the polling subroutine.

Compilation of the computer points list was initiated prior to the selection of the computer system. This was possible since the determination of significant process variables by type, number, and location is primarily dictated by the control philosophy requirements. Of course, specific computer data such as software addresses and scanning interval were added to the list as soon as this information was available.

Before the control room design could be firmly established, all required computer functions had to be defined. After consultation and discussion with plant management, the following computer services were considered to be valuable and desirable for complete float line control.

1) *Monitor:* Generation of data for process operating guidance and establishing a real-time status check of process operating parameters.

2) *Control:* Providing automatic adjustments and corrections to critical process points during operational disturbances through closed loop control action. To insure continuous control, even in the event of computer failure, a completely independent backup capability was developed for every process point under closed loop control.

3) *Logging:* A method for recording process alarms, process alterations by operating personnel made through the process operator's console, and programming revisions made to the direct digital control program by the system programmer.

4) *Reporting:* Generation of production summaries, graphic trend recording, and process point history. This function was specified to be flexible so that plant operating management could select only the process variables of interest to them at any particular time. This decision eliminated the time consuming task of extracting meaningful process data from a complete and lengthy point list summary during occasions when a specific operating problem occurred on the float glass line.

5) *Data Analysis:* This function can be utilized effectively only when adequate computer memory is available to be used on a time shared basis with the real-time control program. It provides a method for performing statistical analysis and averaging of input data, and implementing process simulation and modelling programs for float line improvement studies.

PROCESS COMPUTER INPUT AND OUTPUT SIGNAL SPECIFICATIONS

Development of the extensive points list greatly simplified the planning of computer input and output terminal assignments so that adequate capacity could be assured to accommodate the variety of signals used in the control system.

Similarly, definition of the functions expected of the computer installation dictated the numbers and type of peripheral equipment needed to provide the desired services. In both instances, provision was made for a limited amount of expansion in both the signal handling capability of the computer and peripheral equipment performance.

A predominant characteristic that distinguishes the process control computer from data processing equipment is the unique ability to accept a large assortment of process signals and transform them into standardized digital

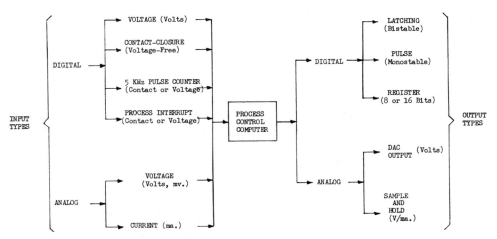

Fig. 3.   Signal handling capability of the Ford Glass Plant process control computer.

levels suitable for computer logic circuitry. Although the variety of signals that can be processed is theoretically limitless if suitable interface equipment can be designed, the number that can be practically accommodated is limited by economic factors and equipment complexity considerations.

During the Ford Motor Company Glass Plant installation, the choice of signal types available in the selected computer system was generous enough to satisfy the majority of process instrumentation and transducer equipment requirements. The number and types of signals directly acceptable by the computer were specified as follows (see Fig. 3).

Input Signal Types

Digital:

1) *Voltage level sensing:* positive voltage level to indicate a logic 1; negative voltage level for designating a logic 0.

2) *Contact closure:* Closed voltage-free relay or switch contact to indicate 1; opened contact to indicate 0.

3) *Pulse counter:* A positive going voltage pulse initiates one count in an 8- or 16-bit counter. Maximum frequency rate of 5 kHz was acceptable without alteration.

4) *Process interrupts:* A contact closure or voltage sensing signal to provide a computer program interrupt when a process condition requires software service.

Analog:

1) *Voltage:* High-level, bipolar analog voltage inputs with range of 0 to ± 5 volts. Low-level, bipolar analog voltages inputs varying in range from ± 10 to 500 mV. The low-level inputs utilize a time shared differential amplifier with preselected voltage gains to raise each input to the ± 5-volt level required by the analog to digital converter.

2) *Current:* Inputs providing 4–20-mA signals are transformed to high-level voltage inputs of ± 5 volts suitable for input to analog to digital converter. A 250-ohm precision resistor is used to change the current value into a corresponding voltage level.

In conjunction with the analog signal capability, a method for synchronizing the digital conversion of analog inputs was available in standard computer hardware. However, this feature had to be requested as a supplementary option to the basic system.

The choice of computer outputs was also adequate to permit operation of most process valves and output transducers without the need for extensive interfacing. The following list illustrates the large variety available for system planning.

Output Signal Types

Digital:

1) *Latched output:* A bistable solid-state ON-OFF control (flip-flop) for operating various devices such as relays, solenoids, lamps, small motors, and alarms. Output capability was limited to 48 volts dc at 0.45 ampere.

2) *Pulse output:* A solid-state monostable device which provides an ON level for a specific time interval. This output was useful for control applications that required initiating an output action and providing an automatic reset of the starting pulse. Signal specifications were limited to a minimum pulse duration of 3 ms and a maximum voltage output of 48 volts dc at 0.45 ampere.

3) *Register output:* A solid-state binary word output comprised of up to 16 bits of digital information transferred in parallel upon receipt of either a software command from the computer program or a request from an external hardware device.

Analog:

1) *Digital to analog conversion:* A transformation of digital data into a corresponding analog voltage for use by analog amplifiers, sample-and-hold circuits, and recording instruments. Two choices of resolution were available for use in the system. One of the options available was a 10-bit resolution output with a voltage range of 0 to $+4.995$ volts. The other was a 13-bit resolution output with a voltage range of 0 to $+4.9994$ volts or 0 to -5.000 volts.

2) *Sample-and-hold amplifier:* A voltage-to-current output converter which provides for analog voltage signal

retention after the computer samples analog input points during the polling interval. This unit also converts the voltage value to a proportional current output to drive process transducer equipment.

Process Computer Peripheral Equipment

To provide the process operating personnel with a suitable and effective device for communicating with the process computer a process control operator's console was designed and incorporated as an integral part of the entire float glass control system. However, the basic console design was modified to expand the process monitoring capability as requested by the plant management. Fortunately, the physical layout of the console provided adequate spare capacity to permit installation of additional hardware without disturbing the original design. Some of the physical modifications made to the operator's console were as follows.

1) Wiring of spare push-button lights to implement a computer monitored sensor calibration software program.

2) Addition of miniature audible alarm devices to provide local and remote indications of computer failure or excessive delays in the control software program.

3) Modification of the console cabinet to reduce the heat buildup above the console power supply assemblies. This action was prompted by erratic performance of the electronic control circuits used by the visual readout panel. Recent designs of the operator's control console have circumvented this problem by judicious hardware layout and use of electronic components that can withstand higher ambient temperatures.

To provide permanent records of daily production activity and control loop changes made by process operators, two low-speed desk size printers were installed near the process control console for the convenience of the process control operator.

One of the printers was programmed to operate on an exception basis, that is, to print a message only when a process change is made or an alarm limit has been exceeded. The other printer was programmed to operate upon requests from the control console keyboard. These requests included items such as a report on the real time status of any variable being monitored or controlled and a printed description of any code number assigned in the system.

A desk size printer-keyboard was provided specifically for use by the system programmer to make and record simple alterations to the direct digital control program. Although the keyboard could be used for data entry, it required software support which consumed valuable computer memory storage. Consequently, the choice was made to use the central processor unit panel for limited data entry and the printer-keyboard unit was subsequently limited to performing a recording function. Other peripheral devices at the disposal of the system programmer were as follows.

1) A card reader and punch unit which is used for initialization of the software system, program reloads, and major revisions or additions to the direct digital control program.

2) A disk storage unit which is used as supplementary storage for relevant but not critical information such as code description data and process point history. In addition, an updated version of the direct digital control program and the loop record table is transferred automatically from the computer core to the disk every 15 minutes to assure recovery of the latest process operating data in case of computer failure.

3) A high-speed line printer which is used for printing out voluminous data such as process point history and extensive program listings.

Although the computer manufacturer provides the necessary cabling to electrically connect all peripheral devices to the computer main frame, the user must specify cable lengths and connector environmental requirements. Furthermore, the user must also provide the necessary power outlets for the desk size, low speed printers, and the computer main frame.

Control Room Design and Layout

To insure reliable and continuous operation of the process control computer and its associated peripheral devices, provisions for adequate control of environmental conditions must be considered in the early stages of the overall physical planning effort. Essentially the hardware required to maintain the ambient within limits suggested by the computer manufacturer may consist primarily of a dual air conditioning system with reserve capability and switchover control.

In the Ford Motor Company Dearborn Glass installation the main air conditioning unit was supplemented by a smaller adjacent unit of approximately half capacity. Both units are operated continuously, side by side, using separate controls. The smaller unit has sufficient capacity to maintain the room environment at higher, but acceptable, temperature levels in the event the main unit is inoperative during periods of maintenance or repair.

Utilization of a dual air conditioning system is undoubtedly more expensive, but the assurance of continuous and reliable system performance will more than justify the increased cost. To provide a guide for facilities planning of the computer area, the supplier recommended and encouraged a design target of 75°F and 50-percent relative humidity controlled within 5 percent of the nominal value.

Other factors that were considered during the control room planning phase included the following items.

1) *Control Room Lighting:* Recessed fluorescent lighting fixtures were used with three independent switch circuits to permit control of incident illumination levels. This versatility in control of the ambient lighting conditions is especially valuable during critical operating periods when numerous process variables must be monitored or controlled simultaneously.

2) *Safety Provisions:* To provide for operator and equipment protection during emergencies the following items were specified in detail.

a) *Electrical power emergency shutdown devices, such as power disconnect switches, circuit breakers, and emergency switchgear:* These were indicated by type, number, and location.

b) *Fire extinguishers:* These (Class *C*) were rated for electrical fire service and specified by type, number required, and location within the room (15-pound carbon dioxide units were used in the Ford float glass installations).

c) *Floor support and covering:* The supporting structure for the free-access raised floor design specified for the control room was required to withstand an average load of 75 pounds per square foot. The floor covering was carefully selected to prevent electrical charge shock hazards to personnel and static noise transients to operating equipment.

3) *Human Engineering Considerations:* The design and arrangement of furniture and personnel equipment was planned as thoroughly as possible to induce a high level of process operator efficiency. Such items as the plant public address system, office telephone, and adequate desk space were located within convenient and easy reach of the process operator. In addition, comfortable and efficient working heights were established and specified for all operator controlled equipment used in the system.

4) *Electrical Power Distribution:* After the voltage and current needs were determined for each electrical component in the system, adequate feeder and branch circuits were designed to fullfill the complete power requirements of the control room. Specific engineering details were outlined for such items as circuit breakers (number, size, and location), grounding methods (to conform to local code requirements), equipment connector design, input power isolation transformers, and automatic switching networks for activation of reserve standby power at substation units during localized power faults. (This involved the design of high power sequencing and interlock circuitry.)

Frequent meetings were held between glass plant engineering personnel and computer physical planning specialists to define system objectives, establish realistic installation schedules, and review progress during actual implementation of the control system.

All pertinent details of the project were discussed in the early meetings so that sufficient time was available to resolve problems without jeopardizing the established installation schedule. For example, one such detail requiring early mutual agreement was the allotment of floor space for computer service parts and equipment.

Auxiliary Control Equipment Planning

To provide operating personnel with a versatile and effective control facility, supplementary recording and monitoring equipment was planned into the system con-figuration. Proficient utilization of this additional equipment has enabled process operators to perform manual control adjustments simply, quickly, and accurately. Consequently, as a convenience to operators, the proximity of manual controls was the prevailing factor in all decisions related to the physical layout of control room facilities. After careful scrutiny of the float glass process to determine critical operating areas, the following equipment was selected for operating management to help them study the float glass process and establish an effective control philosophy for optimizing plant operation.

1) Two 2-pen trend recorders for plotting up to four process variables simultaneously. These recorders have proven to be very useful for generating graphical histories and studying the interaction of several related variables during process changes or disturbances.

2) Two television monitors for selectively choosing the outputs of any two of seven video cameras installed at critical locations in the process. This arrangement provided the process operator with a valuable tool to visually check on the real time operational status of crucial process areas.

3) A video tape recorder for taping of significant process events to be replayed at a later time for review or education of process personnel. The recorder is wired to accept either of the two television video signals upon command from a remote control panel. In addition, an audio channel is available for adding vocal comments to the visual transcription. Other functions of the remote control panel include selection of the process monitoring television cameras and setting of trend recorder chart speed. The control panel was placed adjacent to the process operator's console within easy reach of the operator.

Process Signal Wiring

All input signal lines emanating from the process into the computer backplane utilize twisted pair wiring. Thermocouple signal lines that enter the compensating reference terminal network in the computer are composed of continuous, splice-free, homogeneous, twisted pair extension wires. Adherence to this practice throughout the installation eliminated temperature measurement inaccuracies which could be attributed to spurious potentials generated external to the thermocouple junction.

Low-level analog signals are transmitted in shielded, twisted-pair wires to protect the lines from external electric fields. In some cases several inputs located close to each other in the process were connected to a common signal cable consisting of multiple, twisted pair wires with an overall shielding jacket. To achieve effective shielding of low-level signals from externally generated noise, all shields are insulated from building and computer frame ground. A special shield termination network was developed and used to implement a single point grounding system. Specifically, this effort required the design and construction of a shield bus-bar for installation in the computer backplane. The type of design used in the Ford Glass computer installa-

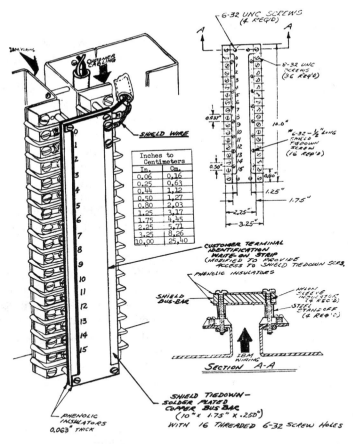

Inches to Centimeters	
In.	Cm.
0.06	0.16
0.25	0.63
0.44	1.12
0.50	1.27
0.80	2.03
1.25	3.17
1.75	4.45
2.25	5.71
3.25	8.26
10.00	25.40

Fig. 4. Shield termination design for digital inputs.

tion is shown in Figs. 4 and 5. Although other shield terminating techniques were possible, this design was chosen because it offered the following advantages.

1) It provided a separate tie point for each shield wire to facilitate wire removal or changes and present an uncluttered and orderly arrangement of shield wiring.

2) It provides a method for insulating all shields from frame or machine ground to preserve single point grounding integrity. (A method for interconnecting bus bars was provided in the design.)

3) It incorporated an effective shielding network without disturbing any existing computer wiring.

4) It presented a low impedance path to shunt externally generated noise transients to a single ground point.

All analog and digital circuit grounds were tied to the shielding network at one insulated point within the computer cabinet. This point was then connected to a copper grounding rod which is located within 50 feet (15.2 m) of the computer system. This rod is approximately 5/8 inch (1.5 cm) in diameter and 12 feet (3.5 m) in length. The rod was driven into the earth below the control room to insure a resistance to ground of 3 ohms (3×10^9 EMU) or less as recommended by the computer manufacturer.

A simplified schematic of the single point grounding network used in the Ford Glass installation is shown in Fig. 6. Note that the computer system frame ground and circuit common wiring are isolated from building ground

and terminated at a single point on the specially installed grounding rod.

The conspicuous absence of problems caused by process electrical noise has verified the prudence of meticulous planning and effort that was expended during the early stages of physical planning.

Since digital signals operate at higher voltage levels which are less susceptible to electrical noise influences, twisted pair wires without shielding jackets were adequate in most of the installations. However, due to the dynamic nature of pulse counter signals (up to 5 kHz rate) the twisted pair wires connecting each input to the process source are shielded individually. This decision was intended to protect low level analog signals from radiation of pulse counter wiring and, in turn, immunize the pulse counter signals from adjacent power line transients.

Most of the input signal wire was stranded, twisted pair, size no. 22 AWG. Each wire was covered with a polyvinyl jacket, except in high-temperature environments where fiberglass insulation was specified. When shielding was utilized, an insulation over the shield jacket was required to prevent accidental ground of the shield along its routed path out in the process area.

Cable length requirements were established as early as possible to accommodate the typically long lead times which are common when purchasing large quantities of electrical wire from suppliers.

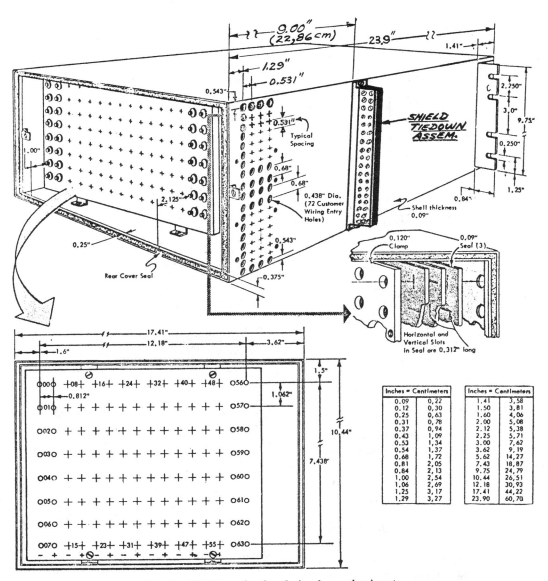

Fig. 5. Shield termination design for analog inputs.

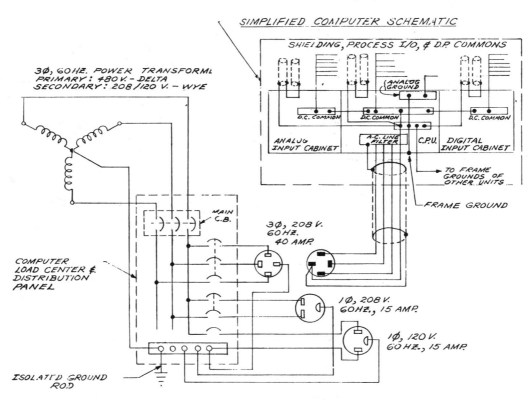

Fig. 6. Computer system isolated grounding schematic.

Conclusion

It has been noted that the successful installation and operation of a process control computer system is predicated upon a shrewd and complete physical planning effort.

Each system, of course, must be specifically planned and installed to satisfy the particular requirements of the plant management who are responsible for continuous and efficient operation of all plant facilities. The ultimate success of the venture, as in any similar undertaking, will heavily depend upon the diligence and dedication of the personnel assigned to the physical planning task. Nevertheless, to assist those who contemplate installation of a process control computer system, the following general recommendations should be considered prior to establishing specific objectives.

1) Organize a working group whose primary functions will be to define project goals, develop schedules, and implement the actual installation of the entire process control system.

2) Establish and maintain good communication with plant personnel who will be responsible for operation of the equipment. This can be effectively accomplished by including a plant representative as a regular and active participant in the working group.

3) Determine and define any specific interfacing that must be provided to achieve compatibility between the control system and process equipment.

4) Survey the process environment to determine requirements for signal wire protection against temperature, electrical noise, and physical abuse.

5) Where possible, standardize on input signal levels and types to simplify wiring and reduce cost.

6) Develop and implement a low-impedance, single-point grounding network for process signal shielding if one is not provided by the computer supplier.

7) Establish and use a simple and distinct wire identification and signal coding system. This is necessary to avoid confusion, errors, and delays during routing and termination of signal wiring.

8) Outline a step-by-step checking procedure for all process signal wiring to minimize wiring errors and reduce delays in the installation schedule. Although this effort can be time consuming, it will prevent serious malfunctions in the process later when the control system is placed on line. Existence of a well-developed wire identification scheme will prove to be a real asset at this point.

9) Devote sufficient effort to such mundane items as operator convenience, furniture arrangement, and control room lighting. Although the significance of these factors may not be readily apparent, they do in fact have an influence upon the operational efficiency of the control system.

Obviously many planning details, initially unforeseeable, must be resolved prior and during the actual physical installation. However, time devoted to development of a well-defined preliminary plan which includes specific objectives and schedules will ultimately reward the user with a more reliable and efficacious process control system.

ACKNOWLEDGMENT

The author wishes to thank all Ford Motor Company Glass Division personnel who have supplied assistance, encouragement, and cooperation in the publishing of this paper. Appreciation is also extended to Divisional Management for the opportunity to actively participate in the process control computer installation and operation.

REFERENCES

[1] P. D. Griem, Jr., "Direct digital control of a glass furnace," *Ceramic Age*, vol. 82, pp. 22–24, 26, February 1966.

[2] D. H. Taeler, "Float glass is computerized," *Ceramic Age*, vol. 84, pp. 30–35, May 1968.

[3] J. E. Talbot, "Process computers show much versatility in recent startups at Mobil Oil, Ford Motor, and the Syntex Research Center," *Instrumentation Technol.*, vol. 14, pp. 11–14, July 1967.

[4] H. L. Feldman, "Minimizing process computer maintenance," *Instrumentation Technol.*, vol. 15, pp. 60–66, January 1968.

[5] J. W. Bernard and J. F. Cashen, "Direct digital control," *Instruments and Control Systems*, vol. 38, pp. 151–158, September 1965.

[6] V. A. Pards and J. M. Vance, "Guide to computer specifications," *Control Engrg.*, vol. 13, pp. 99–104, September 1966.

[7] J. C. Rhodes, "The computer–instrument interface," *Control Engrg.*, vol. 13, pp. 105–109, September 1966.

[8] R. A. Harris, "The computer–actuator interface," *Control Engrg.*, vol. 13, pp. 110–113, September 1966.

[9] J. L. Kern, "The computer–operator interface," *Control Engrg.*, vol. 13, pp. 114–118, September 1966.

[10] N. H. Roos and J. W. Manston, "Design and operational experience with a direct digital control installation," Paper 65-WA/AUT-9, presented at the 1965 American Society for Mechanical Engineers Conf., Chicago, Ill.

[11] E. S. Savas, *Computer Control of Industrial Processes*. New York: McGraw-Hill, 1965.

[12] R. W. Borut, "The control panel from spec to job site and how to stay on schedule," *Instrumentation Technol.*, vol. 15, pp. 35–40, July 1968.

[13] P. N. Budzilovich, "Electrical noise: its nature, causes, solutions," *Control Engrg.*, vol. 16, pp. 74–78, May 1969.

[14] J. W. Lane, "How on-line computer projects go wrong," *Control Engrg.*, vol. 16, pp. 111–114, June 1969.

[15] R. S. Davis, "Defining roles in computer control," *Instrumentation Technol.*, vol. 14, pp. 35–36, December 1967.

The In-Betweens of DDC Design to Startup

NORMAN ROISTACHER AND DAVID M. STEELMAN, MEMBER, IEEE

Abstract—The construction of a modern-day cement plant is a significant undertaking involving the coordination of many resources to develop an operation that must be profitable for many years to come. One of the major investments associated with the construction of the plant is that related to the purchase of suitable control equipment. The development of a digital computer system from purchase to startup is described in this paper.

Today's plant control system, utilizing a digital computer, represents a purchase investment five times greater than that justifiable ten years ago. Users recognize the need for such sophisticated systems, however, and they must strive to optimize their investment. How can this function be best achieved in light of the digital system and plant complexities? Experience indicates that the success of a digital system purchase starts long before the final purchase order is released. The real key lies within the initial "request for proposal."

PROJECT DEVELOPMENT

THE USER should initially select several suitable vendors based on their past performance on similar projects. The vendors are then provided with a basic system specification, stringent in nature, for quotation preparation. The quotation request should include necessary process-control diagrams, flow charts, and instrumentation schematics. From this information, the computer vendors can prepare a detailed proposal, fully outlining their inherent capabilities. Part of the proposal should be a very complete section containing adder and deletion prices for analog inputs, digital outputs, recorders, alarms, trending equipment, backup stations, etc. Based on the initial proposals submitted by the vendors, a careful evaluation

Paper 69 TP 53-IGA, approved by the Cement Industry Committee of the IEEE IGA Group for presentation at the 1969 IEEE Cement Industry Technical Conference, Toronto, Ont., Canada, May 13–15. Manuscript received June 24, 1969.
N. Roistacher is with the Lone Star Cement Corporation, Greenwich, Conn. 06830.
D. M. Steelman is with the Leeds and Northrup Company, North Wales, Pa. 19454.

of their capabilities can be performed, and further insight gained as to how the system can be modified or expanded, and for how much. Upon completion of the evaluation, a purchase order or letter of intent can then be issued to the most suitable vendor. From this point on, the digital system specification becomes a joint effort with the vendor to optimize the total process-control capital investment. The initial proposal will serve as a document to establish "ground rules" for future design work, related to the final digital control system. Such a program was implemented to develop the direct digital control system subsequently discussed.

After initiation of the letter of intent, both the user and vendor must develop project teams to coordinate system development. In particular, the user's project team was fashioned along the following lines:

1) instrument project engineer—responsible for project coordination to ensure correct electrical and instrumentation design for the particular application;

2) systems analyst and process engineer—responsible for the development of the process programs in cooperation with the vendor;

3) computer technician—responsible for the proper installation of the computer system including field devices, interconnection wiring, and calibration;

4) contract representative—responsible for updating system prices relative to the total instrumentation project.

Along similar lines, the vendor established a project team to facilitate design and construction, in keeping with the user's ultimate desires. The team was organized to work efficiently within its own company framework, yet be able to communicate readily with the ultimate user. Vender team organization was formulated as follows:

1) project coordinator–analog engineer—responsible for total project coordination, selection of analog interface equipment, alarm systems, etc., for the entire process;

Reprinted from *IEEE Trans. Ind. Gen. Appl.*, vol. IGA-5, pp. 766–772, Nov./Dec. 1969.

346

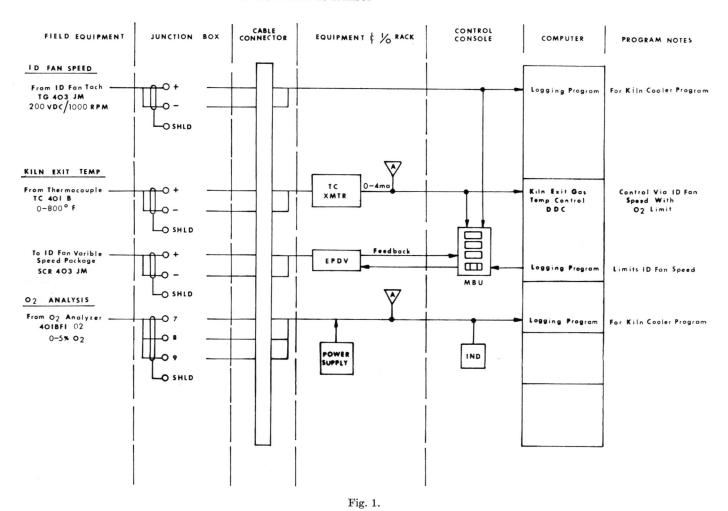

Fig. 1.

2) digital engineer—responsible for digital system design to ensure compatibility with the process interface systems;

3) program coordinator—responsible for total system program development;

4) systems application engineer—responsible for all commercial aspects relative to the project and unique equipment recommendations for special project applications.

The two teams met frequently during the initial stages of the project. Of immediate importance was the development of a comprehensive control system commensurate with the information presented in the basic proposal. All the requirements of the total plant control philosophy were now freely discussed. Through this complete exchange of information, the expertise of both teams could be directed toward the total system development. The user could express his interests reative to the desired control philosophy. This information, coupled with the vendors' in-depth knowledge of the particular system's capabilities, could be effectively directed to produce the most comprehensive system, in keeping with the initial budget requirements.

For example, as discussions developed, systems installation was carefully reviewed. What could the vendor provide that would reduce installation time, yet in the long run be economically feasible? The final result of this investigation was the modification of standard terminal cabinets, so that they could be shipped to the job site several months before the total system delivery. This permitted the user to install, wire, and calibrate all primary elements prior to the computer's arrival. Additionally, all end devices could also be similarly installed and tested. The installation problems were hereby reduced by prudent use of prefabricated cables and appropriate terminal cabinets. This approach permitted complete testing of the computer in the vendor's plant, while the field devices were being installed, checked, and connected to the special computer input–output terminal cabinets. The end result was a minimum system installation time.

Another important function of the team during the initial development stages was to coordinate the flow of drawings and information between the user and the construction contractor. To facilitate this facet of the project, one cardinal rule was observed: develop the entire system fully, produce conceptual drawings, check, then approve the final design for all parties related to the project. Approximately eight months were spent on this phase. No formal drawings were produced, and no steel or other necessary system parts, were ordered at that time. Only initial conceptual drawings (Fig. 1) were developed to provide the following information in a concise form:

1) All system inputs:
    type (current, pulse, voltage, etc.)
    signal level
    quantity
    originating source
    tag number, etc.
2) All system outputs with description:
    type (current, pulse, voltage, etc.)
    signal level
    quantity
    originating source
    tag number, etc.
3) Hardware and location in system:
    type of system backup
    panel mounted equipment
    rack mounted equipment
    field mounted equipment.

Development of conceptual drawings provided an excellent means of system coordination. The vendor could start internal project coordination and establish the best construction schedules, using standard CPM techniques. Concurrently, the user could recheck his own requirements and ensure that the other vendors were producing the desired capital equipment compatible with the ultimate computer system. Once all aspects were coordinated via the conceptual control diagrams, the various vendors could then start producing toward a common goal.

The conceptual drawings were also designed to serve as a system description for the programming effort. From these diagrams the programmer could readily determine the function of each particular control loop and develop the necessary process control programs. The programming aspects of the project became greatly simplified through use of the conceptual drawings. Without question, the time spent during the initial phases of the project prevented major design problems from occurring later on during the construction phases of the project.

As followup to the system development effort, particular attention was paid to the in-plant training and intensive system testing. The latter is particularly important, due to the extreme complexity of such a system. Special test programs were developed during system design that would eventually provide the necessary tests, yet simultaneously permit in-plant training of customer personnel in small logical steps.

System Test Program

The objective of system testing is multifold. In general, it serves to verify concepts, construction, operation, and ultimately obtain customer acceptance. System testing also generates such intangibles as familiarization with the equipment by the customer, maintenance and installation personnel, plus reduced field startup time and reduction of the ever-present risk of upsetting the ultimate process.

The total program for acceptance of the direct digital control computer consisted of hardware test, software test, on-site test, and system availability.

With a large digital system, the factory hardware test takes on special importance, as it represents the last chance to uncover particular problems before shipment to the site. Let us take a close look at the significance of good factory testing.

The final factory test is conducted utilizing the best professional engineering talent, proper tools, and test equipment, plus readily available parts for efficient diagnosis and repair. A good rule of thumb states that a factory defect can be traced and corrected in approximately 1/4 the time required to correct a similar defect in the field; therefore the degree of system testing is directly proportional to the ultimate system startup date.

The hardware test is primarily concerned with the system performance. Results of component quality control cannot be extrapolated as a substitute for the same degree of rigorous system quality control. The same logic applies to tests necessary to confirm reliability in the basic subsystems, i.e., alarms, system backup, input–output, etc. Eventually the entire group of subsystems must be tested as a fully integrated process controller in the factory, not at the user's plant site. The final full system test must be designed to concentrate on interaction effects without the interference of subsystem problems. Any final test must, therefore, closely approach field operating conditions, i.e., temperature, humidity, type of inputs, outputs, and sampling rates.

Depending on the system under consideration, certain portions must be more carefully scrutinized than others. The purpose of this discussion is not to relate all the micro tests performed, but provide a philosophy of testing that can be judiciously applied to most digital control systems.

System Testing Analysis

Any specific system can be broken up into logical parts, based on the major classifications of hardware and software. Table I resulted from an analysis of the systems-engineering and program requirements.

If we take a close look at the complete digital system, it appears analogous to a road map, where the cities represent basic pieces of hardware, and the roads represent the major interconnection wiring. The basic pieces of hardware, or subsystems, would represent the operator's console, typewriters, graphic panel, and individual panel sections relating to specific portions of the plant operation.

A basic first-level testing system should be applied to all of the individual subsystems. Wherever practical, the subsystem performance should be verified without extensive interconnection to other subsystems. All circuits should be checked with standard voltages and simulated inputs and outputs. Contact state change, digital outputs,

TABLE I

Hardware				
Process			Computer	
Analog Loops	Motor Control	Alarming	Main Frame	I/O
Primaries Transmitters Controllers End elements	Starters Sequences	Sensors	Central processor Bulk memory Program console Program I/O	Peripheral I/O OP console Maintenance panel DI system DO system AI system AO system

Software		
Intrinsic	Executive	Extrinsic
Memory transfers Arithmetic Logical Foreground/background	Timing Interrupt Calendar	Peripheral I/O OP console Maintenance panel DI system DO system AI system AO system

Systems Program

Logging   Control   Alarming

and bit patterns may be verified with simple equipment such as light boxes, buzzers, voltohmmeters, etc. Analog equipment need only be checked for overall performance, not for calibration.

The basic purpose of first-level testing is to verify the design concept, wiring, the operation of the individual subsystems in a cause and effect relationship. This form of system testing is based on the assumption that the individual instruments, relays, switches, etc., have been inspected or calibrated prior to installation in the subsystem.

The next level of testing may be regarded as a limited overall test. The test, commonly referred to as second-level testing, involves the interconnection of the basic subsystems to facilitate a limited overall system test. During this particular test only representative loops of each configuration need be checked. In conjunction with the limited second-level test, a very careful ring out of the entire system must be performed to ensure that all loops will perform as well as those individually checked out.

Up to this point we have discussed the basic hardware subsystems, Simultaneously, test personnel must perform the necessary steps to adequately evaluate the system central processing unit (computer mainframe).

The computer itself is somewhat more complex than the other subsystems, however, it can also be checked out on a subsystem basis. A program capable of exercising the computer hardware is entered into core memory. Utilizing the input–output typewriter, program console, and maintenance panel, the test engineer can perform an in-depth evaluation of the computer hardware. The final result is directed toward confirming that the central processing unit is suitable for interconnection to the basic control subsystems. Particular tests performed during this stage are diagnostic in nature and encompass the following functions: diagnostic control program, digital input test,

digital select test, digital output test, digital event test, digital-to-analog converter test, analog input multiplexer uniformity test, thermocouple open-circuit detection test, clock test, power-failure detection test, teletype diagnostic test, output counter test.

The final facet of in-plant testing involves complete checkout of the computer software. Program testing is a highly customized matter, in that at least three levels of in-depth tests are required. The first test is the debugging of the programs in order that the computer system will in fact accept them. The second level is a verification that the programs will perform the cause and effect relationship for which they are written. And finally, the third level is the interaction of programs running consecutively in real time.

The first level of program testing generally only requires a mainframe and its associated tape or card editing equipment. A compatible computer can be used, although familiarity with the actual system computer is desirable. The second level of cause and effect verification will be performed on the computer system, computer system with hardware system, and computer system with analog simulation. Tests on the computer system itself verify that the proposed on-line program can run the computer input–output and peripheral equipment. Diagnostic or first-level testing only verifies that the computer system is capable of running if properly programmed.

Tests utilizing the hardware system are of a customized nature. In general, they represent input–output relationships which are easier to generate with real hardware, as opposed to simulated inputs such as toggle switches and simulated outputs. Software and hardware in this category typically are plotters, multilamp displays, operators consoles, visual devices, etc.

Tests utilizing an analog computer simulation facility are similar to the second-level testing for the system hardware, in that entire loop actions are simulated. The analog computer is wired to act as the user system, and the programmed digital computer as the plant controller. Here again, only representative loops are tested. This testing ultimately verifies the programming and algorithms, as they would react to the actual process. Unfortunately, the possibility of total program interaction cannot be entirely verified by these methods until the field startup. In general, the cost of entire plant simulation by analog and digital techniques becomes prohibitive.

The final testing of the digital system will ultimately take place at the user's plant site. At this time, complete interconnection with the process is finally achieved and the inherent characteristics of the process submitted to the digital control system. At this point, individual loops are brought on to test the computer's capability for individual loop control. After all system loops have been checked out for complete compatibility, the process is ready for computer control.

Most digital computers supplied today have some optimizing means for controlling the process. Although these programs are in the digital controller, they cannot be employed until reasonable process control is achieved so that proper tuning techniques can be employed. Initial tuning of the optimizing programs can be achieved in a relatively short period of time; however, the user does not reap the full benefits of the digital computer system unless he continually tries to improve upon the optimizing programs. This is an on-going function but truly substantiates the basic benefit of a digital system, its built-in flexibility.

As the digital system is being constructed, programs should be conducted to ensure that the user is thoroughly trained in the areas of programming and system maintenance.

Training Program

The direct digital control system contains a storehouse of information contributed during the course of design by engineering and operating personnel responsible for project completion.

A comprehensive training program was instituted to supplement the technical knowledge of personnel in programming, maintenance, and operation of the direct digital control system. The training program was divided into three major categories: system analysis, system maintenance and system operation.

System Analysis

The system analysis training program was tailored for programmers and process engineers and was administered in two phases, fundamental and advanced.

In the fundamental phase, prior knowledge of programming or digital techniques was not a prerequisite. The topics covered a general introduction to digital computers, flowcharting techniques, coding, and problem definition

oriented toward digital computer solutions. Emphasis was placed on developing a programming style directed toward producing simple well-annotated programs.

The personnel selected for this course were those directly responsible for the analysis and programming of the computer. Appropriate backup personnel were necessary to provide in depth experience at various levels in the company, supplemented by other personnel, knowledgeable in programming techniques for short-term and long-range development purposes.

In the advanced phase, emphasis was placed on developing experience in programming of the computer system. The ultimate purpose was to achieve an independent ability to make major modifications to the system programs. The personnel taking these courses, having completed the fundamental phase of training, could then apply their knowledge of the process to the computer system and its operation.

The course topics covered the computer instruction repertoire, symbolic assembly, auxiliary memories, floating-point techniques, and simple executive control of real-time programs. Supplementing this phase were topics covering the specific application of our own process as it relates to the programs. Also, time was allotted for operating personnel to assist the vendor in the programming of selected portions of the system programs and to provide technical assistance in defining the interface requirements between plant operation and the system program.

System Maintenance

The maintenance training program was designed for technical personnel responsible for keeping the computer system in continuous operation by superior trouble-shooting techniques and preventive maintenance. The goal was achieved through two phases of course administration, fundamental and advanced.

The fundamental phase was specifically given to prepare maintenance personnel who have had no previous maintenance experience in digital computer systems. However, it is desirable that the technician have a technical school level of knowledge in electronics with some experience in the use of voltmeters, oscilloscopes, etc. An extensive background in analog electronics (radio, television, analog controllers, analog computers, etc.) is not of great value and is less important than a strong aptitude for logical analysis. The courses placed emphasis on the development of an orderly trouble-shooting procedure, based on the computer diagnostic system using the computer as a tool to diagnose troubles.

Topics included the diagnostic system, logic circuits and diagrams, Boolean algebra, computer timing, core memory timing, etc. Supplementing these courses was a general familiarization with the technology and hardware of the new computer system orientation as to cement plant operation, and field trips to other similar installations, wherever possible.

In the advanced phase, the training was developed as the class hypothetically assembled and debugged a generalized system. The lectures were reinforced by laboratory exercises performed on a reduced operating scale system. The process of locating a fault was shown to be one of signal tracing, using the diagnostic programs to generate the signals plus the computer maintenance panel for control and display.

The training in programming and maintenance was started at an early stage, so that personnel could be assigned to the design team as early as possible. The goal was to complete formal training at the computer vendor's plant in time for system checkout and participation in the vendor factory testing team.

SYSTEM OPERATION

With the advent of more sophisticated cement plants and rising costs for labor and equipment, operation of the modern-day cement plant requires training for operating and supervisory personnel in the correct, and most efficient methods of operation.

The new computerized cement plant replaced an obsolete facility in the same location; therefore supervisory and operating personnel were selected from the existing operation. Where there are no existing facilities, operating people must be recruited from the local population and possibly be supplemented by experienced operators from existing plants in other locations.

It became apparent that an extensive training program was required for operating personnel at our new plant. In order to effect a smooth transition from construction to startup, a preliminary but thorough familiarization with the computerized plant was necessary. In this case the training concept called for utilization of supervisory personnel from the old plant to become involved not only in training sessions, but also in checkout and startup procedures. These same personnel were utilized to help teach classes, as well as attend them. There is no better way to learn a subject than to teach it.

The central control operators had been chosen from the old plant personnel after passing qualification tests designed by our personnel department and approved by the plant union through meetings and discussions.

Training sessions were held while the old plant was in continuous operation, and this required considerable extra study-hours on the part of the supervisory personnel. For supervisory personnel, classes were conducted for two hours each day, five days per week. For the central control operators training was conducted for eight hours per day, five days per week.

Various training techniques were used, such as the drawing of material flow diagrams from memory for all plant areas. This was the basis for an early understanding of the physical plant layout, making it possible to proceed to more detailed training sessions on the theory of process control, machinery function, and construction. This was

Fig. 2.

Fig. 3.

performed concurrently with plant tours to inspect machinery and to actually examine equipment for answers to questions not fully explained in class.

It was necessary to commence control-room training before delivery of the consoles and computer. Therefore, full-sized wooden models of the consoles were constructed (Fig. 2). All equipment, such as pushbuttons, meters, and controller recorders were pictured in their proper locations. By using wooden models, the fundamentals of central control room operation was facilitated, especially machinery startup sequences. Emergency and alarm situations were simulated, and training included the proper procedures to correct emergency situations. Following each week's classes, test were administered to gauge the trainees' comprehension and our teaching effectiveness, and to provide a review of principles taught to all personnel.

This phase of the program aided in giving the participants a feeling of having contributed personnally to the functional success of the new plant. It cannot be stressed too strongly that this training program should not only start prior to plant startup, but continue thereafter on a regularly scheduled basis. Although the success of this program cannot be fully evaluated until the new plant is in full production, we feel certain that job performance will be enhanced by personnel training and knowledge of the process.

CONCLUSION

From design to startup a comprehensive program was initiated to bring forth the ideas, thoughts, and concepts of all who were to be involved with the final system installation and operation.

The time spent during the conceptual design stages enabled a system to be produced with a bare minimum of construction modification. Field devices were installed, connected, and completely tested when the central computer control system was delivered. After the arrival of the computer and its peripheral equipment (see Fig. 3), less than two weeks were required to completely set up the equipment and interconnect all units. The training program gave all operating personnel a "hands-on" feeling during installation, and subsequently, towards system operation.

The familiar questions are now being asked: Will the system work? Can we efficiently operate and control such a complex system? What benefits will be derived? The answers to these questions are at present being written.

ACKNOWLEDGMENT

The authors wish to thank E. Buttiker, Chief Process Engineer, Lone Star Cement Corporation, and J. E. Steinmann, Senior Project Engineer, Leeds and Northrup Company, for their contributions.

Computer-Controlled Petroleum Production Systems

WALLACE E. BLOCK AND JAMES A. BODINE, MEMBER, IEEE

Abstract—Use of computer control in the operation of production facilities has expanded rapidly in the past few years. Standard Oil Company of California completed its lastest such project, the automation of platforms Hope and Heidi in the Santa Barbara Channel, in mid 1967. The equipment, which uses an 8K computer control program together with a supervisory control system, permits unattended operation of the remote facilities. This paper discusses the project design details, startup, and operating history, emphasizing both hardware and software aspects of the system. Two unique operating routines, computed well-test sequences, and leak detection to test manifolds, are discussed in detail. Based on the Hope–Heidi experience and background from previous projects of a similar nature, the authors discuss their philosophy of automation. The needs for user and vendor coordination of their system responsibilities and thorough documentation are defined. Emphasis is placed on the advisability of forming a user hardware–software team to handle system engineering and programming "in-house." Particular importance is placed on the specification phase of a process-control project and the need to extract detailed technical data from the vendors in the bidding phase to ensure optimum and economic selection of a system to do a particular job. The discussion of software specifications and the concept of a user team to implement the project should prove useful to the oil producing industry. The concepts discussed are, however, applicable to the implementation of any industry's computer control program.

HOPE–HEIDI AUTOMATION SYSTEM

HOPE AND HEIDI are oil production platforms located in 140 feet of water in the Santa Barbara Channel about 3 miles off the Southern California coast. The platforms were operated manually using around the clock coverage for about 18 months before the automation facilities were installed. Justification for the automation system was based on reducing the coverage from 24 hours to 8 hours per day and effecting a corresponding reduction in the crew boat contract. In addition, an increase in oil production was anticipated since well testing would be more accurate and because application of flow–no-flow sensors could lead to reduced well downtime.

HARDWARE

The automation system consists of an onshore process computer, a supervisory control master station, two offshore remote stations, and associated process equipment. The system handles the routine operations of 75 producing wells and provides for 90 remote control functions; 450 alarm, status, or flow indications; and 16 test data accumulators. The equipment is shown in block diagram form in

Paper 68 TP 128-IGA, approved by the Petroleum and Chemical Industry Committee of the IEEE IGA Group for presentation at the 1968 IEEE Petroleum and Chemical Industry Technical Conference, Dallas, Tex., September 9–11. Manuscript received December 26, 1968.

The authors are with Standard Oil Company of California, Western Operations, Inc., La Habra, Calif.

Fig. 1. The overall cost was $250 000 including $35 000 for system programming and debugging, and $20 000 for engineering and checkout.

The computer and the supervisory control equipment operate independently of each other except when reporting an event or when commanding or interrogating a device or sensor on the platform. The computer is an 8K process control machine with two teletype input–output units and a relay interface to the supervisory control system. The supervisory control and telemetering system is solid-state digital equipment capable of implementing sufficient field functions to accommodate the two existing platforms plus as many as seven additional platforms of equal complexity. The supervisory control equipment is a scanning system which continually checks for changes in monitored conditions at each of the remote platforms.

The system can be operated in either computer or manual mode. In computer mode all commands and recording of alarms and data are handled automatically by the program, and all field information is passed directly through the supervisory control equipment to the computer for processing without being displayed for operator action. The control, monitoring, and data capabilities associated with computer-controlled testing and surveillance are also available in manual mode, but all actions and calculations must be performed by an operator. Manual mode is intended primarily for standby service when the computer is off-line, although remote control of connected platform devices can be performed at any time from the master station. Normally, only limited functions, such as fog horn on-off or platform shut-in, are initiated manually while in computer mode. Fig. 2 shows a detailed schematic diagram of system operations.

The onshore power supply consists of a 480-volt three-phase rectifier–inverter. The supply voltage is rectified to 125 volts dc then inverted to provide 110–220-volt 60-Hz power to the computer. The supervisory control equipment is fed at 125 volts dc from a 480-volt three-phase dc power supply. Onshore backup power is provided by station-type lead-acid storage batteries, float charging on the output of the 125-volt dc power supply. In the event of a power failure, the battery system continues to provide power to the supervisory control equipment and, through a static switch, provides no-break power to the input of the inverter system to serve the computer. Fig. 3 is a block diagram of the onshore power system.

The offshore power system consists of station-type lead-acid batteries, float charging on the output of a 48-volt dc power supply, which also provides the normal power to the remote station units.

Reprinted from *IEEE Trans. Ind. Gen. Appl.*, vol. IGA-5, pp. 403–410, July/Aug. 1969.

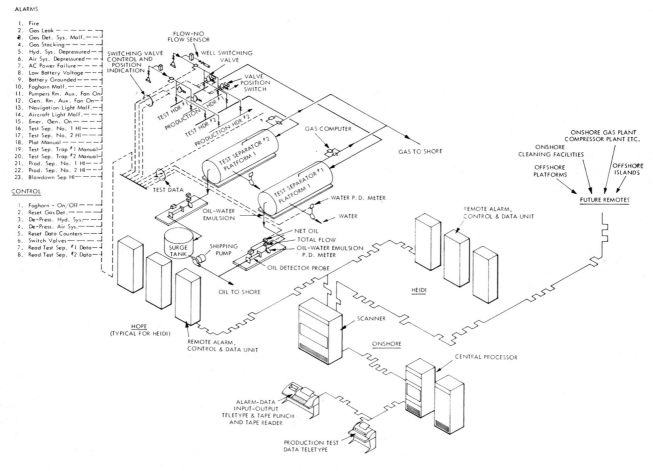

Fig. 1.   Block diagram of Hope–Heidi automation system.

SOFTWARE

Computer-mode operations of the platform production facilities are controlled by an 8100-word (24-bit) all-core program. The real-time supervisory portion of the program is a modified version of the vendor's standard monitor program. This "minimum-monitor" culminated a joint user–vendor effort to eliminate standard features not required for Hope–Heidi. The resulting supervisory program required less than 2400 words of storage versus more than 4000 words required by the vendor's standard monitor.

The system interface and control programs were written by Socal. The logic for automatic control of the production facilities and the various operator input—output programs were developed and coded by a petroleum engineer on loan from the production staff. Nearly 90 percent of the control program was written in FORTRAN as part of a continuing development of nonmachine-oriented oil field automation routines. The use of FORTRAN necessitated development of special assembler language routines to provide communication between the monitor and the supervisory control master station. These routines were written by a professional programmer from the corporation staff.

Production automation requires that considerable data be stored for each well in the system. In order to fit the data for 75 wells, in addition to the interface, control and monitor programs, into 8K of core, it was necessary to pack the well data; that is, to store more than one data entry in a single word. By using FORTRAN call statements and assembler language pack and unpack routines, all information pertinent to a single well is stored in six words. Without packing, 19 words would have been required. Fig. 4 shows the final configuration of the well data words. Additional storage was saved by arranging well data words in core so that their location identified platform and header assignment as opposed to including this information explicitly in the well data array. There are draw backs to these core-saving shortcuts. For example, program flexibility and ease of expansion are compromised and programming becomes more complicated and more expensive.

Most of the automatic control programs and operations are outlined Fig. 2. The routines required for automatic, unattended well testing are the most extensive and complex in the entire program. One of the routines is used to "compute" the next well for test. This represents a radical departure from standard procedure where a pro-

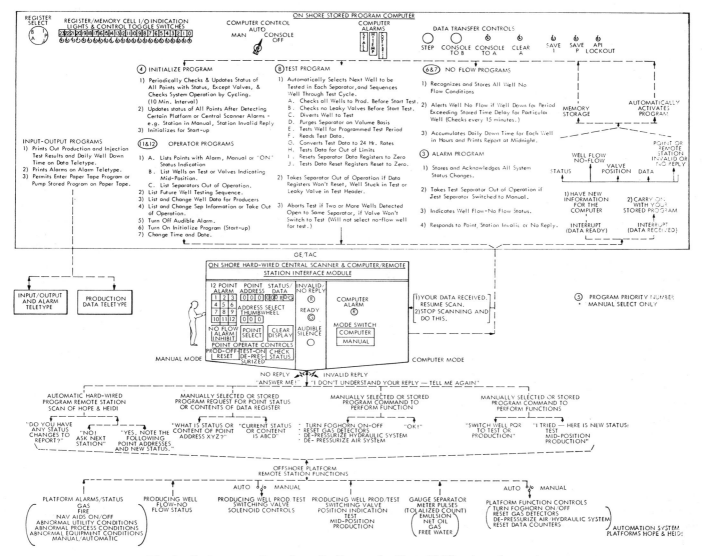

Fig. 2. System operation schematic diagram for Hope–Heidi automation system.

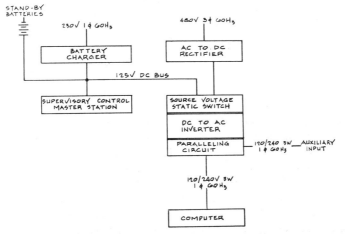

Fig. 3. Block diagram of Hope–Heidi onshore power system.

Word	Bit Pos.	Data Item	Units	Limits
NWELL1	23-12	Well Number	-----	1-999
	11-8	Trap Number	-----	1-?
	7-4	Producing Method Code	-----	8-10
	3-0	Producing Zone Code	-----	1-15
NWELL2	23-12	Last Net Oil Prod. Rate	B/D	0-4095
	11-6	Well Gauging Time	HRS	1-24
	5-0	Days Desired Between Gauges	Days	1-25
NWELL3	23-12	Last Gross Prod. Rate	B/D	0-4095
	11-6	Days Since Last Gauge	Days	0-63
	5-0	Temp Storage for Days Since Last Gauge	Days	0-63
NWELL4	23-12	Last Emulsion Prod. Rate	B/D	0-4095
	11-6	Max. Allow. % change Net Oil	%	0-60
	5-0	Max. Allow % change Gross	%	0-60
NWELL5	23-0	No-Flow Alarm Time (minutes since alarm first sensed)	min	0-527
NWELL6	23-12	Emulsion Meter Factor	factor	0-4
	11-6	Down Time for this Day	HRS	0-24
	5-0	No-Flow Delay Alarm Time	Hrs*10	1-60

WELL DATA STORAGE WORDS

Fig. 4. Hope–Heidi well data word array.

ITEM	1966-67 DEC-APRIL	1967 APRIL-JUNE	JULY-AUG	SEPT-NOV	DEC	1968 JAN-MARCH	APRIL	SUMMARY
COMPUTER SYSTEM								
NUMBER OF OCCURENCES	1	1	2	0	0	0	1	5
TOTAL DOWNTIME (HOURS)	120	260	240	0	0	0	16	636
MTBF (HOURS PER PERIOD)	2900	1700	1000	(2200)	(3000)	(3200)	5500	2400
% AVAILABILITY	96	88	86	100	100	100	99.9	95
SUPERVISORY CONTROL SYSTEM								(APRIL NOT ON)
NUMBER OF OCCURENCES	50	1	3	0	0	1	0	5
TOTAL DOWNTIME (HOURS)	200	4	120	0	0	7	0	137
MTBF (HOURS PER PERIOD)	80	1600	350	(2200)	(3000)	3000	(3000)	1700
% AVAILABILITY	75	99.7	92	100	100	99.7	100	98.5
SUPERVISORY CONTROL FUNCTIONS								
NUMBER OF OCCURENCES		0	12	1	0	7	3	23
TOTAL DOWNTIME (HOURS)		0	48	4	0	21	6	79
MTBF (HOURS PER PERIOD)		2200	120	(2200)	(3000)	550	250	400
% AVAILABILITY		100	96	99.6	100	99.5	97.5	

Fig. 5. Operating history of Hope–Heidi automation system.

duction foreman manually develops a monthly testing schedule. In this routine, well selection is more straightforward. The foreman simply indicates how often he would like a well tested, once every twenty days, for example. This desired test frequency and the number of days since the well was last tested are stored in the well data array. The routine selects that well for testing which has the largest ratio of days-since-last-test to days-desired-between-tests. This algorithm has several advantages over manual scheduling. Well test schedules are continuously optimized within the limits prescribed, and if test time for the month differs from that required, selections are made on a logical basis. The foreman can use a simple operator input program to override the computed schedule if it is necessary to test a particular well out of its normal sequence.

The well-testing routines are complicated by numerous checks made under program control to ensure valid test results. These checks are concerned primarily with verifying that production of only the well on test is entering the separator and that each test starts with the data accumulators set to zero. A unique feature of these checks is a test for leaky manifold valves which utilizes the signal from a test header no-flow sensor. The sensor is set to report a leak exceeding five barrels per day through the header.

Operating History

Platforms Hope and Heidi were put on automation in December, 1967, and operator coverage was reduced from three shifts to a single daylight shift. After December 1967, the platforms were operated with reduced coverage except for brief periods of drilling or workover activity when policy dictated that a production operator be on the platform. There have been single-function electronic failures and sensor malfunctions, none of which disabled the system or necessitated operator coverage on the platforms. Maintenance on the system presently is being handled on a contract basis. Plans have been completed to modify this contract and to arrange for company personnel to perform the majority of the electronics maintenance.

Equipment downtime history is shown in Fig. 5. The frequency of system shutdowns has steadily diminished and system availability since acceptance in October, 1967, has exceeded 99.9 percent. Records of well test performance indicate that the testing equipment itself has been in operation (i.e., testing wells) slightly more than 99 percent of the time. Based on the records to date, future overall availability should be 99.9 percent, or higher, with 2000 hours mean time between failures (MTBF) on system failures and a minimum of 500 hours MTBF on function failures.

Computer failures have been infrequent and are attributable to normal burn-in or digital logic elements or drift in component characteristics. There have been three major shutdowns. These were due in one case to possible damage during a move, in another to a highly sensitive and intermittent short circuit in a multiwire connector on the computer output buffer, and in the third case to a component failure shortly after delivery.

Supervisory control system failures were frequent during the first five months. These were not unexpected since the equipment was delivered before it had undergone a complete factory checkout. These failures included short circuits, component infant mortality failures, cold solder joints, wiring errors, design errors, etc. In April, 1967, the vendor completed a retrofit on the design problems and performed a comprehensive system checkout. Since that time, failure rate has decreased notably.

Individual control function failures are not as critical as a supervisory control system or computer failure since they affect a single function and do not necessarily require immediate attention. Failure rate on these elements has not been as low as that for the overall system. No alarm nor critical control units have failed. The majority of the failures since retrofit have occurred in the pulse accumulators. Program bugs were a problem during the first three months of operation, but these have since been eliminated. Many of the bugs were introduced while making program modifications after the system was installed. Operator errors, initially a problem, have steadily decreased, and the most likely or frequent of these errors are now protected against by program logic.

CONTROL SYSTEM PROJECT IMPLEMENTATION

Philosophy

Once it has been decided to "automate" a process, the next concern should be who is going to do the job and how best to accomplish the desired functions efficiently, economically, rapidly, accurately, and reliably.

Automation of an existing, or even a new process, provides the operators and engineers with a fresh opportunity to decide how it *should* be done, even to the point of questioning how it has been done. In normal operations, changes or improvements in methods, materials, and operating philosophy are continual; but of necessity, these day-to-day changes result in only a gradual revision of the process. Automation of a process, on the other hand, generally causes an abrupt discontinuity in the method of operation.

The opportunity to take advantage of this discontinuity is too frequently ignored and an automation project is often considered a success if it simply does exactly what the operator did previously. This is the safe and easy approach, but it is not the right approach nor is it the economic one. Simply automating existing manual steps (that is, duplicating the manual and mental operations of the human operator with machinery) does not make use of the capabilities of control equipment to optimize a process as to speed, yield, and accuracy. While attempting to capitalize on this opportunity, however, operators and engineers must also recognize the weaknesses of automation. The main weakness is, of course, that an automated facility can handle only those conditions for which it was programmed.

The goal, then, should be to automate in such a manner as to take full advantage of the control and process equipment and to compensate for its weaknesses. Neither can be accomplished unless the design considers the automation equipment, the computer program, and the process to be automated. Most users have been willing to take on the task of the process and the automation equipment but default in the case of the software. The usual approach has been to have the vendor provide the program. What normally happens is that a team of vendor programmers invades the plant to ascertain how it is operated manually. They then withdraw to develop a program that simply duplicates the actions of the human operators. These vendor programs generally have several failings. They do not take advantage of the user's control equipment; they provide useful features which are not applicable to the particular installation, but which use up valuable core space; they are written in assembler language and are not completely understood by anyone within the using company; and therefore hinder program maintenance, updating, and expansion; and finally, since they are in a machine-oriented language, they cannot be reused at a future installation unless the same type of computer is provided.

Our experience indicates that the best solution is for the user to form a project team consisting of a hardware and a software specialist, both of whom are familiar with the plant operations. This team working together with experts on specific problem areas, can then specify, select, and oversee an installation which blends the process, the automation equipment, and the computer program.

RESPONSIBILITIES OF THE USER'S TEAM

The team's first responsibility is to define the hardware functions and software requirements. This should be done by the user team since they are the ones who know what is required for the specific project, what short-cuts, if any, can be taken, and what features are unacceptable. Vendors, even though they maintain special petroleum production sales or engineering groups, simply do not understand or appreciate the individual applications or operating requirements.

Prior to purchasing equipment the user team must derive a system design that is compatible with the operating conditions and requirements and is economical in the use of available hardware. Once the system design is complete, the next step is to inform the prospective vendors of the equipment requirements and of their responsibilities were they to be selected to provide the equipment. This constitutes the specification phase of a project and entails the preparation of four interrelated documents.

Instructions to Bidders

The instructions to bidders should be presented as a mandatory guide for preparation of system proposals. It should define a minimum list of critical items in the specifications to be considered and commented on by the vendors in their proposals. It should also outline the required formats for the text of the proposal and the presentation of the proposed system prices. The electronic package covered by the bid is the most critical and frequently is the most expensive single item in a system. It is also an item that significantly affects other costs related to system engineering, software designs, and start-up. Accordingly, the instructions to bidders should request sufficient technical, not sales, description to permit a detailed engineering review of the equipment design, fabrication, and operating features.

The instructions to bidders constitute one of the more important aspects of the specification phase. By requiring a specific bid format with comments on critical criteria, the user can establish a uniform base from which to evaluate the proposals. By effective questioning and by requiring detailed answers, the user can also be reasonably assured of selecting the optimum system for the project. The bid phase is critical and entails more than simply gathering competitive prices on equipment that can be made to do the job plus a few sales brochures on how the vendor proposes to accomplish the job. The user must be wary, for the hardware configuration, message structure, and operation with the associated software carry a high impact on the overall system cost and on its eventual failure or success.

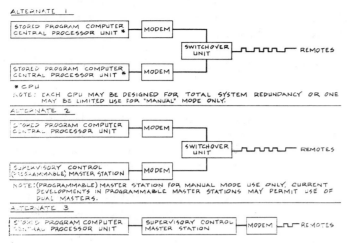

Fig. 6. Equipment configurations for automation systems.

General Specifications

The general specifications should include definitions of the vendor's system responsibilities, equipment configurations, standards of fabrication, operating modes and displays, equipment reliability and testing, warranties, terms of payment, documentation and maintenance training. These specifications, of necessity, should be written to match the operating requirements and minimum standards of the specific industry. Operating modes and standards for an electric utility or cement plant, for example, are simply not the same as, the many times are not suitable for, the "oil patch."

Special or custom requests regarding control equipment tend to create great furor among the vendors. However, assuming the specifications have been carefully prepared with adequate knowledge of the state-of-the-art and field operating requirements, it is important to get what is wanted; i.e., in accordance with specifications, even at added expense. Generally a user includes custom items for specific reasons and expects to pay for the nonstandard items. It is the user's prerogative to decide whether he can afford the costs, not the vendor's. This does not preclude however, an alternate proposal for a standard system, as long as the vendor submits a base proposal, in accordance with the specifications.

For example, a computer-controlled production system may be configured in a variety of ways. Oilfield operations are primarily continuous processes so it is desirable to provide some form of redundant capability in the central or master station equipment for operation during periods of repair or program maintenance. The back-up facility should enable continuous monitoring of field devices and permit manual interrogation and remote control. Some form of selectable, representative or multipurpose displays, as opposed to an extensive point-by-point graphic display, will generally suffice to permit operation during a shutdown period. It is, however, desirable to include some form of printout of field changes rather than to have to continually man the facility to monitor alarms. These requirements lead to three possible equipment configurations, as shown in Fig. 6. Alternatives 1 and 2 are the most desirable, since alternative 3 provides no true redundant backup. The advent of small, special purpose computers and programmable master supervisory stations plus the special requirements of oilfield automation make alternatives 1 and 2 both technically feasible and economically attractive.

Functional Specifications

The functional specification should actually outline the scope of the entire operation and define the design and operation details for the specific installation, i.e., what form and number of field inputs, number and type of control functions, output data formats, etc. Consequently the project design must be nearly complete before a system even goes out for bid. The functional specification must also designate the specific operating environment, communications link and power system characteristics, hazards to equipment or personnel, and vendor responsibilities.

Software Specifications

The software specifications must outline the software (stored program) requirements of the specific project. The need for software specifications has seldom been recognized, and the logic capabilities required to make optimum use of the hardware has been left to the discretion of the vendor. It is imperative that the user recognize this need and be prepared to specify the software as well as the hardware requirements.

In general, the vendor should be required to furnish general-purpose supervisory or executive routines (monitor) which will permit real-time automation activities specified by the user. If user programs are to be coded in FORTRAN, the vendor must be required to provide facility to compile and assemble these routines. The vendor's supervisory routine must be FORTRAN-oriented so that no assembler language is required in the calling sequence.

There are a few recommended, minimum, and readily attainable, special requirements for a FORTRAN-oriented production automation software system. The specifications should require the following.

1) The executive (monitor) program provided by the vendor must include:

    a) interface communication between supervisory control equipment and user's FORTRAN programs;

    b) interface communication between input–output devices and user's FORTRAN programs;

    c) facility to reintailize a program system with a minimum loss of data so that it can be restarted at any time;

    d) facility for a clock-calendar routine that may be interrogated by user's FORTRAN programs (this routine must automatically indicate changes of day, month and year and be so designed as to forestall losing time counts under any conditions except power off and program stall);

e) facility for bootstrap loading;

f) off-line routines to read machine language records from input devices (self checking), dump core in machine language onto output device, list core on printer, compare records on tape to those in core, and list those that do not match;

g) facility to activate FORTRAN routines from input devide;

h) facility to enter data at input device;

i) facility to schedule execution of FORTRAN routines based on predetermined priority, predetermined time intervals, special priorities based on time or order determined at execution time;

j) facility to pack and unpack data by using a FORTRAN call statement (this routine must be general with respect to the number and location of the bit positions to be packed or unpacked).

2) The vendor shall also be required to indicate in his bid:

a) the total storage capacity (core and secondary) required by the executive (monitor) routines including all facilities specified in the section above;

b) the location and availability of computers which can be used by user to compile assemble, and debug the FORTRAN programs;

c) the cost (per 1000 statements) to compile and assemble user's FORTRAN programs;

d) the availability of documentation, including operating instructions, write-ups, and flow charts, of the supervisory (monitor) routines (delivery of this documentation must be made within a specified time after the contract is awarded);

e) the availability of documentation of the telemetering equipment as it relates to programming (this documentation to be delivered with the documentation on the supervisory program);

f) the availability of debugging time on user's hardware at the vendor's factory (the vendor should be required to temporarily wire computer and telemetering equipment together for a programming system checkout using simulated inputs).

Responsibilities of the Vendor

Sophisticated users today demand vendor performance on a system level, and they are willing to pay for this performance. They expect when a contract is signed, however, that the system-level performance be conducted by the vendor. Often this has not been the case, and the users have had to constantly remind the vendors of their responsibilities and, in many cases, have had to perform the very systems integration and follow up the vendors were being paid to do.

One vendor, active in both defense and industrial fields, included their corporate systems philosophy in a recent bid proposal. This philosophy covers nearly all the aspects of what is required to ensure adequate vendor performance on

a system level and is one which any vendor in the "systems" business can profitably employ. It is also a philosophy or level-of-performance that a user should demand of the system vendor, even at added cost to the bid. To paraphrase, it reads as follows. An adequate management system must be based on the following principles.

1) Management organization for a given project must aim at the development of the best possible system. It must be quickly responsive to possible changes in customer requirements so that the program can be achieved on time and at minimum cost.

2) Project organization and operation must be integrated under one technical and administrative project manager.

3) The project manager must be directly accountable to company management for customer liason and satisfaction and be responsible to the customer for contract performance.

4) Plans, before and after contract award, must be prepared by the same staff which is responsible for and performs the work. These plans must be expressed in meaningful form and approved by both company management and the customer.

Coordination

The success of a project cannot be laid solely to the user's specifications, nor can the blame for failure be laid entirely upon the vendor. As engineers, the user's and vendor's first responsibility, once project goals and specifications have been defined and agreed to, is to follow up on the application of the equipment to the process. All too often we fail to resolve even the obvious problems which occur during system design, fabrication, and installation, many times due to changes in personnel, but more often due to poor coordination because it is not expedient at the time.

Project coordination requires a joint user-vendor effort beyond the scope of the normal purchasing-marketing relationship. There is a continuing need, through final acceptance, for joint engineering review meetings. Results of these meetings must be thoroughly documented and followed up.

The coordination responsibilities of the user project team carry on even further. The responsibilities of these systems engineers, which began with the request for bids, ends only after a period of successful operation not, as is often believed, with the completed installation. The user team must follow up and coordinate with the using organization to ensure successful turnover and efficient operation.

Conclusions

The goal of an automation project is to control a process in an optimum and economic manner utilizing modern techniques and devices. Consequently, system equipment and logic must be designed around the specific process requirements, rather than merely mechanizing existing procedures step by step.

Projects of this nature involve three mutually inter-related aspects: the process or operation to be automated, the associated automation hardware, and the computer software necessary to marry the process and the hardware. Since a single individual is seldom sufficiently familiar with all phases to implement these needs, it is necessary to assign a user team consisting of a hardware specialist and a software specialist, both of whom are expert in the process to be controlled. The hardware man should act as the project manager responsible for the overall project implementation as well as the hardware and functional requirements. The software man should be responsible for developing and programming the control-function logic. Jointly this team must develop the initial specifications covering required bid data, hardware quality, functional requirements, and software capabilities.

The user should purchase the system vendor's assembler language monitor program and write his own control and operator programs. These user programs should be coded in a general-purpose easy-to-read language. For example, the Hope–Heidi programs were written in FORTRAN but supported with a few assembler-language bit-manipulation routines which can be called by FORTRAN.

In order to ensure a smooth installation, the system vendor must be changed with and must accept and implement system responsibility for the electronic hardware and computer executive software. Vendor system-level responsibility must be under total management of a single project leader. Thorough and accurate system documentation by the user and the vendor is essential. Unfortunately, many users do not realize the fallacy of inadequate documentation until after the project team is disbanded and the vendor has other interests.

Static tests of equipment and program logic during checkout are essential, but they are not a substitute for the dynamic operations of the field installation. Even the dynamic tests are not a substitute for actual operations.

Field followup during the first year is essential. Even a well-designed system can still go astray, and without adequate follow-up, a potentially successful project is doomed to failure.

Author Index

Subject Index

R

Radiation therapy planning, 189
Remote terminals,
  see computer communications, peripherals

S

Sampled control systems,
  predictive compensation, 254
Sensors, 98
Servo A/D converters, 79
Shop and material control, 145
Signal conditioning,
  line-sharing systems, 121
Simulation,
  predictive compensation of sampled systems, 254
Software, 47
  communication executives, 75
  computer installation planning, 335, 346, 353
  direct digital control, 67
  process control, 56
  terminal control, 319
  see also programming
Spectrometry, 109
  see also neutron spectrometers, ultraviolet spectrometers
Storage,
  see data storage, memory access
Strain gages, 98
Successive-approximation A/D converters, 79
Supervisory control,
  output signals, 102
  petroleum production system, 353
Switching systems,
  see data communication, message switching

System design,
  control computer installation, 335, 346, 353
Systems engineering, 215

T

Tachometers, 98
Telephone systems, 307
Terminal control,
  see data terminal control
Terminals,
  see computer communications, peripherals
Temperature transducers, 98
Testing,
  see automative component testing
Time and attendance reporting systems, 145
Time-delay systems,
  predictive compensation, 254
Transducers, 98

U

Ultraviolet spectrometers,
  data acquisition and processing, 102
Universal monitoring and control systems, 121

V

Velocity transducers, 98

W

Warehouse operations, 280, 287

Editors' Biographies

James D. Schoeffler (S'54–M'58–SM'64) received the B.S. and M.S. degrees in electrical engineering from Case Western Reserve University, Cleveland, Ohio, and the Sc.D. degree in electrical engineering from the Massachusetts Institute of Technology, Cambridge, Mass.

Since 1960 he has been with Case Western Reserve University, where he is presently Professor of Engineering and a Member of the Control of Complex Systems Group of the Systems Research Center. He also directs the Systems Engineering Laboratory, where his work involves on-line data acquisition and control computers and facilities for simulation and computer aided design. His research and consulting activities are in the area of systems engineering, including computer aided design, digital, analog, and hybrid simulation, applied control theory, and the implementation of on-line data acquisition and control systems. He has developed special purpose programming languages for real time systems which are particularly well suited to minicomputer applications. In these areas he has served as a Consultant to many companies, including one year leave with the IBM Corporation designing on-line control systems for the paper industry.

Dr. Schoeffler is a member of the Association for Computing Machinery, the Simulation Council, and several honorary organizations.

Ronald H. Temple (S'65–M'68) received the B.A.Sc. and M.A.Sc. degrees from the University of Toronto, Toronto, Ont., Canada, and the Ph.D. degree in systems engineering from Case Western Reserve University, Cleveland, Ohio.

He is with the Automation Division, General Electric Company, Lynn, Mass., where he is Manager, Advanced Automation Technology. His interests and background are in the area of the design and implementation of new systems utilizing minicomputers for process control and monitoring.

Dr. Temple is a member of the Association for Computing Machinery and the Instrument Society of America.